CHRIST IN CHRISTIAN TRADITION

VOLUME TWO: PART ONE

Christ in Christian Tradition, Volume One, From the Apostolic Age to Chalcedon (451) by Aloys Grillmeier S.J. was first published by A. R. Mowbray & Co. Limited in 1965 with a second, revised edition in 1975

CHRIST
IN CHRISTIAN
TRADITION

VOLUME TWO

From the Council of Chalcedon (451)
to Gregory the Great (590–604)

PART ONE

Reception and Contradiction
The development of the discussion about Chalcedon
from 451 to the beginning of the reign of Justinian

by
ALOYS GRILLMEIER, S.J.

translated by
PAULINE ALLEN
&
JOHN CAWTE

John Knox Press
ATLANTA

Imprimi potest: P. HANS ZWIEFELHOFER S.J.,
Praep. Prov. Germ. Sup. S.J.
Monachii, die 25 iunii 1985
Nihil obstat: PATRICK McKINNEY S.T.L.
Imprimatur: DANIEL LEONARD V.G.
Birmingamiae, die 4 octobris, 1986

The *Nihil obstat* and *Imprimatur* are a declaration that a book
or pamphlet is considered to be free from doctrinal or moral
error. It is not implied that those who have granted the *Nihil
obstat* and *Imprimatur* agree with the contents, opinions or
statements expressed.

Library of Congress Cataloging-in-Publication Data
(Revised for vol. 2)

Grillmeier, Aloys, 1910-
   Christ in Christian tradition.

   Translation of: Jesus der Christus im Glauben der
Kirche.
   Bibliography: v. 1, p.   -579.
   Includes indexes.
   Contents: v. 1. From the apostolic age to Chalcedon
(451) / translated by John Bowden — v. 2. From the
Council of Chalcedon (451) to Gregory the Great
(590-604) / translated by Pauline Allen & John Cawte —
   1. Jesus Christ—History of doctrines—Early church,
ca. 30-600.   I. Title.
BT198.G743   1975   232'.09   75-13456
ISBN 0-8042-0492-6 (v. 1)
ISBN 0-8042-0493-4 (v. 2)

PREFACE

In spite of significant monographs on the subject, post-Chalcedonian christology of the patristic period still cries out for a comprehensive elucidation and exposition. Numerous editions of sources, though these are still far from being complete, now make available the traditions of the old Oriental Churches. Yet in Western writing on the history of doctrine these traditions are discussed only too briefly or passed over completely. Hence the lack of a comprehensive exposition of post-Chalcedonian christology is felt all the more keenly. In order to establish an overall view of the demands and the possibilities of a general sketch of the period from 451 to ca 800, a sketch which even at this time must still remain provisional, we have included in Part One a comprehensive section entitled *Ad Fontes*, which we find reveals in surprising fashion the structure of post-Chalcedonian christology. Here it is shown how strongly the discussion about the great Synods of the early Church, those of Nicaea and Ephesus, but most of all about that of Chalcedon, promoted for the purpose of argument the rise of the literary genres of proof or their application to christology. For this reason we have ventured the sub-title: 'Formengeschichte of the Chalcedonian and post-Chalcedonian sources'. Practically all the forms of theological argumentation which one had previously found practised especially in the Western Scholasticism of the Middle Ages are already present in the time from 400 to 800, and not only in the Byzantine Church, but just as much in the old Oriental, anti-Chalcedonian patriarchates. The West could also learn 'method' from the East. In order to make manifest the conclusion that we have reached, we shall present the analysis of sources unabridged, not for readers in a hurry, but for interested researchers and students. This is also intended to stimulate them to supply corrections and supplements to what has been offered.

Evidence of what is held in common by the Churches should not, however, in the first instance be the preserve of *théologie savante* or be on the level of speculative christology, but it should rather be in the common possession of faith and proclamation. For this reason in the continuation of this work the concrete faith in Christ of each individual region of tradition and of each individual Church will be depicted. One is delighted to have established that despite all the differences, conditioned as they are culturally and intellectually, the great regions of the *orbis christologicus*, whether Eastern or Western, are one in their faith in Christ, especially on the basis of baptismal kerygma and the every-day faith of the Churches. Thus this second volume cannot escape having a decided ecumenical relevance.

Once again my special thanks are due to the many friends who have already been named in the first volume. My thanks are due also in no small way to the *Deutsche Forschungsgemeinschaft,* which from the very beginning promoted this work by granting the necessary funds for an assistant. For this volume Dr. Hans-Joachim Höhn has given unstintingly of himself, and it is thanks to him that this first half-volume has been published more quickly than was expected. Particular thanks must go to Pauline Allen and John Cawte who undertook the demanding task of translating the continuation of this work. In the course of this translation I have come to appreciate immensely their scholarly accuracy and understanding of the problems involved, as well as their personal commitment in seeing the project through to a happy conclusion. Thanks are also due to the publishers, A. R. Mowbray & Company, for venturing to publish the continuation of this work, which once again is burdened with so many scholarly details. I am especially obliged to Mrs Eva Jesse.

St. Georgen, Frankfurt-Main   21 June 1985

CONTENTS

PART TWO
EXPOSITION

ABBREVIATIONS

AbhAkW Bln   *Abhandlungen der Akademie der Wissenschaften zu Berlin, Göttingen,*
GöttHeid Münch   *Heidelberg, München*
AbhD   Abhandlungen des Deutschen Archäologischen Instituts, Abtei-
ArchInstK   lung Kairo, Wiesbaden 1, 1962ff.
AbhKundeMorgl   *Abhandlungen für die Kunde des Morgenlandes,* Leipzig 1, 1857ff.
ACO   Acta Conciliorum Oecumenicorum, ed. E. Schwartz, Argentorati-
                Lipsiae-Berolini; T. IV, vol. 1 ss. ed. J. Straub (1971ff); series
                secunda ed. R. Riedinger (1984ff.)
AHC   *Annuarium Historiae Conciliorum,* Amsterdam 1, 1969ff.
ALW   *Archiv für Liturgiewissenschaft,* Regensburg 1, 1950ff.
AmerJourTheol   *The American Journal of Theology,* Chicago 1, 1897–24, 1920
AnGreg   *Analecta Gregoriana,* Romae 1, 1930ff.
AnBoll   *Analecta Bollandiana,* Paris-Bruxelles 1, 1882ff.
AngTheolRev   *Anglican Theological Review,* New York 1, 1919ff.
AnLovBiblOr   Analecta Lovaniensia Biblica et Orientalia, Louvain 1, 1934–20,
                1947
ANTIΔΩPON   ANTIΔΩPON. *Hulde aan/Hommage à Maurits Geerard.* Vol. 1 (Wet-
                teren 1984)
ASS   Acta Sanctae Sedis, Romae 1, 1865–44, 1908
Aug   *Augustinianum,* Romae 1, 1961ff.

BAC   Biblioteca de autores Cristianos, Madrid 1, 1947ff.
BGAMBO   Beiträge zur Geschichte des Alten Mönchtums und des Benedikti-
                nerordens, Münster 1, 1912
BHTh   Beiträge zur historischen Theologie, Tübingen 12, 1950ff.
BiblMus   Bibliothèque du Muséon, Louvain 1, 1929ff.
Bibl. SS   Bibliotheca Sanctorum, Roma 1961–1969
BKV²   Bibliothek der Kirchenväter, Kempten 1, ²1911ff.
BLE   *Bulletin de Littérature Ecclésiastique,* Toulouse, NS 10, 1899ff.; 20,
                1899 (=3rd ser. 1); 30, 1909ff. (=4th ser. 1)
BM   *Benediktinische Monatsschrift,* Beuron 1, 1919ff.
BSAC   *Bulletin de la Societé d'Archéologie Copte,* Le Caire 1, 1938ff.
Byz   *Byzantion,* Bruxelles 1, 1924ff.
ByzSlav   *Byzantinoslavica,* Prague 1, 1929ff.
ByzZ   *Byzantinische Zeitschrift,* Leipzig-München 1, 1892ff.
BZ   *Biblische Zeitschrift,* Freiburg–Paderborn NS 1, 1957ff.

Cath   *Catholica,* Paderborn 1, 1932ff.
CCG   Corpus Christianorum, series graeca, Turnholti 1, 1977ff.
CCL   Corpus Christianorum, series latina, Turnholti 1, 1953ff.
CCT   A. Grillmeier, *Christ in Christian Tradition.* Vol. 1: From the Apost-
                olic Age to Chalcedon (AD 451) (London–Oxford ²1975)
CFHB   Corpus Fontium Historiae Byzantinae (DOP Series), Washington
                D.C. 6, 1972ff.
Chalkedon I–III   A. Grillmeier-H. Bacht (ed.), *Das Konzil von Chalkedon. Geschichte*
                und Gegenwart, 3 vols (Würzburg 1951–1954, ⁵1979) (=unchanged
                reprint of the 4th ed. with a new Foreword).

ChrAnt	Christianisme Antique, Paris 1, 1978ff.
COD	Conciliorum Oecumenicorum Decreta, ed. Istituto per le scienze religiose, Bologna, curantibus J. Alberigo et al., consultante H. Jedin (Bologna ³1973)
Coleman-Norton, *State & Church*	P. R. Coleman-Norton, *Roman state and Christian church. A collection of legal documents to A.D. 535*, Vols 1–3 (London 1966)
CollCist	*Collectanea Cisterciensia*, Seourmont 1, 1939ff.
Conc	*Concilium*, New York–London 1, 1965ff.
CPG	Clavis Patrum Graecorum, vols I–III, Turnhout 1979ff
CSCO	Corpus scriptorum christianorum orientalium, Roma etc. 1903ff.
CSEL	Corpus scriptorum ecclesiasticorum latinorum, Wien 1, 1866ff.
DAGL	*Dictionnaire d'Archéologie Chrétienne et de Liturgie*, Paris 1, 1924ff.
DHGE	*Dictionnaire d'Histoire et de Géographie Ecclésiastiques*, Paris 1, 1912ff.
DOP	*Dumbarton Oaks Papers*, Cambridge, Mass. 1, 1941ff.
DS	H. Denzinger, *Enchiridion Symbolorum Definitionum et Declarationum de rebus fidei et morum*, quod primum edit Henricus Denziger et quod funditus retractavit . . . Adolfus Schönmetzer, 36 ed. emendata (Barcelona–Freiburg–Rom 1976)
DSp	*Dictionnaire de spiritualité, ascétique et mystique*, Paris 1, 1932ff.
DTC	*Dictionnaire de Théologie Catholique*, Paris 1903–1972
EcumRev	*The Ecumenical Review*, Lausanne 1, 1948–1949ff.
ÉglThéol	*Église et Théologie*, Paris 1, 1960ff.
EngHistRev	*The English Historical Review*, London 1, 1886ff.
ÉO	*Échos d'Orient*, Bucarest etc. 1, 1897–1898—39, 1940–1943
EphThLov	*Ephemerides Theologicae Lovanienses*, Louvain 1, 1924ff.
EstEcl	*Estudios Eclesiasticos*, Madrid 1, 1922ff.
EvTh	*Evangelische Theologie*, München NS 1, 1946–1947ff.
FCLDG	Forschungen zur christlichen Literatur- und Dogmengeschichte, Paderborn 1, 1900–21, 1938
FHG	Fontes historiae religionum ex auctoribus Graecis et Latinis collecti, Bonn 1, 1920ff.
Fiey, *Jalons*	J. M. Fiey, *Jalons pour une histoire de l'église in Iraq* (Louvain 1970) (CSCO Subsidia Tomus 36)
FrancStud	*Franciscan Studies*, New York 1, 1924ff.
FRLANT	Forschungen zur Religion und Literatur des Alten und Neuen Testamentes, Göttingen 1, 1903ff.
FrThSt	Freiburger Theologische Studien, Freiburg–Basel–Wien 1, 1910ff.
FS	Festschrift
FTS	Frankfurter Theologische Studien, Frankfurt 1, 1969ff.
GCS	Die Griechischen Christlichen Schriftsteller der ersten drei Jahrhunderte, Berlin 1, 1898ff.
Greg	*Gregorianum*, Roma 1, 1920ff.
Grumel, *Regestes*	V. Grumel, *Les Regestes des actes du patriarcat de Constantinople*, 3 vols (Bucarest 1932–1947)

HDG	Handbuch der Dogmengeschichte, Freiburg–Basel–Wien 1956ff.
HE	*Historia Ecclesiastica*
HistJb	*Historisches Jahrbuch der Görresgesellschaft*, München–Freiburg 1, 1880ff.
HThR	*The Harvard Theological Review*, Cambridge, Mass. 1, 1908ff.
HTS	Harvard Theological Studies, Cambridge, Mass. 1, 1916ff.
Irén	*Irénikon*, Amay-Chevetogne 1, 1926ff.
ITS	Innsbrucker Theologische Studien, Innsbruck-Wien 1, 1978ff.
JAC	*Jahrbuch für Antike und Christentum*, Münster 1, 1958ff.
JdChr	A. Grillmeier, *Jesus der Christus im Glauben der Kirche*. Vol. 1: Von der Apostolischen Zeit bis zum Konzil von Chalkedon (451) (Freiburg–Basel–Wien ²1982)
JEH	*Journal of Ecclesiastical History*, London 1, 1950ff.
JÖB	*Jahrbuch der Österreichischen Byzantinistik*, Wien 1, 1952ff.
JRel	*The Journal of Religion*, Chicago 1, 1921ff.
JRS	*Journal of Roman Studies*, London 1, 1911ff.
JTS	*Journal of Theological Studies*, Oxford etc. 1, 1899ff., NS 1, 1950ff.
JW	*Regesta Pontificum*, ed. 2a auspiciis G. Wattenbach curavit S. Loewenfeld-F. Kaltenbrunner-P. Ewald, Tomus (Lipsiae 1888)
KKTS	Konfessionskundliche und Kontroverstheologische Studien, Paderborn 1, 1959ff.
KLL	*Kindlers Literatur Lexikon* (Zürich 1965–1974)
Kl.Pauly	*Der Kleine Pauly. Lexikon der Antike*, 5 vols (ed. K. Ziegler-W. Sonnleitner) (Stuttgart 1964–1975)
KlT	Kleine Texte für theologische und philosophische Vorlesungen und Übungen (Bonn 1906)
KlWbChrOr	*Kleines Wörterbuch des Christlichen Orients* (ed. J. Aßfalg-P. Krüger) (Wiesbaden 1975)
KuD	*Kerygma und Dogma*, Göttingen 1, 1955ff.
LQF	Liturgiewissenschaftliche Quellen und Forschungen, Münster 1, 1909–32, 1957ff.
Mansi	*Sacrorum Conciliorum nova et amplissima Collectio* (ed. J. D. Mansi), 31 vols (Florence 1769ff.)
MémTrav	Mémoires et Travaux, Lille 1, 1905ff.
MGH	Monumenta Germaniae Historica ab a. 500 usque ad a. 1500, Hannover–Berlin 1, 1877ff.
MünchThSt	Münchener Theologische Studien, II. Syst. Abt., München 1, 1950ff.
Mus	*Le muséon*, Louvain 1, 1882–34, 1921ff.
NHSt	Nag Hammadi Studies, Leiden 1, 1971ff.
NovTest	*Novum Testamentum*, Leiden 1, 1965ff.
NRT	*Nouvelle Revue Théologique*, Louvain 1, 1869–72, 1940ff.
OCA	Orientalia Christiana Analecta, Roma 1, 1935ff.
OCP	*Orientalia Christiana Periodica*, Roma 1, 1935ff.

ÖAKR   *Österreichisches Archiv für Kirchenrecht*, Wien 1, 1950ff.
ÖkRund   *Ökumenische Rundschau*, Stuttgart 1, 1952ff.
OLP   *Orientalia Lovaniensia Periodica*, Leuven 1, 1970ff.
OrChr   *Oriens Christianus*, Leipzig 1, 1901–41, 1941; Wiesbaden 42, 1953ff.
OrLovAn   Orientalia Lovaniensia Analecta, Leuven 1, 1970ff.
OrSyr   *L'Orient Syrien*, Paris 1, 1956–12, 1967

PatrStud   Patristic Studies of the Catholic University of America, Washington
                1, 1922ff.
PatSorb   Patristica Sorbonensia, Paris 1, 1957ff.
PG   Patrologia Graeca, ed. J.-P. Migne (Paris 1857–1886, etc.)
PL   Patrologia Latina, ed. J.-P. Migne (Paris 1844–1855, etc.)
PLS   Patrologia latina supplementum Paris 1, 1958–5, 1970
PO   Patrologia Orientalis, ed. R. Graffin–F. Nau, Paris 1, 1907ff.
PRE   *Realenzyklopädie für protestantische Theologie und Kirche* (3rd ed.)
                Leipzig 1, 1896–24, 1913
PTSt   Patristische Texte und Studien, Berlin 1, 1964ff.
PWK   *Paulys Real-Encyklopädie der classischen Altertumswissenschaft.* Neue
                Bearbeitung. Vols 1–6 ed. G. Wissowa (Stuttgart 1894–1909); vols
                7–35 ed. W. Kroll (Stuttgart 1912–1937); vols 36ff. ed. K. Mittel-
                haus-K. Ziegler (Stuttgart–München 1947–1972)

RAC   *Reallexikon für Antike und Christentum*, Stuttgart 1, 1950ff.
RAM   *Revue d'ascétique et de mystique*, Toulouse 1, 1920ff.
RevBén   *Revue Bénédictine*, Maredsous 1, 1884ff.
RevBibl   *Revue Biblique*, Paris–Jerusalem 1, 1891ff; NS 1904ff.
RevEgypt   *Revue Egyptologique*, Paris 1, 1881ff.
RevÉtArm   *Revue des Études Arméniennes*, Paris 1, 1920–11, 1933; NS 1, 1964ff.
RevÉtAug   *Revue des Études Augustiniennes*, Paris 1, 1955ff.
RevÉtByz   *Revue des Études Byzantines*, Paris 1, 1943ff.
RevÉtGrec   *Revue des Études Grecques*, Paris 1, 1888ff.
RevHistRel   *Revue de l'Histoire des Religions*, Paris 1, 1880ff.
RevThom   *Revue Thomiste*, Paris NS 1, 1918ff.
RHE   *Revue d'Histoire Ecclésiastique*, Louvain 1, 1900ff.
Richard, *Opera* M. Richard, *Opera Minora*, 3 vols (Turnhout-Leuven 1976–1977)
Minora
RivArcCr   *Rivista Archeologica Cristiana*, Città del Vaticano 1, 1924ff.
RivStorLettRel *Rivista di Storia e Letteratura religiosa*, Firenze 1, 1921ff.
ROC   *Revue de l'Orient Chrétien*, Paris 1, 1896ff.
RömHistMitt   *Römische Historische Mitteilungen*, Graz–Köln 1, 1956ff.
RömQ   *Römische Quartalschrift für christliche Altertumskunde und für Kirchenges-
                chichte*, Freiburg 1, 1887ff.
RSPT   *Revue des Sciences Philosophiques et Théologiques*, Paris 1, 1907ff.
RSR   *Revue des Sciences Religieuses*, Strasbourg–Paris 1, 1921ff.

SbAkw Bln Gött *Sitzungsberichte der Akademie der Wissenschaften zu Berlin, Göttingen,*
Heid Münch   *Heidelberg, München*
SC   Sources Chrétiennes, Paris 1, 1944ff.
Schwartz, PS   E. Schwartz, 'Publizistische Sammlungen zum Acacianischen
                Schisma', *AbhAkwMünch* NF 10 (München 1934)
Seeck, *Regesten* O. Seeck, *Regesten der Kaiser und Päpste für die Jahre bis 476 n. Chr.*
                Vorarbeit zu einer Prosopographie d. christlichen Kaiserzeit (Stutt-
                gart 1919)

SpicFrib	Spicilegium Friburgense. Texte zur Geschichte des kirchlichen Lebens, Freiburg/Schweiz 1, 1957ff.
SpicSLov	Spicilegium Sacrum Lovaniense, Louvain 1, 1922ff.
ST	Studi e Testi, Città del Vaticano 1, 1900ff.
Subs. hag.	Subsidia hagiographica (=suppl. *AnBoll*), Bruxelles 1, 1886ff.
SymbOsl	*Symbolae Osloenses*, Oslo 1, 1922ff.
StudAns	*Studia Anselmiana*, Roma 1, 1933ff.
StudMon	*Studia Monastica*, Montserrat 1, 1959ff.
StudÖR	Studien des Ökumenischen Rates, Genf 2, 1965ff.
StudPat	Studia Patristica, Berlin 1, 1957ff. (=TU 63ff.)

TD	Textus et Documenta (ser. theol.), Roma 1, 1932ff.
TF	Texte zur Forschung, Darmstadt 1, 1971ff.
ThéolHist	Théologie Historique, Paris 1, 1963ff.
TheolPhil	*Theologie und Philosophie*, Freiburg 41, 1966ff.
Thiel	A. Thiel, *Epistulae romanorum pontificum genuinae et quae ad eos scriptae sunt A. S. Hilaro usque ad Pelagium II.* T. 1. A. S. Hilaro usque ad S. Hormisdam (Brunsbergae 1868)
ThLZ	*Theologische Literaturzeitung*, Leipzig 1, 1876ff.
ThQ	*Theologische Quartalschrift*, Tübingen–Stuttgart 1, 1819ff.
Trad	*Traditio.* Studies in Ancient and Medieval History, Thought and Religion, New York 1, 1943ff.
TR	*Theologische Revue*, Münster 1, 1902ff.
TravMém	*Travaux et Mémoires*, Paris 1, 1965ff.
TRE	*Theologische Realenzyklopädie*, Berlin 1, 1977ff.
TU	Texte und Untersuchungen zur Geschichte der altchristlichen Literatur, Leipzig 1, 1882ff.
TZ	*Theologische Zeitschrift*, Basel 1, 1945ff.

VC	*Vetera Christianorum*, Bari 1, 1964ff.
VigC	*Vigiliae Christianae*,Amsterdam 1, 1947ff.

WdF	Wege der Forschung, Darmstadt 1, 1956ff.
WUNT	Wissenschaftliche Untersuchungen zum Neuen Testament, Tübingen 1, 1950ff.
WZUnivRostock	*Wissenschafiliche Zeitschrift der Universität Rostock*, Rostock 1, 1951ff.

ZÄS	*Zeitschrift für Ägyptische Sprache und Altertumskunde*, Berlin 1, 1863–78, 1943; 79, 1954ff.
ZDMG	*Zeitschrift der Deutschen Morgenländischen Gesellschaft*, Wiesbaden NS 1945–1949ff.
ZKG	*Zeitschrift für Kirchengeschichte*, Gotha–Stuttgart 1, 1877ff.
ZKTh	*Zeitschrift für Katholische Theologie*, Innsbruck–Wien 1, 1877ff.
ZMR	*Zeitschrift für Missions- und Religionswissenschaft*, Münster 1, 1938ff.
ZMW	*Zeitschrift für Missionswissenschaft*, Münster 1. 1911–27, 1937
ZNW	*Zeitschrift für die neutestamentliche Wissenschaft und die Kunde der älteren Kirche*, Berlin 1, 1900ff.
ZPE	*Zeitschrift für Papyrologie und Epigraphik*, Bonn 1, 1967ff.
ZSavSt.K	*Zeitschrift der Savigny-Stiftung für Rechtsgeschichte*, Kanonist. Abt., Weimar 1, 1911ff.
ZSem	*Zeitschrift für Semitistik und verwandte Gebiete*, Leipzig 1, 1922–10, 1935
ZThK	*Zeitschrift für Theologie und Kirche*, Tübingen 1, 1891ff.

PART ONE

LAYING THE FOUNDATIONS

SECTION ONE

THE SCOPE OF OUR ENQUIRY

I. THE STARTING-POINT

THE historical starting-point for our enquiry is the Council of Chalcedon (451) and its teaching concerning the person of Jesus Christ.

Following, then, the holy Fathers, we all with one voice teach that it should be confessed that our Lord Jesus Christ is one and the same Son, the Same perfect in godhead, the Same perfect in manhood, truly God and truly man, the Same [consisting] of a rational soul and body; *homoousios* with the Father as to his godhead, and the Same *homoousios* with us as to his manhood; in all things like unto us, sin only excepted; begotten of the Father before ages as to his godhead, and in the last days, the Same, for us and for our salvation, of Mary the Virgin *Theotokos* as to his manhood;
One and the same Christ, Son, Lord, Only-begotten, made known in two natures [which exist] without confusion, without change, without division, without separation; the difference of the natures having been in no wise taken away by reason of the union, but rather the properties of each being preserved, and [both] concurring in one person (*prosopon*) and one *hypostasis*—not parted or divided into two persons (*prosopa*), but one and the same Son and Only-begotten, the divine Logos, the Lord Jesus Christ; even as the prophets from of old [have spoken] concerning him, and as the Lord Jesus Christ himself has taught us, and as the Symbol of the Fathers has delivered to us.[1]

Let us give prominence to one formulation: Jesus Christ—one person, one *hypostasis* in two natures.

In the course of history, and the ebb and flow of religious parties, such a pronouncement takes on a significance which perhaps was not at all intended for it by its authors. The Fathers of Chalcedon might well have believed that their formula had indicated the *via media* between a christology of division and one of fusion, between Nestorius and Eutyches; they had hoped to have rid the world of a problem which for twenty-five years had pressed relentlessly for a solution. Had that hope been realised the formula of Chalcedon would have passed quietly and unobtrusively into the confession and theology of the Church without drawing attention to itself. A host of other topics for preaching and theology would, as time went on, have been ventilated with equal vigour, so long as no fresh controversy had emerged.

Events turned out otherwise. Chalcedon became a stumbling-block, the starting-point of a schism which from then on was to

[1] ACO II 1, 2 p. 129–130.

split the imperial Church, and which even beyond the lifetime of the Byzantine empire itself would continue to afflict the Church—right up to the present. As a result, the formula and christology of Chalcedon would be discussed in as forceful a way as the *homoousios* of Nicaea (325) and, indeed, even more intensively. It was unavoidable that a certain narrowing of outlook occurred in preaching and theology, which at least could have hindered, even if in fact it did not, the harmonious build-up of a total kerygma and theology, especially in the East where the strife was hottest. The formula and teaching of Chalcedon absorbed the attention of the old imperial Church, whether we look at Emperors, Popes, bishops, the monks or the theologians, or finally the mass of Church people. Yet, both before and after the Council, there was a life inspired by faith in Christ which neither needed the formula of Chalcedon for its existence, nor was directly enriched by it. This was because the Church possessed and lived the *content* or the *matter* of this teaching, namely, faith in the one Christ, true God and true man, even though it was not expressed in more advanced philosophical terms. Such faith drew its vitality from a picture of Christ which could not be fully comprehended in the formula of 451 about the person of Christ. This is shown by the fact that the content, though not the formula, of Chalcedonian faith was actually the common property of the opposed parties in the post-Chalcedonian era. The interpretation of Monophysite christology will confirm this. The Churches which then broke away from the Byzantine imperial Church and from the Great Church were, and are, more at one with her than they themselves knew or know.

As the Fathers of Chalcedon understood it, the static-sounding statement about the being of Christ had the purpose of securing for a dynamic EVENT or ACT—God's event or act of salvation—its content and significance. Hence what was done in 451 was rather like what happened at the Council of Nicaea in 325. On the earlier occasion the declaration about the oneness in being of the Son with the Father had been built into the framework of an older symbol, which in its structure was planned completely on the model of salvation history. Its insertion here did not destroy this structure. At Chalcedon, admittedly, there was really a certain shift of emphasis. The more static element in its definition formed, outwardly or in terms of content, the greater part. Yet this too was fitted into a scheme of the economy of salvation which in the last resort was nothing other than that of the Nicene Creed. To appreciate this fact one needs to take into account the whole context of the development which begins at Nicaea and continues through Ephesus (431), the

Union of 433 and its Symbol, and the foundation of the Council of 451. At Chalcedon itself the most important sentence of the Definition was ultimately this:

> Our Lord Jesus Christ is one and the same Son ... begotten of the Father before ages as to his godhead, and in the last days (ἐπ'ἐσχάτων δὲ τῶν ἡμερῶν), the Same, for us and for our salvation, of Mary the Virgin *Theotokos* as to his manhood.

The new statements which were added by Chalcedon were to establish clearly only this: who it is that is to come, and what he signifies for us men and for our history. The static, ontic statement about the person of Christ remains, in the intention of the Fathers, a statement about salvation. It is soteriology, a kerygma of salvation. We shall have to examine whether in the course of the dispute over the Fourth Council this soteriological atmosphere in the Church and in her theology has evaporated. For in the wake of the quarrel about Nicaea— not necessarily as a result of the Council itself—this atmosphere became thinner in the sphere of trinitarian theology. For the view of the one God, Father, Son, and Holy Spirit in the economy of salvation gave way to a consideration of the immanent Trinity, as especially the investigations of J. A. Jungmann and his students have shown.[2]

It is true that the purpose of the formula of Chalcedon was to direct the Church's faith towards the Bringer of salvation, and so to let the presence of salvation be illuminated in his person. But then a development was at hand which is still a burden to christology: the divorce between the person and the work of Jesus, between 'christology' and 'soteriology'. Did this cleavage openly show itself in the patristic period, or is it only the product of later systematic theology? That is a question we shall have to discuss. Whatever the answer to this may be, one thing is assured for the theology of that period by the focusing of attention of Chalcedon—a christocentric emphasis which persisted to the end of the patristic age.

If we have to consider the aftermath of a christological Council on the basis of its central formula, we still want to attempt to see the christological problem in all its breadth, and this in the full context of the Church's faith and life. This aftermath reaches to our own time. For it pertains to the nature of the Church's tradition that each of its phases lives on in the ones to come. With this statement we broach the question of the binding character of the doctrine of Chalcedon.

[2] J. A. Jungmann, *Die Stellung Christi im liturgischen Gebet* (Münster [1]1925; [2]1962): in addition, H. Engberding, 'Das chalkedonische Christusbild und die Liturgien der monophysitischen Kirchengemeinschaften', *Chalkedon* II, 699–733.

2. THE QUESTION OF THE BINDING CHARACTER OF CHALCEDON, OR OF THE RECEPTION OF CHALCEDON

The Problem of Hermeneutics

The question of the validity or the binding character of the doctrine of Chalcedon, which is being posed acutely again today, can be treated under a twofold aspect: firstly under the theme of its 'reception' and then under the heading of 'hermeneutics'. Both are closely interconnected.

(a) The reception of the Council of Chalcedon in the Church

The history of a dogma or a council does not end with its ratification by Church authority or by the Fathers of the council. It is only after this that the process of 'ingrafting' in the Church begins, and that by way of 'reception' or the acceptance of the council. One can understand by reception various procedures or modes of behaviour vis-à-vis a doctrine or a council.[3] It is often understood in a canonical sense, and on the basis of this interpretation a process of reception is either denied or admitted. That is to say that, when a council—as for instance in the Roman Catholic view of it—enjoys such authority that acceptance by the faithful is not a decisive condition for its validity, there is in this canonical sense no scope for an act of reception. It is rather different in the Greek Orthodox Church, where a synodal act, if it is to be valid, must first obtain this acceptance by the faithful. Unfortunately, this canonical notion or reception was the reason that Catholics writing on the history of doctrine were not aware of the whole breadth of the process of reception as it actually took place. Only now is it being realised more and more that at that time the consciousness of a 'formal authority' on the part of a council was still in an embryonic stage, or that it had a different structure from what it had in the Tridentine understanding of things.[4] A council had first of all to prove itself legitimate and valid by the fact that it enshrined the biblical and ecclesiastical *paradosis*. This had to be proved through a comparison of its statement with the truth that had been handed on. It was in this way, for instance, that Athan-

---

[3] Cf. F. Wolfinger, 'Ecumenical Councils and the Reception of their Decisions', *Conc* 167 (7/1983) 79–84; idem, 'Rezeption—ein Zentralbegriff der ökumenischen Diskussion oder des Glaubensvoll-zuges?', *ÖkRund* 27(1978) 14–21; idem, 'Die Rezeption theologischer Einsichten und ihre theologische und ökumenische Bedeutung. Von der Einsicht zur Verwirklichung', *Cath* 31(1977) 202–233; M. Garijo, 'Der Begriff der "Rezeption" und sein Ort im Kern der katholischen Ekklesiologie', P. Lengsfeld/H.-G. Stobbe (Ed.), *Theologischer Konsens und Kirchenspaltung* (Stuttgart 1981) 97–109; H. Müller, 'Rezeption und Konsens in der Kirche. Eine Anfrage an die Kanonistik', *ÖAKR* 27(1976) 3–21; A. Grillmeier, 'Konzil und Rezeption', idem, *Mit ihm und in ihm. Christologische Forschungen und Perspektiven* (Freiburg-Basel-Wien ²1978) 303–334 (lit.).

[4] Cf. the investigations of H. J. Sieben which are mentioned further below.

asius understood the function and validity of the Council of Nicaea. The assistance of the Holy Spirit revealed itself in this agreement of a synod with the tradition. This idea of 'inspiration' became more and more independent, and, together with the emphasis on the consensus of the Fathers of a council, it became a *topos* for the foundation of the authority of a council, for its binding force and irrevocability. The struggle for the Council of Chalcedon necessitated the growth of such a 'formal' conciliar authority. Yet we still catch a glimpse of the old conception that a council is legitimate because it preserves the *paradosis*. When, for instance, Leo the Great calls on the opponents of Chalcedon to test for themselves its agreement with tradition (for him it was an obvious fact) he bears witness to the old idea. But whoever accounts for the legitimacy of a council in this way can 'receive' it on its own showing without needing recourse to formal authority.

(i) *Legal and kerygmatic preconditions for reception*

Whether a council is accepted as legitimate on the strength of its material or its formal authority, still the process of reception is not at an end. More is involved. Reception, as an act of the whole Church, presupposes first of all the promulgation and proclamation of the council throughout the world. The Emperor and the Bishop of Rome, but also all the bishops of the imperial Church, had a decisive part to play. We can call this promulgation and proclamation the 'legal' and 'kerygmatic' pre-conditions or reception. By studying this proclamation we shall be able to see how Emperor, Pope and bishops themselves understood the conciliar decision of Chalcedon and thus how they have 'received' it intellectually, or how they went on to interpret it beyond what the Fathers of the Council themselves perhaps intended by it.

Even on the level of proclamation the language of Chalcedon, which came into being through an amalgamation of various traditions, encountered obstacles. It collided with traditions and 'language games' which were tied to a region and which provided no basis for reaching an understanding of it. Already at Chalcedon itself the 'language of two natures' was confronted with the 'language of one nature', and this confrontation was intensified in the provinces of the East. The conflict and the rupture were inevitable, since no one managed to uncover the common content of faith lying behind the forms of language which were so various and contradictory. To have been in a position to analyse the formula of faith on the basis of the distinction between language and content would have required theological reflection on the kerygmatic proclamation and its formulas.

Unfortunately, the training required for this was present in very few cases. Consequently the unity of belief which at that time actually existed beneath the various formulations could not be indicated. For this reason it happened that more and more it was simply authority, the Emperor's and the Pope's, that was brought into the fray to carry through the 'reception' of Chalcedon. In most parts of the imperial Church, however, the proclamation of the Council's decisions was accepted without particular difficulty. The faith of Chalcedon, already in being *de facto*, was 'received' as the kerygma of the Council.

A particular circumstance demands closer attention. Chalcedon was, like all ecumenical councils of the time, a synod of the imperial Church. The decisions of a council became imperial law. How does one assess this fact in the reception of Chalcedon? Does it mean that an authority is brought into play which has not competence in matters of faith and acts simply out of considerations of power? Would Nicaea, Ephesus and Chalcedon have been enforced without the help of the imperial Church or political pressure? This factor has been rated so highly by some ecclesiastical historians and historians of doctrine that the whole achievement of the Council's decisions and consequently of the christological dogma has been made to depend on it. We must bring the question into the open, even if for our period, i.e. for the post-Chalcedonian age, it is simplified by the following consideration. Imperial power or politics worked to a great extent against, rather than for, the Council from the moment the Emperor realised that its formula of faith was not furthering the unity of Christians, but serving rather to divide them. It was only during this struggle, waged especially by the Roman Pontiffs against the Emperors, that the purely ecclesiastical responsibility for the preaching of the faith became properly clear. So long as the system of the imperial Church carried the Council, this ecclesiastical responsibility was camouflaged rather than brought into the limelight. In any case we shall have to consider what significance, positive or negative, the structure of the imperial Church had on the *reception* of the Council's decisions and its character. In doing this we can outline briefly once more the rôle of politics in the *production* of the formula of faith.

(ii) *The reception of the Council of Chalcedon in theological reflection*

A new phase in the reception or intellectual assimilation of the Council is marked by the philosophical and theological reflection on the formula and doctrine of the Fourth General Council. It was evoked by the open opposition of Monophysite and Diphysite formulas and traditions. Here an early type of 'scholasticism' came into being, the function of which must be judged in its entire course of development. What service did it render to the mutual understanding of the divided parties or to the deepening of the christological understanding of faith within the Church? Fresh research since about 1909, which was able to elucidate this process accurately, has also been able to stimulate more recent christology; above all it has opened up the possibility for ecumenical discussion to be resumed with the Churches that broke away after Chalcedon.[5] Perhaps the most important result of the trinitarian, christological 'scholasticism' of the fifth and sixth centuries was the discovery of the concept of 'person', which was highly fruitful not only for theology but also for philosophy and the history of thought. In the discussion about the fullness of Jesus' humanity, or about the 'one' or 'two' wills in Christ, or about the one or two modes of operation in him, important anthropological problems came to be spoken about. Then for the first time the theme of the 'autonomy' of created being in concurrence and cohesion with divine being made itself heard. Thus the development of the fifth and sixth centuries should not be assessed simply as a 'scholastic' aberration of patristic theology.

(iii) *The spiritual reception of the doctrine of Chalcedon*

Even the most abstract and speculative theology must be in the service of an understanding of the faith, and ultimately of the life of the Church. This life unfolds itself, together with the liturgical and sacramental life, in the domain of piety or of spirituality. Our question is whether there is a form of devotion to Christ and of mysticism in relation to Christ which is inspired and engendered by Chalcedon, or, perhaps we should say, by the portrait of Christ which it presented. A history of christological doctrine cannot baulk this problem, even if, with A. von Harnack, one regards it as already settled by the very nature of the Chalcedonian formula of faith. According to him Chalcedon

sounded the death-knell for the faith of the Eastern Church. Its four bald, negative determinations—'unmingled, unchangeable, indivisible, inseparable'—with which everything is supposed to be said, are, according to the sentiment of the classic theologians of the Greeks, profoundly irreligious. They lack warm concrete substance; they make the bridge from earth to heaven into a line narrower than the hair on which the votary of Islam one day hopes to enter paradise.[6]

[5] See *Konzile und die Ökumenische Bewegung*, ed. by L. Vischer = *StudÖR* 5 (Genf 1968); *EcumRev* 22(1970) nr. 4.
[6] Cf. CCT I [1]483; I[2] 545.

An answer to such a judgement cannot be given, in the way that von Harnack does, purely on the basis of the formula. The *whole* train of development after Chalcedon must be examined for the force which it exerted as an inspiration of christological spirituality. By this approach one can remain completely open to the possibility that it was not theology which influenced piety, but that on the contrary a fervent religious tradition had lent a certain Cyrillian depth to strict Chalcedonian christology. Perhaps the best answer to the question between Chalcedonian christology and spirituality is to be found in Maximus the Confessor, in whom the whole spiritual tradition of the Greeks lives afresh and is reconciled with the christology of Chalcedon. This enquiry might well be extended to the question about a wider cultural influence on the part of the Council—for instance on sacred art, or even on the Byzantine political conception of the imperial Church, and lastly on the Byzantine image of the world. Critical examination is of course needed before we can venture on such perspectives. In such a venture one has to be on one's guard against treading the dangerous path of forcing a system on the theology of history. It is only too easy to discover the 'unmingled' and 'inseparable' of Chalcedon everywhere and to make them the master-key which will unlock all theological and philosophical secrets. All the same the relation between God(head) and man(hood) in Christ as understood by Chalcedon is the model and supreme case of the relationship between 'God' and the 'world' in general—a matter which had already come under debate at Nicaea in the face of Arianism. Finally, Christianity itself intends to be and to offer a *Weltanschauung*. Is not therefore the doctrine of the incarnation, beside and together with the Christian belief in creation, the foundation-stone of this?

(b)   *The question of the hermeneutics of the Chalcedonian statement*

The Graeco-Byzantine christology or the christology of the early Church seems to us today as strange as the world of that time, which rises before us only in the pages of our history books, out of the documentary remains that have come down to us. Is the theological content of the Chalcedonian statement so closely bound up with the means of theological expression conditioned by that period, especially with the language of Greek philosophy, that when we strip off its linguistic and conceptual dress the content itself is lost? The question is not a new one. Under the slogan of the 'Hellenisation of Christianity' it has a history of hundreds of years behind it; and it presents itself today in all its urgency under the heading of 'hermeneutics'.[7] It is a question of the 'historicity' of revelation and the truth of salvation in their broadest aspects, as conditioned by language and concept, by man's picture of the world and his outlook on it. The urgency is more than ever apparent owing to the much-invoked change from the 'object' to the 'subject', which seems to bar access, once and for all, to the theology of the early Church, especially for the period with which we are dealing here. In fact, with post-Chalcedonian christology we stand at the peak of the process in which Greek ideas and Hellenistic belief in an 'objective' world were taken over. This poses two questions. 1) Was the original kerygma preserved intact at Chalcedon? 2) Is this original kerygma, *by virtue of* Chalcedon, binding on us too? In other words, given that the original Christian kerygma was embedded in such a time-bound system of concepts and picture of the world, and insofar as this was not already a definitive falsification of it, is it still possible for us today to analyse this embedded kerygma in such a way that we can salvage something permanent in it for *our* 'system'? Does the urgency of the hermeneutical problem today mean that the 'conditioned nature' of the theology of the post-Chalcedonian period is to be regarded in such a way that its positive value for us is to be set at zero? The answer to such questions presupposes a discussion of the problem of hermeneutics in general, and we cannot go into it here. Moreover, there is at present no unified position, whether in Protestant or in Catholic theology. Certain guiding principles which we shall follow here may be indicated. 1. We admit the relativity of linguistic and conceptual expression which attends any view of the person of Christ. We want to be open for the 'historicity' of the doctrine about Christ wherever it is determinable. It must be possible, however, to recognise the Church's *conviction of faith* behind the time-bound form and the historically conditioned picture of the world. 2. The theology of that time even has a certain value in helping us to perceive the difference between 'content' and 'form' in the statement about Christ, viz. in the dispute between two dialectically opposed theologies, whose common intention became clear in the course of debate, despite all the antithesis of formulas. Some spoke of 'one' nature, others professed 'two'. Yet for both sides there was one Christ, true God and true man, undivided and unmingled. Just because this common content of faith, though it exhibited widely differing nuances and accents, could be detected beneath mutually exclusive formulas, the difference between language or expression and the intended content was brought to the awareness of theologians.

[7] Cf. A. Grillmeier, 'Moderne Hermeneutik und altkirchliche Christologie', idem, *Mit ihm und in ihm* ([2]1978) 489–582.

Thus for the first time it became possible to gain a certain 'distance' from the formulas, as had happened similarly at the Synod of Alexandria in 362. 3. These historical observations deserve to be gathered carefully, for with them is addressed the current question concerning whether the Chalcedonian formula is capable of change. For it is precisely now that the suitability of concepts is being discussed. 4. Our prime task throughout shall be to arrive at the permanent 'meaning' of the post-Chalcedonian development, i.e. its positive contribution to the Church's statement about Christ. This lies assuredly not in any 'scientific' product of men's labours at that time, but in the 'understanding of faith' which must be sought behind all forms of time-bound expressions.

3. The 'Epochs' of the Development after Chalcedon or the Question of Establishing 'Periods'

Our task is to investigate all the factors or causes of development after Chalcedon and to establish what changes they produced in the doctrine relating to Christ. These factors include the influence of Popes and bishops, Emperors and theologians, the local Churches with their monks and laity. According as the various groups move into the foreground or recede from it, the more significant the realities they establish are for the destiny of Chalcedonian faith, the more they characterise the individual phases or segments of this history.[8] But first there are two interlinked questions to be asked. 1. How long, in a strict sense, does the discussion of the Chalcedonian *formula* or the validity of the *Council* as such continue? 2. How long is it a question of the christological *doctrine* as such, even if Chalcedon is not at issue in a particular way? The immediate aftermath of the Council of 451 lasts just as long as the formula or the validity of the Council as a whole is still expressly under debate. From this point of view the Second Council of Constantinople (553) constitutes a marker; for between 451 and 553 nothing else is at issue but the formula of Chalcedon. Since, however, the Council of 553 was contested precisely on the score of its stance on Chalcedon, the aftermath of this Synod too belongs to that of Chalcedon itself. Only after the later dispute, which specially affected the West up to the death of Gregory the Great (604), had been settled, did the discussion about the validity of Chalcedon come to a stop. The answer to the second question includes, in the East, the Monothelite and Monenergist struggle, with its various phases and councils; in the West, Adoption-

---

[8] On this problem see the collection of studies edited by P. E. Hübinger, *Zur Frage der Periodengrenze zwischen Altertum und Mittelalter* = WdF LI (Darmstadt 1969).

ism in Spain and the reaction to it in the Frankish kingdom are also to be included. It is true that in the seventh century in the disputes about the 'one' or the 'two wills' (or energies) in Christ the Council of Chalcedon becomes the starting-point and the norm of the solution, particularly through Maximus the Confessor; certainly through the teaching of the 'one *energeia*' the Chalcedonians and the Monophysites ought to be reconciled. But it is not once again a question of the acceptance or rejection of the 'formula' of 451. Nevertheless we have to do here with a new phase of the Chalcedonian 'doctrine'. For at this stage, against the illogicality of the Monothelites, the fundamental principles of Chalcedon, which concerned only the person of Jesus Christ and the relation of divine and human nature in this person, are extended to the question of the will and of activity. Considerably more tenuous is the link to Chalcedon in the crisis in the West, precipitated by the Spanish Adoptionists.

So much for a first general view of the epochs and phases marking the period of the christological history which we are to explore. In the years from 451 to 680–1 in the East and to around 794 (the Council of Frankfurt) in the West the christological problem is, albeit with unequal intensity, the almost exclusive topic of debate. During this period we can roughly distinguish two major epochs. 1. The age of the immediate discussion about the formula of Chalcedon and about the validity of the Fourth General Council. It embraces also the stages before and after the Council of Constantinople in 553, approximately to the death of Gregory the Great (604). 2. The time when the question of christology (or more accurately of the 'person of Jesus Christ') was broadened to that of the 'two wills' and the divine and human modes of operation in Christ, known to us as the Monothelite and Monenergetic struggle: this broadly covers the seventh century. The eighth century witnesses the so-called Adoptionist controversy. This was confined to the West and had nothing to do with the problem of the seventh century. Though it can point to a real connexion with Ephesus and Chalcedon, it arose and died down under no special influence from the East. It can be reckoned as a side-issue rather than a sequel. The iconoclastic struggle of the eighth century in the East is the true sequel, reminiscent in some ways of the christological warfare of past centuries. There emerges, above all, the figure of the theologian who aimed at a first synthesis of Greek theology and consequently also of christology: John Damascene. The first and second epochs are divided by a cataclysmic event of enormous consequence, the Arab invasion. This was to be of great moment for the Churches that broke away after Chalcedon, and was not without its effect on christological development in Spain. Volume II of our work will deal with the period from 451 to 604, and Volume III with the years 604-c. 800.

The two epochs fall into unequal subdivisions; they also differ in their importance. From 451 to 604 (if we may span so wide an interval) the strife was more fierce, more concerned with fundamental issues and more kaleidoscopic than it was in the East in the seventh century or in the West in the eighth century. Christologically and ecclesiologically the basic principles of Christianity were at stake, if still within an imperial Church framework. The year 519 is an important dividing-point. This is the year in which, after a period of uninterrupted crisis, the validity of Chalcedon was confirmed, following the death of the Emperor Anastasius I (518), through the recognition of Pope Hormisdas' formula by Justin I. In the period between 451 and 519 we shall see the intense struggle between Popes and Emperors over the interpretation of Chalcedon, which finally led to the so-called Acacian schism between Rome and Constantinople; we shall witness the massive development of '*mia physis* theology' under the leadership of the foremost theologian of the age, the Patriarch Severus of Antioch, but also the first powerful efforts from the pro-Chalcedonian theologians. The Emperor Justinian and his wife Theodora, with her Monophysite sympathies, usher in the second phase of this first epoch; the convulsion of the empire by the 'quarrel about the Three Chapters and Origenism' reached its climax at the Council of 553. Between a strict Chalcedonian and a strict Cyrillo-Monophysite christology there now stands the so-called 'Neo-Chalcedonianism', which set out to be a mediating theology, and which had already taken shape during the first phase before 519. At the same time the Monophysite party was able to build up its own hierarchy. The split in the Byzantine imperial Church was complete, and no imperial politics could now reverse the situation, however the world empire of Rome might make a last grand political bid for unity at the time of the conquests of Belisarius and Narses. After 553 the West went off on its own way 'theologically'. Between 553 and 604 we find the West united in a single-minded but uncomplicated trust in Chalcedon. The shift of the Monothelite problem from East to West around 649 was only a minor interlude. In the East John Damascene will at last achieve a relatively sober *dénouement* after two centuries of heated strife; Thomas Aquinas will one day be his interpreter to the West. The most brilliant figure of the Greek Church, Maximus the Confessor, had lost his tongue not only in a physical sense. His writings, which are the most inspired expression of Chalcedonian christology, the supreme synthesis of the Christian Greek spirit, passed into oblivion after his condemnation.

SECTION TWO

THE PRESENT STATE OF RESEARCH

1. General Studies

For the period of christological teaching with which we are dealing only a few general studies from which we can still work are available. With one exception they have been made obsolete by the progress of research, especially since the oriental sources were opened up and the relevant Byzantine studies inaugurated. The best attempt at a comprehensive treatment is still J. A. Dorner, *Entwicklungsgeschichte der Lehre von der Person Christi von den ältesten Zeiten bis auf die neueste*, Part II: *Die Lehre von der Person Christi vom Ende des vierten Jahrhunderts bis zur Gegenwart* (Berlin 1853). The post-Chalcedonian age is presented in the second section: *Die Sicherstellung und folgerichtige Durchführung der chalcedonischen Lehre von den zwei Naturen. Vom chalcedonischen bis zum Frankfurter Concil 794* (pp. 150–330). Chapter 1 of the second section deals with Diphysitism in its struggle with Monophysitism (451–553); chapter 2 of this section reviews the Monothelite controversies of the seventh century. It also includes John of Damascus and the Greek mystics. Chapter 3 treats Adoptionism and the Council of Frankfurt (794).

In substance, the fundamental lines of development, as this stems from the dialectic of 'two natures' and 'one nature', are fairly aptly described; but no complete picture of the groupings of post-Chalcedonian christology emerges. The sources are only slightly evaluated. The assessment of Aristotelianism is questionable. The philosophical background of the development is inadequate. In essential points the work has been superceded by later research into Monophysitism, Monothelitism and Byzantine theology.

2. Special Handbooks on the History of Doctrine

On the whole these are no more helpful than Dorner's work. Here one can name D. Thomasius, *Die christliche Dogmengeschichte als Entwicklungs-Geschichte des kirchlichen Lehrbegriffes*. Volume 1: *Die Dogmengeschichte der alten Kirche. Periode der Patristik*, 2nd edition by N. Bonwetsch (Erlangen 1886). The remarks on the post-Chalcedonian period remain very general (pp. 370–392).

F. Loofs, *Der Leitfaden zum Studium der Dogmengeschichte*, 6th edition by K. Aland (Tübingen 1959) is more thorough, characteristic of the style of the author. §§ 38–40 deal with our period. Unfortunately the new edition does not take into account all the more recent research into Chalcedon, even in the bibliography. Nothing is said about the development of Neo-Chalcedonianism, which is indispensable for a total picture of christology. Even the fundamental works of J. Lebon (the first of which appeared in 1909) are not mentioned. In contrast Leontius of Byzantium, in accordance with the literary-historical assumptions of F. Loofs, is placed at the centre of post-Chalcedonian christology. Yet Loofs perceives the impact after Chalcedon of Cyrillian christology, the characteristic features of which he sees sanctioned for the territories of the empire by Justinian and the Council of 553. Too little attention, however, is paid to development in the West.

A. von Harnack's well-known *Lehrbuch der Dogmengeschichte* Volume 2 (^{5}1931)[9] deals with the Monophysite struggles and the Fifth Council (pp. 400–424), and also with the Monenergist and Monothelite controversies, the Sixth Council and John Damascene (pp. 425–436). Von Harnack emphasises the distinction between the history of doctrine and the history of theology; he excludes the latter from his account (cf. pp. 406 and 407, n. 5). He refers a great deal to the researches of F. Loofs and G. Krüger and their sources (Tillemont, Walch, Gieseler, Dorner, Baur, Hefele). The original sources are not much scrutinised, at any rate when he discusses J. C. Gieseler and his work on the Monophysites. J. Lebon's famous dissertation from the year 1909 was still unknown to Harnack.

A comprehensive survey of our period in the manuals of the history of doctrine which is still most useful has been supplied by R. Seeberg, *Lehrbuch der Dogmengeschichte*, Volume 2: *Die Dogmenbildung in der Alten Kirche* (Erlangen ^{3}1923). By contrast with Harnack, Seeberg arrives at a more positive appraisal of the Council of Chalcedon:

> That the personal unity (in Christ) must not be a merging of the two natures, and that the existence of both natures ought not to annul the unity of the personal life—such was the result of the Synod of Chalcedon. By it not only was Monophysitism driven out of the Church, but the positive problem of how the *one* Christ is to be conceived in his twofold form was deeply stamped into the Church's thinking. Chalcedon maintained the *problem* of christology, but did not remove it. One may compare it to the plan of a building, not to the building itself. It set the task of

---

[9] For a detailed assessment of this work of A. von Harnack and above all of the famous work *Das Wesen des Christentums* (Leipzig 1899/1900; Jubilee edition: Stuttgart 1950) see K. H. Neufeld, *Adolf von Harnack—Theologie als Suche nach der Kirche* = KKTS 41 (Paderborn 1977), esp. 66.84. 102–142; idem, *Adolf Harnacks Konflikt mit der Kirche. Weg-Stationen zum 'Wesen des Christentums'* = ITS 4 (Innsbruck 1979).

comprehending the divinity and humanity in Christ as real and yet as a unity but it did not teach how to realise this unity in expression and thought. Again, Chalcedon is to some extent like a result declared in advance, as distinct from the completed balance sheet. Thus it was useful as a criterion for christological speculation, but it could not unite the existing antitheses. It called for union, but did not attain it. However, this is one of those cases, not rare in history, where a good deal less might have been accomplished (266f.).

The books mentioned so far make use of the compendium, still helpful, of C. W. F. Walch, *Entwurf einer vollständigen Historie der Ketzereien, Spaltungen und Religionsstreitigkeiten, bis auf die Zeiten der Reformation*, parts 6, 7 and 8 (Leipzig 1773, 1776, 1778). In our work too the various parts will be made use of in the appropriate places. One is greatly helped by the excellent posthumous work of W. Elert, edited by W. Maurer and E. Bergsträsser, *Der Ausgang der altkirchlichen Christologie. Eine Untersuchung über Theodor von Pharan und seine Zeit als Einführung in die alte Dogmengeschichte* (Berlin 1957). The focus in these collected monographs is on the period of Monothelitism. Nevertheless the first part contains surveys on the history of the problem which to a large extent depict the development after Chalcedon in its fundamental features.

In an extensive joint effort the attempt was made in A. Grillmeier-H. Bacht (ed.), *Das Konzil von Chalkedon. Geschichte und Gegenwart*. Vol. I–III (Würzburg [1]1951–1954; [5]1979) to work out the significance of the Council from the point of view of dogmatic theology and Church history. The articles in Volumes I and II of this work which deserve our attention will be mentioned in the relevant sections. A synthesis from the standpoint of Byzantine theology and Orthodox tradition is now furnished by J. Meyendorff, *Le Christ dans la théologie byzantine* (Paris 1969). The question of the person of Christ is not consistently pursued, but for all that it is inserted into wider perspectives (Ps.-Dionysius, spiritual teaching, cosmic dimensions of salvation in Maximus the Confessor, the iconoclastic controversy).

In the more recent general accounts of the history of doctrine—for instance, B. Lohse, *Epochen der Dogmengeschichte* (Stuttgart [1]1963, [4]1978) and J. Pelikan, *The Christian Tradition. A History of the Development of Doctrine. Vol. 1* (Chicago/London 1971) 266–277—naturally only a very brief survey is given of the period after Chalcedon.

In A. M. Ritter, 'Dogma und Lehre der Alten Kirche', C. Andresen (Ed.), *Handbuch der Dogmen- und Theologiegeschichte. Bd. 1* (Göttingen 1983), esp. 270–283, the reception of the Council of Chalcedon up to the Sixth Ecumenical Council of Constantinople (Constantinople III [680/681]) is treated rather in a series of highlights. The most important milestones and controversies are certainly expounded, but what is principally lacking is an analysis of the further penetration of the Chalcedonian concept of hypostasis, which is imperative for an assessment of the later christological and trinitarian discussions (Maximus Confessor, Leontius of Byzantium, Dionysius the Areopagite).

The feature which characterises our attempt, in contrast to the works mentioned, consists in the fact that we do not pursue the whole breadth of the development of Christian faith and doctrine, but only that development which centres on the person of Jesus of Nazareth, while we pay attention as well to what radiates from that centre. To begin with, it is absolutely essential to draw a total picture of post-Chalcedonian christology up to 800, because before the publication of modern editions of sources such a picture could only be distorted and fragmented. Even today this deficiency is not yet completely remedied. A decisive gain during our century is the opening up of the *oriental* sources, which for the first time makes something like an *ecumenical* history of faith possible, insofar as it is only now that the individual Churches can be depicted in the tradition which is proper to each of them. With the growth of the ecumenical spirit and dialogue in our time we have also acquired the spiritual attunement to experience the faith of the separated Churches from within, and only from that position to pass judgement on their mutual closeness or distance. With such a procedure oriented to *reconstruction* we abandon the objectifying point of view of an observer in favour of the perspective of one who participates, at least virtually, in the discussions and controversies in the individual Church regions and periods. With J. Habermas[10] we would like to consider this approach as an hermeneutical principle. Unity and differences are not grasped in a presentation which abstracts, but from the concrete history of the individual Church regions in East and West. Admittedly this cannot happen without some overlapping and repetition. In this way, how-

---

[10] J. Habermas, 'Objektivismus in den Sozialwissenschaften', idem, *Zur Logik der Sozialwissenschaften* (Frankfurt ^{5}1982) 541–607: 'For meanings, whether they be embodied in actions, institutions, products of labour, words, contexts that come about through co-operation, or documents, can only be disclosed "from within". Symbolically pre-structured reality forms a universe which remains hermetically sealed, even unintelligible, to the eyes of an observer. The social world in which we live opens itself only to a subject who makes use of his competence to speak and act by assuming interpersonal relationships. He gains entry by reason of the fact that he participates, at least virtually, in the communications that take place between members, and so he himself becomes a member, at least potentially' (ibid., 550). Cf. on this theme also idem, *Theorie des kommunikativen Handelns* (Frankfurt 1981) Vol. 1, 152–203; Vol. 2, 182–228; idem, 'Rekonstruktive vs. verstehende Sozialwissenschaften', idem, *Moralbewußtsein und kommunikatives Handeln* (Frankfurt 1983) 29–52; idem, *Vorstudien und Ergänzungen zur Theorie des kommunikativen Handelns* (Frankfurt 1984) 11–126, 363–379. On the theological relevance of this approach, cf. also H.-J. Höhn, *Kirche und kommunikatives Handeln. Studien zur Theologie und Praxis der Kirche in der Auseinandersetzung mit den Sozialtheorien Niklas Luhmanns und Jürgen Habermas'* (Frankfurt 1985) 159–163.

ever we want at the same time to let each of the old Oriental Churches know how we in the West think about them, and thus make a contribution to ecumenical understanding.

It is against this background that the author wishes the following studies on the history of the impact of the Council of Chalcedon to be read, then also as a contribution to the contemporary discussion about the presuppositions for and conditions of a proper inculturation of the kerygma of Christ into the Churches of the 'Third World'.[11] In our survey of the period after Chalcedon we are interested in determining, as comprehensively as is historically possible, the relevant factors inside and outside the church, the most important supporters and opponents, centres and forms of development which had a lasting influence on the reception of the Council's doctrinal definition. But this is not our sole concern. We are equally interested in the theological question, how the Church's preaching can hold its ground in circumstances which are always different and in which the cultural, social and political factors are constantly changing, with the question how this can happen without the Gospel experiencing assimilation of such a kind that would endanger its identity, or vice versa without the Christian faith taking root in such a way that would lead to an uprooting of cultures which had previously been intact. On account of remarkable analogies with this contemporary problem it is precisely the struggles hither and thither about the dogma of Chalcedon that offer a particularly rich area of work. Here the border lines of such an inculturation can be ascertained in exemplary fashion. It is an inculturation in which the Church's preaching and man's response in faith (e.g. in doctrine, liturgy, spirituality and discipline), bearing the stamp of a particular culture or becoming concrete in it, are so enacted that what is common and binds them together comes to the fore, in spite of and against the background of the incontrovertible differences.

---

[11] Cf. from the constantly growing literature on this topic: J. Mühlsteiger, 'Rezeption—Inkulturation—Selbstbestimmung. Überlegungen zum Selbstbestimmungsrecht kirchlicher Gemeinschaften', ZKTh 105(1983) 261–289; H. B. Meyer, 'Zur Frage der Inkulturation der Liturgie', ZKTh 105(1983) 1–31; H. Waldenfels, 'Von der Weltmission zur Kirche in allen Kulturen', Die Kirche Christi—Enttäuschung und Hoffnung (Im Auftrag des Direktoriums der Salzburger Hochschulwochen hrsg. v. P. Gordan)(Graz-Kevelaer 1982) 303–350; Z. Alszeghy, 'Cultural adaptation as an internal requirement of faith', Greg 63(1982) 61–85; A. A. Roest Crollius, 'Inculturation and the meaning of culture', Greg 61(1980) 253–274; idem, 'What is so new about inculturation? A concept and its implications', Greg 59(1978) 721–738; A. Sanon, 'The Universal Christian Message in Cultural Plurality', Conc 135(5/1980) 81–95; D. Amalorpavadass, 'Evangélisation et culture', Conc (éd. fran.) 134 (avril 1978) 81–92.

SECTION THREE

AD FONTES

THE FORMENGESCHICHTE OF THE CHALCEDONIAN AND POST-CHALCEDONIAN SOURCES OF CHRISTOLOGY UP TO JOHN DAMASCENE

If we do not take into account the exodus of the Nestorians, the communal life of the Church had been one up to the Council of Chalcedon. But with this Council a discussion began which not only influenced that communal life, but for the first time made evident the structure of Christian theology as this would be practised at least until the ninth century. Even before the content of this discussion is considered, this twofold effect can be observed in the literary categories involved, i.e. in the *genera litteraria* of the sources, both in their individual form and in their mutual relationships. Certainly many of these genres had their origin in the period before Chalcedon, particularly in the fourth century, the richest catchment-area for theological thought in the following period. In this regard the fourth century was even more important than Cyril of Alexandria (d. 444), who, with the stature that he attained in the Nestorian dispute and with the dynamism that radiated from him, determined in commanding fashion from that time on theological and christological discussion. Instrumental in this was a particular *genus litterarium*, to the creation of which Cyril himself had contributed, the florilegium.

When we illustrate the new situation with regard to sources, it must not be forgotten that Holy Scripture, particularly the New Testament with its christology or major christological passages, always exercised its influence as well. But no new exegetical method was discovered. It was only that the proof from Scripture acquired younger siblings who wanted to sit at the same theological table and seemed for a while to demand the larger portion, which, however, must never be claimed from the 'first-born'.

As the first *novum* we may cite the synodal *acta*, which as a literary genre have their *Sitz im Leben* in the character given to the early Church synods by the fact that they were synods of the imperial Church. Because with Chalcedon these *acta* are preserved in a fullness not previously known, if we leave aside the sparse records of the events at the Council of Ephesus (431), they were able to display their efficacy as such in the Church's own theological life. Their effectiveness was strengthened, because in the theological dispute concerning the decisions of the Council there were created around the *acta* reference works with relevant texts, works which E. Schwartz appositely characterised as 'publizistische Sammlungen'[*]. In the dispute about the Council of Nicaea (325) Athanasius of Alexandria had already begun with such documentation. The clarification of the proceedings of the Council of 381 has demanded much effort. Cf. E. Chrysos, 'Die Akten des Konzils von Konstantinopel I (381)', *Romanitas-Christianitas. Untersuchungen zur Geschichte und Literatur der römischen Kaiserzeit* = FS. J. Straub (ed. G. Wirth) (Berlin-New York 1982) 426–435. The evaluation of such works is not easy, as they are dominated more or less by the selective or even 'fashioning' spirit of the parties concerned; but such evaluation produces great results. A helpful key to this is provided by E. Chrysos in his recent article: 'Konzilsakten und Konzilsprotokolle vom 4. bis 7. Jahrhundert', *AHC* 15 (1983) 30–40, which sets the tone for further research. He emphasises the fundamental difference of *acta* material in conciliar *acta* and minutes of councils, in accordance with the division of synods into legal and non-legal proceedings. This distinction is to be respected, even when in what follows we speak simply of 'synodal *acta*'.

The synopses of councils already belong to the genre of historiography of councils.

The next group to concern us is works of church history, which is not newly created as a genre, but which certainly found a new area of application. To this category also belong chronicles and hagiographical works dealing either with individual lives or collections of short biographies, the heroes and heroines of which represent the theological parties extremely effectively and in a manner close to the people. The discovery of a new oil-field in our technological era can be compared to the opening up of the rich area of the florilegia, i.e. the anthologies garnered from the writings of the Fathers, which became the fashion in the conciliar era we are considering. More and more they shaped the structure of theological proof. For this reason it is important here to show the extent of this literary genre so to speak materially, because only in this way will the relationship of the proof from Scripture and the Fathers be discernible. Related to these genres are the so-called catenae, i.e. collections of exegetical passages from the Fathers which present a new presence of the Bible

---

[*] Throughout this volume we shall retain the German expression, both because the expression itself has become a technical term and because a concise English equivalent of the adjective used is not available. The sense in which it is employed by Schwartz to describe these collections of documents relating to a synod or council indicates that these documents were journalistically selected and arranged in such a way that they could serve as propaganda for the politics of a particular religious party or group. *Translators' Note.*

in the authority of the interpretation of the Fathers. Admittedly in many respects they could dry up the initiative of exegetical efforts in a later period, if not simply cause it to die out.

From mutual polemic the catalogues of heretics and heresies grew; more than any other genre mentioned here these ran the danger of becoming clichés. We conclude with the collections of definitions of concepts (*definitiones*), which in as far as the history of method is concerned have a special significance, as, in accord with the value that is placed on them, they make fruitful the relationship of theology and philosophy, or the relationship between the proof *ex auctoritate S. Scripturae sive Patrum* and the *argumentum ex ratione*, or else dissolving this relationship could place it, together with the genre of the *aporiai* (ἐπαπορήματα), in question.

PART I

Collections of synodal *acta* and 'publizistische Sammlungen'. Cf. CPG IV: Concilia; Altaner-Stuiber, *Patrologie*, 9.A., VII, §§58–64.

'Since the Church, when it was assumed into the organism of the empire, became an institution of the empire, it became the custom to take official minutes of the proceedings of the synods in the same way as the proceedings of the Senate, the courts, the imperial consistory, etc.' (E. Schwartz, *ZNW* 25(1926) 44). It is a long way, however, from the taking of minutes of the *gesta* to their being worked up into collections. To be distinguished from collections with the synodal *gesta* as their main object are the 'publizistische Sammlungen', which present an extended documentation.

(A) Collections of synodal *acta*
I. Collections made by orthodox Chalcedonians

1. We possess an excellent edition in the *Acta Conciliorum Oecumenicorum*, begun and continued by E. Schwartz and finished by J. Straub, *Concilium Universale Constantinopolitanum sub Iustiniano habitum* = ACO IV, 1 (Berolini 1971). This edition is continued by the 'Kommission für die Herausgabe einer 2. Serie der Acta conciliorum oecumenicorum', under the direction of H.-G. Beck, B. Bischoff, H. Hunger and J. Straub. In this series has appeared the critical edition of the Lateran synod of 649, *Concilium Lateranense a. 649 celebratum*, ACO II, 1, ed. R. Riedinger, (Berlin-New York 1984). The same editor will also publish the *acta* of the second great dyothelete synod of Constantinople (680/1).

On the edition of E. Schwartz: In his edition Schwartz was the first to emphasise that the conciliar *acta* from Ephesus (431) to Constantinople (553), and beyond that, are transmitted in collections which, like their translations, can betray a different stance on the decisions of a council. Compilation, editing and adaptation of the documents, the person of the compiler, their place of use constitute history. For this reason the collections as such must be edited and not torn apart. See the excellent analysis of the complete work of Schwartz by R. Schieffer, *Index Generalis Tomorum I–IIII*, pars prima: Indices Codicum et Auctorum (Berolini 1974); CPG IV—a survey of all the works published by Schwartz on the history of councils (besides ACO) in idem, *Gesammelte Schriften* Bd. 4 (Berlin 1960) 329–344; see ibid. 343–344 for a table of contents of ACO, as far as published at the time. For criticism of Schwartz' edition see V. Grumel, *ByzZ* 35 (1935) 412–423; 38 (1938) 439–451; P. Peeters, *AnBoll* 1932–1934; 1936–1938. For the period after Chalcedon the synods of Constantinople in the years 519, 536 and 553 are particularly important (see Schieffer, Indices, 518–520).

On the edition of the second series of ACO see R. Riedinger, 'Aus den Akten der Lateran-Synode von 649', *ByzZ* 69 (1976) 17–38: a study which even on its own is a testimony to what significance knowledge of the *acta* of a council came into existence can have for the council itself. See especially 37 f.; idem, 'Die Lateinischen Handschriften der Akten des VI. Konzils (680/681) und die Unzialkorrekturen im Cod. Vat. Regin. Lat. 1040', *Römische Historische Mitteilungen* 22 (Rom-Wien 1980) 37–49; idem, 'Zwei Briefe aus den Akten der Lateransynode von 649', *JÖB* 29 (1980) 37–59. The edition of this second series has begun with ACTA CONCILIORUM OECUMENICORUM *sub auspiciis Academiae Scientiarum Bavariae edita Series secunda Volumen primum. Concilium Lateranense a. 649 celebratum* edidit Rudolf Riedinger (Berolini 1984). On the edition see A. Grillmeier, *TheolPhil* 60 (1985) 289–293. In the third volume of our work we shall have recourse to this series.

2. Older editions of conciliar *acta* and their significance

Their value varies greatly. In part, too, they can conceal rathei than reveal important data concerning the composition and transmission of the synodal *acta*. They take their beginning with J. Merlin in the year 1524 (Paris) and are continued by Crabbe, Surius, Nicolini and Bollanus, Baluze, Hardouin and Coleti, down to the *Sacrorum Conciliorum nova et amplissima Collectio* of Joannes Dominicus Mansi, 31 vols, published in Florence 1759–1798.

A useful history of these editions is given by H. Quentin, *Jean-Dominique Mansi et les grandes Collections conciliaires. Étude d'Histoire littéraire suivie d'une correspondance inédite de Baluze avec le Cardinal Casanate et de lettres de Pierre Morin, Hardouin, Lupus et Montfaucon* (Paris 1900). Important and sometimes sharp criticism is contained in the *Praefationes* of the ACO by E. Schwartz. To use the old editions (Mansi) the reader should consult the *Tabulae* Comparationis Veterum Editionum et Regestorum in R. Schieffer, *Index Generalis Tomorum* I–IIII, pars prima = ACO IV 3, pars prima, 539–579.

The following works offer a selection of texts in accordance with recent critical research:

(a) *Enchiridion Symbolorum Definitionum et Declarationum de rebus fidei et morum* quod primum edidit H. Denzinger et quod funditus retractavit auxit notulis ornavit A. Schönmetzer S. J., ed. 36 emendata (Barcelona-Freiburg-Rom 1976); (b) *Conciliorum*

Oecumenicorum Decreta curantibus J. Alberigo, J. A. Dossetti, P.–P. Joannou, C. Leonardi, P. Prodi consultante H. Jedin, ed. 3 (Bologna 1973).

3. Modern translations of conciliar *acta*

Éphèse et Chalcédoine. Actes des Conciles. Traduits par A.-J. Festugière (Textes-Dossiers-Documents 6) (Paris 1982); *Actes du Concile de Chalcédoine. Sessions III–IV* (La Définition de la Foi). Traduction française par A.-J. Festugière. Préface par Henry Chadwick (Cahiers d'Orientalisme IV) (Genève 1983).

II. Old translations of synodal *acta* from 431 to 553

That the *acta* of councils also in themselves could be meant as propaganda will become clear through a large enterprise, the Latin translations of the *acta*, which were brought about by the so-called Three Chapters controversy, or at least received their definitive form from it. Since the investigations of E. Schwartz there are not two, but three forms which are to be distinguished:

1. In Constantinople there came into being the *versio antiqua* of the *acta* (c. 550), as it was called by S. Baluzius (Siglum Φ^a). By comparison with the Greek *acta* we find here no collection of letters before the first session and after the second session. Session XVI is also missing. Here the Latin translation of the *Canones Chalcedonenses* of Dionysius Exiguus is used, traces of which can be identified in Pope Pelagius II, Gregory I, Martin I, in Gaul during the time of Hinkmar of Rheims, and also in Thomas Aquinas (ACO II 3, 1, VII–VIII).

2. The *Versio antiqua correcta* (Φ^c), besides containing the synodal *acta* (see below), was enriched by the *Epistularum ante gesta collectio* and had a revised text of the *acta* (cf. ACO II 3, 1, VII–VIII).

3. The deacon Rusticus revised this translation in 564 and edited it in the sense that an exemplar of his recension remained in the monastery of the Sleepless Monks in Constantinople, where new copies could be made or the correction of old manuscripts undertaken. The Latin scholia, which Rusticus added to his translation of the *Acta Chalcedonensia*, cited by Schwartz in ACO II 3, 1–3 ad loc., are collected in PLS IV 546–597. The Latin *acta* of Ephesus in 431 also owe their existence to the Three Chapters controversy. These translations are reproduced in the *gesta* in more or less abbreviated form. See the accurate survey and collection of parallel Greek and Latin texts in Schieffer, ACO IV 3, 1, 521–527; CPG 8675–8867.

Besides the Ephesian section of the *Synodicon* of Rusticus = *Collectio Casinensis*, ACO I 3–I 4, we have the *Collectio Palatina* = ACO I 5, 1–215. B. Nisters, TQ 113 (1932) 119–137, wished to place this collection between 500 and 519 and attribute it to one of the Scythian theologians favourable to the *Henoticon* of the Emperor Zeno. Arguments to the contrary in V. Schurr, *Die Trinitätslehre des Boethius im Lichte der 'skythischen Kontroversen'* = FCLDG 18, 1 (Paderborn 1935) 180–181. E. Amann, 'L'affaire Nestorius vue de Rome', RevSR 23 (1949) (5–37 etc.) 8–17, however, extricated elements which we could describe as 'neo-Chalcedonian', and looked for the compiler in the sphere of influence of the Scythian monks, taking the *terminus post quem* of the origin as 553. A similar milieu, if a different author, is proposed by him for the *Collectio Turonensis* (*a Rustico Diacono in Casinensem redacta*), ACO I 3, and the *Collectio Veronensis*, ACO I 2 of the *acta* of Ephesus. Amann stresses the strong representation of the Roman Curia (art. cit., 17–23). Here the neo-Chalcedonian additions are missing. For a description of the various collections see Schieffer, ACO IV 3, 1, 80.

III. Synodal *acta* of the Churches which separated after 431 and 451

Prefatory note: on the synodal *acta*, collections of canons and symbols, which are connected with the Council of Nicaea, see Altaner-Stuiber, *Patrologie* §63; further W.-D. Hauschild, 'Die antinizänische Synodalsammlung des Sabinus von Heraklea, in: VigC 24 (1970) 105–126; the counterpart to Athanasius, *De synodis*; instructive document for the self-image of the homoeusian party.

1. The east Syrian (Nestorian) Church

(a) From the *acta* of the Synod of the Katholikos Yahbalaha, dating from the year 420, can be perceived that the east Syrian Church had a kind of *Corpus Iuris* before 410, which, however, consisted of western canons. See below Chabot, 12 f.; Text 276 ff. (French).

(b) Collection of Nestorian synods of dogmatic and canonical content:

J.-B. Chabot, *Synodicon orientale ou Recueil de Synodes Nestoriens* publié, traduit et annoté par J.-B. Chabot (Paris 1902); Syriac text, 17–252; French trans., 253–524; based on the Syriac MS of the B.N. Paris, MS 332 (syr.), and MS K VI, 4, Mus. Borgian., Rome. This collection must have come into being in the early years of the patriarchate of Timothy I (780–823). The last synod to be included in it is that of Ḥenanīsō II (775); the important synod of Timothy (790) does not appear. In total thirteen synods are documented, and the quasi-synod of Barṣawma (484) is mentioned (Chabot 308–309; see further 3ᶜ Partie, I. Appendice, 525–539). The synod of 790: op. cit., Appendice IV, 599–608. Chabot was unaware of the German translation of MS Borg., Rome, by O. Braun, *Das Buch der Synhados* (Stuttgart-Wien 1900), which corresponds to Chabot, 253–524, allowing for the supplements made from B.N. MS syr. 332. Canonical material predominates, but the actual positions of the Nestorian churches are discussed and must be evaluated in our presentation (cf. Chabot's index, 688, *Hérétiques*, where as well as Apollinarians, Eutychians, Severans and Theopaschites, the supporters of Ḥenana appear; *Incarnation*, where also in Chabot's third part solutions to objections against the doctrine of the Nestorians are proffered).

2. The west Syrian (Jacobite) Church

The west Syrian (Jacobite) church had a collection of conciliar canons, which was translated in 501 from the Greek and is transmitted in BM Add. 14.528, ff. 1–151: Wright, *Catalogue* II, 1030–1033, nr. DCCCCVI. The canons preserved are those of Nicaea in 325, Ancyra in 314 (?), Neo-Caesarea (cf. Mansi II 539), Gangra in 343, Antioch in 341, Laodicea (c. 365) (Mansi II 563), Constantinople in 381, Chalcedon in 451—the latter with 27 canons, without the twenty-eighth, which is missing in the Syriac collections. Cf. MS BM Add. 14.529 (seventh/eighth century).

E. Schwartz, 'Die Kanonessammlungen der alten Reichskirche', *Gesammelte Schriften* 4 (Berlin 1960) 159–275, composed in 1936. Further important discoveries have been published by A. Vööbus, *Syrische Kanonessammlungen: Ein Beitrag zur Quellenkunde* I. *Westsyrische Originalurkunden* 1, A–1, B, CSCO 307 and 308 (Subs. 35 and 38) (Louvain 1970); id., *The Synodicon in the West Syrian Tradition* I, CSCO 367 (T), 368 (V) (Louvain 1975). Cf. Introduction to the Synodicon: 6. Legislative Florilegia (see below).

These sources are to be taken into consideration for the recognition of Chalcedon through the inclusion of canons (minus the twenty-eighth); this recognition comes to the fore also in individual Fathers.

(B) 'Publizistische Sammlungen' of the Chalcedonian party

Prefatory note: Since it has only recently been published, we mention here a collection concerned with the Council of Ephesus (431), which was originally composed in Greek at Alexandria soon after the Council, but which was translated around 500 into Ethiopic and is preserved as such. See B. M. Weischer, *Qērellos*, Bd. I, *Afrikanistische Forschungen* (Glückstadt 1973); Bd. III, *Äthiopistische Forschungen* 2 (Wiesbaden 1977); Bd. IV, 1, *Äthiopistische Forschungen* 4 (Wiesbaden 1979). The original collection runs this far. See the survey in *Qērellos* IV, 3 (Wiesbaden 1980) 7, nr. 1–18.

I. *Collectio Novariensis de re Eutychis:* instigated by Leo I in 450: ACO II 2, 1; cf. praef. V–VIII; II 4: praef. XLI; II 3, 1: praef. The Roman archives supplied the documentation.

II. Collections of letters: Leo I had made one or more collections of his own letters which were connected with Chalcedon. Cf. ACO II 4, praef. XXX–XXXI. This, the first collection, contained documents up to 17.8.458. The *Collectio Avellana*, which will be dealt with shortly below, contained later letters of Leo. While the latter is preserved, the other old collections are lost, although they survive in later collections. Cf. ACO II 4, I–XXX; V. Grumel, *ByzZ* 35 (1935) 412–415; 38 (1938) 439–451, concerning the edition of the corresponding Greek collections of letters in ACO II 1, 1 and 2. According to Grumel the Greek translator of Leo's letters had their original and authentic text as his exemplar, but shortened the text and omitted parts of it.

III. *Collectio Vaticana rerum Chalcedonensium:* ACO II 2, 2, 1 [93]–27 [119]. This comes next chronologically, if, as Schwartz believed, it attained its definitive compass only under Pope Hormisdas. Composed for Roman purposes, it contains official letters of emperors, extracts from conciliar *acta* (the second [third], sixth and eighth [seventh] sessions), and five letters to Leo. Julian of Cius and Maximus, Patriarch of Antioch, sent the greater part of the documents to Rome after they had been translated into Latin.

IV. *Collectio Sangermanensis:* ACO II 5. In the first part is contained the important *Codex Encyclius* of Emperor Leo I (457–474) in the Latin translation of Epiphanius (see further below), and in the second part the *Breviarium* of the deacon Liberatus of Carthage: ACO II 5, 98–141 (see below on 'Heresies').

V. *Collectio Veronensis, C. Berolinensis, C. Avellana* (CA): the first two are edited by E. Schwartz, PS3–58, and 60–117; CA: ed. O Guenther, *Epistulae Imperatorum,*

Pontificum, aliorum inde ab a. 367 usque ad a. 553 datae = CSEL 35 (Vindobonae 1895–98). See further ACO II 4, XIV.

The *Coll. Veron.* played its part in the Acacian schism in that it was fiercely written to stir up opposition to the balance of power politics of Pope Anastasius II (496–498), the successor of Gelasius I (492–496), thereby fostering the continuation of the schism. Another collection, which today as such is lost, *Collectio X*, would supplement the *Coll. Veron.*, which was soon enlarged. The existence of X can be postulated from the striking relationship between *Coll. Berol.* and CA, which both drew on X independently. Cf. Schwartz, PS 283 f. with a reconstruction of X. The CA was a private collection from the second half of the sixth century; X was a 'semi-official product of the politics of Hormisdas' (PS 287).

Together with other important documents, the *Coll. Veron.* was later to become an instrument for the schismatic movement in the diocese of Aquilea which was directed against the Council of CP (553). Cf. PS 263, where the documents are enumerated, the MSS of which were produced in Verona in the sixth century. Here we can detect a sharp, pure Chalcedonian tendency, which is directed against the Emperor Justinian. Cf. C. H. Turner, *Ecclesiae occidentalis monumenta iuris antiquissima* (Oxford 1907), vol. 2 I, p. VIII–IX, for a presentation of the struggle of Aquilea and Verona against the Fifth Council. Schwartz, PS 161–170, tabulates the 133 items in the three collections and gives his interpretation of their historical order.

VI. *Collectio Novariensis de uno e trinitate in carne passo*, Cod. XXX, ff. 73–92, of the Biblioteca Capitolare, Novara, ed. E. Schwartz, ACO IV 2, 63–98; cf. Schieffer, ACO IV 3, 1, 30. This is concerned with the Theopaschite controversy and with the advance of neo-Chalcedonian theology towards Rome. On the dating see V. Schurr, *Die Trinitätslehre des Boethius* (see above A II, 3) 185–197. See below under 'Florilegia'.

VII. *Collectio Palatina*, Bibl. Vaticana, Palat. lat. 234, s. IX, ff. 1–93; ACO I 5, 1–215; Fr. Glorie, *Maxentii aliorumque Scytharum monachorum necnon Ioannis Tomitanae urbis episcopi Opuscula*: CCL, vol. LXXXV A (Turnholti 1978); Schieffer, ACO IV 3, 1, 63.

Before the edition of the *Collectio Palatina primaria* by Schwartz: ACO I 5, 1–181, this collection was attributed to Marius Mercator, who wrote between 418 and 431. This John, whose *Disputatio de Nestorianis et Eutychianis* was attached as an appendix, was considered to be Bishop of Tomi, who was still alive after Ephesus (431) and in 449 had subscribed a synod of Constantinople before Bishop Alexander. The collection derives, however, from a Scythian monk of the sixth century, who brought it to a close in the lifetime of a certain Bishop John of Tomi, thus between 530 (534) and 550. In the *Coll. Pal.* this Scythian monk had not only collected the writings of others (Marius Mercator, etc.), but had composed several works himself and added them to the collection:

1. *Disputatio XII capitulorum Cyrilli Alexandrini et sic dictorum Nestorii Anti-anathematismorum*: CCL, vol. LXXXV A, 195–213.
2. A *Refutatio quorundam Nestorii dictorum*: ibid., 214–224.
3. His *Epilogus* concludes the collection: *ibid.*, 231–234. In this, however, he promises to present a *Sermo (disputatio) contra Nestorianos* to Bishop John of Tomi, who is still living. This document, which does not belong to the original *Palatina*, was found and edited for the first time by Dom Morin. The original version was discovered first by R. Weijenborg, who put it at the disposal of Fr. Glorie for the latter's edition (in CCL, vol. LXXXV A, 234–239 both versions are edited, immediately following the *Coll. Pal.* nr. 56–57). The question concerning the *Coll. Pal.* has thus found a definitive explanation.

VIII. *Collectio Sabbaitica contra Acephalos et Origenistas destinata. Insunt Acta Syno-dorum Constantinopolitanae et Hierosolymitanae A. 536*: ACO III (Berlin 1940). The last document included in this collection is the edict of Emperor Justinian against Origen, which was published in February, 542 in Jerusalem and addressed to Patriarch Menas, Pope Vigilius, Patriarch Zoïlus and Patriarch Peter. Cf. praef. ACO III, pp. VIII–XI. This *Collectio* also contains forged letters to Patriarch Peter the Fuller of Antioch, of which there exist three recensions:

(1) the oldest with seven letters, edited (*a*) by Schwartz in PS (1934) based on a *Coll. Vaticana*, pp. 125–140 (Greek); new edition (*b*) in the appendix of the ed. of *Coll. Sabbaitica*: ACO III (1940), 217–231;

(2) Latin edition with eight letters in the CA (Guenther) nr. 71–78;

(3) *Coll. Sabbaitica*: ACO III, 6–25. This is the latest recension, with ten letters.

On the subject, namely the *Trishagion*, see Schwartz, ACO III, praef. XI–XIIII; PS 287–300.

(C) Monophysite and Nestorian 'Publizistische Sammlungen'

I. Monophysites

1. E. Schwartz, 'Codex Vaticanus gr. 1431 eine antichalkedonische Sammlung aus der Zeit Kaiser Zenos' = *AbhMünchAkW*, Philos.-philolog. u. hist. Kl. XXXII. Bd. 6. A (München 1927). Cf. Schieffer, ACO IV 3, 1, 53 (Lit.). According to Schwartz 96, the compiler's attitude is one of 'unconditional condemnation of Chalce-don'. He does not, however, belong to the extremists: 'His way of thinking corres-ponded to the attitude of Peter Mongus, whom the extremists, especially the monks, forced to curse the Synod by threatening him with deposition. Peter, however, had no intention of agreeing to break off communion with the bishops who acknow-ledged the *Henoticon* as norm but who did not curse the Chalcedonian stance'. This was later to bring Severus of Antioch to a harsh judgment on Peter Mongus. The time of composition is therefore the end of the 480's, when Peter had to defend himself against the separatists. According to Schwartz the compiler was 'an Alexan-drian cleric, probably incited by the Patriarch himself' (ibid. 136). The collection is particularly important because it contains three significant documents: the Encycli-cal of the usurper Basiliscus, his Antencyclical, and the Edict of Zeno, which was soon to be described as the *'Henoticon'* (nr. 73–75); see below on Evagrius and Zacharias Rhetor.

2. *The Book of Letters*, in Armenian: Girk' t'łt'oç, Matenagrowt'iwn naxneaç, in the series Sahak mesropean matenadaran, vol. 5 (Tiflis 1901). M. Tallon, *Livre des Lettres (Girk' t'łt'oç). Ier Groupe: Documents concernant les relations avec les Grecs* = Mél. de l'Univ. Saint Joseph, T. XXXII, Fasc. 1 (Beyrouth 1955); L. Frivold, *The Incarnation. A Study of the Doctrine of the Incarnation in the Armenian Church in the 5th and 6th Centuries according to the Book of Letters* (Oslo-Bergen-Tromsø 1981), with partial edition and English translation (eight passages).

II. Nestorians

A Nestorian Collection of Christological Texts, Edited and translated by Luise Abra-mowski & Alan E. Goodman, Vol. I Syriac Text, Vol. II Introduction, Translation and Indexes (Cambridge 1972). This work will be presented below under 'Florilegia'.

(D) Synopses of Councils

Under the term synopses of councils we understand lists of councils or synods presented in summary fashion, in more or less correct historical sequence with a concise summary of their scope.

Lit.: J. A. Munitiz, 'Synoptic Greek Accounts of the Seventh Council', *RevÉtByz* 32 (1974) 147–186; H. J. Sieben, *Die Konzilsidee der Alten Kirche* (Paderborn etc. 1979), Ch. V 344–380: Aspects of the concept of a council according to council synopses from the sixth to the ninth centuries. We shall content ourselves by referring to this work.

The chief work which served as a model is the so-called *Synodicon Vetus*; Sieben, op. cit. 372–373: 'In chronicle style the compiler gathers reports concerning councils, from the Council of the Apostles to that of the ninth century against Photius and Ignatius. Councils before Nicaea are treated more schematically than those after Nicaea . . . What is new here in comparison with previous collections, if one wishes thus to describe the texts discussed in the preceeding extracts, is in the first place the inclusion in principle of heretical collections. In this is undoubtedly manifested a more evident prominence of pure historical interest than in earlier collections. Furthermore to this corresponds also an exceptionally concise, indeed often very pertinent, characterisation of the theme of the council' (373). Edition: *The Synodicon Vetus, Text, Translation, and Notes* by J. Duffy and J. Parker = CFHB, Series Washingtonensis (Dumbarton Oaks, Washington D.C. 1979). In vol. II of our work we are concerned with nr. 92–127, pp. 81–107. See, however, J.-L. van Dieten, 'Synodicon Vetus. Bemerkungen zu einer Neuausgabe', *AHC* 12 (1980) 62–108.

For his work H. J. Sieben investigates three other groups of conciliar compilations:

1. Passages and chapters concerning councils (346–356).
2. Anonymous synopses of councils (356–365).
3. Synopses transmitted under the author's name (365–372).

Part II

Works on Church history and hagiography about or after 451 up to the close of the patristic period.

The significance of these works for our investigation does not need to be stressed. It is important within this genre to specify individual subordinate categories.

Bibliography: F. Winkelmann, 'Geschichtsschreibung in Byzanz', *WZUnivRostock* 18 (1969) 475–481; idem 'Kirchengeschichtswerke im oströmischen Reich', *ByzSlav* 37 (1976) 1–10, 172–190; idem, 'Rolle und Problematik der Kirchengeschichte in der byzantinischen Historiographie', *Klio* 66 (1984) 257–269; J. Irmscher, 'Geschichtsschreiber der Justinianischen Zeit', *WZUnivRostock* 18 (1969) 469–474; Altaner-Stuiber, *Patrologie*, VII, §§58–63; *KlWbChrOr*: 'Geschichtsschreibung'. Winkelmann distinguishes four categories—I. Historical monographs, which treat contemporary history. II. Chronographies, i.e. handbooks of world history which begin with creation or with Adam and continue to the time of the writer. III. Church Histories. IV. 'The nuanced and complicated area of hagiography'. The latter three categories are particularly influenced by Christianity.

(A) Historical monographs

To this category we reckon: 1. the work of Procopius (6th century); 2. continuation by Agathias (for the years 552–558), Menander (for the years 558–582), Theophylact Simocattes (for the years 582–602).

(B) Chronographies

The first Christian chronographies derive from Julius Africanus (d. after 240), Hippolytus (d. 235), Eusebius (d. 339); in Byzantium historiography proper is preferred, but there too the chronography flourished, between 642 and 1071. In the Christian Orient, among Syrians, Armenians etc., the chronography dominates.

I. In the East

1. Byzantine chronicles of world history

(a) John Malalas, a Syrian from Antioch and a contemporary of Emperor Anastasius I; he lived until the time of Justin II. His *Chronicle* in 18 books comes down to the end of the reign of Justinian I, probably as far as 574. Books 1–17 are well disposed towards monophysites; the chronicle of the city of Antioch has been incorporated. Book 18 focuses on Constantinople.

Ed. L. Dindorf, Bonn 1831; PG 97, 64–718; H. Gärtner, 'Malalas', *Kl. Pauly* 3; H. Hunger, *Die hochsprachliche profane Literatur der Byzantiner* I (München 1978) 320ff.; English trans. *The Chronicle of John Malalas. A Translation*, Australian Association for Byzantine Studies. Byzantina Australiensia 4, forthcoming.

(b) *Chronicon Paschale*, which probably originated in Byzantium. This work, which continues until the year 629, has independent value only for the latter decades. Cf. Altaner-Stuiber, *Patrologie*, 235, 6.

(c) Theophanes Confessor, Byzantine monk and chronicler, b. ca. 760 in Constantinople, d. 818 in exile as an iconodule. His *Chronographia* extends from 284–813 and was composed in the years 810–814. Alongside calculations of years from creation and from the birth of Christ he places the year of the Byzantine Emperor's reign, that of Persian and Arabian monarchs, of the Popes and the four patriarchs, as well as the reckoning of the year according to indictions. The *Chronography* is particularly important for the seventh and eighth centuries, for which, apart from Nicephorus, Theophanes is the only source (agreements with Malalas, Procopius and Agathias). In the ninth century the *Chronography* was translated into Latin by Anastasius Bibliothecarius. Ed.: C. de Boor (Leipzig 1883–1885; reprint Hildesheim 1963).

(d) Nicephorus, Patriarch of Constantinople (b. ca. 750, d. 828).(i) *Breviarium,* or Ἱστορία σύντομος; 'A typical chronicle in the manner of the Chronography of Theophanes, and one of the best works of this genre . . . . According to Krumbacher, Nicephorus and Theophanes, without being mutually dependent, took over a great deal from an older source unknown to us' (A. J. Visser, *Nikephoros und der Bilderstreit* [Haag 1952] 80–81).

(ii) *Chronography,* or Χρονογραφία σύντομος.

Ed.: C. de Boor, *Nicephori archiepiscopi Constantinopolitani opuscula historica* (Teubner, Leipzig 1880) 3–77; 81–135; included is the *Vita* of Ignatius the Deacon written by Nicephorus (139–217).

(e) John Zonaras, who lived from the last quarter of the 11th century to the mid-12th century; a high court official in Constantinople, he subsequently became a monk and composed the extensive world chronicle (Ἐπιτομὴ ἱστοριῶν) from creation to 1118 AD. He gives no account of contemporary history. From the foundation of Constantinople onwards he is interested only in the eastern half of the Empire. Ed.: L. Dindorf, 6 vols (1868–1875). Vols 7–9 in Cassius Dio, ed. Boissevain I (1895). See *Kl. Pauly* 5, 1551–1553.

2. Melkite chronicles
    (a) Agapius of Mabbog, Arabic world chronicle (10th century).
    (b) The Arabic chronicle (to 938) of the Melkite Eutychius of Alexandria: 'The String of Pearls' (early secular history, Church history from the time of Christ to 938, with slavish imitation of Byzantine chronography): PG 111, 907–1156; L. Cheiko: CSCO 50 (1906); idem et alii: CSCO 51 (1909). See further G. Graf, *Geschichte d. christl. arab. Lit.* II = ST 133 (1947) 32–34, who points out Eutychius' fondness for heresiology (Nestorians, Jacobites).

3. Syrian–Jacobite chronicles
    (a) *Chronicon Edessenum*, from the end of the 6th century. Important information concerning bishops and buildings of Edessa: ed. and tr. I Guidi, *Chronica minora*, CSCO 1, p. 1–13, (T), 2, p. 1–11 (V); L. Haller, TU 9, 1 (1892). See J. B. Segal, *Edessa, 'The Blessed City'* (Oxford 1970) with 'Select Bibliography'.
    (b) *Chronicon anonymum pseudo-Dionysianum vulgo dictum* (774/5): J.-B. Chabot, CSCO 91 (1927) (T), 121 (1949) (V). Pp. 167–174 contains the *Chronicle* from Chalcedon to the *Henoticon* of Zeno; pp. 174–233 a monophysite chronicle of the period from 495–507 ('Time of affliction for Edessa, Amid and all Mesopotamia'). W. Wright published this part (Syriac with English trans.) with the title: *The Chronicle of Josua the Stylite* (Cambridge 1882). The third section in this chronicle extends from Emperor Zeno to the death of Justinian (565), in which the second part of the *Church History* of John of Ephesus is taken over almost verbatim. Syriac ed. only in Chabot, CSCO 104 (1933). See Ortiz de Urbina, *Patr. Syr.* 211f.; on 'Josua' see H. Gelzer, 'Josua Stylites und die damaligen kirchlichen Parteien des Ostens', *ByzZ* 1 (1892) 34–49.
    (c) Jacob of Edessa (Bishop of Edessa ca. 684). His *Chronicle* is a free reworking of that of Eusebius, which he continued to the year 710 (Bk. 11, ch. 17). Ed. in *Chronica minora*, CSCO 5 (T), 261–330; 6 (V), 197–255; English trans. by E. W. Brooks, *ZDMG* 53 (1899) 261ff.
    (d) *Chronicum miscellaneum ad AD 724 pertinens*, ed. Brooks, tr. Chabot: CSCO 3 (T), 77–155; 4 (V), 63–119 (with a description of synods from the third to the fifth centuries from monophysite viewpoint on 116–119).
    (e) *Chronicon ad AD 846 pertinens*, ed. Brooks, tr. Chabot, CSCO 3 (T), 157–238; 4 (V), 123–180 (period after Chalcedon on 162ff.).
    (f) Michael the Great (b. ca. 1126/27, d. 1199), world chronicle to the year 1194/5. In 21 books, this transmits older works and individual documents, and influences Barhebraeus; in the 13th century a shortened Armenian revision was made. Ed. J.-B. Chabot, *Chronique de Michel le Syrien* I–IV (Paris 1899–1910).
    (g) Barhebraeus (=Gregory Abu-l-Farağ) (b. 1125/6, d. 1286), *Chronography*. This work encompasses both universal history and Church history, lists the main events of the OT, the early Church, of the Jacobite and Nestorian Church up to 1285/6; the continuator brings the work down to 1492/3. Michael the Great is used extensively. J. B. Abbeloos-Th. Lamy, *Chronicon ecclesiasticum*, 2 vols (Lovanii 1872, 1877) (with a Latin trans. which is in need of correction); cf. J. M. Fiey, *Jalons*, 14–16, who calls attention to the significance of Barhebraeus, particularly for the Church history of Iraq, but detects a credulity concerning miracles in the East, as well as 'la surenchère par rapport à l'antiquité et aux gloires du rite, la partialité en faveur des correligionnaires' (16).

4. Syrian-Maronite chronicle

Theophilus of Edessa (d. 785), *Chronicon Maroniticum*, preserved only in fragments. Sole source for the report of a Maronite-Jacobite discussion on religion. Ed. Brooks, CSCO 4, 35f.; W. Hage, *Die syrisch-jakobitische Kirche in frühislamischer Zeit* (Wiesbaden 1966) 7.

5. Syrian-Nestorian chronicles

(a) The much discussed '*Chronicle of Arbela*' = History of the Church of Adiabene under the Parthians and Sassanians, ed. and trans. A. Mingana, and attributed by him to Mšiḥa Zhā (name in Ebedjesu, *Catalogi scriptorum nestorianorum*: Assemani BO III, 1, 216); ed. in *Sources Syriaques* I (Mossoul–Leipzig 1907) 1–168; for criticism see J. M. Fiey, 'Auteur et date de la Chronique d'Arbèles', *OrSyr* 12 (1967) 265–302, with a certain correction in idem, *Jalons*, 10, n. 27. Fiey suspects that 'Mingana himself is the author, but does not convince S. Brock. See Fiey, op. cit.: 'Même si l'avenir devait prouver que l'original de la *Chronique* était une compilation médiévale, nous sérions de même loin de Mšiḥa Zhā et du VIᶜ siècle'.

(b) Simon Barquāyā, translator of a Greek chronicle (between 590 and 628), which in the following period remained authoritative for Nestorian circles (Baumstark 135f.).

(c) John bar Penkāyē, *Chronicle* of the world (to 686), 'a peculiar work in 15 books, embracing the mean between a world chronicle and theologically oriented philosophy of history' (Baumstark 210).

(d) '*Chronicon Anonymum*' of a Nestorian monk from the 7th century. Ed. Chabot: CSCO 5 (1905/1955) 371–378 (T); CSCO 6 (1907/1955) 299–304 (V). For an appraisal of the *Chronicle* see 297.

(e) *Eliae metropol. Nisibeni opus chronologicum* (d. after 1049): Part I: E. W. Brooks, CSCO 62*, 1 (1910/1954) (T); 63*,1 (V); Part II: Chabot, CSCO 62** (T); 63** (V) (1909/1910). In the first part the *Chronicle* is continued down to the year 1018; the second part contains chronological tables. This chronicle 'is composed of individual pieces, furnished with a precise indication of sources, and gains thus "the character of an arsenal of fragments of ancient Syriac historical writing"' (Baumstark 287) (W. Hage, art. cit., 6).

(f) The *Chronicle of Seᶜert*, composed shortly after 1036 in Arabic and only partially preserved: (i) with information concerning the years 251–422; (ii) concerning the years 484–650. The compiler is a Nestorian, who wrote his universal *History* with the help of older, partly Syriac, sources. He has a special interest in the events of ecclesiastical history. Ed. A. Scher, *Histoire Nestorienne. Chronique de Seᶜert*: PO IV, 3 (1908) 213–313; V, 3 (1910) 217–344; VII, 2 (1911) 95–203; XIII, 4 (1919) 435–639. Cf. J. Aßfalg, art. 'Chronik von Seᶜert', *KLL* I (Zürich 1965) 2568; J. M. Fiey, *Jalons*, 21 and passim, where an intensive study of this chronicle is highly recommended. The same sources are drawn on in this chronicle as in the *Liber turris* (see below). This explains the almost identical passages in both works.

(g) Simon of Sanqlāḅād, *Chronicon*: a handbook of computations in the form of questions and answers, including the Church's calendar of feastdays; Baumstark 310, with MSS and lit.

(h) *Chronicon Anonymum*, dating from the beginning of the Muslim period (perhaps from 670–680) and dealing with the period of the last Sassanians (from 590 to the Muslim conquest). This chronicle contains documents of great importance both for civil and ecclesiastical history of the time. Ed. I. Guidi, *Chron. Anonym. de ultimis regibus Persarum*, Syr.: CSCO 1 (*Chron. minora*) (1903) 15–39; Lat.: CSCO 2, 13–22; German: Th. Nöldecke, *Die von Guidi herausgeg. Syrische Chronik übers. u. commentiert* (Wien 1893).

6. Armenian chronicles

Cf. J. Markwart, 'Die Chroniken der armenischen Hs. Eğm. 102,' in R. Helm, *Hippolytus Werke* IV = GCS 36 (Leipzig 1929) 394–448. The third part is important: Armenian chronicle from AD 686/7, a Church history arranged according to Emperors' reigns from Caesar to the second year of the reign of Justinian II (686); pp. 35–80 of the MS. Chalcedon is treated at length, as too is the monothelite controversy. The compiler is a convinced monophysite. Trans. by A. Bauer, ibid., 449–552.

Shorter periods of Armenian history from the fourth to the eighth centuries were described by writers who were in part contemporary with the events: Faustus of Byzantium (originally in Greek); Lazar of Pharp; the so-called 'Agathangelus'; Elischē; Sebeos and Leontius. More comprehensive Armenian historical works, some of them world chronicles, were compiled by Moses of Chorene (5th–8th centuries?), Thomas of Arzruni and the Catholicos John IV (both 10th century). Cf. W. Hage, *KlWbChrOr*, art. 'Geschichtsschreibung', nr. 7; J. Aßfalg, 'Die christlichen Literaturen des Orients', *KLL* VII, 72–74. nr. 7.

7. Georgian chronicles

The Chronicle of Iberia; cf. C. Toumanoff, 'Medieval Georgian Historical Literature (VIIth–XVth Centuries)', *Trad* 1 (1943) 139–182, nr. 14, p. 161; a more detailed description on pp. 173–174; id., *Trad* 5 (1947) 340–344. M. Tarchnišvili, 'Sources arméno-géorgiennes de l'histoire ancienne de Géorgie', *Mus* 60 (1947) 29–50; J. Aßfalg, 'Die christlichen Literaturen des Orients', *KLL* VII (65–77) 74–76.

8. Ethiopic chronicles (translations)

(a) The *Chronicle* of the Coptic bishop John of Nikiu, a monophysite born at the time of the Arab conquest of Egypt, is preserved only in Ethiopic. The work is of great importance for the history of Egypt. We have used the English trans. of R. H. Charles, *The Chronicle of John, Bishop of Nikiu, translated from Zotenberg's Ethiopic Text* (London 1916).

(b) *Chronicle* of John Madabar, Bishop of Nikiu, translated from Arabic into Ethiopic (1602): a history of the world down to the Arab conquest of Egypt. The author is a contemporary of the Byzantine epoch which was drawing to a close. The work is valuable in that 'descriptions of the Arab conquest from the Christian side are very rare'. Cf. W. Müller, 'Äthiopische Chroniken', *KLL* I (1964) 232–236; W. Hage, art. 'Geschichtsschreibung', *KlWbChrOr*, nr. 6.

II. In the West

Cf. Altaner-Stuiber, *Patrologie* §59, I. nr. 16; II. nr. 10–15.

1. Tiro Prosper of Aquitania, *Chronicle of the world* (to 455).
2. Cassiodorus (d. ca. 580), *Chronicle of the world* to the year 519. Ed. Mommsen, MGH AA XI, 2, 109–161; *History of the Goths*, preserved only in the abridgment of Jordanes: Mommsen, MGH AA V, 1, 53–138.
3. Victor of Tunnuna (d. after 566), *Chronica*; the second part, dealing with the years 444–566 has survived. Ed. Mommsen, MGH AA XI, 2, 184–206. See G. C. Hansen, *Theodoros Anagnostes, Kirchengeschichte*: GCS (Berlin 1971).
4. Continuation of Victor of Tunnuna by John, Abbot of Biclar (d. ca. 621), *Chronica*, dealing with the years 567–596. Ed. Mommsen, op. cit., 207–220.
5. Marius, Bishop of Avenches (d. 594), *Chronica* dealing with the years 455–481. Ed. Mommsen, op. cit., 225–239.
6. Isidore of Seville (d. 636): (a) *Chronica maiora* (to the year 615). Ed. Mommsen, op. cit., 391–506; (b) *Historia Gothorum* (West Goths, to the year 625), with two

appendices dealing with Vandals and Suevi. Ed. Mommsen, op. cit., 241–304; B.
Steidle, *BM* 18 (1936) 425–434 (West Goths).

(C) Ecclésiastical historiography
I. Chalcedonian oriented historians
1. In the Greek-speaking region

(a) Theodore Lector (Anagnostes)
  (i) *Historia tripartita* (4 books), written ca. 530, in which Socrates, Sozomen
  and Theodoret are reworked. Only the first two books have been transmitted directly; Books 3 and 4 have been lost.
  (ii) *Church History* = continuation of *Hist. trip.* to 527 in 4 books; this survives
  only in fragments. As a substitute we have an *Epitome* of Church history
  which originated at the beginning of the 7th century, and which, while
  it cannot replace the lost work, is preserved in substantial extracts in Byzantine chronographies. In conjunction with the extracts from Theodore
  Lector the epitomator had also the longest extracts from John Diakrinomenos. Ed. G. C. Hansen, *Theodoros Anagnostes, Kirchengeschichte* (Berlin
  1971).

(b) Evagrius Scholasticus, *Church History*, written after 594 and embracing the
period between 431 and 594. Evagrius is intent on writing a Chalcedonian continuation to the works of Eusebius, Socrates, Sozomen, and Theodoret. In Evagrius
we have once more a high point in the writing of Church history. He shows a
critical attitude to his sources, which are archives in Antioch and Constantinople,
Malalas, Eustathius of Epiphania (to 502/3), Zacharias Rhetor (whose outline and
structure he follows in Books 2–3), Procopius (especially in Book 4 for wars against
Persians, Vandals and Goths). Evagrius' orthodoxy is vouched for by Photius, *Bibl.*
cod. 29: Henry I, 17, 33ff.

Significance: Evagrius is important for post-Chalcedonian history because he provides the text of three imperial edicts as well as Greek texts from the *Codex Encyclius*
of Emperor Leo I and extracts from the *Gesta Chalcedonensia*. He inclines towards
neo-Chalcedonism.

Attitude: God guides developments. The emperors are key figures, and his narrative
is divided into periods corresponding to their reigns. The largely negative evaluation
of Justinian is influenced by Procopius' *Secret History*, although direct use of this
work and the *De aedificiis* cannot be proved. Heresies are considered in a nuanced
manner. In *HE* II 2 Evagrius rejects the charge of Zacharias Rhetor (*HE* III
7) that Nestorius took part in the Council of Chalcedon. In contrast to Zacharias
he provides the text of the Antencyclical of Basiliscus; Zacharias' attacks on the
bishops who subscribed this document are opposed (III 9). Evagrius also uses
letters of Severus of Antioch. F. Winkelmann, *ByzSlav* 37 (1976) 176: 'The close
connection between imperium and orthodox established Church is for him self-
evident and raises no problems'. This also explains why the narrative is divided
into periods by events in the history of Byzantine Emperors, and the large amount
of political material.

Edition: J. Bidez-L. Parmentier, *The Ecclesiastical History of Evagrius with the Scholia*
(London 1889; reprint Amsterdam 1964); French trans. by A.-J. Festugière, *Évagre*
Histoire Ecclésiastique, Byz 45, 2 (1975) 187–471 with appendices. Monographs: P.
Allen, 'Zachariah Scholasticus and the *Historia Ecclesiastica* of Evagrius Scholasticus',
JTS 31 (1980) 471–488; eadem, *Evagrius Scholasticus the Church Historian* = SpicSLov

41 (Louvain 1981); V. A. Caires, 'Evagrius Scholasticus. A literary analysis', *ByzF*
8 (1982) 29–50; G. F. Chesnut, *The First Christian Histories: Eusebius, Socrates,
Sozomen, Theodoret and Evagrius* = ThéolHist 46 (Paris 1977); see further F. Winkelmann, *ByzZ* 74 (1981) 60–63, with supplementary bibliography.

(c) Nicephorus Callistus Xanthopulus, *Church History*, composed around 1320
in 18 books. Books 15–18 present the period between 451 and 610; for an analysis
see Gentz-Winkelmann (see below). Nicephorus offers a compilation of various
sources. F. Chr. Baur: 'He recapitulated ecclesiastical historiography in its entirety
within the Greek Church' (cited in Gentz-Winkelmann VI). His research into his
sources is, however, uncritical—he is a 'loyal and extremely compliant son of his
Church' (Gentz-Winkelmann, op. cit., 6). For all that he has investigated the references given in the continuous, extensive sources which he used—the works of Church
history, chronicles; he examines letters, synodal *acta*, liturgical books, lives of saints
(in this he has particular expertise). 'The writing of ecclesiastical history means here
the choir of all the old witnesses, a polyphonic choir which has been purified according to orthodox viewpoints. Nicephorus' aim is the synthesis which edifies and
constructs, but not critical analysis' (Gentz-Winkelmann, op. cit., 19). The course
of presentation is determined by Evagrius, from whom, however, Nicephorus takes
over only barely the half of his material (ibid., 144). Text: PG 145, 557–1332; 146,
9–1274; 147, 9–448. Analysis: G. Gentz-F. Winkelmann, *Die Kirchengeschichte des
Nicephorus Callistus Xanthopulus und ihre Quellen* = TU 98 (Berlin 1966).

2. In the Latin-speaking region

(a) Cassiodorus, *Historia tripartita*. Following the example of Theodore Lector,
Cassiodorus had the monk Epiphanius first of all translate the *Church Histories* of
Socrates, Sozomenus and Theodoret into Latin and then rework them into a *Historia
tripartita* (12 books). For our period this work is not of direct use, because it ends
with Theodosius II and Proclus of Constantinople. It did, however, have a considerable effect in the Middle Ages. For an appraisal see R. Helm, art. 'Cassiodor', *RAC*
2 (1954) 925.

(b) The *History of the Goths* mentioned above, which is preserved only in the
epitome of Jordanes, was intended in its original form to give a historical foundation
to Theodorich's plans for amalgamation, i.e. the reconciliation of Goths and Romans.
'In any case, Jordanes, who is not an Arian but a catholic Christian and in that
respect therefore without resentment, sees in the changed circumstances in the relation with the Eastern empire the opportunity of his people. Indeed, he wishes to
compose his historical work less to their glory than to the glory of the victor',
thus in the sense of the politics of Justinian. Cf. J. Irmscher, art. cit., 472; B. Luiselli,
'Cassiodoro e la storia dei Goti', *Convegno Internazionale Passaggio dal mondo antico
al medio evo da Teodosio a San Gregorio Magno* (Roma, 25–28 maggio 1977) = Accademia Naz. dei Lincei. Atti dei Convegni Lincei 45 (Roma 1980) 225–253.

(c) Gregory of Tours, b. ca. 540, d. 594 (593?), *Historia Francorum*, composed after
573. Book 1 offers a survey of world history down to 400; Books 5–10 deal with
contemporary history, for which Gregory uses his own records, in opposition to
pagans and Arians. Edition: Krusch-Levison, MGH, script. Merov. 1², 1937f.; Latin
text with German trans. by R. Bucher, *Gregorii Epi. Turonensis Historiarum Libri
Decem*, 1. Bd., B. 1–5; 2. Bd., B. 6–10 (Darmstadt 1955, 1956). Of the Eastern
Councils only 'Nicaea' is mentioned, by which the canons of Gangra in 340 are
meant. There is only scant information to be found about Justinian.

II. Monophysite oriented historians

1. '*History of the Alexandrian Church*', preserved only in Coptic fragments, written originally in Greek. T. Orlandi, *Storia della Chiesa di Alessandria, Testo copto, traduzione e commento*, vol. II: *Da Teofilo a Timoteo II* (Milano–Varese n.d.), Coptic 12–57; Latin 60–90. The work served as a source for Severus of Ašmunein, *Historia Patriarcharum Ecclesiae Alexandrinae*, ed. & trad. B. Evetts, PO I, and also for Theophanes, John of Nikiu and Zacharias Rhetor.

2. Zacharias Scholasticus, *Church History*, written in Greek; as a totality the work has perished. Zacharias provided his own experiences for contemporary Church history, in particular for the years 450–491, and then in Palestine and Egypt, which can be supplemented by Thedore Lector, Basil Cilix and John Diakrinomenos. The author came from Maiouma near Gaza; cf. Severus of Antioch, *ep.* 34: Brooks, PO 12, 269–278; John Rufus, *Plerophories*, PO 8, 128. He became later Bishop of Mitylene, and a Chalcedonian before 536. On the man and his work see M. M. Colonna, *Zacaria Scolastico, Ammonio* (Napoli 1973) 15–20. Of the work in Greek, composed between 492–495 in Constantinople, there remain only excerpts in the *Church History* of Evagrius, Books 2–3. The complete work is preserved in an epitome, which an anonymous Jacobite monk from Amid in Armenia reworked in 569 and composed in Syriac, incorporating his own *Church History* of 12 books in Books 3–6. From Book 7 onwards the author is cited as ps. Zacharias Rh. (cont.). Book 7 treats the rule of Emperor Anastasius I, Book 8 the period of Justin I (518–527), Book 9 the period of Justinian (527–565). Complete Syriac edition: J. P. N. Land, *Anecdota Syriaca* III (1870) 2–340; German: K. Ahrens-G. Krüger, *Die sogenannte Kirchengeschichte des Zacharias Rhetor* (Leipzig 1899); English: *The Syriac Chronicle known as that of Zachariah of Mitylene*. Translated by F. J. Hamilton and E. W. Brooks (London 1899); Syriac–Latin, *Historia Ecclesiastica Zachariae Rhetori vulgo adscripta* (with a fragment from the *Church History* of Dionysius of Tell Maḥrē): Syriac: CSCO 83–84 (1919.1921); Latin: CSCO 87–88 (1924). On the biographical works see below. P. Allen, 'Zachariah Scholasticus and the *Historia Ecclesiastica* of Evagrius Scholasticus', *JTS* NS 31 (1980) 471–488.

3. John Diakrinomenos: a monophysite, as the nick-name attests; between 512–518 he wrote a *Church History* in 5 books about the period from 429 to Emperor Anastasius I (491–518); fragments edited in G. C. Hansen, *Theodoros Anagnostes*.

4. John of Ephesus (b. 507, d. after 588); further information in E. W. Brooks, CSCO 106, I and (better) Honigmann, *Évêques et Évêchés* 207–215. From 540 John was in Constantinople; in 541 he travelled to Egypt; in 542 he was given by Justinian the commission of converting pagans, which he retained until 572. The terms were that he convert the pagans to Chalcedonian belief; cf. Michael Syr., IX 24: Chabot I 287–288; II 207: 70,000 pagans were brought by John to the Chalcedonian belief, 'parce que le saint qui les convertissait jugeait qu'il valait mieux qu'ils quittassent l'erreur du paganisme même pour le chalcédonisme'. In 558 John was consecrated Bishop of Ephesus by Jacob Baradaeus, but he never visited that city. The *Church History* was concluded in or about 588: P. Allen, 'A New Date for the Last Recorded Events in John of Ephesus' *Historia Ecclesiastica*', *OLP* 10 (1979) 251–254.

The *Historia Ecclesiastica* was composed in three parts: parts 1–2 are lost; part 3 begins with the year 571; part 2 can be largely reconstructed from the *Chronicon anonymum pseudo-Dionysianum vulgo dictum*, ed. I.-B. Chabot, CSCO 91 and 121 (1927.1949) and from Michael Syr. Part 3, Book 1 begins with ch. 3; there is a lacuna from the middle of ch. 5 to the middle of ch. 9, etc. See Brooks, CSCO 106, II. All gaps can be filled from Michael Syr. and the *Chronicon an. 1234* (ed. Chabot, CSCO 81 and 109). Book 4 is valuable for the history of the evangelisation of Nubia and Ethiopia. John writes polemically against everything that deviates from monophysism, but for all that shows a tolerant attitude. Edition and trans.: E. W. Brooks, *Johannis Ephesini Historiae ecclesiasticae pars tertia*, T: CSCO 105 (1935); V: CSCO 106 (1936); incomplete German trans.: J. M. Schönfelder, *Die Kirchen-Geschichte des Johannes von Ephesus* (München 1862).

5. Dionysius of Tell Maḥrē, Patriarch from 818–845; author of a *History* in two parts and 16 books dealing with the period from 582–842, which is preserved only in fragments: Assemani, BO II, 72–73; CSCO 88, 149–154. A substantial part is taken over from Anonymous, *Chronicon an. 1234*. See further Ortiz de Urbina, *Patrologia Syriaca*, §152.

III. Nestorian oriented historians

See E. Degen, 'Daniel bar Maryam, ein nestorianischer Kirchenhistoriker', *OrChr* 52 (1968) 45–80; ibid. on the origin of the writing of Church history among the Nestorians, which is to be found in Syrian *acta* of martyrs and in saints' lives: 'From this literary genre the writing of Church history among the Nestorians developed, without being quite separate from it' (ibid., 49). Syriac historiography, however, in its turn, derives from Eusebius, whose work was translated into Syriac early (oldest MS dates from 462). The Nestorians also used Theodoret and Socrates.

1. Basil Cilix, Presbyter of Antioch; cf. F. Winkelmann, *ByzSlav* 37 (1976) 181 n. 121. According to Photius, *Bibl.* 42, who knew only two of the three parts of his *HE*, Basil included many documents. Basil treated the period from 450–540 in three books. Cf. R. Janin, *DHGE* 6 (1932) 1127, nr. 70.

2. Barḥadbešabba of ʿArbaia (late 6th century), *Historia sanctorum Patrum qui propter veritatem persecutionem sustulerunt*: ed. F. Nau, PO XXIII, 177–343 (Part I); PO IX, 490–631 (Part II). F. Winkelmann, op. cit., calls the work 'a religious history of heroes'. There is no objective presentation; Satan is the real driving force of developments within Church history. The heretics are his pupils. Nonetheless the work is important as a supplement to other sources and as characterising the historical compositions among the Nestorians. Counterparts to it are *The History of the Alexandrian Church* and Severus of Ašmunein, *History of the Patriarchs of Alexandria* (see above). For our period after Chalcedon only the last two chapters, 31–32, are important: PO IX 588–615 (Mar Narsai); 616–631 (Mar Abraham). On Narsai see also PO IV, 381–387; PO VII, 114ff. (*Chronicle of Seʿert*). Cf. L. Abramowski, *Untersuchungen zum Liber Heraclidis des Nestorius* = CSCO 242, Subs. 22 (Louvain 1963) 33–73.

3. Daniel bar Maryam (7th century), *Church History* in 4 vols., which has perished apart from a few fragments. Cf. E. Degen, art. cit. Daniel provides information concerning the period from Jesus to ca. the mid-fifth century.

4. Further lost works dealing with Nestorian *HE* from the 7th–9th centuries, inventarised in Ebedjesu of Nisibis at the beginning of the 14th century. See J.-M. Fiey, *Jalons* 9–11; also 12–13: these are works which J.-B. Chabot decided were sources which ps. Dionysius of Tell Maḥrē and Michael the Syrian used.

IV. Armenian ecclesiastical historiography

Cf. W. Hage, art. 'Geschichtsschreibung', *KlWbChrOr* 141f.; J. Aßfalg, 'Die christlichen Literaturen des Orients', *KLL* VII, 72–74. For us two works are important:

(a) Agathangelus, supposed composer of an Armenian historical work which tells of the miracles of Gregory the Illuminator and the Christianisation of Armenia. The work is that of an anonymous writer at the end of the 5th century, who originally used independent writings. Cf. G. Garitte, *Documents pour l'étude du livre d'Agath-angelos* = ST 127 (Città del Vaticano 1946); M. van Esbroeck, 'Un nouveau témoin du livre d'A.', *Revue des Études Arméniennes* NS 8 (1971) 13–167; G. Lafontaine, *La version grecque ancienne du livre arménien d'Agathange*, Éd. critique (Louvain-la Neuve 1973) (Lit.); *Agathangelos History of the Armenians*. Translation and Commentary by R. W. Thomson (Albany 1976) (Lit.: 504–515). See S. Brock, JTS 32 (1981) 273–274.

(b) The *Diegesis* or *Narratio de rebus Armeniae*; cf. G. Garitte, *La narratio de rebus Armeniae*. Éd. critique et commentaire = CSCO 132 = Subs. 4 (Louvain 1952) 357: 'La *Diegesis* raconte, du pointe de vue chalcédonien, l'histoire de l'Église arménienne dans ses rapports avec l'Église byzantine depuis le concile de Nicée jusque vers l'an 700; ainsi que l'annonce le titre, elle expose comment l'Église armé-nienne, d'abord en communion avec l'Église grecque, se sépara d'elle lors du concile de Dvin, où fut anathematisée la doctrine de Chalcédoine, et comment elle retomba dans le schisme après chacune des unions realisées ensuite, sous Justin II, sous Maurice, sous Héraclius et sous Justinien II.'

(c) *Moses Khorenats ʿi: History of the Armenians*. Translation and Commentary on the Literary Sources by R. W. Thompson (Cambridge, Mass. 1978).

(d) Trans. of Socrates, HE; cf. P. Peeters, 'A propos de la version arménienne de l'historien Socrate', in idem, *Recherches d'histoire et de philologie orientales* = Subs. hag. 27 (Bruxelles 1951) I, 310–336. For the Iberians Socrates has 'un intérêt de premier ordre' (335f.).

V. Georgian ecclesiastical history

See above on 'Chronicles'.

D. Hagiographical works

Prefatory note 1: On the significance of this literary genre see F. Winkelmann, 'Geschichtsschreibung in Byzanz', *WZUnivRostock* 18 (1969) 479, who emphasises the wide diffusion of this genre as a consequence of the use of hagiographical works in liturgies, and their inclusion in liturgical and homiletical collections. Hagio-graphical works portray most of all the life of the lower classes and areas removed from cultural centres. For us additionally there is the particular point that we gain an insight into the missionary expansion in the post-Chalcedonian period, especially that of the monophysite Churches. At the same time we can produce occasional examples of christological baptismal catechesis which has no confessional narrow-ness.

Prefatory note 2: It is the attitude to the Council of Chalcedon which, more often than christological reference, is expressed. Christology is revealed directly in monas-tic literature particularly through reference to the *Imitatio Christi* and the *Mysteria vitae Jesu*, but also through the incorporation of fundamental christological-soterio-logical ideas, even if in an unsophisticated manner. A methodologically significant study is that of J. Roldanus, 'Die Vita Antonii als Spiegel der Theologie des Athanasius und ihr Weiterwirken bis ins 5 Jahrhundert', *TheolPhil* 58 (1983) 194–216. Roldanus shows that Athanasius' *Vita Antonii* served as model for two Latin *vitae*: (a) Jerome's *Life of Hilarion* (391 AD) and (b) the *Vita Martini* of Sulpicius Severus (d. 397). In the Greek-speaking region the *Vita Antonii* must have been known (a) to the composer of the Greek *Vita Pachomii*; (b) to Callinicus, who wrote the *Vita Hypatii*. Next R. makes the most important observations: (a) positive: the *Vita Antonii* is permeated with the christological 'theology' of Athanasius; (b) negative: this point

of view has been quite overlooked in the *Vita Martini* and the *Vita Hypatii*. Cf.
J. Fontaine, *Sulpice Sévère, Vie de Saint Martin* I–III: SC 133–135 (Paris 1967–1969);
on the relationship with the *Vita Antonii*: Introd., 33–38 (without the point of view
of Roldanus); G. J. M. Bartelink, *Callinicos: Vie d'Hypatios. Introduction et Notes*
= SC 177 (Paris 1971), based on 4 MSS; another French trans.: A.-J. Festugière,
Les moines d'Orient II (Paris 1961), based on the text of the Bonn Corpus (2 MSS).
See also G. Garitte, 'Reminiscences de la Vie d'Antoine dans Cyrille de Scythopolis',
Silloge bizantina in onore di Silvio G. Mercati (Roma 1957) 117–122; K. Holl, 'Die
schriftstellerische Form des griechischen Heiligenlebens', *Gesammelte Schriften* II
(Der Osten) (Tübingen 1928) 249–269; M. Tetz, 'Athanasius und die Vita Antonii.
Literarische und theologische Relationen', *ZNW* 73 (1982) 1–30; reference to christology on pp. 13, 15f; 20–21, 30; G. J. M. Bartelink, 'Die literarische Gattung der
Vita Antonii. Struktur und Motiv'. *VigC* 36 (1982) 38–62. On the Syriac transmission
see R. Draguet, *La Vie primitive de S. Antoine conservée en syriaque*. Discussion et
trad. = CSCO 417/418; Scr. syri 183/184 Louvain 1980). For a critique of Draguet,
who denies that the *Vita Antonii* is an authentic work of Athanasius, cf. the review
of G. Couilleau, *CollCist Bulletin* 46 (1984) 347–348. – J. Gribomont , 'Panorama
des influences orientales sur l'hagiographie latine', *Aug* 24 (1984) 7–20.

Prefatory note 3:
(a) Reference works on sources and literature:
A. Ehrhard, *Überlieferung und Bestand der hagiographischen und homiletischen Literatur
der griechischen Kirche*, 1. Teil: *Überlieferung*, t. I–III = TU 50–52, 1–2 (Leipzig
1937–1952); 2. Teil: *Bestand* (unpublished).
Bollandists:
Acta Sanctorum (AASS), *collecta . . . a Sociis Bollandianis*, 3a edit. (Paris 1863ff);
Bibliotheca hagiographica graeca, 3e éd. Fr. Halkin (BHG³) = Subs. hag. 8a (Bruxellis
1957);
Auctarium Bibliothecae hagiographicae graecae (BHGᵃ), par Fr. Halkin = Subs. hag.
47 (Bruxellis 1969); BHG³, Préface V–XII: III. Appendix VI: Patrum Vitae,
Paterika, Gerontika, 191–214; Appendix IV: Narrationes animae utiles. On christ-
ology see ibid., Appendix VII, nr. 1–117: Orationes et homiliae de festis Christi,
215–249;
Bibliotheca hagiographica latina (BHL) I–II = Subs. hag. 6 (Bruxellis 1898–1901;
ed. altera 1949;
Bibliotheca hagiographica orientalis (BHO) = Subs. hag. 10 (Bruxellis 1910);
H. Delehaye et al., *Propylaeum ad Acta Sanctorum Decembris* (Bruxellis 1940) (com-
mentary on the *Martyrologium Romanum*);
Idem, *Synaxarium Ecclesiae Constantinopolitanae* (Bruxellis 1902). Other *synaxaria*:
PO 1 (Ethiopic); 1, 3, 16 (Arabic-Jacobite); 5, 6, 15, 16 (Armenian). See H.-G.
Beck, *Kirche und theologische Literatur im byzantinischen Reich* (München 1959) s.v.
Hagiographie, and further P. Peeters, *Le tréfonds oriental de l'hagiographie byzantine*
= Subs. hag. 26 (Bruxelles 1950); in particular p. 165—Traductions et traducteurs
dans l'hagiographie orientale à l'époque byzantine, pp. 165–218.
(b) Bibliography on christological interpretation (*imitatio Christi* etc.): K. Heussi,
Der Ursprung des Mönchtums (Tübingen 1936); S. Schiewitz, *Das morgenländische
Mönchtum* I–II (Mainz 1904–1913), III (Mödling b. Wien 1938); M. Viller–K.
Rahner, *Aszese und Mystik in der Väterzeit* (Freiburg i. Br. 1939); O. Rousseau,
Le rôle important du monachisme dans l'Église d'Orient, OCA 1958, 33–55; U. Ranke-
Heinemann, *Das frühe Mönchtum. Seine Motive nach den Selbstzeugnissen* (Essen 1964),
Ch. VI, 83–100: Das Motiv der Nachfolge; S. Frank, ΑΓΓΕΛΙΚΟΣ ΒΙΟΣ =
BGAMBO 26 (Münster i. W. 1964) 1–11; C. D. G. Müller, 'Was können wir aus

der koptischen Literatur über Theologie und Frömmigkeit der Ägyptischen Kirche lernen?', *OrChr* 48 (1964) 191–215; P. Nagel, *Die Motivierung der Askese in der alten Kirche und der Ursprung des Mönchtums* = TU 95 (Berlin 1966); T. Baumeister, 'Die Mentalität des frühen ägyptischen Mönchtums. Zur Frage der Ursprünge des christlichen Mönchtums', *ZKG* 88 (1977) 145–160; H. Crouzel, 'L'imitation et la 'suite' de Dieu et du Christ dans les premiers siècles ainsi que leurs sources gréco-romaines et hébraïques', *JAC* 21 (1978) 7–41.

See further the complete series of studies by W. Voelker on the doctrine of perfection: Philo (1938), Clement of Alexandria (1957), Origen (1931), Gregory of Nyssa (1955), ps. Dionysius the Areopagite (1958), Maximus Confessor (1965), John Climacus (1968) and Symeon the New Theologian (1974).

(c) More general literature: D. J. Chitty, *The Desert a City. An Introduction to the History of Egyptian and Palestinian Monasticism under the Christian Empire* (Oxford 1966) (on Egypt and Palestine); G. M. Colombas, *El monacato primitivo. Hombres, hechos, costumbres, instituciones* I = BAC (Madrid 1974); K. S. Frank (ed.), *Askese und Mönchtum in der Alten Kirche* (Darmstadt 1975); A. Guillaumont, *Aux origines du monachisme chrétien. Pour une phénomenologie du monachisme* (Begrolles en Mauges 1979). France: Université de Paris X, Centre de recherches sur l'Antiquité . . . : 'Hagiographie, culture et société', IVᵉ–XIIᵉ siècles. Actes du Colloque organisé à Nanterre et à Paris (2–5 mai 1979), *Études Augustiniennes* (Paris 1981), esp. F. Dolbeau, p. 11–31.

In what follows, the main hagiographical sources on the subjects 'Chalcedon' and 'Christology' are presented according to the entities to which they belong (patriarchates, geographical classification).

I. Egypt and the Coptic Church

1. General Literature:

M. Lequien, *Oriens Christianus in quatuor patriarchatus digestus*, vol. II: Patriarchate of Alexandria (Paris 1740) 329–666; E. R. Hardy, *Christian Egypt, Church and People* (New York 1952); M. Cramer, *Das christlich-koptische Ägypten. Einst und heute. Eine Orientierung* (Wiesbaden 1959).—R. Janin, *Les Églises orientales et les Rites orientaux* (Paris 1935³); W. de Vries, *Rom und die Patriarchate des Ostens* (Freiburg–München 1963); Asiz S. Atiya, *A History of Eastern Christianity* (London 1968): Part I: Alexandrine Christianity. The Copts and their Church, p. 11–166; M. Naldini, *Il Cristianesimo in Egitto. Lettere private dei papiri dei secoli II–IV* (Firenze 1968); C. D. G. Müller, 'Zeittafeln zur Kopt. Kirche', *KlWbChrOr* (1975) 396–397; M. P. Roncaglia, *Histoire de l'Église en Orient (Études et Matériaux). Egypte. Histoire de l'Église Copte* (Beyrouth 1985ff.)

2. Series of hagiographical works

(a) On the history of the patriarchs: B. Evetts, *History of the Patriarchs of the Coptic Church of Alexandria* = PO 1 (1907) 100–214; 381–518; PO 5 (1910) 1–215; Severus ben el-Moqaffa', *Historia patriarcharum Alexandrinorum*, ed. C. F. Seybold = CSCO 52, 59 (Arab. 8, 9) (1904–1910); German· C. F. Seybold, *Ibn al Moquaffa. Alexandrinische Patriarchengeschichte von S. Marcus bis Michael I. (61–767)* (Hamburg 1912); R. Renaudot, *Historia Patriarcharum Alexandrinorum Jacobitarum a D. Marco usque ad finem saeculi XIII* (Paris 1713); J. Maspéro, *Histoire des patriarches d'Alexandrie depuis la mort de l'empereur Anastase jusqu'à la reconciliation des églises Jacobites* (Paris 1923); see further A. Jülicher, 'Zur Geschichte der Monophysitenkirche', *ZNW* 24 (1925) 17–43.

(b) Monastic literature (biographies of monks)

Palladius, *Historia Lausiaca*: lists of sources and editions in BHG³ 1435–1438v; CPG 6036; Anonymous, *Historia monachorum in Aegypto*: Greek ed. A.-J. Festugière, Subs. hag. 34 (Bruxellis 1961), without cognisance of MS Vat. gr. 2592; see P. Canart, *Mus* 75 (1962) 109–129; Latin: Rufinus, PL 21, 387–462; French: A.-J. Festugière, *Les moines d'Orient* IV/1: Enquête sur les moines d'Égypte (*Hist. mon. in Aeg.*) (Paris 1964); K. S. Frank, *Mönche im frühchristlichen Ägypten* (Düsseldorf 1967); *Apophthegmata Patrum*: lists of sources and editions in CPG 5560–5615; PG 65, 71–440.

3. Significant individual *vitae* of monks and patriarchs

(a) Pre-Chalcedonian period

In the first place Pachomius must be mentioned. See the extensive bibliography in A. Veilleux, *La Liturgie dans le cénobitisme Pachômien au quatrième siècle* = *StudAns* f. LVII (Romae 1968), XVII–XVIII: Sources. A.-J. Festugière, *Les moines d'Orient* IV/2: La première vie grecque de saint Pachôme (Paris 1965); see too now F. Halkin, *Le Corpus Athénien de Saint Pachôme avec une traduction française par A.-J. Festugière* (Genève 1982) (=Cahiers d'Orientalisme II). H. Bacht, *Das Vermächtnis des Ursprungs. Studien zum frühen Mönchtum* I–II (Würzburg 1972.1985).

(b) Chalcedonian and post-Chalcedonian periods

(i) Shenute the Great of Atripe (d. 466): BHO, Subs. hag. 10 (1910) 235ff. *Vita auctore Besa*, Coptic: I. Leipoldt et W. Crum, *Sinuthii archimandritae vita et opera omnia*, I. *Sinuthii vita bohairice*: CSCO 41 (T), 129 (V); III: CSCO 42 (T), 96 (V); IV: CSCO 73 (T); 108 (V) (H. Wiesmann); a Syrian extract from the *vita* of Shenute, ed. F. Nau, *Revue Sémitique* 7 (1899) 356–363; 8 (1900) 153–167, 252–265. According to I. Guidi, the work was very probably written in the Jacobite Šurian monastery in the Nitrian desert for the Syrian–Jacobite Church. Since it is a question of an excerpt, one has been inclined to infer that there was no interest in the *Vita* as a whole; cf. J. Leipoldt, *Schenute von Atripe und die Entstehung des national-ägyptischen Christentums* = TU 25 (1904) 1–214; on Besa's biography see §2, p. 12–16: 'no great historical value'. A bibliography on Shenute is to be found in P. J. Frandsen-E. Richter Ærøe, 'Shenoute: A Bibliography', in D. W. Young (ed.), *Studies Presented to Hans Jacob Polotsky* (Beacon Hill 1981) 147–177. Cf. C. D. G. Müller, art. 'Schenute', *KlWbChrOr*, s.v. 'Schenute' (who died in 466 at the earliest, but took no part in the discussions around Chalcedon). Shenute writes polemically against Melitians, Arians, Manichaeans (thus Leipoldt §17, whose verdict on Shenute's christology is very negative: 'Christ-less piety'. Unfortunately he is followed by A. Veilleux, 'Chénouté ou les écueils du monachisme', *CollCist* 45 (1983) 124–131.) To be noted are new texts: (1) L. Th. Lefort, 'Catéchèse christologique de Chenouté', *ZÄS* 80 (1955) 40–45; evaluated by H.-F. Weiss, 'Zur Christologie des Schenute von Atripe', *BSAC* 20 (1969) 177–209. (2) T. Orlandi, 'A Catechesis against Apocryphal Texts by Shenute and the Gnostic Texts of Nag Hammadi', *HThR* 75 (1982) 85–95. This text is an exhortation from the period after Ephesus. See Unione Accademia Nazionale, Corpus dei Manoscritti Letterari, where the text has been published (1985). See CCT II, 2.

(ii) Patriarch Dioscorus (444–451; d.454 acc. to Copts): BHO, Subs. hag. 10, 60; M. Cramer-H. Bacht, 'Der antichalkedonische Aspekt im historisch-biographischen Schrifttum der koptischen Monophysiten (6.-7. Jh.)', *Chalkedon* II, 315–338, with special observations on F. Nau, 'Histoire de Dioscore Patriarche d'Al., écrite par son disciple Théopiste', *Journal Asiatique* 10 = NS 1 (1903), 1–108 (Syriac), 241–310 (French); F. Haase, *Patriarch Dioskur I. von Alexandrien nach monophysitischen Quellen* (Breslau 1908) 141–233. Haase defends the authenticity of the work, which is argued for also by K. Khella, 'Dioskoros I. von Alexandrien. Theologie u. Kirchenpolitik', *Les Coptes, The Copts, Die Kopten*, vol. 2 (Hamburg 1981) 9–282 (Part I); vol. 3 (1982) (Part II). According to E. Honigmann, 'Juvenal of Jerusalem' = *DOP* 5 (1950) 265 with n. 1; idem, *Byz* 16 (1944) 68, n. 133, the *History of Dioscorus* is to be appraised as a sort of 'historical novel, written only after 518 and therefore not by Theopistus, the (supposed) deacon of the patriarch'. This *History* is heavily dependent on John Rufus, Bishop of Maiouma, the author of the *Plerophories*: PO 8, 1–208. Cf. E. Schwartz, 'Johannes Rufus ein monophysitischer Schriftsteller', *SbHeidAkW*, Phil.-hist.Kl. 1912, 16 (Heidelberg 1912).

During the excavations in the so-called Cellia there was found a Coptic inscription with the date of the death of Dioscorus, 7 Thoout = 4 Sept., without an indication of the year (454). Cf. F. Dumas-A. Guillaumont, *Kellia I. Kom 219* (Le Caire 1969) 102, nr. 11. According to R. Kasser, *Kellia Topographie* = Recherches Suisses d'Archéologie Copte, Vol. II (Genève 1972) 55–59, this inscription should not be considered as being contemporary with the death of Dioscorus. On the other hand, Kasser admits that the year of death was indicated in Cellia only from the end of the seventh century onwards. Because of the renown of Patriarch Dioscorus, however, (argues Kasser) the inscription also could have been added later than 454. But was this renown so great? Cf. B. Evetts, *History of the Patriarchs of the Coptic Church of Alexandria*, PO 1 (Paris 1907), ch. XIII, p. 443–444, 'Dioscorus'. On p. 444 we read that until the composition of this *Vita* 'no biography of the holy patriarch Dioscorus has been found'. Cf. too R. Barset, *Le synaxaire arabe jacobite* (Rédaction Copte) Texte arabe: PO 1 (Paris 1907) 236–238 (Dioscorus); J. Forget, *Synaxarium Alexandrinum, pars prior* = CSCO 78 (V) (Romae 1921) 8–10.

(ii) *Panegyricus* of Patriarch Dioscorus on Macarius of Tkôu, ed. F. Amélineau, *Monuments pour servir à l'histoire de l'Égypte chrétienne aux IVᵉ et Vᵉ siècles* (Paris 1888) 92–164; previously translated by E. Revillout, 'Les récits de Dioscore, exilé à Gangres, sur le concile de Chalcédoine', *RevEgypt* 1 (1881) 187–189; 2 (1882) 21–25; 3 (1883) 17–24. According to ps. Theopistus, *Life of Dioscorus*, Macarius accompanied the Patriarch to the Council of Chalcedon. Cf. Cramer-Bacht, *Chalkedon* II, 320f. For a critical assessment of this *Panegyric* see J. Leipoldt, TU 25 (1908) 17–18; different in F. Haase, *Patriarch Dioskur I. von Alexandrien*, 166ff.

(iv) Fragments of a biography of Timothy Aelurus, (two parchment leaves from Wādi-n-Natrūn, now in Cairo), dependent on the *Vita* of Peter the Iberian, the *Plerophories* of John Rufus and the *HE* of Zacharias Rhetor. Cf. M. Cramer-H. Bacht, *Chalkedon* II, 316.

(v) Fragments of a *Vita* of Abraham, the abbot of Pbôu, a monophysite Pachomian called to Constantinople under Emperor Justinian. Particulars in Cramer-Bacht, *Chalkedon* II, 334f., with note.

(vi) Encomium on Apa Apollo, a monk under Abraham in the Pbôu monastery, composed by Bishop Stephen of Khnês (Heracleopolis Magna) in the year 823. The suffering of the orthodox under Emperor Justinian is portrayed. Cf. Cramer-Bacht, *Chalkedon* II, 335f.

(vii) *Vita* of Daniel of Scete (preserved in Greek, Coptic, Syriac, Ethiopic and Arabic) dating from the time of Justinian. Cf. CPG 7363. Short extract in Cramer-Bacht, *Chalkedon* II, 328. Daniel's opposition to Chalcedon stirred up agitation in Scete, upon which he withdrew into the Delta to Tamok and founded a small monastery.

On the communal life of Chalcedonians and anti-Chalcedonians in the area of the so-called Cellia after 451, each group having its own church, see A. Guillaumont, Ch. I, 'Histoire du site des Kellia d'après les documents écrits', in F. Dumas-A. Guillaumont, op. cit., 1-15, esp. 8–9.

(viii) *Vita* of Samuel of Kalamon (from the time of Emperor Heraclius, 610/1–641). See Cramer-Bacht, *Chalkedon* II, 329–334, with partial trans. of the unedited Coptic *Vita* of the Pierpont-Morgan Collection, New York. The *Vita* is important for the behaviour of the monks under Emperor Heraclius (the period after 627 saw the suppression of anti-Chalcedonians in Egypt by Byzantium).

(ix) Patriarch Benjamin I (626–665). See H. Brackmann, 'Zum Pariser Fragment angeblich des koptischen Patriarchen Agathon. Ein neues Blatt der Vita Benjamins I.', *Mus* 93 (1980) 299–309, with complete bibliography on Benjamin I (in particular by C. D. G. Müller). Lit.: P. van Cauwenbergh, *Étude sur les moines d'Égypte depuis le concile de Chalcédoine jusqu'à l'invasion arabe* (Paris-Louvain 1914); H. Bacht, *Chalkedon* II, 193–314; A. Campagnano, 'Monaci egiziani fra V e VI secolo', *VetChr* 15 (1978) 223–246.

II. Palestine–Sinai

C. Renoux, 'Hierosolymitana. Aperçu bibliographique des publications depuis 1960, I–II', *ALW* 23 (1981) 1–29; 149–175; Aßfalg, *KLL* VII 67-68. Both Chalcedonian and anti-Chalcedonian sources are particularly important here.

1. Chalcedonian hagiographical works

(a) Cyril of Scythopolis, born around 523; in 544 he became a monk in the monastery of Euphemius, in 555 a hermit in the 'New Lavra' of St. Sabas, where he died around 558. BHG (see below); CPG 7535–7541; Altaner-Stuiber, *Patrologie*, §61, 5; E. Schwartz, *Kyrillos von Skythopolis* = TU 49, 2 (Leipzig 1939); French: A.-J. Festugière, *Les moines d'Orient* I–II. III/1–3 (Paris 1961–1963).

(i) *Vita* of Euthymius (BHG 647–648b); Schwartz, op. cit., 3–85; Festugière III/1, 53–157.

(ii) *Vita* of St. Sabas (BHG 1608); Schwartz, op. cit., 85–200; Festugière III/2, 9–154.

(iii) *Vita* of John the Hesychast (BHG 897); Schwartz, op. cit., 201–222; Festugière III/3, 13–34.

(iv) *Vita* of Cyriacus (BHG 463); Schwartz, op. cit., 222–235; Festugière III/3, 39–52.

(v) *Vita* of Theodosius (BHG 1777); Schwartz, op. cit., 235–241; Festugière III/3, 57–62.

(vi) *Vita* of Theognius (BHG 1787); Schwartz, op. cit., 241–243; Festugière III/3, 65–67.

(vii) *Vita* of Abramius (BHG 12); Schwartz, op. cit., 243–247 (*partim graece*); Festugière III/3, 73–79.

(b) Theodore of Petra, *Vita Theodosii coenobiarchae prope Hierosolyma* (d. 529) (BHG[3] 1176); H. Usener, *Der hl. Theodosius. Schriften des Theodoros und Kyrillos* (Leipzig 1890), 3–101; French: Festugière, op. cit. III/3, 103–160; see further the important work of J. O. Rosenqvist, *Studien zur Syntax und Bemerkungen zum Text der Vita Theodori Syceotae* = Acta Univ. Upsaliensis. Stud. Graeca Upsal. 15 (Uppsala 1981), esp. Part II (87ff.).

(c) John Moschus (b. mid-6th century, d. 619 in Rome) (BHG[3] 1441–1442; CPG 7376). *Pratum spirituale*, PG 87, 2852–3112. See E. Mioni, *DSp* 8 (1974) 632–640. John was in Jerusalem, Egypt, Sinai and Antioch. The *Pratum spirituale* contains over 300 edifying tales and miracles from the lives of ascetics who were in the main contemporaries.

(d) John Moschus and Sophronius of Jerusalem, *Vita Iohannis eleemosynarii* (lost); cf. CPG 7647, with reference to other sources.

(e) Anastasius Sinaita (d. soon after 700), *Narrationes*. Cf. CPG 7758.

2. Anti-Chalcedonian *Vitae*
(a) Peter the Iberian (b. 409, d. under Emperor Zeno).
(i) John Rufus, *Vita* of Peter the Iberian, written in Greek but preserved only in Syriac. Ed. and trans.: R. Raabe, *Petrus der Iberer. Ein Charakterbild zur Kirchen- und Sittengeschichte des 5. Jhts. Syr. Übersetzung einer um das Jahre 500 verfaßten griechi-schen Biographie* (Leipzig 1895). See E. Schwartz, 'Johannes Rufus ein monophy-sitischer Schriftsteller', *SbHeidAkW*, Philos.-hist. Kl. 1912, 16 (Heidelberg 1912). According to Schwartz, p. 19, John Rufus is also the author of the *Plerophories*: F. Nau, PO 8, 1–183. Cf. D. M. Lang, 'Peter the Iberian and His Biographers', *JEH* 2 (1951) 158–168.

(ii) Zacharias (incert. orig.), a Syriac *Vita* of Peter, which is preserved only in a double Georgian version. N.Y. Marr, Georgian text with Russian trans. (St. Peters-burg 1896). According to Lang, art. cit, the Georgian version, despite all its deforma-tions and mutilations, is the lost *Vita* of Peter, written by Zacharias Scholasticus, which is preserved only in fragments. These fragments are to be found in E. W. Brooks, CSCO 7/8 (Parisiis 1907) 18, 11–12. Against this theory see P. Devos, *AnBoll* 70 (1952) 385–388, who stresses rather the similarity between the Georgian and Syriac *Vita* (ed. Raabe), despite all their differences. See too P. Devos, 'Quand Pierre l'Ibère vint-il à Jérusalem?', *AnBoll* 86 (1968) 337–350; L. Perrone, *La chiesa di Palestina*, Index s.v. Pietro Iberico (326).

(b) Isaiah of Gaza (Scete?): CPG 7000; see L. Regnault, *DSp* 7 (1971) 2083–2095; idem, 'Isaïe de Scété ou de Gaza', *RAM* 46 (1970); D. J. Chitty, 'Abba Isaiah', *JTS* NS 22 (1971) 47–72; Zacharias Rh. (Scholasticus), *Vita Isaiae* (BHO 550; CPG 7000), ed. E. W. Brooks, *Vitae virorum apud Monophysitas celeberrimorum* = CSCO 7/8 (Parisiis 1907) 1–16 (Syr.), 3–10 (Lat.). The authenticity of the work is denied by R. Draguet, CSCO 293 (1968) 98*–115*; it is defended by P. Devos, *AnBoll* 93 (1975) 159 n. 2. Isaias Gazaeus (Scetensis?), *Asceticon*, ed. tr. R. Draguet, CSCO 289–290; 293–294 (Louvain 1968); cf. CPG 5555. Draguet disputes the authenticity of the work (CSCO 293, 85*–126*) and wants to attribute it to a certain Isaiah of Scete. According to L. Regnault and D. J. Chitty, art. cit., Isaiah of Scete is identical with Isaiah of Gaza. Cf. the *Vita* of Zacharias, Brooks CSCO 8 (V) 3: Isaias, '*cum corpore Aegyptius esset, animae autem nobilitate Hierosolymitanus*'. In the work the adoration of the Holy Cross is given prominence (p. 5); of importance is also the reference on p. 7 to instances of conflict in Palestine at the time of Peter the Iberian concerning the double *consubstantialitas Christi*. On the christology see L. Perrone, *La chiesa di Palestina*, 286–295; H. Keller, 'L'abbé Isaïe-le-Jeune', *Irén* 16 (1939) (113–126) 117–125, with reference to the *Asceticon*. On the *Vita* and the *Asceticon* see A. Guillaumont, 'Une notice syriaque inédite sur la vie de l'Abbé Isaie', *AnBoll* 67 (1949) 350–360; idem, *L'Ascéticon copte de l'Abbé Isaie* (Le Caire 1956).

(c) Anonymous, *Narratio de obitu Theodosii hierosolymitani et Romani monachi*. Ed. of Syriac text by J. P. N. Land, *Anecdota Syriaca* 3, 341–343; Latin in E. W. Brooks, *Vitae virorum apud Monophysitas celeberrimorum*, CSCO 7/8 (T.V., 15–19); German: Ahrens-Krüger, *KG des Zach.Rh.* (Leipzig 1899) 257–263, with n. 384/5.

III. Syria and Mesopotamia (Chalcedonian and post-Chalcedonian period)

1. Individual biographies: Ortiz de Urbina, *Patrologia Syriaca* 200–205:
(a) Two biographies of Barṣawma (archimandrite):

(i) Samuel, a *vita* preserved in Syriac and translated into Ethiopic.

(ii) Abraham, supposed teacher of Barṣawma, who recounts his pupil's deeds. Both *Vitae* are suspect.

(b) John (Joḥanan) Bar Kursos, Bishop of Tella (482/3–6.11.538); *Vita* of Elias, his pupil; ed. trad. H. G. Kleyn, *Het Leven van J. van Tella door Elias* (Leyden 1882) (c. vers. neerland.). John was important in establishing the monophysite hierarchy by the ordination of priests. His *formula fidei* survives in BM Add. 14.549, s. VIII—IX. Also unedited is a commentary on the *Trishagion*: Vat.Syr. 159. XIX°.

(c) Biographies of Severus, Patriarch of Antioch (512–518) (d. 538); ed. tr. M. A. Kugener, PO 2, 203–400.

(i) John of Beth-Aphthonia, *Vita Severi*, ed. tr. idem, PO 2, 207–264.

(ii) Zacharias Rhetor, *Vita Severi*, ed. tr. idem, PO 2, 7–115; see further W. Bauer, 'Die Severus-Vita des Zacharias Rhetor', *Aufsätze u. kl. Schriften* (Tübingen 1967) 210–228.

(iii) Athanasius of Antioch, *The Life of Severus Patriarch of Antioch*. ed. tr. E.-J. Goodspeed et W. E. Crum, PO 4 (Paris 1908) 591–718 (Ethiopic trans. from Arabic; original was, however, probably Greek).

(iv) A. Vööbus, 'Découverte d'un memrā de Giwargi, Évêque des Arabes sur Sévère d'Antioche', *Mus* 84 (1971) 433–436 (mention of works of Severus).

(v) K. E. McVey, *The Memra on the life of Severus of Antioch. A Critical Edition of the Syriac Text* (Cambridge, Mass. 1977).

(d) *Vita* of Jacob Baradaeus (d. 578). See Ortiz de Urbina. *Patr. Syr.* §111; ed. E. W. Brooks, PO 19, 228–268 with English trans. A. van Roey, 'Les débuts de l'Église jacobite', *Chalkedon* II, 339–360.

(e) Old biography of Aḥudemmeh (d. 575): Ortiz de Urbina, *Patr. Syr.* §116; ed. F. Nau, PO 3, 1–51. Aḥudemmeh was first a Nestorian, then monophysite. Jacob Baradaeus handed over to him the mission to the Arabs in Mesopotamia. He had a philosophical formation and utilised Aristotle in particular: *Opuscula de anima, De unione animae et corporis*, ed. F. Nau, PO 3, 97–120.

(f) Leontius of Neapolis, *Vie de Syméon le Fou et Vie de Jean de Chypre*. Édition commentée par A.-J. Festugière en collaboration avec L. Rydén = Bibl.archéol.et histor. t.95 (Paris 1974); L. Rydén, *Das Leben des heiligen Narren Symeon von Leontios von Neapolis* = Acta Univ. Upsal. Stud. Graeca Upsal. 4 (Uppsala 1963): idem, *Bemerkungen zum Leben des heiligen Narren Symeon von Leontios von Neapolis* = Acta Univ. Upsal. Stud. Graeca Upsal. 6 (Uppsala 1970).

2. Collections of *vitae* from the area of Syria

(a) *Théodoret de Cyr, Histoire des moines de Syrie*, ed. tr. P. Canivet-A. Leroy-Molinghen = SC 234: 'Histoire Philothée' I–XIII; SC 257: 'Histoire Philothée' XIV–XXX. Traité sur la Charité (XXXI) (Paris 1977, 1979). J. Gribomont, 'Théodoret et les Vies des Pères', *RivStorLettRel* 61 (1981) 161–172. Geographically Theodoret included Northern Syria with Antioch and its province, Chalcis (with prov. Chalcidensis), Apamea (with prov. Apamensis), Cyrrhus (with prov. Cyrrhensis), part of the prov. Euphratensis and Osrohëne, i.e. the area from the gulf of Cilicia to Edessa in Mesopotamia. See P. Canivet, SC 234, 11 with reference to idem, *Le monachisme syrien selon Théodoret de Cyr* (Paris 1977) §107. The most southerly monastic community mentioned by Theodoret lies in Lebanon, near Emesa (XVII 2–4); the Palestinian monks are ignored. Several monks come from Pontus (influence of Basil the Great), from Galatia (IX, 1), from the area of Cilicia and from Euphratesia.

For Theodoret, Moses is the model author of hagiographical works; he wrote them not with the Egyptian knowledge that he commanded, but through divine inspiration. Cf. *Hist. rel.* I 1: SC 234, 160.

Of the monks who were Theodoret's contemporaries, three play a special rôle in the history of the post-Chalcedonian period.

(i) Jacob, pupil of Maron, from near Cyrrhus: *Hist. rel.* XXI: SC 257, 70–123; BHG³ 777, p. 256; Canivet, *Monachisme syrien* §143–146.

(ii) Simeon Stylites the Elder (b. 390 in Cilicia, d. 24.7. or 2.9.459), founder of stylite asceticism. BHG³, 1678–1688; *Auctarium* 175; CPG 6640–6650; *Hist. rel.* XXVI: SC 257, 158–214. Canivet, op. cit., §74. All texts concerned with Simeon Stylites can be found in H. Lietzmann-H. Hilgenfeld, *Das Leben des hl. Symeon Stylites*, TU 32, 4 (Leipzig 1908). Stern criticism of this edition is made by E. Honigmann, 'The Monks Symeon, Jacobus and Baradatus', in idem, *Patristic Studies* = ST 173 (Città del Vaticano 1953) 92–100, nr. XIII, esp. 93, n. 4. As well as the *Vita* composed by Theodoret we have:

(1) *Vita* written by Antonius in Greek, for which Theodoret is used: TU 32, 4. Cf. Honigmann, op. cit.

(2) Syriac *Vita* based on BM Add. 14.484. Trans.: TU 32, 79–188; according to Honigmann, op. cit., Vat. Syr. 117 would have been a better basis; reference in ibid. to P. Peeters, 'Syméon Stylite et ses premiers biographes', *AnBoll* 61 (1943) 29–71; reprint in id., *Le tréfonds oriental de l'hagiographie byzantine* = Subs. hag. 26 (1950) 93–136; criticism in M. Richard, 'Théodoret, Jean d'Antioche et les moines d'Orient', *Opera Minora* II, nr. 47. A.-J. Festugière, *Antioche païenne et chrétienne. Libanius, Chrysostome et les moines de Syrie* (Paris 1959), XII; Le premier stylite, Syméon l'Ancien, 347–401 (with French trans. of *Hist. rel.* XXVI, based on the Greek text of TU 32; see the Note additionelle, 418–423).

(iii) The monk Baradatus: *Hist. rel.* XVII: SC 257, 216–222; BHG³ 211, p. 75. On the name see Canivet, *Monachisme syrien*, §182f. See below Ch. III. Lit.: S. Ashbrook, 'Syriac hagiography: an emporium of cultural influences', J. H. Eaton (ed.), *Horizons in Semitic Studies* (Birmingham, University of Birmingham 1980) 59–68.

(b) John of Ephesus, a Syrian b. c. 507, d. after 588 (see above Part I, C 4): *Historiae beatorum Orientalium,* ed. with English trans. by E. W. Brooks, PO 17 (1923) 1–304; 18 (1924) 513–698; 19 (1925) 151–227; cf. Ortiz de Urbina, *Patrologia syriaca* §115, p. 166–167; D. Stiernon, *DSp* 8 (1974) 484–486 s.v. The design of the work is reminiscent of Palladius, *Historia Lausiaca,* and of Theodoret, *Historia religiosa.* It was written in 566 and expanded in 567/8. Over 70 persons are introduced, who are all contemporaries of the author. The district of Amid receives preference. Stiernon writes, op. cit., 485: 'Tantôt, c'est un récit biographique assez complet; tantôt, une anecdote merveilleuse ... Tout le récit baigne dans un climat admiratif. Nulle part quelque instant sur la doctrine'. This is somewhat too black and white.

(i) The significant *Vita* for us is nr. X; Mar Simeon the Bishop, the Persian debater: PO 17, 137–158, from the time of Emperor Anastasius:

(1) Reference to Simeon's knowledge of scripture and the Fathers and to his skill as a debator against the Nestorians, who are dominant. Cf. 148–149.

(2) Vivid contemporary picture of the early history of Christianity in Persia: the Schools of Bardesanes and Manes are widely disseminated; the school of Edessa and the influence of Bardesanes and of Marcion (138–139).

(3) Missionary activity of Simeon from Ctesiphon to Constantinople (140–142).

(4) Double christological attack of the monophysite Simeon (later bishop of Beth Arsham) against Eutychian-Manichaeans and against Nestorians (as we shall often encounter).

(ii) We find countless references to the turn of events after the death of Emperor Anastasius I (518) and the reform of Justin and Justinian, but also to the counter-action of the Empress Theodora and the promotion of the monophysite mission. See PO 17, 187–213; 18, 526–540; 607–623; 624–641; 676–684. There is an encomium of five patriarchs, who are in exile because of their opposition to Chalcedon (PO 18, 684–690): Severus of Antioch, Theodosius of Alexandria, Anthimus of Constantinople (Patriarch from 535–536, then deposed, but hidden in the palace), Sergius and Paul.

(iii) Doctrinal allusions: Mar Simeon: PO 17, 149–150 (the transcendence of Jesus in contrast with the Nestorian 'Adoptianism').

(iv) *Vita* XVI (PO 17, 229–247): Simeon the mountain hermit. Good indications of the state of Christianisation in the mountainous region in the neighbourhood of Melitene. A good example of a baptismal catechesis, which offers common doctrines without monophysite peculiarities (239–240) (around 515 AD). Cf. the personal assignment of John of Ephesus to convert the heathen (above Part II, C I 4).

Bibliography
(a) On the piety of Syrian monasticism:
A. Vööbus, *History of Asceticism in the Syrian Orient*, I. *The Origin of Asceticism. Early Monasticism in Persia.* II. *Early Monasticism in Mesopotamia and Syria*, CSCO 184, 197 = Subs. vols 14, 17 (Louvain 1958, 1960).
G. M. Colombas, O.S.B., *El monacato primitivo* = BAC (Madrid 1974) 119–153 (Ch. IV: El monacato siriaco), with criticism of A. Vööbus, op. cit., esp. on the evaluation of the 'biografia bastante, fantástica' of Rabbula of Edessa (d. 436); Colombas, op. cit. 137, n. 34, with reference to the worthwhile study of G. G. Blum, *Rabbula von Edessa. Der Christ, der Bischof, der Theologe*, CSCO 300 = Subs. 34 (Louvain 1969).
E. Beck, 'Ein Beitrag zur Terminologie des ältesten syrischen Mönchtums', in B. Steidle (ed.), *Antonius Magnus Eremita* (Rom 1956) 254–267; J. Gribomont, 'Le monachisme au sein de l'Église en Syrie et en Cappadoce', *StudMon* 7 (1965) 7–24.
(b) On the stylites see the various introductions to the biographies in H. Delehaye, *Les Saints Stylites* = Subs. hag. 14 (Bruxelles-Paris 1923):
(i) Symeon the Elder: Ch. I, p. I—XXXIV; see CPG 6640–6650.
(ii) Daniel, Symeon's pupil, on the Bosphorus: XXXV–LVIII; French trans. of the *Vita* in A.-J. Festugière, *Les moines d'Orient* II, 93–171 (with chronology).
(iii) Symeon the Younger (d. 592); Delehaye LIX–LXXV; H.-G. Beck, *Kirche u. theol. Lit. i. byz. Reich* 397 with sources and literature; CPG 7369.
(iv) Alypius; Delehaye LXX–LXXXV. Alypius travels to Chalcedon to erect a chapel in honour of St. Euphemia; thus in *Vita* I, §10–11 and *Vita* II; different details in Antonius of Hagia Sophia (BHG³ 66d), ed. F. Halkin, Subs. hag. 38: *Inédits Byzantins d'Ochrida, Candie et Moscou* (Bruxelles 1963) 167–208.
On the spread of the stylites' way of life see Delehaye, ibid., Ch. VII, p. CXVII–CXLIII: 'Les stylites à travers les âges'. The main areas were Syria, Palestine, Mesopotamia (among Semitic people); to a lesser extent they were found in the Greek-speaking area: Cilicia, Paphlagonia, Caria, Bithynia; there were isolated stylites also in Georgia, Thrace, Macedonia and Egypt. See further I. Peña, P. Castellana, R. Fernandez, *Les Stylites Syriens* (Milano 1975) 79–84. The stylites too were split into Chalcedonians and anti-Chalcedonians: ibid., 65–67, with reference to John Moschus, *Pratum spirituale* ch. 29 and 36: PG 87³, 2876C–2877A; 2884C–2885C. Monophysite stylites were present especially in North Syria. Chalcedonians forced

to descend from his pillar Mar Ze'ora, who was known as far away as Rome: Michael Syr., *Chron.* IX, 23: Chabot II, 197b–199b.

IV. The Nestorian east Syrians

See J. M. Fiey, *Jalons* 8–31: II. Sources et leur valeur; esp. 18ff.

1. Patriarchs

(a) *Liber turris* (Le livre de la tour) received its original form from Mâri b. Sulaymân (12th cent.), and was reworked in the 14th cent. by ʿAmr b. Matta of Tirhân and by a priest from Mossul, Slîwa (or Salîba) b. Yôḥannân. From this work H. Gismondi took the chapter *De Patriarchis Nestorianorum* and published it: *Maris Amri et Slibae De Patriarchis Nestorianorum Commentaria ex codicibus vaticanis edidit et latine reddidit ...*, 2 vols (Rome 1896, 1899) (Arabic and Latin). See the reference to J. S. Assemani, BO, and Le Quien, *Oriens christianus* II.

(b) *Vitae* of Catholicoi and Martyrs. See Fiey, *Jalons* 23–25.

2. Monks

(a) Iso'dnâh, Metropolitan of Baṣra (prob. c. 860–870), *History* of the founders of monasteries in the Persian and Arabian empires, better known under the name *Liber castitatis*. Here we find a succession of 140 short notices concerning 'all Fathers who founded monasteries in the Persian and Arabian empires and wrote books on the monastic life, and about holy metropolitans and bishops, of whom some founded schools, others wrote books on religious life and again others founded monasteries in the East ...' a short form of the *Liber castitatis* (probably the oldest form) is found in many MSS as 'Hymn to the Saints' (Fiey, op. cit., 18).

For an analysis of the work see J. M. Fiey, 'Icho'dnah, Métropolite de Baṣra, et son œuvre', *OrSyr* 11 (1966) 431–450.

(b) *The Book of Governors* (also wrongly called *Historia monastica*) (Fiey, op. cit., 19). This is also to be distinguished from the work just mentioned. Only Books I, II, IV and V bear out the title and represent the real work. In Book III general history is introduced. Book VI is a separate work and probably older. Under the title 'History of the monastery of Rabban Cyprian' it fuses two distinct monographs and a general preface, which is of the greatest significance for the early history of Assyrian monasticism.

Edition: *The Book of Governors, by Thomas, Bishop of Marga*, Chaldean with English trans. by E. A. Wallis Budge, 2 vols (London 1893); J. M. Fiey, loc. cit.

(c) The *Biography of Rabban Bar ʿEta* (d. 628), written after 661. Cf. Fiey, *Jalons* 24: the *Vita* allows us to define more clearly the beginnings of the Assyrian monasticism of Abraham the Great, gives us more specific details concerning Sahdona, about the contemporary bishops of Nineve, the conflicts between west and east Syrians; cf. further Fiey, *OrSyr* 11 (1966) 1–16, with corrections in idem,' 'Isô'yaw le Grand', *OCP* 35 (1969) 305–333; 36 (1970) 5–46.

(d) History of the monastery of Mâr Sawrišô' of Beṭ Qôqâ, text and French trans. by M. Mingana, *Sources Syriaques* (Mossoul-Leipzig 1907) 177–271. This text is important for the history of monasticism.

Literature on East Syrian monasticism: J. M. Fiey, *Jalons*, Ch. V, 100–112; id., *L'Assyrie chrétienne*, vol. II (Beyrouth n.d.) 821–827: Le monachisme assyrien; E. Degen, 'Daniel bar Maryam', *OrChr* 52 (1968) (45–89) 46–48; A. Vööbus, *History of Asceticism in the Syrian Orient*, vol. I 2 = CSCO 184, Subs. 14 (Bruxelles 1958) 173–325, esp. Ch. IV, 288ff.: Advance of Monasticism in the Fifth Century, 1. Leading Personalities.

3. Martyrs and Confessors

(a) *History of the holy Fathers who were persecuted on behalf of the truth.* The work gives an account of the Nestorian church from its beginning to Abraham, the leader of the school of Nisibis (d. 569). Text in F. Nau, *L'histoire de Barḥadbešabba ʿArbaia*, PO XXIII (Paris 1932) (Part I), IX (Paris 1913) (Part II); German: G. Hoffmann, 'Auszüge aus syrischen Akten persischer Martyrer', *AbhKundeMorgl.* VII, 3 (1880) 43–60.

(b) Biography of the martyr Isoʿsawran (d. 620), written by the Catholicus Isōʿyaw III. Ed. with French summary by J.-B. Chabot, *Nouvelles archives des missions scientifiques et littéraires*, VII (1897) 485–584: the newly converted (to monphysism) try to convert the confessor in prison.

4. Biographical material in Mar Barḥadbešabba ʿArbaya, *Cause de la fondation des écoles*, Syriac and French in A. Scher, PO IV, 317–404 (Paris 1907). Cf. Fiey, *Jalons* 26 on the question of the author. In the work we find a dithyrambic on Ḥenana.

V. Armenian and Georgian hagiography

On the general position and special significance of this hagiography see P. Peeters, 'Traductions et Traducteurs dans l'hagiographie orientale à l'époque byzantine', in idem, *Le tréfonds oriental de l'hagiographie byzantine* = Subs.hag. 26 (Bruxelles 1950) 165–218; on Armenia, ibid., V, 188–198; on Georgia, ibid., VI, 198–213; idem, 'Les débuts du christianisme en Géorgie d'après les sources hagiographiques', *AnBoll* 50 (1932) 5–58; 54–58 on Peter the Iberian. M. Tarchnišvili, 'Sources arméno- géorgiennes de l'histoire ancienne de Géorgie', *Mus* 60 (1947) 29–50.

On the sources:

1. S. Der Nersessian, 'Le synaxaire arménien de Grégoire VII d'Anazarbe', *AnBoll* 68 (1950) 261–285; P. Peeters, 'Pour l'histoire du synaxaire arménien', *AnBoll* 30 (1911) 5–26. For editions see PO 5, 6, 15, 16.

2. Individual *vitae*

Koriun, *Description of the Life and Death of the holy Teacher* Mesrop (a name common from the 8th century onwards; oldest sources: Mastocʿ) (b. 360, d. 440). The work was composed shortly after 453. German trans. by S. Weber, BKV², vol. 47 (with introduction), 185–231; selected speeches, from a collection of 23, have been added.

VI. Constantinople

H. Delehaye, *Synaxarium Ecclesiae Constantinopolitanae* (1902): H.-G. Beck, *Kirche und theol. Lit. im byz. Reich* (1959) 267–275; *The Byzantine Saint. University of Birmingham Fourteenth Spring Symposium of Byzantine Studies* ed. by S. Hackel = *Studies Supplementary to Sobornost* 5 (London 1981); S. Brock, 'The Byzantine Saint—A Report on the Fourteenth Spring Symposium of Byzantine Studies at the Univerity of Birmingham', *Sobornost* 2 (1980) 75–76. See *ByzZ* 74 (1981) 424–429.

1. Devotion to St. Euphemia.

F. Halkin, *Euphémie de Chalcédoine. Légendes Byzantines* = Subs.hag. 41 (Bruxelles 1965); idem, *Recherches et Documents d'hagiographie Byzantine* = Subs.hag. 51 (Bruxelles 1971).

2. Maximus Confessor (ca 580–662) and the monenergist-monothelete controversy.

W. Lackner, 'Zu Quellen und Datierung der Maximosvita (BHG³ 1234)', *AnBoll* 85 (1967) 285–316.

S. Brock, 'An Early Syriac Life of Maximus the Confessor', *AnBoll* 91 (1973) 299–346.

J. M. Garrigues, 'Le martyre de saint Maxime le Confesseur', *RevThom* 76 (1976) 410–452.

R. Bracke, *Ad Sancti Maximi Vitam. Studie van de biografische documenten en de levensbeschrijvingen betreffende Maximus Confessor (ca 580–662)*, Diss. Katholieke Universiteit te Leuven (Leuven 1980). In his evaluation and chronological assessment of the *Vita s. Maximi* Bracke comes to other conclusions than W. Lackner and S. Brock, and situates the oldest recensions of the Greek *Vita* in the period between 680 and 700. See, however, the review by J.-L. van Dieten, *ByzZ* 75 (1982) 359–361.

Further information on hagiography in the period of the monenergist controversy is to be found in H.-G. Beck, *Kirche u. theol. Lit. im byz. Reich*, 459–467. Particularly important is the 'famous *Hypomnestikon*' dedicated to the suffering of Anastasius Apocrisiarius and Pope Martin I (Beck 462–463).

3. Iconoclastic period

See H.-G. Beck, op. cit., 506–514; A. J. Visser, *Nikephoros und der Bilderstreit. Eine Untersuchung über die Stellung des Konstantinopler Patriarchen Nikephoros innerhalb der ikonoklastischen Wirren* (Haag 1952) 9–11 (various *vitae* of martyrs and confessors). See ibid. 49–56 for a list of contents of the *Vita Nicephori*: PG 100, 41–160; C. de Boor, *Nicephorus, Opuscula Historica* (Lipsiae 1880) 139–217. In Ch. 7 of this *Vita* (PG 100, 91ff.; de Boor, 169–206) is found a 'theological discussion [concerning image-veneration] in the form of an extensive disputation between Saints and Emperor Leo the Armenian' (Visser, op. cit., 50). The *Vita Antonii* gave the inspiration for this manner of presentation in that it contains an integral homily.

Summary of Part II

Cf. F. Winkelmann, *ByzSlav* 37 (1976) 183–190. The significance of the works of ecclesiastical historiography for the description of the history of christological belief must be briefly characterised.

1. *Positive*: Together with chronicles and hagiographical works, the ecclesiastical histories offer (a) important material for situating the development of faith in general and comprehensive terms (i.e. the fundamentals for marking the external framework and divisions of epochs or phases of the course of development); (b) significant doctrinal documents; and (c) criteria for the hermeneutic of these documents. With regard to this hermeneutic it must be noted that the subject-matter of ecclesiastical historiography, the Church, is interpreted above all from the idea of 'orthodoxy'. That results in a closer relationship to the history of doctrine or faith. The principle of 'orthodoxy' holds for both Chalcedonians and anti-Chalcedonians, because each party considered itself orthodox and the representative of the true Church (cf. Winkelmann 186). Orthodoxy was always regarded as the goal of development. Because in our period the Byzantine imperial Church experienced for the first time within the borders that existed up to 451 a division that was spreading further and further, criteria of 'orthodoxy' had to be found which were independent of the Constantinian principle: 'Unity of the faith (of the Church) is the foundation of the well-being of the Empire'. This was the difficulty

facing the Church historians; it was also their embarrassment to the extent that they wanted to include the history of faith in their descriptions of ecclesiastical history.

2. *Negative*: There were various factors that also made it difficult for the representatives of the Great Church to interpret and account for their own history of faith. These were the following: (i) the close link between 'imperial Church' and '*imperium Romanum*' (cf. Winkelmann, ibid.); (ii) the religious status of the Emperor, which was also never questioned by the religious party which happened at that time to be suppressed by the state; (iii) the unexplained 'autonomy' of Church and state, each for itself and in the context of their necessary relationships; and (iv) the amalgamation of competences in decisions relating to faith. But it was precisely the crisis of the imperial Church after Chalcedon which forced the necessary clarification of competences and of authority in questions of faith to be undertaken; included in this too was the relationship of Church and state. We shall encounter theoretical and practical attempts to do this, but they are to be found least of all in the works of ecclesiastical history. The *Church Histories*, however, show clearly that knowledge gained theoretically would not be maintained in practice. The Acacian schism and the Justinianic era are classic examples of this type of inconsistency.

PART III

Christological florilegia from Chalcedon to the iconoclastic controversy.

As early as the post-Nicaean period, and then especially in the confrontation which had Chalcedon (451) as its acme, proof from the Fathers was cultivated in the literary genre of the florilegia, which had their model in the pre-Christian philosophical schools. In their variety they provide a mirror-image of the different phases of theological confrontation from the fourth century up to the iconoclastic controversy in the eighth century.

Comprehensive surveys: Th. Schermann, *Die Geschichte der dogmatischen Florilegien vom VI.–VIII. Jahrhundert* = TU 28, 1 (Leipzig 1904) (largely superceded); G. Bardy, art. 'Florilèges', *Catholicisme* 4 (1956) 1360–1364; H. Chadwick, 'Florilegium', *RAC* 7 (1969) 1131–1160; cols 1131–1143: pre-Christian, pagan florilegia; cols 1143–1160: Christian florilegia (collections of testimonia, biblical and patristic anthologies, catenae); joint article 'Florilèges spirituels', *DSp* 4 (1964) = (a) H.-M. Rochais, 'Flor. latins', cols 435–460 (literary genre, terminology); (b) P. Delehaye, 'Flor. Médiévaux d'éthique', cols 460–475; (c) M. Richard, 'Flor. grecs', cols 475–512. Richard published what for us is the most important research: (1) 'Notes sur les florilèges dogmatiques du Ve et du VIe siècle', Actes du VIe Congrès International d'Études byzantines

I (Paris 1950) 307–318 = *Opera Minora* I, 2; idem, 'Les florilèges diphysites du Vᵉ et du VIᵉ siècle', *Chalkedon* I, 721–748 = *Opera Minora* I, 3.

(A) Pre-Chalcedonian origins
I. Trinitarian florilegium

Cf. M. Richard, 'Les florilèges diphysites', *Opera Minora* I, 3, 722–723; M. Tetz, 'Zur Edition der dogmatischen Schriften des Athanasius von Alexandrien', *ZKG* 67 (1955/6) 1–28; idem, 'Zum Streit zwischen Orthodoxie und Häresie an der Wende zum 4. u. 5. Jahrhunderts', *EvTheol* 20 (1961) 354–368.

According to M. Tetz, ibid. 360, the beginning to the new literary genre of theological proof was made by Basil, *De Spiritu Sancto* ch. 29: PG 32, 200B–209C: 'From Basil of Caesarea we have the first well-defined florilegium that is preserved'. With Basil the 'explicit proof from the Fathers' in the form of the florilegium was inaugurated (ibid. 361). This fact is worth mentioning, even if it is not a question of christology in the strict sense. Still, the new genre did not take long to be applied to christology.

II. Christological florilegia of the pre-Chalcedonian period

1. The path to the christological florilegium in the strict sense was trodden by the followers of Bishop Marcellus of Ancyra, and then in the *Expositio fidei ad Athanasium* of the deacon Eugenius of Ancyra, the significance of which M. Tetz has exposed: 'Markellianer und Athanasios von Alexandrien', *ZNW* 64 (1973) 75–121; 115 on the florilegium.

2. As the next example of the new method M. Tetz, *EvTheol* 20 (1961) 355 f., names the *Contestatio Eusebii*, by which the procedure against Patriarch Nestorius of Constantinople was set in motion. Tetz gives a German translation of this appeal (ibid., 355 f), based on ACO I 1, 1, 101 f. Immediately before the Council of Ephesus the new procedure of theological proof repeatedly receives the imprint of the chief opponent of Nestorius, Cyril of Alexandria, and his imitator, Theodotus of Ancyra.

3. Florilegia of Cyril of Alexandria and Theodotus of Ancyra: without intending an exact chronological sequence, we mention first the *Libri V contra Nestorium* of Cyril (ACO I 1, 6, 13–106; CPG 5217). Book I opens with the *Capita excerpta ex Nestorio*, next comes an anthology of 'heresies' of Nestorius, as Cyril encountered them in his texts (ACO, loc. cit., 1–9; cf. Loofs, *Nestoriana* 353–358). The rest of Cyril's work is an enormous biblical counter-proof from the OT and NT. According to A. van Roey, art. cit., Theodotus of Ancyra imitated the methodology of Cyril, and in doing so used Cyril's citations from Nestorius. He wrote *Three Books against Nestorius*, which are preserved only in Syriac and have yet to be edited. Book I and part of Book II are missing. Cf. CPG 6131. His homily against Nestorius has come down to us: ACO I 1, 2, 71–73, and is edited in Ethiopic with a German trans. in M. B. Weischer, *Qērellos* IV 1, 42–53. Significant too is the florilegium of Cyril in the *Oratio (Prosphoneticus) ad Arcadiam et Marinam augustas de fide*: ACO I 1, 5, 62–118, where we find pronouncements of nine well-known theologians and Fathers of the fourth–fifth centuries (pp. 65–68), including texts of ps. Athanasius. Indeed, emphasis lies again on the 'immense literary mosaic to present the correct doctrine concerning Christ' (70–118). This florilegium is also preserved in Ethiopic in the so-called *Qērellos* (II). Cf. B. M. Weischer, 'Das christologische Florilegium in Qerellos II', *OrChr* 64 (1980) 109–133, where the evaluation just given can be found. Of great influence was the so-called *Florilegium Ephesinum* of Session I in 431: ACO I 1, 2, p. 39, 0–45, 3, which, expanded by other testimonies,

returns in the Session of 22 July, 431: ACO I 1, 7, p. 89, 26–95, 18. The testimonies of the recognised Fathers and the extracts from Nestorius were juxtaposed, which revealed the latter's 'heresy'. Cf. ACO I 1, 2, 45–52. Other florilegia of Cyril are to be found in the *Apologia XII Capitulorum contra Orientales*: ACO I 1, 7, p. 36, 33–37, 23; 45, 20–31; 64, 1–65, 4.

4. Florilegia of Augustine in the West: Vincent of Lérins compiled a collection of citations from Augustine in order to combat Nestorianism, and sent it to Pope Sixtus III (432–440). See J. Madoz, *Excerpta Vincentii Lirinensis* (Madrid 1940): text edition 101–132; cf. 152, the inventory of texts from Augustine. See below on Eugippius.

5. Theodoret of Cyrus, two florilegia: (*a*) In the *Pentalogus* (432 AD), Book IV, preserved only in Pope Gelasius, *de duabus naturis*, ed. Schwartz, PS 96–106 (complete or partial ?). Cf. now L. Abramowski-A. E. Goodman, *A Nestorian Collection of Christological Texts. Cambridge University Library MS. Oriental 1319*, vol. I–II (Cambridge 1972); A. Grillmeier, JdChr I², 707, n. 15; see below Part III C IV. The Cambridge MS contains in VI a florilegium with testimonies which occur in Gelasius, one group of which has parallels in the *Eranistes* and one of which has not (see below). Should the parallels not covered by the *Eranistes* belong to the *Pentalogus*, it would be proved by the Cambridge florilegium that Gelasius did not take over the entire *Pentalogus* florilegium. (*b*) In the *Eranistes* (c. 447–448). See G. H. Ettlinger, *Theodoret of Cyrus Eranistes* (Oxford 1975). The title is nicely translated by C. Andresen, *TZ* 37 (1981) 319 as 'Lumpensammler' (rag-and-bone man); cf. the French 'chiffonnier'. Ettlinger investigates these collections in section II: The patristic citations, pp. 9–35. The text contains three florilegia: fl. I: pp. 91–111; fl. II: pp. 153–187; fl. III: pp. 220–252. From these florilegia are derived many later collections. After 451 the florilegium which Leo I added to his *Tomus ad Flavianum* was included in the *Eranistes*. Cf. M. Richard, *Opera Minora* I, 3, 723–725.

6. A Greek florilegium from christological homilies of the fourth and fifth centuries on the birth of Christ (Paris. gr. 1491). This has been referred to already in CCT I, 520 n. 1 (Proclus).

7. The collection of passages from the Fathers which Eutyches added to his *libellus fidei*, which, together with a letter and other documents, he sent to Rome after the Synod of Constantinople in 448. The collection contained the texts supposedly deriving from Roman Popes, which were sought for in vain in Rome (ACO II 2, 1, 34–42, nr. 7–12; cf. JdChr I², 735).

(B) Florilegia at the Council of Chalcedon

I. The florilegium of 451, taken from the *Eranistes*: ACO II 1, 3, 114, 4–116, 2.

II. The florilegium of Pope Leo I, added to the *Tomus I* when this was sent for the second time to Constantinople (Greek only in ACO II 1, 1, p. 20, 7–25, 6).

(C) Florilegia in the conflict concerning Chalcedon between 451 and 600

I. Pro-Chalcedonian florilegia between 451 and 500

1. To *ep.* 165 (AD 458) to Emperor Leo I, which is called the *Tomus II*, Pope Leo I added an expanded version of the florilegium appended to the *Tomus I*: ACO II 4, p. 119, 15–131, 17; Schwartz, 'Cod. Vat. gr. 1431', p. 71, 4–85, 22.

2. *Florilegium Cyrillianum*: cf. further Schwartz ACO I 1, 1, XII–XVI. This is a collection made in Alexandria by several authors and wrongly attributed to a writer Dorotheus, which contains 244 extracts from 30 works of Cyril. It was intended to provide evidence that Cyril agreed with the formula 'two natures after the union' (in Christ). In about the year 482 it was taken to Rome by John Talaia and given to Pope Simplicius. It fell into the hands of the Chalcedonian ('Nestorian') John Gazophylax, who sent it to the Patrician Appion to cure him of the error of Severus of Antioch and to convince him that Chalcedon was in agreement with the doctrines of Cyril. Here we have the most important theological florilegium of the pro-Chalcedonian variety. During his sojourn in Constantinople in the years 508–511, Severus of Antioch made a critical examination of the florilegium and rejected it. It is transmitted to us directly, but incompletely, in three Greek MSS; cf. R. Hespel, *Le florilège Cyrillien refuté par Sévère d'Antioche. Étude et édition critique* = .BiblMus 37 (Louvain 1955) 55–56; the florilegium is transmitted indirectly in Vat. Syr. 139 = the *Philalethes* of Severus, Syriac with French trans. ed. by R. Hespel, *Sévère d'Antioche, Le Philalèthe*: CSCO 133 (T), 134 (V) (Louvain 1952); a collateral transmission is found in the texts of excerpted works: 37 passages cannot be found in *opera* edited up to now. Of these P. E. Pusey identified the direct transmission of 33 texts and edited them from two MSS: *Sancti Patris nostri Cyrilli archiepiscopi Alexandrini in D. Johannis Evangelium*, III (Oxford 1872) 476–489, ch. 76–90; 549: ch. 120; 583–585; ch. 121; 493–497: ch. 181–191; 511–512, 525–526: ch. 192–196. R. Draguet succeeded in identifying the remaining four passages, ch. 73 and 178–180. For a critical Greek edition of all passages see now R. Hespel, op. cit., 103–216; from ch. 231 Greek in apparatus only. See ibid., 217–233: Notes critiques. There existed also a second *Florilegium Cyrillianum*, which is not preserved.

3. The florilegium in the appendix to the *Tractatus de duabus naturis* of Pope Gelasius (see above under Theodoret).

Summary:

(1) Before 500 we have thus two kinds of anthologies: one in which a single author (whether pro or contra) is excerpted (Cyril; Nestorius, Augustine).

In this connection we may refer also to the Augustine *Encyclopedia* of Eugippius (d. after 533), and to his *Excerpta ex operibus S. Augustini* (unsatisfactorily edited by P. Knoell, CSEL 9, 1858 f; cf. CPL 676). M. M. Gorman, 'The Manuscript Tradition of Eugippius' "Excerpta ex operibus Sancti Augustini"', *RevBén* 92 (1982) 7–32; 93 (1983) 7–30. The author remarks in vol. 92: 'Eugippius seems to have been the first important Augustinian scholar in Italy of whom we have reliable and extensive notice and the *Excerpta* is a unique document for the diffusion of Augustinian doctrines in Italy in the century following the death of the bishop of Hippo' (19). In some passages Eugippius is in harmony with the florilegium of Augustine by Vincent of Lérins, already mentioned (cf. Madoz, *Excerpta* 45–46), but for the rest he has no christological ambitions (see the list of chapters in CSEL 9, 5–33). The greatest importance is to be ascribed to the *Florilegium Cyrillianum* before 500, where the definition of Chalcedon is found: ACO II 1, 2, p. 126, 7–130, 11. From it would be cited the essentials of the narrower definition, especially the controversial formula 'one hypostasis in two natures' (test. 4–10), and placed beside texts from the *Letter to Succensus* of Cyril. Cyril's *mia physis* formula, naturally, does not appear. Here would be given the textual basis to resolve the tension between Chalcedon and Cyril.

(2) Characteristics of diphysite florilegia up to 500: they are still taken from the original works of the Fathers; cf. Richard, *Chalkedon* I, 728–733; Ettlinger, *Eranistes* 23–30, on Theodoret. In this period inauthentic texts are used only seldom. The most momentous case had occurred in 431, when Cyril of Alexandria took over Apollinarian forgeries. Theodoret has two texts from ps. Athanasius, and attributes a *chresis* from Didymus to Eustathius of Antioch. Leo I has a citation from Origen under the name of Basil.

II. Pro-Chalcedonian florilegia between 500 and 600

Preliminary note: Towards the end of the *Henoticon* period (482–518) we have to assume the existence of patristic collections that were probably anonymous and which took the place of florilegia before 500. They were then in general use and were intended to facilitate the defence of Chalcedon by means of the opinions of the Fathers—this in a period when, according to M. Richard, it was dangerous to own a copy of the *Tome* of Leo or the *Eranistes* of Theodoret. The texts were, however, no longer taken from the original works of the Fathers, but contained in ready-made collections. Severus protested against this. These sixth-century collections are certainly based on florilegia from the fifth century, but they use mostly only certain groups of texts. Western authors, like Ambrose, Augustine and Hilary, are more strongly represented. The pre-Nicene Fathers are omitted. On the difference between strict Chalcedonian and neo-Chalcedonian collections see our later discussions.

1. Neo-Chalcedonian florilegia
(a) Nephalius of Alexandria
Under Peter Mongus of Alexandria, who accepted the *Henoticon* of Emperor Zeno, Nephalius belonged to the opponents of the Patriarch, to whose weak stance he took exception (c. AD 482). In 507, however, Nephalius became a Chalcedonian. In Palestine he was the instigator of the movement against Severus, the subsequent patriarch of Antioch, then the founder of a monastery in the vicinity of Maiuma. Severus was driven out with his monks. Nephalius delivered a public address against Severus, a defence (*synegoria*) of the Council of Chalcedon, which probably later circulated in written form. Cf. Zacharias Rh., *Vita Severi*, ed. M.-A. Kugener, PO 2, 103 f., with John of Beith Aphthonia, *Vita Severi*, Kugener PO 2 (207–264) 232. Severus addressed himself to this apologia: *Orationes ad Nephalium*, ed. J. Lebon, CSCO 119 (T), 120 (V), in which he is said to have 'torn apart' the charges of Nephalius 'like a spider's web' (PO 2, 232). The most extensive section of the *Apologia* of Nephalius was a diphysite florilegium, in which he demonstrated that earlier Fathers had spoken of 'two natures': Gregory Nazianzen (PG 37, 180), Proclus of Constantinople (PG 65, 681, 684, 689; see JdChr I², 727–730; John Chrysostom, in a homily on the ascension of Christ, for which, however, according to S. Helmer, no verification can be found. Nephalius could well have referred to the homily on the ascension by Diadochus of Photike, PG 65, 1141–1148, in which precisely the point is made of which Severus speaks in *Ad Nephalium*: CSCO 120, 34 f. Of course Cyril's *First Letter to Succensus* had also to be used (CSCO 120, 15; 22); Helmer (see below) 155, n. 298. On Nephalius' florilegium see C. Moeller, 'Un réprésantant de la christologie néochalcédonienne au début du sixième siècle en Orient: Néphalius d'Alexandrie', *RHE* 40 (1944/45) 73–140; and further M. Richard,

'Le néo-chalcédonisme', *Opera Minora* II, 56; C. Moeller, 'Le chalcédonisme et le néochalcédonisme en Orient de 451 à la fin du VIᵉ siècle; *Chalkedon* I(1951) 638–720; 670–671 on Nephalius. Cf. M. Richard, *Opera Minora* I, 3, 733, 743; S. Helmer, *Der Neuchalkedonismus, Geschichte, Berechtigung und Bedeutung eines dogmengeschichtlichen Begriffes* (Bonn 1962) 151–159; see 154 on Nephalius' florilegium; P. T. R. Gray, *The Defense of Chalcedon in the East (451–553)* (Leiden 1979) 105–111, with some corrections to the authors just mentioned.

(b) John of Caesarea, Presbyter and Grammarian

(i) *Apologia Concilii Chalcedonensis*, ed. M. Richard, *Iohannis Caesariensis presbyteri et grammatici Opera quae supersunt* = CCG 1 (Turnhout-Leuven 1977); nr. 70–118, p. 28–46 for the florilegium. Many scholars would attribute to this John the Grammarian the *Florilegium Cyrillianum* and regard him as the opponent of Severus in the latter's works *Philalethes* and *Apologia Philalethis* (latter ed. by R. Hespel, CSCO 318–319, Louvain 1971). R. Draguet, *Julien d'Halicarnasse et sa controverse avec Sévère d'Antioche sur l'incorruptibilité du corps du Christ*... (Louvain 1924) 50–73, has, however, proven definitively that the *Florilegium Cyrillianum* and its refutation by Severus cannot have anything to do with John the Grammarian. The *Apologia Philalethis* is, moreover, a work written against Julian. With our author Severus is at loggerheads only in the work *Contra impium grammaticum*. See the ed. (Syriac) and trans. (Latin) by J. Lebon, *Severi Antiocheni liber contra impium Grammaticum. Oratio prima et secunda*: CSCO 111–112 (T. and V.); *Orationis tertiae pars prior*: CSCO 93–94 (T. and V.); *pars posterior*: CSCO 101–102. After the *Apologia* of John there comes a florilegium, the design of which can be recognised, even if Severus is not citing all testimonies. Cf. M. Richard, op. cit., XIV and XXIV; the texts cited are nr. 70–118, pp. 28–46. John is rebuked by Severus for having taken the greater part of his texts from older florilegia, which Severus himself did not know. Thus John is the most ancient witness to ready-made (lost) florilegia, with which the adherents of Chalcedon engaged the monophysites at the turn of the sixth century (op. cit., XXVII). John is one of the first representatives of so-called neo-Chalcedonianism, which will be dealt with in its own right below. Thus with A. de Halleux, who is in disagreement with M. Richard, we may also account for John's connection with the so-called Synod of Alexandretta in Cappadocia (between 514 and 518). See A. de Halleux, 'Le "synode néochalcédonien" d'Alexandrette (ca 515) et l' "Apologie pour Chalcédoine" de Jean le grammairien', *RHE* 72 (1977) 593–600.

(ii) By the same author: a florilegium in his treatise *Adversus Aphthartodocetas*, which survives only in incomplete fashion in a MS from Ochrid, Musée nat. 86, pp. 206–212. Some pages of the florilegium are lost. Ed. M. Richard, op. cit., 69–78; florilegium on 71–78 with 25 testimonia. See below on Leontius of Byzantium. (Related to this attitude against the Aphthartodocetists in a certain sense is the stance of John the Grammarian against Manichaeism, which Richard, op. cit., XXX–XXXI, XLI–XLIV, regards as highly significant. In this investigation Richard was able to avail himself of four *opuscula*, including the *Disputatio cum Manichaeo*, which the editor M. Aubineau, however, regards with some uncertainty, without coming to a definitive decision about them. Cf. Aubineau's introduction 109–116).

(c) Florilegia of the neo-Chalcedonian Scythian monks of Maxentius. These florilegia play an important rôle in the endeavour to attain the neo-Chalcedonian blend between the Chalcedonian two-nature teaching and the *mia physis* formula of Cyril, and to have the *'unus e Trinitate crucifixus est'* recognised by Rome too. To this end the compilers of the florilegia take up explicitly the opening words of the Chalcedonian definition: *'Sequentes igitur et nos sanctissimos patres confitemur'* (cf. CCL LXXXVA, 7, 60–61). We have two florilegia:

(i) One in the *Libellus fidei* of Maxentius: ACO IV 2, 3–10, recently edited by F. Glorie: CCL LXXXVA, 5–25, composed in the period between 25.3 and 29.6.519 On 29.6.519 Pope Hormisdas raised the objection against the monks sent to Rome by Maxentius to the effect that *'unus de Trinitate'* was to be found neither in synods nor in the Fathers. Maxentius, however, wanted to prove the opposite, with 15 texts from Augustine, Leo's Tome, Gregory Nazianzen, ps. Athanasius, *Contra Apollinarium*, Cyril of Alexandria and Proclus and Flavian of Constantinople, which he had preserved through contacts in Constantinople. With the exception of the third anathema of Cyril, none of these texts occurs in a previous diphysite florilegium. F. Glorie, CCL LXXXVA, XXIV–XL, reports on the activity of the Scythian monks in a masterly fashion.

(ii) The florilegium in Anonymous, *Exempla ss. Patrum, quod unum quemlibet ⟨licet⟩ ex beata Trinitate dicere*: ACO IV 2, 74–96, from AD 519/520 (*Coll. Novariensis*). Cf. V. Schurr, *Trinitätslehre des Boethius im Lichte der 'skythischen Kontroversen'* = FCLDG 18, 1 (1935) 127–197; B. Altaner, 'Zum Schrifttum der "skythischen" (gotischen) Mönche. Quellenkritische und literar-historische Untersuchungen', *HistJb* 72 (1953) 568–581. The florilegium is a source of a letter of Justinian (*Ep.* 196 of the CA from 9 July, 520). It is mentioned in the preface of Dionysius Exiguus' translation of the Tome of Proclus of Constantinople. Containing 100 excerpts from the Fathers, chiefly from Latin works, it is compiled by a Latin speaker, not translated from the Greek, for the use of Pope John I (523–526), who took over not a few passages in a letter which has been lost. See Schwartz, ACO IV 2, XVI–XVII; cf., however, CPL 1685.

(d) Ephrem of Amid (Patriarch of Antioch 526–544)

See CPG 6902–6916; Photius, *Bibliotheca, cod.* 228–229: Henry 4, 114–174; J. Lebon, 'Éphrem d'Amid, patriarche d'Antioche', *Mélanges Ch. Moeller* 1 (Louvain 1914) 197–214; M. Richard, *Chalkedon* I, 738–739 = *Opera Minora* I, 3; S. Helmer, *Der Neuchalkedonismus* 185–195; A. Grillmeier, art. 'Éphrem d'Amid', *DHGE* 15 (1963) 581–585; P. T. R. Gray, *The Defense of Chalcedon in the East* 141–154.

We are concerned here with four tractates, which Photius analyses in *cod.* 229: Henry 4, 126 ff.: (i) a defence of the *Second Letter to Succensus* of Cyril: Henry 126–135; (ii) answers to the questions of Anatolicus Scholasticus: Henry 135–142; (iii) in particular an *Apologia* for the Synod of Chalcedon: Henry 142–159; (iv) a work addressed to Eastern monks who wanted to become Severans: Henry 159–174. Ephrem recognised the problem of showing the agreement between Cyril of Alexandria and Chalcedon and tried to resolve it in the neo-Chalcedonian sense. In doing this he follows the basic idea of the great *Florilegium Cyrillianum*, although M. Richard assumes that he used it for only seven or eight texts. Cf. R. Henry, op. cit., 4, 143 n. 1. Ephrem cites approximately 100 passages from the Fathers more or less literally, in which 38 authors, including heretics, are excerpted. Cyril is represented with 30 works. Ephrem also accepts the Apollinarian forgeries as genuine, as if he were completely lacking in critical judgement.

The Cod. Marc. gr. 573, ff. 44^r–47^r (s. XII) contains, as S. Helmer, op. cit., 251–252, reports, a text (or an *opusculum*? cf. CPG 6907) called 'Twelve Orthodox Chapters'. (In the Cod. Marc. these twelve chapters occur at the end of a patristic florilegium joined to a work entitled 'Agreement between what has been said by blessed Bishop Cyril and the Sacred Scripture with the definition of faith of the holy Synod of Chalcedon'.) They are attributed to Patriarch Ephrem of Antioch. Helmer has edited the pronounced neo-Chalcedonian text (op. cit., 262–265). Following these twelve chapters in their turn are testimonies from the Fathers 'concerning the inseparable unity of the two natures in Christ', which are supposed to prove the teaching of the martyr-bishop Adda of Persia. Helmer gives no more precise information concerning the florilegia. Ephrem's works were in their turn excerpted by Anastasius of Sinai (see below; cf. *Viae Dux*, ed. K.-H. Uthemann = CCG 8, Index Fontium, 405–406.

(*e*) Eulogius (Melkite Patriarch of Alexandria 580–608) (cf. CPG 6971–6976; S. Helmer, *Der Neuchalkedonismus*, 236–241; J. Darrouzès, art. 'Euloge', *DHGE* 15 (1963) 1388–1389). Apart from a few fragments, Eulogius is known to us particularly from the *Bibliotheca* of Photius: *cod.* 225–227: Henry 4, 99–114; *cod.* 230: Henry 5, 11–33. The fragments attributed to him in the *Doctrina Patrum* have been critically established by M. Richard, which is now noted in the second edition of F. Diekamp. Cf. *Doctrina Patrum de Incarnatione Verbi. Ein griechisches Florilegium aus der Wende des 7. und 8. Jahrhunderts*, 2. Auflage mit Korrekturen und Nachträgen von B. Phanagourgakis hrsgg. von E. Chrysos (Münster 1981): p. 374 on p. 69, XIV; p. 381 on pp. 193–198, 205–206; p. 382 on pp. 214–216, 220. M. Richard, *Iohannis Caesariensis. Opera* = CCG 1, XVIII, gathers 83 testimonia from the surviving fragments, but these represent only a small part of the Patriarch's patristic documentation. He is a neo-Chalcedonian and has garnered his testimonies largely through his own reading of the Fathers, which puts him a step above most writers of works belonging to this genre. His favourite authors are Cyril of Alexandria and the great Cappadocians. He used, however, an earlier collection, and, what is more, monophysite authors as well. Cf. M. Richard, *Opera Minora* I, 3, 745. On the large number of lost works see CPG 6976.

2. Leontius of Byzantium, his florilegia, and their relationship to later collections

On Leontius of Byzantium see Richard, *Chalkedon* I = *Opera Minora* I, 3, 739–740; B. E. Daley, *Leontius of Byzantium: a critical edition of his works with Prolegomena* (Diss. Oxford 1978). B. E. Daley was kind enough to put his text at my disposal in advance. With his work the unsatisfactory preliminary studies of Torres (Latin trans.) and the description of J. P. Junglas and R. Devreesse, cited in Richard, op. cit., 739, nn. 60–61, are superceded. Cf. Daley, Introduction III. The Florilegia. We shall follow Daley's exposition here.

(*a*) *Contra Nestorianos et Eutychianos* (*CNE*), analysed by Daley, Introduction III 1. The florilegium has three sections with three introductions by Leontius: section I is intended to provide proofs from Basil and Gregory Nazianzen for his definitions of *physis* and *ousia, hypostasis* and *prosopon* (test. 1–7). Section II (test. 10–63) provides texts on the 'two natures in the one hypostasis' in Christ, from ps. Justin to Isidore of Pelusium. Section III (test. 64–88) contains texts from Cyril and Paul of Emesa (= Union of 433; test. 72–73) as testimony to the diphysite position. Test. 8–9 are better placed between test. 60 and 61.

Significance: the florilegium is important for our knowledge of the source material used between 500 and 540 and now lost, as well as for research into the text. Of the 88 testimonia there are 19 which do not otherwise survive in Greek. Nr. 78 is the first witness to Cyril's lost *Commentary on the Hebrews*.

(*b*) *Contra Aphthartodocetas* (*CA*): the florilegium contains 27 testimonia. Nr. 26 is a second witness to Cyril's *Commentary on the Hebrews*, mentioned above. See Daley, Introduction III 2. Edition under Text, nr. 4.

Significance: We have a testimonium from ps. Dionysius, *De Div. nom.* (nr. 1). The florilegium demonstrates a particular relationship with the anthology of Severus of Antioch and his work against Julian of Halicarnassus, and with the essay of John of Caesarea against the Aphthartodocetists. According to Daley, Severus and Leontius possibly drew on a (Chalcedonian) florilegium against the *incorruptibilitas* of the earthly body of Christ. Test. 25 comes from the diphysite *Florilegium Cyrillianum*, mentioned above. Cf. Hespel, *Le florilège Cyrillien* 127–128.

(c) *Deprehensio et Triumphus super Nestorianos* (*DTN*); cf. M. Richard, 'La tradition des fragments du traité Περὶ τῆς ἐνανθρωπήσεως de Théodore de Mopsueste', *Mus* 56 (1943) 55–75 = *Opera Minora* II, nr. 41; B. E. Daley, op. cit., Introduction III 3.

DTN contains a florilegium of 62 texts in four sections, in which it is the author's intention to prove a continuous tradition between Paul of Samosata and Nestorius:

Section I (test. 1–36): Extracts from Theodore of Mopsuestia, namely from the lost work *De Incarnatione* (test. 1–29), *C. Apollinarem* (test. 30–35), *Com. in ps. 8* (test. 36). For the *De Incarnatione* we have here the oldest witness, and the only testimony to the Greek text.

Section II (test. 37–41): Diodore of Tarsus (sole witness to the Greek text).

Section III (test. 42–55): nr. 42 comes from the *Contestatio Eusebii* (see above). Test. 43–45 are short extracts from Paul of Samosata and Nestorius, partly with texts which agree with the *Contestatio Eusebii*.

Section IV (test. 56–62) is a later addition, because test. 56, 58, 61 and 62 are found in the same order and length in the *Doctrina Patrum*. The latter work is not dependent on Leontius. Daley provides a summary of all 62 lemmata.

Origin: With Richard, Daley shows that the Theodore-Diodore florilegium used by Leontius and his contemporaries is essentially the same as that which Cyril used towards the end of the decade 430–440 when he wrote against both 'Antiochenes'.

Influence: What connection is there with the important florilegia of the Three Chapters controversy? (1) A connection with the florilegium of the Second Council of Constantinople (553), *Actio IV* = ACO IV 1, 44–70; see Schieffer, Index generalis: ACO IV 3, 1 s.v. Theodorus, Diodorus ep. Tarsi (with reference to M. Richard 207); (2) With the *Constitutum I* of Pope Vigilius = *Collectio Avellana* (CA) nr. 83, p. 230–320, of 14 May, 553. Both florilegia are practically identical. Their connection with Leontius of Byzantium is described in more detail by Richard, *Opera Minora* II, 41, p. 56, who concludes: 'Ces coïncidences ne s'expliquent que si Léonce et le compilateur anonyme des florilèges de Vigile et du Concile ont prise à une même collection des fragments ou, si l'on veut, à deux exemplaires plus ou moins complets d'une même collection'.

(d) *Adversus Fraudes Apollinistarum* (*AFA*): The whole text is a florilegium from works of Apollinarius, furnished with introduction and conclusion, as well as a transition to texts 2 and 3. The first two numbers belong to the same smaller Apollinarian florilegia: the *Capita Apologiae* of the Apollinarist Valentinus, in which there are twelve texts, and the work of Timothy of Beirut, *Ad Homonium*, in which twenty-four extracts from Apollinarius are presented. The two disciples of Apollinarius are at loggerheads. Timothy seems to have taught that the human flesh of Christ, on its assumption by the Logos, actually became consubstantial with the Father. Valentinus, however, was decidedly against this teaching. But each tries to verify his position from the texts of the master. Now, for his refutation Leontius claims to be exploiting the works of Apollinarius themselves, although this seems to be the case only in nr. 3, the rest of the texts being but excerpts. He wants to prove that the famous Apollinarian forgeries, appearing under such names as Athanasius, Gregory Thaumaturgus, Pope Julian (and Felix), can be unmasked as such by means of the comparative texts of the Apollinarians. In the introduction Leontius seems to indicate that the creators of these forgeries are Eutychians or adherents of Dioscorus, who wished to support their own heresy through the forgeries, and that they assigned genuine Apollinarian texts to the names of three famous orthodox Fathers. However, the forgeries had already been perpetrated before Ephesus, by Apollinarians who succeeded in fooling Cyril of Alexandria.

(e) The florilegia of Leontius and other contemporary anthologies

Negative conclusions: The investigation of comparative texts in Leontius and other authors throws a strange light on theological works of the period. Cf. Daley, Introduction LXII–LXIII: (1) With John of Caesarea (see above) there is a common denominator of six or seven texts (Richard, CCG 1, frag. 59, p. 25). (2) In three of his works (see Photius, *Bibl.* 229: Henry 4, 126–174), Ephrem of Amid has eight exact and two possible agreements with Leontius. (3) Emperor Justinian I, *Contra Monophysitas* and *Confessio rectae fidei*, has five exact agreements, and thirteen longer versions of texts which Leontius uses. (4) Leontius of Jerusalem, *Contra monophysitas*: PG 86, 1769–1901, a work almost contemporary with *CNE*, does not equal the quality of the collections of *CNE*, for all the extent of the florilegium in four parts (cf. PG 86, 1817C–1820B; 1820B–1841A; 1841A–1849C; 1852B–1876C). Only four exact agreements with *CNE* can be ascertained. For three longer and four shorter excerpts we must look to a common source. Cf. Richard, *Chalkedon* I, 741 = *Opera Minora* I, 3.

(f) Later florilegia and Leontius of Byzantium
Cf. M. Richard, *Chalkedon* I = *Opera Minora* I, 3, 744–745; Daley, Introduction LXII–LXIII.

(i) *Negative*: Leontius is not to be attributed with an anti-Julianist florilegium, discovered and partly published by M. Richard: 'Le florilège du Cod. Vatopédi 236 sur le corruptible et l'incorruptible', *Mus* 86 (1973) 249–273 = *Opera Minora* I, 4. This florilegium dates from the late sixth or early seventh century (see below).

(ii) *Positive*: A direct dependence on Leontius is to be assumed in (1) *De Sectis, Lectio (Actio) IX*. Cf. M. Richard, 'De sectis et Léonce de Byzance', *RHE* 35 (1939) 695–723 = *Opera Minora* II, 55, esp. 711–712. There are eleven exact agreements with Leontius. (2) Also to be mentioned is Pamphilus Theologus (after 560). Cf. M. Richard, *Chalkedon* I, 744; 'Léonce et Pamphile', *RSPT* 27 (1938) 27–52 = *Opera Minora* III, 58; S. Helmer, *Der Neuchalkedonismus* (Bonn 1962) 225–235; cf. CPG 6920. The florilegium from *Quaestio VI* derives partly from Leontius (Richard, art. cit., *RSPT*, 43). In *Quaestio VIII*, on the other hand, he avails himself of a monophysite florilegium, which Emperor Justinian also uses. Nonetheless, Pamphilus contributes also the fruit of his reading of ps. Dionysius the Areopagite, the Cappadocians, and perhaps Aristotle as well. (3) Furthermore, Leontius is used by Patriarch Nicephorus of Constantinople (806–815) in his *Antirrhetici* II and IV; still to be investigated is the florilegium in the unedited work *Apologia fidei orthodoxae* (2 MSS in the Bibl. Nat., Paris: Cod. Coisl. 93; Cod. Paris. 1250). In the second part are refuted the testimonia of which the iconoclasts availed themselves. Cf. A. J. Visser, *Nikephoros und der Bilderstreit* (Haag 1952) 83; C. von Schönborn, *L'icône du Christ. Fondements théologiques élaborés entre le Ier et le IIe Concile de Nicée* (325–787) = Paradosis 24 (Fribourg 1976) 203–217. (4) Also to be mentioned are two anonymous collections: in Cod. Marc. gr. Z 573, ff. 30r–47v, with nine texts from *CNE* and five shorter versions of the same texts; Cod. Lenin. gr. 131, Moscow (Fund. 339), ff. 15v–47v, with 34 exact agreements and ten shorter citations of the same texts. See Daley, Introd. LXXXX, n. 365: 'Fully half of the 106 texts in this florilegium are apparently derived from Leontius's CNE and CA'. (5) Anastasius Sinaita, *Viae Dux*: the numerous references which especially from Book X onwards seem to owe something to the testimonia of Leontius in *CNE* are worth attention. In the edition of K.-H. Uthemann, *Anastasii Sinaitae Viae Dux* = CCG 8 (Turnhout-Leuven 1981) 427–428, these are noted. But a direct dependence cannot be demonstrated. We observe something remarkable in Anastasius of Sinai, who wrote in the second half of the seventh century: certain parts of the *Hodegos*, for example, were composed at the latest in 686/689, but probably, however, before the Sixth Ecumenical Council of Constantinople in 680/1, and the work was put together between 686 and 689. Yet, apart from indirectly, there is no discussion given of the problem of one or two energies, or one or two wills in Christ—monophysism still takes first place. Thus Anastasius' florilegia belong intrinsically to this polemic. Cf. *C. Monophysitas*, (ed. Mai), in PG 89, 1180C–1189D (flor.); cf. Uthemann, op. cit., CCVIII, n. 72. On Anastasius' attitudes to monotheletism see ibid., n. 73 (for the years 692/94 and 701). The relationship of the *Hodegos* to a large number of florilegia is made note of very thoroughly by Uthemann, Index fontium, 413–416.

3. Florilegia stemming from the dogmatic activity of Emperor Justinian I (527–565) in the years 527–553 and at the Council of Constantinople (553).

(a) Two attacks against Origen and Origenism:

Edictum contra Origenem: ACO III, 189–214; CPG 6880 (AD 543). The florilegium is found on pp. 197–207, and contains testimonia from Peter of Alexandria, Athanasius, Basil, Gregory of Nyssa, Cyril of Alexandria, the anti-Origenist Synod of Alexandria in 400. Following the conclusion to these witnesses (pp. 207–208) are 26 citations from Origen from the *Peri Archon*: ACO III, p. 208, 26–213, 10; Index gen. ACO IV 3, 1, 387–391. Cf. H. Görgemanns-H. Karpp, *Origenes Vier Bücher von den Prinzipien* (Darmstadt 1976) 44–45: 'What is said in the edict itself about the teaching of Origen rests on the citations, not on an independent knowledge of 'De Principiis'. All pronouncements concerning Origenist teaching which go beyond the content of the citations seem to relate more to contemporary Origenism than to Origen himself. The same holds true for the subsequent 10 anathemas. However, it appears that this form of Origenism still approaches very closely that on which the first Origenist controversy was centred (ref. to A. Guillaumont, *Les 'Kephalia Gnostica' d'Évagre le Pontique* = PatSorb 5 (Paris 1962) 132 f.; 141 f.) and which was directly concerned with the works of Origen himself'. In Canon X of the edict *De recta fide* of AD 551 (CPG 6885 = IV 9343) Origen is still not mentioned. 'Not until the documents of 553 does a doctrine make its appearance that is definitely from another author, Evagrius of Pontus, and which can be clearly distinguished from the genuine Origen . . .' (cf. Görgemanns-Karpp 822–824).

(b) On the condemnation of Origenism at the Council of Constantinople in 553 see A. Guillaumont, op. cit., 133–170; M. Richard, 'Le traité de Georges Hiéromoine sur les hérésies', *RevÉtByz* 28 (1970) 239–269 = *Opera Minora* III, nr. 62; J. Straub, ACO IV 1, XXVI–XXIX; cf. CPG 9352; 6886: *Epistula Iustiniani ad synodum de Origene*. On the appended anathemas see F. Diekamp, *Die Origenistischen Streitigkeiten im sechsten Jahrhundert und das fünfte allgemeine Concil* (Münster 1899) 90–96; they were condemned by the Fathers of the Fifth Ecumenical Council and by Pope Vigilius before the beginning of the actual deliberations on 5 May, 553, though in a proper synodal decree. In Canon XI = Canon X of AD 551 Origen is expressly mentioned. A. Guillaumont, op. cit., 133–170, establishes that the *Cephalaia Gnostica* of Evagrius were the chief source for the 15 anathemas (cf. A. Grillmeier, JdChr I², 565). Excerpts from the *Capita Gnostica* will certainly have been made.

(c) Florilegia in three dogmatic writings of Justinian I. Cf. E. Schwartz, 'Drei dogmatische Schriften Justinians' = *AbhMünchAkW* NF 18 (München 1939; Milano 1973²): CPG 6878, 6882, 6885.

(i) *Contra Monophysitas*, a letter to Alexandrian monks: Schwartz, op. cit., 7–43. This is an attempt to show the monks the agreement between Chalcedon on the one hand and Athanasius and Cyril on the other; thus it corresponds to the main purpose of the *Florilegium Cyrillianum* presented above (Part III B III 2). Justinian and his helpers try to use only those works which are accepted by monophysites. Of pseudonymous works there are represented only the *Two Books against Apollinarius* of ps. Athanasius, *De incarnatione et c. Arianos* of ps. Athanasius (Marcellus of Ancyra), *C. Eunomium IV* of ps. Basil (Didymus? See JdChr I[2], 529, n. 2). Severus accepted all these works as genuine. The extensive florilegium in this letter of Justinian receives from Richard, *Chalkedon* I, 742 = *Opera Minora* I, 3,742, the label 'manifestement de bonne qualité'.

Contents: 40 citations from Cyril of Alexandria, but only a small number of these is taken from the works themselves (e.g. in the case of the two *Letters to Succensus*). Perhaps Justinian knew the *Florilegium Cyrillianum*, mentioned above; it is probable, however, that he used the second Cyril florilegium, of which Richard found traces in Ephrem of Amid and Leontius of Byzantium.

23 citations from Athanasius, either taken from the works directly or from an otherwise unknown collection.

21 texts from other Fathers, partly names which are found here for the first time in a florilegium.

Next come heretical texts, first from Paul of Samosata and Nestorius (§§28–55); texts on the 'one composite nature' of the Severans, for which fragments from the works of Apollinarius and Polemon are cited as evidence (cf. Lietzman 108–116; §§59–67, 71–75).

A second series of monophysite texts contains excerpts from Severus, *C. Nephalium*, texts from Manes (§§89–92), from Dioscorus and Timothy Aelurus (§§93–107) as being the fathers of the Acephaloi and successors of Apollinarius, Manes and the Docetists.

By way of refutation texts from ps. Athanasius, Gregory of Nyssa, Cyril and Ambrose are then cited.

For the first time we have a florilegium of christological concepts (cf. Schwartz, op. cit., 36, §169 ff.), namely *physis, ousia, morphe, hypostasis*, with testimonies from ps. Athanasius, *C. Apol.* 2, 1, Chrysostom, Basil, Cyril (*Thesaurus*), and both Gregories. The Apollinarius texts are interpolated (§§182–3, 190–1).

A new group of texts validated the *Trishagion*: Schwartz 41, §§193–197. §200, loc. cit., 43 shows the complete dogmatic procedure in which Justinian sets the example: scriptural proof, Church dogmas, traditions of the Fathers, the four Councils, and, as contrast, the teachings of the heretics.

(ii) *Epistula contra tria capitula*: Schwartz, op. cit., 47–69; AD 549/50. *Purpose*: to lead Chalcedonians to make certain concessions to the monophysite archenemy. The defenders of the Three Chapters are aimed at. Twenty-one testimonia are cited, of which only one possibly comes from the *Florilegium Ephesinum* (= Basil). Twenty others are taken from original works. The number of Latin testimonia points to the addressees, Pope Vigilius and his companions. Augustine is cited, and an African synod (PL 67,206), according to which dead heretics too could be anathematised (cf. 68, nr. 75–78). Furthermore, it is claimed that Pope Celestine and Ephesus (431), as well as Leo the Great and Chalcedon (451), had accepted the Twelve Anathemas of Cyril (62, nr. 55). In any case the 'Three Chapters' (Theodoret, *ep.* 142; eight fragments from Theodore of Mopsuestia; the letter of Ibas to Mari the Persian) are guilty of Nestorianism, and their defenders are wanting with regard to the right belief of the Church (62, nr. 55).

(iii) *Rectae fidei confessio*: Schwartz, op. cit., 72–111; elucidated on p. 116 f. The document was posted in the church of Hagia Sophia in the year 551. It contains eleven citations, two of which come from Cyril's *Contra Theodorum*. On Justinian's tractate, with which he opened the offensive against the Three Chapters in 544/5 (Schwartz) or 543/44 (E. Stein), see E. Schwartz, 'Zur Kirchenpolitik Justinians' = *SbMünchAkW* (1940) 32–72; in the appendix (73–81) the fragments of Facundus of Hermiane are to be found.

(*d*) The patristic texts in the *acta* of the Second Council of Constantinople (5 May–2 June, 553) (concerning the Three Chapters). See CPG 9332, 9358–9360; ACO IV 1; ACO IV 3, 1, 519–520. In *Actio* IV of 13 May, 553: ACO IV 1, 39–72 excerpts from the works of Theodore of Mopsuestia were read out. In *Actio* V of 17 May, 553: ACO IV 1, 73–136 passages from Theodore were once again read publicly, together with texts from Cyril to refute them. In nr. 31–35, p. 94–96 there follow extracts from Theodoret; in nr. 36–89 are texts dealing with the problem of whether Cyril spoke of 'Theodorus bonus', which would be the equivalent of recognition. From nr. 93 onwards texts are again taken from Theodoret, with passages supporting the opposite position (p. 130–136). In *Actio* VI: ACO IV 1, 137–182 Ibas of Edessa and his Letter to the Persian Mari are taken to task; the letter is read out and answered by other documents. In spite of these numerous excerpts, M. Richard, *Chalkedon* I, 743 = *Opera Minora* I, 3,743, sees here no real florilegium. From his treatment of dogmatic florilegia he also excludes Facundus of Hermiane, *Pro defensione trium capitulorum*, and Pelagius Diaconus, *In defensione trium capitulorum*, on the grounds that their argumentation is more historical than dogmatic. Nonetheless we shall bring them to bear on our presentation. See above, B. E. Daley on Leontius of Byzantium (Influence), and further Richard, *Opera Minora* II, 41, p. 56. The works of the deacon Rusticus in defence of the Three Chapters have already been cited in Part I A. On his working conditions in the library of the monastery of the Sleepless Monks see M. Tetz, *Eine Antilogie des Eutherios von Tyana* = PTSt 1 (Berlin 1964) XXXIX f.; on the Monks' significance for the history of literature see L. Abramowski, *ZKG* 73 (1962) 417 f. (notices of the works of R. Riedinger).

III. Anti-Chalcedonian monophysite florilegia

In Part III, A II, nr. 7 above we have made mention of a florilegium of Eutyches with the so-called Apollinarian forgeries, which turn up time and again in the group of florilegia under consideration. This group still requires comprehensive investigation. Cf. A. Baumstark, *Geschichte der syr. Literatur* 176 f., who refers to 'biblical florilegia' (esp. 176, n. 4: a christological-biblical florilegium); Ortiz de Urbina, *Patrologia Syriaca* §112, with reference to the biblical florilegium of Cod. BM Add. 12.154 (s. VIII–IX); cf. Wright II, 986, esp. 904–1015 (*Catenae Patrum*). See too CPG IV (*Catenae*). The monophysites of the fifth century (the anti-Chalcedonian collection of Cod. Vatic. gr. 1431 with two examples; Timothy Aelurus), and ps. Caesarius too (sixth century) have a particular fondness for the *Ancoratus* of Epiphanius. Cf. R. Riedinger, *Pseudo-Kaisarios* (München 1969) 285–294.

1. Florilegia from Timothy Aelurus (Patriarch of Alexandria 457–460; 475–477)

(*a*) Florilegia against Chalcedon. The most extensive florilegium of this kind is found in his *'Refutation of the doctrine propounded at the Synod of Chalcedon'*, transmitted only in Armenian, ed. K. Ter-Mekerttschian-E. Ter-Minassiantz (Leipzig 1908), although it survives in a shortened form in Syriac in Cod. BM Add. 12.156, f. 1ra–29vb: *A* [treatise] *of Timotheus against the Diphysites*; cf. Wright, *Catalogue* II, DCCXXIX, 639–642, with details of the Fathers cited. Cf. J. Lebon, 'Version arménienne et version syriaque de Timothée Élure', *Handes Amsorya* 11–12 (1927) col. 713–722; idem, *RHE* 9 (1908) 677–702. Both florilegia are analysed by E. Schwartz, 'Codex Vaticanus gr. 1431 eine antichalkedonische Sammlung aus der Zeit Kaiser

Zenos' = *AbhMünchAkW* XXXII, 6 (1927): Armenian florilegium 98–117; Syriac florilegium 117–126, with supplement to F. Cavallera, 'Le dossier patristique de Timothée Aelure', *BLE* IV, 1 (1909) 342–359. Both florilegia begin with the Apollinarian forgeries (Schwartz, op. cit., 98 f., nr. 1, 10, 12, 13, 14; Syriac 117 ff.). Pre-Nicaean Fathers are also represented; cf. ibid., 98 f., nr. 3, 7, 8, 11. Athanasius, ps. Athanasius, and Epiphanius (Ancoratus) are cited extensively. *Nota bene*: this first book of Timothy is to be distinguished from his *'Tractate with the refutation of the Definition of Chalcedon and the Tome of Leo'*, in Cod. BM Add. 12.156, ff. 39b–61a, of which 39b–42a are edited by F. Nau in PO 13, 218–236; of the Syriac version of the work mentioned above Nau, ibid., 202–218, has edited ff. 11a–13b. This second tractate, too, is followed by a florilegium (ff. 69a–80a), which goes under the name *Florilegium Edessenum anonymum* and will be discussed in its own right. On the contents of ff. 61b–68b see Wright, op. cit. 643–644.

(b) Letters of Timothy Aelurus with an anti-Eutychianist florilegium: Cod. BM Add. 12.156, ff. 29b–39b contains a collection of letters (and Credos), ed. R. Y. Ebied–L. R. Wickham, 'A Collection of Unpublished Syriac Letters of Timothy Aelurus', *JTS* NS 21 (1970) 321–369. The first letter is addressed to the city of Constantinople. Cf. Ebied-Wickham 329–330 (analysis); Syriac text and English trans., ibid., 333–337 (ff. 30a–32a), esp. 351–357. The appended florilegium is intended to be thematic, and is extremely valuable ecumenically speaking. For this reason it will be discussed in detail.

It should be observed that Timothy Aelurus thus conducted a war on two fronts with his publications and florilegia, a war which later Severus of Antioch continued on other levels.

2. *Florilegium Edessenum anonymum (syriace ante 562)*, ed. I. Rucker = *Sb-MünchAkW*, Phil.-hist. Abt. 1933, 5 (München 1933). In Cod. BM Add. 12.156, ff. 69rc–80rb there follows a monophysite florilegium which Rucker regards as a further development of the older tradition found in Timothy (op. cit., XVI). It comprises five parts: (1) Mary is Theotokos; (2) Jesus Christ is true God; (3) the Son of God is one, consubstantial with the Father and son of the Virgin; (4) through his birth in the flesh the Logos has consequently a capacity for suffering and death; (5) Christ is identical with the Logos of God. If excerpts from pre-Nicene Fathers are typical of florilegia before 500, then the *Florilegium Edessenum* is particularly rich in this respect (containing at least 18 texts from Ignatius of Antioch, Polycarp of Smyrna, Clement of Rome, ps. Clement, Hippolytus, Methodius and [ps.] Melito of Sardis; among the Nicene and post-Nicene authors we find Julius of Rome, Serapion of Thmuis (unique in florilegium literature, apart from the florilegium in the Cod. Vat. gr. 1431; see below). An older source has probably been used.

3. A double anti-Chalcedonian florilegium in Cod. Vat. gr. 1431. This codex is a collection of most diverse pieces (see above, Part I C I). The double florilegium is R I and R II: Schwartz nr. 65, text 28–33; explanation 96–132, in which the comparison with the florilegia of Timothy Aelurus, transmitted in Armenian and Syriac respectively (see above), is made; nr. 66, text 33–49; explanation 132. Nr. 65 is for the most part taken from the florilegium of Timothy preserved in Armenian, which has as its intention the refutation of the two-nature doctrine of Chalcedon; an exception is nr. 13, which is an Apollinarian forgery. Nr. 66, with 67 testimonia, is assembled in order to prove that the Fathers proclaimed unanimously that body and godhead in Christ were indeed separated; 'from them, however', it runs, there was 'only a single Christ in a henosis physike in an unseparable manner'. The testimonies are taken chiefly from Cyril and Athanasius, then from Gregory Nazianzen, Basil, Ambrose, Epiphanius, John Chrysostom, Amphilochius of Iconium, Theo-

philus of Alexandria and Proclus of Constantinople. *De Sectis* 8: PG 86, 1257, is directed against Erechthius of Antioch in Pisidia, who is named in nr. 65, §1—but see Schwartz, 'Cod. Vat. gr. 1431', 97: no bishop of this name existed. The anthology of nr. 66 is more extensive and independent than that of nr. 65. There are points of contact with Theodoret, Gelasius and the *Florilegium Chalcedonense* in §§21 and 32. Dependence on a certain collection cannot be proved. In both florilegia we have a war waged on two fronts: nr. 65 is directed against Chalcedon, nr. 66 against the Eutychians, where the limit is given 'to which two natures must be admitted, namely to the pure intellectual, not to the actual, separation' (Schwartz, 'Cod. Vatic. gr. 1431', 132). Against Lebon, *Le monophysisme sévérien* 334–412, Schwartz thus believes that he can prove that the Cyrillian teaching 'from the two natures which are present not actually but only in intellectual contemplation' was revived first not by Severus, but previously in the period after Zeno's *Henoticon*. Factually this may be true, but this terminology is not found in so many words in florilegium R II.

4. Two florilegia of Bishop Philoxenus of Mabbog (d. 523)

(*a*) *Letter to the monks of Senoun*, ed. A. de Halleux, CSCO 231/2 (T.V.); ibid., 232, XI–XIV, with an analysis of the letter. (i) In one florilegium we find the theme life and death of God, with citations from Gregory Nazianzen, Basil, Gregory of Nyssa, Athanasius and Ephrem (trans. 26–29; see apparatus); (ii) the other has the theme of one nature after the union, with citations from ps. Gregory Thaumaturgus, ps. Julius, ps. Athanasius, Cyril of Alexandria, ps. Basil and Ephrem (trans. 29–50; to 50–60 is attached a dogmatic interpretation, which in both florilegia can follow various texts).

(*b*) Florilegium in the 10 Mēmrē against Habīb (end of mēmrē 10); diss. 1–2: PO 15, 439–542; diss. 3–5: PO 38, 478–632; diss. 6–8: PO 39, 448–752; diss. 9–10: PO 40, 202–350; Florilegium: PO 40 (in prep.). On the mēmrē see A. de Halleux, *Philoxène* 228–233; idem, 'Une clé pour les hymnes d'Éphrem dans le ms. Sinai syr. 10', *Mus* 85 (1972) 171–199; F. Graffin, 'Le florilège patristique de Philoxène de Mabboug', *OCA* 197 (1974) 267–290. We can distinguish five groups of texts with five subjects:

(1) 'One of the Trinity, the God-Logos, has come down and dwelt in the Virgin', with 36 citations from Ephrem.

(2) 'God became man without change', with 7 citations from Ephrem, then 8 others from John Chrysostom; 7 from Cyril of Alexandria, 9 in total from Eusebius of Emesa, Athanasius, Atticus and Basil.

(3) 'Mary is really the Mother of God': here is the most extensive part of the florilegium, taken from 10 Fathers, among whom are Alexander of Alexandria and Theophilus of Alexandria, one *chresis* from each of whose works appears only here. Ephrem is represented by 7 citations, and exacts a long explanation from the excerptor for his formula of 'two natures' (Graffin, art. cit., 274 f.).

(4) 'There is (in Christ) not one and then another (Greek: allos kai allos), but only the one God-Logos'. All numbering should be excluded from Christ. Here there are 3 citations from Athanasius and Basil, 23 from Ephrem, between 4–6 from each of Chrysostom, Eusebius of Emesa, Cyril and Gregory Nazianzen.

(5) 'God has suffered, has died and has been crucified': 40 citations come from Ephrem alone, while 6 other Fathers receive only 34 between them (Chrysostom, Eusebius, Athanasius, Basil, Gregory Nazianzen and Cyril of Alexandria). See Graffin, art. cit., 276–278.

With the 104 citations from Ephrem, taken from almost all of his major works, one is reminded of the great *Florilegium Cyrillianum*, which has already been treated (see above B III 2). The differences are certainly greater than the similarities. Not all citations are verified (see Graffin 283–290). The Philoxenus florilegium thus furnishes a number of *inedita* for Ephrem. It is not said how Philoxenus achieved the 104 citations from Ephrem from the total of 226. Perhaps he came upon extracts in one of the monasteries where Ephrem was read and revered. Cf. A. de Halleux, *Philoxène* 324, n. 28, who also emphasises that Philoxenus' erudition did not match that of Severus of Antioch. The majority of the witnesses whom he cites belong to the classic monophysite collections (ibid., 323, with R. Draguet). De Halleux, ibid., 460, n. 2, stresses that the Julianist controversy is not to be found in the subject-matter of our florilegium. The debate concerning the corruptibility or incorruptibility of Christ's body began in 510 in Constantinople, when Philoxenus had already left that city (ibid., 59–60). The controversy between Julian of Halicarnassus and Severus in Egypt in 520 was no longer comprehended by Philoxenus (d. 523). On the relationship of Philoxenus to Julianist anthropology and soteriology see A. de Halleux, op. cit., 503–504.

5. Patristic florilegia in Severus (Patriarch of Antioch 512–518) (CPG 7022–7081)

Among the anti-Chalcedonian theologians it is Severus who exhibits the greatest knowledge of the Fathers. Connecting series of texts, which up until now we have met frequently, are seldom to be found. The citations are mostly set in a commentary.

(a) *Sévère d'Antioche, Le Philalèthe*, ed. R. Hespel = CSCO 133 (T), 134 (V) (Louvain 1952). The *Philalethes* is the altercation with the famous *Florilegium Cyrillianum*. Severus takes all the testimonies one by one, or in groups, in the order in which they are cited, and each time follows this with a dogmatic commentary which itself often grows into a florilegium and is intended to prove that all the testimonies from Cyril, taken in their proper extent and context, do not prove an agreement with Chalcedon but far more with monophysite christology. The various passages from the Fathers in the *Philalethes* are cited in the Index of CSCO 134, 298–301. In the Cyrillian florilegium both parties had texts which should have been not the foundation of diversity in their doctrines but the basis of unity. A great 'ecumenical' chance was wasted.

(b) The florilegia in *Severus Ant., Liber contra impium Grammaticum. Oratio prima et secunda*: ed. J. Lebon: CSCO 111–112 (Lovanii 1938), text and Latin version; *Orationis tertia pars prior* (1929) text and Latin version = CSCO 93–94; *Orationis tertiae pars posterior* (1933) text and Latin version: CSCO 101–102, reprint 1952. Cf. CPG 7024. The patristic citations of Severus, which acquired great influence and ousted other florilegia, for example the *Florilegium Edessenum*, are listed in CSCO 112 (V) 10*–22*. *Contra Grammaticum* III, cap. 41 is important. Here we find *chreseis* from Ignatius of Antioch, Polycarp, ps. Clement (II Clem), Irenaeus, the Synod of Antioch against Paul of Samosata (AD 268), Cyprian, Gregory Thaumaturgus, ps. Felix, Peter of Alexandria, Athanasius, ps. Julius (the Apollinarian forgeries), the three Cappadocians, and Amphilochius of Iconium; in addition Cyril of Jerusalem, Gelasius of Caesarea in Palestine, John Chrysostom, Theophilus of Alexandria, Epiphanius, Antiochus, Severian of Gabala, Atticus, Cyril, Proclus and Theodotus of Ancyra (26 extracts in all). According to its type this selection belongs to the period before 500; the emphasis on the Apollinarian forgeries is a monophysite peculiarity.

(c) *Severi Antiocheni Orationes ad Nephalium eiusdem ac Sergii Grammatici epistulae mutuae*, ed. J. Lebon (Lovanii 1919) = CSCO 119–120 (text and Latin version). See the patristic citations in vol. 120, 5*–9*. Ignatius of Antioch is represented again, with Irenaeus and the Apollinarian forgeries (7 passages from Apollinarian works); Cyril of Alexandria has the greatest share; Dioscorus I and the *Henoticon* are also mentioned.

(*d*) The patristic citations in the anti-Julianist polemic of Severus. The controversy began in 510 in Constantinople, was taken up again in about 520 in Egypt, and ended in 527, as far as the protagonists Severus and Julian of Halicarnassus were concerned. In 528 Paul of Callinicum completed the translation of the works of Severus against Julian into Syriac. See R. Hespel, *La polémique antijulianiste*:

(i) I = CSCO 244–245 (Louvain 1964); see 245, pp. 239–242 for the patristic citations. Cyril of Alexandria has the largest share; apart from him we find Ignatius of Antioch, Irenaeus, Julius of Rome, John Chrysostom, Athanasius and Theophilus.

(ii) IIA = CSCO 295–296 (Louvain 1968) = *Contra Additiones Juliani*;

IIB = CSCO 301–302 (Louvain 1969) = *Adversus Apologiam Juliani*; indices of patristic passages on pp. 135–136. The majority of the citations comes from Cyril of Alexandria; we encounter also ps. Dionysius and Timothy Aelurus (see above 1b: the letters of Timothy, esp. 'The Letter written to Alexandria from Gangra concerning the excommunication of Isaiah and Theophilus').

(iii) *Apologia Philalethis* = CSCO 318–319 (Louvain 1971). Hespel, p. V, speaks of the 'innombrables citations patristiques'. The testimonies are listed in ibid., 124–126. Most of them come from Cyril and Severus himself (from the *Philalethes* and polemic against it). Otherwise all the other names are known to us.

6. Other Severan florilegia directed against the Julianists

(*a*) 'Le florilège du Cod. Vatopédi 236 sur le corruptible et l'incorruptible', exact description and partial edition by M. Richard, *Mus* 36 (1973) 249–273 = *Opera Minora* I, 4. (The promised continuation has not as yet been published). The attribution to Leontius of Byzantium is regarded by Richard as a disguise. We are dealing with a collection of monophysite (Severan) origin. The florilegium is divided into five chapters, of which chapters 2 and 5 are badly placed:

Chapter 1: a biblical florilegium in three sections, with a short commentary.

Chapter 2: a long extract from a letter of Severus of Antioch to Timothy III, Patriarch of Alexandria (517–535).

Chapter 3: Even before the Fall, Adam was mortal and corruptible by reason of his nature, but through grace he received the gift of immortality—this is shown by testimonia from the Fathers (260–262; 27 testimonia in all).

Chapter 4: Against the foolish Docetists, with two passages from the Fathers, from Gregory of Nyssa and Cyril, and a confession of faith (ibid., 263).

Chapter 5: After the resurrection (for the first time) the body of the Lord is incorruptible, i.e. not subject to suffering and death. Then follow 47 citations from the Fathers and an appendix with another four passages. What the promised continuation would have offered is not said (cf. 262–273). Richard appeals often to the edition of R. Hespel, *La polémique antijulianiste . . .*, from where without doubt a certain number of patristic citations comes (Richard, ibid., 250).

(*b*) M. Richard, *Opera Minora* I, 3, 747, regards the third part of the florilegium of the Cod. Laur. IV, 23, nr. 79–103, as directed against Julian of Halicarnassus. Likewise M. Tetz, *ZKG* 67 (1955/56) (1–28) 27, n. 58. See the text in E. Schwartz, 'Der s.g. Sermo maior de fide des Athanasius' (cited above in Part I B I) 32–37. It is thus to be assigned to the mid-sixth century.

(*c*) A longer collection in Syriac of 100 or 99 chapters against the Julianists is contained in BM Syr. MSS 857–858, 863, and in a shorter version in 857; see Wright, *Catalogue* II, 929–933, 958–961; 939–941; 947–948 (MS Add. 14.532, ff. 36a ss.; MS Add. 14.533, ff. 52 ss.; MS Add. 12.155, ff. 180b–181b). Cf. Baumstark, *Geschichte d. syr. Lit.* 176 f. The bulk of these collections came into being on Aramaic soil, with the use of Greek florilegia in translation. For the particulars see Baumstark.

7. Florilegia against the Agnoetes (Themistians)

The opposition to the Julianists, with the demonstration of the 'corruptibility' of Christ's body, led to a new discussion and split among the Severans. Themistius (cf. CPG 7285–7292), pupil of Severus and deacon of Patriarch Timothy II of Alexandria (520–526), concluded: if Christ is 'corruptible', he is also 'unknowing'. He established the sect of the Themistians, which was opposed to the Theodosians, i.e. the majority of Severan monophysites. By catholics and Severans Themistius was condemned as 'Nestorian', as we learn from Patriarch Theodosius II (monophysite) (532–538) and Patriarch Eulogius (580–608) (neo-Chalcedonian). According to Photius, *Bibl. cod.* 230: Henry 5, 57 ff., in this question Eulogius despatched many patristic citations to Pope Gregory I. Cf. J. Darrouzès, art. 'Euloge', *DHGE* 15 (1963) 1388–1389.

8. Florilegia in the Tritheist controversy

Sources and treatment are listed in H. Martin, *La controverse trithéite dans l'empire byzantin au VIe siècle* (Diss. dactyl. n.d. Louvain); idem, 'Jean Philopon et la controverse trithéite du VIe siècle', *StudPat* 5 = TU 80 (1962) 519–525; G. Furlani, 'Un florilegio antitriteistico in lingua siriaca (An Italian translation by G. Furlani of extracts from the Antitritheite Florilegium contained in Br. M. Add. 14532, fol. 194a–207b)', *Atti del Reale Istituto Veneto di Scienze, Lettere ed Arti* 83 (1924) 661–677; this part is now newly reworked and, together with the fragments from Philoponus, edited and translated by A. van Roey, 'Les fragments trithéites de Jean Philopon', *OLP* 11 (1980) 135–163; cf. idem, 'Fragments antiariens de Jean Philopon', *OLP* 10 (1979) 237–250; idem, 'La controverse trithéite jusqu'à l'excommunication de Conon et Eugène (557–569)'. *OLP* 16 (1985) 141–165; idem, 'La controverse trithéite depuis la condemnation de Conon et Eugène jusqu'à la conversion de l'évêque Élie', *Von Kanaan bis Kerala*. FS J. P. M. van der Ploeg (Kevelaer 1982) 487–497; R. Y. Ebied, A. van Roey and L. R. Wickham, *Peter of Callinicum. Anti-Tritheist Dossier* = OrLovAn 10 (Leuven 1981). (This collection belongs not to the literary genre of the florilegium but to that of 'publizistischen' documentation.)

The Tritheist heresy came into being among the Jacobites, growing out of the misunderstanding of the formula of the 'one incarnate nature of the God-Logos'. By reason of the fact that this formula was poorly integrated into the trinitarian formula of the three *hypostaseis* (this being the consequence of the synonymous use of *physis* and *hypostasis*), the Son appeared to be contrasted with the Father and the Holy Spirit both according to *physis* and *hypostasis*. The patristic use of 'nature' and 'essence' was erroneously interpreted, such that both concepts were applied separately to each of the divine persons. The confusion began with John Ascotzanges in about 557. He and his followers were, however, unable to think out their initiative to its logical conclusion, which saved them from real polytheism.

(a) Tritheist florilegia

(i) Ascotzanges himself compiled a florilegium before the death of Theodosius, Patriarch of Alexandria (d. 566 in Constantinople): Michael Syr., *Chron.* IX 30: Chabot 2, 252.

(ii) A florilegium, compiled about 570, according to John of Ephesus, *HE* III 10: ed. Chabot CSCO 105 (T), 106 (V), 197. Its purpose: 'afin que ... ils montrassent—du moins ils le croient—que tous les Pères eux aussi introduisent et enseignent comme eux le nombre des natures et des ousies' (from Martin, *La controverse trithéite* 158; cf. 143). The florilegium had a strong influence.

(iii) John Philoponus and the argument from the Fathers.

John reversed the relationship between the argument from authority and philosophical deduction. Taking the monophysite *mia physis* formula as his starting-point, he argued with assistance of Aristotelian logic. The patristic witnesses were used in an auxiliary rôle. This reversal is pursued by no Christian theologian so resolutely as by Philoponus. A different opinion is found in K.-H. Uthemann, 'Syllogistik im Dienst der Orthodoxie. Zwei unedierte Texte byzantinischer Kontroverstheologie des 6. Jahrhunderts', *JÖB* 30 (1981) 103–112, esp. 106, who wants to see this reversal first in Leontius of Byzantium, *Contra Nestorianos et Eutychianos* III 41: PG 86, 1, 1380B7–9; ed. Daley op. cit., and to see deduced there 'from first principles' (by which he would understand the pure Aristotelian *archai*) 'everything—even the mystery of Christ'. But here the Leontius text has been wrongly interpreted, as the remainder of the text shows.

With his work *De Trinitate*, composed in the years 567–568, John Philoponus wrote the document of the sect. Cf. H. Martin, 'Jean Philopon...', *StudPat* 5 = TU 80 (1962) 519–525. The book is preserved only in 15 fragments in a Syriac translation. A further six fragments derived from a book *Contra Themistium*, in which Philoponus likewise defended his teaching on the Trinity. It is a long way from Ascotzanges' proof based on authority to the strict logical system of the philosopher of Alexandria. The latter, however, must have known the patristic proofs of the florilegium mentioned by John of Ephesus. He cites it occasionally (cf. H. Martin, op. cit., 522, n. 1). Photius, *Bibl. cod.* 75: Henry 1, 153–154, says that Philoponus, in his 'Biblidarion', by which we must understand the *De Trinitate*, gathered together extracts from Fathers like Gregory Nazianzen, Basil and Cyril of Alexandria. 'But these citations themselves never hit the godless target which he intended... He believed himself capable of spreading mistrust concerning the mysteries of our Theologia (i.e. the Trinity)'. A useful summons to a critical attitude towards an exuberant growth of the genre of the florilegium!

(b) Florilegia of the opponents of the Tritheists

(i) Florilegium in the speech of Patriarch Theodosius of Alexandria held in 564 in Constantinople, ed. Chabot, *Documenta ad origines monophysitarum illustrandas*: CSCO 17 (1909) (T); 113 (1909) (V), 26–55; florilegium on p. 29 ff. See H. Martin, *La controverse trithéite* 25, who observes that this tractate, which would serve the orthodox as a basis for all further polemic against their Tritheist opponents, was in reality a very long tractate which Theodosius expounded in Constantinople.

(ii) Florilegium in the second work against the Tritheists, ed. Furlani, PO 14, 737–747, with the title: 'On the fact that the Tritheists gather proofs from the holy Fathers to show that they speak of substances and natures'. According to Martin, op. cit., 143, we have here the counter-florilegium to that mentioned by John of Ephesus (see above, Part II C II 4). It is to be dated after 587.

(iii) The third florilegium is that in Cod. BM Add. 14.532, ff. 194ra–207va, first translated by G. Furlani and now newly reworked by A. van Roey. It is the third part of a more extensive collection which has parallels in Cod. Add. 14. 533, ff. 73a–89a. The whole work is entitled 'Volume with testimonies of the holy Fathers against various heresies'. See Wright, *Catalogue* II, 955–967. In the first part the monophysite florilegium attacks the 'two natures' of Chalcedon (Wright 955–958), in the second part it attacks Julian of Halicarnassus, in the third part, the Tritheites (Wright 961–964, c), with texts from Philoponus, such that A. van Roey can now give a description of it, as will be shown in brief.

(iv) *Florilegium anti-Philoponianum*: Cod. BM Add. 14. 532, ff. 194^r–207^v (= Add. 14. 538, ff. 104^r–145^r), with the title: 'Tomus which briefly shows the contrast between Johannes Grammaticus (= Philoponus) and his adherents and Holy Scripture and the holy Fathers' (cf. A. van Roey, *OLP* 11 (1980) 137–163).

Whilst the anti-Tritheist Jacobites answered the Tritheists in a like vein—thus setting one proof from authority against another, without analysing the concepts and proceeding to philosophical argumentation—the Aristotelian Philoponus, who likewise took the *mia physis* formula as his starting-point, now put Aristotelian logic in the first place. The testimonies from the Fathers were used in the second place. In his book *On the Trinity* (567/8), the Alexandrian wrote the chief document of the sect (H. Martin, *StudPat* 5 = TU 80 (1962) 519–525). Altogether A. van Roey discerns 30 fragments (without considering the classification of particular passages), coming from the *De Trinitate, De Theologia, Contra Themistium*, from a letter to a co-religionary, and works of uncertain origin. Philoponus himself must have known the patristic testimonies in the florilegium mentioned by John of Ephesus. He mentions the florilegium in passing (cf. H. Martin, op. cit., 522, n. 1; 524, with reference to Photius, *Bibl.* 75). It is less well known that Philoponus was the originator of a schism because of his theory of the resurrection which touches on christology. See A. van Roey, 'Un traité cononite contre la doctrine de Jean Philopone sur la résurrection', ΑΝΤΙΔΩΡΟΝ 123–139, where an edition of a Cononite florilegium is given. In the second volume of the same Festschrift J. Paramelle gives the Greek fragments of the refutation of Philoponus, *De resurrectione*, composed by Conon and Eugenius. Here, too, a florilegium is published, which does not agree with that published by A. van Roey, loc. cit. Because of his significance for the change in the method of christological-theological argumentation, Philoponus will demand our attention in our presentation itself.

9. Monophysite florilegia of secondary importance (Coptic, Armenian, Arabic, Syriac)

(a) Coptic monophysite collections
(i) The priceless Pearl
(ii) The Confession of the Fathers
Cf. G. Graf, 'Zwei dogmatische Florilegien der Kopten', *OCP* 3 (1937) 49–77, who refers repeatedly to Cyril of Alexandria, *De recta fide ad reginas*. Here too we find Apollinarian forgeries. Cf. G. Graf, 'Unechte Zeugnisse römischer Päpste für den Monophysitismus im arabischen "Bekenntnis der Väter"', *RömQ* 36 (1929) 197–233.

(b) Armenian collections
See J. Lebon, 'Les citations patristiques grecques du "Sceau de·la Foi"', *RHE* 25 (1929) 5–32. Lebon speaks of "une de *sommes* de l'ancienne théologie arménienne" (p. 32). Here we have an important testimonium of Emperor Anastasius I (451–518) (see below), as well as the Apollinarian forgeries, citations from ps. Dionysius, Dioscorus of Alexandria, the *Henoticon* of Zeno, but also pre-Nicene Fathers such as Hippolytus and Irenaeus, and the unknown "Erechthius of Pisidia", who is quite often mentioned (on the name see Le Quien, *Oriens Christianus* I (1740) 1038; PO 13, 162).

(c) Collections in Arabic
Cf. G. Graf, *Geschichte der christlichen arabischen Literatur* II (Città del Vaticano 1947) 296–297: in the twelfth century Abu 'l-Ḫair ibn aṭ-Ṭaiyib had dogmatic collections of great proportions ('a dogmatician of style'!). A patristic florilegium against monophysites and monothelites is also contained in Arabic in the Cod. S. Sepulcri, Jerus. Ar. 12, ff. 217ᵛ–281ᵛ, with citations from Leo the Great and Ambrose. Cf. Graf, op. cit., 494.

(d) Anonymous Syriac florilegia (Baumstark, *Geschichte d. syr. Lit.* 176–177)
(i) A collection originally in nine chapters, of which are preserved chapters six to nine in Cod. BM Add. 14.535: Wright, *Catalogue* II, 796–798: a refutation of the 'Nestorians'.
(ii) A Tract in defence of Monophysite doctrines: 'Demonstration, or Evidences, concerning the Dispensation of the Messiah' (15 chapters). For an analysis see Wright II, 978–979 (Cod. BM Add. 12.154).

(iii) A whole series of diverse patristic collections on the doctrine of the Trinity, on the incarnation, on the teaching of Julian of Halicarnassus, either under more general titles or without a general description is contained in Cod. BM Add. 12.155: Wright II, 921–955.

IV. Florilegia of the post-Chalcedonian Nestorians (east Syrians)

On the patristic citations of Nestorius himself see A. Grillmeier, JdChr I², 713, n. 10. On Syriac-Nestorian literature see A. Baumstark, *Geschichte der syr. Lit.* (Bonn 1922) 100–139; I. Ortiz de Urbina, *Patrologia Syriaca* (Romae 1965), part II, 115–153, on Nestorian theology. See above, Part I C II and Part III A II 5: L. Abramowski & A. E. Goodman, *A Nestorian Collection of Christological Texts*, Vol. I Syriac, text, Vol. II Introduction, Translation and Indexes = University of Cambridge Oriental Publications 19 (Cambridge 1972); L. Abramowski & A. van Roey, 'Das Florileg mit den Gregor-Scholien aus Vatic. Borg. Syr. 82', *OLP* 1 (1970) 131–180; L. Brade, *Untersuchungen zum Scholienbuch des Theodoros Bar Konai* = Gött. Orient-forsch. I. R. Syriaca 8 (Wiesbaden 1975).

1. The Cambridge Florilegium, Univ. Libr. Or. 1319 (= Flor. Cambr.): see Abramowski-Goodman op. cit., section VI, trans. 75–88. In its present form VI is an anonymous abridged translation of a refutation, originally in Greek, of the Twelve Anathemas of Cyril. See the analysis in ibid. XXXVIII–XLII. A list of the lemmata is given in ibid., 75–88, with notes.

(a) Theological peculiarity: The Flor. Cambr. gives an insight into the christology of the compilers and excerptors, despite the abridgements which it has undergone. Technical terms, with the exception of 'two natures', are avoided. The incomprehensibility and ineffability of the incarnation and of the unity of the two natures in Christ are stresseu repeatedly. The expression 'synapheia' is not used in the text as it has come down to us. During the refutation of Cyril's fourth Anathema the 'union of sonship' is spoken of. The compiler writes of the union of the 'two whole natures' (refutation of Anathemas 2 and 6). Their goal is to connect the God-Logos with the 'whole human being', and the result is 'the one Son'. This is 'our faith'! 'One prosopon' is not mentioned, and the division of the Son into two *prosopa* is rejected (refutation of Anathemas 3 and 4). 'Hypostasis' is used only of the Trinity. The 'orthodox' rejects the reproof of the two hypostases teaching which was raised by Cyril in Anathema 3. In doing this Cyril disguised his opposition to the two nature teaching.

> 'The author therefore does not hold up two christological hypostases, he belongs to the large group of theologians who took a long time to become accustomed to the use of the word hypostasis in christology at all, no matter if it were one or two hypostases. We know of Greek-writing Antiochene theologians of this kind in the fifth century, and the Syriac diophysite church maintained its reserve officially until 612 as the conciliar creeds in the *Synodicon Orientale* testify' (op. cit., vol. II, XLI).

(b) Section VI was thus compiled originally in Greek—about 433, as the reference to Hebr. 12, 14 suggests (cf. JdChr 1,707, n. 15). The translation into Syriac followed after a time, for the older, unrevised translation of Cyril's *Anathemas* was still in use.

(c) The collection as a whole goes beyond the purpose of VI. Cf. the analysis of Abramowski-Goodman, op. cit., vol. II, XVII–XIX. It represents the teaching of two *hypostaseis* and one *prosopon*, as this became the official Nestorian doctrine in 612, championed in particular by Michael Malpana, Ḥenanisho the monk and

Babai the Great. They were opponents of Ḥenana and his christology, and, too, of his exegesis. 'The texts of our collection witness to the Nestorian dogmatical war on two or three fronts within their own church and against the neighbouring churches', Chalcedonians and monophysites included (ibid., XIX). In its present form the collection comes from the period of the revival of strict Nestorianism under Catholicos Timothy I (d. 823) (ibid., XVIII).

2. The florilegium of 612 (= Flor. 612): J.-B. Chabot, *Synodicon Orientale ou recueil de synodes nestoriens* (Paris 1902); text: p. 575, 23–578, 25; trans.: p. 592, 31–615, 23; 597, 24–598, 23. 'The florilegium of 612 is the patristic underpinning of the credo that the Persian diophysite bishops handed over to the King of Kings in Persia in 612' (L. Abramowski & A. van Roey, art. cit., 133, n. 6). The authorities appealed to are John Chrysostom, Gregory Nazianzen, Athanasius, the Synod of Constantinople in 381, Pope Damasus, Basil, Gregory of Nyssa, Atticus of Constantinople Justinian, Amphilochius of Iconium and Ambrose. See below on Flor. Greg.

3. The florilegium of 680 (= Flor. 680): J.-B. Chabot, op. cit., text: 242, 11–244, 5; trans. 510, 1–513, 10. It is embedded in the letter written in 680 by the Catholicos Giwargis to the priest Mina.

4. The florilegium with the scholia on Gregory (= Flor Greg.): ed. and trans. Abramowski-van Roey, art. cit.

(a) *Contents*: The florilegium contains 89 citations, of which 22 testimonia exhibit points of contact with Antiochene and Nestorian florilegia—with Flor. 612, Flor. Cambr., Flor. 680, with the *Eranistes*, Gelasius, the Flor. Ephesinum 14 (= ACO I 1, 2, p. 43 f.). The bulk of the citations remains without parallels; a lost florilegium on Andreas of Samosata is not taken into account by the editors. Also excerpted is ps. Athanasius, *Sermo maior de fide*, which under this name circulates as a florilegium from the *Epistula ad Antiochenos* of Marcellus of Ancyra. Here we find:

(i) Citations from Gregory Nazianzen, which, together with passages from Chrysostom, form the chief constituent of the florilegium. 'The commentary on the Gregory fragments proves that the christology of the Theologian, despite its utterances concerning the unity of the natures in Christ and the apotheosis of human nature, which were eminently serviceable for the monophysite opposition, had to be preserved as authority also for the strict Antiochene aspect of Nestorian theology. This is because the commentary could otherwise yield those diphysite expressions so treasured by Theodoret' (Abramowski-van Roey, art. cit., 137 f.).

(ii) Citations from Chrysostom. These point in another direction (ibid., 138): 'Ḥenana, leader of the School of Nisibis from ca 570, replaced the canonical authority of the exegete Theodore of Mopsuestia by that of Chrysostom. At the same time the direction which Ḥenana took in christology championed the teaching of one hypostasis. In our florilegium the Chrysostom excerpts are selected so deliberately that the distinction of both natures in Christ is emphasised. In 86, against the Greek text, Theodore's favourite expression *participatio* even appears. From all of this one can conclude that a claim had to be made on Chrysostom by orthodox Nestorians against the deviation and heresy of Ḥenana and his party within the Nestorian camp. The eight citations from Chrysostom with which the Flor. 612 opens (see above) have precisely the same function there; in 612, under the influence of Babai the Great, the christology of two *hypostaseis* became official Nestorian teaching. The taking over of these citations in our florilegium is thus not only gratifying in a formal sense, but corresponds thoroughly to their original purpose. The conflicts within the Nestorian camp with regard to christology continued until the time of the Catholicos Timothy I (d. 823)' (Abramowski-van Roey, art. cit., 138).

(iii) The scholia: Of the 36 extracts from Gregory, 7 are furnished with scholia (nūhōrō, *elucidatio, commentarius*). The sole interest of the writers of the scholia is christology (ibid., 138). Nr. 62a is written polemically against the monophysite *physis synthetos* (ibid., 139). Jacobites and Nestorians alike attempted to lay claim to Gregory Nazianzen for themselves and to compose commentaries on him (in the eighth and ninth centuries this was particularly true of the Nestorians).

(D) Florilegia in the monenergist and monothelite controversy and in the question of the veneration of images

I. Florilegia in defence of 'one energy' and 'one will'

Here we can only be tentative. Monenergists and monothelites wished to be Chalcedonians (i.e. to accept the formula of the one hypostasis in two natures), and tried to seek a compromise with the champions of the *mia physis* formula. Three groups of florilegia are to be distinguished:

1. In his *Disputatio cum Pyrrho* (PG 91, 333A), Maximus Confessor mentions the fact that Sergius of Constantinople had requested an anthology on the question of the 'one energy' from the Paulinian George of Arsas, in order to use it to work for the unity of the Church. The text is lost. Cf. Grumel, *Regestes* I², nr. 280, for the year 618 (617?).

2. A Syriac MS, BM Add. 7192 (s. VII–VIII) (F. Rosen and J. Forshall, *Catalogus codicum manuscriptorum qui in Museo Britannico asservantur*, pars prima, 3 vols., (London 1838–1871) 83–84, nr. 51) contains on ff. 51–78 a collection of six shorter texts of which four are specifically anti-dyothelite.

3. Cod. BM Add. 14.535, ff. 1–20 has a florilegium which is regarded as monophysite-anti-Nestorian by Wright II, 796–798, and likewise by A. Guillaumont, *DOP* 23/24 (1969/70) (39–66) 52; S. Brock, 'An Early Syriac Life of Maximus the Confessor', *AnBoll* 91 (1973) 299–346, shows, however, that the florilegium is monothelite.

II. Anti-monenergist and anti-monothelite florilegia

1. The florilegium against monenergist teachings in Sophronius of Jerusalem, *Epistula synodica ad Sergium Constantinopolitanum*: PG 87³, 3148–3200 (Mansi XI, 461–510). According to Photius, *Bibl.* 231: Henry 5, 64 f., this *ep.* is addressed to Pope Honorius. In it Sophronius had a collection of patristic texts to testify to the two energies in Christ. According to Stephen of Dor: Mansi X, 896A, Sophronius collected 600 *testimonia* in two books, at the end of which Eulogius of Alexandria (580–607) was represented. See C. von Schönborn, *Sophrone de Jérusalem* = ThéolHist 20 (Paris 1972) 100–101. See R. Riedinger, *ÖAkW*, Sb. 352 Bd., 13, n. 8.

2. Maximus Confessor (b. ca 580, d. 13.8.662); Lateran Council (649); Third Council of Constantinople (680/1).

On the *Vita* of Maximus see above, Part II D VI 2; on both synods see E. Caspar, 'Die Lateransynode von 649', *ZKG* 51 (1932) 75–137; R. Riedinger, (a) literature listed in Part I A above; and (b) id., 'Griechische Konzilsakten auf dem Wege ins lateinische Mittelalter', *AHC* 9 (1977) 262–282; idem, 'Lateinische Übersetzungen griechischer Häretikertexte des siebenten Jahrhunderts', *ÖAkW*, Sb. 352.Bd., 5–82; idem, *Concilium Lateranense a. 649 celebratum*: ACO series secunda, vol. I (Berolini 1984), esp. introduction IX–XXVIII.

(a) Florilegia in the works of Maximus Confessor:

(i) *Op. theol. pol.* = CPG 7697, 15: PG 91, 153–184. In about 646 Maximus sent to Stephen of Dor a florilegium which, according to Sherwood, *Date-List* nr. 87, must be described as 'the most extensive florilegium due to Maximus'.

(ii) The florilegia listed in CPG 7697, in *Opuscula* 23, a–c and 26–27 are spurious. On nr. 26 see M. Richard, 'Un faux dithélite ou traité de S. Irénée au Diacre Démétrius', *Polychronion* = FS F. Dölger (Heidelberg 1966) 431–440 = *Opera Minora* III, 65. On *Opusculum* 26: PG 91, 276B–280B, see K.–H. Uthemann, *OCP* 46 (1980) 340, n. 155.

(b) Florilegia at the Lateran Council (649) (CPG 9402):

(i) Secretarius V: *Testimonia Patrum* = Mansi X, 1071–1108; now in R. Riedinger, ACO ser. II^a, vol. 1, 256(257)–314(315): Maximus and his Greek assistants selected from the orthodox Fathers testimonia which in the *acta* of the Lateran Synod are more numerous, although sometimes shorter, than in the *acta* of the Third Council of Constantinople (Riedinger, ÖAkW, Sb. 352 Bd., 12); idem, ACO ser. II^a, vol. I, introduction XVIII–XIX.

(ii) *Testimonia Haereticorum*: Maximus and the Greek monks also produced a florilegium of heretical works: Mansi X, 1113–1121; see now R. Riedinger, ACO ser. II^a, vol. 1, 320(321)–334(335), including a passage from an Easter homily of the Arian Lucius (Mansi X 1113CD = ACO ser. II^a, vol. I, 320(321) = *Doctrina Patrum* 9 XV: Diekamp 65 = CPG 2535, which could have been known only to Eastern theologians. The bulk of the texts comes from Theodore of Pharan. There is an important piece of evidence in J. Pierres' two volume Roman dissertation, of which only the second part is devoted to Maximus: II *Sanctus Maximus confessor princeps apologetarum synodi Lateranensis anni 649 (Pars historica)* (Romae 1940): *Maximus ad colligendum Florilegium sess. V syn. Later. aliquid ipsemet contulit* (pp. 27*–51*). Pierres shows that 27 of the 161 testimonia of the Lateran *acta* are found also in Maximus, and he is of the opinion that the Latin *acta* constitute the minutes of the conciliar proceedings in the usual sense (cf. R. Riedinger, ÖAkW, Sb. 352 Bd., 13, n. 8).

(iii) A florilegium with six testimonia in Riedinger, ACO ser. II^a, vol. I, p. 84,1–90,26; see further p. XVIII.

(iv) *Florilegium dyotheleticum* in Cod. Vat. gr. 1455 (a. 1299), ff. 165^r–176^r; ed. princeps R. Riedinger, op. cit., 425–436; see ibid., XI, with a reference to J. Darrouzès, 'Notes de littérature et de critique', *RevÉtByz* 18 (1960)179–194. For Riedinger this florilegium is a new argument for the Greek origin of the Lateran *acta*. It contains 81 testimonia. Riedinger observes: 'The total number of these testimonia has thus increased from 161 in Mansi to 166 ... If one counts as well the 81 testimonia of the *florilegium dyotheleticum* (425–436), this makes 247 passages which were selected by the compilers of the Greek text of the *acta* as evidence. As the author index shows, in the Lateran *acta* there are extracts from some 150 different works, deriving from about 70 authors—a respectable arsenal that presupposes not only theological knowledge and theological discernment, but also the possession of source material, at least in the form of older florilegia' (op. cit., XVIII).

(c) Florilegia at the Third Council of Constantinople (680/1) (CPG 9416 ff.):

(i) In *Actio* IV, in connection with the reading out of his letter, we find the florilegium of Pope Agatho: Mansi XI, 257–265 (CPG 9423).

(ii) *Actio* X: *Testimonia Patrum orthodoxorum*: Mansi XI, 393–440 (CPG 9424). *Testimonia haereticorum*: 440–449. Many 'heretics' are cited who could not be used in the *acta* of the Lateran Council, namely the letters of Sergius of Constantinople and of Pope Honorius. The 11 texts cited from Theodore of Pharan are due to Maximus Confessor, who had selected them before the year 649. For these 11 texts there are thus 'two separate traditions today, of which each goes back to the seventh century' (Riedinger, *ÖAkW* 13–14; idem, *AHC* 9 (1977) 257–258).

3. The *Florilegium Achridense* in Cod. 86 of the Mus. Nat. of Ochrid, thus named by M. Richard, who discovered it: 'Le traité de Georges Hiéromoine sur les hérésies', *RevÉtByz* 28 (1970) 239–269 = *Opera Minora* III, 62; for a table of contents of the MS see ibid., 241; nr. 11 (pp. 133–212) is a *Florilegium theologicum capitulis XXV distributum*. Some extracts are edited by M. Richard: (1) 'Quelques nouveaux fragments des Pères anté-nicéens et nicéens', *SymbOsl* 38 (1963) 76–83 = *Opera Minora* I, 5; (2) 'Un faux dithélite...' (see above on Maximus); (3) M. Richard–M. B. Hemmerdinger, 'Trois nouveaux fragments grecs de l'Adversus haereses de saint Irenée', *ZNW* 53 (1962) 252–255. The florilegium contains 9 dyothelite texts (cf. *Opera Minora* III, 65, 438), but most of them are of the pseudepigraphical variety. Richard, ibid., 439, speaks of 'a complete propaganda literature' which was composed in the seventh century to defend the orthodox teaching of two wills in Christ. In *Chalkedon* I, 732, Richard had already described the 'dogmatic forgery' as a weapon which was normally used by a persecuted minority. According to Richard, this observation also fits the *Florilegium Achridense* and the orthodox party with the teaching of 'two energies' and 'two wills', which encountered difficulties not only with the monophysites but also with the power of the imperial state and Byzantine ecclesiastical authority. Anonymity and pseudepigraphy created possibilities for the defence of orthodoxy. People placed themselves under the patronage of a Justin, an Hippolytus, and of men down to John Chrysostom and Cyril of Alexandria. In Richard's eyes, research into these pseudonymous passages will make critical editions of the older Fathers easier on the one hand, and on the other it will furnish a picture of the reaction to monenergism and monotheletism. But this is a more difficult task than working on the florilegia of the period between 451 and 553.

4. A christology in the words of the Fathers: the *Doctrina Patrum*.

Cf. F. Diekamp (ed.), *Doctrina Patrum de Incarnatione Verbi. Ein griechisches Florilegium des 7. u. 8. Jhs.* (Münster 1907), 2. Aufl. mit Korrekturen und Nachträgen von B. Phanourgakis, hrsgg. von E. Chrysos (Münster 1981). The new editors decided in favour of the opinion of J. Stiglmayr, 'Der Verfasser der Doctrina Patrum de Incarnatione', *ByzZ* 18 (1919) 14–40, i.e. in favour of Anastasius Apocrisiarius, the pupil of Maximus Confessor, as author. Cf. R. Riedinger, art. cit., *AHC* 9 (1977) 257: 'This comprehensive florilegium is so closely tied to the surviving works of Maximus and to the lists of testimonia of the Lateran Synod and of the Sixth Council, that one can well understand the authorship of Maximus' pupil, Anastasius Apocrisiarius'. Both Synods work with the material prepared by Maximus (ibid., 258). In the edition of Diekamp the *DP* yields 977 citations, of which 143 are biblical, 751 patristic, synodal or ecclesiastical, and 83 are culled from heretical works. Apart from ch. 1 and ch. 25, the first 30 chapters attack monophysite and monothelite doctrine. See the details in Diekamp XXXVI. On the relationship of the *DP* to Leontius of Byzantium and his *CNE* cf. B. E. Daley, op. cit., Introduction, n. 367: 14 testimonia in *CNE* correspond exactly to texts in the *DP*; another 14 texts from the *DP* are longer extracts from the same passages, and a further 13 are shorter versions. From this it follows that there is no direct connection with Leontius, but more with the sources of Leontius. Maximus is thus in the foreground. According to Diekamp, however, it is the *DP* which is probably the link between Leontius, *CNE* and Euthymius Zigabenus (op. cit., LXXXV, LXXVI). Daley, op. cit., Introduction n. 368 points to the *Libellus fidei* of John Maro (probably dating from the mid-seventh century, surviving only in Syriac and still unedited), which again is connected with the *DP* not in its own right but by virtue of its sources.

III. John Damascene and his florilegia

See K. Holl, *Die Sacra Parallela des Johannes Damascenus* = TU 16 (Leipzig 1897) 261–262; M. Richard, art. 'Florilèges Grecques', *DSp* 5 (1964) 476–486: Florilèges Damascéniens.

Edition: B. Kotter, *Die Schriften des Johannes von Damaskos* = PTSt 7, 12, 17, 22 (Berlin–New York 1969, 1973, 1975, 1981), with corresponding analyses. Cf. CPG 8040–8127.

After Maximus Confessor (*Opusc. theol. et polemica*), it is John Damascene who exhibits the greatest patristic learning. Cf. K. Holl, op. cit., 391. For the present it must remain open whether John gathered his material merely from florilegia like the *Doctrina Patrum*, or from original works. B. Kotter (see below), in any case, notes in the apparatus not only the original work but also, when applicable, the occurrence of a passage in the *DP*. K. Holl is less circumspect.

1. The *Hiera* (or *Sacra Parallela*)

On the various recensions see CPG 8056. We are at the acme of Greek (spiritual) florilegium literature. Dogma is incorporated into ethics to a small extent only. Cf. the gaps in the table of concordances between the *Sacra Parallela* and the *Expositio fidei*. Unfortunately in these excerpts John Damascene did not incorporate christology in the sense of 'ethics as imitation of Christ'. 'At two points only does dogma enter the picture at all: the dogma of the Trinity and the teaching of judgement to come form the framework in which the whole work is placed. But the former . . . is made the principle of ethics as little as the latter' (Holl, op. cit., 392). 'Within the work itself he [John Damascene] does not pass over christology, but treats it as if he lived in the second century; he devotes to it a single chapter, the content of which is "the prophecies concerning Christ our God"' (idem, *Fragmente vornicänischer Kirchenväter aus den Sacra parallela* = TU 20, 2 (Leipzig 1899) XIV). A section dealing with the Holy Cross can also be mentioned. The connection with Maximus Confessor is discussed by Holl in TU 16, 277–278.

2. The florilegium in the *Expositio fidei*

Cf. B. Kotter, *Die Schriften des Johannes von Damaskos. II. Expositio fidei* = PTSt 12 (Berlin–New York 1973) XXVIII: 'In this work John Damascene is a compiler of great flair, but he is also a superior compiler, for whose dogmatic assessment not only the evidence of the sources is needed, but also the selection, the omissions, the occasional remarks etc. are of decided importance' (H.-G. Beck, *Kirche u. theol. Lit. i. byz. Reich* (München 1959) 480). For John's treatment of his sources we really need a critical edition of the Fathers he used. However, B. Kotter, op. cit., XXIX draws a picture of a provisional nature: in the first place comes ps. Cyril, *De trinitate*, seventh century: PG 77 1120–1173, who almost exclusively provides the material for chapters 1–11, 48, 77 and 91.

> Gregory Nazianzen: 194 passages concerning the Trinity, christology etc.
> Athanasius of Alexandria: 92 passages concerning the Trinity
> Cyril of Alexandria: 73 passages on christology and the Trinity
> Maximus Confessor: 70 passages on wills and energies in Christ
> Nemesius of Emesa: 70 passages on anthropology and psychology
> Gregory of Nyssa: 49 passages on the Trinity and *energeia*
> Ps. Dionysius the Areopagite: 38 passages on the name of God and the angels
> John Chrysostom: 18 passages (without emphasis).
> See *Expositio fidei* III–IV, nr. 45–81: Kotter, op. cit., 106–180 on christology.

3. Extracts on the *Trishagion* in the *Epistola de Hymno Trishagio* (CPG 8049). Kotter, *Schriften* IV, 304–332, in which a florilegium of Anastasius, the abbot of the monastery of Euthymius, is preserved as proof that the *Trishagion* does not bear on the Trinity, but on the Son. See Kotter's introduction, op. cit., 290–294; 294 for an analysis of the florilegium.

4. The florilegium in *Contra Jacobitas*: Kotter, *Schriften* IV, 102–103: 34 citations from the Fathers, of which more than half (22) are in the *Doctrina Patrum*; 13 citations from Leontius of Byzantium, *CE* I; but the florilegium is related most closely to the *DP*.

5. Florilegia on image-veneration in each of the three speeches on images: *Contra imaginum calumniatores orationes tres*, ed. B. Kotter = PTSt 17 (Berlin–New York 1975) 24–33. For an analysis of the florilegium see ibid., 27 ff. Kotter remarks that there are well-ordered anthologies for all three speeches, but in particular for *or.* I–II (which perhaps had been put together previously?). 11 lemmata are also in the *DP*, 20 in the Second Council of Nicaea. Here John Damascene always appeals to the original sources, never to intermediary ones. Probably there existed an arsenal of texts for the defenders of the veneration of images. A certain relationship with the *DP* is probable.

Literature: *St. John of Damascus, On the Divine Images. Three Apologies Against Those Who Attack the Divine Images*, translated by D. Anderson (Crestwood, N.Y. 1980). Unfortunately this is not based on Kotter's new edition. The appended florilegia are drastically shortened, because they are 'so repetitious and obscure' (op. cit., 7–12); Abbot Chrysostomos and M. G. Chapman, 'St. John Damascus and Iconoclasm: The First Apologetic Discourse', *Kleronomia* 11 (1979) 263–272.

Postscript to *Part III*: the *Erotapokriseis*

We shall not go into the literary genre of the *Erotapokriseis* or *Questions and Answers*. H.-G. Beck, *Kirche u. theol. Lit.* 91 describes them as 'general catechisms' (exegetical, philosophical, theological in a practical way). They often contain extracts from the Fathers, but cannot be put on the same footing as the dogmatic florilegia. They provide a good insight into popular theology (cf. Beck, op. cit., 444).

Well-known examples: 1. Ps. Athanasius, *Quaestiones ad Antiochum*: PG 28, 597–700, to which 2. Anastasius of Sinai, *In Hexaemeron*: PG 89, 581–1078 exhibits striking similarities. 3. Ps. Caesarius, *Erotapokriseis* will be important for us. It has been investigated by R. Riedinger and will be published by him. Cf. id., *Pseudo-Kaisarios, Überlieferungsgeschichte und Verfasserfrage* = Byz. Archiv 12 (München 1969), esp. the question of sources, 283–300. 4. Patriarch Photius, *Amphilochia*, is a significant work which is the counterpart to his *Bibliotheca*: PG 101; see Beck, op. cit., 523.

Literature: G. Heinrici, 'Zur patristischen Aporienliteratur' = *AbhSächsGesWiss* Bd. XXVII, no. XXIV (Leipzig 1909); idem, 'Griechisch-byzantinische Gesprächsbücher u. Verwandtes aus Sammelhandschriften', ibid., Bd. XXVIII, Nr. VIII (Leipzig 1911). See A. Ehrhard, in W. E. Crum, *Der Papyruscodex saec. VI–VII der Phillipsbibliothek in Cheltenham, Kopt.-theol. Schriften* (Straßburg 1915) 131–171; G. Bardy, 'La littérature patristique des "Quaestiones et responsiones" sur l'Écriture sainte', *RevBibl* 41 (1932) 210–236, 341–369, 515–537; 42 (1933) 14–30, 328–352; Beck, op. cit., Index 'Erotapokriseis'; P. O'Connell, 'The "Patristic Argument" in the Writings of Patriarch St. Nicephorus I of Constantinople (+828)' = *StudPat*

11 (Berlin 1972) 210–214. The *Erotapokriseis* are related to, but not identical with, the older literary genre of the dialogue. On this see M. Hoffman, *Der Dialog bei den christlichen Schriftstellern der ersten vier Jahrhunderte* = TU 96 (Berlin 1966), esp. 4–5 with n. 4.

Part IV

Catalogues of heretics and of brief presentations of heresies.

The phenomenon of heresy led within orthodoxy to particular literary genres, which appear with increasing clarity as catalogues of heretics and of brief presentations of the errors they championed. They are the negative counterpart of the series of Fathers, who are taken as a guarantee of the right faith, and they correspond thus in many ways to the orthodox florilegia or to synopses of councils. The more the sense of tradition on the side of orthodoxy is developed, the more readily is formed the image of a coherent tradition for heresy too. Every heretic's name has, so to speak, a glutinous strength in it, which gathers other names about it to make a vertical and horizontal consensus, just like in the orthodox tradition. Heresies, like Christian orthodoxy, must have their Fathers.

Such catalogues or registers of heresies have their positive significance, as we shall see time and again, but they have also their greater danger. Nowhere in theology is the inclination towards cliché as close as here, and at the same time also the endangering of justice and the consolidation of misunderstanding. The history of the post-Chalcedonian period unfortunately offers richly illustrative material for this observation.

(A) Literary forms and antecedents

The catalogues of heretics or heresies which we encounter in post-Chalcedonian christology have various subsidiary or secondary forms. All of these have their models or antecedents in the pre-Chalcedonian period.

I Various forms

1. Catalogues of names
2. Catalogues with a short description
3. Inventories connected with anathemas or with formulas of abjuration. These can refer to a single name with a description of the person's particular errors, or to several names with or without a presentation of their errors.

II Models

1. Catalogues of names

Simple 'lists of heretics' in the period before Chalcedon are short, when they are to be found at all. As the history of the faith proceeds, so too does the list grow.

2. Catalogues with a short description or with longer refutations

(a) The *Refutatio omnium haeresium*, also called *Elenchus* or *Philosophoumena*, which comes to be ascribed to Hippolytus. The work, which was composed between 222 and 235, treats Gnostic heresies (Books 5–9). Together with original Gnostic texts, the writer also used the *Adversus haereses* of Irenaeus of Lyons in his work. The *Syntagma*, a treatise written before the *Refutatio*, names 32 heresies, of which the last is that of Noetus.

(b) The model and source of many later presentations is Epiphanius of Salamis with his *Panarion* (*Medicine-cabinet*, also cited as *Haereses*), written between 374 and 377 and dealing with 80 heresies. A later extract from the *Medicine-cabinet* is the *Anakephalaiosis* (*Recapitulatio*), which was made before 428 since Augustine used it in his work *De haeresibus* (CCL 46, 283–345). Edition: *Epiphanius, Panarion*, ed. K. Holl, (a) *Haer.* 1–64, GCS *Epiphaniuswerke* II; (b) *Haer.* 65–80: GCS *Epiphaniuswerke* III, ed. H. Lietzmann. *Anakephalaiosis sive eorum quae in Panario dicta sunt summa comprehensio*: PG 42, 833–885. It is significant that a corpus of Epiphanius' works existed in Coptic: E. Lucchesi, 'Un corpus épiphanien en copte', *AnBoll* 99 (1981) 95–99.

(c) Theodoret of Cyrus (d. ca 466), *Haereticarum fabularum compendium*. The first four books present many heresies from the Antiochene point of view, beginning with Simon Magus and ending with Nestorius and Eutyches (Books I–IV: PG 83, 336–437).

(B) The most important collections of the post-Chalcedonian period
I Catalogues and collections of heretics and heresies

1. Monophysite oriented presentations of christological heresies are found scattered in countless works. As a sample we may call attention to several authors and works:

(a) Philoxenus of Mabbog (d. 523): this author names Manes, Marcion, Eutyches (a list found likewise in Chalcedonian writers), Theodore of Mopsuestia, Diodore of Tarsus, Theodoret of Cyrus, and in particular Nestorius (see too under the Three Chapters controversy). Cf. E. A. W. Budge, *The Discourses of Philoxenus Bishop of Mabbôgh* (1894) vol. II, C—CXXXVIII; PO 13, 248–251.

(b) The Armenian collection of texts known under the title of 'Seal of Faith of the holy catholic Church, of our holy orthodox and inspired Fathers', Armenian text edited by K. Ter-Mekerttschian (Etschmiadsin 1914). Cf. J. Lebon, 'Les citations patristiques grecques du "Sceau de la foi"', *RHE* 25 (1929) 5–32. Lebon suspects that John the Mayragomier, a representative of Julianist christology, was the compiler of the collection; the time of composition would be connected with the Synod of 616. On p. 366, 20–371, 13 of the Armenian edition we find, according to Lebon, art. cit., 31, an 'explanatio ad declarationem et reprehensionem haeresium', i.e. a long series of anathemas against the heretics of old, among whom both Leo I and Severus of Antioch are included.

(c) The Armenian 'Book of Letters' (Girk' t'łt'oç) (Tiflis 1901) contains in the letter of the Catholicos Babgen to the orthodox in Persia a comprehensive survey of heretics, namely Arius, Diodore of Tarsus, Theodore of Mopsuestia, Nestorius, Theodoret of Cyrus, Ibas, Eutychus (= Eutyches), Paul of Samosata, Acacius of Nisibis, Barsumas, and Babai (op. cit., 49 f.). The reply of the Syrians to Babgen enumerates Marcion, Apollinarius, Manes, and Severus of Antioch (op. cit., 53). Cf. L. Frivold, *The Incarnation. A Study of the Doctrine of Incarnation in the Armenian Church in the 5th and 6th Centuries according to the Book of Letters* (Oslo-Bergen-Tromsø 1981) 149–160. See ibid., 160 on the split of the monophysites into Julianists and Severans.

(d) Not to be forgotten is the pre-Chalcedonian heresiology (ca 430) of Eznik of Kolb, *Vier Bücher über Gott* (Gegen die Irrlehren: Heiden, Perser, griechische Philosophen und Marcioniten). German trans. by S. Weber, BKV² 57 (1927).

2. Nestorian oriented presentations

(a) Barḥadbešabba of 'Arbaia has in his *Church History* (Part I: ed. F. Nau, PO XXIII, 177–333) 186–199, a section on heresies which have divided the Church. After Sabbatians, Simonians, Marcionites, Borborians, Daisanites, Manichaeans and Paul of Samosata (a Judaiser), he labels also as Nestorians Cyrillians and Severans. In the latter, as in the Arians (Eunomians), Satan has particularly shown his might.

3. Chalcedonian oriented collections

Cf. M. Aubineau, 'Un recueil "de haeresibus": Sion College, Codex Graecus 6', *RevÉtGrec* 80 (1967) 425–429. Aubineau stresses the worth of this collection, which in its original form perhaps derives from Patriarch Photius.

(a) Theodore of Raithu (end of the sixth century) gives in the first part of his work *Praeparatio* a list of heresies much like a catalogue, which extends from Manichaeism to Severus of Antioch; ed. F. Diekamp, *Analecta Patristica* (OCA 117) 185–222, esp. 187–200; CPG 7600.

(b) The *De Sectis*, written by an unknown author and previously ascribed erroneously to Leontius of Byzantium, treats in chapters IV–VI heresies from Apollinarius to the Three Chapters controversy under Emperor Justinian; ed. PG 86, 1193–1268, esp. 1217–1237; CPG 6823.

(c) Timothy, a presbyter in Constantinople around the year 600, endeavours in his work *De receptione haereticorum* to provide detailed definitions in order to give an exact picture of each heresy which he deals with. Timothy, too, incorporates into the list of christological heresies the representatives of Manichaeism; ed. PG 86, 12–68; CPG 7016; M. Aubineau, *RevÉtGrec* 80 (1967) 426 nr. 3.

(d) The *Epistula synodica ad Sergium* of Sophronius, Patriarch of Jerusalem (634–638), contains a catalogue of heresies, which, besides an extensive summary of heresies connected with the theology of the Trinity, also investigates special christological heresies. This compilation comprises the main heresies from Eutyches to Theodore of Mopsuestia; ed. PG 87, 3148–3200, esp. 3186B–3195D; CPG 7635; M. Aubineau, *RevÉtGrec* 80 (1967) 426, nr. 2.

(e) George, a monk and presbyter in the seventh century, compiled a catalogue of heresies. The work was published in 1900 by F. Diekamp in an incomplete version in *ByzZ* 9 (1900) 14–51. Diekamp dated the work to 638/639. Through his significant find of the Codex 86 in the National Museum of Ochrid, M. Richard was in a position to offer an almost complete version of George's work on heresies. George begins his treatise on heresies with the representatives of Gnosis (Manes) and closes his descriptions, which, *inter alios*, make mention of Nestorius, Eutyches and Dioscorus, with the teaching of the Tritheists, Aphthartodocetists and Agnoetes; ed.

M. Richard, 'Le traité de Georges Hiéromoine sur les hérésies', *RevÉtByz* 28 (1970) 239–269 = *Opera Minora* III, 62.

(*f*) A work of uncertain origin ascribed to Anastasius the Sinaite deals with the starting-points of heresies and the councils which were summoned against them. This *De haeresibus* contains a presentation of christological heresies which begins with the Gnostic teaching of Simon Magus and Marcion and ends with a treatment of the opposition to heresy of Sophronius, Patriarch of Jerusalem (cf. 3d); ed. J. B. Pitra, *Iuris ecclesiastici Graecorum historia et monumenta* II (Romae 1868) 257–271; cf. CPG 7774. The *De haeresibus* can be dated to the years between 692–695.

(*g*) The second part of the chief work of John Damascene (650–754), the *Pēgē gnōseōs*, contains a history of heresies, which relies heavily on the model of the *Anakephalaiosis* from the corpus of Epiphanius of Salamis. In his *Liber de haeresibus* John adds Greek philosophy, Judaism and Manichaeism to the list of heresies. The inventory of Christian heresies in the strict sense extends down to the Donatists and monothelites; ed. B. Kotter, *Die Schriften des Johannes von Damaskos* IV, PTS Band 22, (Berlin 1981), 1–67. Cf. M. Aubineau, *RevÉtGrec* 80 (1967) 426, nr. 1.

(*h*) The *Doctrina Patrum*, edited by F. Diekamp, contains several catalogues of heresies and citations from heretical works. One catalogue sets forth the opposition of the decrees of the Council of Chalcedon to contemporary heresies (174–179), a second section comprises a catalogue of heresies in the stricter sense (266–272), and a third passage deals with the heresies of monenergism and monothelitism (302–315).

(*i*) From the pen of Germanus I, Patriarch of Constantinople between 715 and 730, comes the collection of heresies *De haeresibus et synodis*. Germanus, too, begins his treatise on heretics with representatives of Gnosis like Simon Magus, Manes and Marcion; ed. PG 98, 40–88; cf. M. Aubineau, *RevÉtGrec* 80 (1967) 426, nr. 5.

(*k*) In his letter to Pope Leo III, Nicephorus I, Patriarch of Constantinople from 806–815, furnishes a catalogue of christological heresies. In this connection, besides Arius, Macedonius and Apollinarius, he mentions the names of Nestorius, Eutyches, Dioscorus, Theodore, Origen, Didymus, Evagrius, and others; ed. PG 100, 169–200, esp. 192–193. Cf. M. Aubineau, art. cit., 427, nr. 7 and 13.

II Formulas of abjuration with anathemas

The peculiarity of these anti-heretical texts lies in their liturgical use, i.e. in the act of solemn and public abjuration (*euchologion*). The longest and most detailed formulas concern the Manichaeans, together with whom the Paulicians are also spoken of, although they are not labelled with this name.

Cf. Ch. Astruc, W. Conus-Wolska, J. Gouillard, P. Lemerle, D. Papachryssanthou, J. Paramelle, 'Les sources grecques pour l'histoire des Pauliciens d'Asie mineure' = *TravMém* 4 (1970) 189: 'L'histoire, encore à faire, des rituels d'abjuration (comme collection)...'; many references for the period of iconoclasm are given by J. Gouillard, 'Le synodikon de l'Orthodoxie édition et commentaire', *TravMém* 2 (1967) 1–316.

1. Latin formulas of abjuration

(*a*) Anathemas in the so-called *Commonitorium* (*Instruction*) of St. Augustine, ed. J. Zycha: CSEL 25, 980,4–982,3; German in *Die Gnosis*. 3. Bd.: *Der Manichäismus.*

Unter Mitwirkung von J. P. Asmussen, eingeleitet, übersetzt und erläutert von A. Böhlig = *Bibl. d. Alten Welt* (Zürich-München 1980) 293–295; nr. 8, p. 295 is christological.

    (*b*) The Augustinian formula of the year 398: Adam, KlT 175, VIII, 61, p. 90.

    (*c*) The large Latin formula of abjuration (*Prosperi Anathematismi*) (AD 526): Adam, KlT 175, nr. 62, pp. 90–93. Sentences 1–9 and 18–19 = sentences 1–8 and 9–10 in the *Commonitorium* of Augustine. Sentence 9 is christological.

2. Greek formulas of abjuration or anathemas

    (*a*) ⟨Zacharias Rhetor⟩, *VII Cephalaia* with anathemas against the ungodly Manichaeans, discovered by M. Richard and edited from Codex Athon. Vatopedianus 236, ff. 127ʳ–129ᵛ: *Iohannis Caesariensis Presbyteri et Grammatici Opera quae supersunt* = CCG I (1977), XXXIII–XXXIX. According to Richard this text is 'une des meilleures sources byzantines sur le Manichéisme et l'ancêtre des formules d'abjuration médiévales' (op. cit. XXXII). Part of the contents is known from the extensive Greek formula of abjuration (see below). At the end there is a formula to be signed.

    (*b*) Short Greek formulas of abjuration (fifth century) from the *euchologion* of the patriarchate: A. Adam, KlT 175, 93–97 (nr. 63).

    (*c*) Long formulas of abjuration (ninth century): ibid., 97–103 (nr. 64).

    (*d*) The longest formula of abjuration: PG 1, 1461C–1469D (directed against the Paulicians from 1468B–1469D); PG 100, 1321B–1324B.

    (*e*) Paris. Coisl. 213, ed. Ch. Astruc et al., op. cit., 199–203 (in addition 187–189).

    Corresponding to the negative formulas of abjuration and the anathemas in the liturgical context are the benedictions of the orthodox. Also to be remembered is the inclusion or exclusion of names in the diptychs, which we encounter often in the post-Chalcedonian period. Further texts in M. Aubineau, *RevÉtGrec* 30 (1967) 426–428, nr. 6, 10, 11, 18, 19.

PART V

Collections of definitions of concepts and *aporiai*

A new step in the history of post-Chalcedonian christology and in theology itself is made with the appearance of *collections of definitions* and *of anthologies of christological aporiai*. We stand at the point of contact between theology and philosophy, or, more concretely, before the attempt to investigate christological statements according to the laws of Aristotelian logic and syllogisms, and to bring this means into polemic. From the *Proparaskeue* of Theodore of Raithu (see below) it becomes clear that as early as the first half of the sixth century a knowledge of the elements of logic, of the kind of the *Categories* of Aristotle and the *Eisagoge* of Porphyry, was considered as essential. The mutation can be made plain from two famous works of our period: while the *Doctrina Patrum* is still a 'dogmatic florilegium', in the *Dialectic* of John Damascene we have a 'philosophical florilegium' (Roueché 65; see below).

Bibliography on the new situation:

M. Roueché, 'Byzantine Philosophical Texts of the Seventh Century', *JÖB* 23 (1974) 61–76; H.-G. Beck, 'Bildung und Theologie im frühmittelalterlichen Byzanz', *Polychronion* = FS F. Dölger (Heidelberg 1966) 69–81; K.-H. Uthemann, 'Syllogistik im Dienst der Orthodoxie. Zwei unedierte Texte byzantinischer Kontroverstheologie des 6. Jahrhunderts', *JÖB* 30 (1981) 103–112; G. Ruhbach, 'Klerusausbildung in der Alten Kirche', *Wort und Dienst* = *Jb.d.K.Hochschule Bethel*, NF 15 (1979) 107–114.

Two new literary genres

1. Collections of definitions. The more that contrary formulas were discussed in the controversy after Chalcedon, the more one had to refer to definitions of concepts that were related to these. But the philosophical branch of the *enkyklios paideusis*, too, aroused the desire for compendia of logic in Greek, in particular as school textbooks. We do not have to decide here which cause was the more important. It also cannot be determined whether such collections were part of a course of theological instruction. Always, however, it was only the most fundamental elements of logic that were taken over. Whoever wanted to make a careful study of logic had to have recourse to other sources. M. Roueché describes the user of the anthologies to be cited here in these words: 'He was a Christian, studying in a Christian milieu, probably to a theological end, and was probably the same student for whom the *Doctrina Patrum* was written' (*JÖB* 23 (1974) 64). In order to produce these 'very short manuals' of Aristotelian logic, recourse was had to the Alexandrian Aristotelians about 600 AD: (a) to *David*, a Christian neo-Platonist from Armenia (sixth century): his commentary on the *Categories* of Aristotle is preserved for us completely only in Armenian (unedited); there are fragments in Greek. Complete in Greek are the *Prolegomena*, i.e. his introduction to philosophy, and a commentary on the *Eisagoge* of Porphyry, ed. A. Busse, CAG 18, 2 (1904); (b) to *Elias*: ed. A. Busse, CAG 18, 1 (1900); (c) to *Stephen of Alexandria, In librum Aristotelis de Interpretatione Commentarium*, ed. M. Hayduck, CAG 18, 3 (1885). Something analogous to what happened with the florilegia of the Fathers after 500 began to occur here also: 'logical compendia had widely replaced the lectures of the Alexandrians in schools and libraries' (Roueché, art. cit., 67). These collections of definitions were utilised particularly in the monothelite controversy.

The Syrian tradition, which also has recourse to the Alexandrian authors already mentioned, bears witness as well to the broad dispersion of these collections of definitions. Cf. A. Baumstark, 'Syrische Kommentare zur Eisagoge des Porphyrios', in idem, *Aristoteles bei den Syrern vom V.–VIII. Jh., Syr. Texte I* (Leipzig 1900) 182–189.

Forms of such collections (Roueché 63): they range from simple

collections of excerpts, in the main destined for the friends of the
compiler, to elaborate compilations which were intended to serve
the whole gamut of introductory logic. Thus we have:

(a) the simple excerpt;

(b) excerpts ordered according to logical *topoi* ('perhaps slightly
rewritten with examples'); the comprehension of the material was
made easier by meaningful arrangement and the selection of examples;

(c) 'Collections of collections', i.e. a compilation of several shorter
collections which were destined in the first instance for students.
At this level we are dealing with texts used in schools.

The subject matter of such collections could be: the distinction
of essence, nature and hypostasis; epistemological definitions for the
meaning of the *horoi*; conceptual distinctions of the levels of being,
of human and divine being, definitions of *actio* and *passio* ... The
connexion with the christological starting-point remains more or less
preserved (Uthemann, *OCP* 46 (1980) 308).

2. Anthologies of christological *aporiai* (ἐπαπορήματα)

These are 'compilations of syllogistic rebuttals which endeavour
to prove to the opponent the conceptual illogicality, the self-contra-
diction, even the absurdity of his dogmatic formulations'. One hap-
pily 'fixed on a univocal identity of the conceptual formulation and
of what was intended in the confession, this not being without
influence on the formation of 'orthodoxy', as this was present at
the end of the seventh century, e.g. in the writings of Anastasius
of Sinai or Ps. Cyril, and in the eighth century in John Damascene'.
K.-H. Uthemann, 'Syllogistik im Dienst der Orthodoxie. Zwei
unedierte Texte byzantinischer Kontroverstheologie', *JÖB* 30 (1981)
(103–112) esp. 107.

(A) Collections of definitions

I. Sixth century

1. Anastasius of Antioch (559–598), *Capita philosophica* (CPG 6945), ed. K.-H.
Uthemann, 'Die "Philosophischen Kapitel" des Anastasius I. v. Ant. (559–598)'.
OCP 46 (1980) 343–366, according to Uthemann the 'oldest' extant collection (ibid.,
308).

2. Even before this a start had been made to place together various definitions
of one and the same (word and) concept:

(a) Ephrem of Antioch (527–545), Definitions of the *Epistula ad Acacium philoso-
phum* (CPG 6906; ed. S. Helmer, *Der Neuchalkedonismus*, 271–272; 273–274); see
also the *Florilegium Achridense* (Uthemann, art. cit., 308, n. 4). They belong to the
'etymological tradition'.

(b) The lost collection of definitions of Rusticus Diaconus which he purportedly
compiled in 565 during the Three Chapters dispute, while he was staying in the

monastery of the Sleepless Monks in Constantinople; cf. Altaner-Stuiber, *Patrologie*, 465; A. Grillmeier, *Chalkedon* II, 820–821.

II. Transition from sixth to seventh centuries

Theodore of Raithu, *Praeparatio* (CPG 7600), ed. F. Diekamp, *Analecta Patristica* = OCA 117 (1938) 173–227 (christological context).

III. Seventh century

1. Anastasius of Sinai, *Hodegos* II, 1–8 (CPG 7745): ed. K.-H. Uthemann, CCG 8 (1981) 23–75. Anastasius emphasises the christological context through 'shorter digressions' (Uthemann).

2. Maximus Confessor, *Opuscula* (CPG 7697; PG 91)
   (a) PG 91, 149–151: CPG 7697, 14: *horoi diaphoroi*
   (b) PG 91, 213–216: CPG 7697, 18: *horoi henoseos*
   (c) PG 91, 260–264: CPG 7697, 23
   (d) PG 91, 280–285: CPG 7697, 27
   (e) *In Isagogen Porphyrii et in Categorias Aristotelis*: CPG 7707, 34 and 7721, following M. Roueché, 'Byzantine philosophical texts of the Seventh Century', *JÖB* 23 (1974) (61–76) 74–76; in addition, S. L. Epifanovič in Uthemann, *JÖB* 30 (1981) 107, n. 12, on the sections named in CPG 7707, 21–25.
   (f) Ps. Maximus Confessor: Roueché, art. cit., 61; nr. 2 and 4 are certainly related to the *horoi diaphoroi* and *horoi henoseos* mentioned above; they are found together with the genuine works in the codices; possibly they stem from the literary remains of Maximus, in any case before John Damascene.

3. *Doctrina Patrum*, cap. 33 (CPG 7781): 'Collection of definitions', ed. Diekamp, 249–266, with alphabetical arrangement and broader theological purpose; they are logically established arguments against monothelitism; only somewhat later are they added to the work; but 'it [the chapter] is no way out of place there' (M. Roueché, art. cit., 64). These definitions are based ultimately on the *Categories* of Aristotle and the *Eisagoge* of Porphyry. 31 definitions come from the *Capita philosophica* of Anastasius of Antioch; the definitions which precede each section also appear in the *Definitiones Patmenses* (K.-H. Uthemann, *OCP* 46 (1980) 335–336).

4. *Definitions Patmenses*: with this term Uthemann, art. cit., characterises 'that alphabetically ordered collection of roughly 1000 definitions, whose oldest witness, even if not the best preserved, ... is the *Codex Patmensis* 263, ff. 120–189, which is to be dated to the tenth century'. Excerpts from the second chapter of the *Hodegos* are taken over in this, and sometimes with the lemma An(astasii); the *Capita philosophica* of Anastasius of Antioch, however, are not known to this compiler (Uthemann, art. cit., 335–336, n. 140–141).

5. *Definitiones Marcianae*: Cod. Marc. gr. 257 (622) ff.250ᵛ, 247–248 (incompletely preserved). Cf. Uthemann, *OCP* 46 (1980) 332f. Of the 82 definitions preserved 20 are to be found in the collection of definitions of the *Doctrina Patrum*. 7 *horoi* stem from the *Capita philosophica* (long version) of Anastasius of Antioch.

6. A collection concerned with the distinction of *ousia* and *hypostasis* (Uthemann, *OCP* 46 (1980) 333–335) in the Codex Laurent. IX, 8 (s. XI) ff.304–305. See as well Eutychius of Constantinople (sed. 552–565.577–582), *De differentia naturae et hypostaseos* (armeniace) (CPG 6940); ed. P. Ananian, 'L'opusculo di Eutichio patriarca di Costantinopoli sulla "Distinzione della natura e persona"', *Armeniaca. Mélanges d'études arméniennes* (Venise 1969) 316–382, with an Italian translation.

IV. From the seventh to the eighth centuries

John Damascene, *Institutio elementaris. Capita Philosophica* (*Dialectica*) ed. B. Kotter,

PTSt 7 (Berlin 1969), Ch. η' περὶ ὁρισμοῦ, pp. 57–60. On the scope of this work see Kotter, p. 55. According to Roueché, *JOB* 23 (1974) 65, we have 'almost a philosophical florilegium'.

V. Collections of definitions in Syriac

The Jacobite and Nestorians as well could not escape the necessity of producing manuals with definitions. Let us mention two examples:

1. for the Jacobites:

Jacob of Edessa (633–708); I. Ortiz de Urbina, *Patrologia Syriaca*, 129, pp. 177–183. His *Enchiridion* deals with the concepts *ousia, hypostasis, natura, species, persona*; ed. G. Furlani, *Rend.Acc.Naz.Linc.* s. 6, vol. 4 (1928) 222–249; Italian translation, idem, *Studi e Materiali di Stor. delle Rel.* I (1925) 262–282.

2. for the Nestorian east Syrians:

Michael Bad(h)ōqā, pupil of Henana at the school of Nisibis, but then in opposition to his teacher. He is the author of a work against the Jacobites, and the compiler of a collection of definitions and distinctions. Ed. and Italian translation with commentary G. Furlani, '"Il libro delle definizioni e divisioni" di Michele l'Interprete', *Atti d. Reale Acc.Naz.Linc.* s. 6, vol. 2 (1926) 5–194. On the author and his work see ibid., 189–194. In *definitio* XCIII concerned with "hypostasis", Michael writes polemically against the Jacobites as well as against the Chalcedonians. He has worked together two sources in particular, the *Book of definitions* of Aḥudhemmeh and a part of the *Book of scholia* of Theodore bar Konai. See the analysis in Furlani 190–191. Michael deals with logic, physics, anthropology and theology. The theological part especially is endebted to Theodore. The whole philosophical and theological genealogy (with Gregory of Nyssa, the Alexandrian commentators on Aristotle, etc.) is presented (p. 193).

(B) Anthologies of christological *aporiai*

I. *Aporiai* of John of Caesarea (CPG 6856.6861):

1. John of Caesarea, *Capitula XVII Contra Monophysitas*: ed. M. Richard, CCG I, 61–66. K.-H. Uthemann, 'Antimonophysitische Aporien des Anastasios Sinaites', *ByzZ* 74 (1981) 11–26, demonstrates that the *Cephalaia* 12–17 are not from John of Caesarea, but are to be attributed to Anastasius of Sinai. For they are to be found in 15 anti-monophysite *aporiai* of Anastasius, transmitted in two recensions, which in part are at variance; hence the use of the *Capitula* of John of Caesarea is not to be assumed. Thus Uthemann already in his review of Richard's edition, *ByzZ* 73 (1980) 70–72.

2. Idem, *Syllogismi Sanctorum Patrum* (against the Manichaeans): ed. M. Richard, CCG I, pp. 131–133.

II. Leontius of Byzantium

Epaporemata or '30 Chapters against Severus', ed. F. Diekamp, *Doctrina Patrum* c. 24, II, 155–164. The *epaporemata* are 30 concise theses, of which the first 14 are little more than syllogisms; the other 16, however, are more discursive. They are wholly in the *DP*, partly in Euthymius Zigabenus, *Panoplia dogmatica* XVI: PG 130, 1068B7–1073B12. According to B. E. Daley, who will publish a new edition of Leontius, the old title ran: 'Proposals and Definitions (ὁριστικά) offered as Objections against those who Deny the Double Reality of the Divine and Human Nature in the One Christ'. Later '30 Chapters against Severus' (as above). It was perhaps the best known work of Leontius in the Byzantine world (Daley).

III. Eulogius of Alexandria (sed. 580–608), *Dubitationes Orthodoxi* (fragments), in the *DP*, c. 24, I, 152–155: CPG 6971, 23b (inter *Opera Maximi Confessoris*).

IV. Two related sources from the sixth century

1. The Ἐπαπορήματα πρὸς Ἰακωβίτας of the convert Probus, in Cod. Oxon. Bibl. Bodl. Roe 22, ff. 549ᵛ–550ᵛ; Cod. Vat. gr. 1101, ff. 193ᵛ–194; now edited by K.-H. Uthemann, 'Syllogistik im Dienst der Orthodoxie. Zwei unedierte Texte byzantinischer Kontroverstheologie des 6. Jahrhunderts', *JÖB* 30 (1981) (103–112) 110; Uthemann was not able to identify the person of Probus. This has been achieved by J. H. Declerck, 'Probus, l'Ex-Jacobite et ses ΕΠΑΠΟΡΗΜΑΤΑ ΠΡΟΣ ΙΑΚΩΒΙΤΑΣ', *Byz* 53 (1983) 213–232, with a new edition of the text 229–231. Consequently the ex-Jacobite Probus is identical with the Probus who was bishop of Chalcedon at the end of the sixth century and the beginning of the seventh. See now K.-H. Uthemann, 'Stephanos von Alexandrien und die Konversion des Jakobiten Probos, des späteren Metropoliten von Chalkedon', *After Chalcedon* = OrLovAn 18 (1985) 381–399.

2. Anonymous *Capita XII syllogistica* in Cod. Vat. gr. 2220, ff. 83–84ᵛ, ed. K.-H. Uthemann, art. cit., 111–112.

PART VI

Sacred Scripture in christology between 451 and 800

THE CATENAE

For a special reason we address ourselves last of all to sacred Scripture and its impact in the period after Chalcedon. The appearance of the new *genera litteraria* in the theological literature of the time could create the impression that sacred Scripture had retreated into the background. (1) But individual passages of Scripture retained their impact; Joh 1, 14, for instance, under pressure from the theologians who supported a christology of union, gained a supreme significance (e.g. in Philoxenus of Mabbog). (2) There were still homilies on biblical passages and pericopes, and (3) there were also commentaries.

In the period we are considering, however, a new *genus litterarium* came into existence or was able to unfold exceptionally: the catenae. 'On appelle "chaînes" les manuscrits bibliques où le texte sacré est accompagné de citations exégétiques juxtaposées, provenant des commentateurs des six premiers siècles, avec leurs attributions respectives; celles-ci sont évidemment sujettes à caution et varient d'ailleurs souvent d'un document à l'autre' (F. Petit, *TU* 115 (1955) 46).

Because the catenae are closely related to the florilegia, one might be inclined to expect that they would become, in a similar way, a tool of the polemic for and against Chalcedon. In this sense M. Richard believed that he had discerned a 'monophysite' catena (CPG

IV, C 13). This position, however, cannot be upheld. The well-known catenae, even that of Procopius of Gaza, furnish nothing for a typical post-Chalcedonian christology, but indeed a great deal for the history of texts, especially for the 'Greek' Severus of Antioch (see G. Dorival).

ON THE BIBLIOGRAPHY

CPG IV (1980) 185–259;

F. Petit, *Catenae graecae in Genesim et in Exodum: I. Catena Sinaitica* = CCG 2 (1977) with an important introduction and bibliography;

eadem, 'Les Fragments grecs du livre VI des Questions sur la Genèse de Philon d'Alexandrie', *Mus* 89 (1971) 93–150;

eadem, *Philon d'Alexandrie, Quaestiones in Genesim et Exodum. Fragments grecs*, éd. F. Petit = Les Oeuvres de Philon d'Alexandrie, 33 (Paris 1977);

eadem, 'Les chaînes exégétiques grecques sur la Genèse et l'Exode. Programme d'exploration et d'édition', *StudPat* XII = TU 115 (Berlin 1975);

eadem, 'Une chaîne exégétique peu connue: Sinai gr. 2. Description et analyse', *Studia codicologica* = FS M. Richard, II = TU 124 (Berlin 1977) 341–350 (further literature in the text);

G. Dorival, 'Nouveaux fragments grecs de Sévère d'Antioche', *ANTIΔΩPON I*, 101–121, where he makes important methodological remarks on the evaluation of catenae (for the Greek Severus of Antioch);

idem, 'Aperçu sur l'histoire des chaînes exégétiques grecques sur le psautier (Vᵉ–XIVᵉ siècles)', *StudPat* 15 (1984) 146–169.

H. J. Sieben, *Exegesis Patrum. Saggio bibliografico sull' esegesi biblica dei Padri della Chiesa* = Sussidi Patristici 2 (Roma 1983).

SUMMARY

1. We are faced with the phenomenon that for centuries, to all intents and purposes from ca 431 to ca 800, the *christological question* so dominated theological discussion that, if we do not consider the controversy about grace in the West, the whole synodal life of the imperial Church, as well as that of the Churches separated from her, was sustained by it.

2. In this discussion some new literary genres were formed or developed further; these served more or less completely the christological question. To be named here in particular are the *synodal documentation* and the *publizistische Sammlungen* which go together with it, the extremely comprehensive *florilegia*, and finally the *catalogues of heresies*, the collections of *definitions* and the *Epaporemata*; this is hardly true, however, of the catenae.

3. Relatively independent of this development was hagiographical literature as such. But the more the history of Christianity between

Nicaea and 954 (schism) was centred on the Byzantine imperial Church, the more ecclesiastical historiography of all inner-Christian tendencies and in all its forms also took up the christological problem. From it we have to take the dates, important documents and the factors behind the development. Even *hagiography* is included.

4. Developments which in particular shaped the way of things to come find expression in:

(a) the *florilegia*: they present in theology the proof from authority, a proof which for the first time was developing in all its strength. This proof from authority either takes its place beside the proof from Scripture or produces this anew with sayings from the Fathers. Florilegia belong to the area of our sources which is still the least researched, edited and evaluated. The new genre, which arose from the commitment of the Church and theology to 'tradition', is so abundantly represented that it has penetrated all the Churches and shows all the theological developments within all the groups. Consequently a survey, as complete as possible, would have to be given of this genre, even though here too evaluation can occur only on the basis of particular collections of testimonies (on the catenae see above Part VI).

(b) the *collections of definitions and aporiai*: the problem of the relationship of *faith* and *reason*, of *theology* and *philosophy*, of the proof *ex auctoritate* and that *ex ratione*, is extremely prominent, this again occurring because of the christological discussion.

5. Even on the basis of the emergence and the reciprocal relation of the literary genres introduced here some fundamental insights result for our overall presentation, without yet consideration being given to the christological content itself. Two points are to be noted: (a) the stratification of proclamation and reflection. The same structure is evident everywhere. Even in remote areas which were relatively isolated, as was the case particularly in the Syrian region, simple missionary kerygma and theology working with philosophical means proceeded simultaneously. The hagiographical sources are particularly enlightening here. Homiletic and liturgical texts also have their place in the presentation. (b) A parallel development, even when this is chronologically varied, can be discerned from Constantinople to Ethiopia, and from the Greek-speaking region to Syria and Persia, Armenia and Georgia. The Latin-speaking region displays relative independence, an impression which will be reinforced particularly when the areas of Spain and Gaul, and of England, Ireland and Scotland are discussed. The lower Danube region facilitated greater communication between the Greek-speaking and the Latin-speaking areas.

PART TWO

EXPOSITION

CHAPTER ONE

A MATTER OF HIS OWN WORK: EMPEROR MARCIAN AND CHALCEDON (AFTER 451)

AN early Church council was far from enjoying the kind of publicity which attended the Second Vatican Council in our own time. Before the doctrinal and canonical results of the Church assembly in 451 could be made known in the furthest corners of the imperial Church, a longer *tempus utile* was required than for the conciliar decisions of our day. Emperor Leo I could ascertain this with his questionnaire to the bishops about the Council of Chalcedon, as we shall see later. In the heart of Asia Minor, seven years after the end of the Synod, some bishops still knew nothing, or not very much, about what it had transacted.[1] On the basis of these reflections, one thing should be stressed: even after an imperial synod on such a scale the life of the Church continued for a time to go its accustomed way, at least in circles that were not directly drawn into the controversy which soon arose. Only for the leaders of the imperial Church—the Pope and the Emperor—and for a limited group of bishops and theologians and a rather larger number of monks did this Council become the central point of spiritual life and 'political' activity, so that something like a narrowing of outlook could come about and nothing in the world seemed to exist apart from the question: one or two natures in Christ. Historians of doctrine should not be tempted to judge the awareness of the Church as a whole by such voices nor to see the problem concerning Christ reduced to the dimensions of these formulae. Hence it must be our endeavour to consider all forms and utterances of belief in Christ throughout the post-Chalcedonian era, even those which do not bear the Council's imprint. Unfortunately we must regard what history has bequeathed to us as a partisan selection. We can only redress the balance by remembering that the broader background of Church life and faith was there all the while, even if its witnesses do not speak as clearly as those involved in the controversies that were taking place at the front of the stage.

Chalcedon was no people's council, as Ephesus (431) had been able to become. The Council Fathers were not escorted to their lodgings with a torchlight procession, as twenty years earlier. After the

---

[1] *Codex Encyclius*, Alypius, Bishop of Caesarea in Cappadocia: ACO II 5, pp. 75–77 (see below).

Council was over, the bishops also did not of their own accord make a collective move to have their own work accepted, as one might have expected when the first voices of opposition made themselves heard. It was Emperor Marcian, Empress Pulcheria and Pope Leo who had to seize the initiative in defending the Council. Activity was stronger at first on the imperial side, for Leo's attitude to Chalcedon was plainly inhibited by the so-called Canon 28 which ran counter not only to his views on Church politics but also to his ecclesiological ideas. A special inducement was needed to kindle his enthusiasm for the doctrinal work of the Synod (with which he fully agreed and which he believed was not in danger). But, when this occasion arose, he proved himself for close on a decade the unyielding *Defensor fidei Chalcedonensis*.

I. IMPERIAL PROMULGATION, DEFENCE AND INTERPRETATION OF THE COUNCIL OF CHALCEDON

The Emperor's activity in support of the Council of Chalcedon naturally reached its first peak with his participation in the decisive sixth session of 25 October, 451, in which the definition of faith was adopted. No less important, however, were the acts of promulgation proclaiming the decisions as imperial law. But in these there is already talk of opposition and of the threat of sanctions, which soon had to be invoked. It was not long before Chalcedon became a battle-ground and the efforts of Pope and Emperor on its behalf a 'struggle for the Council'. In all these documents and measures for the promulgation and defence of the Council we want to look particularly for the Emperor's own interpretation of the *fides Chalcedonensis*. We are concerned not only with the validity of Chalcedon for the imperial Church, but, above all, with the truth which it enshrined.

It is of great importance to ascertain what the Emperor expected from the Council. He delivered himself on this subject during the sixth session of 25 October, 451, in the presence of the Empress. The purpose he had in view for the Council was as follows: the light of truth concerning the Christian religion is to be cleared of all cloud of error

and in the future no one shall dare to speak about the birth of our Lord and Saviour except as handed on to posterity by the apostolic preaching and the teaching, concordant therewith, of the 318 Fathers of Nicaea, and attested also by the letter of the holy Leo, Pope of the city of Rome and incumbent of the Apostolic See, to Flavian of blessed memory, Bishop of Constantinople.

The victory of 'truth' is the goal of Marcian's efforts:

Following the example of the pious Emperor Constantine it was our wish to be present at the Synod to strengthen the faith and not with an eye to exercising any power (*ad fidem confirmandam, non ad potentiam aliquam exercendam*), that the world might no longer be torn apart by perverse convictions. . . . The goal of our endeavour is that the whole people should reach unity of mind through the true and holy teaching, and return to the same religion and confess the true catholic faith, as you shall expound it in accord with the teachings of the Fathers.[2]

Just as from Nicaea until that time (i.e. until the day of the quarrel started by Eutyches) the truth of the faith was lit up by the elimination of error, so too this new Synod was to dispel the clouds that had gathered in those last years. The parallel drawn between Nicaea and Chalcedon shows that the Emperor was fully awake to the significance of the hour. This will also have its effect on his attitude to the validity of the Synod.

After the bishops had wound up their commission by finally signing the new formula, the Emperor once again took the forum to make sure of their unanimous assent to the definition that had just been read out. This was witnessed to and proclaimed in a longer acclamation. From that time forward the Emperor banned any public meeting of disputation on matters of faith, and imposed heavy sanctions on violations of this order.[3]

On 7 February, 452, the Emperor issued a Constitution which proclaimed the Council's decision as imperial law and conferred imperial Church validity on it. His words have the echo of a triumphant general's harangue at a victory parade:

What we had most earnestly and anxiously wished for has come to pass. The struggle over the law (*lex, nomos*) of orthodox Christians is ended; at last the remedy for sinful error has been found, and difference of opinion among the peoples changed to full agreement. From the various provinces the venerable bishops have come to Chalcedon at our command and, by a clear definition, have taught what observance is to be followed in the worship of God.[4]

The unanimous decision of so many bishops leaves no room for further uncertainty. Day has now dawned. It is utter madness to crave in broad daylight for artificial light (*commenticium lumen*). The truth has been discovered; one who seeks further is a seeker after lies.

The Constitution thus forbids any more public meetings and discussions about the Council's decision. Anyone who does not keep this law will be punished, for he is not only going against a clear definition

---

[2] *Marcian. imp., alloc. ad concil.*: ACO II 2, 2, nr. 4, p. 6, 4–10; Greek: ACO II 1, 2, nr. 4, pp. 139–140.
[3] ACO II 2, 2, nr. 6, pp. 16–17 (Latin); ACO II 1, 2, nr. 12–14, pp. 155–156 (Greek).
[4] *Marcian. imp., constitut. ad syn. Calchedonensem*: ACO II 2, 2, nr. 8, p. 21, 31–22, 4 (Latin); ACO II 1, 3, nr. 23, pp. 120–121 (Greek).

but profaning the Christian mysteries before Jews and pagans. The rest will be banished, or other penalties will be imposed on them by the courts. 'Therefore everyone must observe what has been determined by the holy Synod, and entertain no further doubts'.[5]

Another Constitution follows on 13 March, addressed to the pretorian prefect Palladius.[6] The Emperor argues from the unity of the four imperial synods held up till then. This is important. The new Synod stands in full agreement with Nicaea, with the Council of Constantinople in 381 and with Ephesus, the Council at which Celestine, Bishop of Rome, and Cyril of Alexandria found the truth and Nestorius was condemned. Now Eutyches and his errors have been subjected to scrutiny, that he may be able to do no more mischief. Everything has been ordered for the faith in such a way as to leave no room for doubt or criticism in the future. All future discussion of religion is banned by edict, since no individual can fathom such mysteries after so many bishops with all their striving and long prayer have been able to find out the truth only with help from God.[7] The Emperor is already aware that some persist in dissent and hold gatherings and disputations. Those whom respect for orders could not improve should really be corrected by punishments. But punishment is once more deferred, though the order already given is renewed with fresh emphasis for the future; if a man does not abide by it, the statutory penalties will be put into effect and justice will take its course.

For one must follow Chalcedon, because after painstaking search it has defined what the three above-mentioned Synods, obedient to apostolic faith, have appointed for the observance of all men.[8]

There are two further supplementary Constitutions of 6 and 18 July, 452.[9] The first of these deals with the rehabilitation of the memory of Flavian, the late bishop of Constantinople, and with the new ratification of the Council of Chalcedon. The very outcome of the Council is also a victory for Flavian himself.[10] Accordingly the

---

[5] Ibid., p. 22, 21–23: *universi ergo quae a sancta synodo Calchedonensi statuta sunt, custodire debebunt, nihil postea dubitaturi.* Further disputation after this edict (*edictum, diatagma*) is not only sin against God, but also subject to the statutory and judicial sanctions of the state.

[6] ACO II 2, 2, nr. 9, p. 23 (Latin); ACO II 1, 3, nr. 22, pp. 119–120 (Greek).

[7] ACO II 2, 2, nr. 9, pp. 20–23: *quoniam unus et alter tanta secreta invenire non posset, maxime cum summo labore et amplissimis orationibus tot venerabiles sacerdotes nisi deo, ut credendum est, auctore ad indaginem veritatis non potuerint pervenire.* The Emperor's idea of a council is revealed here.

[8] ACO II 2, 2, nr. 9, p. 24, 2–4.

[9] ACO II 1, 3, nr. 24 and 25, pp. 121–124 (Greek); ACO II 3, 2, nr. 107 and 108, pp. 89–93 (Latin).

[10] ACO II 3, 2, nr. 107, p. 90, 12–16: 'Then followed that (event) which the godhead bestowed on his deserving ones: that a venerable Synod of almost countless bishops (*sacerdotum*) convened at Chalcedon. It both examined carefully the faith under the authority of blessed Leo, Bishop of the eternal city Rome, and laid the foundations of religion (*religionis fundamenta*) as well as also conferring on Flavian the palm of a holy life and death in glory'.

Constitution which Theodosius II had issued against him after the Synod of Ephesus (449) is annulled; so too the unjust sentence pronounced on Eusebius (of Dorylaeum) and Theodoret is to be lifted. On the other hand, the refutation of Eutyches is again, in the second Constitution, made the centre of the interpretation of the Council which boasts of such a great number of Fathers and takes up the entire tradition.[11]

Thus from the side of the imperial Church the Synod of Chalcedon was declared valid in every way. But, as the Emperor had already intimated, only a few months after the end of the Council considerably large centres of resistance can be detected. Such adversaries are at work even in Constantinople.[12] From the imperial decree, addressed to Palladius and other leading officials of the empire for promulgation, one can discover the method of combatting heretics which Marcian has in mind to employ against the opponents of the Council. First of all, the Eutychians are to be denied all opportunity of setting up a hierarchy. They may not ordain bishops, priests, clergy of any kind or bestow these titles, just as Eutyches himself has been deprived of his priestly name and dignity. If this regulation is violated, ordainers and ordained are to forfeit all their goods and be banished. They have no right of assembly, of founding monastic communities or building monasteries. They cannot bequeath or inherit property, and are admitted to only a limited form of military service. Fellow-members of Eutyches' monastic community who fall away from the true practice of religion and follow his teaching against the Council shall undergo all the penalties fixed in this or in previous laws (against the Apollinarians and Manichaeans especially); for

---

[11] ACO II 3, 2, nr. 108, p. 91, 9–19: 'First of all countless bishops from almost all the world who were gathered at Chalcedon eliminated the impious fabrications (*improba . . . commenta*) of the aforementioned Eutyches, and at the same time those of the Synod which had been held for his sake [at Ephesus (449)], this following the definitions of the holy predecessors, either those which were formulated at Nicaea by 318 [Fathers] or the explanations which were made subsequently by 150 bishops in this august city [Constantinople] or at Ephesus 431, where the error of Nestorius was excluded under the presidency of Celestine, the Bishop of the city of Rome, and Cyril, the Bishop of the city of Alexandria. Thus what was defined in accordance with the early discipline (*iuxta pristinam disciplinam*) by the venerable Synod of Chalcedon shall, according to our earlier and present decision (*censuimus atque censemus*), be preserved totally with that faith with which we worship God. For it is utterly consistent to preserve with the utmost reverence the definitions of the 520 bishops [Chalcedon] which worship God with pure intention and which took place according to the rules of the Fathers for the benefit of the sacrosanct faith of the orthodox . . .'. It is to be noted that at Chalcedon the *teaching* of Eutyches was condemned, not once again his person, because he was regarded as already condemned (on 22 November, 448 by the Synod of Constantinople, and further by Leo's Tome and by Anatolius on 21 October, 450).

[12] It is no doubt in Constantinople that we have to seek for those who are mentioned in the constitution '*Venerabilem Catholicae*' (ACO II 2, 2, nr. 9, p. 23, 23ff.) (Latin); (ACO II 1, 3, nr. 22, p. 119) (Greek); and likewise those supporters of Eutyches who are named in the correspondence of 18 July, 452 to Palladius ('*Divinae semper*') and on whom special sanctions are imposed: ACO II 3, 2, nr. 108, pp. 90–93 (Latin); ACO II 1, 3, nr. 25, pp. 122–124 (Greek). Seeck, *Regesten*, 397 falsely has as the date 28 July, 452.

example, with regard to writings: where such are found, they are to be burnt and the authors and distributors of these works deported.

We mean to remove from all men the possibility of teaching this unfortunate heresy, as has been stated in previous edicts issued by Our Highness; anyone seeking to teach forbidden doctrines (*illicita*) shall be punished with death (*ultimo supplicio coercebitur*). Those, however, who listen to such criminal teachers with the intention of emulating them shall be penalised with a fine of ten pounds in gold. Thus all forms of sustenance (*materia, prophasis*) are taken away from the error, when it can find neither teachers nor hearers.[13]

Eutyches' immediate circle of fellow-monks and followers is the target of this edict. Admittedly not all his friends in Constantinople are encompassed by this legislation. In Leo I's letters other names occasionally crop up, but these are of no great importance here. At any rate Marcian pursues the line of imperial Church legislation against heretics, the theological significance of which we have still to consider, once we have surveyed the anti-Chalcedonian movement as a whole. In the pages which follow we are concerned to clarify the rôle of Emperor Marcian and his intentions in the post-Chalcedonian controversy. What in these is conditioned by the imperial Church? In what way is he the witness to genuine tradition? (On the basis of his position, this rôle cannot be denied him from the outset). Was his procedure in the struggle for Chalcedon theologically up-to-date for the purpose of achieving his real goal, viz. securing the unity of the imperial Church through the one faith? Beyond Constantinople, the Emperor has to operate above all in two theatres of the Church battle: in Jerusalem and in Alexandria.

II. MARCIAN AND THE UPRISING IN JERUSALEM

The impulse towards a greater movement against Chalcedon came from the monks in and around Jerusalem, whose leader was the monk Theodosius.[14] Even before the Council had ended, this man, who had already provoked major disturbances at the scene of the Council, rushed back to Palestine, to announce there that the Council had declared itself for Nestorianism.[15] Juvenal, the Archbishop of Jerusa-

---

[13] *Marcian. imp., De confirmandis quae a s. synodo Calchedonensi contra Eutychem et eius monachos statuta sunt*: ACO II 3, 2, nr. 108, pp. 90–93 (Latin); ACO II 1, 3, nr. 25, pp. 122–124 (Greek).

[14] Cf. H. Bacht, *Chalkedon* II, 244–255. The Emperor himself reports in detail about Theodosius in his letter to Macarius, the abbot-bishop of the Sinai monastery: ACO II 1, 3, nr. 29, pp. 131–132.

[15] Cf. Zacharias Rh., *HE* III 3, ed. Brooks: CSCO 87 1, 107–108; Cyril of Scyth., *Vita Euthymii* 27, ed. Schwartz 41f.: Festugière, *Les moines d'Orient* III, 1, pp. 95–96. R. Devreesse, *RSPT* 19 (1930) 257, is of the opinion that Eutyches himself fled to Jerusalem and there stirred up resistance to Chalcedon. Cf. H. Bacht, *Chalkedon* II, 244, n. 6; E. Honigmann, 'Juvenal of Jerusalem', *DOP5* (1950) 211–279, esp. 249–251. This flight, however, did not take place. See A. Grillmeier, 'Eine Flucht des Eutyches nach Jerusalem?', *ROMANITAS-CHRISTIANITAS. Untersuchungen zur Geschichte und Literatur der römischen Kaiserzeit* (= FS J. Straub), ed. G. Wirth (Berlin-New York, 1982) 645–653.

lem, who had formerly always been on the side of the Alexandrian party,[16] had been accosted on his return to Caesarea by an excited crowd of monks and laymen calling on him to revoke his assent to Chalcedon. Even during the course of the Council (apparently after the decisive session of 25 October, 451), when Juvenal had put his signature to the new formula of faith, a form of abjuration, containing anathemas on the Council, on Leo of Rome, and on Juvenal himself, was handed around to be signed.[17] According to Zacharias Rhetor, Juvenal cried out to the monks: '*Quod scripsi, scripsi*'.[18] To which they replied: 'Then we repudiate you, because you have broken your oath and your promises'. Juvenal then went back to the Emperor, while the monks made their way to Jerusalem where they set up Theodosius as bishop. All the episcopal sees in Palestine were

[16] At the Council of Ephesus (431) Juvenal was regarded as the second leader of the Cyrillian party. In 449 he backed Eutyches; at the so-called Latrocinium he was, after Dioscorus and with Thalassius, one of the three leaders. On 8 August, 449, he was the first among the 113 bishops who voted for the rehabilitation of Eutyches. He even called him 'completely orthodox' (*orthodoxotaton*) (cf. ACO II 1, 1, p. 182, 11–15). He voted with Dioscorus for the deposition of Flavian and of Eusebius of Dorylaeum (ibid., p. 192, 3–10) and further for that of Ibas of Edessa and of Theodoret of Cyrus. 'It is therefore quite safe to assume that Juvenal's leading role at the side of Dioscorus highly impressed the Palestinians. Two years later, after the Council of Chalcedon, their attitude proved that the one-sided and mistaken conception of Cyrillian theology, which we now call "Monophysitism", had almost entirely conquered the country. At this time Juvenal far surpassed the archbishops of the other prominent sees in seniority' (E. Honigmann, op. cit., 237). In 449 Juvenal had been a bishop for at least 27 years, Dioscorus for 5, and Leo the Great for 9 years. For a short time Juvenal could extend his jurisdiction to three other provinces: Phoenicia I and II and Arabia (until 451). Before his departure for Chalcedon Juvenal still refused to add his signature to the Tome of Leo, '. . . had ridiculed the ungodliness which it contained, and testified before all clergymen and monks that the doctrine expressed in it was Jewish and worthy of Simon Magus, and that those who consented to it deserved to be excommunicated' (ibid., 240). Leo reacted in several letters to Anatolius of Constantinople. In *ep.* 85 (ACO II 4, p. 44, 33–34) we read: 'At this Synod [= Ephesus (449)] Dioscorus showed his malevolence, Juvenal, however, his inexperience (*imperitia*)'. A harsh judgement on a bishop who had been so many years in office! This '*imperitia*' recalls Leo's judgement on Eutyches (ACO II, 1, p. 24, 20–21; Honigmann, op. cit., 240, n. 26). At the Council of Chalcedon Juvenal, together with Dioscorus, was at first the main guilty party. Juvenal, Thalassius and other accomplices from 449 emphasise, however, that they played only the secondary rôle. After Thalassius and Eustathius of Berytus had acknowledged the confession of faith of Flavian, who was condemned in 449, as orthodox, finally Juvenal also professed himself to be in favour of the rehabilitation of Flavian, and with all the Palestinian, Illyrian and four Egyptian bishops deserted Dioscorus; only six Egyptian bishops appear to have remained definitively with him. Cf. L. Perrone. *La chiesa di Palestina e le controversie cristologiche* (Brescia 1980) 90.

[17] It is preserved in monophysite texts which F. Nau edited from Syriac manuscripts: PO 13, 237–238: 'I, Anastasius, priest of Jerusalem, anathematise the ungodly creed that comes from that ungodly Council which is presently (maintenant) gathered at Chalcedon on the ground of its ungodly and foreign teachings which are opposed to apostolic faith but are found there; likewise those who support them or signed them and participated there [at the Council]; [I anathematise] too the ungodly letter of Leo, the Bishop of Rome, and the teachings which it contains—they are also foreign to catholic faith, and the renegade Juvenal because he adheres to these [teachings] and added his signature to them; [I anathematise] as well those who are in community with him and think like him and the ordinations which he has performed since his offence. I anathematise anyone who acknowledges (reçoit) Bishop Juvenal on account of his thought about God. Without being constrained to do so, I have signed this with my own hand'. This formula no doubt stems from the time of Juvenal. For after his death it would have hardly any sense in this form. According to Honigmann, *DOP5* (1950) 251, n. 24, the presbyter Anastasius is mentioned by Cyril of Scythopolis, *Vita Euthymii* 30: Schwartz 49, 3; he later became patriarch (458–478).

[18] Cf. *HE* III 3, Hamilton-Brooks 50; Brooks, CSCO 87, p. 107, 34.

given to Theodosian supporters, that is to say to Monophysites.[19] The orthodox rallied round the monk Euthymius who, though also courted by Theodosius, withdrew into the Rubâ desert with his loyal followers and remained there until the new bishop was expelled (i.e. until the middle of 453).[20] Thus Theodosius had not only the mass of the people and monks behind him, but also enjoyed the favour of the Empress Eudoxia who was residing at that time in Jerusalem. The way towards all these happenings had undoubtedly been paved by Juvenal's earlier attitude of friendship towards Dioscorus. We need not look for an heretical trend behind them, only for a traditionalism clinging fondly to the acknowledged Cyrillian teaching. There was no real intention of defending Eutyches. Blame must be laid at the feet of Theodosius, for, after hastening away from Chalcedon, he spread far and wide the news that Chalcedon had reached a 'Nestorian' definition—thus the teaching of the two sons and two persons in Christ. The smear-campaign was so great that by the time of Juvenal's arrival at Caesarea a disturbance had broken out, leading to the murder of Bishop Severianus of Scythopolis and his entourage by hired assassins. With such tidings Juvenal was able to make an impression on the Emperor.[21] The rioters had now to fear the consequences, and they turned to Empress Pulcheria to intercede with the Emperor. This prompted the letters which give us our first insight into the way the Council was understood on the imperial side immediately after its conclusion.

In the *Collectio Sangermanensis* are transmitted various letters of Marcian and his wife Pulcheria, and also of Patriarch Juvenal of Jerusalem, which take a position on the question of faith in Jerusalem (Aelia).[22] Ostensibly—says Marcian—the monks had turned to the Empress as suppliants (*sub schemate precum*) that she might plead their cause with the Emperor, but in reality an impious and lawless purpose (*impia et dei legibus Romanaeque rei publicae contraria intentio*) lurked behind their action. He says they ought to practise their monastic *hesychia* and obey the teachings of the bishops (that is the Council) instead of arrogating to themselves the rank of teachers. Standards

---

[19] Zacharias Rhetor reports on Peter the Iberian in *HE* III 4, Hamilton-Brooks 51–52; Brooks CSCO 87, p. 108, 9; he was made the bishop of Maiuma-Gaza. Cf. E. Honigmann, op. cit., 249–251.

[20] Cyril of Scythopolis, *Vita Euthymii* 27, ed. Schwartz 42–45. Cf. S. Vailhé, 'Saint Euthyme le Grand, moine de Palestine (376–473)', *ROC* 12(1907) 298–312. 337–385; 13(1908) 181–191. 225–246. 389–405; 14(1909) 189–202. 256–263.

[21] Cf. Evagrius, *HE* II 5; Bidez-Parmentier 52, 1–9.

[22] *Exemplar epistulae sancitae a Marciano sacratissimo imp. ad archimandritas et monachos reliquos habitantes in Aelia et circa eam*: ACO II 5, nr. II, pp. 4–7; *Pulcheria sacratissima et piissima pp. aug. archimandritis et reliquis monachis in Aelia* etc.: ibid., nr. III, pp. 7–8. The letters are almost identically worded and come from the same secretary. Greek: ACO II 1, 3, pp. 124–129, nr. 26 and 27. They were written before 21 March, 453, because on this date Leo M., *ep.* 115 and 117, already refers to the action of Marcian. Cf. E. Honigmann, op. cit., 253.

are inverted if monks set themselves up as the norm of complete knowledge about faith, in the place of the writings of the apostles and prophets and the traditions of the Fathers. Instead of remaining in their monasteries they have become violent overlords of Jerusalem and murderers. They were quite right in condemning Eutyches (a statement which is of importance for the study of Monophysitism) but in Theodosius they had chosen a still greater scoundrel for their leader. He thought like Eutyches, who with his eagerness for the madness of Valentinus and Apollinarius spelt unrest for the Churches and disorder for the cities and became the instigator of every monkish iniquity.

After the monks have thus been put in the wrong, they are given a piece of imperial advice. The Emperor knows that the novelty (*novitas*) of the 'two natures' is the reason for their inner unrest. But they are not entitled to set themselves up as critics of such doctrines for they cannot comprehend the subtlety (*subtilitatem*) of the matter. What, after all, is meant by 'nature'? It is not the content of a lofty philosophical concept, but it has a simple meaning available to all: 'We, indeed, taking up the teachings of the Fathers, understand by "nature" "truth" (*nos autem patrum suscipientes doctrinas naturam intellegimus veritatem*)'.[23] The Council's business was merely to eliminate all trace of docetism with regard to the manhood of Christ.

For this is our common thought and word: our Lord Jesus Christ is one and the same truly God and truly man... [reference to Gal 4,8: *sed tunc quidem nescientes ⟨Deum⟩ servistis eis qui natura non sunt dii*] that is, in ignorance [of the true God] they served those who are in reality no gods; so that he made it plain that nature (*natura, physis*) is truth.[24]

Nature has thus no strict philosophical connotation. As a statement of fact, this is correct. Yet the content of the Chalcedonian statement is played down here to some extent. For Chalcedon has certainly fulfilled a function in the history of philosophical conceptions by distinguishing between *hypostasis* and *physis*. In Christ, the unity is to be stated of the *hypostasis*, the difference is to be stated of the *physis*, the nature. In the last resort this distinction must be established conceptually, even if the Council aimed at this determination rather than really achieved it.[25] The Emperor grants that nothing is to be found in the Nicene Creed about natures (φύσεων). For at that time this question had not yet arisen, and the faith in Christ's true manhood had not yet been challenged by any new teaching (*novitas*). The

[23] ACO II 5, p. 6, 5–6; Greek: ACO II 1, 3, p. 126, 14: by *physis* we understand *alêtheia*.
[24] ACO II 5, p. 6, 8–12; ibid., II 1, 3, p. 126, 16–19. Pulcheria says this in almost the same words in nr. III (Latin), or nr. 27 (Greek).
[25] Cf. A. Grillmeier, CCT I², 543–550; JdChr I², 753–764.

Emperor does not realise that the foundations of the teaching on account of which Eutyches was condemned had at that time already been laid: namely that *Logos-Sarx* christology which admits no full manhood of Christ. Nicaea had found nothing remarkable in that: its eyes were fixed only on the question of the Logos.[26] Just as the monks had accepted the Nicene *homoousios*, and raised no difficulty over the fact that in the Symbol of Chalcedon the same term was applied to the humanity of Christ (a deliberate stab at Eutyches)[27], so they had no reason to fight shy of accepting the word 'nature'. For they were accustomed to using it in many different ways (indeed, even in their formula of the one nature of the Word made flesh). With this line of argument the Emperor by-passes the monks' real difficulty. What alarms them is not the use of the word 'nature' as such, but the talk about the 'two' natures—for this meant for them acknowledging two sons and two Christs.[28] That inference is, however, rejected. It does not correspond to the truth. Chalcedon also condemned such teachings. The Emperor's claim is just, but here it misses its mark. Precisely at this point it was necessary to make it intrinsically understandable. This would have meant that Marcian would have had to explain the Chalcedonian distinction between *hypostasis* and *physis* and thus resolve the alleged opposition of '*mia physis*' and '*duo physeis*'. For the monks understood by *physis* (and *hypostasis*) a concrete individual nature, perfect and hence self-contained. If one were to say of Christ that he is in two natures, this would have meant for them that he was strictly an uncombined duality. But he is 'one'. For this reason there can be only *one physis*.

Unhappily, by resorting to violence, the monks had openly put themselves in the wrong before all the world. Had they argued only with theological reasons, they might have been able to prove what even the Emperor was prepared to recognise as a reason for rejecting the Chalcedonian formula: conscientious objection! For that period there seems to be an unusual expression of freedom of conscience in the words which Marcian, no doubt out of political shrewdness, addressed to the monks:

> Our Clemency in no way imposes on anyone the necessity of signing anything or giving assent against his own will. We have no desire to drive others by terror or violence along the road to truth, unlike you, who have lately dared to perpetrate many acts of violence—with sword and cruelty, injuries and torture—against respectable and high-born women, that they might agree to your perverse teachings,

---

[26] Cf. idem, CCT I², 153–166; JdChr I², 283–299.
[27] Cf. idem, CCT I², 283–299, 547; JdChr I², 756. ACO II 1, 1, p. 142, nr. 516; T. Camelot, *Chalkedon* I, 237.
[28] ACO II 5, p. 6, 23–24; ACO II 1, 3, p. 128, 30–33.

loudly anathematise the holy Synod and Leo, the holy Patriarch of the Apostolic See of Old Rome, and the holy Fathers, and then confirm all this by their signatures....[29]

The monks should remember their complaints about the brutal Samaritans, against whom the Emperor had decreed penalties after a judicial enquiry. They should remember too the stern measures recently taken against Eutyches and his followers (on 18 July, 452—see above). The monks of Jerusalem should obey these instructions, remain in their monasteries, devote themselves to prayer, and abide by the ordinances of the Fathers. If they repent of their wrongdoing, the Emperor would in no way begrudge them his pardon—on the intercession of the Patriarch Juvenal, who had requested this letter to them. Marcian was also ready to consider the petitions lodged by various monasteries, and to stop any disturbance caused to the monks by the quartering of soldiers and horses, just as previously he had never had the intention of issuing orders which would inconvenience their monasteries or their sanctuaries.[30]

These letters of Marcian and Pulcheria have the following theological arguments in common. 1. In spite of the reproaches of the monks and all other opponents of the Council, Chalcedon is no innovation since, like the earlier Synods of Ephesus and Constantinople, it simply endorses and recapitulates the Council of Nicaea. The Nicene Creed is mentioned in all these documents[31], though not (as at Chalcedon itself) quoted literally. What is decisive in this Creed is that it confesses the incarnation of the Son of God.[32] Here already the lie is given to Eutyches, for the true human nature of him who was born of Mary is expressed. 2. In more or less explicit terms the separation by Nestorius of the manhood and godhead in Christ and the transmutation by Eutyches of the manhood of Christ into the godhead are repudiated. 3. In the longer documents (such as Marcian's letters to the monks of Sinai or to the Synod of Palestine, or even Pulcheria's letter to Bassa) turns of phrase from the Symbol of Chalcedon are slipped in without attention being drawn to the fact—those that say: one and the same is fully God and fully man, without division, without separation, without change. 4. In none of these allusions to the Chalcedonian Symbol is the key-formula of the 'one hypostasis in the two natures' to be found. The employment of the word *physis*

[29] ACO II 5, p. 6, 33–41 (Latin); ACO II 1, 3, p. 127, 6–12 (Greek).
[30] ACO II 5, p. 7, 20–24 (Latin); ACO II 1, 3, p. 127, 33–37 (Greek).
[31] Cf. the documents nr. 26, 27 and 29–31 in ACO III 1, 3, p. 126f., 128, 132, 134f.
[32] Cf. *Marcian. imp. ad archimandr.* (= nr. 26 in ACO II II 1, 3), here following ACO II 5, p. 6: 'Our Tranquillity (*tranquillitas*) followed the Creed of the 318 Fathers in the preceding period. I shall believe and confess in the future that our Saviour Jesus Christ was born of the Holy Spirit and of Mary the virgin and *Theotokos*'.

and the formula of the two *physeis* are mentioned only briefly—not to expound their more precise connotation, but to paraphrase what they express: *physis* is 'reality'. The accent invariably lies on a formulation in which faith in the incarnation of Christ is stated without special concepts, and, what is more, as a *tradition* which goes back beyond the two Councils of 431 and 381 to Nicaea, and thence to the Apostles. This procedure is noteworthy, insofar as the Emperor had demanded that the Council produce its own formula of belief while the Fathers wanted to content themselves with the documents which had already been handed on, or while Leo placed emphasis on his Tome. Marcian in effect is now making the position of these Fathers his own starting-point—only, however, with the aim of easing the path to Chalcedon for the obstinate monks. This gambit is justified, even if it leads to no final solution so long as the opponents of Chalcedon are not given detailed proof that the two-nature formula is compatible with Ephesus and Nicaea. 5. The picture of the Nestorian and Eutychian heresies and of the 'heretics' themselves is clear-cut, and as such will not be discussed further. Eutyches stands in the direct line of succession from Valentinus, Apollinarius and the Manichaeans. It also does not matter very much that Marcian knows that (some of) his addressees dissociate themselves from Eutyches.[33] As long as not every link with the leaders of the uprising in Jerusalem is broken, in the Emperor's eyes one professes the Eutychian heresy. The historical development of 'heresy' after Chalcedon must all the while be taken into account if one is to assess the scope of the Chalcedonian doctrine and its function in history.

Undoubtedly connected with the Emperor's letters from Constantinople is a synodal letter of Juvenal and several other bishops of the Patriarchate of Jerusalem to the priests, archimandrites and monks of Palestine who are under the Patriarchate.[34] In this the position is restated. Obviously reference is made to the intrigues against Chalcedon, by allusion to false testimony and to David's complaints about sneaky persecutors. The calumny referred to is directed particularly against the Council of Nicaea and the '*magnum et universale concilium nuper congregatum Chalcedone*'. Yet the faith of these Councils rests on the apostolic tradition, as expressed above all in Peter and in his confession at Caesarea Philippi. If Juvenal here quotes Mt 16, 16–18, still it is not for the purpose of calling to mind the Pope of Rome and his authority, but the Church as a whole which rests on that

---

[33] *Marcian. imp.*, ibid., ACO II 5, p. 5, 17–19: 'Our Devoutness wonders why you imposed the anathema on Eutyches, and in doing so you did well. But you have put yourselves in the hands of Theodosius who is worse than all others because he thinks like Eutyches...'.
[34] ACO II 5, nr. IV, p. 9.

confession, and to its faith which, attested by the apostles and councils, remains always the same until the end of the world: 'to which
nothing can be added, nor anything subtracted'.[35]

III. MARCIAN AND ALEXANDRIA

Marcian's greater anxiety was in the long run Alexandria. We have
in effect already encountered Alexandrian influence in tracing the
spiritual ancestry of Juvenal and the past history of the monk Theodosius, who seems to have been in close cooperation with Alexandria,
at least after 448.[36] Behind all this stands the figure of Cyril of Alexandria himself. Because initially a pro-Chalcedonian patriarch had been
appointed in place of Dioscorus, peace could be maintained longer
in Alexandria than in Palestine. But there too the opponents of the
Council were not inactive. Pope Leo mentions in a letter of 11 May,
455, transmitted only in the Collectio Grimanica, that Emperor Marcian had despatched the decurio John to Egypt.[37] This man was especially well qualified for his mission because on the Emperor's own
testimony he had been present at the Council and thus was very
well acquainted with the proceedings of the Council and with the
questions of faith that were treated there.[38] Even in Alexandria violent
opposition to the Synod of Chalcedon was put up—and this by
Timothy Aelurus and his supporters. Monks in the vicinity of Alexandria were their first victims. Vis-à-vis the Alexandrians, Marcian
justifies his own belief and sets the Council squarely in the Alexandrian tradition of an Athanasius, a Theophilus and a Cyril, by which
Eutyches and the Apollinarian teaching taken over by him had been
condemned. Thus the Synod of Chalcedon represents no innovation:
it stands by the Council of Nicaea, without diminution or addition,

---

[35] ACO II 5, nr. IV, pp. 9, 13.

[36] Cf. E. Honigmann, op. cit., 249: 'Since Zacharias Rhetor asserts that Theodosius had "struggled
for years for the faith" and "was known for his zealous veracity", I suppose that he was the same
as the "well-known monk" of this name who, according to a remark of the priest and protonotarius
John made in the second session of the "Robber-Synod", had arrived with others at Alexandria
a year before (448) and agitated there against Theodoret of Cyrrhus and Domnus of Antioch' (reference
to Zach. Rh., HE III 3; John of Bēth Rufinā, Vita Petri Iberi, ed. R. Raabe, p. 52 [53]).

[37] Cf. ACO II 1, 3, p. 130, 33; Seeck, Regesten, 401, places this despatch at the end of 454,
referring to the letter of Leo just mentioned; he does not make reference to the document which
Marcian gave to be taken along. This letter opens the Collectio Sangermanensis, ACO II 5, nr. I,
pp. 3–4; Greek: ACO II 1, 3, p. 129, nr. 28, without any indication of date. On the authenticity
of Leo's letter 141, ACO II 4, nr. 85, cf. C. Silva-Tarouca, Nuovi Studi, 158, 178. According
to him this letter is not authentic because it is only attested in the Grimanica, furthermore it is
of uncertain date and has elements that stand in contradiction to Leo's ep. 142. For the monk Carosus
is portrayed in letter 141 differently from the way he is in the genuine letter 142. It is possible
to resolve this difficulty by accepting that there are two monks of this name, as Schwartz proposes,
ACO II 5, p. 77. Cf. H. Bacht, Chalkedon II, 141, n. 38; L. Perrone, La chiesa di Palestina, 90,
n. 2.

[38] Marcian. imp. Alexandrinis: ACO II 5, p. 4, 16–19.

and it condemns Nestorius. The imperial letters and the recently proclaimed edicts addressed to the Alexandrians should convince everyone of that. The Emperor states his personal faith in such a way
as to make it a repudiation of Nestorianism—a fact which ought
to set the minds of the Alexandrians at rest. The new formula of
the 'two natures', no doubt for psychological reasons, is avoided.[39]
Marcian's conception of the imperial Church betrays itself when he
exhorts the Alexandrians to unite themselves with the

holy and catholic Church of orthodox believers, which is *one*, as the venerable
definitions of the Fathers also teach us. By such conduct you will save your own
souls and do what is pleasing to God.[40]

Here again the Emperor displays his unquestioning faith in Chalcedon. With the Council all doubt had as a matter of course to be
banished from the world. The two-nature formula itself plays no
great part; indeed, it is not mentioned at all. The doctrine of Chalcedon
is repeated in paraphrase form, just as the Council itself had done
with the formulations of previous councils. There is an interesting
reference to Apollinarian forgeries, doubtless the first of its kind.
Chalcedon has destroyed the ungodliness of Eutyches; but Dioscorus
has followed in his wake,

and certain others who did not hesitate to introduce books of Apollinarius among
the people, by giving them the names of holy Fathers, that the understanding of
simple folk may be wholly subjected to lies.[41]

   Equation of the Alexandrian (= Cyrillian) christology with Apollinarianism also accounts for the strong tone adopted by Marcian in
his final letter to Palladius concerning Chalcedon.[42] The Emperor's
first Constitution against Eutychianism and Apollinarianism has
proved insufficient.

The citizens and inhabitants of Alexandria have been so infected by the poison
of Apollinarius that it has become necessary to re-draft the old regulations into
a new law....

---

[39] *Marcian. imp.* ibid.: ACO II 5, nr. I, p. 4, 3–9: 'I believe that our Lord and Saviour Jésus
Christ, the only-begotten Son of God, equally eternal and one in being with the Father, became
man for our sake and for our salvation, was born of the Holy Spirit and Mary the virgin and
Theotokos, is as one and the same God and true man, never anyone else (*non alium et alium*) but
one and the same, never divided, or separated or changed (*convertibilem*). Those, however, who
say or have once said that there are two sons and two persons, we also loathe, and impose the
anathema on them'.
[40] ACO II 5, nr. I, p. 4, 12–15.
[41] *Marcian. imp. ad Alexandrinos*...: ACO II 5, p. 3, 30–32; Greek: ACO II 1, 3, nr. 28, p.
130, 14–16. Marcian employs the word ἐξανδραποδίζειν, to make a slave of, to subjugate. By
the 'names of the holy Fathers' are meant Athanasius, Felix and Julius, if one takes the well-known
texts in H. Lietzmann, *Apollinaris von Laodicea und seine Schule* (Tübingen 1904) 292–322.
[42] *Marcian. imp., Palladio pp.*, 1 August, 455: ACO II 2, 2 (*Collectio Vaticana*), nr. 15, pp. 24–27.
The passage cited: ibid., p. 24, 23–25.

In his appraisal of the events at Alexandria there now follows a new demonstration of the identity existing between Eutyches, Dioscorus and Apollinarius. Their teachings are characterised as heretical, and the Nicene-Alexandrian tradition (Athanasius, Theophilus and Cyril), which had also been represented at the Councils of Constantinople (381), Ephesus (431) and Chalcedon (451), is set up in opposition to them.[43] The supporters of Dioscorus should therefore be visited with every penalty laid down in the earlier Constitutions (see above). Had Marcian possessed a more exact knowledge of the Alexandrian tradition, he would have learnt to his surprise that in regard to the 'soul of Christ' or the 'perfect humanity' of Christ Athanasius stood closer to Apollinarius than did the Alexandrian opponents of Chalcedon. He would have been equally taken aback by the fact that Cyril too had succumbed to Apollinarian distortions and that it was he who had secured for them a right of acceptance in orthodox tradition by taking over their *mia physis* formula, while at the same time also interpreting it in an orthodox sense. On the other hand Marcian can point—with greater right than to Athanasius and Cyril—to the Synod of Constantinople,[44] and to Theophilus of Alexandria whose christology was the closest to Chalcedon, closer than that of the other Alexandrians named. Here then careful distinctions would have had to have been made, if the Emperor wanted to convince the Alexandrians that Alexandrian tradition and Chalcedon did not contradict each other. The same is true of the other line constructed, that concerning the heresies. Marcian's equation of Eutychians and Apollinarians on the one hand, and of Eutyches and the supporters of Dioscorus on the other was a step full of consequences on Alexandria's path towards schism.[45] In common with Cyril the Alexandrians acknowledged a 'soul' of Christ (in the place of which the Apollinarians had set the Logos) and also the true corporality of the Lord. From Cyril they also inherited the *mia physis* formula, which they took

[43] ACO II 2, 2, p. 24,27–25,9: those in Constantinople or Alexandria or in all the dioceses of Egypt or in various other provinces (the opposition to Chalcedon is thus already rather broadly dispersed) 'should know that they are heretical Apollinarianists; for Eutyches and Dioscorus have followed the criminal sect of Apollinarius'.

[44] The Synod of Constantinople (381) found little favour with the Alexandrians, admittedly not on doctrinal grounds, but on account of Canon 3 of this Synod, which anticipated the so-called Canon 28 of Chalcedon on the precedence of Constantinople.

[45] Cf. also the further words of Marcian: ACO II 2, 2, p. 25, 13–18: 'The Apollinarians, i.e. the Eutychians, are admittedly different in what they are called, but they are bound together in the malice of the heresy. The name is certainly not the same, but the sacrilege is the same, whether they are now in this august city [Constantinople] or within the dioceses of Egypt, and they do not believe as the previously mentioned venerable Fathers believed, nor do they maintain community with the venerable man and Bishop of the city of Alexandria, Proterius, who holds the orthodox faith...'. Here all the opponents of the Council from Constantinople to Alexandria are lumped together as Eutychians.

for an expression of orthodox christology. They dissociated themselves more and more from Eutyches, although the latter wanted
to be nothing other than a Cyrillian, true with little understanding
or success. The hub of all the misunderstandings is thus ignorance
of Cyril, whose relationship both to the line of tradition (in Marcian's
sense)—Nicaea, Athanasius, Constantinople, Theophilus of Alexandria, Cyril, Ephesus—and also to the line of 'heresies' (again in Marcian's sense) ought to have been clarified. Unhappily we find no
trace of any inclination to go back to the texts. Sentence is passed
according to the label already attached. For this reason no further
discussion against Chalcedon must be allowed. This confirms the
untheological arrogance of the Emperor. In the letter to Palladius,
that is to say in the Constitution *Licet iam sacratissima*, we read again
long lists of penalties prescribed against the Apollinarians (i.e. the
Eutychians).[46] This is the last of Marcian's letters bearing on the Alexandrian Church which has come down to us.

It is evident that the christology of Chalcedon was tailor-made
for the Emperor. The Chalcedonian concepts and distinctions, the
'adiairetôs—asynchytôs', the doctrine of the two natures, the whole
picture of Christ, seem to correspond to his clear, orderly mentality
and uncomplicated character. His simple clarity of mind cannot
understand the restless urges of the Monophysites. Above all they
do not fit into the picture of religious order which he would like
to have for the empire and which it is his commission to protect.
That the goal which Marcian set for the Council of Chalcedon was
to favour the imperial Church is no secret. But did he not manipulate
the Council, and the Church's faith, in such a way that the formula
of Chalcedon is simply his own work and not that of the bishops?
Did he not misunderstand, because he could not see beyond his own
ideas, the theological intent of those who opposed the Council, and
thus contributed to having them branded for evermore as heretics?
What is his own interpretation of the Council of Chalcedon, and
is this interpretation a witness for the Church—or merely a game
of politics? To begin with this last question: even if the Emperor
was pursuing a political interest in his quest for unity of faith, he
still left it to the bishops to formulate this faith. Even if the bishops
felt themselves under pressure to shape a new formula, which without

[46] ACO II 2, 2, nr. 15, pp. 24–27, esp. p. 26, 21–25: 'Furthermore no permission (*facultas*) is
to be given to any Eutychian or Apollinarian to convene meetings (*coetus*) publicly or privately
or to form circles (*circulos*), to dispute about the heretical error and to lecture on the perversity
of an atrocious doctrine (*facinorosi dogmatis*); as well no one shall be allowed to dictate (*dictare*) or
write or edit or publish (*emittere*) anything against the venerable Synod or Chalcedon or to produce
other writings about it'. For violations deportation or fines are prescribed. Once again writings
which defend the Eutychian 'dogma' are ordered to be burnt.

pressure from the Emperor they would not have attempted, still the content of the result is not simply a reflection of the Emperor's will. Anyone able to trace the purely theological trends of development prior to Chalcedon recognises at once that the Emperor's view of the incarnation can be explained from beginning to end by the tradition of Constantinople, Antioch and Old Rome. Finally, it is quite clear from the interpretation which Marcian gives to the Council of Chalcedon that he himself cannot have discovered the decisive formula which established the use of the terms *hypostasis* and *physis*. It is precisely this *novum* in the Chalcedonian determination of language—the distinction of *hypostasis* and *physis*—that can indeed be explained from pre-Chalcedonian theology, but not from the Emperor's own theologising. Marcian never tries to argue or to express his meaning by the use of these new terms. It is clear that he has not fully grasped the theological import of this determination of language, though he has grasped something essential in it: viz. that by the two *physeis* is expressed the truth of the divine nature and the reality of the human nature of Christ. Marcian has an extremely simple conception of the error of Eutyches and the representatives of the *mia physis* formula in general: they deny the reality and truth of Christ's human nature or the truth and reality of the incarnation. The heart of the matter is for him that *physis* means truth, reality, *veritas*. In line with Church tradition extending from the apostles to Nicaea, Constantinople and Ephesus, he espouses the truth of the incarnation. If he champions the formula of the 'two *physeis*', then it is through, and on behalf of, this tradition.

There is a political motive of course, for he sees that the well-being of the empire stands or falls with his responsibility for the unanimous acceptance of the formula of faith approved by the Council. For the sake of imperial interests he makes himself the servant of unity in faith. That is why injuring unity of faith incurs the imposition of sanctions. Here is the weak point of the imperial Church system and the danger inherent in the Emperor's policy. What ought to have been received in a purely theological and spiritual way could, however, in the last resort be imposed forcibly, even if the Emperor in some of his utterances had renounced compulsion. What could have been tolerated as a special theological tradition and explained correctly was, through a superficial understanding of the *mia physis* formula, interpreted as a heresy and saddled with the odium of being a repudiation of faith. For this, admittedly, the theologians were responsible, and their failure should not be laid at the Emperor's door. We shall often have to revert to this question.

That the other side, however, incurred great guilt by first treading the path of violence and open resistance sharpened the Emperor's actions and reactions decisively. In Alexandria armed force had to be employed to dislodge the shrewd and pacific Proterius from the episcopal throne (November, 451). The murder of this bishop on 29 (28?) March, 457 was an unpardonable step by the monophysite party. Marcian, however, had nothing to do with that. We now turn to his measures on behalf of Chalcedon which brought in Leo of Rome as his ally in the fight against the Monophysites.

I.V. MARCIAN—THE MEMBERS OF THE SYNOD OF CHALCEDON— LEO I OF ROME

Emperor Marcian and the Patriarch Anatolius had communicated the Council's decisions to the Bishop of Old Rome in a letter of 18 December, 451, together with a complaint about his legates' opposition to the so-called Canon 28.[47] To Leo too Marcian betrays the same certainty over the work done that breathes through his 'Constitutions' (see above).

What we sought we have found, and fulfilment has been granted to our wishes: religious desire has found faith in religion and, doubtless by God's authorship, that which His Majesty implored has been defined.[48]

Against the enemies of religion (Eutyches) he has no grievance, nay he is grateful to them that they were the occasion for a deeper search for God and of a greater knowledge of him. Leo too should rejoice at the victory of the faith (*victoria fidei*). Marcian sees Christ as the conqueror decked with the laurel wreath at the Council, and for that reason it was his own wish to be present in spite of campaigns in the field and affairs of state. Now peace has been vouchsafed and restored to the Churches, for all that appertains to catholic faith and truth has been resolved. The Emperor points out that Leo was involved in this success, because his letter (to Flavian) met with universal agreement. A feeling of insecurity is present, nevertheless, in the Emperor's further words, because he now begs for Leo's assent to the promotion in rank of the Bishop of Constantinople, aware as he is that the papal legates have opposed this conciliar request.[49] The Patriarch Anatolius also stresses in his letter to Leo the unanimous

---

[47] *Inter ep. Leon. ep.* 100, 101: ACO II 4, nr. 114, pp. 167–168 (Marcian); nr. 115, pp. 168–169 (Anatolius) (Greek: ACO II 1, 2, nr. 15, pp. 52–54).

[48] *Marcian., ad Leon. ep.*: ACO II 4, nr. 114, p. 167, 5–7.

[49] ACO II 4, nr. 114, p. 167, 24–33: 'It has also been resolved (*statutum*) to keep firmly to what the 150 holy bishops, under the divine (*divo*) Theodosius the Elder, had decided about the precedence of the venerable Church of Constantinople and which now the Synod of Chalcedon has adopted in respect to the same matter: namely, that the bishop of the city of Constantinople has second place after the Apostolic See [of Old Rome], because this magnificent city is called the second Rome (*iunior Roma*). May your Holiness bestow your assent also on this part [of the conciliar decision], although the venerable bishops who came as representatives of Your Piety (*religio-*

acceptance of the Council's definition and its agreement with Leo's letter to Flavian. Dioscorus, the cause of the trouble, has been routed. Leo, therefore, cannot withhold his assent. Anatolius shows himself piqued, and justly so from the Eastern standpoint, at the utter intransigence of Leo's legates in the question of the precedence of Constantinople.[50]

Similar feelings about the task accomplished echo finally from the report of the Synod itself which was forwarded to Leo after its conclusion.[51] The Synod has discharged the Lord's apostolic commission (Mt 28, 19–20), just as Leo himself has also become the interpreter of the words spoken to Peter (Mt 16, 16). At the Council each man did not present his teaching for himself in secret; but in *one* spirit, in full unanimity they set forth the confession of faith. The Council was like 'a communal circle of friends', a joyous royal banquet, rich in spiritual delights, which Christ, through Leo's letter, had prepared for all the guests. 'We believed we saw the heavenly bridegroom holding conversation with us'.[52] Leo, however, was present in the

nis) to the holy Synod opposed it. With violence they attempted to prevent anything being enacted at the Synod about the venerable Church [of Constantinople]. But we hope that the divine favour will be given to what, if all of the bishops are in agreement (*concordantibus toto orbe sacerdotibus*), will be of advantage to the whole Roman republic'. We shall not enter into more detail on the problems of the so-called Canon 28. Two clues emerge from the text we have just cited: in and for itself the precedence of Constantinople was for the East a more or less acknowledged state of affairs since the Council of Constantinople. The following factors are decisive for Leo's attitude to the Council: 1. in his opinion the content of Chalcedon was in effect his Tome to Flavian; 2. his legates had assented to the dogmatic part of the Council; 3. these refused, however, to give their assent to the so-called Canon 28. These three presuppositions determine Leo's attitude to the Council, and this never changed. On the problem of the so-called Canon 28 one can refer to: T. G. Jalland, *The Life and Times of St. Leo the Great* (London 1941) Chs. 13 and 14; E. Hermann, 'Chalkedon und die Ausgestaltung des konstantinopolitanischen Primats', *Chalkedon* II, 459–490; A. Michel, 'Der Kampf um das politische oder petrinische Prinzip der Kirchenführung', *Chalkedon* II, 491–562; H. M. Klinkenberg, 'Papsttum und Reichskirche bei Leo d. Gr.', *ZSavSt.K* 38(1952) 37–112; W. de Vries, 'Die Struktur der Kirche gemäß dem Konzil von Chalkedon (451)', *OCP* 35(1969) (63–122) 109–111; in French: idem, *Orient et Occident* (Paris 1974) (101–160) 139–149; J. Vierhaus, *Das Alte und Neue Rom* (Castrop-Rauxel 1964) 12ff. (Extract from an unpublished dissertation at the Gregorian University 1963).

[50] Anatolius *ad Leon.* (inter epp. *Leon.* 101): ACO II 1, 2, pp. 52–54, nr. 15 (Greek); PL 54, 981C–983A (Latin): '... they reject the Synod, they disturb the assembly and throw it into confusion, because they pay no regard to this see [of Constantinople] and do everything to bring injustice both to me as well as to the most holy Church of Constantinople'. The Synod now brings the decree to Leo so that he will give it his approbation: 'For the see of Constantinople also has your apostolic cathedra as its father; it binds itself in a special and outstanding way to you so that through your care for it all can recognise that for a long time you have truly thought about its advantage and also now have the same care for it ... So we earnestly entreat that both propositions (*unaquaeque propositio*) [the definition of faith as well as Canon 28] receive the appropriate answer. Bishop Lucian, beloved of God, will explain everything to you, because he himself was present at the holy Council and with the utmost discretion did everything in his power to support our enthusiasm for the faith (*summa cum prudentia pro virile parte adlaborans nostro studio erga fidem*' (ibid., 983 BC).

[51] *Relatio S. Synodi Calchedonensis ad b. papam Leonem*: ACO II 3, 2, nr. 109 (translation of Rusticus), pp. 93–95; in another Latin translation, ibid., pp. 96–98 with the signatures of the Fathers affixed; Greek: ACO II 1, 3, nr. 21, pp. 116–118.

[52] The images of the 'circle' and the 'royal banquet'—despite all the differences of application—call to mind the depiction of the relationship of the Emperor Constantine to the members of the Synod of Nicaea given by Eusebius, *Vita Constantini* II 61–III 24. Cf. H. J. Sieben, 'Die Konzilsidee des Eusebius von Caesarea oder der hellenistische Einfluß', idem, *Die Konzilsidee der Alten Kirche* (Paderborn etc. 1979) 424–465.

persons of his legates and presided over the assembly as the head over the members (*tu quidem sicut membris caput praeeras in his qui tuum tenebant ordinem*). The Emperor took on himself the part of Zoro-babel-Jesus and protected those who through their teachings carried out the rebuilding of the Church of the new Jerusalem (Ezra 3, 2–8). But outside the fold Dioscorus had offered himself as prey to the prowling lion. He had plotted to excommunicate even Leo to whom the guardianship of the Lord's vineyard had been entrusted, because the Pope was exerting himself for the unity of the Church's body.[53] The Council wanted to give Dioscorus the possibility of coming to his senses and to make him the victor over his supporters, in order that the full unanimity of the Council might be ensured. But he appealed to the law of his own conscience (*sed ille in semet ipso inscriptam convictionem conscientiae habens*) and rejected the three legitimate demands to appear before the Council. Thus the wolf was stripped of his sheep's clothing which he had previously worn only as a dis-guise. The solitary tare had been rooted up; the bishops had carried out their task—to plant, and to uproot. Having to cut off one (branch) had been for them an occasion of sorrow, but the fullness of the benefit attained, on the other hand, a cause for joy. Leo had been present in spirit to the Council Fathers and, as it were, visibly through his representatives—and thus had participated in the work of the Synod. These words express the same conviction that is to be found in the letters of Marcian and Bishop Anatolius: unity of faith has been re-established in the Church, and peace restored.

After the Fathers had thus laid sufficient stress on what was needed to ensure Leo's unqualified assent, they believed that they were in a position to make their second request too with confidence: the request for recognition of their statement about the precedence of the episcopal see of Constantinople.

We make known to you, however, that we have also taken a decision on (ὡρίσα-μεν) another matter for the sake of the ordering of Church relations and the stability of Church decisions, and in the knowledge that Your Holiness also, as soon as you are cognisant of it, will sanction and endorse it: we have, namely, by a synodal decision, confirmed the already longstanding custom (*consuetudinem, quae ex longo iam tempore permansit*) which the holy Church of Constantinople has followed in consecrating the metropolitans of the Asian, Pontic and Thracian provinces. In this we have not so much bestowed anything on the see of Constantinople as cared for the right ordering of the metropolitan cities, because on the passing away of a bishop disturbances frequently spring up, since clergy and people are left without guidance and bring Church order into confusion.[54]

---

[53] ACO II 3, 2, p. 94, 12–14: *et post haec omnia insuper et contra ipsum cui vineae custodia a salvatore commissa est, extendit insaniam, id est contra tuam quoque dicimus sanctitatem, et excommunicationem meditatus est contra te, qui corpus ecclesiae unire festinas.*

[54] *Relatio S. Synodi . . .*: ACO II 1, 3, nr. 21, p. 118, 3–11 (Greek); ACO II 3, 2, nr. 109, p. 97, 27–36 (Latin).

Why are the reasons given for a seemingly self-evident and obvious matter so exhaustive? Presumably the behaviour of the papal legates during the negotiations over Canon 28 had made the Fathers aware that on the side of Old Rome this solution was by no means considered to be so self-evident and harmless. From the Eastern point of view there were thoroughly reasonable grounds for a new ordering of Church relationships: the time-honoured custom reaching back to the Council of Constantinople, and the confirmation of that Council by Theodosius I. The Easterners tried to forestall the objection that the see of Constantinople wanted to make itself independent of the bishop of Old Rome:

> To reassure you that we have granted no privilege, pursued no vendetta, but rather were led by God's guidance, we have, as an earnest of our sincerity and as a step towards attaining the ratification of and assent to our transactions, laid before you the whole persuasive power of our course of action.[55]

Leo had a different view of things. This was based on principle and gave little consideration, if any, to the actual situation of the Eastern Churches. He took his stand on a tradition which was not known in the East and did not tally with the form of the canon of Nicaea (Canon 6) as held there.[56] The East went by the imperial maxim that ecclesiastical precedence should be ordered in accord with the civil rank of the episcopal cities (see above, n. 3). The papal position, on the other hand, would allow a higher jurisdiction to be allocated to any particular see only on the basis of apostolic origin. This principle had many drawbacks from an administrative point of view, but it also had the advantage, within an imperial Church system, of calling attention to the peculiar characteristic and source of Church authority.

---

[55] Ibid., ACO II 3, 2, p. 95, 34–37.

[56] Cf. W. de Vries, 'Die Struktur der Kirche' (above n. 49) 90; in French, idem, *Orient et Occident*, 128: 'In the sixteenth session [of Chalcedon], during which the legates protested against Canon 28, at the command of the commissioners that both parties should present the canons on which they based themselves, Paschasinus cited Canon 6 of Nicaea in the interpolated Roman version: "The Roman Church has always had the primacy (τὰ πρωτεῖα)". The secretary Constantine read out the same canon in its Constantinopolitan version without the Roman addition'. Cf. ACO II 1, 3, p. 95, nr. 16 and 17; Leo refers to Canon 6 of Nicaea in *ep.* 106 *ad Anatol. ep.*, of 22 May, 452: ACO II 4, nr. 56, pp. 60–61; *ep.* 119 *ad Maxim. Antioch. ep.*, of 11 June, 453: ACO II 4, nr. 66, pp. 73–74. For the West cf. C. H. Turner, *Ecclesiae Occidentalis Monumenta Iuris Antiquissima* I, 1, 2 (Oxonii 1904) p. 121, in addition p. 148. 151. See further the so-called *Decretum Gelasianum* which, according to the present state of research, is a collection of the sixth century (made by a cleric in North Italy or South Gaul), but contains decrees of various ages and different origins. It encompasses five parts. The third part concerns the primacy of the Bishop of Rome and the precedence of the sees. *Est ergo prima Petri Apostoli **sedis** [sedes] Romanae Ecclesiae, non habens maculam neque rugam nec aliquid eiusmodi* (Eph 5, 27). *Secunda autem **sedis** [sedes] apud Alexandriam beati Petri nomine a Marco eius discipulo atque evangelista consecrata est . . . Tertia vero **sedis** [sedes] apud **Anthiociam** [Antiochiam] beatissimi Apostoli Petri habetur honorabilis, eo quod illic primus (primitus) quam Romae venisset habitavit et illic primum nomen Christianorum novellae gentis exortum est* (cf. Acts 11, 26) (Text from DS 351). According to C. H. Turner, E. Schwartz and others this part is to be traced back to Pope Damasus; E. v. Dobschütz, TU 38, 4 (Leipzig 1912) and P. Battifol, *Siège Apostolique* (359–451) (Paris 1924) 146f. are of a different opinion; cf. A. Michel, *Chalkedon* II, 503–509.

Still, it was not unalterable, and should have been applied flexibly for the sake of ecclesiastical peace. But on this matter Leo became ever more intransigent and this influenced to some extent also his doctrinal stand.

CHAPTER TWO

RECOGNITION, DEFENCE AND INTERPRETATION OF THE COUNCIL OF CHALCEDON BY POPE LEO I

I. The Phases in the Activity of Leo I after Chalcedon

In the following descriptions we shall place the accent on theological questions and developments. In order to be able to understand Leo's actions and reactions, however, these must be inserted into the whole compass of external events. A decisive turning-point was the death of the Emperor Marcian (26 January, 457), with whom the Pope worked harmoniously to have the doctrinal decision of the Council of 451 recognised, even if the two of them could not agree on the question of the so-called Canon 28. At this point this *first phase* of development after Chalcedon comes to a close. It includes the Palestinian rebellion led by the monk Theodosius, an event that was a cause of pain both to the Emperor and to the Pope. Leo showed his involvement not only in letters, but also in his *sermones* in Rome, as these are available in the Collectio II for the period from Christmas 452 to Christmas 453. Only in the autumn of 452 had he learnt of the insurrection of the monks.

For Leo, the *second phase* of the difficulties after Chalcedon begins with the new Emperor, Leo I (457–474). The Council was not the new ruler's 'own work'. With regard to the Church assembly he was clearly much more unengaged than Marcian was. More and more the forces that were working against the Council rallied together. Behind the new Emperor stood the *magister militum praesentalis*, Flavius Adaburius Aspar, who was Roman general from 424 to 471 (i.e. until his assassination). Already influential under the Emperor Marcian, he had procured the throne for Leo I and swayed the Emperor's politics more and more in an anti-Chalcedonian direction.[1] Timothy Aelurus became the focus and driving force of the anti-Chalcedonian movement. He had been consecrated bishop uncanonically in opposition to the Patriarch Proterius (451–457).[2] On 28 March

---

[1] Aspar's support for the Monophysites is mentioned by Theophanes, *Chron.*, A.M. 5952: ed. de Boor I, 112; cf. Zacharias Rh., *HE* IV 7: Hamilton-Brooks 74. Cf. E. Stein, *Geschichte des spätrömischen Reiches I* (Wien 1928) 520–539; French: *Histoire du Bas-Empire*, tom I, éd. par J.-R. Palanque (Desclée De Brouwer 1959) 351–364, 588–592; T. G. Jallard, *The Life and Times of St. Leo the Great* (London 1941).

[2] Theophanes, *Chron.*, A.M. 5950: de Boor I, 110, 24ff. Zacharias Rh., *HE* IV 1: Hamilton-Brooks 64–66; he emphasises that the consecration took place against the will of Timothy.

(?) Proterius was murdered and Timothy Aelurus took over the patriarchal see of Alexandria (457–460), until he was deposed and banished.[3]

To this period belong the following letters of Leo: *ep.* 144 of 1 June, 457 to Julian of Cius, and three further letters of 11 July: *ep.* 145 to the Emperor Leo, *ep.* 146 to Anatolius of Constantinople, and *ep.* 147 to Julian of Cius. When news of the murder of Proterius had reached Rome at the same time as reports about efforts to summon a new council and about the pro-monophysite lecturing activity of the priest Atticus in Constantinople, Leo increased his engagement in defence of the Council of Chalcedon, as the letters 148–153 testify. To Bishop Julian of Cius were sent several copies of an encyclical, dated 1 September, 457, which were to be forwarded to the most distinguished metropolitans of the East through the mediation of the Emperor.[4] From this encyclical it follows that in Leo's opinion Chalcedon stands or falls with the stance of the bishops, not so much with that of the Emperor or other authorities.[5]

In *sermo* 96 Leo allows his congregation to be privy to the events in Alexandria, which he had already learnt about before 11 July. (A. Chavasse, CCL 138A, pp. 593–595, is of the opinion that this sermon could have been delivered between the writing of *ep.* 156 (1 December, 457) and of *ep.* 164 (17 August or 1 September, 458) in which the Alexandrian affair is dealt with. Thus *sermo* 96 would date from 25 December, 457. Cf. ibid., 592). It is certain that he often returned to this topic.

On his side, Emperor Leo tried to postpone the summoning of a new council as long as possible. On the advice of the Patriarch Anatolius he wanted, however, to appease the opposition with two concessions, one following rapidly on the other. (1) He addressed to the metropolitans a circular in the form of a questionnaire (the *encyclia*), by means of which he intended to seek the bishops' opinions about the timeliness of a council, the validity of Chalcedon and the legitimacy of the occupation of the patriarchal see of Alexandria by Timothy Aelurus. At this time Emperor Leo was still neutral in respect

---

[3] Theophanes, *Chron.*, A.M. 5950: de Boor I, 110, 32ff. Zacharias Rh., *HE* IV 2: Hamilton-Brooks 66.

[4] In *ep.* 153 *ad Aetium*, the former Archdeacon of Constantinople and at this time Coadjutor to Bishop Julian of Cius, the patriarchs of Antioch and Jerusalem are named as special addressees of the encyclical. The copy destined for Antioch (Patriarch Basil) is preserved in *ep.* 149, and the other as *ep.* 150, addressed *a pari* to Euxitheus of Thessalonica, Juvenal of Jerusalem, Peter of Corinth and Luke of Dyrrhachium.

[5] Cf. Leo M., *ep.* 149.150: ACO II 4, nr. 90.91, p. 98, 6–7: during all the Alexandrian hubbub 'let not the common faith be found either anxious or luke-warm in any of us' (*ne in quoquam nostrum communis fides aut trepida inveniatur aut tepida*); ibid., 1. 18–20: neither the Emperor, nor the Patricius Aspar, nor the senate will allow the heretics to attain their goals, if they do not see the bishops vacillate: '*si pastorales animos in nullo viderint fluctuare*'.

to either party. Pope Leo replied to the *encyclia* with *ep.* 156, 157 and 158 which were addressed respectively to the Emperor, to Anatolius and to the exiled Egyptian bishops who were staying in Constantinople. The Pope did not lay the blame for the *encyclia* on the Emperor himself, but on Anatolius. (2) Emperor Leo was occupied with the thought of organising a religious discussion in Constantinople between the supporters of Eutyches or Dioscorus and a deputation from the Bishop of Rome. The Emperor despatched a certain Philoxenus to Rome; as messenger of the Bishop Anatolius went the deacon Patricius. Anatolius did not have the fortitude to dissuade the Emperor from this course. Leo reacted in *ep.* 162 to Emperor Leo which he handed over to Philoxenus (21 March, 458), and as well in *ep.* 163 to Anatolius (23 March, 458) which he entrusted to Patricius.[6] Each messenger had possibly also two further letters to take to Constantinople (*ep.* 160 to the Catholic bishops and clergy from Egypt, and *ep.* 161 to the priests, deacons and clergy of Constantinople).

The Pope was strongly averse to the idea of a religious discussion, as he was to disputations in general, and rejected it on grounds of principle. In these letters Leo's stand with regard to the immutability of the decision of the Council developed distinctly. He showed himself prepared, however, to send a delegation to Constantinople to represent his position before the Emperor. The legates were to administer milk of instruction to the simple children of the Church, but not to seek dealings with heretics. On 17 August, 458 a delegation proceeded to Constantinople. By way of credentials the two bishops, Geminianus and Domitianus, took the *ep.* 164 with them. In this letter Leo once again opposed disputations in matters of faith. Reminiscent of the early Church's discipline of penance is the instruction that acceptance into the Church could be conceded to contrite supporters of Eutyches and Dioscorus, but only after complete satisfaction or penance had been performed. But Timothy Aelurus, the suspected murderer—Leo calls him *parricida*[7]—is conceded no form of ecclesiastical penance. He can only entreat God for clemency. Thus, even in the event of his conversion, the *pax cum ecclesia* would no longer be granted to him. Conjointly with *ep.* 164 the Emperor is

---

[6] Leo M., *ep.* 163 *ad Anatol. ep.*: ACO II 4, nr. 116 was overlooked in the body of the edition by Schwartz and subsequently included in the *praefatio* to ACO II 4, p. XXXXIV.

[7] Five letters of Leo are concerned with the events in Egypt. These are preserved in the so-called *Collectio Avellana* (= *CA*), ed. O. Guenther I-II, CSEL 35 (Vindobonae 1895 and 1898). They are the letters 169–173, or nr. 51–55 in Guenther. Here are to be found the sharpest statements of Leo about Timothy Aelurus. See Ch. IV below. In some *sermones* (*tractatus*) of the Second Collection, Leo also deals with the events around Proterius and Timothy. We discuss this more fully below, following the edition of A. Chavasse, *Sancti Leonis Magni Romani Pontificis tractatus septem et nonaginta* = CCL CXXXVIII and CXXXVIIIA (Turnholti 1973). (See below n. 105.)

sent the principal document of Leo's christology in the post-Chalcedonian period, *ep.* 165, the so-called Second Tome, which will be
discussed in detail below.

Causa finita?

When at the beginning of 452 Leo's legates returned to Rome and
reported to him about the Council, the Pope's attention was apparently drawn more to the so-called Canon 28 than to the doctrinal
decision of the Synod. This was no doubt the reason that the Pope
remained silent about the Council for a fairly long period. In four
letters—to Emperor Marcian, to Empress Pulcheria, to the Archbishop of Constantinople and to Julian of Cius, all dating from 22 May,
452[8]—Leo let it be known that for him the real goal of the Council,
the reason for its being summoned, was perfectly accomplished.[9]
Hence there is no talk of a ratification properly speaking. In the
East, however, a reaction was expected. It caused a sensation that
there was no response to the document of the Fathers of Chalcedon
which was available for reading out in all the Churches. The opponents of the Council made capital out of this and spread uncertainty
about whether Leo approved the Council at all. Thus on 15 February,
453, Emperor Marcian appealed to Leo[10] to proclaim as quickly as
possible by means of a letter his full public approval of the Synod
of Chalcedon, so that there would no longer be any doubt about
the verdict of the Pope.[11] In this request it is not a matter of initiating
legislative recognition properly speaking, but rather of a psychological and propagandist undertaking to which Leo should contribute.
The expectation of the Emperor shows in any case the extent of Leo's
authority. Leo's reaction is palpable in a bundle of letters despatched
to the Emperor, the Empress, Julian of Cius and—this is the central
document—to the 'sancta synodus apud Calchedonem habita'. The various
ways in which Leo formulates his thought in these letters show reaso-
nably clearly how he understands his approbation and to what it
relates. In his reply to Emperor Marcian, Leo enlarges on the fact
that there can be no doubt at all about the agreement of the Apostolic
See with the Council's decision with regard to faith, for all the

---

[8] Leo M., *ep.* 104–107: ACO II 4, nr. 54–57, pp. 55–62.

[9] Leo M., *ep.* 104 *ad Marcian. aug.*: ACO II 4, nr. 54, p. 55, 27–28: 'when these things, on
account of which such a great gathering of bishops had been organised, had been brought to a
good and desirable conclusion...'; p. 57, 4: 'The heresy has been destroyed by God who worked
through you'. He wrote in a similar manner to Pulcheria and Anatolius.

[10] *Marcian. aug. ep. ad Leon.*; in Greek: ACO II 1, 2, nr. 19, p. 61 (*Coll. epp. B*)

[11] ACO II 1, 2, nr. 19, p. 61, 24–27: 'therefore will Your Holiness despatch as soon as possible
a special letter (*idia grammata*), through which you make clear that by it the Synod of Chalcedon
is confirmed in the most manifest way, so that those who are infatuated by hopeless things can
no longer have any suspicion about the decision of Your Holiness'.

members of the Synod (thus including the papal representatives) gave their signature to that '*fides*' which he had propounded in accordance with the pattern of apostolic teaching and the tradition of the Fathers; furthermore, through Bishop Lucensius he had addressed letters to the Emperor and to the Bishop of Constantinople which quite openly proclaimed that he approved the decisions which the Synod had enacted concerning Catholic faith.

Since the devout will of Your Piety is to be obeyed in every respect, however, I have gladly given my assent to the synodal conclusions, which regarding the confirmation of Catholic faith pleased me; a decree of Your Kindness may now direct that this [my *sententia*] comes to the notice of all bishops and Churches.[12]

The Pope formulates it in a similar way in the letter 'to the Synod held at Chalcedon'.[13] Actually his assent to the Council's definitions is already known to everybody; in fact this is clear not only from the work itself of the (synodal) agreement (*hoc autem non solum ex ipso beatissimae consensionis effectu*; Greek: ἐξ αὐτοῦ τοῦ ἔργου τῆς μακαρίας συναινέσεως), but from his letters to Bishop Anatolius, if only the latter had been willing to communicate the reply of the Apostolic See to the other bishops. Now, however, all the brethren (i.e. the bishops) and the faithful should know not only through the bishops (legates) who took his place at the Council, but also through his own express approbation of the synodal proceedings, that Leo unites his own assent with that of the Council Fathers, admittedly purely and solely in the matter of faith which was exclusively the purpose of the Council.[14] The so-called Canon 28 is expressly excepted from

[12] Leo M., *ep.* 115 *ad Marcian. aug.*, 21 March, 453: ACO II 4, nr. 61, p. 68, 1–5; cf. p. 67, 22–27: 'about this (i.e. with regard to the assent of the Apostolic See) there was no occasion to doubt, because the consent of all the signatories was given to that faith which in accordance with the pattern (model, *forma*) of apostolic teaching and the tradition of the Fathers had been issued by me (= *Tomus ad Flavianum*), and because through my brother, Bishop Lucian (according to Silva-Tarouca, "Lucensius" is to be inserted in the text), I addressed such letters to Your Majesty and to the Bishop of Constantinople which make it clear that I ratify what had been defined about *catholic faith* at the aforementioned Synod'.

[13] ACO II 4, nr. 64, pp. 70–71; in Greek: ACO II 1, 2, pp. 61f., *Epist. Coll. B*, nr. 20 (21 March, 453).

[14] Leo M., *ep.* 114 *ad synod. Chalc.*: ACO II 4, nr. 64, p. 71, 2–8: '. . . so that all the brothers and the hearts of all the faithful may know that I have joined my own *sententia* with yours (*vobiscum*) not only through the brothers who functioned as my representatives, but also through approbation of the synodal acts (literally: the synodal events: *gestorum synodalium*), admittedly only in the sole matter of faith (*in sola . . . fidei causa*), a fact which must often be repeated, on account of which a general council had been summoned on command of the Christian ruler as well as with the consent of the Apostolic See, so that after the condemnation of the deliberately incorrigible heretics there would no longer remain any doubt at all about the true incarnation of our Lord Jesus Christ. Thus whoever at any time should have dared to defend the perfidy of Nestorius or to advocate the ungodly teaching of Eutyches or Dioscorus [the equation of these is to be noted] shall be separated from the community of catholics and shall no longer share in the body whose truth he denies, dearest brothers'. Cf. *ep.* 116 *ad Pulcher. aug.*: ACO II 4, nr. 62, pp. 68–69; *ep.* 117 *ad Julian. ep.*: ibid., nr. 63, pp. 69–70. The propagandist point of the approbation of Leo which was desired by Marcian becomes evident here: Leo addressed a letter to all the members of the Synod of Chalcedon, 'through which I wanted to demonstrate (*demonsrarem*) that I gave my *placet* to what was decided by our

this assent. It was in Anatolius that Leo saw the cause of the conciliar attempt to revise the status of the Patriarchate—an attempt that Leo deemed unfortunate.[15] In the confrontation that is beginning, Leo's post-Chalcedonian notion of a council or his view of the timeliness, validity and immutability of conciliar decisions manifests itself. In this framework the Christian doctrine of Chalcedon, i.e. its validity and immutability, is to be seen. The more acutely both are apprehended, the more unequivocally the opponents of the Council and its christological formula are designated as heretics. Here we come to the three questions which have to do with Leo's post-Chalcedonian teaching and policy.[16]

II. Leo's Notion of a Council in the Light of the Confrontation over Chalcedon

1. Leo I and the notion of a council

We shall deal first of all with the framework[17] of Leo's post-Chalcedonian christology, his conception of a council in general. What significance does this framework have for the preaching and handing on of the doctrine concerning Christ? One has the impression that the Pope argues and acts pragmatically in the question whether a council should be summoned. A council is not something to be considered uncritically. Hence, in assessing a council, there seems to be an important difference between whether it is a matter of a *concilium convocandum* (a council to be summoned) or of a *concilium iam convocatum* (a council already summoned). After Ephesus II (449) Leo has a marked aversion to, or rather, apprehension of general[18] councils. Obviously there is no complete guarantee of a successful outcome.

holy brothers about the rule of faith, for the sake of those, namely, who in order to conceal their own perfidy want it to appear that the decisions of the Council are weak and in doubt, because they are not strengthened by any *sententia* of my consent" (p. 69, 12–15). Leo learnt that the reading out of the 'letter to the members of the Synod' of Chalcedon was carried out from Julian of Cius, as he writes in *ep.* 127, 9 January, 454. He complains, however, that his protest against Canon 28 was not made known in the same way.

[15] Cf. Leo M., *ep.* 104, *ad Marcian. aug.*, 22 May, 452: ACO II 4, nr. 54, p. 55, 28ff., in particular p. 56, 13–17: 'may the city of Constantinople have its glory, as we desire, and under the protection of the hand of God may it enjoy a long rule of Your Clemency; however, *one* is the sight of secular things (*ratio rerum saecularium*), the *other* that of divine things, and without that rock which the Lord laid as a foundation no construction will be stable. Whoever lusts after things which are not his due loses those things which are'. Leo does not do justice to the person of Anatolius or to the actual state of affairs. But he senses rightly the political component in the ecclesiology of Anatolius.

[16] On the pre-Chalcedonian christology of Leo, see CCT I², 526–550; JdChr I², 734–750.

[17] Cf. H. J. Sieben, *Die Konzilsidee*, 103–147 (Leo the Great); M. Wojtowytsch, *Papsttum und Konzile von den Anfängen bis zu Leo I.* (440–461). *Studien zur Entstehung der Überordnung des Papstes über Konzile* = Päpste und Papsttum 17 (Stuttgart 1981) 304–350. Our presentation considers the conciliar idea of Leo under the aspect of his christology.

[18] Leo's trust in regional synods, particularly those of the West, is unreserved. Cf. H. J. Sieben, op. cit., 104–112.

Even Church assemblies can be manipulated, as Leo saw in the case of Ephesus. However, he recognises that these are ways of deciding questions of Christian faith and ecclesiastical order. As in the study of the whole development of the notion of a council, so too in a study of Leo, one must distinguish between the function attributed to a council in the life of the Church, the authority it has and how this is established. The function which falls to a council is nothing other than the transmission of the evangelical and apostolic tradition. Its legitimacy and authority are gauged by this standard.[19] The gospel and the apostolic teaching are fundamentally the unchangeable norm on which the Church has to rely.[20] This teaching is deposited in the Apostles' Creed, which Leo, in common with the tradition dating from the fourth century, traces back to the apostles themselves.[21] To deny the Creed means to contradict the gospel. Thus Chalcedon is also to be appraised on the basis of the fact that there it became manifest 'that in conformity with evangelical and apostolic tradition we must all adopt the one, unvarying confession regarding the incarnation of our Lord Jesus Christ'.[22] It is sufficient here to have given a fundamental indication of this decisive notion in Leo's understanding of a council. We shall encounter it again quite often in different variants. Every (legitimate) council, Chalcedon also, is at the service of the paradosis. Because it preserves and transmits this, it must be upheld. This is the original conception propounded by Athanasius, the defender of Nicaea, of the legitimacy and task of that Council in 325.[23] Gospel—apostle or apostolic teaching—Apostles' Creed—Nicaea and its Creed—Leo's own Tome to Flavian—Chalcedon: all

[19] Cf. A. Lauras, 'Saint Léon le Grand et la Tradition', *RSR* 48 (1960) 166–184, in particular 178ff.; H. J. Sieben, op. cit., 132–143.

[20] Cf. Leo M., *ep.* 82, *ad Marcian. aug.*, 23 April, 451: ACO II 4, nr. 39, p. 41, 24–26: '... because it is not allowed to be at variance with the evangelic and apostolic teaching, not even in one word, or to think about the divine scriptures in any other way than that which the blessed apostles and our Fathers learnt and taught (*didicerunt atque docuerunt*)'. Cf. the other passages in A. Lauras, art. cit., 172–178.

[21] Cf. Leo M., *Tr.* 62 (16 March, 452): Chavasse CCL 138A, p. 337, 1.30–31: 'this rule of faith which we have received in the very beginning of the creed through the authority of apostolic instruction...'. Cf. A. Lauras, art. cit., 181, with reference to Pope Siricius, *ep.* 42, 5; Cyril of Jerusalem, *Catech.* V, 12; Augustine, *De symbolo ad catech.* 1; *serm.* 224, 1 and the well-known works of research on the creeds (see below with regard to *ep.* 165 and to Vigilius of Thapsus). H. de Lubac, *La Foi chrétienne. Essai sur la structure du Symbole des Apôtres* 2 (Paris 1970²) 23–59; J. N. D. Kelly, *Early Christian Creeds*, (London 1972³) 6–13.

[22] Leo M., *ep.* 102 *ad eppos Galliae*, 27 January, 452: ACO II 4, nr. 53, p. 53, 22–25. See the text below in n. 27.

[23] Cf. H. J. Sieben, op. cit., 24–67 (Athanasius). The authority of Nicaea is the authority of apostolic tradition. The Apostles' Creed is in the Nicene Creed. Cf. Leo M., *ep.* 54 *ad Theodos, aug.*, 24 December, 449: ACO II 4, nr. 9, p. 11, 18–21: '...it cannot be doubted that we believe in all purity and assert constantly this which also the venerable Fathers once gathered at Nicaea in accord with the faith of the creed [= the Apostles' Creed, which was not known, however, to the Eastern Fathers] declared with most sacred authority must be believed and confessed'. Were Eutyches to accept the Apostles' Creed in its fullness, he would not stray from Nicene faith. *Ep.* 31 *ad Pulcheriam aug.*: ACO II 4, nr. 11, p. 14–15: '...if, however, that short and perfect confession of the catholic

constitute one line. Here there is nothing to be taken away or added.[24] There is no doubt that Leo is charged by his opponents with being an innovator, especially on account of his *Tomus ad Flavianum*. Even Vigilius of Thapsus in Africa knows that Leo is accused of having another creed than that which all the faithful hold.[25] The point in question was a sentence from his letter to Flavian in which he cited the Apostles' Creed.[26] Leo no doubt cites the Nicene Creed in his Second Tome, *ep.* 165 to Emperor Leo (see below), to meet these reproaches. For his own part, however, he also emphasises the fundamental immutability of the Apostles' Creed and its importance for the right orientation of the faithful. He can do this, because the Gospel is enshrined within it.[27] The faithful will continue without error if they hold fast to the Creed (the baptismal creed).[28] The essential reason

creed, which is characterised (*signata*) by having just as many sentences as there are twelve apostles, be fitted out with such heavenly defences (*munitione caelesti*), all opinions of the heretics could be cut down by its sword alone. If Eutyches had wished to accept the fullness of this creed with a pure and simple heart, he would have deviated in no way from the decrees of the most sacred Nicene Council, and he would understand that which was decreed by the holy Fathers, so that no manner of thinking and no word raises itself against apostolic faith which is only one'.

[24] On Leo's formula of tradition, cf. A. Lauras, op. cit., 170, n. 18–21. In *ep.* 162, *ad Leon. aug.*, 21 March, 458: ACO nr. 101, p. 106, 17–18, Leo quotes a phrase of his imperial namesake: 'because, as you said devoutly and correctly, perfection admits no increase, and fullness no addition (*perfectio incrementum et adiectionem plenitudo non recipit*)'.

[25] Vigilius Thaps., *C. Eutych.* IV 1: PL 62, 119B: 'all the faithful (*fidelium universitas*) profess to believe in God the Father almighty, and in Jesus Christ his only Son our Lord. In this chapter he (Leo) is on that account blamed unjustly, because he did not say "in one God the Father and in one Jesus Christ his Son" in accord with the decree of the Council of Nicaea'. Vigilius refers to the Apostles' Creed, which was not known in the East: 'but at Rome and before the Synod of Nicaea had convened, from the time of the apostles until now, . . . the creed is handed over in this way [cf. the expression "*traditio symboli*"]; the words do not signify any prejudice where the sense remains intact'. We shall have to return to this important sentence many times.

[26] Leo M., *Tomus I* = *ep.* 28 *ad Flavian. ep.*: ACO II 2, 1, pp. 24–32, here according to Silva-Tarouca, TD 9, p. 21, v. 14: '. . . insofar as all the faithful profess to believe in God the Father almighty and in Jesus Christ his only Son our Lord who was born of the Holy Spirit and the virgin Mary'. The opponents state that all the faithful confess differently from Leo. The difference, however, concerns only the wording. The Eastern Churches do not know the Apostles' Creed. Cf. the Bellerini in PL 54, 855D–856. 1195D–1160C.

[27] Cf. Leo M., *ep.* 102 *ad appos Galliae*, 27 January, 452: ACO II 4, nr. 53, 22–29: '. . . and rightly we emphasise (*cognoscimus*) that we made known to our oriental brothers and fellow-bishops that in accordance with evangelic and apostolic tradition there was for all of us one confession without distinction (*una . . . et indiscreta confessio*) regarding the incarnation of our Lord Jesus Christ; through no disputations of heretics can it be maintained that we think anything else about the truth of the highest salvific mystery (*de summi et salutiferi sacramenti veritate*) than what we have learnt and teach (1) from the preaching of the holy Fathers and (2) from the authority of the unchangeable creed by which the universal Church now condemnds Eutyches and had previously condemned Nestorius. Whoever has decided to adhere to their unbearable impieties (*non ferendis impietatibus*) cuts himself off from the body of Christian unity'.

[28] Leo M., *Tr.* XXIV (from 443): Chavasse, CCL 138, p. 115, 130–138 (PL 54, 207B): 'remain constant in that faith which you confessed before many witnesses . . . If anyone, however, preached to you anything other than what you have learnt, let him be anathema . . . and whatever happens to be read or heard that is against the rule of the catholic and apostolic creed hold it to be utterly deadly and diabolical'. *Tr.* 46, 3 (1 March, 453): Chavasse, CCL 138A, p. 272, 84–85: 'hold fast to that in your soul which you learnt in the Creed'. On the other hand, heretics are those who oppose the Creed: *Tr.* 96 (25 December, 457): Chavasse, CCL 138A, p. 594, 26–27 (PL 54, 466C): . . . *et instituto a sanctis apostolis simbolo repugnantes*. The Manichaeans are those whose stupidity can be summarised as follows: '*tota apostolici veritate symboli sublata*'. Eutyches, for example, as an old

that Chalcedon and its doctrine regarding the incarnation also possess an immutable authority is that this Council has the function of a witness. In this function it takes its place in the line of accredited witnesses to this very doctrine, namely on the basis of its agreement with all the witnesses before it. The gospel, the apostolic teaching, Nicaea and the tradition of the Fathers live on undiminished in it. Leo is conscious that one has only to read and understand these witnesses in order to establish this agreement. Thus Chalcedon's authority as a witness can be tested by every Christian. Nevertheless, Leo is forced by the controversy over it to adduce more and more reasons to ensure for the Fourth Council its quality as a witness. Thus it is in the controversy about Chalcedon that Leo's notion of a council grows. From the outset, however, he takes pains to win for himself such influence at the Council in order to guarantee this witnessing function. Here his Petrine notion interlocks with his understanding of a council.

2. General Council and the Petrine-idea

Leo is most in favour of a council when he succeeds in implementing his fundamental propositions on the position of the Bishop of Rome as the successor of Peter, and in seeing these guaranteed in the accomplishment of the council. For by these means a surety is given that a council can be a witness to apostolic tradition.[29]

First of all this concerns the *summoning* of a council. Because this question has been sufficiently clarified, we do not need to go into it here. Leo acknowledged the right of the Emperor to summon a council, even if he emphasised the participation of the Apostolic See by referring to its *consensus* (*assensus*),[30] without ascribing to this

man did not understand even the rudiments of the Creed which every candidate for baptism knows.: *ep.* 28 (First Tome): Silva-Tarouca TD 9, p. 21 v. 11 (ACO II 2, 1, p. 25): '*qui ne ipsius quidem symboli initia conprehendit et quod per totum mundum omnium regenerandorum voce depromitur, istius adhuc senis corde non capitur*' (?).

[29] For the following, cf. W. de Vries and J. Vierhaus (above, ch. I, n. 49). In comparison with the work of H. M. Klinkenberg cited above, the writings of these two authors measure Leo's own ideas against those of the conceptions in the East and the actual procedure of the Fathers of Chalcedon. Leo's idea of Roman participation at the Council (as depicted by Klinkenberg, it is far too strongly emphasised) and what was reality for the East (as described by de Vries and Vierhaus) are in part sharply opposed. On the Petrine idea, cf. T. G. Jalland, op. cit. (above, n. 1) 64–85, where he gives a special evaluation of Leo's *sermones* and the sources of ecclesiastical law; P. Stockmeier, *Leo I. des Großen Beurteilung der kaiserlichen Religionspolitik* (München 1959) § 21, 205–211; ibid., 164–167 and critique of Klinkenberg's overemphasis of the Petrine idea and underestimation of the Council.

[30] The instances are given by W. de Vries, op. cit., 65–66; in French in: idem, *Orient et Occident* (Paris 1974) 102–104. Prominence is given to *ep.* 114 (21 March, 453): ACO II 4, nr. 64, p. 71, 5–7: '... a general Council, assembled both by the command of the Christian rulers and with the consent of the Apostolic See...'. Cf. W. Kissling, *Das Verhältnis zwischen Sacerdotium und Imperium nach den Anschauungen der Päpste von Leo d. Gr. bis Gelasius I. (440–496). Eine historische Untersuchung* (Paderborn 1920) 40–85, who refers back to the fundamental study of F. X. Funk, 'Die Berufung der ökumenischen Synoden des Altertums', *Kirchengeschichtliche Abhandlungen und Untersuchungen I* (Paderborn 1897) 39ff.; P. Stockmeier, op. cit., § 15, 156ff., strongly emphasises the Emperor's

assensus a significance that would be constitutive for the legality of the summoning.

Leo showed more interest in gaining influence over the *object* of the conciliar deliberations and in determining the proceedings at the council itself. But here also one must distinguish between desire and reality. Leo had no intention of allowing a long debate at the council over the orthodoxy of Eutyches or Dioscorus.[31] He wanted 'to suggest' the details to the Emperor through his special legates.[32] At the centre of the Pope's thoughts was his view that the question of faith had already been settled *positively* by his *Tomus ad Flavianum*, and *negatively* by his condemnation of the Council of Ephesus (449). Just how highly Leo estimated his Tome is revealed in a letter of 1 September, 457 to Julian of Cius, even after this Tome had become more and more a bone of contention in the post-Chalcedonian dispute.

I am amazed at the calumnous madness which would have it that in my letter, which has found the agreement of the whole world, there is something obscure, so that these are of the opinion that it must be set forth more clearly; its proclamation, however, is so easily comprehended and so substantiated that it is capable of no addition, either to its meaning or to its language. For what was written by us at that time shows itself to be taken from apostolic and evangelic teaching.[33]

right to summon a council, taking as his starting-point particular terms, such as *velle, iubere, constituere, praecipere*, which are used in this context and leave the Pope little scope. The imperial *auctoritas* is taken by Leo absolutely seriously.

[31] Leo M., *ep.* 82 *ad Marcian. aug.*, 23 April, 451: ACO II 4, nr. 39, p. 41, 28ff.: 'it is unjust beyond measure that through the folly of a minority (*paucorum insipientiam*) we are called back to conjectured opinions (*ad coniecturas opinionum*) and to wars of fleshly disputes (*ad carnalium disputationum bella*), as if in renewed discussion it were a matter of investigating whether Eutyches thought irreligiously and whether Dioscorus judged wrongly, he who struck himself with his condemnation of Flavian of holy memory and forces all more simple souls to tumble with him into the same disaster. For many of these who, as we know, are already converted to the remedies of satisfaction and request pardon for their inconstant vacillation (*de inconstanti trepidatione*) it is not a question of what faith must be held, but how their requests may be met'. Thus it should be a question of reconciliation only for those who turn away from Eutyches and Dioscorus. Leo has a horror of doctrinal debates. Cf. Leo, *ep.* 90 *ad Marcian. aug.*, 26 June, 451: ACO II 4, nr. 47, p. 48, 25–29. But it is precisely here that Leo desires an 'order' from the Emperor to uphold the '*antiqua Nicaenae synodi constituta*'! Is it worth it, however, to summon a council for the sake of something so closely circumscribed? As far as he was concerned, Leo himself at that moment would have answered immediately in the negative.

[32] Ibid., p. 41, 35–38: 'Hence whatever I think pertains to the benefit of the cause will be proposed more fully and opportunely (*plenius atque oportunius suggeretur*) to the devout care which you deign to have for the proclamation of the Synod through a delegation which with the grace of God will arrive at Your Clemency forthwith'.

[33] Leo M., *ep.* 152 *ad Iulian. ep.*: ACO II 4, nr. 93, p. 99, 18–22. Several times Leo speaks about falsifications with which his letter was circulated: *ep.* 130 *ad Marcian. aug.*: ACO II 4, nr. 74, p. 84, 13–16: 'it is said that the cunning vileness of certain heretics falsified ... my letter, so that by substituting certain words or syllables that could maintain that I was one who accepted the Nestorian heresy (*ut ... receptorem me Nestoriani erroris assererent ...*)'. In his edition of the post-Chalcedonian letters of Leo, C. Silva-Tarouca (p. 139) refers to the letter, dating from 497, of the Alexandrian apocrisiarii in Constantinople, which is transmitted in the CA (CSEL 35, 468–473) and which was delivered to the Roman legates in Constantinople. It deals with the falsification of the Greek translation of the Tome. On this see *Chalkedon* II, 67–70. Also in *ep.* 131, 10 March, 454, Leo speaks of these falsifications as occurring in the translation: '*fallaci interpretatione*' (ACO II 4, nr. 77, p. 87, 5ff.). The alleged Nestorianism of the Letter is intensified. For this reason Julian of Cius is to see to a new translation which, furnished with the imperial seal, is then to be sent to Alexandria, so that there the Tome may be read out to the Christian people.

Consequently, the Council was intended only to accept this doctrinal letter without any discussion whatsoever. This was the only way in which the question of faith was to have been handled at the Council. In this sense Leo could write in his letter to Anatolius of Constantinople early in 452 that the Council had been held to eradicate heresy and to confirm the faith.[34] For all that, the question of faith was still given pride of place. Furthermore, what mattered to Emperor Marcian was a solution in a concrete form, viz. a new formula of faith which was to be discussed and put to the vote.[35] When the papal legates emphasised in opposition to this proposal that the previous definitions of Nicaea, Constantinople and Ephesus (431) together with the *Tomus Leonis* were sufficient to express the content of faith validly, they made their judgement on the basis of the uncontested Western faith in the incarnation, which needed no new formulation. What mattered to the Emperor, however, was a new formula which would correspond to the Eastern situation. The new formula was seen from the typical position of the imperial Church: it was to be a *formula of unity* which the whole Church in all the provinces of the empire could accept. The Alexandrians saw this project as an infringement of the agreement reached at Ephesus (431) that no new formula of faith was to be made.[36] There was a second cause of annoyance for them: Chalcedon declared that the *Tomus Leonis* was in agreement with the previous councils. Even if no new formula of faith had been forged, the Alexandrians would still have had a reason for rejecting the Council.

Just as there was clear difference between the Emperor and the Pope in determining the object of the Council, so there was also a difference of opinion with regard to the question of presidency at the Council. On the basis of his Petrine-idea, Leo had his own notions. On account of his experiences with Ephesus (449), Leo had become unexpectedly mistrustful of ecumenical synods, or better, ecumenical synods held in the East. He wanted to be on the safe side, and hoped to gain this security by having his legates preside. Before the Synod of 449, the Pope had been satisfied to have his legates participate.[37] Certainly, he had not made the presidency of

---

[34] Leo M., *ep.* 106 *ad Anatol. ep.*, 22 May, 452: ACO II 4, p. 60, 12–13. See below. Cf. *ep.* 160 *ad eppos et clerum Egypt.*, 21 March, 458: ACO II 4, nr. 100, p. 108, 5–7.

[35] Cf. the firm declaration of the imperial commissioners at the beginning of the fourth session a declaration certainly inspired by the Emperor: 'we are of the common opinion that a more exact investigation must be carried out ... into the orthodox catholic faith'. (ACO II 1, 2, p. 92). Nevertheless the Emperor recommends the more modern way, discussion.

[36] Cf. Can. VII: 'the holy synod has decreed that no one is permitted to produce or draw up or compose another faith (another creed of faith) apart from that defined by the holy Fathers who were gathered at Nicaea with the Holy Spirit'. (COD 1973³, p. 54, 16–55, 7).

[37] Cf. Leo M., *ep.* 33 *ad Synod. Ephesin.* (449): ACO II 4, nr. 12, p. 16, 2–3: '... I have sent (our brothers Julius, Renatus, Hilarus, Dulcitius) to participate (*intersint*) in my place in the holy

his legates a question of law, as the behaviour of his legates at the
Council testifies.[38] In fact, it was only once that Paschasinus presided,
and then in the third session.[39] Nevertheless, Leo firmly maintained
that his legates at the Council should have preserved the right of
presidency uninterrupted. This can only be a matter of 'interpreting'
the proceedings, and not of an historical, legal reality. Leo saw the
rôle of his legates within the theological perspective of his Petrine-idea
and of his conviction that the council has the Holy Spirit when 'Petrus'
meets with the bishops in questions of faith.[40] For all that the Pope
saw the participation in the Council as providing the necessary control. Where his representatives had given their assent, the work of
the council was definitive. Their assent is his approbation. This conception is very pointedly expressed in his letter to the bishops of ·
Gaul at the beginning of 452, thus immediately after the Council,
and in another letter to Theodoret of Cyrus, if this second letter
is genuine. In the first letter Leo informs the bishops of Gaul that
judgement was passed on Dioscorus by synods presided over by

gathering of your fraternity and to determine with you in common *sententia* what shall be pleasing
to the Lord...'. *After* this Council Leo is more cautious. After 449 no council ever again receives
an advance on trust from his side.
    [38] Leo M., *ep.* 89 *ad Marcian. aug.*, 24 June, 451: ACO II 4, nr. 46, p. 47, 34–48, 2: 'but because
some of the brothers [at Ephesus II], which we say not without sorrow, were unable to maintain
catholic constancy against the whirlwinds of falsehood, *it is appropriate (convenit)* that the said brother,
my fellow bishop (Paschasinus) preside over the synod in my place...'. This *'convenit'* is to be
noted. With regard to this, W. Kissling, op. cit. (see above, n. 30) 61, rightly says: 'thus Leo demands
a chairmanship at the Synod not on principle as a right to which he is entitled. But on the other
hand he does not simply request it, but for particular reasons he resolutely insists on it. Hence
at the third (more correctly, second) session he demands his delegates can say the Pope commissioned them
to have the chair in his place'. H. Gelzer, 'Die Konzilien als Reichsparlamente', *Ausgewälte kleine
Schriften* (Leipzig 1907) 142–155, would like to translate *praesidere* by 'to take first place' rather than
by 'to have the chair'. Cf. ACO II 1, 2, p. 8, 29: τὴν ἡμετέραν βραχύτητα ἀνθ'ἑαυτοῦ ταύτης
τῆς ἁγίας συνόδου προεδρεύειν ἐπέτρεψεν. Latin: Actio III, ACO II 3, 2, p.18: *nostram parvitatem
huic sancto concilio pro se praesidere praecipit....* Thus Leo ascribes to himself a certain claim of rightness
for the chairmanship at the Council without pressing it as a matter of law or being able to press
it at all at that time. Cf. also *ep.* 93, ACO II 4, nr. 52, p. 52, 10–11, where Leo writes to the
bishops who were for the time being gathered at Nicaea that he himself was not able to be present
at the Synod; but they should regard his emissaries as chairmen: *qui ab apostolica sede directi sunt,
me synodo vestra fraternitas aestimet praesidere....* Finally, *ep.* 103 to the bishops of Gaul: ACO II
4, nr. 112, p. 155, 18–19: *nam fratres mei qui vice mea Orientali synodo praesederunt ...* (see below).
On account of his experiences in 449, Leo thus intensified his demands without going as far as
he could. Hence one must not translate the '*praesidere' after 449* by the '*interesse' of 449*, as P. Stockmeier
does with reference to H. Gelzer (op. cit., 167).
    [39] Cf. W. de Vries, *OCP* 35 (1969) 73–76 = idem, *Orient et Occident* (Paris 1974) 111–114, with
reference to P. Battifol, *Le Siège apostolique*, 537, who is to the point when he states: 'the eighteen
high state officials, who represented the Emperor at the Council, did not have simply the commission
of being present at the sessions and caring for order, but they led the discussions. They did not
take part in the voting, but they presided, over the heads of the papal legates'. On the position
of the Emperor in the imperial Church, see R. Haacke, *Chalkedon* II, 96–101, with literature;
J. Gaudemet, *L'Église dans l'Empire Romain (IVᵉ–Vᵉ siècles)* (*Histoire du Droit et les Institutions de l'Église
en Occident, III*) (Paris 1958) § 3: Les Conciles, pp. 451–466. The statements of the latter are in
part very unguarded.
    [40] Leo M., *ep.* 89 *ad Marcian. aug.*, 24 June, 451: ACO II 4, nr. 46, p. 47, 28–30: (Leo speaks
of the despatch of his legates to the new council and their rôle in settling the dispute about faith,
a settlement based on his own position): ... *quoniam catholica fides quam instruente nos spiritu dei per
sanctos patres a beatis apostolis didicimus et docemus, neutrum sibi miscere permittit errorem.*

his legates in his place. He adds to this letter the text of the record of the condemnation of the Alexandrian bishop by his legates. This record, however, is given by Leo in a translation which differs markedly from the one which the deacon Rusticus later prepared from the Greek *acta* (ACO II 1, 2, p. 29, 14–20). On account of the significance of the variations, we give the final sentence of both forms of the text in parallel columns.

Leo M., *ep.* 103, ACO II 4, nr. 112, p. 156, 21–26

Unde sanctus ac beatissimus papa *caput universalis ecclesiae* per vicarios suos, sancta synodo consentiente, Petri apostoli *praeditus dignitate* qui ecclesiae fundamentum et petra fidei, caelestis regni ianitor nuncupatur, episcopali eum [D.] dignitate nudavit, et ab omni sacerdotali opere fecit extorrem. *Superest*, uti congregata venerabilis synodus canonicam contra praedictum Dioscorum proferat iustitia suadente sententiam.

('Whence the holy and most blessed Pope, *head of the whole Church, possessing the dignity* of the apostle Peter who is called the foundation of the Church and the rock of faith, the door-keeper of the heavenly kingdom, through his representatives, with the consent of the holy Synod, stripped him [Dioscorus] of his episcopal dignity and suspended him from every sacerdotal work. *It only remains* that the gathered venerable Council pronounce a just sentence on the said Dioscorus'.)

Rusticus, ACO II 3, 2, p. 46, 21–25

unde sanctissimus et beatissimus *archiepiscopus magnae senioris Romae* Leo per nos *et per* praesentem sanctam synodum *una cum* ter beatissimo et omni laude digno Petro apostolo, qui est petra et crepido catholicae ecclesiae et ille qui est rectae fidei fundamentum, nudavit eum tam episcopatus dignitate quam etiam et omni sacerdotali alienavit ministerio. Igitur sancta haec et magna synodus quae placent regulis, super memorato Dioscoro decernet.

('Whence the most holy and most blessed *Archbishop of great older Rome*, Leo, through us *and through* the present holy Synod *together with* the apostle Peter, worthy of all praise, who is the rock and base of the catholic Church and the foundation of right faith, stripped him [Dioscorus] of his episcopal dignity, as well as removing him from all sacerdotal ministry. Therefore, let this holy and great Synod in accord with the rules [canons] pass judgement on the said Dioscorus'.)

The two forms differ noticeably. In his text Leo gives an edge to the words of his legates (as given in the Greek text and the translation of Rusticus), which already express the primacy of the Bishop of Old Rome clearly enough. His own position was emphasised by the insertion that the Pope is 'head of the universal church'. Furthermore, the equal status of the legates and the synod in the original text was changed, with a slight alteration of language, into the subordination of the latter to the former. Finally, in the linguistic form adopted by Leo, the Petrine principle is applied more decisively to the Pope than happens in the formulation of the legates.

The relationship of council and Pope as understood by Leo would

be even more clearly formulated, were the disputed letter to Theodoret[41] already mentioned genuine:

> [The Lord] did not permit us to suffer any harm in our brothers [the members
> of the Synod], but what he had previously defined by our ministry (*ministerior defina-
> verat*) he confirmed through the assent of the whole brotherhood, in order to show
> that what was previously formulated by the first of all sees and had received the
> approval of the world truly proceeded from him, so that in this also the members
> may be in agreement with the head.[42]

If the letter to Theodoret, at least in this passage, were genuine,
Leo would be saying that God has defined the true faith through
the mouth of the Pope and given his grace to the Council so that
it knew the definition of Rome to be prompted by God, or to stem
from God, though admittedly mediated through Leo as an instrument. In fact, such sentences point ahead to the time when the canonical foundations of the rights of the Roman primacy would be laid.
Certainly such words were spoken from a purely Western standpoint

---

[41] On the question of the authenticity of Leo M., *ep.* 120, 11 June, 453, to Theodoret, let us
briefly say the following. E. Schwartz and T. G. Jallard, op. cit., 340ff., accept the letter as genuine
without further ado. C. Silva-Tarouca, TD 20, p. XXXIV–XXXVIII with reference to the Ballerini,
designates it as 'spuria'; idem, *Nuovi Studi*, p. 81f.; 155ff.; he places the edition of this letter in
an appendix to TD 20, pp, 169–175. P. Stockmeier, op. cit. (see above, n. 29) 165, n. 151, follows
Silva-Tarouca, but is unaware of the dissertation of H. M. Klinkenberg, *Römischer Primat und Reichskir-
chenrecht* (Diss. Köln 1950) (typescript); in this there is an excursus on the question of the transmission
and authenticity of the letter, viz. *ep.* 120, pp. 146–164. According to Klinkenberg, who investigates
the manuscript tradition anew, the beginning and the end of *ep.* 120 in their present form are certainly
genuine, and this includes also the sentence cited above; cf. idem, *ZSavSt.K* 38 (1952) (37–112)
93 with n. 128; H. Arens, *Die christologische Sprache Leos des Großen. Analyse d. Tomus an d. Patriarchen
Flavian = FrThSt* 122 (Freiburg-Basel-Wien 1982) 37–51. H. J. Sieben, *Die Konzilsidee der Alten
Kirche* (1979) 126ff., n. 75, is critical of Klinkenberg's thesis. The question is taken up
anew by R. Schieffer, 'Der Brief Leos d. Gr. an Theodoret von Kyros (CPG 9053)', ΑΝΤΙΔΩΡΟΝ
I 81–87. Schieffer is undoubtedly successful in settling the question. He leaves it open whether
'it is possible to delimit exactly a (certainly very slight) "genuine core"' (84). He insists, however,
on Leo's reference towards the end of the letter to an appended exemplar of his letter to Maximus
of Antioch (11 June, 453) (JK 495) (ACO II 4, p. 81, 19–27; Silva-Tarouca, TD 20, p. 174, 148–175),
and says: 'Perhaps JK in its original, genuine form was hardly more than a brief accompanying
letter to this copy, which then over a century later in an utterly changed situation was extended
to an ostensible witness defending the orthodoxy of Theodoret' (ibid., 85). Schieffer can produce
good reasons for the fact that *ep.* 120 in the text of the Grimanica must be placed in the dogmatic
discussions of the sixth century (see below on the Three Chapters Dispute), indeed after 553 'when
the opposition against the decision of 553 was limited geographically to northern Italy, especially
Aquileia, and when its literature exhausted itself in more or less successful historical fictions' (ibid.,
84). E. Schwartz let the opportunity slip of applying his hermeneutical knowledge of the origin
and purpose of 'publizistische Sammlungen', here the Grimanica, to the question of *ep.* 120.

[42] See Leo M., *ep.* 120: ACO II 4, p. 78, 24–27. Is this forcing of the teaching authority of
the Pope really to be ascribed to Leo himself? The idea that either Christ or Peter is himself active
in his representative is otherwise only present in an inauthentic letter, the '*Quali pertinacia*' addressed
to the bishops of Gaul, which is edited by G. Gundlach in *MGH Epistulae III*, pp. 90–91 (PL 54,
1237): 'with what obstinacy Hilarius, the Bishop of Arles, fled our decision, your holy brotherhood
is not ignorant. Whence we regard it as just that the Bishop of Arles did not expect the great
moderation in judgements of the prince of the apostles *which he always displays in power through
his vicars*'. H. J. Sieben, *Die Konzilsidee der Alten Kirche*, 126ff., n. 76 and 77, points emphatically
to the fact that Leo avoids the word *definire*, the *terminus technicus* for conciliar decrees and imperial
edicts, and with his *Tomus* brings to bear primarily *material*, not *formal* authority.

and must not be taken on the basis of the 'assensus' of the Fathers in 451.

One finds, however, also 'in the letters to the Pope from the East . . very positive statements about the primacy and even about its Petrine foundation. At the same time, however, we must take into account the actual proceedings of the Council to guard against conclusions that go too far'.[43] In the section of the (inauthentic) letter of Leo to Theodoret already quoted, the Pope binds the Petrine doctrine to the idea of the assent of the 'whole world'. Here Leo certainly stands in the tradition of the theologians who in the discussion about Nicaea attempted to provide a foundation for its truth and authority. He himself, one must admit, does not enter expressly into the question, but he does take over some elements of a theory of the council which was developing. Hence attention must be called to these elements, because for Leo they lay the foundation for the authority and validity of the Council of Chalcedon and its christological doctrine. In spite of his mistrust of every council,[44] the Pope could enter the fray very vigorously on behalf of councils already concluded and conciliar decrees already passed. This was particularly the case when the Alexandrian party disputed the validity of the Council of Chalcedon and demanded a new one. For him the Council of Nicaea held a special position. After this Council had prevailed in the fourth century, it gained a new significance in the christological conflict of the fifth and sixth centuries. One can see this first of all in the struggle

---

[43] W. de Vries, 'Strukturen der Kirche...', OCP 35 (1969) 98. Ibid., 98–111 (cf. idem *Occident et Orient* (Paris 1974) 136–149), deals with 'Primacy from the Eastern viewpoint' and comes to the conclusion: 'the primacy is no doubt more clearly recognised at Chalcedon than at other councils. But even here Rome (with its further claims) could not carry the day. The consciousness of the collegial authority of the bishops at the Council was too strong for this' (111). When de Vries, ibid., says that the so-called Canon 28, despite the well-known difficulties from Leo's side, became 'immediately the law in force in the East', one may take this statement further. This Canon was in practice the law in force since 381. Only in the West one had been unaware of this. According to *ep.* 105 ad Pulcher.: ACO II 4, nr. 55, p. 58, 23, Anatolius points to a sixty-year old tradition, which Leo did not want to acknowledge. But the Alexandrians also ignored the Council of 381. Cf. E. Honigmann, 'Juvenal of Jerusalem', *DOP* 5 (1950) (211–279) 236f., 247, where Honigmann indicates the principal reason for Leo's rejection of Canon 28: Anatolius cannot make of Constantinople an 'apostolica sedes'; Leo M., *ep.* 104 ad Marcian. aug., 22 May, 452: ACO II 4, nr. 54, p. 56, 19. In our analysis of the *Codex encyclius* we shall return to this question.

[44] Cf. Leo M., *ep.* 119 ad Maxim. Antiochen. ep., 11 June, 453: ACO II 4, p. 74, 9–12: 'subripiendi enim occasiones non praetermittit ambitio et quotiens ob occurrentes causas generalis congregatio facta fuerit sacerdotum, difficile est ut cupiditas improborum non aliquid supra mensuram suam moliatur appetere, sicut etiam de Ephesena synodo...'. Leo means Juvenal's attempt at the Council of Ephesus (431) to extend his jurisdiction. Leo found the same ambition in Anatolius and his efforts on behalf of the so-called Canon 28. One is reminded of Gregory Nazianzen, *ep.* 130 ad Procopium: 'it is my decision to flee all gatherings of bishops, because I have not yet seen a council that had reached a happy conclusion and brought an end to our troubles, rather than increasing them. One experiences there only chicanery and disputes about precedence which surpass anything that one could say ... And if one were to have the audacity to reprimand the bishops, still they would rather accuse him of lack of faith than be brought to the renunciation of evil' (translated from J. Barbel, *Gregor von Nazianz, Fünf Theologische Reden*, (Düsseldorf 1963), 18–19).

against Nestorius, as the proceedings of the Council of Ephesus show,[45] but then also in the confrontation with the Alexandrians who ascribe more and more significance to the Council of 325 and who see *their* christology established in it (according to the pattern of Ephesus (431)). For Leo, particularly on the level of ecclesiastical politics, Nicaea became the symbol of immutability. When the attempt was made from Constantinople to press the claim of patriarchal priority on the basis of the great number of council Fathers at Chalcedon—greater than the number at Nicaea!—Leo was not impressed. Though another synod produce just as high a number of council Fathers, Nicaea is and remains, for all that, unchangeable.

No council should flatter itself on the increased number of the assembly. No number, no matter how high, of priests (*sacerdotum* = bishops) should dare to compare itself with or take precedence over those 318 bishops, because the Synod of Nicaea had been held with such a great privilege bestowed by God that everything which stands in opposition to its decree loses all authority, even if the ecclesiastical tribunals (*ecclesiastica iudicia*) were held with more or fewer synodal members.[46]

The Pope, together with Empress Pulcheria, would go even so far as to declare as invalid (*unita nobiscum vestrae fidei pietate in irritum mittimus*) agreements of bishops (*consensiones episcoporum*) which contradict the sacred canons of Nicaea. With the authority of the blessed apostle Peter he would 'annul' (*cassamus*) them in one general definition and thus obey in all ecclesiastical matters the laws which the Holy Spirit through the 318 bishops had ordered to be observed peacefully by all priests (bishops).

Although compared with them ever so many decide something different from what they decided, whatever differs from the ordinances enacted by them deserves no consideration at all.[47]

---

[45] Cf. A. Grillmeier, CCT I², 484–487; JdChr I², 687–691.

[46] Leo M., *ep*. 106 *ad Anatol. ep.*, 22 May, 452: ACO II 4, nr. 56, p. 60, 16–21; cf. *ep*. 104 *ad Marcian. aug.*: ACO II 4, nr. 54, p. 56, 20–22. Leo does not indicate how he knows of Nicaea's special right. The only special right that is demonstrable is that of its reception which had been particularly reflected upon and fought for. Nicaea had a special significance for Rome, insofar as the Canons of the Council of Serdica (342), which dealt with the right of appeal to the Bishop of Rome, were later passed off as Canons of the Council of Nicaea. Cf. F. X. Funk—K. Bihlmeyer—H. Tüchle, *Kirchengeschichte I* (Paderborn ¹²1951) § 64, 1. In our context, however, Canon 6 of Nicaea (in the interpolated Roman form mentioned above), which settles the order of precedence of episcopal sees, is decisive. See above ch. I, n. 56.

[47] Leo M., *ep*. 105 *ad Pulcher. aug.*, 22 May, 452: ACO II 4, nr. 55, p. 58, 33–59, 4. Cf. *ep*. 119 *ad Maximum Antioch. ep.*: ACO II 4, nr. 66, p. 74, 8–9: 'and it will be easier for contracts of whatever agreement to be dissolved (*consensionum pacta dissolvi*) than for the rules of the said canons to be infringed'. What deviates from Nicaea can never find the assent of the Apostolic See (p. 74, 29–30). From the viewpoint of the imperial Church, did Leo undertake too much, if he believed—even with the assent of Pulcheria, should she be able to be reached—that he could exercise a right of annulment against a conciliar decision that did not meet with his favour? He could refuse his assent, but he could not 'annul' it. It is striking that the demands which he made simultaneously to Marcian and Pulcheria are formulated more strongly in his letter to Pulcheria than they are in his letter to Marcian.

The notion of a council is the only thing of interest to us here. Nicaea is utterly irrevocable, even when it is only a question of the regulations of Church law. Even a synod such as Chalcedon can change nothing in this regard.

Leo can thus understand the competence and the significance of Chalcedon in a relative sense. But the motivation for this comes only from Canon 28. When it is a matter of the *causa fidei*, he can emphasise unequivocally the immutability of this Council as well; he does this when he sees that the Alexandrians or the Emperor are striving for a new council in order to repeal the last. To want to repeal Chalcedon would also mean making Nicaea invalid. Leo emphasises this connexion, because the Alexandrians lay claim to the Council of 325 for themselves and play it off against Chalcedon.[48] Thus the Fourth General Council appears more and more as being of equal standing with the First Council, and this happens for the very reason that both synods stand in the same relationship to their authentic source: the evangelic and apostolic tradition.[49] In one of his last letters, *ep.* 164, Leo rounds off his conception of Chalcedon, and more or less of councils in general, even if other letters need to be consulted to complete the picture.

What is well regulated must in no way be revoked. For to want to quarrel still about such legitimate and divinely inspired ordinances is not a sign of a peaceful spirit, but of one that is rebellious. ... For if one is at liberty to discuss human convictions constantly [afresh], then there will never fail to be those who dare to militate against the truth. [Leo indicates the futility of false rhetoric.] ... The holy Synod of Chalcedon has been celebrated by all the provinces of the Roman empire with the consensus of the whole world (*quae ab universis Romani orbis provinciis cum totius mundi est celebrata consensu*) and is completely one with the decrees of the most holy Nicene Council. Because now the holy Synod of Chalcedon has separated all the ungodliness of the Eutychian doctrine (*Eutychiani dogmatis*) from the body of the catholic community, how can one of the fallen have the intention of returning

[48] Cf. Leo M., *ep.* 156 *ad Leon. aug.*, 1 December, 457: ACO II 4, nr. 97, p. 102, 25–27: 'in no way could it happen that we could have sentiments against the holy Synod of Nicaea, as the heretics lie (about us) who pretend (*configunt*) to hold (*tenere*) the faith of the Council of Nicaea'. On this, *ep.* 164 *ad Leon. aug.*, 17 August, 458: ACO II 4, nr. 103, p. 112, 30–34: 'For whoever is so forgetful of Christian hope and his own salvation that, in order to contort the most sacred Council of Nicaea, he ventures to violate the evangelic, apostolic decree of the holy Synod of Chalcedon, this person ... we condemn'. It was certainly not the intention of the Alexandrians to destroy the teaching of Nicaea. According to Leo, however, they deny the truth of the incarnation, and hence annul the Council.

[49] Leo M., *ep.* 162 *ad Leon. aug.*, 21 March, 458: ACO II 4, nr. 99, p. 106, 30–32: 'those who do not follow the definitions of the venerable Synod of Nicaea or (*vel!*) the rules of the holy Council of Chalcedon are in no way to be reckoned as catholics, for it is clear that the holy decrees of both (synods) proceed from the evangelic and apostolic source'. Immediately following this, Leo expresses the parity of both councils: '... about the things which both at Nicaea and at Chalcedon were defined in accord with God's good pleasure, we do not dare to enter into negotiations (*tractatus*), as if those things were doubtful or weak (*infirma*) which so great an authority had decided through the Holy Spirit (*quae tanta per sanctum spiritum fixit auctoritas*)'.

to the peace of the Church before he is cleansed by perfect satisfaction (*perfecta satisfactione*) [cit. I Joh 4, 2: *Omnis spiritus qui confitetur . . .*]? Full of respect and with tenacity we must hold to the former instruction of the Holy Spirit, lest—if a debate of such things [i.e. the decisions of the Council] be permitted—authority be withdrawn from what has been defined under divine inspiration (*ne dum talium disceptatio ammittitur, his quae divinitus definita sunt, auctoritas derogetur*). In well-founded peace may the faith ratified at Chalcedon be preserved in every part of your empire and in the whole world. Whoever separates himself from our community and from unity is unworthy of the name of Christian.[50]

Several reasons for the '*auctoritas*' of Chalcedon are named here— beyond the decisive one that this Council (just as Nicaea) contains the evangelic and apostolic teaching.[51] Although Leo is convinced that strictly speaking every believer could establish the agreement between council and apostolic teaching, he names further reasons for the authority of Chalcedon. Two reasons stand in the foreground: (1) the Council had the assistance of the Holy Spirit, his *inspiratio*; (2) through this inspiration the Fathers came to a *consensus*. A further reason is only intimated: the notion of the *repraesentatio* of the whole Church, which must be seen, however, in connexion with the notion of *consensus*. This is not considered more closely. It would have to be seen above all in the framework of the structure of the imperial Church. One question will deserve attention: how do all these special reasons given for the *auctoritas* of the Council of Chalcedon relate to the one decisive reason—its evangelic, apostolic quality?

(a) The Council and the *inspiratio* of the Holy Spirit

Numerous letters centre on this topic. Whatever may take place against Chalcedon (e.g. in Alexandria) 'cannot signify a prejudice against the Synod of Chalcedon; that which through the instruction of the Holy Spirit has been defined for the salvation of the whole world must remain inviolate'.[52] Indeed, at 'this Council which was assembled by the Holy Spirit everything was laid down in definitions so comprehensive and perfect that nothing can be added to or removed from this rule which issued from divine inspiration'.[53] But how did the Pope know about this inspiration or about the assistance

[50] Leo M., *ep.* 164 *ad Leon. aug.*, 17 August, 458: ACO II 4, nr. 103, p. 110, 33–112, 2.

[51] Leo refers to the fact that the Emperor should restore the original state of affairs in Alexandria and the freedom of this Church by installing a bishop who observes the decisions of Chalcedon and thus also agrees with the 'evangelic discipline': *antistes illic Calchedonensis synodi statuta custodiens et concordans evangelicis disciplinis . . . ordinetur* (ibid., p. 112, 21ff.).

[52] Leo M., *ep.* 144 *ad Iulian. ep.*, 1 June, 457: ACO II 4, nr. 106, p. 138, 35–37: . . . *quae instruente spiritu sancto ad totius mundi salutem definita sunt, inviolata permaneant.*

[53] Leo M., *ep.*, 145 *ad Leon. aug.*, 10 July, 457: ACO II 4, nr. 87, p. 96, 4–6. Cf. *ep.* 147 *ad Iulian. ep.*: ACO II 4, nr. 89, p. 97, 21–23 (agreement of this definition from divine inspiration with apostolic and evangelic teachings); *ep.* 149 and 150 *ad Basilium Antioch. ep.*: ACO II 4, nr. 90/91, p. 98, 23–24 (emphasis on the inspiration of the Council, with regard to which any *novitas* no longer has any place): 'because, something which must be emphasised time and time again, the whole Christian religion is thrown into disorder when anything that was decided at Chalcedon

of the Holy Spirit? Certainly he had received this confidence from ecclesial tradition, and in particular from the synodal practice of the Western Church.[54] But we must again bear in mind that Leo is convinced that the assistance of the Holy Spirit is guaranteed to a council through *his* mediation (i.e. his mediate or immediate participation) as the successor of Peter. His letters 89 and 120 (if the latter is authentic: see above) have shown this. In any case, as Leo's reaction to Ephesus (449) shows, it is unthinkable for him that a synodical decision which came into existence against the assent of the apostolic see of Rome could have the assistance of the Holy Spirit.

(b) The Consensus Patrum

A special guarantee of the validity and efficacy of a conciliar decision is its unanimity. From the very beginning, this—as a moral attitude—was accepted as a characteristic of the Christian community (cf. Act 2, 46; 5, 12). The bond between *consensus* and truth had already a strong non-Christian tradition, before it was utilised for the interpretation of the councils. The catch-phrase of this tradition is '*consensus omnium gentium*'.[55] Aristotle was the one who established the recognition of universal thought. The Stoics and the Epicureans, with their doctrine of the inner perception which resides in the nature of man, added the detailed psychological foundation of the *consensus*.

The nature of man which is grasped in the self-perception of the I is the same in every man. Hence it produces only one sole decree, one sole law, one sole state in which the spirit of cosmopolitanism reigns. This changed attitude towards the world and man rests upon a new doctrine of human community, viz. the doctrine of the natural relationship of all men, the οἰκείωσις-doctrine.[56]

Admittedly, in Leo's writings hardly any connexion with ancient philosophy can be discerned. To the extent that the notion of *consensus* is found in his writings, it has been mediated through the Church.[57]

---

is destroyed *(convellitur)*'. On the principle that nothing may be added to the Council or taken from it, cf. Dt 4, 2 Vulg.: *addere-auferre*; Isidor of Pelusium: PG 78, 1163: 'the holy Synod which met in Nicaea is to be followed, without anything being added or subtracted; for, inspired by God, it "dogmatised" the truth' (quoted from H. J. Sieben op. cit. (see n. 17), 220). Here Sieben also deals with the idea of the inspiration of the Council with reference to G. Bardy, 'L'inspiration des Pères de l'Église', *RSR* 40 (1952) 7–26, in particular 23–25.

[54] Cf. H. J. Sieben, op. cit., 220–221.

[55] Cf. K. Oehler, 'Der consensus omnium als Kriterium der Wahrheit in der antiken Philosophie und der Patristik. Eine Studie zur Geschichte der Allgemeinen Meinung', idem, *Antike Philosophie und Byzantinisches Mittelalter. Aufsätze zu Geschichte des griechischen Denkens* (München 1969) 234–271; R. Schian, *Untersuchungen über das 'argumentum e consensu omnium'* = Spudasmata 28 (Hildesheim 1973); G. Sauter, 'Consensus', *TRE* 8, 182–189. On the more recent theological discussion of the concept of consensus see G. Sauter, 'Konsens als Ziel und Voraussetzung theologischer Erkenntnis', P. Lengsfeld/H.-G. Stobbe (Ed.), *Theologischer Konsens und Kirchenspaltung* (Stuttgart 1981) 52–63; J. Wohlmuth, 'Konsens als Wahrheit? Versuch einer theologischen Klärung', *ZKTh* 103 (1981) 309–323; P. Højen, 'Wahrheit und Konsensus. Ein Beitrag Ökumenischer Theologie zum Verhältnis zwischen Wahrheit und Geschichte', *KuD* 23 (1977) 131–156.

[56] K. Oehler, art. cit., 243. On Aristotle, ibid., 237–241.

[57] Cf. the witnesses named by K. Oehler: I Clement, Irenaeus, Hippolytus, Cyprian and others.

To be sure, a typically Roman element makes its appearance, when Leo compares the indissolubility of the canons of Nicaea with the inviolability of any agreement whatever: *'quarumlibet consensionum pacta'*. It is only the association of ideas that is important here. One must not be seduced into interpreting Nicaea, for example, as *'consensionum pactum'*. The point of comparison, the tertium comparationis, is the stability. But the bond between 'council' and *'consensus'* is intrinsic, being all the more significant the more a council really brings together the representatives of the Christian *oikumene* or of the *orbis Romanus*. Hence the notion of *consensus* is tied to that of *repraesentatio*, even if Leo does not use this term in this context. For Leo, the ideal *consensus* is attained when bishops from all the provinces have gathered at a council, and are at one in the unity of the decision.[58] It is significant that in this context Leo refers to the gospel as the unifying point for the whole *orbis terrarum*. Unity in the evangelic and apostolic tradition is the necessary goal of all conciliar endeavour. Thus Leo has traced the notion of *consensus* back to its authentic ground—the ground which dominates his idea of a council.[59]

The reader may be reminded briefly of the fact that the valuation of the so-called acclamations[60] was a classical element in the notion

[58] Leo M., *ep.* 105 *ad Pulcher. aug.*, 22 May, 452: ACO II 4, nr. 55, p. 57, 26–30: 'once the whole earth had been confirmed in unity of faith and the hearts of all the bishops (*sacerdotum*) had been directed to the same opinion (*in eundem sensum directis*), it was best that beyond those things on account of which the holy Synod had been assembled ... nothing contrary to such a great good should be introduced' (viz. the so-called Canon 28). But in contrast to Leo, Anatolius had also emphasised the unity of the decision for this canon (in *ep.* 101: ACO II 1, 2, nr. 15, p. 53, 36–54, 6). Only the papal legates did not join in. Particularly in his pre-Chalcedonian letters to Marcian and Anatolius, Leo had spoken of the representation of all provinces at the coming Council. Thus in *ep.* 83 *ad Marcian. aug.*, 9 June, 451: ACO II 4, nr. 41, p. 43, 11–14: '... we also demanded that there be a synod (*synodum fieri*), but the plight of the present time in no way allows the bishops of all the provinces (!) to gather, for those provinces, from which especially (*maxime*) (bishops) are to be summoned, are disturbed by war, thus hindering them from leaving their Churches, (hence above all the bishops of North Italy and Gaul): cf. *ep.* 89 *ad Marcian. aug.*, 24 June, 451: ACO II 4, nr. 46, p. 47, 15–20: 'we believed that Your Clemency would meet our desire and, in view of the present plight, would order that the episcopal synod be postponed to a more suitable time, so that the bishops could be summoned from all the provinces and there would be a truly universal council'. The same request is found in *ep.* 90 *ad Marcian. aug.*, 26 June, 451: ACO nr. 47, p. 48: *ep.* 91 *ad Anatol. ep.*, 26 June, 451: ACO nr. 48, p. 49: '... for when could we send (messengers or invitations) through all the various and distant provinces, so that there could really be a universal council?'.

[59] K. Oehler, op. cit., 257f. establishes a connexion between the idea of *consensus* and Christian thought on tradition: 'the argument of tradition is also held consistently by Hippolytus ... On the unity of truth rests the unity of the true, apostolic teaching, and on the latter rests the unity of the Church. Whoever cuts himself off from her, whether it be in his concrete way of life or in his teaching, deviates from the indivisible truth whose bearer is solely the one, indivisible Church. In its structure this principle calls to mind the formulation of Seneca (*Dial.* 7, 8, 6): *summum bonum esse animi concordiam; virtutes enim ita esse debebunt, ubi consensus atque unitas erit: dissidentia vitia*. This ethical concept of *consensus* held by Seneca has entered as well into early Christianity's awareness of Church politics and the economy of salvation'. For Leo, however, something else is certainly to the fore: the one truth and the aspect of the question concerned with the politics of the imperial Church (see below).

[60] E. Peterson, Εἷς Θεός. *Epigraphische, formgeschichtliche und religionsgeschichtliche Untersuchungen* (FRLANT N.F. 24) (Göttingen 1926) Sections III and IV: 141–227; Art. 'Akklamationen' by T. Klauser, *RAC* I (1950) 216–233; K. Oehler, op. cit., 253.

of *consensus*. In fact we also find acclamations in the history of Chalcedon, namely by the bishops and by the people. They are the expression of the *consensus* inspired by the Holy Spirit. But already in the history of the Roman Emperors they were of great significance.[61] In connexion with the Synod of Ephesus (449) two witnesses report acclamations inspired by the Holy Spirit—though in contrary senses. The *acta* which have been passed down in Syriac naturally present Dioscorus in a good light. When it was a question of the deposition of Bishop Ibas of Edessa, twelve monks from this city first of all gave an account of the acclamations against the bishop given by the people before the imperial officials for days on end. At the Synod itself, when Ibas was condemned and deposed, the Council broke into loud shouting. Dioscorus interpreted with his statement: 'That was the Holy Spirit screaming through you'.[62] Indeed, loud crying out was the distinguishing mark of the influence of the Holy Spirit—without doubt, an enthusiastic, mantic element. It is of interest to note that Leo also attributed the influence of the Holy Spirit to those who dissented from Dioscorus. At the Council of 449, the acclamations of the orthodox people of Constantinople were reported to Leo in Rome. By these acclamations he discerned that the faithful of Constantinople had not succumbed to the Manichaean error of Eutyches.[63] That is probably the sole demonstrable point of contact between Leo and the classical *consensus* doctrine. Even the 'transmission' of acclamations has its parallels in the history of the emperors. According to *Cod. Theod.* VIII 5, 32, the messengers of such attestations by the people may even use the imperial post. All statements of *consensus* at a council should not, however, be interpreted in a mantic or enthusiastic manner. Normally *consensus* is the factual outcome of the *sententiam rogare*, i.e. the straightforward expression of differing opinions. Even when partisan passion plays a rôle, the bishops speak along the lines of their theological traditions.

Institution and enthusiasm can, moreover, be closely connected. First of all it is possible to establish the institutionalisation of even such a dynamic factor as the acclamations. There are many indications

---

[61] Cf. E. Peterson, op. cit., 145, who gives an example from Cassius Dio (75, 4 Boissevain) from the year 193; he experienced spontaneous, simultaneous and unanimous acclamations of the people, and comments on these as follows: 'thus they were roused to enthusiasm by a divine breath ... For otherwise so many thousands of men neither would have begun all at once, like a practised choir, to shout the same thing, nor would they have shouted faultlessly, like one who has practised'. Cf. K. Oehler, op. cit., 253f. For the transfer of this conception of enthusiastic acclamation to the proceedings of a council and other gatherings, cf. E. Peterson, ibid., 144–152.

[62] Cf. J. Fleming, *AbhGöttGW*, Phil.-hist. Kl. N.F. Bd. XV, 1 (Berlin 1917) 15–19; 57, 10–12. On κράζειν, cf. Rom 8, 16; Gal 4, 6.

[63] Cf. Leo M., *ep.* 59, *ad cives Constant.*: ACO II 4, nr. 34, p. 34, 5–11: *gaudemus et in sanctae plebis acclamationibus, quarum ad nos exempla delata sunt, omnium vestorum probamus affectum ...* etc. Cf. Leo M., *ep.* 61: ACO II 4, nr. 27, p. 28; cf. on this the comments of the Ballerini in PL 54, 1224, n. 35 and 36.

that from the middle of the third century at the latest the number
of times an acclamation was repeated was recorded in the senate
minutes. There is documentary evidence for this practice from the
first half of the fifth century.[64] This repetition, which could easily
be produced by a clever manager, is not to be appraised in the first
instance as anything other than, for example, the 'curtain-calls' for
a play. But in a religious act, such as a council, one is quickly prepared
to trace the acclamation and its intensity back to the Holy Spirit.
For this reason the idea of the inspiration of such events needs to
be tested critically. This does not mean that acclamation, as a simple
abbreviated form of voting, is inadmissable. The value of a conciliar
vote is determined finally by the depth of the theological discussions
and by the freedom of the vote.

3. The immutability of the Chalcedonian decisions

The way in which all the various reasons for the *auctoritas* of the
Council of Chalcedon are ordered into a single whole in Leo's view
can be understood by a look at the 'result'. With his emphasis upon
the inspiration of the Council and its unanimity, Leo's final goal
is this: in the struggle for the recognition of the Synod, it should
be set down as immutable and irrevocable. Against the voice of the
Holy Spirit any *novitas* is out of order. In comparison with a world-
wide *consensus* no particular opinion counts anymore. Fullness permits
no increase. What has been well worked out requires no subsequent
work. Finally, whoever will not hear the community of the Church
or the voice from above should withdraw from the Church and live
according to his own opinions. The questions have been so unambiguously explained 'that what has been established in all the past centuries in accord with the gospel of Christ and the truth of apostolic
teaching by one faith and one understanding can no longer be destroyed by any further undertaking'.[65] Chalcedon has entered into

---

[64] K. Oehler, op. cit., 253. The Roman Synod of 13 March, 495, where Gelasius was acclaimed
as *vicarius Christi*, offers an example of the counting of acclamations. Cf. Gelasius I, *ep.* 30, 15:
Thiel 447.

[65] Leo M., *ep.* 145 *ad Leon. aug.*, 10 July, 457: ACO II 4, nr. 87, p. 96, 11–13: ... *ut quae secundum
evangelium Christi et praedicationis apostolicae veritatem omnibus retro saeculis una fide unaque intelligentia
roborata sunt, nulla ulterius possint actione convelli.* In further letters from this time he speaks in the
same way: *ep.* 152 *ad Iulian. ep.*, 1 September, 457: ACO II 4, nr. 93, p. 99, 17–18: Emperor
Leo will certainly intervene, *ne bene finita atque composita aliqua possint novitate violari. Ep.* 153 *ad
Aetium presb.*, 1 September, 457: ACO II 4, nr. 94, p. 99, 35–37: 'with regard to the mystery
(*sacramentum*) of catholic faith (= the incarnation), it is not for us to engage any longer in conflicts,
because nothing can be investigated more diligently or defined more truly'. Chalcedon signifies
a conclusion. In *ep.* 156 *ad Leon. aug.*, 1 December, 457: ACO II 4, nr. 97, p. 102, 2–7, besides
the assistance of the Holy Spirit, the importance of the Church's teaching authorities is also given
prominence. If we give in to the endeavours inimical to Chalcedon, 'we shall appear to root up
that which has been well established and at the whim of heretical request to weaken the authorities
which the universal Church has embraced. and hence seem to set no criterion for Churches in
conflict, but to expand the permission given to rebel rather than to calm conflicts'. Leo combines
with this the Petrine idea and emphasises the coherence in tradition with Nicaea, which the opposition

the unchangeable tradition of the Church, and can never disappear from it.

In the post-Chalcedonian letters of Leo we see thus that in the confrontation with the Alexandrian opposition Chalcedon is more and more 'built up' as the 'immutable and irrevocable Council'. With this development there occurs a precedent which affects not just the narrower history of the Fourth General Council, but the Church's understanding of councils in general. This concerns the Church's becoming aware of the rôle which Chalcedon has in the paradosis with regard to the true incarnation of the Son of God. Leo's thought always begins with this central point. He knows that the *causa fidei* which was endangered by Eutyches is guaranteed by the decision of faith of 451. For this reason the Pope no longer has to say much about the Council—his long silence proclaims this. The Council has already fulfilled its function, and the Church has really no need to look to this Council as such. The Church could simply continue to live her paradosis with regard to Christ according to the teachings of the Fathers, in particular of Nicaea. But the opponents who wished to eliminate the Council used as a lever the question of the legitimacy and orthodoxy of the Council as such. As Chalcedon had led to the liquidation of Ephesus (449), so now again the Council of 451 should be put into liquidation. For this reason Leo directs his thoughts to the legitimacy of Chalcedon, its irrevocability and its validity. Naturally, his intention is focused, as it was before, on the proclamation of faith or the content of the conciliar statement. But now he defends it by shoring up conciliar authority as such. This protective

claim for themselves (p. 102, 25–27). *Ep. 157 ad Anatol. ep.*: ACO nr. 102, p. 109, 37–38: the Egyptians work for a new synod. Whoever assents to these 'machinationes' 'will separate himself from the community of the catholic Church, for in accord with divine inspiration there is a conviction (*sententia*) with regard to faith in the incarnation of the Lord and with regard to the protection of the Synod of Chalcedon of the universal Church, and particularly in our regions (*partibus!*) the evangelic doctrine is so strongly held that it is considered a great sacrilege to deviate from apostolic tradition even in the slightest'.

Finally the concept of *auctoritas* comes in here: *ep.* 160 to the Egyptian refugees who were sojourning in Constantinople: ACO II 4, nr. 100, p. 108, 7ff.: 'for of those things defined, which the authority of such a great synod and the most Christian of princes sanctions and which the assent of the Apostolic See confirmed, nothing need be discussed, lest it seem that something be made void (*infringi*) in an unlawful way . . .'. *Ep. 161 ad Clerum Constant.*, 21 March, 458: ACO II 4, nr. 101, p. 108: if a discussion (*disceptatio*) is allowed over Chalcedon, its authority is withdrawn. According to C. Silva-Tarouca, *Nuovi Studi*, 183, the authenticity of the letter is suspect in part. *Ep.* 162 *ad Leon. aug.*, 21 March, 458: ACO II 4, nr. 101, p. 106, 5–11: '. . . whatever has been devoutly and fully (*plene*) defined must not be called again into any discussion, lest we ourselves appear at the whim of those condemned (*ad arbitrium damnatorum*) to have doubts about the things which in everything accord with the authority of the prophets, the gospels and the apostles. Whence if there are some who dissent from these things which are heavenly constituted, let them be left to their own opinions and let them leave the unity of the Church (*ab unitate Ecclesiae . . . discedant*) with that perversity which they have chosen. For it is in no way possible that those who dare to contradict the divine mysteries may associate with us in any *communio*'. On the Emperor's new plans for a council, which Leo energetically rejects in *ep.* 162, cf. T. G. Jallard, op. cit. (above n. 1), 388.

rôle is emphasised so much that Leo in no way reflects upon the theological advance which the Council had brought to the interpretation of the incarnation. In other words, the Pope never attempts to show the significance that Chalcedon has in taking a new step in the linguistic and conceptual formulation of faith in the incarnation. Or to put this in modern terms, the necessity of a hermeneutic for a conciliar formula that is so shocking is not seen. The linguistic, conceptual element of the new conciliar formula is not analysed. It is not interpreted for the opponents, nor is it appraised for the intrinsic legitimation of the Council; it is merely 'affirmed'. A hermeneutic would have been the only way to make it clear that the new formula of faith could also do justice to the theological concerns of the Alexandrians. On their side the Alexandrians were just as little capable of presenting their concerns hermeneutically as Leo was. Only a hermeneutic would have been able to build a bridge of understanding between the kerygma of the incarnation, as Chalcedon intended to pass it on and passed it on, and the increased emphasis on the formal authority of the Council which surrounded the new formulation of faith. Because the 'pontifex' did not grasp that he should build this bridge of understanding, Leo conducted his battle for Chalcedon with the 'anathema', a weapon that was too severe. He laid the ground for 'Chalcedonian orthodoxy', by which the opponents were separated out as 'heretics'. The strong authoritative emphasis on the validity of the Council was a substitute for a theological method which was lacking at that time. This was a deficiency under which not only Leo but also the Church of that period laboured. It must be said to Leo's credit that silence with regard to the propagation of the monophysite formula in the whole of the West and in many parts of the East would have unleashed boundless confusion in the Church. Unfortunately a new element was added; in this struggle for truth the machinery of the imperial Church was introduced. This meant that the problems were dealt with 'from outside' in a twofold fashion: not only by ecclesiastical authority, but also by sacral, state authority. Thus one must situate Leo's conception of a council and his fight for Chalcedon within the structure of the imperial Church, insofar as he recognised and used this itself as a factor in the solution of Chalcedonian questions.

4. *Leo's conception of a council situated within the structure of the imperial Church*

In all the endeavours of the Pope to exert his influence within or against the system of the imperial Church, he still remained tied to the thought of this imperial Church. In fact, he used this framework to advocate the validity and immutability of the Council of

Chalcedon which he defended. It is only in this respect that we have to discuss the imperial Church, which in the history of doctrine must be taken very seriously. For it is precisely on account of the institution of the imperial Church that the old dogmas come under the suspicion of owing their existence to a structure or to the functioning of a machinery, and not to the dynamism of the paradosis within the Church. The Emperor's occupation with theological questions met with Leo's complete approval, in as much as, indeed, because the protection of orthodox faith seemed to be guaranteed to him. If the Emperor acts on behalf of the Church, this is also to the advantage of the empire.[66] Leo's trust in the rôle of the Emperor can only be understood on the basis of a conception which encompasses Church and state. The world, history, human welfare, Church and state are conceived from the viewpoint of God, who uses the Roman Emperor for the purpose of allowing the whole human race to participate in his *providentia*. From this point of view it seems quite natural to attribute to the ruler functions which are proper to the Church. The connexion between religion, faith, Church and the secular domain is so close that the secular order is also interpreted from the viewpoint of religion (i.e. from the viewpoint of God through the mediation of the Emperor). As it were the Church is interpreted as only a specific and concrete realisation of this sacral dimension which encompasses everything. The Emperor stands at the summit of the pyramid under which the human race and the Church are safe. One God, one religion, one Emperor, one Church, calm within and without in 'ecclesial and royal peace'.[67] This one sacral order can be threatened by only two enemies: by heretics and by barbarians.[68] Hence the Emperor must fight against both.

A fair amount of old Roman tradition and a considerable part of

---

[66] Leo M., *ep.* 140 *ad Iulian. ep.*, 6 December, 454: ACO II 4, nr. 83, p. 94, 15–17: Julian of Cius is to convey the appropriate suggestions to the Emperor at the right time (*oportunas suggestiones*), 'because in many experiences we have proved that it is the faith of the most glorious *augustus* that he is convinced that he serves his kingdom most when he particularly applies himself to work for the integrity of the Church'. *Ep.* 142 *ad Marican, aug.*, 13 March, 455: ACO II 4, nr. 86, p. 95, 12–13: Leo does not cease to pray for the welfare of the ruler, 'because the Church and the Roman *res publica* are greatly taken care of by God through your welfare'. *Ep.* 146 *ad Anatol. ep.*, 10 July, 457: ACO II 4, nr. 88, p. 96, 30–31: *et Romana res publica et religio Christiana* should rejoice at the virtues of the new Emperor Leo. Similarly, *ep.* 147: ACO II 4, p. 97, 28–29: the security of the empire is the calm of the Church.

[67] Leo M., *ep.* 154 *ad eppos. Egyptiorum*: ACO II 4, nr. 96, p. 101 (suspect according to C. Silva-Tarouca, *Nuovi Studi*, p. 158, 184): *ecclesiastica pace et regia*! In this passage ecclesiastical peace is placed before *pax regia*, and this twofold protection holds good for the *mysterium* of the divine economy of salvation or the mystery of the incarnation. In *Tr.* LXXXII, 1 (22 June, 441): Chavasse CCL 138A, p. 509, 1.30, Leo speaks of the *pax christiana*. See H. Fuchs, 'Augustin und der antike Friedensgedanke', *Neue Philolog. Untersuchungen 3* (Berlin 1926) 214–223.

[68] Leo M., *ep.* 82 *ad Marcian. aug.*, 23 April, 451: ACO II 4, nr. 39, p. 41, 17–21: 'for a twofold trust throughout the whole world between Christian princes will strengthen harmony with the support of the Spirit of God, because the advance in love and faith makes the power of both weapons insuperable, so that with God propitiated through unity in confessing (*per unam confessionem*), at the same time both heretical falsehood and barbarian hostility are destroyed'.

the ideology of Middle and Neo-Platonism were rife in the imperial Church of Constantine, a fact which only a few of the Fathers before Leo were aware of, or better, which only a few theologians grasped.[69] The one sacral conception of the world and of the empire bound the secular and ecclesiastical orders into a unity. The deposit of Middle and Neo-Platonism in the world-order of Constantine led logically to the Emperor's interpretation of himself as the radiance of God and the bearer of divine power.

> The Emperors are not only ἐκλογὴ τῆς τριάδος, but πρόβλημα τῆς τριάδος, θεοπρόβλητοι. The Emperor lives and governs as the radiance of God.[70]

The idea of empire and universal unity which dominated the thought of Constantine has since his time coincided more and more with the realisation of Christianity. Constantine's letter to Alexander and Arius[71] is evidence of his genuine interest in religious questions. He is shocked that 'a mere idle wrangle about words'[72] threatens to shatter the unity which he greatly desires. For this reason he entreats the clergy:

> Thus give me back peaceful days and carefree nights. Division among the people of God, among my fellow worshippers, would cost me the tranquillity of my life. ... Through your harmony, then, open the way for me to be able to glorify and praise the All-High for the unanimity and freedom of all.[73]

Though Constantine did not grasp the significance of the doctrinal disputes, he did interpret Christianity as a unanimous unity in order to build the unity of the empire on this basis. He paved the way for the state-church, a way that would sometimes bring the Emperor and bishops together and sometimes also set them against each other. It is remarkable that Nicene orthodoxy could give greatest approval to the Emperor's control over the Church precisely when in point of fact this control violated the nature of the Church to the utmost. This happened on 28 February, 380 when Emperor Theodosius I published his famous act of imperial legislation dealing with the matter of Nicene faith. By imperial law Theodosius I determined the faith of his subjects, restricted the rights of those who would not

---

[69] Cf. H. Rahner, Kirche und Staat im frühen Christentum. Dokumente aus acht Jahrhunderten und ihre Deutung (München 1961) 13–15; G. Pilati, Chiesa e Stato nei primi quindici secoli (Roma-Parigi-Tournai-New York 1961) 31–43.

[70] O. Treitinger, Die oströmische Kaiser- und Reichsidee (Darmstadt ²1969) 38.

[71] In Eusebius, Vita Constantini (= VC) II, ch. 64–72: ed. F. Winkelmann, GCS Eusebius I 1 (Berlin 1975) pp. 74–79, German in H. Dörries, 'Das Selbstzeugnis Kaiser Konstantins' (AbhGöttAkW, Phil.-hist. Kl., 3.F., Nr. 34) (Göttingen 1954) 55–58; see ibid., 286–328: (Constantine's) idea of Church; cf. M. Vogelstein, Kaiseridee-Romidee und das Verhältnis von Staat und Kirche seit Constantin = Hist. Unter. 7 (Breslau 1930) 64.

[72] Cf. H. Dörries, op. cit., 7.

[73] Eusebius, VC, ch. 72, 1–3: Winkelmann, op. cit., 78, 13–79, 2: German in H. Dörries, op. cit., 58. Constantine finds the quarrel of the bishops more disastrous for the empire than a war: VC III, 12, 2: Winkelmann, op. cit., 87, 11–13.

accept this faith, and threatened them with more penalities.[74] This act was an immediate expression of the Emperor's will, arrived at without previous cooperation of a synod or of the bishops as representatives of the Church. It has been rightly observed that neither before nor after this has there been such a typical representative of autocratic government who imposed his will in this way on the Church as state-church, as Emperor Theodosius I. No imperial document that would become a bone of contention in the history of the Church after Chalcedon, such as the Encyclical of Emperor Basiliscus or the Henoticon of Emperor Zeno, was so composed without any contact with bishops, as was the law of Theodosius I. Even Emperor Justinian I wanted to screen his interventions in doctrinal questions by synods and councils.[75]

At the basis of every intervention by an Emperor in questions of faith was the idea that through the unity of faith the unity of the empire and its well-being would be ensured. Constantine and his successors expected that the bishops and the Church would do their duty of conducting the state over internal dangers. Then the discord in faith threatened to annihilate the 'ecumenical' plan. The idea of alliance between the ecumenically conceived empire and the ecumenical Church gave signs of being shattered.[76] The plight of

[74] Cod. Theod. XVI 1, 2: Mommsen 833; given here in the English translation of C. Pharr, The Theodosian Code and Novels and Sirmondian Constitution (Princeton 1952) 440: 'it is Our will that all the peoples who are ruled by the administration of Our Clemency shall practice that religion which the divine Peter the Apostle transmitted to the Romans, as the religion which he introduced makes clear even unto this day. It is evident that this is the religion that is followed by the Pontiff Damasus and by Peter, Bishop of Alexandria, a man of apostolic sanctity; that is, according to the apostolic discipline and the evangelic doctrine, we shall believe in the single Deity of the Father, the Son, and the Holy Spirit, under the concept of equal majesty and of the Holy Trinity'. (Cf. Cod. Iust. I 1, 1; Sozom., HE VII, 4). 'We command that those persons who follow this rule shall embrace the name of Catholic Christians. The rest, however, whom We adjudge demented and insane, shall sustain the infamy of heretical dogmas, their meeting places shall not receive the name of churches, and they shall be smitten first by divine vengeance and secondly by the retribution of Our own initiative (motus), which We shall assume in accordance with the divine judgement'. For the early history of legislation against heretics, see A. H. M. Jones, The Later Roman Empire vol. I, 284–602, vol. II, 950–956 with footnotes, vol. III, 323–325. The first edict on the persecution of heretics is in Eusebius, VC III, 64–65: GCS Eusebius I, 111–113. Cf. C. Pharr, op. cit., XVI title 5, 450–463 with the legislation from 326 to 435. To be noted in particular is a sentence from the decree of 22 February, 407 (Honorius Augustus) Cod. Theod. XVI 5, 39, 1 (Pharr 457): 'in the first place, indeed it is Our will that such heresy (Manichaeans, Phrygians, Priscillianists) shall be considered a public crime, since whatever is committed against divine religion redounds to the detriment of all'. C. Pharr remarks in note 85: '. . . this is the fundamental principle on which was based the persecution of Christianity by the pagan Emperors and the persecution of heresy and paganism by the orthodox Christian Emperors. The Emperors were also influenced by their desire to promote the unity of the Empire, n. I.'. See also Cod. Iust. I 5.

[75] W. Enßlin, 'La politica dell' imperatore Teodosio agli inizi del suo governo', Nuovo Didaskaleion 2 (1948) (5–35), 18: 'lo stesso Giustiniano, in questioni ecclesiastiche che toccavano la fede tornò sempre alla soluzione del concilio, oppure, come nella introduzione della formula teopaschitica, fece mettere in evidenza la colloborazione della Chiesa in un modo assolutamente speciale nella pubblicazione della sua costituzione' (with reference to Cod. Iust. I 1, 8). Cf. H. Berkhof, Kirche und Kaiser (Zollikon-Zürich 1947) 64.81; F. Dvornik, 'Emperors, Popes and General Councils', DOP 6 (1951) 3–23.

[76] Cf. M. Vogelstein, op. cit., 72–73.

the state-church lay in the fact that two *universal* notions, which over-
lapped and thus were in competition, stood in juxtaposition. There
were no firm formulations which enabled them to be coordinated
and demarcated. All statements about the reciprocal relationship of
state and Church, whether issuing from the imperial or the ecclesiastical side, show a continuing vacillation.[77] Even when here and there
attempts are made to relate them mutually, an absolute formulation
is never attained. In the terminology of M. Vogelstein, a 'system
of stop-gaps' is created. The importance of precedence for the creation
of law, as was the case in Roman law, is now transferred as well
to Church politics.

Certainly in the West at Leo's time the conception of the Roman
ruler as the unique representative of God on earth was already familiar. Aponius testifies to this in his *explanatio* of the Song of Songs,
in which the problem of the Emperor-Church is clearly manifest.[78]
In his commentary on Sg 7, 5 (*Caput tuum ut Carmelus et comae capitis
tui sicut purpura regis vincta canalibus*), he develops a Christian theology
of the Emperor.

> It is intimated that the head of this people are the Roman kings, those of course
> who have discerned the truth and serve Christ in humility. Like the river of Carmel,
> from them flow forth the godly laws, praiseworthy peace and the illustrious submiss-
> iveness to the worship of the holy Church; ... these are the ones to whom God
> has revealed himself ... With good reason one can understand that they who do
> military service under Christ, the King of kings, are the head of this people, a
> people which has been made God's daughter from a daughter of the ruler of this
> world. For the devout kings who hold the place of God on earth are considered
> the head of the Christian people to such an extent that by their authority they
> restore the body of Christ to health, should it have been sick through heretical
> infection or persecution, provided that they themselves are of sound faith; of course,
> should they themselves be sick, [the body of the Church] will be weakened by
> them.[79]

The position of the Emperor in the imperial Church—as it had
become accepted since Theodosius I—is addressed by Aponius in

[77] The vacillation is clearly to be seen in the rich evidence produced by W. Kissling, op. cit.
Cf. M. Vogelstein, op. cit., 94.
[78] Aponius, *Explanatio in Canticum Canticorum*, ed. H. Bottino-J. Martini (Rome 1843); reprinted
in PLS I, 799–1031; according to a probable assumption, Aponius wrote in Italy between 405
and 415, no doubt in Rome, 'whose ecclesiastical precedence he repeatedly emphasises' (Altaner-
Stuiber, *Patrologie*, Freiburg 1966, 457).
[79] Aponius, *Explan. in Cant. Cant.*, ed. cit., 201–202. Only the last sentences of the above text
are quoted in their Latin form: *qui verissima ratione sub Christo rege regum militantes, omnium capiti
Christo coniuncti, caput huius plebis intelliguntur, quae ex filia principis mundi, Dei effecta probatur. Nam
in tantum religiosissimi reges vices Dei agentes in terris, caput christianae plebis esse noscuntur, ut, si quando
morbo haereticae contagionis aut persequutionis, Ecclesiae corpus coeperit infirmari, ipsorum auctoritate ad
pristinam sanitatem reformetur, si sani fuerint in fide, aut si insani, per ipsos infirmari necesse sit.* Does
the author refer to a concrete situation? Is this important for dating the commentary? The image
of the Emperor was, however, already in a critical state at the time of the Arian conflicts. Cf.
Lucifer of Cagliari (361), *De regibus apostolicis* I 3–6.10.11: CSEL 14, 35–64; H. Rahner, op. cit.,
142–149.

all its problematic: the Emperor has true authority to cleanse the Church of heresy. It is also possible that he can be infected with heresy, and thus make the Church ill. Even if, in the writing of Aponius, the Petrine idea is clearly enough present and the primacy over the whole Church is proper to the bishops as the *vicarius Petri*,[80] the Emperor still obviously stands at the apex of the visible world which is subject to God. In this respect the *vicarius Dei* surpasses even the *vicarius Petri* (or *Christi*, as is the usual expression in the Roman Synod of 13 March, 495). In 451 this notion still dominated, uncontested. 'What Constantine still refused, perhaps because in devout awe he may have glimpsed an endangering of his mercy through an excess of statements about his greatness as a ruler, Emperor Leo I, as far as we can tell, accepted without objection. In a synodal letter of the bishops of the Hellespont, which is preserved only in Latin translation, the salutation reads: *Piissimo et Christianissimo terrae domino possidenti caeleste regnum perpetuo Augusto imperatori Leoni*[81] (To the most devout and most Christian lord of the world, who possesses the heavenly kingdom, the eternal Augustus and Emperor Leo). Matching this is a letter of the bishops of Paphlagonia, which dates from the same time: *Piissimo et Christianissimo amabili imperatori et regnum caelestium possidenti Augusto Leoni*[82] (To the most devout and most Christian Emperor, who is worthy of love and possesses the heavenly kingdom, Augustus Leo).'[83]

Pope Leo fundamentally accepts this image of the imperial Church,

---

[80] Cf. M. Maccarone, *Vicarius Christi, Storia del titolo papale* (Lateranum, N.S. 18) (Romae 1952) 41–43, with reference to A. von Harnack, 'Christus praesens—Vicarius Christi. Eine kirchengeschichtliche Skizze' (*SbBerlAkW*, Phil.-hist. Kl. 34 (1927) 415–446), who wants to prove that '*vicarius Christi*' is substitute for the much older concept '*Christus praesens*', and was employed in contrast to the Emperor's title of '*vicarius dei*'. In its Christian usage '*vicarius dei*', as a characterisation of the Emperor, is to be traced back to the application of Prov 8, 15 (*per me reges regnant, per me principes imperant*) to the imperial Church. It is found for the first time in Ambrosiaster, *Lib. quaest.* c. XCI 8: CSEL 50, 157, 19–25: . . . *rex enim adoratur in terris quasi vicarius Dei, Christus autem post vicariam impleta dispensatione adoratur in caelis et in terris*. Ibid., c. CVI 17: p. 243, 17–20: *habens imperia dei, quasi vicarius eius*. Cf. commentary on Rom 13, 6: *principi suo, qui vicem dei agit*. Cf. W. Enßlin, *Gottkaiser und Kaiser von Gottes Gnaden*, 81–82; Eusebius, *Tricentennial Oration* 3, 6 (GCS, Eusebius I 202, 2) introduces Christus (*hyparchos*) as the governor for the true mighty king in heaven and the *Emperor* as the governor for this mighty king on earth. Enßlin, ibid., refers to a suggestive passage in Ennodius, *Vita Epiphanii* 71: CSEL 6, 349, 6ff.: 'thanks be to the almighty Lord who instilled his peace into the heart of the Emperor and willed that he be the vicar of his power for mortals after the fashion of heavenly sovereignty' (. . . *quem ad instar superni dominatus vicarium potestatis suae voluit esse mortalibus*). In his letter of convocation for the Council of Ephesus (431), Theodosius II characterises himself as mediator between God and man: 'the well-being of our empire depends on religion: each of these stands in a close relationship to the other. Thus the true religion is endebted to justice, and the state is endebted to both. Because we have been set by God to rule and are the natural bond between the religion of our peoples and their temporal fortune, we preserve the unimpaired harmony of both orders and uphold it by serving as mediator between God and man' (ACO I 1, 1, p. 114f.).

[81] From the so-called *Codex Encyclius* (*CE*), which we still have to investigate more closely: ACO II 5, p. 84, 12f.

[82] ACO II 5, p. 86, 9f.

[83] W. Enßlin, *Gottkaiser und Kaiser von Gottes Gnaden*, 82.

although, perhaps without being fully aware of the consequences, he had already worked out a counter-conception in his Petrine doctrine and in his newly sketched out notion of Rome which has 'Petrus' as its basis. The Pope does not discuss the religious position of the Emperor. Leo, no differently from the people, considers the occupant of the throne as the first after God. Even if we possess no indications that Leo shared the mystical veneration of the ruler which the people appropriated and which found its expression in the ceremonial of the ruler,[84] nevertheless for him there also existed a *harmonia praestabilita* between the power of the Emperor and the universal Church. For both come from God. Thus without doubt Leo accepts an immediate relationship of the Emperor's mission to the *Christian truth* and *tradition*. This also already has its type in the pagan concept of the *princeps*. For it was already claimed that the *princeps* possessed the capability of selecting the right tenet from opposing ones[85] and in this way conducting public affairs properly. It is here that the *auctoritas* becomes effective. Applied in a Christian way this means that since 380 it was presupposed that the Emperor was orthodox. The domain of revelation which is entrusted to the Church and the collection of norms according to which the pagan Emperor also had to steer the world are no longer separate and opposed. The one revelation in Christ, the one faith of Christians are the one source from which Church and state live. According to Leo the Emperor has a special charism to make this source flow for the world—the *inspiration* of the Holy Spirit, howsoever that is to be understood. In his letters to the Emperors Leo used such strong expressions about this inspiration that a whole series of historians has doubted whether these words are to be taken seriously.[86] For that period a general influence of God on the Emperor, as the instrument of his government of the world, is presupposed. The Emperor already has a natural disposition, viz. the *conscientia*, a judging power to weigh up a state of affairs, after which a decision is taken. With this natural disposition of the Emperor is united the special strength of God which Leo designates by related concepts, all of them centering on advice, instruction.[87] But to speak of the *inspiration* of the Emperor makes an even

---

[84] Cf. the two studies of O. Treitinger, *Die oströmische Kaisermacht und Reichsidee nach ihrer Gestaltung im höfischen Zeremoniell* (1938) and *Vom oströmischen Staats- und Reichsgedanken* (1940), now in one volume: Darmstadt ³1969.

[85] Cf. P. Stockmeier, op. cit., 53–54, with reference to Cicero, *De nat. Deorum* 2, 168.

[86] Cf. K. Voigt, 'Papst Leo d. Gr. und die "Unfehlbarkeit" des oströmischen Kaisers', *ZKG* N.F. 10 (1928) 11–17. In addition, P. Stockmeier, op. cit., § 14, 138–152: the Emperor under God's direction; H. Bacht, 'Sind die Lehrentscheidungen der ökumenischen Konzilien göttlich inspiriert?', *Catholica* 13 (1959) 128–139.

[87] Cf. P. Stockmeier, op. cit., 140–152: Leo M., *ep.* 164: ACO II 4, p. 110, 23f. speaks of the *eruditio spiritus sancti*, the lexical meaning of which is enlightment, instruction, teaching, or the

higher claim. With this term one is certainly not to think of the inspiration of scripture (or the inspiration of the Emperor's edicts). We come closer to the mark with 'prophetic inspiration', thus a divine charism which enables a man to communicate divine truth to mankind. The Emperor, as the instrument of the eternal world-order, is dependent on this influence. It also profits the Church.[88] Even if scholars are constantly perplexed by this notion of the Emperor's inspiration, and are tempted to want to dispose of it either as 'Captatio benevolentiae' or diplomacy, or even as 'figures of speech',[89] P. Stockmeier is no doubt correct in writing: 'Perhaps one has, however, to admit that, corresponding to the views of his time, they [the utterances of the Pope] also express the conviction of the Pope'.[90] Today we would say that Leo's views on the inspiration and infallibility of the Emperor fit into the framework of the conception of the world as sacral. The awareness that a clarification was necessary came only slowly, and with difficulty. This happened particularly in the politics with regard to Chalcedon which were pursued by the rulers after Emperor Leo I up until Justinian. Pope Leo himself did not have the burden of coming to terms with imperial decrees favouring the Monophysites. In that situation his conception of the inspiration of the Emperor would have been put most severely to the test. The only restriction which he makes with regard to the Emperor's position in questions of faith concerns the right of preaching, which he would not grant to the laity and monks, but reserved for the representatives of the ordo sacerdotalis.[91] For all that Leo left the Emperor relatively large scope for activity, even with regard to doctrine. He himself speaks of 'docere', but this is probably to be interpreted as 'to admonish' and 'to reprove'. This activity pertains to his right of supervision

---

learning obtained through these; '... without the intervention of mediating organs the Emperor can, as it were, draw the truths of faith from the source' (140f.). Ep. 30: ACO II 4, p. 10, 7–10 speaks of a docere of the Holy Spirit which Pulcheria participates in. Ep. 145: ACO II 4, p. 96, 13–15 uses the word instruere. Through the instruction of the Holy Spirit Emperor Leo can put the circumstances in Alexandria back in order. Similarly ep. 162: ACO II 4, p. 106, 25f.: the Spirit dwells in the Emperor and 'instructs' him. The piissimae aures of the Emperor are directed immediately to God and require no mediation (ACO II 4, p. 61, 12).

[88] Cf. Leo M., ep. 162 ad Leon. aug., 21 March, 458: ACO II 4, nr. 99, p. 105, 16f.: 'for in the exhortations of Your Devoutness it is clear beyond doubt what the Holy Spirit works through you for the salvation of the whole world'. Ep. 165 ad Leon. aug., 17 August, 458 (= the so-called Second Tome): ACO II 4, nr. 104, p. 119, 3f.: 'therefore I have narrated these things with as much brevity as I could so that you will know that our preaching also is united with the faith which has been divinely inspired in you'. Ep. 135 ad Anatol. ep., 29 May, 454: ACO II 4, nr. 79, p. 88, 36–38: the Emperor as guardian of the faith (custos fidei) (1.34) has instruction through the Holy Spirit (eruditio spiritus sancti), and this in full measure.

[89] Stockmeier, op. cit., 148f., reviews the various opinions; he himself takes these statements in Leo seriously and works out a broader basis for the idea of inspiration (150–151).

[90] Ibid., 149.

[91] Leo M., ep. 119 ad Maxim. Antioch. ep.: ACO II 4, nr. 66, p. 75, 2: non tamen permittendum est ut quisquam extra sacerdotalem ordinem constitutus gradum sibi praedicatoris assumat. With this ordo sacerdotalis the bishops are primarily meant.

over the Church which also comprises *'continere'*, *'revocare'* and *'incre-pare'* (i.e. to keep in check, to revoke, to reprimand) as well as the *'cohortatio'* and the *'ammonitio'* (exhortation, admonition).

The secular ruler receives the authorised right to intervene in the religious sphere when abuses occur; in doing this he does not transgress the boundaries of the sphere of government, rather, true to his divinely willed mission, he fulfills from a lofty standpoint his duty as *custos fidei*.[92]

Leo affirms the connexion between the 'one creed' and the *'pax chris-tiana'*. Wherever this creed is disturbed, the Emperor must regard the *'reparatio pacis'* as his duty. For this reason he must ward off equally barbarians and heretics![93]

Finally, this question must be posed: how far did Pope Leo commit himself to the system of the imperial Church for the purpose of shoring up the authority of Chalcedon from without as well? Pope Leo's whole attitude towards the transmission of faith gives no indication that, where the content of faith or the *basis* of faith in the incarnation was concerned, he would have depended on the Emperor's authority. In these matters the Pope appeals exclusively to scripture, the apostolic tradition, Nicaea and the other councils and to important Fathers before him. Moreover, the Petrine doctrine counteracted the principle of the imperial Church. Only very rarely does Leo argue from the fact that the decision of Chalcedon is also protected by the Emperor's authority and that the violation of this authority would entail the sanctions which had been threatened by Emperor Marcian.[94] This appeal to the Emperor's authority is occasioned by the addressee who is likely to become insecure in his fidelity to Chalcedon. Even in response to this Emperor Leo's argumentation is in the last resort theological: a revision of Chalcedon, such as the opposition from Alexandria are striving for, would be an abrogation of Nicaea, and of the gospel and apostolic tradition in general.[95]

Leo's thought is also purely 'theological' when, in the struggle against the Monophysites, he finally considers excommunicating them, i.e. severing them from the Great Church. Because he no longer sees any possibility of maintaining unity with the supporters

---

[92] P. Stockmeier, op. čit., 173; cf. the whole § 16: Emperor and ecclesiastical discipline, 168–173. Cf. Leo M., *Tr.* 36 (Epiphany 451): Chavasse CCL 138, p. 199, with p. CXCII.

[93] Cf. above n. 68.

[94] Cf. Leo M., *ep.* 162 *ad Leon. aug.*, 21 March, 458: ACO II 4, nr. 99, p. 106, 14–17: 'for according to the same apostle (Paul), if "I build up again those things which I tore down, I prove myself a transgressor" (Gal 2, 18) and I subject myself to the conditions of punishment which not only the authority of Emperor Marcian of holy memory, but I myself have confirmed with my consent'. The final reason for calling upon the protection of the Emperor is the *'communis fides'* which the Pope finds, for example, in Emperor Leo. Cf. *ep.* 155 *ad Anathol. ep.*, 11 October, 457: ACO II 4, nr. 95, p. 101, 5.

[95] Leo M., *ep.* 164, 1 September, 458, *ad Leon. aug.*: ACO II 4, nr. 103, p. 112, 30–34. See the text in n. 48.

of Dioscorus and the other opponents of Chalcedon on the basis of the confession of faith, no other course remains open for him save dividing the Church community. Hence he demands that Anatolius of Constantinople sever from the Church clerics who sympathise with the opponents of Chalcedon.[96] The unity of the empire in one faith, always of importance to the Emperors, is without doubt valued very highly by the Pope. He considers this an ideal to be striven for, as he expresses it once again in *ep.* 164 to Emperor Leo. But while the Emperors in the long run were all too clearly ready to buy 'unity' in faith through compromises, the Pope remained consistent and placed purity of faith above a false unity. In this sense, therefore, Leo I abandons the principle of the imperial Church at a decisive point. In a consistent way he wants the Alexandrian Church to know that the following had been decided: anyone deceived by the doctrine of Eutyches who wishes to return to the Church must do penance; but he is able to be reconciled with the Church. Yet whoever will not accept the faith of Chalcedon is unworthy of the name of Christian and must be severed from the Church.[97]

For all that Leo also thinks of protecting the true unity of faith—thus the Nicene-Chalcedonian tradition—by means of imperial power. He also has no scruples about the application of the statutory ordinances which since Theodosius were available for use against heretics; in fact, he demands that the Emperor use them. Thus, for example, more severe measures should be taken against Eutyches, who after his condemnation was still able to remain in his monastery. In various letters Leo demands his banishment to a more distant place in order

---

[96] Leo M., *ep.* 155 *ad Anathol. ep.*, 11 October, 457: ACO II 4, nr. 95, p, 100, 29–31: 'I make it known that it displeases me very greatly that it is said that among your clergy (*inter dilectionis tuae clericos*) there are some who support the perverseness of the opposition and mingle the vessels of anger with those of mercy. Your Diligence should pursue with vigilance the searching out of these and their correction with appropriate severity, so that those whom correction cannot profit one should not refrain from cutting off' (reference to Mt 18, 8.9). Resistance to paganism outside the Church will be ineffective, if a wounding of the Church from within is allowed: 'for we resist in vain those outside the Church, if we are wounded by those who are within in those whom they deceive' (ibid., p. 100, 11–12). Cf. the further letter (*ep.* 157) to Anatolius (without date, and suspect according to C. Silva-Tarouca, *Nuovi Studi*, p. 183): ACO II 4, nr. 102, p. 109, 37–110, 2 (cited above n. 65).

[97] Leo M., *ep.* 164 *ad Leon. aug.*, 17 August, 458: ACO II 4, nr. 103, p. 111, 24–112, 2: 'whence the holy Synod of Chalcedon, which was celebrated by all the provinces of the Roman empire (*Romani orbis*) with the consent of the whole world (*mundi*) and which is one with the decrees of the most sacred Council of Nicaea, cut off all the ungodliness of Eutychian teaching (*dogmatis*) from the body of the catholic community, how can there be a return to ecclesiastical peace for one of those who have fallen unless he has been purified by perfect satisfaction (*satisfactione*)? ... Since throughout all the parts of Your empire and in all the regions of the earth the faith of Chalcedon is confirmed, let it be preserved in well-founded peace and let whoever separates himself from the company of our unity be unworthy of the name of Christian'. Thus the Pope thinks that for the sake of a splinter group the Emperor ought not jeopardise through new discussions the Chalcedonian unity of faith which had already been universally achieved—and hence not endanger as well the imperial ideal of unity. Cf. the conclusion of *ep.* 164 cited above (n. 48).

to prevent any possibility of propaganda from the side of the condemned. Even in Constantinople itself heretics are to be tracked down and brought to fitting punishment.[98] In sundry letters Julian of Cius receives the commission to exercise influence on the Emperor so that resistance is broken and the stubborn opponents of the Council of Chalcedon are treated as enemies of imperial and ecclesiastical peace. The same holds good for Jerusalem as well as for Egypt.[99]

The Pope finally had success. The Emperor submitted *ep.* 165 of the Pope, the so-called Second Tome, to Timothy Aerlurus for his comment. Yet this was in vain. An oral exchange of views was also of no use. Timothy kept to his rejection of Chalcedon and of the letters of Leo. Hence he was finally removed from his episcopal see and banished (first to Gangra, and then to the Chersonese). Perhaps before his death in November 461 Leo was still confident that calm

[98] Thus in *ep.* 134 *ad Marcian. aug.*, 15 April, 454: ACO II 4, nr. 78, p. 87, 38–88, 5: 'because you gladly accept my suggestions for the tranquillity of catholic faith, may you know that it has been pointed out to me by a communication of my brother and fellow-bishop Julian that the ungodly Eutyches is deservedly in exile, but in the very place of his condemnation (*damnationis loco*), in order to deceive harmless people (*innocentes*), pours out against catholic blamelessness (*integritatem catholicam*) much poison of his blasphemies which are full of despair, and with great impudence vomits forth what the whole world shuddered at and condemned. Thus I consider it to be very wise that Your Clemency command that he be transferred to a more distant and concealed spot'. Julian will take care that in the monastery of Eutyches the monks are strengthened in evangelic and apostolic teaching. About Julian, however, we learn that Leo set him as a sentry for the faith (in Cius): *quem in speculis propter fidem illic esse constitui* (p. 88, 8). On the intensification of the exile of Eutyches, see A. Grillmeier, 'Eine Flucht des Eutyches nach Jerusalem?' *ROMANITAS-CHRISTIANITAS. Untersuchungen zur Geschichte und Literatur der römischen Kaiserzeit* (FS J. Straub), ed. G. Wirth (Berlin–New York 1982) 645–653. For Constantinople, see Leo M., *ep.* 155 *ad Anatol. ep.*, 11 October, 457: ACO II 4, nr. 95, p. 100, 29–33: *illud sane . . .* (see the text in n. 96). The word *'investigandis'* is to be noted.

[99] Cf. Leo M., *ep.* 109 *ad Iulian. ep.*, 25 November, 452: ACO II 4, nr. 105, p. 137, 27–30 (for *Jerusalem* Julian receives the following commission): 'You must endeavour to persuade His Clemency that the inciters of these insurrections be kept away from unhealthy gatherings, and not only Eutyches and Dioscorus, but also anyone who eagerly fosters the maddening perverseness should be deposited in such places where they are not able to have intercourse with the fellows of their blasphemies'. In the same vein *ep.* 118 *ad Iulian. ep.*, 2 April, 453: ACO II 4, nr. 65 (according to C. Silva-Tarouca this letter is not authentic, *Nuovi Studi* p. 169) p. 72, 7–14: 'if there are some, who, blinded by their obduracy, have become so mad in their rejected thinking that they would rather rage than be healed, it is the responsibility of the imperial power to see that the disturbers of ecclesiastical peace and the enemies of the body politic (*reipublicae*), which is deservedly praised by Christian rulers, be restrained with particular care (*sollicitius comprimantur*). As we have said, just as it is the responsibility of the imperial power to restrain public tumults and sacriligious uprisings more severely, so it is the responsibility of episcopal authority not to give to the monks any permission to preach against the faith, and to resist with all their might those who dare to claim for themselves what belongs to the bishops (alone)'. The Emperor, however, should be on his guard against the shedding of blood, 'although those who have dared to repudiate both divine and human laws deserve to undergo all kinds of punishment' (ibid., 72, 27–28). On the whole matter, see L. Perrone, *La chiesa di Palestina II*, 1: 'La ribellione palestinese: Calcedonia come "tradimento della fede"', 89–103. With regard to *Egypt* Leo hoped that after the murder of the Patriarch Proterius (457) the Emperor would intervene: *ep.* 145 *ad Leon. imp.*: ACO II 4, pp. 95–96. The Emperor had indeed punished the murderers of the patriarch, but he had left Timothy Aelurus in office. Leo pressed for his deposition. Cf. *ep.* 156 *ad Leon. imp.*: ACO II 4, pp. 101–104: 'for it is glorious for you to destroy the weapons of hostile peoples, how great will be your glory when you free the Alexandrian Church from its raging tyrants' (pp. 103, 35–104, 2). In addition *ep.* 164 *ad Leon. imp.*: ACO II 4, pp. 110–112, 5ff., 24ff. With regard to Leo's experiences in *Rome* we shall go into more detail below.

had returned in this way to the centres of conflict. The Alexandrians and the disciples of Cyril were not won over. The imperial Church stood before its first enduring schism.

Was this state of affairs not due to the very fact that the traditions of the Alexandrian Church, which in themselves were legitimate and whose orthodoxy had been guaranteed by Cyril, had been summoned by an ecumenical council before a tribunal which was incapable of making these traditions comprehensible? Instead they were measured purely against the wording of the formula which may have been familiar to the greater part of the Church, but quite certainly not to the disciples of Cyril. These, however, also took no pains to understand the other side, and chose division. Consequently, the following question must be asked: would it have been easier to preserve unity in faith without an imperial council? Would it not have been better to have left the settling of matters to the individual Churches? The principal failure had already occurred earlier, with Cyril of Alexandria. Unfortunately, he failed to submit his *mia physis* formula and the whole christology built on it to Rome and to explain it. If anyone would have had the authority and the trust necessary for making clear in Rome the unity of faith even in the antithetically opposed formulae, this would have been Cyril. However, he preferred to remain silent. Thus Rome, Constantinople, and even Antioch had not been prepared to deal with the dicta of a man who with the use of these would have failed in an ordinary theological examination.

III. Leo's Chalcedonian and Post-Chalcedonian Picture of Christ

Just as in the pre-Chalcedonian teaching of Leo the *Tomus ad Flavianum*, the so-called First Tome, became the dominant document, so the post-Chalcedonian period has its compendium in the so-called Second Tome, *ep.* 165 to Emperor Leo I, which was despatched on 17 August, 458 but which had already been announced on 1 December, 457.[100] The other christological statements from the post-

---

[100] Leo M., *ep.* 165 *ad Leon. aug.* = the Second Tome (here: T. II) ACO II 4, nr. 104, pp. 113–131 (largely identical with *ep.* 124: ibid., nr. 113, pp. 159–163). Cf. the First Tome: ACO II 2, 1, nr. 5, pp. 24–33. We cite both tomes here according to Silva-Tarouca, TD 9 (Romae 1959, repr.) indicating the ACO in round brackets.

Editions of Leo's letters: ACO II 4, where we follow the numbering of the Ballerini in PL 54. In addition C. Silva-Tarouca, *S. Leonis Magni Epistulae contra Eutychis haeresim, Pars I* (Romae 1934), *Pars II* (1935); idem, *Epistularum Romanorum Pontificum ad vicarios per Illyricum aliosque episcopos Collectio Thessalonicensis* (Romae 1937). There are some further letters in the *Collectio Avellana* (CA: see below). On the state of the text, collections and editions of Leo's letters, see the survey in H. Arens, op. cit., 23–90; J. Martorell, *Mysterium Christi (Léon Magno)* (Valencia 1983). The latter gives a list of Leo's letters and *sermones*, the Latin text of the First Tome with a Spanish translation and a good selection of christological texts from the *sermones*. On the announcement of the Second Tome, see *ep.* 156: ACO II 4, nr. 97, p. 104, 4–5; T. II introduction.

Chalcedonian letters and sermons of Leo should be considered together with this Second Tome. This great theological letter to the Emperor represents the Pope's christological testament with which he put the finishing touch to his struggle for Chalcedon. As was the case with the First Tome,[101] so too here it will be worthwhile attempting a survey of the Second Tome, so that the thought of Leo can be followed more easily.

1. *Analysis of* Ep. 165

(The numbering of verses follows TD 9, with references to ACO II 4 being given subsequently in brackets.)

vv. 1–8 (113, 2–10)	*Introduction:* Through human instruction and from the fullness of the Holy Spirit the Emperor has the pure doctrine. Nevertheless, it is the duty of the Pope to expound the inner appreciation and the faith of the Emperor publicly and to preach (*praedicare*).
vv. 9–46 (113, 11–115, 1)	*First Part:* Invasion of the Church by heresy through Eutyches (9–11) (113, 10–13). Twofold attack on catholic faith: Nestorius and Eutyches. Dialectic of heresies (*haereses contrariae*) (12–37) (113, 13–114, 14). These lies were formerly refuted by the catholic faith, that is by the Council of Nicaea (41) (114, 18–24) with which Leo concurs (42) (114, 25–26). The principal proposition of this faith (43) (114, 26–28): 'He (the Lord), in order to restore human salvation, did not bring the true flesh of our frailty down from heaven with him, but he assumed it in the womb of the virgin-mother'. The burden of proof rests on those who deny the truth of the human flesh. They have to show how they can retain the name of Christian or prove their conformity to the gospel, if either flesh without the divinity (Nestorius) or divinity without flesh (Eutyches) has issued from Mary.
vv. 47–165 (115, 1–119, 2)	*Second Part:* The development of the true faith in the incarnation and in the redemption of Christ.
1. vv. 47–75 (115, 1–29)	Faith in the true humanity and true divinity in Christ is necessary for the true foundation of the redemption. a) Christ 'mediator' (51–52) (115, 5–7); b) Redemption from death only through the death of the 'one' who himself was not subjected to death (53–54) (115, 7–8); c) The riches of the redemption in the blood and sacrifice of Christ (55–75) (115, 8–29) Rom 5, 20; Eph 5, 2; Joh 12, 32; vv. 55–72 (115, 8–27) = *sermo* 64.
2. vv. 76–98 (115, 30–116, 17)	Demonstration of the true divinity and the true humanity of Christ in the person-unity of God and man from the quality of the works (*ex operum qualitate*) (from *sermo* 64, together with Mt 3, 17; Joh 1, 29; 20, 22).

---

[101] See the summary of the First Tome in JdChr I², 739; CCT I², 530.

3. vv. 99–111 (116, 18–32)	Those who deny the humanity of Christ can explain neither the cross nor the resurrection; Lk 24, 39; Joh 20, 27; they have neither deliverance nor redemption: Acts 4, 12; I Tim 2, 6.
4. vv. 112–136 (117, 1–32)	Phil 2, 6–11 as a special proof for the unity of *forma servi* and the *forma Dei*; assertions of majesty and assertions of lowliness in the one Christ, because *forma servi* and *forma Dei* are truly distinct. Joh 5, 26; Mt 26, 38; Joh 1, 1–3.14.
5. vv. 137–149 (117, 32–118, 14)	The mystery of our redemption is worked in the concealment of the majesty of the Word (Logos) in the incarnation.
vv. 150–161 (118, 15–29)	Exhortation that the mystery of the true incarnation is to be accepted according to the witness of the apostles, the teachers of the Church, the martyrs and confessors.
vv. 162–165 (118, 29–119, 2)	Reference to the attached testimonies of the Fathers.
vv. 116–174 (119, 3–13)	*Conclusion:* Reference to the inspiration of the Emperor with which Leo's preaching (*praedictatio*) is combined for common witness to the faith.

2. *The Second Tome and the post-Chalcedonian* sermones *of Leo I*

In post-Chalcedonian christology, *ep.* 165, or the Second Tome, definitely has a special significance not only for superficial reasons and because of its fullness of detail, but also because it is a counterpoint to the First Tome. But rather than isolating this document, we want to situate it within the Pope's preaching activity in Rome. The Pope did not write theoretical doctrinal treatises in the strict sense. The designation of the sermons of the Pope as *tractatus*[102] also does not justify this assumption. Whether letters or *sermones/tractatus*: both ways of expressing an opinion on undecided questions are entirely determined by the situation at the time. Leo is always in a dialogue, either with his Roman audience or with the decisive people in the East and West, Emperors, bishops or his opponents. Mostly he demands that some negotiations or measures be taken. The Emperors, his 'nuntius' (without diplomatic status), Julian of Cius, who was the occupant of the small episcopal see across from Constantinople,[103]

---

[102] On this designation see Chavasse, CCL 138, p. CCXV. Leo's *sermones* are cited according to this edition CCL 138 and 138A, the *tractatus* of the first collection being indicated with Roman numerals, and those of the second collection with their sub-groups with Arabic numerals. Since Chavasse retains the numbering of the Ballerini (also in PL 54) and numbers the lines for each *sermo*, we dispense with references to PL 54 and adhere to CCL 138 and 138A, giving each time the number of the lines. The edition of R. Dolle, *Léon le Grand: Sermons Tome I–IV* (Paris 1949–1973) = SC 22 bis, 49, 74, 200, was also used, but is cited only in individual cases.

[103] Cf. A. Wille, *Bischof Julian von Kios, der Nuntius Leos des Großen in Konstantinopel* (Kempten 1910) 1–8 on Julian's personal data. Leo always writes: '*Ad Iulianum Coensem*'. For a long time it was assumed either explicitly or tacitly that Julian's episcopal see was the island city of Kos; this, however, hardly tallies with the function of a papal representative to the imperial court and to the Bishop of Constantinople. As Julian's episcopal see, Wille has rightly postulated Kios (Cius), which was situated in the immediate neighbourhood of the imperial city.

and other important personages continually receive some commission. The two Tomoi certainly come closest to an express 'doctrinal
treatise'. But for all that they are still letters, addressed to particular
people, tailored to the concrete situation, free from scientific definitions, advancing in the familiar Leonine rhythm,[104] but above all
they are permeated with parts from the *sermones*.

Through the research and the edition of A. Chavasse,[105] the classification of Leo's
sermons (*tractatus, sermones*) into the pre-Chalcedonian and post-Chalcedonian
periods has now been worked out on a scholarly basis. For the period with which
we are concerned we have to deal above all with a series of *tractatus* (designated
by the editor as a second collection) which were delivered in the years 446–461.
Four groups of these must be distinguished.[106]

(1) The *sermones* which refer to the insurrection of the Palestinian monks and
which were delivered between Christmas 452 and Christmas 453. The *tractatus* 28,
38, 46, 64, 65, 66, 79, 91 and 29 belong here. Cf. the important letter 124. Leo
had heard of the rebellion of the monks through a letter (now lost) of Bishop Julian
of Cius. He replied on 25 November, 452, shortly after having met Attila (summer
452). The *tractatus* 79 and 91 in particular reflect this ecclesiastical situation.

(2) The *sermones* 47, 67, 68, 69, 92 and 30 (delivered between 21 February and
Christmas 454). In *tractatus* 47 Leo refers again to the events in Palestine. This group
of *sermones* deals with the opposition against the Chalcedonian Patriarch Proterius
(451–457). To prove that the Pope was a Nestorian, supporters of Eutyches had
falsified Leo's First Tome. The letters 130 (to Emperor Marcian), 131 (to Bishop
Julian of Cius) and 129 (to Patriarch Proterius) are concerned with the same matters.
The themes and language of the confrontation with the Palestinian monks are taken
up again. This is also the case in the letters 134 (15 April, 454) and 135–136 (29
May, 454), but especially in the letter 139 of 4 September, 454, to Juvenal, Patriarch
of Jerusalem, who had been restored to office (ACO II 4, pp. 91–93). Against
the 'Denial of our Lord Jesus Christ in the flesh' which was imputed to Eutyches
(ibid. 91, 1.33–92, 2), the Pope refers to the wholly concrete events of the life
and death of Jesus in the Holy Land.

(3) This group, which includes the *sermones* 12, 26, 36, 44, 18, 27, 37, 45, 62,
63 and 19, is situated before the sermons of the second group, viz. between December
450 and December 452. In particular, *sermones* 18, 27 and 63, together with *sermones*
37, 45, 62 and 19, are a part of the series from 451–452.

(4) This group, which comprises *sermones* 49, 50, 93, 94 and 96, falls in the period
of most grievous political disturbances in the West. From this period we have only
two letters of Leo (13 March, 455 and 1 June, 457; *ep.* 143 and 144). The assault
of the Vandals and famines in Rome, moreover, pushed to the fore the theme of
penance.

---

[104] On the rhythm in Leo's writings, cf. C. Silva-Tarouca in the introduction to the edition of
both Tomes, TD 9, 16–17, with reference to the studies of F. di Capua, 'Il ritmo prosaico in S.
Agostino', *Miscellanea Agostiniana II* (Romae 1931) 607–764; A. P. Lang, *Leo der Große und die Texte
des Altgelasianums* (Steyler Verlagsbuchhandlung 1957); above all H. Arens, op. cit., each time under
the heading: Stilistisches. For an evaluation of the liturgical sources of Leo's christology, see
A. P. Lang. Cf. further B. Studer, 'Die Einflüsse der Exegese Augustins auf die Predigten Leos
des Großen', *Forma futuri. Studi in onore del Cardinale M. Pellegrino* (Torino 1975) 915–930.
[105] See Chavasse, CCL 138 and 138A.
[106] Cf. idem, CCL 138, p. CXCV–CCI. We shall discuss the first collection at the end of this
chapter. Cf. CCL 138, p. CLXXVII–CLXXXI.

Even if the two Tomoi have received particular recognition—the First Tome became the most intensely disputed document apart from the definition of Chalcedon itself—, still one must not for that reason overlook the fact that 'as regards range and completeness of theological explication' (H. Arens) the *sermones* represent the primary text-group within the Leonine corpus.

Does there correspond to the relative uniformity of Leo's writings (in as much as the closeness of the letters and *sermones* is concerned) as far as these have come down to posterity a homogeneous fundamental theological conception? In part this question can be quickly answered. Both before and after Chalcedon Leo's christology is dominated by the event of God's economy of salvation in Christ. It remains 'soteriology'. But we shall still have to examine to what extent the alleged static christology of Chalcedon had been able to leave its stamp on the dynamic, soteriological kerygma of Leo, or to what extent a more static model had superimposed itself on the soteriological, dynamic primary structure. As far as Leo was concerned, how did the two-nature doctrine of the Council and the kerygma of the economy of salvation stand in relation to each other? How strongly, for instance, did the 'reflection' on theological concepts, initiated by Chalcedon, infiltrate Leo's kerygma? Did the Pope notice at all and admit the terminological advance which had been made at Chalcedon, viz. the contrasting of the meaning of *hypostasis* to that of the word *physis*? Was the importance of the formula of the 'one *hypostasis* in two natures', which in the post-Chalcedonian discussion was taken more and more in isolation, perceived at all by Leo, the Latin kerygmatic theologian?

3. *The soteriological kerygma in Leo's post-Chalcedonian christology*

The essential truth which had to be preserved in the struggle against Nestorius and Eutyches (and the Manichaeans) was what was expressed in the Creed, the message of salvation in the incarnation and death of Jesus Christ, the Risen One. In warding off the errors of the separation of the two natures by Nestorius and their mingling by Eutyches, as Leo understood this, soteriological arguments are ultimately decisive. On this point there is no difference between the First and Second Tomes.[107] In both cases the starting-point is the dignity and character of Jesus as mediator.[108] Eutyches can no longer take this biblical word seriously, if he speaks of the 'one nature'. For Christ can only represent and fulfill the 'reality of the mediator' (II 52), because in the 'form of God' he is equal to the Father, and in the 'form of man' a sharer of our reality and destiny. More than

[107] Cf. T. I, 54–88 (27, 2–28, 6) with T. II 49–75 (115, 3–29).
[108] T. I 59 (27, 5f.): T. II 36f.; 109 (114, 12f.; 115, 5f.; 116, 28f.).

the First Tome, the Second Tome offers a stronger emphasis on the death inherited from Adam, which can only be removed by a true divine-human mediator. The so-called mystical doctrine of redemption, which sees in the divine-human unity of Christ the very representation of salvation, is presupposed in both documents. What is new[109] in the Second Tome in contrast to the First Tome is that Leo attributes Christ's work as redeemer to his self-surrender to death (vv. 53–54) and to the shedding of his blood. The latter, however, is expressed in the words of *sermo* 64 (T II, vv. 55–72), in which Christ's redemptive act is characterised (with Eph 5, 2) as a sacrifice (T II, vv. 61–64). What is interesting in the Second Tome is the reason given for the value of the death or of the sacrifice of Christ. In *sermo* 64 Leo presents this sacrifice in such a way that the surrender of the victim is ascribed to the *verus pontifex* who sacrifices his own flesh on the altar of the cross. But including the *sermo* in the Second Tome he adds *et aeternus* to the *verus*. Without doubt here a reference is intended to the divinity of this high priest. One can hardly assume that Leo—similar to Origen—champions a priesthood of the Logos, according to which the decision to surrender the body is transferred to the Logos as Logos. Admittedly, the language is imprecise. For insofar as the text speaks of *aeternus pontifex*, and not of *pontifex in aeternum* (cf. Ps. [110] 109, 4), following this line of thought Christ would be 'priest' already in his pre-existence, and would be active in time as such because he sacrificed his assumed human nature.[110] In that case the *physical* principle of the surrender would be the Word as Word. But Leo is not thinking of that. For he speaks of the 'voluntary suffering of the Lord' (*voluntaria domini . . . passio*).[111] In connexion with the 'eternal high priest', one must also think of the One-made-man, the mediator[112] between God and man. In the Second Tome Leo introduced the *aeternus* into the text of *sermo* 64 with the sole purpose of giving particular emphasis to the holiness of the sacrifice of Christ and to stress participation of divinity and humanity in this sacrifice. The significance of the human death of Christ is

---

[109] One can easily acquire a general view of the difference in terminology between the two Tomes by consulting the index of C. Silva-Tarouca in TD 9, p. 61–70. The study of M.-M. Mueller, *The Vocabulary of Pope St. Leo the Great* = PatrStud. 62 (Washington 1943) is only partly useful. Decisive terms, such as *natura-persona*, are missing entirely. Cf. the severe criticism by A. Lauras, *RSR* 48 (1960) 167f., n. 6.

[110] Cf. T. II 63 (115, 17–18). The apparatus in Silva-Tarouca shows that according to a less valuable tradition *aeternus* has again dropped out. Apart from this passage Leo speaks often of the eternal priesthood of Christ, by which he always means the Incarnate One. Cf. Tr. III, 2: CCL 138, p. 11, 35: *omnipotens et perpetuus sacerdos*; Tr. V, 4: CCL 138, p. 24, 79–80; Tr. V, 3: CCL 138, p. 23, 52–53: *verus et aeternus antistes*.

[111] Leo M., Tr. LV, 2 (8 April, 442): CCL 138A, p. 324, 1.35–36.

[112] On the concept *mediator* see the passages in M.-M. Mueller, op. cit., 13. On the priesthood of the Logos in Philo, Origen, Athanasius, cf. *Chalkedon* I, 64.84–85; on Cyril of Alexandria's different understanding, ibid., 173; CCT I², 476, n. 10; JdChr I², 677, n. 10.

thus also established starting from the divinity of Jesus. But another reason stands out: it is as guiltless that Christ has been killed, because he was conceived, i.e. begotten in a new birth, through the birth from the virgin, as Leo enlarges on this theme in the First Tome (vv. 89–90a) with the use of *sermo* 22.[113] Christ is free from original sin, and therefore not subjected to the *debitum mortis*.[114] Thus the Saviour could also overcome the devil.[115] In any case Leo is certainly at pains in the Second Tome to bring the doctrine of salvation more strongly into play than it was in the First Tome. Thus a greater richness in soteriological language is also to be discerned.[116] The major events in the redemptive life of Jesus are death and resurrection (cf. *sermo* 28, 5; 30, 5; 21, 2). But in the opposition to Eutyches, all the events in the life of Jesus have theological significance, particularly his birth from Mary.[117] Whoever decides with Apollinarius for *una natura* denies the truth of the human flesh and of the soul, and allows the divinity of the Word itself to be changed into flesh and soul.

And to be conceived and born, to be nourished and to grow, to be crucified and to die, to be buried and to rise and to ascend into heaven and to sit at the right hand of the Father ... would be proper only to the divine essence, which, however, retains nothing of them without the truth of the flesh.[118]

But through the true incarnation, the destiny of Christ has become the destiny of all. In him, the true and guiltless man, all are crucified, all have died and been buried, all have risen as well, and this in community with his humanity.[119] Leo's doctrine of redemption thus calls to mind Rom 5 and 6 more than it does Joh 12, 32, which is explicitly cited (v. 10). Through this bond with the humanity of

[113] Cf. T. I 89–90a (28, 6–8): *nova autem nativitate generatus quia inviolata virginitas concupiscentiam nescivit, carnis materiam ministravit; adsumpta est de matre Domini natura non culpa* ...

[114] T. II 53–54 (115, 7–8): *ut mortis vinculum unius praevaricatione contractum, Unius morte, qui solus morti nihil debuit, solveretur.* Cf. vv. 58–59 (115, 11–13).

[115] The idea of the devil's right or of the overcoming of the devil (as the master of mankind through the power of death) by outwitting him is recognisable here. This outwitting is achieved through the assumption of lowly flesh which did not allow the godhead to become visible to Satan. Cf. T. I 26.77.111 (25, 20; 27, 17; 28, 27) with T. II 56 (115, 9–10) or 74–75 (115, 28–29): *qui contra hostem humani generis in carnis nostrae humilitate congressus, his victoriam suam tribuit in quorum corpore triumphavit.* On Leo's terminology for the devil, see M.-M. Mueller, op. cit., 222–223.

[116] What is new in T. II, in contrast to T. I, in the following. 1. For the depiction of our unredeemed condition: *captivitas, chirografum letale* (II 140) (118, 4), *debitum servitutis* (II 59) (115, 13). 2. For the interpretation of Christ's work: *immolatio* (II 63) (115, 18), *pontifex* and *altare*, or *sacrificium crucis* (II 61 and 63) (115, 17f.), *reconciliatio, repropitiatio, redemptio* (but cf. I 173 [31, 24]: *sanguis redemptionis*), *redintegratio* with its derivative forms (II 50.61.63.88) (115, 4–18; 116, 8). The talk of 'blood' (*sanguis*) is significantly stronger (cf. I 173 (31, 24) with II 55.61.111.140) (115, 9ff.; 116, 32; 118,4). 3. For the description of the fruits of the redemption: *reconciliatus, redemptus, redintegratio* with its derivative forms, *renasci, salvare.* While in T. I the cultic consideration of Christ's act of reconciliation is missing entirely, suddenly it is introduced quite strongly in T. II.

[117] Cf. the accentuation of the birth: T. I 23.86.89.90.103 (25, 17–18; 28, 2.6–8.20–21).

[118] T. II 28–30 (114, 4–6).

[119] T. II 69 (115, 25) from *Tr.* 64 (5 April, 453): CCL 138A, p. 392, 76–77: Iesus Christus ... 'in whom all have been crucified, all have died, all have been buried, but also all have been raised...'.

Christ, the true Son of God, redeemed humanity as a whole becomes the body of Christ.[120]

4. The dynamic of salvation history and the two-nature model in Leo's christology

Through his frequent reference to the Apostles' Creed and the Nicene Creed, as in general through his emphasis on tradition, the Pope indicates that his fundamental christological model is the doctrine of the economy of salvation which is expressed in these creeds. Precisely on account of this reason the Nicene Creed is adduced in the Second Tome. One and the same Son of the Father, the subject of the Nicene statements about the true godhead, is also the subject of the incarnation, the humiliation and the exaltation (cf. vv. 41–42). It is here that the work of Chalcedon also fits in:

> What in our days has been laid down at Chalcedon about the incarnation of our Lord Jesus Christ was also determined at Nicaea by that mystical number of Fathers, so that the catholic confession does not believe that either the only-begotten Son of God is in anything unequal to the Father, or that the same [Son], in as much as he became the son of man, did not have the true nature of our flesh and of our soul.[121]

It is not a big step from this stress both on the divinity and on the humanity of Christ within the credal model of the economy of salvation to a more static 'two-nature doctrine'. But such a doctrine is not an end in itself. The impulse for it comes only from Eutyches, and the background of the history of heresy which lies behind him (Manichaeans, Docetists). A certain number of 'technical' modes of expression from the two-nature language seem, indeed, to have found their way into Leo's sermons and letters. But these can hardly be a literal reference to the formula of the 'one hypostasis (person) in two natures'. Inducement for this new language came from the report of Bishop Flavian of Constantinople in his second letter to Leo about Eutyches: 'before the incarnation of our Saviour Jesus Christ—so he [Eutyches] says—there are the two natures of divinity and humanity, but after the union there is only one nature'.[122] In this way Leo received the catch-phrase, which he was able to enlarge upon slightly and without difficulty in his sermons and letters for a simple audience.[123]

The first time we encounter talk of *natura* is in the First Tome

---

[120] Cf. M.-M. Mueller, op. cit., s.v. *corpus*, 89 and 203.
[121] Leo M., *ep.*, 162 *ad Leon. aug.*, 21 March, 458: ACO II 4, nr. 99, p. 105, 34–106, 4. What is interesting in this context is that Leo transfers back into the statement of Nicaea the rejection of Apollinarianism with its denial of a soul in Christ.
[122] *Ep. Flaviani secunda ad Leon.*, *ep.* 26 *inter ep. Leon.*, in Greek in ACO II 1, p. 38, 24–25.
[123] Cf. H. Arens, op. cit., 187–241.

v. 27: 'we could not conquer, of course, the author of sin and death, if He (*ille*) had not assumed our nature and made it his own (*nisi naturam nostram ille susciperet et suam faceret*)'. The assumption of the concrete human nature of Christ immediately affects the whole of humanity, of which we have become members by birth, thus our nature. One will call to mind the 'Christus totus' of Augustine, when Leo says in *tractatus* 63:

> There is no doubt, beloved, that the human nature was taken up by the Son of God in such a close union (*naturam humanam in tantam conexionem a Filio Dei esse susceptam*), so that Christ is one and the same not only in that man who is the first-born of the whole of creation (cf. Col 1, 15) but also in all his saints; as the head cannot be separated from the members, so too the members cannot be separated from the head.[124]

Leo uses the word *natura* twenty-five times in the First Tome; etymologically, the cognate words, the verb *nasci* (v. 22) and the noun *nativitas* (v. 23) are to be bracketed with this. This etymology should always be adverted to, just as the Greek word *physis* (begetting, birth, derivation, origin, source) should be connected with the verb *phyein* (to beget, to develop, to produce) and the Syriac word *kyānā* with the verb *kyn*. When Leo uses the word 'nature', therefore, one must not think immediately of the question about the 'what', the 'essence', 'quiddity', the *ousia*, the *essentia*, but first of all of 'genesis', origin. As has been correctly observed,[125] the concept of nature for Leo is stamped with a meaning that is unfamiliar to us, because the noun *natura* always suggests *nasci* (cf. First Tome, v. 90 *nativitas—natura*). Our humanity is determined by the origin, birth from a human being. There is a tension in the First Tome, v. 90, because on the one hand with Christ *nasci* leads to genuine humanity, and yet on the other hand there was a *nativitas mirabilis*, a wondrous birth, i.e. birth from the virgin. It is precisely this tension which, beginning with the Docetists and up until Eutyches, is repeatedly resolved one-sidedly. But for the very reason that the 'appearance' destroys the incarnation, in Leo's mind the opposite of appearance, i.e. *veritas*, reality is immediately combined with stress on the assumption of our 'nature', as we have observed to be the case with Emperor Marcian. *Natura* is not to be defined philosophically; on the contrary, it gives a kerygmatic, anti-heretical accent which is valid in the first place for the humanity of Jesus Christ, but in its own way for his divinity as well.[126]

---

[124] Leo M., *Tr.* 63, 3 (19 March, 452): CCL 138A, p. 383, 41–45.

[125] Cf. H. Arens, op. cit., 187–241, 453–475.

[126] Cf. ibid., 323–353. That Leo and Marcian (see above) agree in their understanding of *natura* as *veritas*, truth, reality (in contrast to phantasy, appearance) is shown by numerous passages in Leo's writings: for instance, *Tr.* 27, 1 (from the year 451): CCL 138, p. 132, 4: *naturae nostrae veritas*; 1. 18: *in utraque ergo natura*; cf. p. 133, 27: *veritas . . . formae utriusque. Tr.* 28, 4 (from the

Both are important for our salvation. There is also a third: that godhead and manhood are united to each other.[127] But by the application of this word *natura* both to the godhead of Christ as well as to his manhood, the formulation *utraque natura* (each of the two natures) can appear, as is demonstrated in the passages just cited. The paratactical and static impression of Leo's picture of Christ is intensified by this, but it must not be isolated from other structural elements, as will become clearer.

Besides *natura*, the concepts *essentia* and *substantia* are also found in Leo's writings, as has already been shown to be the case in the pre-Chalcedonian period.[128]

(a) *Essentia* (cf. First Tome, v. 20). Leo does not offer any definition for this concept either. This concept also occurs almost exclusively in a theological context. Quite often *natura* can be replaced by *essentia*. In the *sermones*, *essentia* appears twenty-seven times, and in the letters eleven times.[129] Particularly in speech about God both expressions can be combined.[130] But the same can also be said with regard to man, and this means that Leo can use *utraque essentia* christologically: in Christ both essences are united in the unity of the person.[131] Essence is to be understood here in a verbal sense as derived from the root *esse*. As was the case with *nasci-natura*, so here is the relation between *esse* and *essentia* reproduced. This relation is particularly explicit in *tractatus* 27 (from 451) and 28 (from 452).[132]

(b) *Substantia*.[133] Apart from *natura* and *essentia*, the term *substantia* is also employed without there being a 'significant semantic difference'. Here too Leo offers no definition. The following text illustrates how these three expressions can be combined.[134]

'Since we confess the divine nature (*divinam ... naturam*) from the Father and the human substance (*substantiam*) from the mother in the one Lord Jesus Christ, the true son of God and of man, although there was only one person of the Word of God and the flesh, and although each of the two essences has functions in common, the properties of the works themselves (i.e. whether divine or human) are, nevertheless, discernible.'

year 452): CCL 138, p. 141, 65–66: *duarum in Christo naturarum veritatem sub unius personae confessione*; *Tr.* LIV, 1 (5 April, 442): CCL 138A, p. 317, 18–20: *exprimit quidem sub distinctis actionibus veritatem suam utraque natura, sed neutra se ab alterius conexione disiungit* ... In the activity (*actio*) of the one Christ the reality of the godhead and the manhood expresses itself. This emphasis on the 'reality of each of the two natures' is always directed against Eutyches. Important is *Tr.* 96 (25 December, 457) *contra haeresim Eutychis dictus ad populum in Basilica S. Anastasiae*: CCL 138A, pp. 593–595. In this the murder of the Patriarch Proterius is presupposed. Once again *natura* is interpreted by *veritas*. According to Leo the messengers of Timothy Aelurus maintain: 'only the nature of the godhead is present in Christ; he had nothing at all of the reality (*veritatem*) of human flesh, which he assumed, however, from the blessed Virgin'. Leo does not reply with analyses of concepts, but with theological reasons: 'the ungodliness accepts that the humanity (of Christ) is false and names God passible'. Cf. Chavasse, loc. cit., p. 593, 19–20. The 'one nature' of the Alexandrians is for Leo simply the denial of the human reality of Christ, whence also their theopaschism.

[127] Leo M., *Tr.* 69, 5 (4 April, 454): CCL 138A, p. 424, 134–136: 'if the divinity of the Word were not to assume this (i.e. the human nature) into the unity of his person (*in suae personae reciperet unitatem*), there would be no rebirth (*regeneratio*) in the water of baptism, nor would there be redemption in the blood of suffering'.
[128] Cf. H. Arens, op. cit., 187–303 on vv. 16–20 of T. I.
[129] Ibid., 197, n. 81.
[130] Leo M., *Tr.* LXXV, 45ff.; *Tr.* LXXVII, 76ff. (according to Arens, op. cit., 199).
[131] Leo M., *ep.* 84 (9 June, 451): ACO II 4, p. 44, 1–3.
[132] Leo M., *Tr.* 27, 36f.; *Tr.* 28, 8f. (according to Arens, op. cit., 200–203).
[133] Cf. H. Arens, op. cit., 314–323 on vv. 54–55 of T. I.
[134] Leo M., *Tr.* 64, 4 (5 April, 453): CCL 138A, p. 392, 87–91.

Substantia is employed in anthropological[135] and trinitarian[136] contexts. In both spheres it signifies 'existence'. This expression occurs most often in the doctrine of the incarnation, but it is replaced in part by *natura*.[137]

'Accordingly, by *substantia divina* Leo designates the *Deus esse*, and by *substantia humana* the *homo esse*, or, in other words, the being-subsistence of God and the being-subsistence of man.[138] Both, God and man, subsist in the one Jesus Christ; as the incarnate Word of God, he subsists as God and man' (Arens).

(A different view will, of course, predominate in Neo-Chalcedonianism: the one Word God, the one divine hypostasis, subsists, exists in divine and human nature.) To the extent that *substantia* (in the biblical sense) does not express, for instance, possession, property, goods or means, it is interchangeable with *natura*. However, the concrete choice of a word is nuanced with regard to its etymological origin (*nasci-natura, substare-substantia*; cf. *esse-essentia*). 'With respect to its origin, that which exists is called nature, and, with respect to its existing, nature is called substance.'[139] There is still an important sociological aspect to be mentioned: to see the Son of God as 'bound by nature' to the community of mankind is the most sublime motive for highly esteeming human nature simply, and this concretely in every individual man.[140]

5. *The one Christ* una persona

How does the usage of the word *persona* in Leo's christology relate to what we have just analysed? It is not easy to gauge the import of this word; it is certainly not easier after Chalcedon than it was before. What one can establish is that Leo becomes more circumspect in the use of this word through the controversy with the Alexandrians, particularly because of the attacks on his First Tome.[141] His primary interest is also not in terminology and its definition, but in the theological contents which he wants to combine by means of it. What we notice is that he binds together the language of the 'two natures' and the 'one person' in the model of salvation history, as he outlines in *sermo* 65 of 8 April, 453.

Thus although from that very beginning when the Word became flesh in the womb of the Virgin no separation of any kind arose between the divine and the human substance, and in all bodily growth the activities during the whole period belonged to one sole *persona*, still in no way do we mingle that which has become in unseparatedness: from the character of the works we discern what belongs to

---

[135] Leo M., *Tr.* LXXI, 47ff. and so forth.

[136] Leo M., *Tr.* LXXV, 78ff.; *Tr.* XXIII, 51ff.; *Tr.* LXXVI, 30ff.; *Tr.* LXXVII, 17ff.; 115ff. (according to Arens, op. cit., 333, n. 79).

[137] Cf. T. I 54 with *Tr.* XXI: CCL 138, p. 87, 44 (*natura-substantia*); T. I 91 (*unitas*) with *Tr.* XXIV, 3: CCL 138, p. 112, 71 (*substantia*).

[138] Cf. H. Arens, op. cit., 334. Cf. *Tr.* LVI, 1 (28 March, 443): CCL 138A, p. 329, 31–33: *unde oportuit in unum Dominum Iesum Christum et divinam et humanam convenire substantiam* ... Cf. JdChr I², 748, n. 24.

[139] H. Arens, op. cit., 336.

[140] Leo M., *Tr.* IX, (November, 443), p. 35, 59–68.

[141] For the sake of comparison let us draw attention once again to the quite careless presentation of the unity in Christ in *Tr.* XXIII (from the year 442): CCL 138, p. 102–108, which we commented on in JdChr I², 747; CCT I², 537.

which nature. The divine does not encroach upon the human, nor the human upon the divine. Then each of the two came together into one and the same (*in idipsum* = neuter) is such a way that in them neither the peculiarity is taken away, nor the *persona* doubled.[142]

For the theology of the trinity, Leo takes over the distinction between person and nature from the Latin tradition. 'Person' means here: 'non-interchangeability and individuality in the same divine spiritual nature'. Thus Leo says in *tractatus* LXXV, 3: 'Though in the properties of the persons, the Father is other, the Son is other, and the Holy Spirit is other, there is not, however, another godhead or a different nature'.[143] In his christology, where it is a matter of controversies, he avoids combinations such as *persona humana* or *persona divina Christi*. In the christological distinction, there is for Leo only the *natura divina* on the one side and the *natura humana* on the other. In his *sermo* delivered on the occasion of the feast of Epiphany in 443, he had admittedly spoken more freely:

> Finally [the Magi] fulfill their duty with devotion (*cum religione*) and furnish themselves with gifts to show in their adoration that they believe in one Trinity—by honouring the kingly person with gold, the human person with myrrh and the divine person with incense.[144]

The expressions are not to be pressed. For, as *ep.* 119 (11 June, 453) bears witness, Leo knows of the false employment of the concept of person by Nestorius: '*unumque Christum in duos dividens aliam deitatis, et aliam humanitatis voluit esse personam, cum omnino unus idemque sit*' (Nestorius 'divided the one Christ into two and wanted the one to be the person of the godhead and the other the person of the manhood, though, indeed, [Christ] is completely one and the same'.)[145] The two texts are not necessarily opposed. In the first text *persona* is combined each time with an adjective, but in the second, with two abstract nouns. Moreover, Leo sets his own formula over against this second 'Nestorian' formula: '*deitatis humanitatisque persona*'

---

[142] Leo M., *Tr.* 65, 1 (8 April, 453): CCL 138A, p. 395, 12–22.

[143] Leo M., *Tr.* LXXV, 3 (23 May, 443): CCL 138A, p. 467, 53–55. In *Tr.* 28 (from the year 452): CCL 138, p. 142, 74–78, the opposite position is presented, viz. the teaching of the Sabellianists (or the Patripassians?) on the 'trinity': 'because they could not understand the unity in the godhead as (on the assumption) of the unity of persons, thus they maintained the Father is the same as the Son, so that being born and nourished, suffering and dying, being buried and rising belonged to one and the same, who in everything fills both the person of the man and of the Word' (*qui per omnia et hominis personam impleret et Verbi*). 'In the unutterable unity of the trinity, whose works and decisions are common in all things, the person of the Son assumed strictly for himself (*proprie Filii persona suscepit*) the restoration of the human race, so that being born and suffering belong to the Son and not to the Father'. Thus in *Tr.* 64, 2 (5 April, 453): CCL 138A, p. 390, 32f. On the doctrine of the trinity, cf. *Tr.* LXXV, 3 (23 May, 443): CCL 138A, p. 468f., 74–80.

[144] Leo M., *Tr.* XXXIII, 2 (1a ed., 443): CCL 138, p. 172, 41–44: *auro honorantes personam regiam, myrra humanam, ture divinam.*

[145] Leo M., *ep.* 119: ACO II 4, p. 73, 23–24.

(the person in godhead and manhood).[146] With this he intends to say that through the event of the incarnation there was the one concrete subject Jesus Christ in godhead and manhood, as we have already seen expressed in *tractatus* 65.[147] Who this final subject is, is clearly determined in *tractatus* 63, where Joh 1, 14 and II Cor 5, 19 (a soteriological text) are quoted, and where it is then said:

Thus it has been shown that the Only-begotten of the Father Most High established such a consortium with human lowliness that he indeed assumed the substance of our flesh and of our soul; but nevertheless remained one and the same Son of God (*unus atque idem Dei Filius permaneret*).

(It is not he who gained something, but we.[148]) In other words, even if the word *persona* is not used in reference to the Pre-existing One in order to express the unity in the duality of the natures, nevertheless the eternal Son of the Father clearly remains the subject of the incarnation, and hence the final bearer of the manhood of Christ.

That from the viewpoint of Leo the one Christ stands as the 'one person of godhead and manhood' (*una persona deitatis et humanitatis*) is the 'result' of the incarnation. Nevertheless, it remains true that even before the incarnation the Word is *persona deitatis*. For Leo 'persona' is the '*natura*' (*substantia*) with its properties (*proprietates*).[149]

---

[146] Leo M., *Tr.* LXXII, 2 (21 April, 444): CCL 138A, p. 442f., 38–39. Here Leo uses the abstract nouns *deitas-humanitas*, whereas in *Tr.* 47 (21 February, 454): CCL 138A, p. 277, 1.70–72 (*in Christi Dei atque hominis una persona*) he uses the concrete nouns *deus-homo*. Both formulae are incapable of attaining the sharpness of theological expression which Cyril formulated in his *Laetentur* letter on the Formulary of Reunion of the Antiochenes (see JdChr I², 704–706; CCT I², 498–501). For Leo it is not a question of finding the most adequate formula possible for expressing the unity in Christ, but primarily of safeguarding that bond of divinity and humanity in him, which appears necessary and sufficient for grounding our salvation. The different intentions of Cyril and Leo need to be taken in account in reaching a judgment about them.

[147] See above n. 142.

[148] Leo M., *Tr.* 63, 1 (19 March, 452): CCL 138A, p. 383, 1.11–16.

[149] See below the passages on *persona*. Flavian of Constantinople, in his second letter to Leo, had already sketched a similar solution: ACO II 2, 1, nr. 4, p. 23, 13–16: 'the unity of the two natures which come together in Christ does not mingle, as Your Holiness knows, their properties in the unity (*neque ... propriatates suas in unitate confundit*); rather the properties of the natures remain unimpaired (*inlibatae*) in the unity of the natures'. The two natures themselves and their properties remain unmingled. The *anonymous author on Eutyches* also holds this viewpoint. He no doubt wrote in Rome shortly before Chalcedon and describes the following as *traditio fidei*: 'to confess one person of Christ and the two natures of the divinity and the humanity, of the creating and the created, of the assuming and the assumed. These substances or natures are not mingled, but united (*unitae*) and remain undivided in one and the same person and always in the property which is peculiar to each...'. Admittedly the anonymous author in his interpretation of the death of Christ still accepts the separation of the Word from the body, and holds a quite simple christology of indwelling: 'when he was hanging on the cross of suffering and saw that the God who was dwelling in him (*in se*) was going from his body, he cried after him in a sobbing voice and called out in Hebrew: Heli Heli [Mt 27, 46 is cited], although he would raise him after the third day (*quamvis post tertiam diem eum esset resuscitaturus*)' (ACO II 4, p. 148, 33–35). The text reminds one of Hilary, *Comment. in Ev. Matthaei 33*, 6: PL 9, 1074B–1075A) together with *Tract. in psalm. 55*, nr. 12: CSEL 22, 167, 23. Leo himself polemicizes against this false interpretation of the cry of abandonment in Matthew, and that in many *sermones*, which is a sign that the reason for this was still relevant. Did he have our anonymous author in mind? Cf. *Tr.* 67, 7 (28 March, 454): CCL 138A, p. 412f., 130–135: 'that call (*voc ista*), beloved, is teaching, not a complaint. For since there is in Christ *one*

Strictly speaking, there would have to be thus two *personae* in Christ. But both natures enter into each other in such a way that, each without loss of its *veritas* and its *proprietates*, they form an inseparable, unmingled unity. This conception still stems from 442:

> God therefore assumed the whole man and joined himself to him, and him to himself, out of mercy and power, so that each of the two natures inheres in the other and neither changes into the other with the surrender of its properties.[150]

The *una persona*, which Christ is in and through the incarnation, is the result of the unmingled and inseparable penetration of divine and human natures (each with its own properties). Like Cyril of Alexandria, Leo too always sees first the one concrete subject in Jesus of Nazareth. The unity is his starting-point. For the distinction has to be sought for. One can do this successfully, because the natures and their properties are united unmingled. This 'searching' for the distinction is expressed by the Chalcedonian 'recognisable', which refers to the operations by which at one time the godhead, at another

person of God and man (*Dei et hominis una persona ist*) and he could not be abandoned by him from whom he could not be separated, he asks for the benefit of anxious and weak ones, why the flesh which fears sufferings has not been heard'. In the same way *Tr.* 68, 1 (31 March, 454): ibid., 414, 7–12: (in the death of Christ there is no separation), 'because the nature of God and the nature of man have come together into such a great unity that they could neither be severed by torment nor separated by death. For since each of the two substances remains in its characteristics, neither did God abandon the suffering of his body, nor did the flesh make God passible, because the godhead was certainly in the sufferer but not in the suffering (*dolore*) itself'. But already in the sermon of 2 April, 443, Leo had stressed the inseparability of the divinity and humanity of Christ for soteriological reasons. If they were separable, there would be no immortality for us. Thus in *Tr.* LXX, 3: CCL 138A, p. 428, 62–65. Cf. *Tr.* LXXI (3/4 April, 443): ibid., p. 436, 44–49. In several new studies the origin of the *una persona* in Christ in the writings of Leo the Great is researched: (1) B. Studer, '*Una persona in Christo*. Ein augustinisches Thema bei Leo dem Großen', *Aug* 25 (1985) (= Miscellanea di Studi Agostini in onore di P. Agostino Trapè, OSA) 453–487. In particular he shows the connexion with Augustine's 'Letter to Volusianus' (see JdChr I², 600–602; in addition ibid., Index, *persona, una persona*). 'From the survey of Leo's patristic sources it is altogether evident that, apart from the writings of Augustine and texts dependent on him, no immediate sources, including Eastern ones, can be demonstrated for his conception of the *una persona in Christo*' (p. 475). Augustine had developed the concept of the *unitas personae* between 400 and 411 (p. 476). The confrontation with the Pelagians brought about a deepening of this expression, though Augustine did not advance beyond the consideration of the *una persona* as the result of the union of the Son of God with the man Jesus (pp. 482–483). Leo did not proceed further than Augustine, but rather lagged behind (pp. 486–487). (2) For Augustine himself the following work is important: H. R. Drobner, *Grammatische Exegese und Christologie bei Augustinus. Zur Herkunft der Formel una persona* (= Philosophia Patrum 8 (Leiden 1986). The author placed at my disposal the manuscript of his dissertation, Rome 1984. Ambrose, also, like Augustine, reached the term *persona* through grammar and exegesis. *Una persona*, however, cannot be demonstrated in genuine passages. The same is true of Ambrosiaster: by means of the grammatical concept *persona* he arrives at the terminology of the *persona* of Christ, but without emphasising the *una persona*. (3) M.-J. Rondeau, *Les commentaires patristiques du Psautier (IIIe–Ve siècles)*, Vol. II: Exégèse prosopologique et théologie = OCP 220 (Roma 1985) 415–417. Rondeau refers to Jerome's *In Zachariam* II, 6, 9–15 (CCL 76A, 799): *Non iam Iesum dividimus, nec duas personas in una possumus facere persona, sed ipse qui Iesus appellatur ... et Oriens dicitur.* Drobner, too, takes note of this passage and discusses it. M.-J. Rondeau believes that Jerome arrived at the formula *una persona* not through the Apollinarians, as R. Cantalamessa believed, but perhaps through Didymus, on whom he is dependent in his commentary on Zacharias (op. cit., 417).

[150] Leo M., *Tr.* LIV, 1 (5 April, 442): CCL 138A, p. 318, 25–29. For the assumption of the whole man, Leo emphasises here God's mercy and power (*potentia*).

time the manhood is illuminated. That is the meaning of that so much disputed sentence 'agit enim utraque forma...' (each of the two natures acts). The differences between Leo and Cyril can be made clear, however, if the 'natures-christology' of Leo in sermo 72 (21 April, 444) is contrasted with the mia physis formula, as understood by Cyril.

That nature, which lets neither what is his be imprisoned by what is ours, nor what is ours imprisoned by what is his, has assumed us: rather it [the nature] makes the persona of the godhead and of the manhood intrinsically one in such a way that in the economy (dispensatio) of the way of weakness and of power, neither the flesh could be invulnerable through the godhead, nor the godhead capable of suffering through the flesh.[151]

The conception that the one persona is due to the coming together of two natures in Christ is still accepted in 452:

The following is very useful for an understanding [of the suffering of Christ]: certainly the Creator is one thing, the creature something else; the invulnerable God is one thing, the flesh capable of suffering something else; however, the properties of each of the two natures come together in one person, so that—whether it be in humiliation or in a demonstration of power—the humiliation and the glory belong to one and the same.[152]

This text creates the impression that the 'one person' in Christ is a tertium from godhead and manhood. On the basis of the conceptural language, it does not become clear where the point of unity in Christ really is, where the final subject is. In any case, 'two persons' is ruled out: 'Neither of the two substances has retained its properties in such a way that there would be a separation of the persons in them' (non ita proprietates suas tenuit utraque substantia, ut personarum in eis possit esse discretio).[153] What is meant by these properties becomes evident in various sermones. In naming them, Leo is guided by soteriological interests. These interests determine his picture of Christ:

In this lies the healing of our wounds and the elevation from our state of rejection: had so vast a difference (diversitas) not come together into one (in unum), human nature would not have been able to be reconciled with God.[154]

[151] Leo M., Tr. LXXII, 2 (21 April, 444): CCL 138A, 442f., 37–41. The grammatical subject of the assumption is in fact the natura, not the persona (hypostasis); this is also the case further on in the text, § 2: loc. cit., 443, 41–42: suscepit nos illa natura. But this language is conditioned by soteriology: Leo wants to emphasise the binding of godhead and manhood. To have reflected on the subject of the assumption would have been to pass over this point of concern.
[152] Leo M., Tr. 62, 1 (16 March, 452): CCL 138A, p. 377, 1.24–29.
[153] Leo M., Tr. XXIII, 1 (from the year 442): CCL 138, p. 103, 21–23. We are obliged to say here already that Leo employs the word 'mingling' (miscere) to reject the (Nestorian) teaching of indwelling: nec sic creatura in societatem sui Creatoris adsumpta est, ut ille habitator et illa esset habitaculum, sed ita ut naturae alteri altera misceretur (an explanation follows, however): Et quamvis alia sit quae suscipitur, alia vero quae suscipit, in tantam tamen unitatem convenit utriusque diversitas, ut unus idemque sit Filius, qui se, et secundum quod verus homo est Patre dicit minorem, et secundum quod verus Deus est Patri profitetur aequalem (loc. cit., 23–29).
[154] Leo M., Tr. 37, 1 (from the year 452): CCL 138, p. 200, 13–16.

'*In unum*' is to be taken as neuter and not as masculine. God and man have become 'one' in Christ. Finite-infinite, passible-impassible: they are bound in this unity. In a soteriological *sermo* (1 March, 453) we read the following:

> In him are true and numerous testimonies of each of the two natures (*testimonia utriusque naturae*) which in the subliminity of the divine decree come together (*concurrentia*) in such a way that one can recognise by the invulnerable Word and his nondividedness from passible flesh that in everything the godhead shares in the flesh, and the flesh shares in the godhead.[155]

Thus it is not Leo's concern to establish the unity in Christ speculatively, to employ correctly for this the accurate concepts. He has only one task in mind: starting from the necessity of our salvation, to represent the true unity of God and man as the unity of one *persona*, and, in doing this, to stress the distinction in such a way that both the truth of the godhead and also the reality of the assumed manhood are guaranteed. Let us see this expressed once again in the words of *sermo* 62:

> With this rule of faith..., which we received at the beginning of the Creed on the authority of the apostolic teaching, we confess our Lord Jesus Christ, whom we call the only Son of the Father Almighty, and as one and the same also born of the Virgin Mary from the Holy Spirit; we also do not abandon his majesty when we believe the same to be the One who was crucified, who died and who rose on the third day. Everything which in Christ is of God and of man fills at the same time both the manhood and the godhead: and, indeed, in such a way that in the indwelling of the Impassible in the Passible neither is power affected by weakness, nor is weakness overwhelmed by power.[156]

Even in the Second Tome to Emperor Leo, no deepening of the concept of person is to be noted, especially in the light of the fact that in decisive places older sermons are quoted.

> 'Although, therefore, in the one Lord Jesus Christ, the true son of God and man, there is one person (*una persona*) of the Word and of the flesh, which has, unseparated and undivided, activities in common, the properties of these activities are, however, discernible...'[157] '... Although, therefore, from the very beginning when the Word became flesh in the womb of the Virgin there was no division at all between both forms [=natures] and in all bodily growth the activities during this whole period belonged to the *una persona*, thus we do not mingle, for all that, what has been worked in unseparatedness; rather we recognise from the properties of the works to what nature they belong.'[158]

Is it intentional on Leo's part that in this Second Tome the '*agit enim utraque forma*...' of the First Tome, an expression which was horror to the Monophysites, does not reappear? In fact, nothing

---

[155] Leo M., *Tr.* 46, 2 (1 March, 453): CCL 138A, p. 270f., 44–48.
[156] Leo M., *Tr.* 62, 2 (16 March, 452): CCL 138A, p. 377, 30–39.
[157] Leo M., T. II 76–78 (115, 30–32) (from *Tr.* 64).
[158] Leo M., ibid., 94–98 (116, 13–17).

has changed in Leo's conception. His sole intention is to make clear, 'for the sake of our salvation' and not from speculative interest (i.e. not from the rational employment of concepts and analysis), that from the properties of the word one can plainly recognise the following fact: in Christ there are two natures, i.e. two principles of operation, each in its own *veritas*, which are thus capable of mediating divine salvation to sinful flesh, by reason of their union as well as their unseparated activity in common. Both their union and their unseparated activity in common would not be possible, if Christ were divided into two persons, or if in reality either of the two natures is not taken account of. The bodily, human reality of Christ manifests itself on the cross, but also in the resurrection (cf. vv. 99–104, following Lk 24, 39 and Joh 20, 27). For that very reason Christ is the mediator, the foundation of our hope; his name, his blood, his humiliation and exaltation are our salvation and our redemption.[159] Worthy of note is the recapitulatory statement.

Cum ergo unus sit dominus Jesus Christus et verae deitatis veraeque humanitatis in ipso una prorsus eademque persona sit. Exaltationem tamen, qua illum sicut doctor gentium dicit, exaltavit Deus et donavit illi nomen, quod super omne nomen excellit, ad eandem intelligimus pertinere formam quae ditanda erat tantae glorificationis augmento. (Therefore, although the Lord Jesus Christ is one, and in him there is just one and the same *persona* of true godhead and of true manhood, we perceive, however, that the exaltation, by which, as the teacher of the gentiles says, God exalted him and gave him the name which is above all other names (Phil 2, 10–11), belongs to that same form [nature] which would be enriched by such a glorification.)[160]

Jesus Christ is one concrete subject from godhead and manhood. This implies such a unity that the Lord Jesus Christ is strictly one. But this also preserves the unmingledness in such a way that the part which is the recipient in the exaltation, i.e. the manhood, could be enriched on its own, without receiving the godhead as a gift. Leo is not successful in clarifying his concept of person in such a way that from an analysis of it the final bearer of godhead and manhood in Christ could appear explicitly.[161] For Leo to have brought this about he would have needed additional models and expressions, which then in their turn would have called for a new application

---

[159] Ibid., 105–113 (116, 25–117, 10); cf. Acts 4, 12; 1 Tim 2, 6; Phil 2, 6–11.
[160] Ibid., 113–115 (117, 8–12).
[161] Cf. M. J. Nicolas, 'La doctrine christologique de saint Léon le Grand', *RevThom* 51 (1951) (609–660) 638: '... il vient à considérer l'incarnation non plus dans l'instant de sa réalisation, mais dans son résultat qui est l'Homme-Dieu'. Cf. J. P. Jossua, *Le salut, incarnation ou mystère pascal, chez les Pères de l'Église de saint Irénée à saint Léon le Grand* (Paris 1968) 255: 'saint Léon distingue bien la première manifestation de l'incarnation lors de la naissance du Christ à Noël, et l'incarnation comme "structure" ontologique permanente du Christ, qui est à l'œuvre, non seulement dans le mystère de la nativité, mais dans tous les mystéres de la vie du Seigneur' (quoted from H. Arens, op. cit., 342, n. 121).

of *persona* in Christ. We can make this clear best of all by referring
to a commentary on Leo's First Tome. This commentary was composed during the lifetime of the Pope.

6. *The fragment of a commentary of Patriarch Gennadius of Constantinople*

An interesting parallel to Leo's concept of person is found in a
fragment of the 'Eulogy of the Archbishop of Constantinople, Gennadius, on the letter of Leo, the most holy Pope of Rome'.[162] Although
the First Tome (449) is meant here, there are many indications that
this *laudatio* was not composed until after Chalcedon, but still before
the death of Leo I (461). We present the text in translation.

> This is then what Leo wrote . . . For my part, while I applaud his interpretations
> of the orthodox faith, I am at a loss to know how I should praise Leo fittingly.
> Such a vast knowledge of unutterable things, I see as vouchsafed to him by the
> Holy Spirit, so that he also has a penetrating understanding of the mystery of the
> incarnation of the Only-begotten, and as well the capacity to express his comprehen-
> sion clearly.
> Of what he has written here [First Tome] what does not aim at clearing up error
> and at increasing knowledge of the truth? Has he not in his lofty praise of the
> Father and of the Son silenced the Sabellians, Arians and Eunomians? With his
> scripturally based confession to the birth of the eternal Son of the Eternal Father
> from the Holy Spirit and from the Virgin Mary has he not condemned all those
> who dare to call him [Christ] by other names? With his proof that in the worthy
> and truthful way of God the flesh of the Lord assumed reality from the Virgin
> and that from God himself he was animated with the rational spirit of life, has
> he not strengthened the evangelic and prophetic kerygma and dispelled any mere
> appearance and illusion from it? With his preaching of the unmingled preservation
> of the properties of each of the two natures *in the one prosopon of the Son*, has he
> not countermanded those who babble it about that He [the Son] disappeared or
> suffered a transformation? With his confession of the death of the Only-begotten
> has he not praised clearly the impassibility of the divine nature? Has he not explained
> to us clearly the unutterable gift of the humiliation of the Son for us below through
> the incarnation? Has he not through every word of the gospel demonstrated to
> us that Christ is true God and true man . . .?
> But he was not the inventor of new names, but remained with those which were
> to hand from the orthodox Fathers; the words which they advanced attested and
> said to him that 'the Logos became flesh', that He 'took', 'added', 'assumed', (perma-
> nently) 'assumed' (ἐπελάβετο), 'had', 'participated in', 'was united to', 'was joined
> together with', 'had borne', 'had put on', 'was clothed with', 'had hidden himself',
> 'had revealed himself', that He 'has settled', 'has pitched his tent'; that He 'was
> body, temple, instrument', that 'Christ is true God and true man, that in him there
> is both the divine as well as the human nature'; that He 'is eternal and in time,
> passible and impassible, invisible and visible, uncreated and created, infinite and
> finite'; 'that He was in the form of God and became the form of man'; 'eternal
> Son of the eternal Father, and in time the son of a temporal mother'; 'of one being

---

[162] See the text in F. Diekamp, *Analecta Patristica. Texte und Abhandlungen zur griechischen Patristik*
= OCA 117 (Roma 1938) 77–78; on the person of the Patriarch Gennadius, ibid., 54–72; comments
on the eulogy on the letter of Pope Leo to Flavian, ibid., 93–96.

with God and the Father, of the same being as the Virgin Mother'; 'of the same nature, of the same kind', 'of the same divine origin'; (ὁμοφυής, ὁμόφυλος, συγγενής); 'first-fruits', 'yeast', 'head', 'first-born', 'brother'; 'creator and creature', 'raised and rising'; 'having', 'assuming'; 'ruler', 'under the lordship'; 'sending', 'coming', 'returning' (venturus); 'man', 'human being'; 'in fullness of power', 'under the law'; 'equal to God and less than the angels'; 'saviour and saved'; 'indweller and place of the indwelling'; 'listener and the one listened to'; 'sanctifier and sanctified'; 'nourisher and hungering'; 'refresher of the weary and himself weary'; 'strengthening and receiving support'; 'lord'; 'master'; 'redeemer'; 'Christ'; 'God praised above all in all eternity. Amen'.

On the basis of the Greek translation of the First Tome, numerous terms mentioned here can actually be demonstrated to be excerpts from it.[163] The most interesting thing is the reproduction by Gennadius, in fact in question form, of the famous sentence from the First Tome (Latin: vv. 54–55: salva igitur proprietate utriusque naturae et in unam coeunte personam; Greek, ACO II 1, 1, p. 13, 11: σῳζομένης τοίνυν τῆς ἰδιότητος ἑκατέρας φύσεως καὶ εἰς ἓν πρόσωπον συνιούσης): 'Has he not with the unmingled preservation of properties of each of the two natures in the one prosopon of the Son...?' (The Greek reads: οὐ τῆς ἑκατέρας φύσεως ἰδιότητα σῳζομένην κηρύξας ἀσύγχυτον ἐν ἑνὶ προσώπῳ τοῦ υἱοῦ...;[164]) The alteration is striking. The differences, in contrast to the elements in common, must be noted accurately. (1) Both speak of the preservation of the two natures and the one prosopon. (2) The differences between the two forms are: (a) it is probable that with the word 'unmingled' Gennadius refers by this time to Chalcedon; (b) εἰς with the accusative means for Leo that he views the one prosopon as the goal of the coming together of two natures. Moreover, prosopon has no apposition in the genitive, but is used absolutely; (c) according to Gennadius the starting-point is 'the one prosopon of the Son' or 'of the First-born', whereby there is no doubt that the 'eternal Son of the eternal Father' is meant (Diekamp, p. 78, 11.2 and 24). A disappearance or a transformation, as the heretics assume in their interpretation (Diekamp, p. 78. 1.3), is also certainly excluded by him—such is the Patriarch's interpretation of Leo's words. In this 'one prosopon of the Son', the assumed human nature is just as much preserved as the godhead. Gennadius elucidates in this way not just the statement of Leo, but also that of Chalcedon itself. That is to say, the application of the word prosopon (hypostasis) to the Pre-existent One, the Only-begotten of the Father, suggests itself unmistakeably. In this way the Second Person of the Trinity is also introduced conceptually as the 'one

[163] See the Greek translation of the First Tome in ACO II 1, 1, nr. 11, pp. 10–20, particularly from p. 12, 26ff.
[164] Cf. Diekamp, loc. cit., 78, 1–2.

person' who assumes. On this point there is no factual difference from Leo, but there is certainly a terminological difference—and this came about through an interpretation of the First Tome. For fundamentally the same picture of Christ is proper to both defenders of Chalcedon. (3) The picture of Christ that is held in common. Gennadius himself had gone through a process of development.[165] To begin with he was a vigorous opponent of Cyril of Alexandria, and wrote a refutation of the twelve anathemas, a work which is no longer extant. Only isolated fragments of this work have been retained by Facundus of Hermiane and the deacon Pelagius.[166] According to Diekamp, there is nothing extraordinary in the fact that a resolute supporter of Antiochene theology became an ardent defender of Chalcedon. In the commentary of Gennadius on the Letter to the Romans there are

clear indications of Antiochene christology, just as he is closest to the Antiochenes in his type of exegesis. His repeated talk of the adoption (hyiothesia) of Christ, which is the pattern of our adoption, shows that at the time of the composition of this commentary he [Gennadius] did not conceive the unity of God and man as a true unity of person.[167]

That a change took place Diekamp demonstrates by a fragment from the commentary on the Letter to the Galatians (Gal 3, 20):

That is to say, the mediator Christ is the Son of God, one and the same, being at the same time truly God and truly man, who, through his kinship (syngeneia) with both. brings both together into unity in himself (εἰς ἓν συνάγων ἐν ἑαυτῷ τὰ ἑκάτερα).[168]

Could Gennadius' turning away from Antiochene theology have taken place sometime between the composition of the commentaries on Paul? In any case, the commentary on the Letter to the Romans proves to us that at one time the Patriarch Gennadius was not too far removed from Nestorianism. The fact that he was accused of Nestorian tendencies by some when he was still patriarch (Diekamp, p. 68, n. 4) may perhaps have been based on recollections of this commentary.[169] Already in 442 in a commentary on Phil 2, 7 Leo developed ideas on Christ which are similar to those expressed in the words of Gennadius just quoted, and which also allow the concept of person to be placed in context.

---

[165] Ibid., 70–72.
[166] Ibid., 73–76; CPG 5974. The Facundus fragment is now critically edited in CCL 90A (1974), 57–58; for an explanation see Diekamp, op. cit., 85–89.
[167] Ibid., 88. Diekamp refers to the explanation of Rom 1, 7; 6, 4; 8, 16; 11, 16; 15, 5f., following K. Staab, Pauluskommentare aus der griechischen Kirche (Münster 1932) 352, 19ff.; 365, 28ff.; 379, 5ff.; 400, 8ff.; 414, 12ff.; now on this: S. J. Voicu, 'Gennadio di Costantinopoli. La transmissione del frammento In Hebr. IX, 2–5', OCP 48 (1982) 435–437.
[168] Diekamp, op. cit., 89, following Staab, op. cit., 419, 12ff.
[169] Nevertheless, the supporters of Chalcedon were accused simply of Nestorianism.

In their blindness the Arians could not see with the eyes of the spirit (*intelligentiae*) the relationship or the unity of Creator and creature. For they did not believe that the Only-begotten of God is of the same glory and substance as the Father. For they devised for themselves a lesser godhead for the Son from what must be referred to the form of the slave. To show that this form in him does not belong to a separate or another person (*in se non discretae neque alterius esse personae*), this very Son speaks with this very [form of the slave]: the Father is greater than I (Joh 14, 28b), as he also says with this form: I and the Father are one (Joh 10, 30). That is to say that in the form of the slave, which he assumes at the end of the ages for our restoration, he is less than the Father, but in the form of God, in which he was before the ages, he is equal to the Father. In human lowliness he is born of a woman, subject to the law (Gal 4, 4), but remained, however, in divine majesty God the Word, through whom all things came to be. He, therefore, who in the form of God made man, has become man in the form of a slave, but each (*utrumque*) is God by the power of the One assuming (*Deus de potentia suscipientis*), and each is man on account of the humility of the One assumed (*utrumque homo de humilitate suscepti*).[170]

Leo's picture of Christ has a clear centre: the eternal Son of the Father. In the incarnation, two things are true: the divine nature and the human nature; there are not, however, two separate persons in the Incarnate One. The Word *persona*, therefore, emerges for the first time when there is talk of the Incarnate One. The trinitarian 'person' of the Word or the second *persona trinitatis* (cf. *tractatus* LXXV, 53ff.; above n. 130) is not yet *conceived* as the starting-point to anchor the unity of God and man. When, in the text just quoted, Leo characterises Christ as 'one person' (to the exclusion of a second), his view is directed to the concrete Christ, and the 'one person' is the result of the union. Nevertheless, his christology remains a christology from above. In its structure the picture of Christ held by the bishops of West Rome and East Rome is one. This follows very clearly from the many words which Gennadius gathers from Leo's Tome (and his *sermones*) to show that he stands completely in the tradition of the Fathers. Following H. Arens,[171] we wish to supplement somewhat this terminology of union in Gennadius, and to summarise briefly its significance.

First of all, let us establish the fact that Gennadius places his Leonine dictionary between two scriptural passages which were also extremely important for the opponents of Chalcedon: Joh 1, 14 and Rom 9, 5, the latter certainly being understood christologically. Some terms of assumption or union are etymologically an expression of a christology from above: thus 'became flesh' (Joh 1, 14), especially 'to assume, to have, to participate in, to have borne, to have put on, to hide onself, to reveal oneself, to dwell and to pitch a tent (cf. Joh 1, 14), "to become" (body, temple, instrument), to come'.

The following expressions, which also to some extent are rare in Leo, do not

---

[170] Leo M., *Tr.* XXIII, 2 (from the year 442): CCL 138, p. 103f., 30–45.
[171] H. Arens, op. cit., 147–685 (a critique of the text of the Tome).

appear: *coire*, to come together (which also expresses the sexual union of man and wife) (this appears only in the First Tome, v. 55 and *tractatus* XXI, 44); more removed is the word *compositio*, which Leo does not use christologically; the usage of *miscere*, to mix, to mingle, is important: Arens enumerates eighteen places where Leo employs it christologically in various ways. It occurs in *tractatus* XXIII (dating from 442), which we have just cited extensively. Here Eutyches is not yet in the picture, but only Nestorius. The separation into (two) persons (*personarum discretio*) is rejected. So too is the model of indwelling (*nec sic . . . ut ille habitator et illa esset habitaculum*); (when Gennadius speaks of ἐνῴκησεν as an expression of Leo (Diekamp, p. 78, 19), he intends by that nothing other than Joh 1, 14, as 'he pitched his tent among us', which is added immediately, proves. But, on the positive side, Leo proposes *sed ita ut naturae alteri altera misceretur* (but in such a way that the one nature is mingled with the other).[172] In contrast to this, in *ep.* 35 and *tractatus* 65, 16 *non permixtione confusa* (no mingling) is said explicitly.[173] Finally, '*infusa*' is replaced by '*unita*', which Gennadius also quotes explicitly (Diekamp, p. 78, 18).

All in all, Gennadius is open enough to mention also many expressions which among the Alexandrians aroused the suspicion of Nestorianism (the model of clothing, 'to join together', 'to cover with'). Taken as a whole, the commentary of Gennadius explains and interprets the Tome of Leo in the sense of a clear Chalcedonian christology. Strictly speaking it is only biblical language which is adopted, a fact which Gennadius probably also stresses by placing as brackets around his list two scriptural passages which state in very clear terms the godhead of Christ and the *ductus* of the incarnation.

What the commentary of Gennadius on the First Tome has made evident holds true for Leo in his writings as a whole: he remains in the domain of a concrete, non-technical language which is gathered from the Scriptures and the Fathers, as the *testimonia*, which he appended to both his Tomes, also prove.[174] In his christology Leo also remains concrete, insofar as in the *sermones*, but particularly in

---

[172] Leo M., *Tr.* XXIII, 1 (from the year 442): CCL 138, p. 103, 25.

[173] Cf. *ep.* 35 (13 June, 449) to Julian of Cius: ACO II 4, p. 7, 21-22; *Tr.* 65, 1 (8 April, 453): CCL 138A, p. 395, 17 (*Nulla permixtione confundimus*).

[174] The *testimonia* of the Second Tome are an enlarged version of that florilegium which was attached to the First Tome when it was despatched for a second time to Constantinople. Cf. on this M. Richard, 'Les florilèges diphysites du Vᵉ et du VIᵉ siècle', *Chalkedon I*, 721–748 (= Op. *Min.*, I,3) in particular 725–727. All the texts are taken from the tradition prior to Ephesus or from Ephesus itself, and this for the clear purpose of demonstrating the traditional character of Leo's christology. On account of this the motive behind the selection of texts must not be sought in the elements of those extracts concerned with the history of concepts or formulae. Most interesting in this regard is perhaps Chresis V in Hilary, *De Trinitate* 9, 14 (ACO II 4, p. 122), where there is talk of the 'person of each of the two natures' (*utriusque naturae persona*) which we have discovered also in Leo. For the rest the recourse to Hilary, Athanasius, Ambrose, Augustine, John Chrysostom, Theophilus and Cyril of Alexandria, Gregory Nazianzen and Basil of Caesarea is only thought of by Leo as a proof that he stands in a tradition accepted by East and West, a tradition which confesses the true divinity and the true humanity in the one Christ. These *testimonia* are an 'illustration', not an immediate literary 'presentation' of Leo's teaching. See the text of the florilegium in E. Schwartz, 'Codex Vaticanus graecus 1431': *AbhMünchAkW* 32, 6 (1927) 71–85; for an explanation, ibid., 137–143; in addition ACO II 4, 119–131. On an interesting problem of translating a sentence from Cyril of Alexandria's *Scholia de Incarnatione Unigeniti* (ACO II 4, p. 131, nr. XXX; PG 75, 1397C), see M. Richard, op. cit., 726f. with n. 31. On Leo's florilegia cf. M.-B. De Soos, *Le Mystère Liturgique d'après Saint Léon le Grand* (Münster 1958) 6–21.

the two Tomes, he keeps in sight the mysteries of the life of Jesus.[175] The way in which Leo conceives that the unity of God and man in Christ is brought about also remains remote from abstraction: it proceeds from the insight that the Word assumed human reality by divine power (*potentia*). The power of the One assuming (*potentia suscipientis*) is the same power through which the Word created the world (*tractatus XXI, 2*, which dates from 440). The union of God and man in Christ is the consummation of the relationship of the Creator-God to his world, admittedly with a total orientation towards the redemption. Let us see the latter aspect emphasised once again in the words of the Second Tome.

Because, under the appearance of honouring the godhead in Christ, the heretics deny the truth of the flesh, they hold it to be religious to say that in our Redeemer precisely that which saves is not true, although, indeed, according to the original promise the world has been reconciled to God in Christ in such a way that without the Word's condescending to become flesh, no flesh would have been able to be saved.[176]

The personal bearer and terminus of this 'assuming power'— notwithstanding the fact that all activity *ad extra* is exercised by the threefold God in common—is the Word alone, whose own *actiones* are enumerated in *tractatus 64, 4*, which dates from 5 April, 453.[177] This creative power is constantly at work in preserving the union of God and man; indeed, it is more penetrating than the power which keeps body and soul together in us human beings:

For it is much easier for the power of the godhead to preserve this unity of itself with man (*hanc unitatem sui atque hominis*) than it is for the weakness of humanity on its own to maintain the unity of its substances [i.e. the uniting of soul and body].[178]

[175] The mysteries of the life of Jesus, which are to the fore in Leo's writings, are already present in the liturgical cycle of the Church year. See the various titles given in A. Chavasse, CCL 138 with the particular collections of the *sermones*, p. XIVff.; but on this see idem, 'Dans sa prédication, saint Léon le Grand a-t-il utilisé des sources liturgiques?', *Mélanges liturgiques* (offerts au R. P. Dom B. Botte OSB) (Louvain 1972) 71–74; K. Esser, *Das Kirchenjahr nach den Sermonen Leos des Großen* (Diss. Innsbruck 1934); F. Hofmann, 'Die Osterbotschaft in den Predigten Leos d. Gr.', Fischer-Wagner, *Paschatis Solemnia = Studien z. Osterfeier u. Osterfrömmigkeit* (J. A. Jungmann z. 70. Geburtstag) (Freiburg-Basel-Wien 1959) 76–86; J.-P. Jossua, op. cit.; H. Dénis, *La théologie de l'ascension dans les sermons de saint Léon le Grand* (typescript thesis—Lyon 1960) (not used).
[176] Leo M., T. II 145–148 (118. 8–12).
[177] Leo M., *Tr.* 64, 4: CCL 138A, p. 393, 95–111. As revelation of the *potentia Verbi* in the incarnation the following are put forward: virginal conception and birth of Christ, the calling of the Magi by the star, the voice at the baptism in the Jordan, the curing of the sick and the raising of the dead, Christ's revealing of himself that he is equal to the Father (cf. Joh 10, 30). According to Arens, op. cit., Section II, nr. 2.1.5, n. 78–79, *potestas* is also tied to *gloria*. In the *sermones potestas* appears in the singular 71 times, and *potentia* in the singular 55 times.
[178] Leo M., *ep.* 35 *ad Iulian. Coens. ep.*, 13 June, 449: ACO II 4, p. 7, 18–20. From this passage it is clear that the initiative and power for the uniting of godhead and manhood proceed from the Word and that a 'Nestorian' *Bewährungslehre* (the theory that Christ earned exaltation through obedience) may not be read into Leo's writings. There is no sufficient reason for claiming either Leo or Gennadius as witnesses for a so-called 'Antiochene' interpretation of Chalcedon, as P. T. R. Gray, *The Defense of Chalcedon in the East (451–553)* (Leiden 1979) 80–103, does for the latter. (For more details see the chapter on Neo-Chalcedonianism).

This insight into the act of union of God and man in Christ, an act posited once but persisting, goes deeper than any metaphysical formula. It leads to the conclusion that the final subject in Christ is to be sought in the Word himself, a fact which for Leo was present in the incarnational model of the Apostles' Creed and Nicene Creed. The concept of the 'one person' is to be located there. But Leo did not take this final step, although Gennadius already seems to interpret his work along these lines. Ultimately Leo looks at the man Jesus starting from the Word, and sees him borne completely by the creative power of the Logos. One would only need to reverse the point of view to come to the idea of 'to exist in'. In any case, Leo also saw the possibility of arriving at an unsurpassable and inseparable unity in Christ, without surrendering himself to the ambivalence of the *mia physis* of Cyril. He could easily ratify the 'towards the *hypostasis*', as we found this expression in Mark the Monk.[179]

IV. 'THE MADNESS (*INSANIA*) OF VALENTINUS, MANES AND EUTYCHES': AN ECUMENICALLY IMPORTANT PERSPECTIVE OF LEO I IN HIS SECOND TOME (458)

If the immediate antecedents of the christology of Chalcedon be explained by the internal Greek debate about the *mia physis* formula of Cyril and by the struggle of the Antiochenes against the Apollinarianism which they surmised lay behind this formula, then in his Second Tome, dating from 458, Leo established a lineage which points beyond the immediate antecedents of Chalcedon and the Greek world: the bond between Valentinus, Manes and Eutyches. This resulted from his experiences of the dualistic, docetist Manichaeism in Italy (and Africa). The more vehemently Leo reacted against Manes, all the more significantly must the equal treatment meted out to Manes-Eutyches-Dioscorus and Timothy Aelurus affect the relationship between Rome and Alexandria. For this reason we must consider in more detail the encounter of the Roman Pope with Manichaeism,[180]

---

[179] JdChr I², 685, n. 35.
[180] Very useful for understanding Leo's position on the Manichaeism of his time is P. Brown, 'The Diffusion of Manichaeism in the Roman Empire', *JRS* 59 (1969) 92–103, now in idem, *Religion and Society in the Age of Saint Augustine* (London 1972) 94–118. It would seem that C. Callewaert, *S. Léon le Grand et les textes du Léonien* = Extrait de Sacris Eruditi I (1948), finds too many allusions to Manichaeism. We limit ourselves to the more important literature. 1. J. Ries, 'Introduction aux études manichéennes. Quatres siècles de recherches', *AnLovBiblOr*, ser. III., F. 7 = *EphThLov* 33 (1957) 453–482 (I); f. 13 (1959) 362–409 (II). 2. E. Rose, *Die manichäische Christologie* = Studies in Oriental Religions 5 (Wiesbaden 1979) 1–7: Survey of Research. 3. F. Decret, *Aspects du manichéisme dans l'Afrique Romaine. Les controverses de Fortunatus, Faustus et Felix avec saint Augustin* (Paris 1970), produces some excellent material on Western (African) Manichaeism. 4. On the characteristics of Manichaean christology at the time of Leo, cf. T. G. Jallard, op. cit., 56–63. The studies of A. Lauras are important: 1. *Recherches sur le manichéisme à Rome sous le pontificat de Léon le Grand*

and in doing so have recourse once more to the last decades of the fourth century.

Very shortly after the beginning of his pontificate (440–461) Leo had to deal with groups which also laid claim to the name of Christian (see below), but which placed the understanding of Christ in the imperial Church far more fundamentally in question than Nestorius and Eutyches did. Leo himself drew a clear line of demarcation here.

Certainly the other heresies, however dissimilar they may be, are all together rightly to be condemned. For all that, the individual heresies have something of truth in one or other of their parts. Arius propounded that the Son of God is less than the Father and is his creature; from this [Son] the Holy Spirit also with the universe was created. Thus he prepared his perdition for himself in great ungodliness. Although he could not order the eternal and unchangeable godhead into the unity of the trinity, still he did not deny this in the essence of the Father. Macedonius was no doubt far from the light of truth, because he did not accept the divinity of the Holy Spirit; however, he confessed in Father and Son the one power (potentia) and the unity of being. Sabellius let himself become bewildered by an inexplicable error. On the assumption that the unity of substance in the Father and the Spirit is inseparable, he attributed that which must be ascribed to the identity [in essence] to the peculiarity [of the persons]; because he could not understand the true threeness, he believed in only one person with three names. Deceived in the blindness of his intellect, Photinus certainly confessed in Christ the true man who is the same as us in essence, but he did not believe that the very same one was begotten as God by God before all ages. Without constancy in the faith, Apollinarius supposed that the Son of God assumed the true nature of human flesh in such a way that he maintained that in that flesh there was no soul; instead its place was filled by the godhead. If one thus examines all the errors which the catholic faith has condemned, then one finds something which can be separated from what is to be condemned—in one error it will be this, and in another that. In the criminal teaching of the Manichaeans, on the other hand, there is nothing at all that one could even partially tolerate.[181]

(440–461) (Paris 1946, mécanogr.); 2. 'Saint Léon le Grand et le manichéisme romain', StudPat 11 = TU 108 (Berlin 1972) 203–209. Here Lauras clarifies the connexions between Leo and Augustine in the Manichaean question, and in the second place also the relationship of Roman to African Manichaeism. Lauras pleads for a certain independence of Leo with regard to Augustine. The main point here is that Leo insists with particular forcefulness on the docetism of the Manichaeans. In the résumé of Manichaeism which Augustine gives in De haeresibus XLVI—a work that Leo appears to have read—he does not mention this fundamental error (TU 108, 205). Lauras shows both the points of contact as well as the differences of opinion between Leo and Augustine in the Manichaean question (ibid., 205ff.).

On the patristic sources about Manes and Manichaeism in general, see J. A. Fabricius-G. C. Harles, Bibliotheca graeca VII (Hamburg 1801) 315–334; C. Riggi, Epifanio contro Mani. Presentazione di O. Cataudella (Roma 1967) 399–403, 409–419; E. Beck, Ephräms Polemik gegen Mani und die Manichäer im Rahmen der zeitgenössischen Polemik und der des Augustinus = CSCO 391, Subs. 55 (Louvain 1978). We shall have recourse to the works just mentioned in chapters IV and V.

[181] Leo M., Tr. XXIV, 5 (from the year 443): CCL 138, p. 113f., 101–125. Cf. on this Tr. XVI, 4 (12 December, 443): CCL 138, p. 64, 80–88: 'the error (which works in manifold ways) has erected a fortress for itself in the foolishness of the Manichaeans and in it has found a great hall (aula) where it can blithely parade; it has adopted not just the form (species) of a single corruption, rather it possesses a mixture of all errors and kinds of ungodliness'. The Manichaeans, in comparison with Marcion and Valentinus, receive an identical judgement in Serapion of Thmuis, Lib. adv. Manichaeos, cap. 3: PG 40, 901CD. Manes is 'postrema abortio improbitatis' who leaves all others in the shade.

Even though sketched with only a few strokes, Leo's picture of the 'classical' heresies of the fourth century corresponds essentially to the historical reality. Worthy of recognition is his readiness to see good wherever it is present. But why then the harshness and totally negative attitude with regard to the Manichaeans? In contrast to Nestorius, Eutychians and their supporters in Jerusalem and Alexandria, it was only with the Manichaeans that Leo had personal contact. After the sect of Manes expanded in Mesopotamian, Syrian and Egyptian society, it also gained ground in the Latin Church, namely in North Africa, Italy and Spain.[182] The late gnosticism of Manes deserved all the attention of the imperial Church in East and West.

1. The Manichaeans and their relation to Christianity

Quite recently through an important manuscript discovery, the so-called Cologne Mani-Codex (CMC),[183] the long disputed question of the origin of Manichaeism within the history of religions has advanced a significant step further, even if it is not at all clarified definitively. According to the CMC, Manes seems to have belonged to a Christian baptist sect, more precisely the Elchasaites.[184] Consequently, his teaching could be regarded as Christian heresy, which

---

[182] See P. Brown, art. cit. On Africa see F. Decret, op. cit. In addition J. Ries, 'Jésus-Christ dans la religion de Mani. Quelques éléments d'une confrontation de saint Augustin avec un hymnaire christologique manichéen copte', *Augustiniana* 14 (1964) 437–454. On Egypt see CCT II/2.

[183] See A. Henrichs-L. Koenen, 'Ein griechischer Mani-Codex', *ZPE* 5 (1970) 97–216 (= preliminary report); iidem, 'Der Kölner Mani-Kodex. Edition der SS. 1–72': *ZPE* 19 (1975) 1–85; 'Ed. der SS. 73–99': *ZPE* 32 (1978) 87–200; 'Ed. der SS. 99/100–120': *ZPE* 44 (1981) 201–318. Iidem, 'Berichtigungen', *ZPE* 34 (1979) 26; G. J. D. Aalders, 'Einige zusätzliche Bemerkungen zum Kölner Mani-Kodex', ibid., 27–30. The CMC appears to stem from the place where 'Manichaeism first set foot in Egypt', from the region of Assiut, the old Lycopolis where also Alexander of Lycopolis was active, he 'who composed the first polemical treatise against the Manichaeans; according to Epiphanius the first missionary came to Hypsele in the Thebaid, i.e. strictly speaking into a region seven kilometers south-east from Assiut (Haer. 66, 2, 3 [III 17, 16ff. Holl]). When we think of this Manichaean centre south of Assiut, it is easy to imagine how a codex found in this region came into the hands of a rich private person in Luxor; the Greek Mani-Codex appears to come from the original region of the Manichaeans in Egypt'. Thus L. Koenen, 'Zur Herkunft des Kölner Mani Kodex', *ZPE* 11 (1973) 240–241. The CMC is a translation from Syriac: cf. Aalders, art. cit.; R. Köbert, 'Orientalistische Bemerkungen zum Kölner Mani-Kodex': *ZPE* 8 (1971) 243–247. It is interesting that in this region the finds of the Gnostic writings of Nag Hammadi were made. See further CCT II2.

[184] Cf. A. Henrichs-L. Koenen, art. cit., *ZPE* 5 (1970) § V, 141–160: Manes and the Elchasaites; Rose, op. cit., 32–34: dependence of Christian baptists and gnostics. J. K. Coyle, O.S.A., 'The Cologne Mani-Codex and Mani's Christian Connections', *Église et Théologie* 10 (1979) 179–193, in particular 192f., urges caution, however: 'No one today would deny the presence of Christian elements in Manichaean teachings, nor even the possibility that some of these elements go back to Mani himself. But there is not enough to determine that Mani was raised in Christian circles, or that he consciously shared Jesus' teachings *in extenso*, or that he meant to provide Jesus with a strong, let alone central place in the system he devised. When we find texts that appear to indicate otherwise, we have to remember that in all cases they are far removed in time and place from Mani himself and therefore may not be faithful mirrors of Manichaeism's earliest form'. Coyle will thus not accept that 'the Christian roots of Manichaeism have already been proved definitively' (193). Henrichs-Koenen made the attempt in the 'preliminary report', *ZPE* 5 (1970) 158–160, to

would correspond to the testimony of the Church Fathers and also to the statements of Leo I.[185] But perhaps the assertion of E. Rose, as given below, must still be expressed more cautiously.

Henceforth there can no longer be any doubt that the Church Fathers were correct when they unanimously recognised in Manichaeism a Christian heresy; and what is more, they opposed in Manes the arch-heretic of the gnostic late-period, in whom not only the previous heresies coalesced, but also through whom they exercised a profound influence on the catholic Church itself, as well as on subsequent heretical movements.[186]

We cannot decide the question here, whether and how Manes changed from a clearly discernible Judeo-Christian milieu, to which he became more and more strongly opposed, over to the domain of 'pagan-Christian gnosticism'.[187]

compile a list of the agreements between Elchasaitic and Manichaean views. These concerned mainly Manes' understanding of himself as the prophet and final incarnation of Christ, the distinction between a heavenly and an earthly Christ which is duplicated in the distinction between 'Jesus the radiance' and the 'earthly Jesus'. In Manes himself there is an earthly and a heavenly person (syzygos). In spite of all the differences, they also have in common the use of the Christian gospels, asceticism and food taboos and the title presbyter; cf. A. Henrichs, 'Mani and the Babylonian Baptists. A Historical Confrontation', Harvard Studies in Class. Philol. 77 (1973) 23–59; K. Rudolph, 'Antike Baptisten. Zu den Überlieferungen über frühjüdische und -christliche Taufsekten', SbSächsAkW. Bd. 121 (Leipzig 1981), H. 4, 13–17. Cf. also F. C. Baur, Das manichäische Religionssystem nach den Quellen neu untersucht und entwickelt (1831, repr. Göttingen 1928) VI: Manichaeism is 'a cardinal heresy of Christianity'. The Manichaean Faustus congratulates himself on the fact that he is 'today still a Christian' 'thanks to my teacher (praeceptor) Manes and his veneranda fides'. Thus according to Augustine, C. Faust. XIX 5: CSEL 25, 1, p. 501, 1–2. That, however, does not exclude the possibility that between Manes and Faustus Christian elements came into Manes' system.

[185] On the testimonies of the Church Fathers, see E. Rose, op. cit., 19–24. The principal opponents of Manichaeism are (a) Ephraem: see C. W. Mitchell, S. Ephraim's Prose Refutations of Mani, Marcion and Bardaisan, Vol. I (London 1912), Vol. II completed by A. A. Bevan and F. C. Burkitt (London 1921). E. Beck, op. cit., offers an excellent evaluation of Ephraem. In conjunction with this Beck treats the other Greek opponents and Augustine. (b) Epiphanius, Panarion, Haer. 66: CGS, Ep.W. III, pp. 13–132 (K. Holl); C. Riggi, op. cit., offers the same text with improvements, an Italian translation and a good commentary. This text is used here (see also CCT II/2). (c) For the West: Augustine, (i) Contra Fortunatum: CSEL 25, 1, 83–112; (ii) Contra Faustum: CSEL 25, 1, 251–797; (iii) Contra Felicem: CSEL 25, 2, 801–852. It is convenient to consult these and other treatises in: Oeuvres de Saint Augustin (2nd Ser.) Vol. 17: Six traités anti-manichéens, traduction, introduction et notes par R. Jolivet et M. Jourion (Paris 1961) (the Maurist text is followed, this being improved several times in CSEL). Beyond the works in CSEL 25 this volume includes the following: De duabus animabus, Contra Adimantum, Contra Epistulam Fundamenti, Contra Secundinum. Augustine knew only a few works of Manes or of the Manichaeans. See E. Beck, op. cit., 6.

[186] Ibid., I. B. Aland (Ehlers) in particular has worked hard to determine the relationship of Manes to Bardesanes: (1) eadem, 'Bardesanes von Edessa—ein syrischer Gnostiker', ZKG 81 (1970) 334–351; E. Beck, 'Bardaisan und seine Schule bei Ephräm', Mus 91 (1978) 271–333, in particular 324ff., criticises the utilisation of Ephraem, Pr. Ref. I, 122, 32ff. (especially I, 123, 1–14) for gaining Bardesanes' interpretaion of the Genesis passages on the creation of man; (2) eadem, 'Mani und Bardesanes. Zur Entstehung des manichäischen Systems', A. Dietrich (Ed.), Synkretismus im syrisch-persischen Kulturgebiet = AbhGöttAkW, Phil.-hist. Kl. 3.F. 96 (Göttingen 1975) 123–143. Ibid., 126, reference to her Göttingen Habilitationsschrift. There can be no doubt about the dependence of the Manichaean system on that of Bardesanes, in spite of the influence on Manes of numerous syncretistic elements of an additional kind. For example, in Bardesanes the body is still 'neutral with regard to redemption, i.e. irrelevant for redemption'; in Manes it is 'hostile to redemption. The same primeval battle which happened at the beginning of the ages between light and darkness now takes place in every man. From this it follows, however, that salvation can come only from an absolute separation of the natures through the most severe asceticism which must be performed already in this life' (142). B. Aland stresses that the dualism of Manes does not rest 'on the basis

2. *The struggle against Manichaeism*[188]

When the Manichaean mission, proceeding from the Mesopotamian region across Syria, came into contact with the Imperium Romanum, it filled the Roman officials and the local authorities with the old 'dread of the Persians'. This is articulated in the rescript of Diocletian in 297.

We have recently heard that into this [Roman] world, like new [and] unforeseen omens (*prodigia*), the Manichaeans have proceeded from the people of the Persians, a folk inimical to us, or they arose there, and have perpetrated many vile acts (*facinora*); for they bring peaceful people into turmoil and bring the greatest evil to the communities of citizens (*civitatibus*). It is to be feared that, as usual, they will attempt with the advance of time to infect people of innocent nature, the unassuming and peaceful Roman people and our whole continent, with their abominable customs and with the pernicious laws of the Persians, as with the poison of a vile snake.[189]

Christian Emperors issued harsher and harsher laws against the sect.[190] In these there is a fusing of the prejudice of the Roman state

of a completely symmetrical dualism' (131). 'On account of the uniqueness of God which must be safeguarded, it is not possible even for Manes to furnish the darkness in the same way as God, even if this be only formally, i.e. to ascribe to it the same active powers, even if under a negative sign' (132f.). Because light and darkness have been mixed, Bardesanes and Manes come to the conclusion: the world must have been created necessarily. The mingled principles are the material of the world and its purpose is to make possible the liberation of the particles of light (135). In contrast to Bardesanes, for whom darkness is primarily inactive, Manes ascribes to it 'a diabolical initiative of its own ... (he has) ascribed to darkness from the outset its own activity which is determined by greediness, hatred and aggressivity ... It is just more intensified by the light particles which have been snatched...'. [From the exertion of the diabolical powers of the darkness which sees itself in danger of losing its particles of light comes about the creation of man, through which the darkness hopes to remain in possession of the light particles for ever. For the individual man the task arises] 'of helping the soul to its authentic life; mythologically expressed, of purifying it from the darkness which imprisons it. That would be an impossible undertaking, however, without the help of the spirit or the Manichaean *nous*. Spirit is that essential core of man which is already redeemed, which no longer needs redemption. [According to Manes, in the primeval history Jesus shook Adam awake out of sleep and helped him to the knowledge of his true I.] In the earthly man, living here and now, this task is performed by the *nous*' [which according to Alexander of Lycopolis is Christ himself] (141, with n. 73).

[188] Apart from the texts named in n. 185, the most important ones are collected by A. Adam, *Texte zum Manichäismus* = KlT 175 (Berlin 1954: ²1969).

[189] See ibid., nr. 56, p. 83, § 4. In § 6 burning for "*auctores ac principes una cum abominandis scriptis eorum*" is ordered.

[190] Ibid., nr. 57. Cf. E. H. Kaden, *Die Edikte gegen die Manichäer von Diokletian bis Justinian* = FS for H. Lewald (Basel 1953) 55–68. See C. Pharr, op. cit., 16, Title 5: Heretics. The edicts between 372 and 428 are given here. In § 9 (382) it is observed that the Manichaeans do not join in the communal celebration of Easter. In § 18 (389) expulsions are decreed: the Manichaeans are to be driven out of the whole *orbis terrarum* = Roman empire (in contrast to *mundus* = world), out of Africa (§ 35, from the year 399), out of Rome to a distance of 100 miles (§ 62, from the year 425), and out of the range of vision of various cities (§ 64, from the year 425 and § 65, from the year 428; the reason given for this: 'since no opportunity must be left to any of them'). Reproach of *publicum crimen*: § 39, 1.5. In connexion with Leo I what is particularly important for us is Title 18 from 'The Novels of the Sainted Valentinian Augustus (III)', 19 June, 445; cf. Pharr. op. cit., 591. In this novel, which is devoted entirely to the Manichaeans, Valentinian refers to Leo I. 'We are speaking of the Manichaeans, whom the statutes of all the former Emperors have adjudged execrable and worthy of expulsion from the whole world. Their crimes which have been recently detected do not permit Us to disregard them. For what things that are obscene to tell and to hear have been revealed by their very manifest confession in the court of the most blessed Pope Leo,

with Christian doctrinal intolerance (P. Brown). The Christian attitude, however, had first to be formed. P. Brown rightly notes that
in the second century the teachings of Elchasai, from which Manes
started, would still have found in Rome a certain fertile soil. But
after Emperor Diocletian the chances for the influx of new missionary
ideas from the East had changed. A witness for this situation in the
fourth century is Ambrosiaster, who was in contact with Roman
senators and who mentions the decree of Diocletian in his commentary on Paul. Manichaeism is a 'new and unexpected monstrous-birth
from Persia' which was bound to disturb the conservative Romans.[191]

But we are more interested in the situation in the fifth century.
At the time of Augustine and Leo I, the bishops in the West acquired
a quite special rôle, a fact which was decisive for the final overthrow
of the sects.

> For, in the fifth century, the Western provinces of the Roman Empire lay wide
> open to Manichaean propaganda. Pope Leo was genuinely alarmed: the barbarian
> invasions had dislocated the security-system of the Catholic episcopate and had
> paralysed the Imperial authorities ... The para-Manichaeism of the Priscillianists
> had already swept North-western Spain.[192]

Nevetherless time ran out for the missionaries of Manes in the
Western world. P. Brown sees the reason for this in the following
elements, which help us to understand well the rôle of Leo.

(a) The new rôle of the bishops. The 'Western' towns had become
very small, easily surveyable places in the radical change from the
fourth to the fifth century. Falling inwards, these towns were gathered
more and more about their bishops, as for instance Augustine of
Hippo or Gregory of Tours (*Historia Francorum* IX, 6) illustrates.
Nothing could escape their attention. The bishop acquired a pre-
eminent rôle in executing the suppression of the Manichaeans, after

---

in the presence of the most august Senate! Thus even the man also who was said to be their bishop
both betrayed with his own voice and wrote out all the secrets of their crimes...'. Then there
follows once again in 18, 2 the explanation that Manichaeism is a *crimen publicum* (= a crime that
could be prosecuted by any person). Leo I adheres to the limits of these imperial laws. The *Codex
Iustinianus*, ed. P. Krueger, Vol. II (Berolini 1929) continues to tighten up these laws: I 5, § 11:
penalty of death for Manichaeans (law from 487 or 510); particularly severe is Justinian himself
in 527: (a) 12, 2: the complete separation of Manichaeans is ordered; (b) § 12, 3: penalty of death,
which in § 16 is also ordered for relapse into the heresy. Cf. § 18, 2. E. Kaden shows, however,
that Justinian did not consider a general application of these punishments. The laws would serve
as a warning. In the period after Justinian Manichaeism no longer played a rôle in the Byzantine
empire. The motives and the goals of the various imperial laws are well characterised by E. H.
Kaden, op. cit., especially 68.

[191] Cf. Ambrosiaster, *Comment. in XIII epp. Paulinas*, on 2 Tim 3, 6.7: CSEL 81, III (1969)
312, 4–24; the Manichaeans in their art of seduction are particularly to be feared as *importuni, fallaces,
captiosi*. They live in conflict between their inner conviction and their external behaviour with regard
to marriage, social relationships, asceticism and outward affected manner. They gorge themselves,
but give the appearance of fasting by 'a certain art of appearing wan'. The decree of Diocletian
is also mentioned here (1. 10–24).

[192] P. Brown, art. cit., 101.

the government in the West was no longer in a position to press the restrictions on permits for sects or to order a stop to all vagabondage. The Christian community in Rome had put its house more and more in order.

Ascetic eccentricity was clamped into monasteries, and a powerful clergy would pray pointedly that God should protect their flock from ill-kempt ascetic CONFESSORES.[193]

In short, no matter how severe the Emperor's laws could be made, in the West only the local bishop could discover ways of applying them (with the help of the secular arm).[194] Leo I gives us only one proof of this, but this can be corroborated by Augustine's references to similar circumstances in Africa.

(i) A case of legal proceedings against the Manichaeans under Leo I. In *tractatus* XVI, 4, dating from 12 December, 443,[195] Leo gives a report of a judicial equiry which he himself conducted concerning a number of *electi* and *electae*. There were other bishops, priests, Christian men and *nobiles* (probably senators) present. The interrogation produced 'much about the perversity of their teaching (*dogmatis*) and the customs of their feasts'. They acknowledged even an offence on a girl, who was at the most ten years old. All the persons involved in this were present. 'In this way it became abundantly clear that there is no shame to be found in this sect, because there the lie signifies the law, the devil religion, and baseness the sacrifice'.[196] That does not necessarily indicate libertinism, even if both Augustine and Leo point the finger at Manichaean lasciviousness as such.[197]

---

[193] Ibid., 102. See above n. 190: laws for expulsion from Rome etc. Cf. F. Ferrère, *La situation religieuse de l'Afrique Romaine depuis la fin du IVe siècle jusqu'à l'invasion des Vandales (429)* (Paris 1897: repr. Amsterdam 1970) P. IIIe, I: Le manichéisme.

[194] P. Brown, op. cit., 102 with reference to the procedure of Theophilus, Patriarch of Alexandria. On the resistance of the Manichaeans to the imperial legislation (*Cod. Theod.* 16, Tit. V. §§ 35 and 40), see F. Ferrère, op. cit, 294–300. From ignorance about their teaching, however, the Emperors persecuted the Manichaeans above all as 'une société secrète qui fait ombrage au pouvoir' (ibid., 296). The Emperors demanded an '*inquisitio*', but this was not enthusiastically acted on either by pagans, Jews or Christians. With reference to the divine judgement, Leo urges denunciation of the Manichaeans: *Tr.* XVI, 5 and 6: CCL 138, p. 66, 124–128.132–134.137–138. The sequence in time of Leo's *tractatus* and letters on the Manichaean question has been studied by A. Lauras, *Saint Léon le Grand et le manichéisme romain* (see n. 180) 203–205. We indicate the series briefly: *ep.* 4 *ad eppos per Campaniam* etc., 10 October, 443: PL 54, 610A–614B; *Tr.* XVI, 12 December, 443; likewise Christmas 443: *Tr.* XXIV: CCL 138, 109–116; *ep.* 7 *ad eppos Italiae*, 30 January, 444: PL 620B–622A; *Tr.* XXXIV, Epiphany 444 (1. ed.): CCL 138, 178–187; *Tr.* XLII, 12 March, 444 (1. ed); CCL 138, p. 238–250; *Tr.* LXXVI, 6, 11 June, 444 (1. ed.); then follows the *Novel* of Valentinian III, 19 June, 445. The series concludes with *ep.* 15 *ad Turribium ep. Asturg.* against the Priscillianists, 21 July, 447: PL 54, 677–692.

[195] Leo M., *Tr.* XVI, 4: CCL 138, 64f., 90–114; cf. *Tr.* XXIV (Christmas 443): CCL 138, 113, 97–98, where there is talk of the 'recently made confession'.

[196] Ibid., p. 65, 110–114.

[197] Leo M., *Tr.* XVI, 4 (12 December, 443), p. 64, 92–94: *sacra ... apud illos tam obscura quam nefanda*; *Tr.* XXVI, 4 (from the year 443): CCL 138, 113, 99–100: *nec in fide integritatem nec in pudore servantes, ut et in dogmatibus suis impii et in sacris inveniantur obsceni.* What Leo reports also has parallels in Augustine, *de haeresibus*: Adam, op. cit., nr. 49, 2, pp. 65–68. In the matter of

(ii) Leo's letter to the Italian bishops (*ep.* 7, al. 8: PL 54, 620B–622A). The Roman discovery induced Leo on 30 January, 444 to warn the bishops of Italy in a letter that their communities could suffer the same sickness as had now been diagnosed in Rome. Leo was afraid that without his warning the bishops would allow, for instance, the members of the sects who were departing from Gaul to find shelter in their cities as in a hiding-place, 'so that what was wiped out by us here in the capital (*in Urbe*) makes itself at home among you in concealment' (54, 620B).

Our investigation (*investigatio*) has tracked down very many supporters and teachers of Manichaean ungodliness; our vigilance has dispersed [them], our authority and censure punished them. What can be improved, we have brought into order (ibid., 620C).

It was demanded that one abjure Manes, his doctrines and his discipline, and make a confession before the Church, to be signed with one's own hand. Whoever was prepared to mend his ways could stay in the community. In accordance with imperial laws, stubborn people were banished by the public prosecutor. The faithful were informed about the sect. Its 'bishop', who was in Leo's custody (*a nobis tentus*), finally confessed the misdeeds which he had perpetrated in the course of the mystery-like celebrations. These were described in the reports of the trial which Leo enclosed for the bishops. But many heretics had fled. Hence this informative letter delivered by an acolyte.

For otherwise we cannot guide those entrusted to us, if we do not pursue these seducers and seduced with the zeal of faith [after the example] of the Lord (*zelo fidei Dominicae*—no doubt recalling the cleansing of the temple), and cut them off from the healthy with all possible rigour, so that this plague does not expand further (621B–622C).

(b) With the economic development in the Roman empire, Manichaeism lost the *merchant* and hence its best lay-helper. In Christian

concubitus with under-age girls or virgins, about which the tribune Ursus interrogated those guilty and the *Gesta episcopalia* report, it was a case of freeing the divine particles of light which are hidden in the *semen humanum* and must be liberated by the *electi*. '... *turpissimum scelus, ubi ad excipiendum et commiscendum concumbentium semen farina substernitur*' (p. 67, 78–80). Augustine calls this '*non sacramentum, sed <u>exsecramentum</u>*' (ibid., 83). (Leo M., Tr. XXVI: CCL 138A, p. 484, 186 takes over this expression). From this a dish for the *electi* is prepared, *ut purgent Dei sui partem: quam profecto, sicut in omnibus corporibus coelestibus et terrestribus, atque in omnium rerum seminibus, ita et in hominis semine teneri existimant inquinatam. ac per hoc sequitur eos, ut sic eam etiam de semine humano, quemadmodum de aliis seminibus, quae in alimentis sumunt, debeant manducando purgare*' (ibid., p. 68, 98–103). Augustine speaks of the '*horrenda cibi turpitudo*' (p. 68, 106). Because conception contributes to the imprisonment of the particles of light, the Manichaeans recommended contraception. Cf. Augustine, *C. Faust.* XV, 7: CSEL 25, 1, p. 429, 24–430, 4; see on this F. Decret, op. cit., 302. On the external behaviour of the Manichaeans Augustine gives details in *De moribus Ecclesiae catholicae et de moribus Manichaeorum*: PL 32, 1309–1378. Cf. II, c. XIX, n. 68: 1374; n. 70: 1374f. Particular *flagitia* were uncovered in Rome: n. 74: 1376–1378.

romances on the sects—but not only for them—he had played a large rôle.[198] In the West above all, trade declined and the merchant became a local landowner who was subjected to the conditions of his locality. Not until the eleventh and twelfth centuries with the crusades and the social and economic changes brought about by them did a new situation begin to appear in which the founding of Manichaean sects would be revived.

(c) P. Brown suspects an alteration in the situation in Mesopotamia as well, insofar as it was controlled from Persia. Radical gnostic movements had kept this part of the Fertile Crescent in a state of ferment until the sixth century. From here the Manichaean movement could despatch wave after wave of missionaries into the Roman empire. But at the end of the fifth century this source area began to dry up and Manichaeism became 'a Soghdian affair' (P. Brown), if one does not take into account the effects on Armenia, which are, in any case, controversial.[199]

It is our intention to include the christology and soteriology of Manes[200] in our investigation, insofar as they can be of service in elucidating Leo's attitude towards the supposed Manichaeism of Eutyches and his supporters in Constantinople and Alexandria. For this identification had far-reaching 'ecumenical' consequences. Was the *tertium comparationis* sufficient, as Leo assumed, for regarding Eutyches and Manes as equally dangerous? A precise knowledge of the background, which Augustine possessed to a far greater degree than Leo, would have been necessary for entering into dialogue with the opponents of Chalcedon in the East. How difficult this was will be demonstrated for us by Timothy Aelurus himself. Before we investigate the texts of Leo, let us present a 'systematic sketch of the life of hearers (katechumenen) in a Manichaean community' from Augus-

[198] P. Brown, art. cit., 102. Merchants and travellers played a great rôle in all Church groups. The most famous example is Cosmas Indicopleustes (traveller in 'India') who was probably a Nestorian merchant. See W. Wolska-Conus, *La 'Topographie Chrétienne' de Cosmas Indicopleustes*: SC 141.159.197 (Paris 1968–1973). A delightful example is analysed by E. Dinkler, 'König Ezana von Aksum und das Christentum', *Ägypten u. Kusch. Schr. z. Geschichte u. Kultur des Alten Orients* = Mél. F. Hintze, 13 (Berlin 1977) 121–132. Aksum had also Manes in view. Cf. F. Thélamon, *Païens et chrétiens au IV siècle* (Paris 1981) 62–83, with reference to Kephalaion 77: C. Schmidt, *Manichäische Handschriften der staatl. Museen, Berlin*, I, 1–2, *Kephalaia* (Stuttgart 1940) LXXVII, pp. 188.190. Tr. 96, a sermon of 25 December, 457, mentions the arrival of the Alexandrian supporters of Timothy Aelurus, *praecipue negotiatores, ad Urbem*: CCL 138A, p. 593, 15.

[199] P. Brown, op. cit., 102–103. For this reason Brown will no longer accept that at the time of Augustine and Leo the motive for the fear of the Manichaeans was that they were a 'fifth column' of the Persians.

[200] On the christology and soteriology of Manichaeism, see J. Ries, op. cit. (cf. n. 182); the principal work: E. Rose, op. cit., with bibl. (183–186), a report of research, a history of the problem and a critique of the sources for a christology (15–29); E. Feldmann, 'Christus-Frömmigkeit der Mani-Jünger. Der suchende Student Augustinus in ihrem Netz', E. Dassmann and K. S. Frank (eds), *Pietas* = FS for B. Kötting: *JAC*, Comp. Vol. 8 (Münster 1980) 198–216. This article deserves detailed study. It shows that the Manichaean devotion to Christ could impress Augustine until he saw through its intrinsic contradiction. Cf. Augustine, *Conf.* 3, 8 (Feldmann, 215f.).

tine's *ep.* 236 to Deuterius, written after 395. This can help us to fit together the 'fragments' from Leo's writing into a better overall picture.[201]

Those amongst them who are called hearers (*auditores*)

1. [manner of living] eat flesh, till the fields and are, should they desire, married. Those who are called the chosen (*electi*) do none of these things. However, the hearers

2. [imposition of hands] kneel before the chosen, so that during prayer hands can be imposed on them
    a) not only by the presbyters
    b) or the bishops
    c) or their deacons
    d) but by any of the chosen at all.

3. [Veneration of the sun and moon; prayer] The sun and moon
    a) they implore with them
    b) and pray [in this way].

4. [Fasting—common faith—christology]: On Sunday
    a) they fast with them
    b) and with them they believe all kinds of blasphemy (by which the false doctrine of the Manichaeans is cursed).
    c) They deny
        i) Christ was born of a Virgin.
        ii) They confess that his body is not real, but was feigned,
        iii) and consequently his suffering is feigned.
        iv) They also maintain that a resurrection did not take place.

5. [Rejection of the O.T.; cf. Marcion] They slander the patriarchs and prophets. They say that the law mediated through the servant of God, Moses, was not given by the true God, but by an *archon* of the darkness.

6. [Divine substance identical with all souls] Not only the souls of man but also those of animals are, so they believe, from the substance of God and in general parts of God (*partes dei*).

7. [God—people of darkness—fight] They maintain, finally, that the good and true God fought with the people of darkness, and mixed a part of his being with the *archontes* of the darkness;
    [Doctrine of redemption] this part, which through the whole world is defiled and held in bondage, will be purified (so they claim seriously)
    a) [(food taboos) purification through the meal] through the dishes of the chosen
    b) [cosmic] and through the sun and moon,
    c) [damnation] and the part of God which could not be purified will at the end of the world be fettered with eternal and extremely painful bonds...

3. Leo's Idea of Manichaeism

(a) Manes and Jesus

(i) Manes himself intends to be an 'apostle of Jesus', not, however, of the Jesus of the gospels, but of the divine redeemer of the gnostic

---

[201] Text according to Feldmann, op. cit., 199–200, in a simplified version. See Augustine, *ep.* 236, 2: CSEL 57, 524, 12–525, 8 and idem, *de haeres.* 46: CCL 46, 312, 20; Adam, op. cit., 65–70; R. Haardt, *Die Gnosis* (Salzburg 1967) 256–262.

tradition. Hence his christology can first of all be nothing else than 'purely a criticism of the gospel tradition of the Incarnate Saviour'.[202] Leo confirms this in a sermon, delivered on the Feast of the Epiphany in 444, in which he censures the way in which the sects deal with sacred scripture:

> The opponents of truth have repudiated the great and unutterable mysteries of religion [cf. I Tim 3, 16] which, however, is proclaimed by all the witnesses of Holy Scripture, the law that was given through Moses [cf. Joh 1, 17] and the sayings of the divinely inspired prophets; they have damaged even the evangelic and apostolic pages (*paginas*), by taking one away and adding another; for this purpose they have made for themselves many falsified books under the names of the apostles and with the words of the Saviour himself (*confingentes sibi sub apostolorum nominibus et sub verbis ipsius Salvatoris multa volumina falsitatis*), in order by means of them to support their erroneous inventions (*erroris sui commenta*) . . .[203]

(ii) Manes and his adherents are on the basis of their dualism firm opponents of the fundamental message of the true incarnation of the Son of God. Hence at Christmas Leo comes readily to speak of them.

> They deny that he was born bodily of Mary the Virgin; hence because they do not believe in the true birth, they also do not accept any true sufferings; they do not confess him as truly buried, and they deny that he is truly risen.[204]

In the sermon on the Feast of the Epiphany in 444, which we have already mentioned, Leo says:

> They represent Christ with a false body which has nothing solid about it, which shows nothing really to man's eyes, not even in its activities.

It shows only, as Leo goes on to say,

> the empty picture of simulated flesh.

---

[202] E. Rose, op. cit., 35; cf. A. Böhlig, *Die Bibel bei den Manichäern* (Diss. Münster 1947). A careful analysis of the use of the New Testament in Augustine's discussions with Fortunatus, Faustus and Felix is offered by F. Decret, op. cit., 151–182. The whole second part is important: Les questions scripturaires: beyond the NT it is only the writings of Manes which bring the full knowledge of the truth. The hearing of these books leads, as it were, *ex opere operato* into the kingdom of light through the Gnosis. Cf. Decret, op. cit., 116. In 297 Diocletian had already ordered them to be burnt (ibid., 118f.). For this reason Fortunatus and Faustus refrain completely from citing them. Only Felix refers to them as the *auctores* (ibid., 104).

[203] Leo M., *Tr.* XXXIV (from the year 444): CCL 138, p. 184f., 129–139.

[204] Leo M., *Tr.* XXIV, 4 (Christmas 443): CCL 138, p. 113, 89–92. See on this the determined statements of Faustus in Augustine, *C. Faustum*, quoted by F. Decret, op. cit., 279–289. We translate, following p. 281, n. 1, from *C. Faustum* XXIII, 2: CSEL 25, 1, p. 709, 4–11, from which the way in which Faustus deals with the life of Jesus will become clear: (Faustus says to the catholics:) '*your* position, then, is to accept that the Son of God is from Mary, according to *Matthew* from the Jordan [baptism of Christ], *ours* that he is from God [following Joh 16, 28 = I came from the Father and have come into the world (ibid., XII, 1: CSEL 25, 1, p. 329, 13f.)]. If his words are true in this profession of his, Matthew is as much at variance with you as with us. In your eyes he is a little too careful in that the origin from the female sex he ascribes more to the son of David than to the Son of God. Therefore you must admit one of two things: either it was not Matthew who appears to have written this, or you do not have the faith of the apostles'.

Then for Manes the admission of a birth in the flesh is an *iniuria* for the Son of God, whereas for Leo it is a proof of the power of God. Hence, in practice for Manes there is no event in the earthly life of Jesus which is 'true' or of significance for salvation, neither the baptism of Christ, nor his cross, nor the water from the side of Christ. Consequently, 'baptism' as a sacrament of rebirth also ceases, because it is deprived of all the power of grace. 'Amongst them nothing is holy, nothing safe, nothing true'.[205]

It is true that for Manes Jesus remains a pure divine being, but he has various *modi* or functions. He is teacher of man and the conveyor of the gnosis, at one time as an active 'envoy', and then a passive Jesus *patibilis*,

who, under the symbol of the light crucified in matter, intends by his passivity to bring to man's awareness the suffering of the world-soul in the world. The purpose of his instruction and the communication of the gnosis is in both cases to effect in his believers an ethical behaviour which corresponds to it, so that through severe asceticism they show themselves to be placed in the service of the work of salvation.[206]

The gnostic double-being that Christ is has a relation to the world in three phases.

At the commencement of the history of the world stands the luminous or shining Jesus who was sent to Adam at this very beginning, in the middle phase the historical 'prophet of truth', and finally at the end the 'great judge', the cosmic judge of the eschatological drama.[207]

---

[205] Leo M., *Tr.* XXXIV: CCL 138, p. 184; p. 185, 146–148; *Tr.* IX (from the year 443): CCL 138, p. 38, 114–115.

[206] E. Rose, op. cit., 58; F. Decret, op. cit., 284 (with n. 2)–286. In the souls imprisoned in matter and in the whole of nature (Augustine, *C. Adimantum* 22: CSEL 25, 1, p. 181 and often) is enacted in reality the tragedy of Golgotha: 'le *Iesus patibilis* subit vraiment la flagellation et les souffrances du gibet, cette passion que le Maître "impassible" avait semblé endurer pour nous donner la sublime leçon d'espoir: le retour au Royaume bienheureux du Père'. This *Iesus patibilis* acquires particular significance for the Manichaean Felix: CSEL 25, 2, p. 801–852; Decret, op. cit., 291–293. Felix professes only the crucifixion (p. 845).

[207] E. Rose, op. cit., 58. The difficulty of Manes in comparison with Church Christians consisted in determining the Chrestos (thus the Manichaeans of the Greek world) in relation to Jesus of the radiance. 'The acknowledgement of Jesus Christ as Son of God, however, could not occur without some reservations vis-à-vis the Church's teaching, viz. vis-à-vis the dogma of the God-manhood. For Manes there could be here only an either-or: God or man—*tertium non datur*. Were Jesus Christ, however, "the Son of the Greatness" (*Keph.* 12, 20 and often; *filius maiestatis*, Aug., *C. Faust.* XXXXII 7, p. 766, 10) and had he nevertheless, as "his apostles preached" (Phil 2, 7), on his entrance into the world a *morphe doulou* and a *schema hos anthropos* (*Keph.* 12, 24–26), still that could be combined only on condition that he came *choris somatos* (ibid.) . . . (Manes' dualistic presuppositions absolutely precluded him) from limiting the concept *similitudo* to the *caro* determined by the addition of *peccati*, in other words from acknowledging the reality of flesh and blood and denying only its sinfulness or sinful origin: for him body and *hyle* are one; hence a sinless body is a *contradictio in adiecto*; flesh and blood that would come from God is an impossibility to which there can be no exception. The necessary result is the *choris somatos* (by which the denial of the birth of Christ is also expressed)'. Logically one cannot really speak of *docetism* in Manes. He did not accept a positive determination of the earthly appearance of Jesus Christ, but he did not deny it a real substance. It is a question of a 'reception of the Church's understanding of Jesus' for 'missionary purposes'. H. J. Polotsky, 'Manichäismus', *PWK* Suppl. VI (241–272) 268–269. Manes' 'docetism' is different from that of Valentinus.

He who had been sent at the beginning of the world to the first man remains sacramentally present 'in the manner of the mysteries'.[208] E. Rose warns against confusing these different *modi* of Christ, which are clearly distinguished in the system of Manes itself, but which on the other hand are already sacrificed to a 'scholastically ironed out principle of identification' in the *Kephalaia*.[209] Caution must also prevail in determining the rôle of the sun and moon in their relation to (a) Christ.

To represent 'the redemptive function of the sun' as 'intermediate member' to a Christ, viz. to the 'ideal one who was equated with the sun' (Titus of Bostra), is simply not correct, for the sun has no special function as redeemer, because it is merely a means of conveying the redemption, nor is Christ himself 'equated with the sun'. Instead, the sun is the seat of one of his functions, in connexion with which the naming of the moon as the seat of the other function should not be neglected, and the Third Envoy, as the specially favoured macrocosmic power, must always remain implicated.[210]

Full of insight is Rose's reference to the fact that, according to Titus of Bostra, the redemptive functions of the cosmic Christ are assigned to the sun and moon, as *Dei virtus* in the sun and as *Dei sapientia* in the moon (cf. I Cor 1, 24: *theou dynamis—theou sophia*).[211]

But perhaps Leo is close to such an identification (in a different way from Titus of Bostra).[212] For in his confrontation with the Manichaeans in *tractatus* XXXIV, he speaks of their having robbed their believers of the true mystery of the incarnation of Christ and all of the mysteries of the life of Jesus until his return, and of their having taught in the place of these 'a worship of Christ in the sun and moon' (*in sole et luna colere Christum*).[213] In *tractatus* XLII, 5 he reports that the Manichaeans

---

[208] One may read on this the beautiful psalm transmitted in Coptic (nr. 248) from that group which is addressed to Jesus, in E. Feldmann, op. cit., 209–210 (already in A. Böhlig, op. cit., 58f.) and the Coptic psalm for the feast of Bēma and the one to Jesus (both in A. Adam, op. cit., nr. 24 and 25).

[209] E. Rose, op. cit., 60.

[210] Ibid.

[211] Ibid., with n. 27.

[212] *Titi Bostrensis contra Manichaeos libri quatuor*: Lagarde (Berlin 1859), p. 147 (following Rose, op. cit., 60, n. 27). For more information see CCT II/2.

[213] Leo M., *Tr.* XXXIV, 4: CCL 138, p. 185f., 139–156. In these lines we have a succinct counter-outline to the soteriology of Manes, of which Leo, however, knows or has in mind only a part. It is a question of Christ's descent into the flesh, his ascent to heaven in the flesh and second coming. Thereby the whole man, the whole world (not just the divine light part) shall be taken home. In *ep.* 236, 2 Augustine also speaks of the fact that the Manichaeans, *auditores* as well as *electi*, worship the sun and moon; in *C. Faust.* 20, 6: CSEL 25, 1, p. 541, 1–3, he refers, like Titus of Bostra, to the distinct functions of the sun and moon: 'the Father dwells in a mysterious light, but the Son according to his power in the sun, according to his wisdom in the moon'. On the worship of the Manichaeans, see F. Decret, op. cit., 308–309. L. J. van der Lof, 'Manichäische Verbeugungen vor der Sonne auf dem Vorderplatz der Sankt Peterskirche in Rom?', *Numen* 16 (1969) 156–160, doubts whether the bows before the sun in the square in front of St Peter's in Rome had anything to do with Manichaean practices. We shall have more to offer on the theme 'sun-moon' CCT II/2 in connexion with an explanation on a newly compiled exhortation of Shenute.

offer to the luminaries of the heavens a foolish fast, in as much as they had been caught in the act, as on the day of the Lord and Monday they fast in honour of the sun and moon.[214]

There would be a twofold perversity in this, viz. holding days of fast in honour of the stars in general and scorning the day of the resurrection in particular. Behind this would lie in fact the denial of the true birth, true death and true resurrection of the Lord, so that Sunday, the day of rejoicing for Christians, would be made a day of mourning.[215]

(iii) Manes in the rôle of the earthly Jesus. It was logical for this docetism, in which there was no place for the earthly Jesus, that Manes himself should take his place or that the pericopes of the gospels be applied to him. For his supporters he was the 'new Christ', whom the depiction of the twelve year old Jesus (Lk 2, 41–52) and of the hidden life to the age of thirty (Lk 3, 23) fitted. One ascribed to him the choice of the twelve disciples, gave him three beloved disciples, and knew of a sending out of 70 or 72 disciples.[216] Because he did not remain within the borders of as small a land as Judea, however, but came to India and the borders of China, Manes must have appeared superior to the 'Jesus of the gospels'—and this also for the reason that he endured real suffering which could be confirmed historically (even if, properly speaking, he did not suffer death on a cross).[217] Precisely what the Jesus of the gospels (the Chrestos) and even more than ever Jesus in his divine nature could not accomplish, became reality through Manes, as the one who truly suffers,

---

[214] Leo M., *Tr.* XLII, 5 (12 March, 444): CCL 138A, p. 247a, 175–181.

[215] Ibid., 182–187. Leo overlooks here the fact that it was above all the function the sun and moon had in returning the light particles to God that was important for the Manichaeans. 'For the full moon had a religious significance in the Manichaean system. In the first half of the month the light particles redeemed from matter gather in the moon; from the night of the full moon onwards in the second half of the month they are further conducted to the sun. When the moon waxes it is manifest how the redeemed light particles increase, and when the moon is on the wane how they go on to the sun. Thus at the full moon begins the return of the light to the pure light of the sun and to the home of life, so that the night of the full moon symbolises the victory of the light over the darkness'. Thus Henrichs-Koenen (above n. 183), *ZPE* 5 (1970) 123.

[216] Cf. Augustine, *de haeres.* § 46, nr. 6: Adam, op. cit., 70: for this reason Manes himself had twelve disciples, corresponding to the number of the apostles, a number which the Manichaeans even today still maintain. For they have from their *electi* twelve whom they call teachers (*magistri*) and a thirteenth who is their superior (*princeps*). They have moreover seventy-two bishops who are consecrated by the *magistri* and priests (*presbyteros*) who are ordained by the bishops. The bishops also have deacons. The rest are called only *electi* . . .'.

[217] On the alleged 'crucifixion' of Manes, see E. Rose, op. cit., 36. The feast of Bēma, which was observed each year in March with the greatest pomp, was to celebrate of the death of Manes. Cf. Augustine, *C. ep. Fundamenti* 8: CSEL 25, 1, p. 202, 11–203, 4: '. . . your Bēma, i.e. the day on which Manes was killed, you observe by erecting a stage (*tribunal*) which is furnished with five steps, decorated with precious linens and set up and offered for the worshippers . . . For us what was most pleasant at that celebration of Bēma was that it was observed as the feast of Easter'. See the further material in H. C. Puech, *Le manichéisme. Son fondateur, sa doctrine* (Paris 1949) 185, n. 368. Cf. the (supposed) illustration in F. Decret, *Mani et la tradition manichéenne = Maîtres spirituels* 40 (Paris n.d.) 120–121.

the 'apostle' and 'messias'. He was the 'incarnation' of the Son of God and the truly crucified; accordingly, the feasts of Christmas and Good Friday also no longer had meaning for the Manichaeans.

(b) Manes as Paraclete[218]

By taking over this title, Manes laid claim to being the one who completed the message and mission of Jesus. One must not conclude from this, however, that he passed himself off as the Holy Spirit in the dogmatic sense, as the third person of the godhead. But Leo is of the opinion, whether from real information or from mere deduction is here left open, that the Manichaeans 'worship under the name of the Holy Spirit Manes, the teacher of such ungodliness itself'.[219] Leo is even plainer in his address on the feast of Pentecost, 11 June, 444, from which it is clear that the followers of Manes refer Jesus' promise of the Spirit in Joh 16, 13b to the master, in order to emphasise the greatness of the founder they followed.

For they believed that the Holy Spirit appeared in their teacher Manes, and that the Paraclete promised by the Lord did not come earlier than the emergence of this deceiver of the unfortunate, on whom the Holy Spirit of God has so remained that Manes himself was nothing other than the Spirit, who with the help of a bodily voice and tongue leads his disciples into all truth.[220]

All this signifies only that Manes, as Paraclete, is the one who completes the teaching of Jesus, that is, as the earthly teacher of divine truth.

(c) Manichaean asceticism and liturgical practices according to Leo

Whereas at a later period in the Syrian region we hear of a way of following Jesus practised by those who sojourned in the desert, fasted and prayed, in the case of Manes it cannot be a question of a 'following' of the earthly life of Jesus. His asceticism is determined by other principles. The disciples of Manes were obviously capable of making an impression by their affected ascetic behaviour. Thus Leo warns the faithful of Rome: 'No one should be deceived by their [the Manichaeans'] discrimination between foods, their soiled clothing and pale faces'.[221] This is a brief reference to the food taboos of the sect which were also common in Rome. Augustine describes them rather fully in De haeresibus §46.[222] Through the CMC they

---

[218] Cf. E. Rose, op. cit., 37–38; further the Manichaean Felix in Augustine, C. Felicem: CSEL 25, 2, p. 801–852; F. Decret, Aspects du manichéisme, 293–295.
[219] Leo M., Tr. XXXIV, 4 (1a ed. 444): CCL 138, p. 185f., 154–156: et sub nomine Spiritus sancti ipsum talium impietatum magistrum adorare Manichaeum.
[220] Leo M., Tr. LXXVI, 6 (1a ed. 11 June, 444): CCL 138A, p. 480, 127–133.
[221] Leo M., Tr. XXXIV, 5 (1a ed. 444): CCL 138, p. 186, 170–171.
[222] Augustine, De haeres. (about 428), § 46: Adam, op. cit., nr 49, § 3–4, pp. 68–69.

are now comprehensible for us historically.[223] According to Augustine, the disciples of Manes abhor the partaking of flesh, because the divine substance has already fled from the killed animals. They do not eat eggs, because when eggs are opened they become 'dead'. By way of inconsistency they also do not drink milk. Such regulations about food perhaps make a remarkable statement of Leo understandable.

If they nevertheless dare to be present at our mysteries in order to conceal their unbelief (although they do not consider the events of the life of Jesus worth celebrating), then at the 'sacramentorum communio' they hold back so far that they sometimes take the Body of Christ with unworthy mouth in order to remain more securely concealed, but in any event they avoid drinking the Blood of our redemption.[224]

One might think at first that the Manichaeans retained the Jewish prohibition on the partaking of blood. But if one looks at the reason for this prohibition—'the soul, life, is in the blood'—, then this would have to be the very incentive for the Elect of Manes to free the divine particle by partaking of the blood.

Therefore they do not drink wine, because they say it is the gall of the Prince of Darkness; they do, however, eat grapes, but they never take any must, be it ever so new [unfermented].[225]

The establishment of food taboos Manes no doubt had in common with the Elchasaites. However, he differentiates himself from these in the choice of and the reasons for such taboos.

Replacing agriculture in one's garden [which guaranteed purity of food for the Elchasaites], Manes has the regulation that Manichaean office-bearers and *electi* must not pick any produce at all in the fields or from trees, or chop any wood; for in every living thing, even in water and in the earth, the divine particles of light are dispersed. Moreover Manes calls the earth 'flesh and blood' of the Lord. Thus in the Chinese roll of hymns the food which the catechumens bring to the *electi* are described as 'flesh and blood of Jesus'. By eating these foods, the *electi* combine the particles of light which are present in the nourishment with the light which is in themselves, and thus return these to God.[226]

Seen in this way, the participation of some Manichaeans (*electi*) in the Eucharist is not for them a really religious act of salvation, but only a deception of the bishop, and a way of concealing their membership of the sect. Their 'celebration of the Eucharist' is enacted in

---

[223] Cf. Henrichs-Koenen: *ZPE* 5 (1970) 141–160.

[224] Leo M., *Tr.* XLII, 5 (1a ed. 12 March, 444): CCL 138, pp. 247f., 196–205. We shall have more to offer below on the Gnostic and Manichaean understanding of the Eucharist in connexion with abuses which Shenute had to censure in his exhortation (edited by T. Orlandi). See CCT II/2.

[225] Augustine, *De haeres.* § 46, 3: Adam, op. cit., 68, 116–118. The reason that the *electi* eat grapes, but do not drink the pressed must, lies no doubt in the fact that the pressing makes the must 'dead'. A fortiori the fermented must, i.e. wine, is forbidden to them.

[226] Henrichs-Koenen, *ZPE* 5 (1970) 150.

the daily partaking of the foods prepared by the *auditores*; they return to the treasury of heaven the particles of God which are hidden there.

4. *Manichaeism as a doctrine of salvation*

It was as a soteriology, a doctrine of salvation, that Manichaeism developed and achieved its seductive power for the Christians of the Great Church and its missionary effect. It gave to the people to whom it knew how to appeal a way out of the experience that everywhere on earth evil is mingled with good to the detriment of life on earth. The message of Manes took those who were converted to it into a movement which above all had a more comprehensive effect than the Church's message of salvation in Christ and its mediation in faith and sacrament. For in the message of Manes two elements are mingled. On the one hand there are the human primordial experiences which one has in dealing with nature, in witnessing the cosmic event, and of one's own instincts and yearnings; on the other there are the hopes which the message of Christ—however much it may be distorted—was able to arouse and, in Manes' preaching, produce. In the Manichaean myth of creation and redemption, in which gnostic ideas have been incorporated, an enticing vision manifests itself.

On the basis of the traditional model of the gnostic myth, Manes developed his world-drama in three stages or 'periods'. He starts with the original *separation* of light and darkness, then he expounds the reason for and the process of their subsequent *mingling* and their dissociation which proceeds at present, and finally as goal of the world's development—the definitive division of light and darkness, good and evil—is indicated as eschatological goal.[227]

Because Manes wanted to be not only a philosophical theorist but also the mediator of salvation in practice, he had to proclaim an ethical programme which demanded, more than previous gnostic systems, 'the radical renunciation of everything earthly and fleshly as the sole way to this striven after conquest of the power of darkness'. With this demand a subject arose that was able to start a world-wide religious movement:

the liberation of man's light-nature from the fetters of matter. The artificially fashioned, purely gnostic myth of creation and the complicated mystery of redemption can only be understood on the basis of soteriology; this is the case here more than in any other gnostic system. The unity of Manes' doctrine becomes comprehensible without the use of force and re-interpretation, if one attempts to understand it by beginning with its simple, fundamental soteriological ideas. Here we stand in the centre of this late gnostic doctrine of redemption. For this reason it is understandable that in its myth not a small number of saviour-figures appear, whose constant primary task is to set free the light imprisoned in the darkness. The sources testify unanimously that Jesus as interpreted by the Manichaeans takes pride of place

[227] E. Rose, op. cit., 48. See the wealth of information contained in the section 'soteriology' in F. Decret, *Aspects du manichéisme*, 271–309.

among all the saviour-figures. This is why christology also has a distinguished position in the framework of the religion of Manes.[228]

Manes had no intention of displacing Christ from this centre, nor
of imposing his own name on his supporters. He wanted them to
have only the name of Christ, and it is against this that Ephraem
the Syrian protested.[229] In their feeling of superiority, the Manichaeans laid claim to being the true 'Christians' and the only true
Church, whereas the *Catholica* is a community of heretics.[230]

But however much the Manichaeans insisted upon Christ (as God)
and on the name of Christian, one could not delude oneself that
decisive changes in the Church's message of Jesus Christ had not
been undertaken. Even if Leo could only get to know the Manichaean
system from the outside—Augustine had been after all an *auditor* for
ten years, which still did not allow him complete access to the inner
core—, even if the Pope arrived at no genuine understanding of the
food taboos and the worship of the sun and moon, even if he did
not know about the myth of the return of the sparkle of light deposited
in matter and of the return passage of souls into the kingdom of
light through gnosis and asceticism and the whole mechanism of
creation, still he recognised immediately that the docetism of Manes
and the depreciation of the earthly life of Jesus and his mysteries
were the cardinal point of his error. The unity of the history of the
human race and the universality of the vocation of all to salvation
was endangered. Though one may discover a great deal of christology
in Manes, yet E. Rose is correct in his concluding judgement:

There is no doubt that in the great cosmological myth of Manes, which finally
ends in an appeal to self-redemption, the figure of Christ is fundamentally depreciated
and the redemption which occurred once on the cross of Golgotha has evaporated
into a symbol. It is not a history of salvation which brings redemption, but a
knowledge of salvation and the corresponding behaviour. And yet the veneration
of Christ, Christ as interpreted by the Manichaeans, is obviously the centre of the
religion of Manes, because the saving gnosis is bound to his person . . .[231]

[228] E. Rose, ibid., 49.

[229] C. W. Mitchell, op. cit., Vol. I, XCII.

[230] Cf. Augustine, *C. Faustum* XVI, 7: CSEL 25, 1, p. 446, 1–4. Cf. F. Decret, *Aspects du manichéisme*, 148–149. Following Manes' pupil Adimantus, for Faustus the touchstone of true Christianity
is the rejection of the Old Testament. On account of their recognition of it the *catholici* are heretics,
indeed *christianarum haeresium pars maxima*.

[231] E. Rose, op. cit., 181. This soteriological, pedagogical link to Christ's activity as saviour appears
clearly in the Manichaean presbyter Fortunatus. See F. Decret, *Aspects du manichéisme*, 271–278:
cf. CSEL 25, 1, pp. 83–112. Joh 14, 6 and 10, 8 (Jesus the way, the truth and the life) play a
particular rôle in Fortunatus (CSEL 25, 1, p. 86). Christ alone is the liberator, the saviour, the
mediator between the Father and the souls. The real liberator is, however, the *Verbum*, apart from
any incarnation. He is not born in the flesh, but at the beginning of the world. Phil 2, 5–8 is also
interpreted in this regard (*in similitudine hominum factus*, hence not true man). The redeemer through
his 'heavenly *praecepta*' frees from matter those whom he has chosen in accordance with his holy
will. Indeed, it is according to the will of the redeemer that the soul has come into the world,
so that he can free it (Decret, 277). Thus Christ brings the *mandata caelestia*, the *sancta praedicatio*,
commonitio, sancta doctrina. He is thus *magister*, a title that will be of great significance for the newly-
converted Augustine.

Serapion of Thmuis, in his 'Book against the Manichaeans' Ch. 3, already notes this contradictory attitude towards Christ:

... contra Iesum militant, et Iesum invocant. Haec est difficillima omnium improbitas [poneria], nomine Christi appellari, et Christum oppugnare (PG 40, 901/2C).

The reason Leo had been able to make the equation Valentinus—Manes—Eutyches, however, was that the three heresies had been reduced to the lowest common denominator—docetism, i.e. the postulation of an apparent body in Christ. Because in the case of Eutyches these conclusions resulted from a false interpretation of the *mia physis* of Cyril, the chain reaction had to follow: all champions of this formula are Valentinians, Manichaeans, Eutychians, i.e. they are supporters of Alexandrian anti-Chalcedonianism. However much the Alexandrians might dissociate themselves from Eutyches (see below) or Timothy Aelurus might reject the Eutychian extremists from Constantinople and Egypt with all his might, nothing was known of this in the West; instead all the opponents of Chalcedon who followed Dioscorus were reduced to the same denominator.

The bond between Eutyches, Valentinus and Apollinarius had first been manufactured in the East. In two letters to Leo, Flavian of Constantinople had already given a hint of this.[232] Quite soon after the 'Latrocinium Ephesinum' of 449, the Pope associated Eutyches with the Manichaeans.[233] We see that shortly after Chalcedon, Eutyches, Dioscorus and the Manichaeans are on equal footing.[234] At this time Apollinarianism is also condemned by Leo more severely than in the *tractatus* XXIV from 443 (see above). In the Christ of the Apollinarians there was something lacking which certainly pertained to human nature: on the one hand, the (lower) soul and the spirit-soul, but on the other hand bodiliness as well, for this does not stem from woman but resulted from the conversion of the Word into flesh. Apollinarianism was viewed together with Manichaeism and its hostility to the body. This view rests upon the misunderstanding of Apollinarius' talk of the 'heavenly flesh of Christ', although he only intended to emphasise by this expression the close bond between the flesh and the Logos, and the dignity and power of this *sarx*.

It was Eutyches himself who introduced Rome to the so-called Apollinarian forgeries through his *Libellus appellationis*. This is contained in the *Collectio Casinensis*[235] in a Latin translation differing from that of the *Collectio Novariensis*,[236] which was in use in the papal archives. The former translation, made for a *vir nobilis Romanus*, was certainly based on the Greek copy which was in the archives. The translator was a cleric who undertook at the same time to refute the false doctrines of Eutyches, and above all to remove the scandal that a letter of Pope Julius was claimed as a testimony for the heresy of Eutyches. The cleric was sceptical about the letter

---

[232] Flavian., *ep. ad Leon. I:* ACO II 2, 1, nr. 3, p. 22, 11; *ep.* 2, ibid., nr. 4, p. 23, 8.

[233] Leo M., *ep.* 59 (civibus Constantinopol.): ACO II 4, nr. 34, p. 36, 34–37, 2: according to Leo the Manichaeans confess Christ only as 'God'.

[234] Leo M., *ep.* 109, 25 November, 452: ACO II 4, p. 137, 38: Eutyches-Dioscorus; 43: Apollinarius and '*insana Manichaeorum opinio*'.

[235] *Collectio Casinensis:* ACO II 4, nr. 108, pp. 143–151; on this, *praefatio* XIII.

[236] *Collectio Novariensis de re Eutychis:* ACO II 2, 1, pp. 33–42: *Libellus appellationis*.

of Julius or the alleged quotation from it.[237] Apparently this letter had been searched for in the papal archives and not found. The reproach of Apollinarianism against Eutyches could be based on the fact of his acknowledgement of the *mia physis* formula. In the West this formula was ascribed solely to Apollinarius, without its being known that Cyril had adopted and 'domesticated' it.[238]

In an important *sermo* which he delivered at Christmas 457 in the Basilica of St Anastasia, Leo stated what he found to be held in common by the Manichaeans, Apollinarians, Eutyches and finally by all the Alexandrian opponents of Chalcedon. In fact, this sermon was preached after news of the murder of the Alexandrian Patriarch Proterius had reached Rome and Egyptian supporters of Timothy Aelurus were proclaiming their doctrine in Rome.[239] Leo addressed his congregation:

It could not remain hidden from the concern which we show towards you that some Egyptians, above all traders (*negotiatores*), have come to Rome (*ad Urbem*) and defend what at Alexandria is conceded by the heretics in a criminal way. They maintain that in Christ there is [present] uniquely and solely the nature of the godhead, that he [Christ] has in no way the reality of flesh which he assumed, however, from the blessed Virgin Mary. Thus this ungodliness characterises the man [in Christ] as a falsification and God as passible...

(With fatherly and brotherly concern, Leo warns against their giving assent to these 'enemies of the catholic faith', these '*hostes Ecclesiae*', who deny the incarnation of the Lord and attack the apostolic Creed established by the holy apostles.) (Then in § 2 that heretical 'kinship' is established, in which all the opponents of Chalcedon from Eutyches to Timothy Aelurus are assembled.)

Whoever follows that ungodliness in which many before him, as he knows, have been lost, destroys himself by his own obstinacy and in his madness (*insania*) separates himself from Christ. Such a person holds for pious (*religiosum*) and catholic what according to the judgement of the holy Fathers has been condemned, as is well known, in the perfidy of *Photinus*, the foolishness of *Manes* and in the madness

[237] The heading for the reputed letter of the Pope reads as follows: *Incipit exemplar Iulii episcopi urbis Romae, ut asserit Eutychis* (ACO II 4, nr. 110, p. 149, 35); in the explanation of the anonymous author it goes: *nam denique epistula quam dicit Eutychis Iulii quondam episcopi urbis Romae esse, quam etiam ad solatium suae perfidiae, ignoro forsitan falsam, protulit* (ACO II 4, p. 146, 39–147, 1); because Athanasius, Gregory Thaumaturgus and Pope Felix must have allowed their names to be associated with the falsifications, the anonymous author can say in summing up: 'in order to seize the minds of the simple and inexperienced and to draw them to himself, he pretends that the holy men mentioned, authors and proclaimers of the catholic faith, are fellow-travellers in his new and newest perfidy'. The falsifications of the Apollinarians are recognised as such for the first time, but here they are still ascribed to Eutyches. He is the *minister perfidiae* (ACO II 4, p. 149, 28–29). Cf. H. Lietzmann, *Apollinaris von Laodicea und seine Schule* (Tübingen 1904) 292–322.
[238] It is interesting that in the refutation of Eutyches by the anonymous author the word *imprudens/ inprudens* also appears as characterisation of the opposition simply, that label which Leo sticks onto Eutyches. Cf. ACO II 4, p. 146, 37 with T. I, TD 9, vv. 4 and 187. On the line Eutyches-Apollinarius, see also Leo M., *Tr.* XXIV (from the year 443): CCL 138, where in § 5, p. 113f. (as already cited in n. 181) a line of heresies is drawn from Arius through Macedonius, Sabellius, Photinus, Apollinarius to Manes, who discovered the worst of all heresies.
[239] Leo M., *Tr.* 96 (25 December, 457): CCL 138A, pp. 593–595.

of *Apollinarius*, so that now to the detriment of his own soul he assents to an infamy which is at the same time new and not yet condemned, because he denies the mystery of the incarnation of the Lord.[240]

Because Leo saw Eutyches and his supporters, up to and including Timothy Aelurus, in the sphere of influence of Valentinus, Origen, Arius, Apollinarius and above all Manes, one can understand that for him dark clouds were gathering over the whole region around the Mediterranean. '*Ponto nox incubat atra . . .*' (Virgil, *Aeneid* I, 89). From the time the Pope became aware that his silence with regard to the Council of Chalcedon was being exploited by the Eutychians to work against this Council, until the day he died, he never ceased to combat what he saw as the one sole threat to faith in the incarnation.[241] Because he had no success with his admonitions, the idea emerged of severing the Eutychians and all the opponents of Chalcedon from the Church.[242] To be fair, the fact that certain groups of the opponents of Chalcedon were becoming increasingly radical must be taken into account. These groups were no less a cause of concern to the moderate leaders of the Cyrillian party than to the Pope. We shall meet up with them sufficiently later (Ch. IV and Vol. II/2). In fact, in the Mediterranean area the temptations to docetism, which originally had been introduced in the East, became acute time and again. With the decline of Manichaeism in Egypt, North Africa and Italy, the most menacing dualistic-gnostic heresy could be eliminated. As the leading Monophysites dissociated themselves from Eutyches and his radical supporters, clarification was introduced which could also allow the *mia physis* formula to appear less threatening. This decisive point, however, was not seen. Fortunately, it was only after Leo that an attempt was made to prove that the genesis of the formula as such was due to *Manes*. This was in fact stated by subsequent heresiologists. People like Ephraem and Theodoret of Cyrus still knew nothing of it. The latter, who was well informed about Manes,[243] would certainly not have neglected to trace the Apollinarians back to this family tree, if he had had any occasion to do

---

[240] Ibid., § 2: p. 594, 31–38.

[241] The following letters are important: *ep.* 109 (25 November, 452) to Julian of Cius; *ep.* 110 *Marciani imp. ad Leon.* (15 February, 453); *ep.* 113 *ad Iulian.* (11 March, 453); *ep.* 143 (13 March, 455) to Anatolius; *ep.* 144 (1 June, 457) to Julian (ACO II 4, nr. 106); *ep.* 149/150 (1 September, 457) to Basil of Antioch and Euxitheus of Thessalonica; *ep.* 151 (1 September, 457) to Anatolius; *ep.* 155 (11 October, 457) to Anatolius; *ep.* 158 (1 December, 457) to the bishops of Egypt; *ep.* 162 (21 March, 458) to Emperor Leo; in this he speaks of the *rebelles haeretici* (ACO II 4, p. 107, 4). Finally there is T. II (see the heading of section IV).

[242] The most important text for this is *ep.* 162 *ad Leon. Aug.*, 21 March, 458: ACO II 4, nr. 101, p. 106, 8–11. The text appears above at the conclusion of n. 65. Cf. also *ep.* 114 *ad synod. Chalced.*: ACO II 4, nr. 64, p. 71, 2–8 (above n. 14).

[243] Theodoret of Cyrus, *Haeret. fab. comp.* XXVI: PG 83, 377–381; see on this G. Kessler, Art. 'Mani, Manichäer', *PRE* 12 (1912) 193–228; E. Rose, op. cit., 20–21.

this. He knows, of course, what in Manes' picture of Christ is similar to that of the Apollinarians:

> They [= the Manichaeans] teach that the Lord assumed neither a *soul* nor a body but only 'appeared' as man, although he had nothing human about him. Cross, suffering and death happened only as an apparition (*phantasia*) (PG 83, 380C).

The *mia physis* does not surface. It is otherwise in the heresiological demonstrations of the *Doctrina Patrum*. Its author knows that Manes acknowledged Christ only as 'mere God' (*theon psilon*) and hence was condemned by the statement of Chalcedon which says: 'one and the same truly God and truly man' (DP, Ch. 24: Diekamp, p. 175, 21). Just as Marcion, Manes, Valentinus and Eutyches would be hit by the sentence: 'the same in his manhood [has] the same nature as us' (ibid., p. 176, 9–13). With these presuppositions one can conclude logically: Manes knows in Christ only 'one *physis*', i.e. the divine nature. But with this perception one would still be far from the Apollinarian formula properly speaking: 'the one nature of the Word made flesh'. An unjustified reference to Manes is also implied when it is a question of averting the Severan formula of the 'one composed nature of the Logos', as happens in the DP, Ch. 8, *superscriptio*.[244] Among the important monophysite authors, it is only Severus of Antioch who seems to have used the expression *mia physis synthetos* of Christ.[245] To incriminate him, Apollinarius is deliberately named in the heading referred to as the originator of this expression, before him already Manes, and then the Arians and Eutyches.[246] With this expression these heretics would have wanted to eliminate the 'two natures'. Here the exaggeration is so great that one recognises the artificial *conclusio*. The Greeks also produce fragment from the *letters* of Manes. Unfortunately, these can no longer be checked, as the Manes-Coptica which were in Berlin—so far as they had not already been conserved—disappeared without trace after the Second World War. These fragments were employed in the struggle against the Monenergists and Monothelites, as the DP shows.[247] It could be that some meagre genuine remains were assimilated; as a whole these pieces display severe mutilation with regard to both content amd the designation of the addressees.[248] On the basis of

---

[244] *Doctrina Patrum*, cap. 8, *superscr.*: Diekamp, 58, 10–20.

[245] See J. Lebon, 'La christologie du monophysisme syrien', *Chalkedon I* (425–580) 472, in particular 488, n. 92; 489, n. 93. Lebon says here that the one who proposes Severus as author of this formula was certainly Cyril of Alexandria, but that this formula does not occur in his writings. Further details can be found in CCT II/2.

[246] Cf. Apollinarius, *Fragm.* 111: Lietzmann, 233, 28; further *Fragm.* 174, 19: ibid., 274.

[247] These fragments of letters are gathered well in J. A. Fabricius-G. C. Harles, *Bibliotheca Graeca VII* (Hamburg 1801) 315–316: (1) two fragments from *ep. ad Zebenam*, 315 = DP cap. 41, XV and XVI: Diekamp, 306 (against Monenergists and Monothelites); (2) *ep. ad Scythianum*, 316; (3) *ep. ad Saracen. Cudarum*, 316 = DP, cap. 9, XIII: Diekamp, 64; *ep. ad Addam vel Buddam*, 316.

[248] Cf. E. Rose, op. cit. (above n. 180) 20–21.

such sources, one is not justified in concluding to an historical connexion between Manes, Apollinarius, Eutyches and Timothy Aelurus. Unfortunately, this heresiological confusion contributed decisively to the perpetuation of the split between the Churches. In our later presentation (Ch. IV and Vol. II/2) we shall show how the fronts developed in actual fact, and where the genuine dangers were.

CHAPTER THREE

THE RECEPTION OF THE COUNCIL OF CHALCEDON IN THE EPISCOPAL CHURCHES. THE *'ENCYCLIA'* OF EMPEROR LEO I AND ITS ECHO

OUR investigation so far has centred on the imperial and papal position with regard to the Council of Chalcedon and the effort to secure its acceptance. But it was not without reason that Pope Leo had stressed that the Council stood or fell with the stance of the bishops.[1] They above all had to make it their business that the intention of the Fourth Council was made known in their dioceses and its teaching preached. In vast areas of the Church this proceeded without difficulty, because for the faithful there Chalcedon did not present any innovation over against the language to which they were previously accustomed. This is true above all for the West. In the East the situation was different. We well know what emotions the monks and the faithful in Alexandria and Jerusalem, but also in Constantinople, were capable of. In other respects as well the East was not completely at one. Hence it is not unimportant to gain an insight into the reception of Chalcedon. We have a particular help for this purpose, viz. the enquiry of Emperor Leo I already mentioned, his *Encyclia*, which was precisely intended to provide information about the reception of Chalcedon. Nevertheless, this enquiry took place six to seven years after the Synod, so that a certain *tempus utile* was given for reflection on what happened in October 451. It included above all, however, the metropolitans and bishops of the East, the exception to this being Leo I, certainly the most commanding figure of the West. The replies to the imperial enquiry were collected in the chancellery at Constantinople and received the official designation *'Encyclia'* (τὰ Ἐγκύκλια) or also *'Codex encyclius'*.[2] Using it as our starting-point, we want

---

[1] See above, Ch. II, n. 5.

[2] Cf. Evagrius, *HE* II 9: Bidez-Parmentier 59, 25. The letters of the *Codex Encyclius* (in the following =CE) are preserved in the *Collectio Sangermanensis*, edited by E. Schwartz in ACO II 5, p. 9–98, nr. V–XLVIII, in the Latin translation of Epiphanius which was prompted by Cassiodorus. Cf. his *De institutione divinarum litterarum* 11: PL 70, 1123CD; ed. R. Mynors (Oxford 1937). Unfortunately this collection is not complete. The CE is introduced by 1. a foreword by the translator which explains the occasion for and the carrying out of the questionnaire; 2. the letter of Emperor Leo to Anatolius of Constantinople and the metropolitans (in Greek in Evagrius, *HE* II 9: Bidez-Parmentier 59–61); 3. the letter to the Emperor from the Chalcedonian bishops and clergy of Egypt who had fled to the imperial capital after the uprising against Proterius; 4. the letter of the same bishops to Anatolius; 5. the letter to the Emperor by the delegation from Timothy Aelurus. Then there follows the list of the addressees or the recipients of the questionnaire (CE 10–11), and beginning

to form an opinion about the reception of Chalcedon around the year 457/8. For this reason, however, there are various questions about this undertaking and its result which need to be posed. 1. To what extent is the imperial Church of that time encompassed by it? 2. What is the freedom and independence of the episcopal answers vis-à-vis the envoys from Constantinople? 3. What position did the Emperor hold for the bishops in matters of faith? 4. What conception did the bishops have of the authority of the Council of Chalcedon? 5. What insight into the christological work of the Council is expressed in the *Codex encyclius*?

I. How Comprehensive is the Information Gathered?

It was the intention of the Emperor that all metropolitans of the East and West as well as some important representatives of monasticism in the East would be reached by his enquiry. The metropolitans in their turn were to call together their suffragans in order to exchange views on the questions posed in the Emperor's circular, the attitude to Chalcedon and the validity of the consecration of Timothy Aelurus, and to report the result to the Emperor. In the extant form of the *Codex encyclius*, we have the Emperor's letter to Anatolius as a 'specimen' of the enquiry. No doubt this was altered to some extent according to the particular addressees[3], because in this specimen letter there are directions that apply only to Constantinople. The Emperor refers to the so-called *Synodos endemousa* (Home Synod) as this was the custom in the Imperial City. It was to be convened[4] in order to transmit to the Emperor a quick reply to the problems which had been raised.[5] This concrete direction had no significance for the other metropolitans. The letter to Pope Leo, who headed the list of addressees, was certainly altered appropriately, as is discernible from the

---

with nr. 12 the replies. The first letter cited is *ep.* 156 of Pope Leo. With the exception of the letter of Baradatus, this is the only letter which bears a date (1 December, 457). In nr. 13–48 follow the letters which have been preserved. Cf. E. Schwartz, ACO II 5, *praef.* XII–XVI; T. Schnitzler, *Im Kampfe um Chalcedon. Geschichte und Inhalt des Codex Encyclius von 458* (AnGreg 16) (Romae 1938).

[3] Cf, the heading of CE nr. 6: *Exemplar epistulae Leonis Imp. ad Anatolium epm. Constantinopolitanum. hoc modo scriptum est et aliis metropolitanis episcopis.* Cf. the Greek text in Evagrius, *HE* II 9: Bidez-Parmentier 59, 26–29 where the Emperor's intention of including all the metropolitans and bishops of the *oikumene* is expressed more clearly: Ἴσον θείου γράμματος τοῦ εὐσεβεστάτου βασιλέως Λέοντος πεμφθέντος Ἀνατολίῳ ἐπισκόπῳ Κωνσταντινουπόλεως καὶ τοῖς κατὰ τὴν οἰκουμένην ἅπασαν μητροπολίταις καὶ λοιποῖς ἐπισκόποις. According to ACO II 5, p. 11, 7, the Emperor's title reads: *Imperator Caesar Leo piissimus victor ac triumphator maximus semper Augusatus.* Cf. G. Rösch, *ONOMA BASILEIAS* = Byzantina Vindobonensia X (Wien 1978) 165, nr. 35.

[4] ACO II 5, p. 11, 21–23: 'May your Reverence arrange that all the orthodox bishops who are at present residing in the imperial city and also the most reverent clerics meet with you immediately to investigate and discuss everything diligently'.

[5] Ibid., 1. 28–29: 'Let me (*meam pietatem*) know in all haste . . .'.

reply of the Pope.[6] From the various answers of the metropolitans, we know that a metropolitan synod was to be held everywhere, and indeed also as quickly as possible. This direction was presumably not contained in the letter to Pope Leo, as he in no way takes it up in his reply.[7] Rather he draws attention to the promise to Peter, and hence to his Petrine doctrine, according to which in relation to the bishop of Rome a council has only a subordinate and supplementary function, not an unconditionally necessary one.[8] Leo's standpoint on the question of Chalcedon was also that of the whole Latin Church, although the Pope did not deal with that more closely. Leo, aroused and disturbed by the uncertainty which seemed to find voice in the Emperor's *Encyclia*, attempted, fully in accord with his initiative, to strengthen fidelity to Chalcedon by three further letters. There was a letter to the orthodox Egyptian group in Constantinople as well as to the bishop of the Imperial City.[9] The third letter would be, then, the Second Tome, *ep.* 165, to Emperor Leo, which is already familiar and has been analysed.[10] Thus Pope Leo reacted to the enquiry

---

[6] Cf. the *admonitio* of the Ballerini and n. b to *ep.* 156: PL 54, 1127–1128. Perhaps Zacharias Rhetor had before him a specimen letter, such as it went forth to *all* the metropolitans of the East. He reports what led up to the imperial encyclical and then cites a passage from it which he introduces in the following way: 'And he [the Emperor] began to write to the bishops about Timothy and the Synod of Chalcedon, in the encyclical letter, to the following effect: "Do you, without fear of man or partiality, and unbiassed by influence or by favour, setting the fear of God alone before your eyes, and considering that to Him alone you must make your defence and give your account, tell me briefly the common opinion held by you the priests in our dominion, what you think right, after having carefully investigated the transactions of Chalcedon, and concerning the consecration of Timothy of Alexandria"'. (*HE* IV 5; Hamilton-Brooks 69, slightly adapted in this translation). The corresponding sentence, which reads somewhat differently, occurs at the conclusion of the Emperor's letter to Anatolius. Cf. Evagrius, *HE* II 9: Bidez-Parmentier 60, 31–61, 6; ACO II 5, p. 11, 26–32.

[7] That Leo received imperial documents in addition to the encyclical, however, is shown by the fact that he refers to the petitions to the Emperor of the two Egyptian parties: ACO II 4, p. 103, 14–15: 'Entreaties have been presented to Your Piety, copies of which you appended to your letters'. He then mentions the letter of the orthodox and that of the 'heretics'.

[8] Cf. Leo M., *ep.* 156 *ad Leon. aug.*: ACO II 4, p. 102, 19–25 (the Petrine doctrine); on the relationship of primacy and council cf. H. J. Sieben, *Die Konzilsidee der Alten Kirche*, First Part, Ch. III: Leo der Große (+461) über Konzilien und Lehrprimat des Römischen Stuhles, 103–147.

[9] Leo M., *ep.* 158 and 157: ACO II 4, pp. 104–105; 109–110.

[10] On the connexion of Leo's Second Tome (*ep.* 165) with the *Encyclia*, see ACO II 4, p. 104, 3–7 and p. 113, 2–5; Evagrius, *HE* II 10: Bidez-Parmentier 61, 17–24, reports that Emperor Leo forwarded to Timothy Aelurus the Pope's reply to his *Encyclia* though the *silentiarius* Diomedes. Following Evagrius one would have to assume that here Leo's *ep.* 165 was meant. The Syrian editor of Zacharias Rhetor, *HE* IV 5: Brooks 1 = CSCO 87, p. 121, 31–32; Hamilton-Brooks 70, 10–11; Ahrens-Krüger 28, 8–11, gives his presentation more accurately. According to him Emperor Leo forwarded to Alexandria *ep.* 165, which had been translated into Greek. Against this letter Timothy then composed a '*deesis*', the size of a *libellus*, about which Zacharias reports in Book IV (Brooks, pp. 121–123; Hamilton-Brooks 70–73; Ahrens-Krüger 28–31. In the German translation of Ahrens-Krüger the sentence on p. 31, 7–9 is still a part of the text of Timothy and not of the report of the editor. In Brooks, p. 123, 29–30, the punctuation and translation are better: 'Sed quae mihi [= Timothy] *in hac epistula* [= Leo's *ep.* 165] *corrigi debere videntur*'—*quae non exscripta sunt*—'*sunt haec*'. Cf. Hamilton-Brooks 73, 6–7. From the continuation of the text, which again is translated better by Brooks than by Ahrens-Krüger, it is clear that Timothy also dealt with Leo's *florilegium*, the *chreseis*; this, however, has been omitted by Zacharias. The Greek translation of Leo's *ep.* 165 is to be found in E. Schwartz, 'Codex Vaticanus gr. 1431' (*AbhMünchAkW* 32, 6, pp. 56–62; there

of the Emperor with a total of four letters, these being also the testimony of the Latin West to this action.

The testimony of the East is more involved, differentiated and, unfortunately, also incomplete. First of all, we can establish from the list of addressees that, including Leo of Rome, 62 metropolitans and three monks were recorded. Two addressees whose letters are extant were, however, inadvertently omitted.[11] In contrast to these 65 (67) addressees, there are only 34 replies which some 280 bishops or monks signed. According to the report of Photius, *Bibliotheca cod.* 229 (Ephraem of Antioch), 470 bishops or monks are said to be represented by signature.[12] The Latin translation of the *Codex encyclius* concludes briefly: 'end of the letters of the *Encyclia* [= *Codex encyclius*], i.e. of the 500 bishops of the whole world'.[13] The number instanced by Ephraem of Antioch may be the closest to the truth. According to the testimony of Photius, Patriarch Eulogius of Alexandria (580–607) later understood the imperial enquiry in a completely universal sense. In order to silence the ridiculous rumours of the Egyptians propagated after the death of the Emperor Marcian (Chalcedon rejected Cyril, but accepted Nestorius), (Emperor)

Leo had the decrees and acts of the Synod of Chalcedon despatched to the whole world with an *Encyclia* which directed that every bishop and every priest and all who excelled in monastic life confess their faith in writing. Roughly 1600 did this in great haste without even one expressing a divergent opinion, with the exception of Amphilocius of Side who shortly afterwards made known his assent by signing. Included in this number were the great Simeon who as a stylite lived impressively

---

is a commentary in ibid., 137–141). According to Evagrius, *HE* II 10: Bidez-Parmentier 61, 21–24, a copy of Timothy's *libellus* was included in the *Encyclia*, the CE, and with it also Leo's *ep.* 165, as Evagrius says: Ὧν τὰ ἀντίγραφα μὲν σώζεται ἐν τοῖς καλουμένοις ἐγκυκλίοις. Since Leo's *ep.* 165 is dated 17 August, 458, Timothy's reply is in any case the last document to be added to the CE. That *ep.* 165 still belonged to the corpus of the CE is attested to even before Evagrius by the *libellus fidei* of Maxentius and his companions from the year 519, which was presented to a Roman delegation in Constantinople: *beatus papa Leo coactus est diversorum patrum sententiis per illa quae dicuntur encyclia, contradicentium ora obstruere* (ACO IV 2, p. 3, 31–33; ACO II 5, *praef.* XIII). The *florilegium* is evidence of the fact that it is a question of *ep.* 165.

[11] Cf. ACO II 5, *praef.* XIII f.. It is a question of CE 17 and 40. In *praef.* XIII Schwartz corrects the false account he gave in the apparatus pp. 24, 28.

[12] Photius, *Bibl. cod.* 229: PG 103, 988D–989A; ed. R. Henry, *Photius, Bibliothèque, T. 4* (Paris 1965) 142. The Latin text in PG 103, 987D has, no doubt by mistake, the number 370. R. Henry, ibid., n. 3, falsely believes that the number 470 is the number of signatures at the Council of Chalcedon itself. The documentary evidence adduced by him would, of course, have to read: ACO II 1, 2, pp. 141–155, even if there were reference to the Chalcedonian list of signatures. But Henry does not take account of the εἶτα in the Greek text which he correctly renders with 'dans la suite'—thus 'after Chalcedon'. Furthermore, the names of the three monks which are mentioned here, Symeon, James and Baradatus, would have to draw one's attention to the fact that by the number 470 the members of the Synod of Chalcedon cannot be intended. Cf. E. Honigmann, 'The monks Symeon, Jacobus and Baradatus (434, 457–8 AD)', *Patristic Studies* = ST 173 (Roma 1953) 92–100.

[13] ACO II 5, p. 98. This figure is also an indication that all the letters were at the disposal of the translator and the collector of the *Collectio Sangermanensis* as well. '500' as a round figure comes rather close to the number of the *cod.* 229 in Photius.

the angelic life of the hereafter, as well as Baradatus and others who made every effort to follow that way of life to the same degree.[14]

Because it is incompletely preserved, the *Codex encylius* leaves not a few blank spots on a map which could be sketched to illustrate the reception of Chalcedon. With some effort the number of these can be reduced to some extent.[15] In several sources Amphilochius of Side is named[16]; he had declared himself to be against the validity of Timothy's consecration, but also against Chalcedon. According to a remark by Eulogius which cannot be checked, he soon afterwards, however, assented to the Council.[17] In the list of the addressees of the *Codex encyclius* 11, the tenth is given as Bishop Stephen of Hieropolis in Euphratesia. In the *Codex encyclius* itself there is no letter from him preserved. But Cassiodorus must still have seen his letter, for he cites a passage from a letter to Emperor Leo by a Stephen who is not identified more precisely. This passage is found once again in Benedict of Ariane in dependence on Cassiodorus.[18] In fact, we have before us a testimony of a good Chalcedonian christology from the *Codex encyclius*. We have already spoken of the traces of a monastic reaction (which goes beyond the letter of Baradatus).

Thought has been given to why the *Collectio Sangermanensis*, in contrast to the Greek original and the Latin translation corresponding

---

[14] Cf. Photius, *Bibl.* 230: PG 103, 1077C; R. Henry, op. cit., 5, 55. Only the letter of Baradatus is preserved in the CE (21). We are informed to some extent about the letter of Symeon by Evagrius, *HE* II 10: Bidez-Parmentier 62, who quotes extracts, admittedly not from the letter to the Emperor, but from the monk's letter to Basil, the archbishop of Antioch; this letter refers to the *Encyclia* of the Emperor. Hence we learn of the Stylite's attitude to the Council. These three monks are also mentioned in Photius, *cod.* 228, on which R. Henry, op. cit., 4, 123f., n. 2, gives a completely misleading commentary. He is of the opinion that with 'Symeon' the 'Younger' (518/526–592) is meant, but this fits neither Chalcedon nor the CE. The reference can only be to Symeon the 'Elder' (d. 25 August or 2 September, 459). Cf. T. Schnitzler, *Im Kampfe um Chalcedon* (above n. 2), 62–63, where, however, misleading misprints are to be noted.

[15] T. Schnitzler, op. cit., 63–67, follows up witnesses who, beyond the CE in its present state, report further replies to the Emperor.

[16] Cf. above n. 14 (*cod.* 230 in Photius); Zacharias Rhetor, *HE* IV 7: Hamilton-Brooks 73–74; Evagrius, *HE* II 10: Bidez-Parmentier 61, who remarks that Zacharias Rh. inserted the letter of Amphilochius in his collection. Leontius Byz., *C. monoph.*: PG 86, 2, 1841B, cites a sentence from it.

[17] Cf. Ahrens-Krüger in their commentary on Zacharias Rh., *HE* IV 7 (31, 34). Reference is also made there to *Le Quien* I, 998.

[18] Cassiodorus, *Expos. in Ps. 76, g*: PL 70, 549AB: CCL 98, p. 702, 170–177. 'Concerning this passage Bishop Stephen, writing in the *encyclia* to Emperor Leo, says in wondrous words: The Son donned the garment of the body, that is the whole man from the holy virgin, which the Holy Spirit wove in ineffable fashion; his entrance into it is beyond description, his coming out in it is open to understanding. The entrance into the virgin is invisible, the coming out is visible; God the Word entered, what emerged is himself and man'. In *Opusculum II* of Benedict of Aniane (PL 103, 1409B) this passage turns up again with slight changes. Schwartz, ACO II 5, *praef.* XV, has overlooked this quotation in Cassiodorus, and hence also did not recognise Benedict's dependence on him. In Migne, because of false punctuation, the same passage was significantly 'extended' with a content which fits the period of Spanish adoptionism, but not the year 457. If one takes the passage to the extent that it is found in Cassiodorus, Schwartz' judgement of its not being authentic is no longer to the point, as Schnitzler, op. cit., 63f., rightly remarks. That it should be ascribed to Stephen, the metropolitan of Hierapolis, is obvious.

to this, had omitted so many letters. E. Schwartz contents himself with an allusion to the economy of the man 'for whom the collection with so many letters of the same content seemed to be too large and inconvenient'.[19] This reason need not be discounted. But beyond this it can be asked whether the imperial collection itself did not already show a difference between the number of addressees and the letters returned. How is this to be explained? It has been assumed with somewhat too much certainty that a dispensation from writing in their own name could be given to themselves by those bishops who were at that *Synodos endemousa* (Home Synod) which had been recommended by the Emperor to Bishop Anatolius in the Alexandrian affair.[20] But, in that case, one would expect a document of precisely this *Synodus endemousa* (Home Synod) with the signatures of the participants, if it had really taken place. In his own letter of reply Bishop Anatolius mentions only that he has indeed conferred with others, but stresses that he sets forth for the Emperor 'his' opinion.[21] If a 'Home Synod' had taken place, Anatolius would hardly have left it unmentioned after there had been talk of it in the Emperor's letter to him. What is striking is that in the *Codex encyclius* letters of the metropolitans whose sees are in the neighbourhood of the capital city (such as Nicomedia, Chalcedon, Nicaea) are missing. An attempt has been made to explain these gaps by claiming that these bishops could have expressed their *sententia* orally at the imperial court.[22] Such a declaration, however, would certainly have been included in the *acta*. Very probably the imperial officials would have pressed for a written document even in this case, leaving out of consideration the fact that synods were indeed desired for metropolitan sees. In any event the metropolitans also had to supply information about their suffragans which was not practically possible without a synod, or at least not without signatures. How these gaps came into existence thus still remains unexplained.

The lack of a response from Palestine is particularly to be regretted, for, besides Alexandria, Jerusalem had been, indeed, the centre of the disturbances connected with Chalcedon, before Juvenal could carry the day with imperial assistance. It used to be held that the silence of Palestine could be explained by reference to the death of Juvenal which occurred at the time of the despatch of the imperial enquiry (457). But Juvenal is mentioned expressly in the *Encyclia*

[19] ACO II 5, *praef.* XV.
[20] See above n. 4. T. Schnitzler, op. cit., 65, makes this suggestion.
[21] CE 13: ACO II 5, p. 25, 17–18: 'Since I have aptly expounded these things to others, I am now in a better position to be able confidently to make known more clearly my opinion on the matters in hand'.
[22] Thus T. Schnitzler, op. cit., 65.

of the Emperor in 457, and this is the last extant document addressed to him. It would still have reached him, for he died only in July 458.[23] Thus it can be rightly assumed, that

... he [Juvenal] probably answered the Emperor by synodical letter composed by him together with the suffragan bishops of the three Palestinian provinces; but his answer, like many others, is missing in the only two existing manuscripts of the Latin translation of the Encyclical ...[24]

Nevertheless, we know the opinion of the Patriarch of Jerusalem and his suffragans from a synodical letter which immediately precedes the *Codex encyclius* in the *Collectio Sangermanensis*. This *synodica* was certainly composed before the end of 453 or the beginning of 454 at a synod held shortly after the return of Juvenal from Constantinople to Jerusalem.[25] But from that time until his death, Juvenal undoubtedly kept to the profession of Chalcedon made in this synodical letter. It reads the same as the majority of the declarations of Chalcedon in the *Codex encyclius*. Could this perhaps be the reason that the Palestinian reply was not included in the *Codex encyclius* of the *Collectio Sangermanensis*? This synodical letter of 453/454 gives, nevertheless, more information about the state of the reception of Chalcedon in Palestine than a reply sent into the Emperor by a few bishops. From the text of the letter it is to be inferred that the bishops had to struggle hard to gain acceptance for the Council of 451.[26] Opposition from the monks and faithful was still not overcome even in 457/458.

The letters, taken together, could give Emperor Leo sufficient information about the reception of Chalcedon, at least as far as the majority of the bishops in the East was concerned. The decision taken against Timothy was unanimously accepted; only one bishop had declared himself to be against Chalcedon. But it was only toward the end of 459, or even in 460, when the influence of Aspar had declined, that the *dux Aegypti* received the order to banish Timothy from Egypt.[27] The Emperor was certainly not unaware that, apart from the supporters of Timothy in Egypt, there were still some pockets of resistance in monastic circles and among the people. This gives rise to the question, how seriously one is to take the reception of Chalcedon by the bishops? To begin with we shall have to ask about

[23] Cf. E. Honigmann, 'Juvenal of Jerusalem', *DOP* 5(1950) 261; L. Perrone, *La Chiesa di Palestina e le controversie cristologiche* (Brescia 1980) 11, 118.
[24] E. Honigmann, ibid..
[25] Cf. ACO II 5, nr.4, p. 9. Irenaeus of Caesarea, Paul of Paralus and the other bishops of the three Palestinian provinces signed with Juvenal.
[26] On the situation of the Synod of 453/54 cf. E. Honigmann, op. cit., 258f.; L. Perrone, op. cit., 103–116.
[27] Cf. E. Schwartz, 'Publizistische Sammlungen', 178; idem, 'Codex Vaticanus gr. 1431', 128. G. Krüger, *Monophysitische Streitigkeiten*, 101–102.

the inner freedom of the signatories or of the assent given to Chalcedon in the *Codex encyclius*.

II. A MANIPULATED RESPONSE?

The letters of the Emperor and his approach in the questionnaire do not give the impression that he wanted to steer the bishops in a particular direction. The fact that he ultimately demanded that even Timothy Aelurus express his opinion and that he still allowed him to come to Constantinople after his deposition shows that he had the intention of hearing both parties, even leaving aside the pressure from Aspar.[28] It also cannot be confirmed that the imperial *magistriani*, who were sent with the enquiry throughout the whole East, exercised any pressure. But there seems to have been a certain influence on the bishops which came from Anatolius, the Bishop of Constantinople. Liberatus reports in his *Breviarium* that not only did the Emperor despatch his messengers, but Anatolius also sent out the deacon Asclepiades. Through both sets of emissaries the bishops in the provinces would learn what happened in Alexandria.[29] That the 'truth' about Timothy and the events in Alexandria be known everywhere was of particular interest to Anatolius, for he knew that the supporters of the Alexandrian ignored the Council of 381 which had fixed the position of precedence of the bishop of the Imperial City in the East. Through the despatch of his deacon and through a circular to all the Eastern metropolitans and to Pope Leo in Rome[30], Anatolius demonstrated his 'patriarchal rights', and thus must have been interested in putting the Egyptians in a bad light and also in emphasising the Council of Chalcedon, together with the Council

---

[28] Cf. E. Schwartz, 'Codex Vaticanus gr. 1431', 128. In Constantinople the Emperor still wanted to make the last attempt to obtain from Timothy a formula that the government could tolerate. Only when even then Timothy remained intransigent was he banished to Gangra by decree.

[29] Liberatus, *Breviar.* XV: ACO II 5, p. 124, 27-30: '. . . and [the Emperor] sent officials (*magistrianos*) throughout the whole Orient; also Bishop Anatolius sent his deacon Asclepiades so that through all these the bishops who had gathered at Chalcedon would know what had happened at Alexandria'. Cf. *Codex canonum (Collectio Quesnelliana)*: PL 56, 609AB. On the deployment and travel routes of the imperial envoys cf. T. Schnitzler, op. cit., 21-25.

[30] Cf. CE 12 (Anatolius to Emperor Leo): ACO II 5, p. 25, 4-18: 'Also now with regard to the acts of usurpation that were committed in the Alexandrian Church I have not abstained from action, but following the intention of Your most Christian Tranquillity—which desires that the rules of the holy Fathers be not spurned and civil rights be protected—I have done what seemed suitable to me as encumbent of the see of this imperial city. This should be clear to Your Devoutness from what I wrote to the most holy and venerable Roman Pontifex Leo as well as to the venerable metropolitan bishops of every diocese'. It is his intention to deal with the two questions posed by the Emperor, and to do this with all clarity (*clarius . . . meam possim publicare sententiam*), having already expounded these matters to others (*quoniam aliis haec convenienter exposui*). Before this in CE 10 it is said in a summary way that the imperial envoys also received Anatolius' letters to take along with them (ACO II 5, p. 22, 24-25). Zacharias Rh. *HE* IV 8; Hamilton-Brooks 75, also reports that Anatolius wrote to the bishops. Whereas Anatolius' deacon could not go to all the metropolitans, his letter could have a far greater range.

of 381. According to the pro-Monophysite *Church History* of Zacharias Rhetor, the positive response for Chalcedon and the negative response for Timothy which came from the provinces were due precisely to Anatolius.

He himself was the cause of the bishops' assent to what had been concluded at the Synod in their letters to the Emperor. Many from the Senate (σύγκλητος) and many inhabitants of the city cut off contact with Anatolius when they heard this about him.[31]

The statement of Zacharias Rhetor is certainly not to be maintained in this rigour.[32] As the analysis of the letters of the *Codex encyclius* will show, a considerable number of bishops ventured to place a question-mark after the reliability of the reports about Egypt (whether these stem from the Egyptian bishops who had fled to Constantinople or from Anatolius). Some obviously attempted to confirm the events in Egypt or they were inclined to hear the opposition party as well.[33] The examples adduced show in any case that with striking frequency the intention of gaining conscientious information is stated and that the replies of the bishops are considered and restrained. The burden of assessing the situation and of deciding was for this reason handed back to the Emperor: ... *si tamen vera sunt* ...[34]

This gives us some right to take as honest and considered also

---

[31] Zacharias Rh. ibid.; Hamilton-Brooks 75, 20–24.

[32] The feeling of being 'manipulated' is most intensely displayed in the letter of Epiphanius and the bishops of Pamphylia; this letter also shows the greatest reserve vis-à-vis Chalcedon (see below). After the bishops express their opinion, which is certainly none too agreeable to the Emperor, they request benevolence with regard to unguarded statements, and give the following reason for this: *invitati enim, potius autem iussi et, quod maius est, coniurati haec scribere vestrae tranquillitati praesumpsimus* (ACO II 5, p. 60, 4–6). 'Invited'—'commanded'—'bound by oath' imply a moral pressure; does this pressure not emanate from the opponents of the Council or from a group which has 'reservations' with regard to it and to which the bishops adhere, although they perhaps fear the disapproval of the Emperor?

[33] Epiphanius, who has just been mentioned, writes in the following way: 'To speak the truth, with regard to Timothy, insofar as we humble souls (*humiles*) could examine things, ... if the facts about him, so great and of such a kind, which are contained in the entreaties handed over to the authority of Your Tranquillity are ascertained to be true, as the most reverent bishops who suppliantly (*suppliciter*) submit these things affirm ...' (ibid., p. 59, 36–40). The bishops of CE 35 (Cyzicus on the Hellespont: ACO II 5, p. 67, 29–31) also use the following formula with regard to the report of the orthodox from Alexandria: 'if there is truth in these entreaties'; or ibid., p. 68, 3: 'provided, of course, as we have said, that the entreaties do not deviate at all from the truth'. In the same way CE 36: ACO II 5, p. 69, 36–38; CE 37: ibid., p. 74, 34–35; CE 38: ibid., p. 77, 6–11; CE 40: ibid., p. 82, 5–7; 83, 3–5: 'provided these things happened in the way that was said (for we do not know the ins and outs of the matter, living as we do at the very end of Pontus) ...'; CE 41: ibid., p. 85, 18–25; CE 42: ibid., p. 87, 7–8; CE 45: ibid., p. 92, 10–11; the bishops of CE 47: ibid., p. 95, 36–38 say expressly: '... if what is claimed (*deducta*) by the Alexandrians in their accusation tallies with the truth (for words must not be taken from one side)'.

[34] Cf. especially CE 31 (Epiphanius): ACO II 5, p. 59, 41–60, 6: 'For his [Timothy's] whole cause depends on the judgement and decision (*probatione*) of Your Sovereignty and the integrity (*integritate*) of the most holy and supreme fathers [no doubt the senate is meant], whom it is right that we humble souls (*humiles*) should obey on account of their great knowledge and wisdom, capable as they are of judging such things in a subtle manner'.

the position expressed with regard to Chalcedon itself and its reception, even if the theological stand or the content of the christological statement as well is very disappointing.

III. THE BISHOPS HAPPILY ACCEPT THE IMPERIAL CHURCH

The question about the independence of the bishops and their replies in the *Codex encyclius* rises again, however, when we look at the structure of the imperial Church at that time. The letters of the *Codex encyclius* are very instructive for studying the ties of this system and provide an example of the future fate of Chalcedon. If we are to investigate the reception of Chalcedon, we cannot neglect this.

Hardly anywhere else in patristic literature is there to be found together in the one place such a happy acceptance of the imperial Church and homage paid to the Emperor as here in the *Codex encyclius*. In many letters the theology of the imperial Church is more strongly expressed than the doctrine of the incarnation of Christ. The motif of the imperial Church is already intoned in the letter of the orthodox bishops from Egypt, and hence could find an echo in other letters.

To you [the Emperor] we come, for you are animated by a religious spirit; to you, the protector of the human race, to you who show such zeal for Christ.[35]

The same sentiment is expressed often in the description of the crimes of Timothy and is formulated in the request to the Emperor:

We beseech Your Christian Power ... that you do not allow the true faith to be subjected to tyranny, but rather that you avenge the holy rules of the Fathers, the ecclesiastical order, the civil discipline and the harm done to the holy and great councils which were celebrated at various times to strengthen orthodox faith.[36]

Ecclesiastical and civil order, orthodox faith and the common good (*status communis*), the well-being of the people and of the Churches are closely tied in the minds of these bishops—fully in accord with the Constantinian idea of the Empire. While Pope Leo ever more clearly wished to limit the rights of the Emperor in questions of faith (particularly in regard to the *praedicare*), in the letters of the *Codex encyclius* the Imperator occupies the highest place in caring for 'right faith' and 'devotion to God' (*pietas circa Deum*).

Without doubt the teachers of right doctrines and the shining lights of truth which appeared at various times are authoritative for them [i.e. the *recta fides* and the *pietas*

---

[35] CE 7: ACO II 5, p. 12, 21–22.
[36] CE 7: ibid., p. 15, 24–31; cf. the letter of the same bishops to Anatolius, CE 8: ibid., p. 20, 22–27. 32–34, where the outrage of Timothy 'against the holy and undefiled faith and against the holy and venerable rules [canons] and the common discipline, but even more against the status of the holy Churches and against the *res publica* and laws' are described.

circa Deum]; at the summit, however, you stand as the special protector of all, when you take over the plantation inherited by you and appear as its faithful caretaker.[37]

Certainly here there is still a distinction made between episcopal and imperial function. But does it endure? The bishops of *Syria secunda* even apply the Petrine promise of Mt 16, 18 to the Emperor.

Christ, the Lord of all, demonstrated his immense love for the Churches and brought to fulfilment the promise in which according to the gospels it was said to Peter: 'You are Peter, and on this rock I will build my Church, and the gates of hell will not prevail against it', when he encircled Your Tranquillity with the august robe of devout rule. In this there is nothing marvellous; for he indeed is God and he speaks without lies and always shows his promises to be true.[38]

The application of this Petrine promise to the Emperor is made even more pointedly by the bishops of *prima Armenia*. They say that the inventors of their own blasphemous doctrines should also perceive what the holy catholic Church dictates, whose head is indeed Christ, but whose power and foundation, and thus the guarantor of the peaceful exercise of devotion for all, is the Emperor; for he emulates the power of the immovable rock on which the Creator of all built his Church.[39]

Christ the head, the Emperor the power and the foundation of the Church! The rôle of Peter is attributed to the Emperor almost in the way in which in the West Pope Leo lays claim to it for himself. It is understandable that many scholars could succumb to the temptation to speak of 'Byzantine Caesaropapism'. The bishops admittedly did not want to deliver themselves up to the 'political' power, as we understand this today, but to the Emperor as an instrument of a world order, an instrument *inspired* by Christ or the Holy Spirit[40]

---

[37] CE 20 (from the bishops of *Syria prima*): ACO II 5, p. 33, 1–3. In line 10 the bishops speak of the fact that the Emperor possesses divine sagacity and is completely conversant with divine things. The monk Baradatus expresses it similarly in CE 21: ACO II 5, p. 35, 11–17: for the care of all the Churches and all the poor 'God chose Your Devoutness in the whole Roman empire and conferred on you understanding and wisdom ... which go beyond the wise of the world, so that Your Excellence (*divinitas*) may destroy those who live in the basest iniquity and free the just from the hands of the impious'.

[38] CE 22: ACO II 5, p. 38, 32–38.

[39] CE 36: ACO II 5, p. 70, 26–32: 'For many, not understanding the divine scriptures as they are written, have created dogmas of their own blasphemy; may Christ the Lord by his clemency and the sacred sagacity and diligence of Your Devoutness convert them and teach them to preach the word of right truth and to know what the holy catholic Church teaches (*dictat*), whose head is Christ, whose strength and foundation, however, you are in taking as your model the immovable rock of Christ, on which the Creator of all builds his Church and thus bestows rest on all Christians'. The Emperor appears here as the instrument of Christ by which he converts the heretics and teaches them to preach (*praedicare*) the word of right truth.

[40] At the conclusion of the text from CE 31: ACO II 5, p. 70, 34–38, from which we have just cited, we read: 'For we believe that ... every way of truth and every manner is open to Your Devoutness to settle scandals and to lead back discordant members to right faith, with Christ the Lord conducting Your Tranquillity to everything that is good by the inspiration that comes from above (*de super quadam inspiratione*)'.

which they held to be responsible for the Church and state in the same way. The Emperor thus receives here a function which surely affects the inner spiritual essence of the Church and does not just have to do with its 'external sphere'—a distinction which will immediately become thematic. This is clear in the letter of the bishops of Mesopotamia (CE 24). This takes as its starting-point the salvific work of Christ which is enacted or mediated in the revelation of truth and in the foundation and preservation of the Church. In this activity of Christ for his Church, the Emperor receives a place between the *apostles* and the bishops, who are described as *conlaborantes piscatoribus*, fellow-workers of the fishermen.[41] He has to exercise a sacral function. In Emperor Leo, God

> has given to his Churches a successor of this devout rule and an heir of the faith which brings salvation, and to everything under the heavens the most tranquil power of Your Christianness for the strengthening of ecclesial peace which will be salvation for you in hope and faith, and the consolation of the whole earth and of the great number of faithful nations.[42]

Once again there is talk of *praedicatio*.

Constantine and his famous, much-discussed distinction between 'bishop of internal and external affairs' come to mind, when Epiphanius, the metropolitan of Perge in Pamphylia, says to the Emperor:

> Emperor, beloved of God! We know you to be not only the one who cares for external affairs, but with great effort you also bestow peace on the holy Churches of God; thus you should also enjoy that peace, you who struggle on their behalf and conscientiously accomplish everything for them in their entirety, because all who belong to it are bound to the one body of Christ.[43]

---

[41] CE 24: ACO II 5, p. 41, 17–19: 'Not only through the fisherman, his disciples, who announced the great mystery of truth, not with words of human cleverness, but through heavenly wisdom and the tongue of fire of the Holy Spirit did he establish her [the Church] and give her increase; he also advanced the preaching of devotion through pious princes who came later, and through fellow-workers of the fisherman [the bishops]'.

[42] CE 24: ACO II 5, p. 41, 20–24. It was precisely in this preaching (*praedicare*) that Pope Leo did not want to allow the Emperor to share. Cf. above Ch. II, n. 90 and 87.

[43] CE 31: ACO II 5, p. 58, 14–18. Thus there is talk of the Emperor as *extranearum rerum provisor* at the same time as his care for the peace of the Church. Without doubt allusion is made here to Eusebius, *Vita Constantini* IV 24 (Heikel 126): ἀλλ' ὑμεῖς μὲν τῶν εἴσω τῆς ἐκκλησίας ἐγὼ δὲ τῶν ἐκτὸς ὑπὸ θεοῦ καθεσταμένος ἐπίσκοπος ἂν εἴην. On the interpretation of this passage cf. F. Vittinghoff, 'Eusebius als Verfasser der "Vita Constantini"', *RheinMus. f. Philologie* NF 96(1953) (330–373) 365–370; J. Straub, 'Kaiser Konstantin als ἐπίσκοπος τῶν ἐκτός', *StudPat* 1 = TU 63(1957) 678–695. With Valesius and others, Vittinghoff derives τῶν ἐκτός from τὰ ἐκτός (πραγμάτων); Straub, on the other hand, (with Tillemont and others) is for its derivation from οἱ ἐκτός, but as far as the matter itself is concerned he agrees with Vittinghoff who says, op. cit., 368: 'Constantine's task as ἐπίσκοπος τῶν ἐκτός is thus related to the area of the state and politics within which the imperial 'bishop' gains acceptance for the precepts and views of the Christian faith. For the bishops and the Church lack here the means of law and power to transform this domain into something Christian. The Emperor is thus 'bishop' not only for those inhabitants of the empire who are outside the Church, but also for those others who, as members of the Church, are at the same time also members of the Roman state and subjects of the Emperor, and also as Christians are subject to the ordinances and laws of the state'. We do not have to decide the problem of interpreting Constantine's description of himself. The fact that CE 31 obviously interpreted the Greek text as a neuter

According to the opinion of the bishops of *secunda Armenia*, God and the Christian Emperor are sufficient to guarantee the right order of the world and a 'life and way of life which is wonderful and faithful to the law'.[44] The Fathers of the Council of Nicaea appear to them as armour-bearers of Emperor Constantine with whom he wages the Lord's wars against heretics.[45] The whole work of the Council of Constantinople (381) is also ascribed to the successors of Constantine, so that the activity of the members of the Synods of 325 and 381 retreats wholly into the background, or is at least severely restricted.[46] Because Emperor Leo accomplishes his negotiations fully according to the faith and bases himself on apostolic and catholic strength, God has conferred upon him power over the world, and he can guide it in peace.[47]

We conclude with the words of Bishop Agapitus of Rhodes in which the vision of a sacral order is expressed in a way that is simply fascinating.

is, however, to be noted. *Extranearum rerum provisor* is the translation of τῶν ἐκτὸς πραγμάτων ἐπίσκοπος. Vittinghoff, op. cit., 369, draws attention to the chapter heading of *Vita Constantini* IV: ὅτι τῶν ἔξω πραγμάτων ὥσπερ ἐπίσκοπον ἑαυτὸν εἶπεν εἶναι, which stems from a Byzantine editor, but has been taken over already in the earliest manuscripts. Our text in CE 31 is made even clearer by '*extranearum rerum*' being set over against '*sanctarum dei ecclesiarum pacem*'. The '*res extraneae*' would be obligations in the area of the state and politics, obligations which affect Christians and pagans and for which the Emperor is naturally responsible. Emperor Leo, however, is praised for the fact that he also cares for the 'peace of the holy Church of God', hence its internal affairs. In the *Vita Constantini* the view is from within to without; in CE 31 it is from without to within. Thus one needs the Emperor to gain acceptance 'outside' for fundamental tenets of Christianity and for the proclamation of the gospel, and 'inside' to maintain the peace of faith—a statement that is not an insignificant confession and concession! For further information on the interpretation of *Vita Const.* IV 24 see G. Masay, *L' 'épiscopat' de l'empereur Constantin*. Mémoire de licence, Université Libre de Bruxelles, Sect. Histoire, 1967–68 (Bibl. de l'Université); J.-M. Sansterre, 'Eusèbe de Césarée et la naissance de la théorie "Césaropapiste"', *Byz* 42(1972) 131–195.532–594. Masay and Sansterre are for the masculine sense of τῶν ἐκτός. With this phrase Constantine characterised himself as bishop of the pagans, this admittedly at a time when he still had complete trust in the bishops as the ones responsible for the Christians. From November–December 325 in the dispute about Nicaea he let the bishops feel, however, that he was not only the bishop of the pagans, but also the protector of the decisions of the Council. For further information see A. Grillmeier, *Mit ihm und in ihm*, 400f., n. 34. Constantine's characterisation of the Emperor as *sacerdos* or *pontifex* is in line with a sacralisation of the Emperor, although the Emperors Gratian and Theodosius the Great demonstratively abandoned the title *Pontifex Maximus*; cf. R. Schieffer, 'Der Papst als Pontifex Maximus', *ZSavSt.k.* 88 (1971) (300–309) 303, n. 16. Bishop Agapitus of Rhodes says in CE 33: ACO II 5, p. 64, 9–10: vere namque sacerdos et natura imperator existis. R. Schieffer, art. cit., 304, n. 20, produces other instances of this combination, in fact from the period 449 to 451 (also from Rusticus). Cf. ibid. for further literature.

[44] CE 37: ACO II 5, p. 71, 18–21: *legalis et mirabilis vita conversatioque...*

[45] Ibid., l. 4–8: 'For Constantine of happy memory, ruler of the militia of Christ the almighty, with the 318 holy Fathers bearing arms, victorious in the war of the Lord, appeared in full stature before the King of Kings [at his death]; but for a long time in all the Churches of God he enjoys a commemoration which withstands forgetfulness and is praised by every pious tongue'.

[46] Ibid., l. 8–13. According to this paragraph the Emperors sanctioned the decision of 381 and again the Council of Nicaea (325), they confounded the heretics and drove the heretical plague from the Church, and they 'proclaimed' (*adnuntiantes*) the doctrine of the oneness in being of Father, Son and Holy Spirit and their divinity.

[47] CE 41 (from the bishops of the province Helenopontus): ACO II 5, p. 84, 15–17: 'Since you act in the strength of apostolic and catholic faith, God has bestowed on you power over the world which you guide in peace that is pleasing to God'.

It is a gift of first fruits and a pleasing sacrifice that the governor of the world and the ruler of the whole earth under the sun preserves intact the faith in the adorable Trinity, and through his action and his worship also teaches man both to fear God and to imitate such things through which our race is maintained, and to direct his thought to the common state and the order of the whole people. Thus the primary preoccupation and the name of peace should have precedence and importance everywhere. Man should not be like the animals and individually vent his wild rage against his own race.[48]

The dangers involved in being tied in such a way to the system of the imperial Church were not immediately acute at the time when the bishops composed their replies to the enquiry of Emperor Leo, but they could become so at any time. It was also not a case of the Emperor's having given to the bishops the *content* of their letters.[49] Emperor Leo I truly wanted candid information. The risky element in the replies of the bishops resided rather in the fact that the Emperor appeared as the principle of unity of the Church and its doctrine in such an unmistakeable fashion. Hence the ruler functions not as a political principle, but as a religious one.[50] Even for the bishops who thought in the religious sphere, every expression of the Emperor's will had to appear as a revelation of God's will, because of his *sacra maiestas* and the complete sacralisation of his office. In the light of the letters of the *Codex encyclius*, what J. Straub says of the Western Church is valid as well for the East.

The Western Church soon learned to interpret the meaning of the two competing authorities (i.e. of the sacerdotal and imperial authority) in such a way that she herself became a reflection of imperial institutions. Thus Sägmüller was able to characterize 'the Church as Imperium Romanum' in regard to its external appearances, the *ecclesia catholica* which had become the *ecclesia Romana*. Opitz, on the other hand, rightly points out that Constantine intended to integrate the Church community into the universal community of the Roman Empire, to transform the Empire into an *ecclesia*, in which the specifically theological, liturgical and ritual functions were

---

[48] CE 33: ACO II 5, p. 64, 2–7. Here the Emperor receives the title *auriga mundi et princeps totius orbis qui sub sole consistit*. In this context there then follow the words *sacerdos et imperator* of which we have already spoken in n. 43. On the introduction of this idea that the Emperor as the charioteer of the universe receives the reins of Helios, cf. H.-G. Opitz, 'Eusebius von Caesarea als Theologe', *ZNW* 34 (1935) (1–19) 15: 'As God, as the steerer of the universe, holds the reins of the world, so also the Emperor. It is not by accident, and therefore all the more significant, that on the imperial coins, even in the later period, Helios as charioteer or with a whip still appears. This does not need to be evidence of the pagan views of the master of the mint or of the unsubdued paganism of Constantine, but Eusebius himself, the Christian theologian, uses the image to represent Constantine as ἡνίοχος [= auriga] in a Christian sense'. The monarchy of Constantine is the image of God's monarchy over the world.

[49] It is true that quite often one can establish that the arguments of the various letters are the same. It may be that the travelling deacon of Anatolius or the imperial *magistriani* gave reports about synods already held and their lines of argument or even allowed their statements to be examined. Nevertheless, the various letters are not composed according to a model, but are completely individual.

[50] In J. Straub, 'Constantine as κοινὸς ἐπίσκοπος. Tradition and Innovation in the Representation of the First Christian Emperor's Majesty', *DOP* 21 (1967) 39–55, this is particularly clearly emphasised in the discussion of previous research (Jacob Burckhardt, E. Schwartz, among others).

primarily reserved for the *ordo clericorum* (bishops), while the supervision (ἐπισκοπή) of the *populus Christianus* (which was to be identified with the state) was entrusted to the emperor, who ruled on earth as viceregent of God, *vicarius Christi* and κοινὸς ἐπίσκοπος.[51]

The readiness to grant to the Emperor a special rôle in the preservation and realisation of the unity of faith was also conditioned by the positive experiences which the Church had had with important rulers. From the letters of the *Codex encyclius* we heard the praise of Constantine and his successors up to Emperor Marcian, particularly too where there was a reference to settling the Arian troubles. Nevertheless, this 'sacral-imperial' basis of the unity of faith and of the Church was not so much a rock as a volcano whose eruptions could convulse the Church at any time. For the idea of the unity of faith was subordinated to, and not placed above, the other idea of imperial unity. As long as the Church found its own doctrines and traditions reflected in the faith of the Emperor, she was quite happy to regard the ruler as *custos* and *cultor fidei*. But if there was an heretical split, then the Emperor, by reason of the great value placed on the religious–political principle of unity, was constantly tempted to bring about unity, even at the cost of orthodoxy. If for the sake of this over-taxed idea of unity a council was sometimes accepted by the Emperor, sometimes ignored or eliminated, then the bishops had also either to put off the robes of the imperial Church or to join in all the movements of imperial diplomacy with regard to faith: *cuius regio eius religio*! This hither and thither would soon begin for many bishops, if they had not already joined in it from 431 to 457. This struggle would also provide a new opportunity to reflect upon ecclesial and imperial spheres of competence.

This gives us a point of orientation in the question about the reception of Chalcedon in the letters of the *Codex encyclius*. The intention and foundation of assent to Chalcedon could be made in a completely sincere and 'religious' manner, even when the sacral figure of the Emperor had an influence on it. Nevertheless, it was disguised in its *ecclesial* character and exposed to the oscillations of imperial diplomacy in matters of faith. Thus should a bishop place the idea of unity developed by Constantine and enshrined in the imperial Church above the purely ecclesial tradition and its fundamental propositions, then with the further developments in imperial politics, aimed at eliminating the Monophysite split, he would have to determine his nearness to, or distance from, Chalcedon on the basis of what was

---

[51] Ibid., 54–55, with reference to J. B. Sägmüller, 'Die Idee von der Kirche als imperium Romanum im kanon. Recht', *TQ* 80 (1898) 50–80; H.-G. Opitz, art. cit., 1.15. Instead of *vicarius 'Christi'* it would have been better to have said *vicarius 'dei'*. See above, Ch. II, n. 79.

happening in the imperial palace. This precedence given to concerns of the imperial Church vis-à-vis those which are purely ecclesial probably explains best of all the oscillation of the bishops, as we are able to observe this in the further history of Chalcedon. One must not see in this merely a lack of principle, but one must consider at the same time the excessive tie of *conscience* to the sacral authority of the Emperor.[52] This tie affected one's conscience all the more strongly, the more an Emperor wanted to be genuinely religious. In his letter to Emperor Leo, Bishop Julian of Cius touches on this fact and stresses that 'no terror of imperial authority' forced the Fathers of Chalcedon to their decision; Emperor Marcian, fired by spiritual care and love for orthodox faith, endeavoured that the doctrine of the apostles be endorsed by the bishops of the Church.[53] Several bishops draw attention to the opposite circumstances at the so-called *Latrocinium* (Robber Council) of Ephesus (449). In particular, Peter of Myra, who in 449 was still not a bishop but who had at his disposal first-hand reports reaching back to Ephesus I through one of his suffragans, the old Bishop Eudoxius of Choma, compares Chalcedon with the events of 449. In sharp condemnation of the stand of Timothy Aelurus on Chalcedon, he defends the Council and says

that it in no way deviates from the decision of the Fathers gathered at Nicaea, for it was held in accord with God's [will] and [without] fear before men. On whom among the members of the Synod of Chalcedon was violence inflicted as happened to Flavian of holy memory under Dioscorus at Ephesus? Who pressed the pen into the hands [of the bishops], as happened there, and, pointing with the finger to those waiting outside the door, extorted anything, or who had to suffer blows? No one hid himself under the stools to escape the crime of signing. Here (= Chalcedon) we did not hear any innovation, nor could we thus consent to any.[54]

IV. CHALCEDON IN THE STRUCTURE OF CONCILIAR TRADITION

Our investigation into the attitude towards the imperial Church of the bishops of the *Codex encyclius* has revealed that the figure of Constantine and the sacrality of the system of the imperial Church created by him so dominated and formed people's minds that for

[52] Cf. T. Šagi-Bunić, 'Drama conscientiae episcoporum qua fidei iudicum in periodo ephesino-chalcedonensi', *Laurentianum* 9 (1968) 225–266.

[53] CE 34: ACO II 5, p. 66, 34–37: 'For at that time there was no fear of imperial authority, since Marcian of holy and pious memory, crowned with the diadem of divine love and full also of spiritual care, hastened out of a desire for orthodox faith to have the teachings of the apostles (*apostolorum dogmata*) confirmed by those who presided over the Church'.

[54] CE 32: ACO II 5, p. 62, 29–35. Cf. the dispute of Bishop Basil of Seleucia with Dioscorus in *actio* I of Chalcedon: ACO II 1,1 (Greek), ACO II 3,1 (Latin), nr. 851–862, where Basil gives as the reason for his own weakness the blackmailing procedure of Dioscorus.

this reason the fourth century became a kind of classical period in the history of the Church and of theology. This becomes all the more manifest when we examine the way in which the bishops of the *Codex encyclius* assessed Chalcedon. The way in which the councils from 325 to 451 are interpreted by the bishops is revealed in practically all their replies. There is one crucial point towards which everything is oriented: the Council of Constantine, the Council of Nicaea. Almost all the letters of the *Codex encyclius* are pervaded by the following observation: because Chalcedon considered the Council of 325 its proper norm, subtracting nothing from it nor adding anything to it, for this reason it is valid and to be received. This concentration on a point in the history of faith may have been *strengthened* by the Monophysites in Alexandria who wanted to lay claim to Nicaea for themselves, so that at least Ephesus I and II (449) remained uncontested. But this concentration upon Nicaea was not *occasioned* by them. The Church as a whole looked to Nicaea, as we have already seen in Leo of Rome. 'Nicaea in Chalcedon'—this catch-phrase could be given as a title to the whole aftermath of Chalcedon up to the Council of Constantinople (553). Only with the controversy about this Council did the first four synods receive the halo of Nicaea: four gospels— four councils! In the *Codex encyclius* almost everything is oriented towards 325. Even the high-flown designation, which we read again and again in the *Codex encyclius*—'the holy and general Council which gathered at Chalcedon'[55]—should not mislead us on this point. Whoever does not look behind this formula and takes it according to a modern understanding of a council, overlooks the peculiarity of the grading of Chalcedon in the *Codex encyclius*. Only one group of bishops, those from *secunda Mysia* and *Scythia* (CE 19), is an exception. These bishops list the first four general councils chronologically, viz. after the aspect of the heresies which they refuted. The teaching of these four councils is the content of their confession in which they intend to persevere. For Chalcedon, however, they emphasise that it is

a Council celebrated by many holy bishops at the command of the Bishop of Rome, Leo, who is truly the head of the bishops, and of the illustrious Bishop and Patriarch Anatolius, and ratified by two Emperors, a Council which we, together with all the clergy and the Christian people, possess as our property and in which we intend to remain.[56]

[55] Cf. the letter of the Chalcedonian bishops of Egypt, CE 7: ACO II 5, p. 12, 30f.; CE 8 (letter of the same bishops to Anatolius): ibid., p. 18, 26; p. 19, 40; CE 13 (the letter of Anatolius): ibid., p. 25, 29; CE 14 (the letter of the bishops of the province Europa): ibid., p. 27, 5–6: *per dei gratiam Calchedone collectum magnum sanctumque et universale concilium*. Similar expressions occur in other letters.
[56] CE 19: ACO II 5, p. 32, 11–17. We cite lines 15–17: *quod concilium nos cum omni clero et populo Christiano usque ad finem tenentes et possidentes in eo concupiscimus permanere*. The reception of the Council

With regard to the other letters of the *Codex encyclius*, we shall establish two points. 1. One group measures Chalcedon only by Nicaea; thus they acknowledge only a *relative* authority for Chalcedon. 2. The second group, however, is prepared to see in addition to this orientation towards Nicaea Chalcedon's own conciliar function, and thus to ascribe to it as well an authority in itself, an *absolute* value. What is meant by this will have to be determined more closely. Hence both groups are opposed to Timothy and his supporters, whose opinion is expressed in CE 9. For them Chalcedon does not exist, as is the case also with the Council of Constantinople. For them the First General Council is so perfect that its creed needs no interpretation, 'because it is interpreted by itself and proclaims clearly the mystery of devotion'.[57]

The first group. These bishops look through Chalcedon towards Nicaea, as one views a distant object through a telescope, which itself is only the instrument for seeing but not the goal of observation. The reason for 'making an instrument' of Chalcedon is this; it is intended to emphasise that in 451 no innovation was added to the faith, but that only the *fides antiquitus existens*, i.e. the *Symbolum Nicaenum*, was ratified anew.[58] According to Anatolius, the whole task of the Fourth Council consisted in removing the *scandals* against this faith, reimpressing the Creed of Nicaea on the household of the faith (*domesticis fidei*) and interpreting it for heretics, viz. with sanctions, '*cum terrore*'. The two other general Synods between 325 and 451 served the same purpose. At the Council of Chalcedon they were

---

is expressed by the words *tenere* and *possidere*, and is represented as an act of the clergy and of the whole people. Leo, with special emphasis, and Anatolius are named *before* the Emperors. The countries of the lower Danube, the area where the old Roman veterans settled, retained their orientation to West Rome. This is true as well for the Illyrian Marcellinus Comes, who, in his *Chronicle* for the years 379–534, which was composed in Latin in Constantinople, writes with regard to the year 458: 'For the benefit of the Tome of Chalcedon Emperor Leo sent throughout the whole world to all the bishops of the orthodox an individual letter, each similar in wording (*singulas consonantesque ... epistulas*), so that they could indicate to him in their letters of reply what they all thought of this Tome. From all these bishops he received letters which were so much of one accord (*conspirantes ... epistulas*) that one could think that they were dictated at the same time by the mouth of one man'. Cf. T. Mommsen, *Chronica minora* = MGH, Auct. Ant. XI, vol. 2 (Berlin 1894) 87, 9–17. Liberatus, *Breviarium* 15: ACO II 5, p. 124, 30–32, affirms a clear-cut consensus, but one that is motivated by the reference to Nicaea: 'They write back that Chalcedon is to be defended up to the shedding of blood, because it held no other faith than what the Synod of Nicaea established ...'. Cf. also Victor of Tunnuna, *Chronicon*: Mommsen, *Chronica minora* 187, 24–188, 4 (ad annum 468).

[57] CE 9: ACO II 5, p. 22, 1–2.

[58] Anatolius himself, who assuredly did not conceal his interest in the validity of Chalcedon, speaks in this way. Cf. CE 13: ACO II 5, p. 25,34–26,1: 'That Synod [of 451], in order to destroy the scandals which at that time seem to have arisen against the pure faith, did not invent (*innovavit*) another faith, it did not destroy [the faith] which was in existence from of old, it did not add anything to the confession which had been handed down from past times, it did not diminish the faith which is always kept and saves [us], but it prescribed that the Creed of the 318 holy Fathers be kept uncontaminated and inviolate by those who are of the faith (*domesticis fidei*) and be handed on with dire warning (*cum terrore tradi*) to those who are imbued with ungodliness'.

ratified in just this function. Chalcedon's unique characteristic consists in destroying the seeds of the (heretical) weed which had been sown by Eutyches.[59] Anatolius, indeed, calls Chalcedon "*sanctum et universale concilium*' or '*deo amabilis ac venerabilis synodus*'. But it has only a relative significance, viz. to be in the service of Nicaea, and a purely negative task, viz. to destroy newly arisen heresies which had not been condemned by previous councils. Hence the Bishop does not speak also, for instance, of the inspiration of Chalcedon, but only of the fact that it 'was celebrated at the command of the Emperor'[60], which without a doubt should be understood as a hint to the Emperor not to allow a council, summoned by imperial power itself, to fall. Anatolius says nothing about Chalcedon's formula of faith in the realisation of which he, however, shared—even if not with complete success.[61] Of the existence of this formula of faith we would learn nothing from the letter of the Bishop, were we not otherwise informed.

The most important example of an interpretation which is, indeed, positive, but which, however, makes Chalcedon relative with regard to Nicaea is the letter of Bishop Basil of Seleucia (CE 27), one of the most significant witnesses of the history of Chalcedon. He attended all synods from 448 to 451.[62] This bishop, who did not die as some have thought in 458 but only in 468[63], can without doubt be regarded as the most significant mediator between Antiochene and Cyrillian christologies, between diphysite and monophysite christologies. To all appearance he is worthy of little trust, for in 448 he was one of those who condemned the Archimandrite Eutyches, at the Synod of Ephesus (449) he accepted the *mia physis* formula, and at Chalcedon he voted once again with the majority, after he had been rehabilitated. On closer examination, however, as far as the *substance* is concerned, he is consistent; hence in formulating this way and that he is so cautious that he cannot be accused of dishonouring his convictions. On the basis of his christological statements from 448, 449 and 451, one can without too much difficulty make clear to the reader what is common to the different parties in the christological dispute, but also at the same time the vast differences between

---

[59] Ibid., p. 26, 2–4.
[60] Ibid., p. 25, 35: *synodus ex imperiali tunc sanctione celebrata.*
[61] CCT I², 543; JdChr I², 753.
[62] On Basil of Seleucia see CCT I², 525, n. 29; 548f.; JdChr I², 733f.; 756–758; 761; 767–768.
[63] On his year of death cf. E. Honigmann, 'Theodoretus of Cyrrhus and Basil of Seleucia (The Time of their Death)', idem, *Patristic Studies* (ST 173, Vatican 1953) 180–184. Important studies dealing with Basil are: T. Šagi-Bunić, '*Duo Perfecta*' et '*Duae naturae*' *in definitione dogmatica Chalcedonensi* (Roma-Laurentianum 1964); idem, '*Deus perfectus et Homo perfectus*' *a Concilio Ephesino (a. 431) ad Chalcedonense (a. 451)* (Romae 1965); M. van Parys, 'L'évolution de la doctrine christologique de Basile de Séleucie', *Irén* 44 (1971) 493–514 (here there is also further literature); M. Aubineau, *Homélies Pascales* = SC 187, 167–277.

them.[64] How does a man who was involved in the history of Chalcedon in a special way assess it at this particular time?

Basil confesses: 'The intention of the Council of Chalcedon is utterly clear-cut'.[65] (1) It conforms, namely, to the evangelical message; (2) it preserves the Creed of Nicaea intact (it rejects every ungodly interpretation of this Creed and seeks to explore carefully the meaning of its words and to make this clear); (3) it preserves also the decisions of the Council of Constantinople. (Basil names as the principal point on this Council the doctrine of the Holy Spirit and the one nature in the Trinity; he says nothing, however, about the condemnation of Apollinarianism.) (4) Furthermore, he names the main concern for Chalcedon: the extermination of the ungodly and intolerable fancies of the Manichaeans (Eutychians) which are disguised under the appearance of devotion. (5) The explanation of the method of Chalcedon is important. Basil admits that the Council needed 'many reasons and many words to be produced' (*multis enim rationibus eguit illa synodus multisque verbis*). In doing this, however, it had no intention of putting innovations in the place of already clear definitions. Rather through a full 'interpretation' every assault of the 'robbers of truth' on the Creed of Nicaea would be thwarted.[66] The expression '*interpretatio latior*' is significant from the point of view of the history of theology, precisely because the main reproach of the Alexandrians against Chalcedon was that it coined a new formula of faith in violation of the agreement of Ephesus (431). According to Basil, it is in fact not a matter of a new formula of confession, but only of hermeneutical instructions for the interpretation of Nicaea, for which two documents will be of service. One is the *Obloquuntur* letter of Cyril against Nestorius (Second Letter against Nestorius), and the other is Leo's Tome to Flavian. As a third letter the members of the Synod of Chalcedon 'added that letter which, as is well known, was written to the Fathers of the Eastern Church'.[67] Here is meant the *Laetentur* letter of Cyril, containing the so-called Formulary of Reunion which became the model for the christological statement of Chalcedon. But

---

[64] On Basil's christology see below.

[65] Cf. CE 27: ACO II 5, p. 47, 24: *Calchedonensis concilii intentio est valde firmissima*. On the following see especially ibid., p. 47, 24–48, 31.

[66] Ibid., p. 47, 36–37: ... *sed ut interpretatione latiori conamen contra symbolum meditatum latronibus veritatis auferret*. The word '*latrones*' is possibly an allusion to the use of '*latrocinium*' for Ephesus II. The bishops of *Nova Epirus* contrast the brevity of the Creed of Nicaea with the wordiness of the Fathers of Chalcedon (CE 47: ACO II 5, p. 96, 11–14): 'Even if the exposition of faith which was proclaimed (*celebrata*) at Chalcedon runs to many discourses (*plurimis sermonibus extendatur*), nevertheless it is concerned with those which it has demonstrably recalled in what precedes and it is, as it were, the interpretation of those few syllables'.

[67] Cf. CE 27: ACO II 5, p. 48, 25–31. The text of l. 25–26 is confused. See the proposal of Schwartz in the apparatus ad loc. We shall return to the significance of this letter for understanding Basil's position.

the *Obloquuntur* letter receives the strongest stress, certainly because it played a rôle both in 431 and in 451, and hence bound the Council of Ephesus to Chalcedon. Consequently, the Council of Chalcedon cannot be in contradiction to the earlier Council! With the stance adopted here at least the supporters of Timothy with their letter to the Emperor (CE 9) are disclaimed, for they see an irreconcilable opposition between the two Councils. One and the same letter was at the earlier Council the main argument against Nestorius, and at the Council of Chalcedon destroyed the folly of Eutyches. Thus Cyril was the splendour of the Council of Ephesus and the *praeceptor* of the Council of Chalcedon. Cyril agrees, however, with Leo in his Tome against Eutyches.[68]

But in spite of the significance of these documents, the Creed of Nicaea retains its precedence. The letters of Cyril and Leo are to be ranked below this Creed.[69] With them one wanted only to strike home at the pretended Nicene faith of the Eutychians and their concealed Manichaeism. 'More vigilance is necessary with regard to them than with regard to the ungodly cunning of Nestorius'.[70] To be sure the Eutychians confess rightly (in contrast to the 'two sons doctrine' of Nestorius which was inimical to Nicaea) the one and the same Christ,

> but they annul again the characteristics of the two natures which have been united, and they profess neither the passibility of the flesh of the Lord nor the impassibility of the godhead'.[71]

It is only in this passage that Basil goes briefly into the diphysite formula of Chalcedon without making the attempt to build a bridge of understanding for its opponents, although of all the bishops of that time he was perhaps the one best in a position to do so. The Chalcedonian formula of faith is itself in no way positively rated, nor even mentioned. The reading out of the various letters of Cyril

---

[68] Ibid., p. 48, 34–49, 2: 'For the text (*litterae*) of the same letter written by Cyril to the ungodly Nestorius was honoured (*florentes*) at both Councils; at Ephesus it censured the blasphemous Nestorius and at Chalcedon it destroyed the madness [*vesania*, no doubt in Greek *mania*] of Eutyches; and on account of the same words in the *former* Council [Ephesus] Cyril was crowned with the praise of all as the wise father of the Alexandrians, and again at the *latter* Council [Chalcedon] after his death he was proclaimed, so to say, as *praeceptor pietatis*. [The bishops who] gathered at Chalcedon brought forward publicly, apart from the letters (*ex epistulis*) of the most blessed Cyril, nothing else except those words Leo, beloved of God and father of the Church of Rome, addressed to Flavian of holy memory against the madness of Eutyches, in which he is discerned to agree with the statements of the most blessed Cyril'. On this matter cf. P. Galtier, 'Saint Cyrille d'Alexandrie et saint Léon le Grand à Chalcédoine', *Chalkedon*. I, 345–387.
[69] Ibid., p. 49, 2–4: 'And the Synod [of Chalcedon] tendered these [letters] not as if it wanted to contend that they were more valid than the creed of the Fathers gathered at Nicaea ...'.
[70] Ibid., p. 49, 7–8. We have seen that Leo the Great judged Manichaeism in the same way (l. 6–8).
[71] Ibid., p. 49, 10–12.

and Leo is for him of greater significance than the newly created formula of faith itself. These letters are understood by Basil, moreover, only as a testimony for Nicaea and as texts for its interpretation. Hence the whole 'doctrinal work specific to' Chalcedon is its capacity to witness to Nicaea, which has been documented in this way.[72] Solely on account of this connexion with Nicaea, therefore, must Chalcedon be upheld. The same is also true of Ephesus.[73]

Bishop Epiphanius of Perge in Pamphylia, together with the other bishops of this *regio* (CE 31), advocates the relativity of Chalcedon in unquestionably the most powerful manner. No doubt they did not wish to deny to the Council the proper respect.[74] But all the same they wanted to register a certain reserve with regard to Chalcedon. For obviously its effect is a 'division' or 'splitting' of the simple people, which admittedly stems from ignorance. Already in his first letter which is lost, the Bishop had emphasised

that no other doctrine has been transmitted by us to those approaching salvific baptism than that which has been expounded with the grace of the Spirit by the holy Council of Nicaea . . .'[75]

On the basis of this baptismal faith which is sufficient for everybody, this reverence for Nicaea is determined. Indeed, he also accepts Chalcedon, but only as a shield against the heretics, not, however, as an object of instruction (*mathema*) for belief (of the candidates for baptism). The writing of Leo and of the holy Council of Chalcedon was not addressed to the people, who would have been scandalized at it, but only to the bishops so that they could withstand the opposition (or contrary doctrines).

The unity of two natures or substances in the one Christ we find expounded by very many of the holy and famous Fathers who lived with us; but in no way at all do we hand this on as an object of instruction (*mathema*) or as Creed to those who are baptised, but reserve it for the battle against the enemy.[76]

---

[72] Ibid., p. 49, 18–21: 'For the Fathers who celebrated the holy Council of Chalcedon, after the most subtle exposition of these letters, once again took the Creed of the Fathers of Nicaea as the foundation stone (*lapidem*); they decreed that it alone was to be disseminated and preached for the enlightenment of the faithful'. Thus the bishop does not have a clear recollection of the *prooemium* of the definition of 451, just as he does not pay attention to the sanction which is added at the conclusion. Cf. DS 300 and 303.

[73] Ibid., p. 49, 22–24: 'Whoever praises the Council of Chalcedon greatly admires both the Council of Ephesus and the Council of Nicaea; but whoever rejects this Council does not give assent to the laws of those [Synods] either, but merely gives the impression of practising piety'.

[74] CE 31: ACO II 5, p. 58, 29–32. (After Epiphanius explains that he has already written his opinion about right faith and the Council of 451, still at the appeal of the Emperor he has the intention of doing this once again with his suffragans): 'Once again we indicate to Your Majesty that with the grace of God we in no way withdraw from its pious decision (*ab eius pietate*), even if we judge that the division of the simple people is an injury which in some way they suffer out of ignorance'.

[75] Ibid., p. 58, 33–34: *nulla alia doctrina tradita est a nobis accedentibus ad salutare sanctumque baptisma nisi quae a sancto Nicaeno concilio gratia spiritali prolata est . . .*

[76] Ibid., p. 59, 7–10.

Unfortunately the text which follows this exhibits some *lacunae*.[77] Apparently Epiphanius wants Emperor Leo to obtain from Pope Leo a declaration that his letter to Flavian is not a creed or an object for baptismal instruction, just as what the Council itself formulated was not either. These documents serve only to ward off heresies. They have no positive significance. In various respects Chalcedon is here made relative. (1) Nicaea and the confession of faith which is contained in its Creed enter into the full Christian life and lay hold of it totally[78]; a defensive council, such as that of Chalcedon, cannot have the same significance. (Was not Nicaea also the warding off of a heresy?) (2) Nicaea concerns all the faithful. Chalcedon, and in particular Leo's letter, affects only the bishops. (3) The simple faithful can take offence at Chalcedon and its teaching. (4) *Symbolum* or *mathema fidei* for baptismal instruction and the liturgy is alone the *fides Nicaena*.[79] The fruit of Chalcedon does not deserve these titles of honour, nor does it even raise this claim, as is also noted in the *acta* of the Council.[80] (5) The two-nature formula of the Council is played down in its significance: it *can* be accepted, as the explanation of many holy and famous Fathers from the vicinity of the authors of CE 31 shows. But what is said of the Council as a whole is especially true of it: it does not have the significance of (an article of) the Creed. The 'in two natures' is advanced by one of the members of the Synod

---

[77] See E. Schwartz's supplements to the text, ACO II 5, p. 59.

[78] Apart from CE 31: ACO II 5, p. 58, 34–59, 1, the same argumentation is used in CE 9 (the letter of Timothy's party): ACO II 5, p. 22, 6–7; CE 39: ACO II 5, p. 77, 37–78, 2 and finally CE 41: ACO II 5, p. 85, 5.

[79] The bishops of *prima Armenia* in CE 36 also make reference to the literary genre, ACO II 5, p. 70, 15–22: 'Therefore we point out that the definition by the holy Council of Chalcedon was not brought forward as a symbol of faith, but was offered as a definition to destroy the Nestorian madness and to exclude those who are known to deny the salvation that comes from the incarnation of our Lord Jesus Christ, so that all those who suffer on account of this scandal may know that after the orthodox Creed of the 318 holy Fathers we accept neither increment in nor diminution of what has been defined so perfectly by the Holy Spirit and we know no other faith, because this is not the case and we do not wish to hear it, although some say it is the case'. Here Chalcedon has no *positive* doctrinal significance, but only a *negative* one. It is 'horos' = 'definitio' = 'determining', as these words signify. Cf. Lampe, *A Patristic Greek Lexicon*, 975, and in addition 973 ὅρισμα, ὁρισμός. T. Schnitzler, *Im Kampfe um Chalcedon*, 87, is of the opinion that in contrast to these bishops of the East the Synod of Arles (451) 'considers even the writings of St. Leo the Great with the phrase "ut symbolum fidei"'. The synod in question was certainly a Gallic synod of 451, but where it was held is unknown; moreover, the text which Schnitzler has in mind says something else. Cf. C. Munier, *Concilia Galliae A. 314–A.506*= CCL 148 (Turnholti 1963) 107 ff.: Epistola Synodica Episcoporum Galliae ad Leonem papam post Concilium incerto in loco adunatum: 451, 107, 20–31: 'Whoever adds to the writing tablets of the heart the writings of Your Apostolic Dignity [only the Tome to Flavian is meant] as someone who does not neglect the mysteries of redemption does with the symbol of faith and has firmly committed it to memory, so that he is all the more prepared to refute the errors of heretics . . .'. Thus one does not have to conclude from this that the First Tome itself or even the other writings of Leo are designated as 'symbolum'. This Tome certainly deserves the same high esteem as the baptismal Creed does, but it is not designated as such or even employed in this way.

[80] Cf. ACO II 1, 2, pp. 126–130. In contrast to the two *symbola* of 325 and 381 which were read out, the Synod refers to its work as a *horos*, which, however, is intended to make a statement of faith (*circa fidem*). And this *horos* is the faith of the Fathers (ibid., p. 130, nr. 35, 12–13).

only on account of those who deny the incarnation, but the expression was unclear even to many of the Fathers. Hence this formula should also be explained more clearly, admittedly in such a way that no wrong is done to the authority of the Synod.[81] For Chalcedon should remain as it is. Thus these bishops felt that the Synod of 451 was *a new type* of Council which, however, they wanted to recognise only in a limited way. A definition outside of a (baptismal) creed gave them difficulties. Nevertheless Chalcedon has its function in restoring the unity which had been destroyed: the acts of violence against the bishops cease (an allusion to Alexandria), heretics are reduced to silence and everything is guided towards peace in the unity of Christ.[82]

The second group. Characteristic of this group of bishops is that they also consider Chalcedon as an instrument for endorsing Nicaea, but they give attention to this instrument as well and describe it in its special endowment. This means that they reflect upon the formal authority of Chalcedon and divine assistance which in principle the Fathers of 451 enjoy in the same way as the members of the Synod of 325. As the first example of the combination of a *relative* and an *absolute* assessment of Chalcedon, we present CE 30, the letter of the bishops gathered at Sardes.[83] For them what is at stake in the Council of Chalcedon is the 'chief article' or 'summit' of Christian faith. At this

holy and general Council in accordance with the canons (*regulariter*) presided both Leo, the holy and blessed Bishop of great Rome, through the illustrious bishops and clerics whom he despatched there as well as Anatolius, the holy and illustrious Archbishop of the royal city, together with the chief bishops (*summi sacerdotes*) who reached accord with him and passed the same resolutions, together also with many holy bishops of the whole world'.

Hence the bishops gathered at Sardes must also follow in their footsteps and show them respect,

because everything which is acknowledged as a resolution of this aforementioned holy and general Council was decided in devotion and with divine inspiration; we can concur with it, for, indeed, there is no discord between it and the holy and general Nicene Council of 318 Fathers.[84]

---

[81] CE 31: ACO II 5, p. 59, 17–20: '... at the same time also the in two natures [formula] which they used and which can perhaps be recognised as a cause of uncertainty for them [the simple faithful], although it was put forward by the Father [Pope Leo?] on account of those who deny the true incarnation of the God-Logos, should be indicated more openly in these discourses [i.e. the explanations which the Emperor should request of Leo] in such a way, however, that there be no harm done to the holy faith in any respect'.

Epiphanius then produces an important text on 'formulas' in general, having taken as his starting-point the Chalcedonian-Cyrillian dilemma (see below).

[82] Cf. ibid., p. 59, 24–28: 'May Your Power act fittingly, for the Synod will remain as it is ...'. Thus Epiphanius expects everything from a reassuring and clarifying declaration of Pope Leo on the Council of Chalcedon: peace and unity of the Church, the cessation of acts of violence against the bishops, and the silence of heretics.

[83] CE 30: ACO II 5, pp. 56–57.

[84] Ibid., p. 56, 23–34.

In both Church assemblies the Holy Spirit was active, and at the most recent assembly (Chalcedon) ratified what was laid down canonically at the first assembly.[85] Hence it tells against Timothy Aelurus 'that he was not afraid of condemning the Council of Chalcedon'.[86] According to these bishops, the Fourth Council in its function and structure could expound the faith just as well as Nicaea did. For Chalcedon too had the inspiration[87] of the Holy Spirit!

Perhaps Julian of Cius can be considered as the special spokesman of this second group.

I shall also make known to Your Power what I think about the holy Council of Chalcedon. This [Council], of course, in no way departs from the truth, because unanimously under divine inspiration it ratified the faith handed on by the 318 holy and blessed Fathers; it did not introduce any other doctrine, any other creed, any empty formula (non vanam expositionem; the Greek being no doubt κενολογία or κενολεξία) or duality in the only-begotten Son of God; it did not solemnly proclaim any innovation at all; it also agrees in everything with the Council of the 150 Fathers [Constantinople] and the Council of Ephesus, at which presided the thrice blessed and holy Fathers, Celestine, Bishop of the city of Rome, and Bishop Cyril of Alexandria. We beseech Your Power to preserve intact what was decided by Christ about himself through it [the Council]. Where, therefore, such a number of bishops was gathered, where there was the presence of the holy gospels and at the same time frequent prayer, there we believe the master builder of the whole creation was present with his invisible power".[88]

The validity of Chalcedon is hence gauged first of all against the previous conciliar tradition, above all against Nicaea. Positively, this means the ratification of three earlier councils; negatively, all deviations with regard to the First Council are excluded by its teaching. But to this relative point of view is added the absolute reason for the Council's efficacy—at Chalcedon Christ himself was active. He used the Council for the purpose of allowing himself to be spoken about. The Council was especially the place of the activity of the creative power of God, i.e. certainly of the 'Holy Creator-Spirit'. The holy gospels were also present there, i.e. in the work of the Council they were the supreme norm. Through urgent prayer contact

[85] Ibid., p. 56, 34–36: 'For God, who once through those [Fathers of Nicaea] explained the faith canonically (regulariter), has also confirmed it again now through these [Fathers of Chalcedon], because according to the Apostle one and the same Holy Spirit has worked everything (cf. 1 Cor 12, 11)'. The word 'regulariter' is in Greek κανονικῶς. Cf. ad voc. Lampe, A Patristic Greek Lexicon: 'canonically; 1. according to ecclesiastical canon or regulations'.

[86] Ibid., p. 57, 2–3: anathematizare.

[87] Besides CE 30 many other letters speak of this inspiration of Chalcedon: CE 25: ACO II 5, p. 43, 31: Calchedonense concilium divinitus inspiratum; CE 34: ACO II 5, p. 66, 25: Chalcedon ratified the faith of Nicaea divina inspiratione. The same (idem) Holy Spirit (as at Nicaea) was also active at the Council of Constantinople: CE 40: ACO II 5, p. 83, 40. Cf. H. J. Sieben, Die Konzilsidee der Alten Kirche, 258–263.

[88] CE 34: ACO II 5, p. 66, 22–33; here only 1. 30–34 are cited from the Latin text: supplicamus igitur vestrae potentiae ut inviolabiliter conservetis ea quae a Christo per ipsum de ipso bene sunt constituta. ubi enim tantorum erat congregata multitudo pontificum et sanctorum praesentia evangeliorum et frequens simul oratio, illic creaturae totius opificem invisibili virtute credimus fuisse praesentem.

with God and Christ was sought. Finally, the great number of bishops is also a reason for the special presence of the Spirit of God or a guarantee of the orthodoxy of the assembly. Hence there is proposed here a *theology of councils*. Julian reflects on the authority of Chalcedon and of 'councils' in general. The various grounds for this authority have already been named: the presence of Christ and of the gospels, the inspiration of the Holy Spirit, but also the unanimity of so many bishops which came about through the inspiration of the Holy Spirit.[89] Thus there is allusion to the idea of consensus. As a council, Chalcedon receives an autonomy of its own authority which is deduced from its intrinsic functioning as a council. This functioning is not, however, attributed to a 'device', but to the attentive, faithful striving for the illumination of the Spirit through prayer and the study of the gospels. It is not the meeting together of the bishops on its own which ensures success. Behind this emphasis on the faithful, religious endeavour of the Council of Chalcedon no doubt stands the contrasting picture of the violence which Timothy had applied.[90]

Other bishops too seek to establish their view of the validity of Chalcedon by reference to the criterion of the conciliar act itself. Thus the bishops of Pontus Polemoniacus with their metropolitan Euippus speak of the age, the wisdom and the intellectual giftedness of the Fathers of Chalcedon, and also of the inspiration of Nicaea and Constantinople.[91] All other councils are surpassed by Chalcedon on account of the size of the gathering.[92] The Archbishop of Sardes in Lydia, with the members of his synod, sees 'the bishops of the whole world' gathered at Chalcedon.[93] The whole *oikumene* was thus represented.

From all these statements we see that at least in one part of the letters of the *Codex encyclius* the conciliar singularity and autonomy of Chalcedon are reflected upon. There is no doubt that in this second group the relationship to Nicaea is also preserved, but it is not exaggerated or at all played off against the Council of Chalcedon. Why should even Nicaea as a council have an absolutely singular place in the line of the councils? Nowhere was a reason given for this,

---

[89] Ibid., p. 66, 24–25: *fidem traditam . . . consona voluntate divina inspiratione firmavit*, together with l. 31–32: . . . *tantorum . . . congregata multitudo pontificum*.

[90] Ibid., p. 66, 17–20.

[91] CE 40: ACO II 5, p. 83, 36–40: '. . . we say [about the Fathers of 451] that considering the number of those men, mighty in age and wisdom and admirable in all spiritual gifts, beyond all this also glorifying the faith of the devout number whom the Holy Spirit gathered in the city of Nicaea as well as the 150 whom the same Spirit drew together in the Imperial City . . .'.

[92] Thus CE 26 (from the archbishop of Emesa in the province of *Phoenice Libanensis*): ACO II 5, p. 45, 3–4: *de beatis patribus Calchedone collectis, qui superiora quidem concilia multitudine transcenderunt*. Similarly CE 28: ACO II 5, p. 50, 25: *multitudo pontificum*.

[93] CE 30: ACO II 5, p. 56, 29: . . . *sanctissimi totius orbis episcopi*, who all decided the same thing as Leo and Anatolius.

just as we found none either in the writings of Leo of Rome. On the contrary, the more the 'representation' of the whole Church is demanded, e.g. for the status of a council, the more Chalcedon may lay claim to a special position. As no other council had been able to do previously, it was able to speak in the name of the Church. Hence whoever rejected it, placed himself simply at variance with the whole Church. For this reason the wrong enacted by Timothy's party consisted precisely in its having stirred up 'war against the Church'. This is the case, because they waged 'war against such great Councils'.[94]

On the basis of this analysis we can already sketch a clearer picture of the reception of Chalcedon. With the exception of Timothy and of Amphilochius of Side who has been mentioned briefly, none of the witnesses examined rejects the Council; all accept it positively. Even so, the way in which it is accepted is quite different. The slightest degree of reception is present where Chalcedon is seen purely in its auxiliary position to Nicaea, and the Fourth Council is conceded neither its own statement in a doctrinal sense nor its own function or autonomy in the sense of a theology of the councils. The reception is more positive where Chalcedon is realised to be necessary for purging the Eutychian heresy, or as well for the 'explanation', 'interpretation' of Nicaea, or even for the 'revelation'[95] of its intention. For here it is at least conceded that even Nicaea had not achieved everything, for every council is summoned in a particular situation that is peculiar to it alone. Finally, where consideration is given to the intrinsic characteristic of the Fourth Council as the actio Ecclesiae in Christ and the Holy Spirit, the justification of Chalcedon on the level of a theology of the councils is intimated. Accordingly, the way is made clear for an appreciation of the Council for reasons which are no less proper to Chalcedon than to Nicaea. The Council

---

[94] CE 20 (from Basil, Archbishop of Antioch): ACO II 5, p. 34, 18–20: '. . . they have shown themselves to have waged war against the Church, presumptuously rejecting such great Councils, i.e. of the 150 Fathers and of those who gathered at Chalcedon'. The concrete historical circumstances of the Council of 381 are in the meantime forgotten. Cf. CE 35: ACO II 5, p. 68, 8–10: the supporters of Timothy are against the episcopate of the whole world (contrarii cultores . . . sanctorum episcoporum qui in toto orbe consistunt). In CE 45 (from the bishops of prima Galatia): ACO II 5, p. 91, 26–28, it is said that the breach with Chalcedon is not just simply a nominal renunciation of a council, but it is in reality a separation from the college of bishops of the whole world (rebus autem ipsis cuncto totius mundi collegio sacerdotum sine dubio segregantur). In CE 8 (from the Egyptian bishops): ACO II 5, p. 18, 39–19, 2, we read of certain monks excommunicating themselves by their refusal of Chalcedon: et semetipsos, sicut et ille [= Timothy], ex quo Calchedonense sanctum et universale concilium celebratum est, a communione generalis ecclesiae suspenderunt.

[95] Cf. CE 25 (from Dorotheus of Tyrus): ACO II 5, p. 43, 22–26: '. . . we declare that [the Council of Chalcedon] is in no respect or way in opposition to (discordat) the exposition of the holy Fathers gathered [at Nicaea]. Nor is it as though this [Council of 451] were held because the teaching of the predecessors who were at Nicaea had too little content, but so that through the Council of Chalcedon the intention of their exposition may be revealed (revelatur intentio)'. Thus Nicaea needs no supplement; at the most what is needed is a clarification of its statement.

of 325 had admittedly passed the crucial test of the Arian controversy for two generations, and thus had an aura all its own. If one leaves aside the Germanic peoples who had become Arian, that Council no longer had any opposition; this is particularly the case if one looks at the smaller area of the Byzantine empire. Through the conflict of the Nicene Fathers with fanatical opponents and their victory over them, the Nicene faith and Creed were appropriated in a manner which we cannot establish for any other document of faith. The break for the First Council consisted in the fact that it incorporated its statement of faith in a creed which was suitable for baptism and liturgy. It was not without reason that some groups of bishops expressed the sentiment that Chalcedon did not seize the same opportunity and did not secure for itself the same place in the kerygmatic, liturgical and sacramental life of the Church. One can in no way create a 'Sitz im Leben' subsequently. A document with its literary genre is born out of it. Once again, speaking in the sense of the critics of Chalcedon, its document of faith also has its 'Sitz im Leben', yet this place was patently not in the hearts of the believing people, but in the will of the Emperor and in the heads of bishops and theologians. Will the situation ever change for the Fourth Council? We are only at the beginning of our investigation into the reception of this Council.

The question of the reception of this Council in its decisive aspect has not yet come into view. What does the *Codex encyclius* divulge about the *christological* understanding of the bishops, thus about the reception of the content of the Council? For the question of the appropriation or non-appropriation of a council is not so much decided on the basis of the recognition of its formal authority, but rather from the acceptance of the content of its theological statement, in our case of the christology of the Fourth Council. But this again presupposes that first of all a level is attained from which the document of faith of Chalcedon ought to be interpreted. Only a few letters provide evidence that the appropriate presuppositions are present. On these grounds we also have a criterium for gauging how far Chalcedonian christology was actually 'understood'.

V. THE CLASSIFICATION OF METHOD AND THE UNDERSTANDING OF THE CONTENT OF THE CHRISTOLOGY OF CHALCEDON

The endeavour to attain the content of the statement of Chalcedon does not depend only on one's positive or negative attitude to the Council as a whole, but also on one's readiness to apply the *theological method* which in fact was employed—even if only some of the Fathers were aware of it. With an apposite phrase Bishop Euippus (CE 40) characterises the way in which one can approach such a statement of faith: in the manner either of a fisherman or of Aristotle.[96] In other words, one can consider Chalcedon simply from the kerygmatic viewpoint or one can approach it by reflecting upon it in a philosophically trained manner. Most of the letters of the *Codex encyclius* remain on the kerygmatic level in their assessment of the Council. Either they want to reduce the document of faith itself completely to this or they confess their own alienation from the text and classify it accordingly. Only a few bishops are capable of going beyond the kerygmatic assessment of the formula of faith and noticing as well the new step which Chalcedon takes with regard to *language* and the *history of theology*. This distinction will be made evident on the basis of the texts, for in these a portion of the history of faith and theology is revealed.

The consistent kerygmatic attitude of the bishops in the *Codex encyclius* is extremely commendable. It is not 'concepts' (*hypostasis, physis*) which play a rôle, but baptismal instruction and faith. They wanted to continue to model this instruction on the basis of the Nicene Creed. This intention is so strong that no opportunity was afforded to the Fourth Council ever to become the foundation for baptismal catechesis. Everything is measured by the baptismal faith of *Nicaea*.

We have and preserve the faith in which we were born and with which we—this is the prayer of us all—wish to come before the dreadful judgement seat of God; the faith in which we were also baptised and with which we who without merit were called to the office of bishop fill those who receive the grace to believe [= the candidates for baptism].[97]

This baptismal faith rests upon the evangelists and apostles, but it was established in Nicaea. There the bishops defined the apostolic religion perfectly and in the spirit of the apostles, and thus preserved the Church's treasury of faith. The other synods—Chalcedon included—had to be summoned to *ward off* the heresies which had newly arisen and they decreed that this (Nicene) faith was to be preserved intact.[98] The bishops of Paphlagonia emphasise their own fellowship with the 'faithful' on the basis of this evangelical, apostolic, Nicene faith[99], which, however, is preserved at the other councils.

[96] CE 40 ACO II 5, p. 84, 2–3: *haec* [the opinion on Chalcedon] *ergo breviter piscatorie et non Aristotelice suggessimus.*
[97] CE 45 (from the bishops of *prima Galatia*): ACO II 5, p. 90, 24–27.
[98] Cf. ibid., p. 90, 27–39. In order to differentiate the peculiarity of Chalcedon as a council from Nicaea, several letters place emphasis on its goal of countering heresy: CE 29: ACO II 5, p. 52, 35–54, 17 (certainly the longest remarks on this theme); CE 31: ACO II 5, p. 59, 16–21; CE 35: ACO II 5, p. 67, 8ff. and l. 15–21; CE 41: ACO II 5, p. 85, 12–18; CE 45: ACO II 5, p. 90, 34–91, 2 (this letter gives prominence to the necessity for Chalcedon to combat two contrary heresies: *quasi ex quadam diametro utramque redarguens veritatis adversitatem*).
[99] CE 42: ACO II 5, p. 86, 28–36.

Indeed, whoever does not accept these councils, in particular Chalcedon, destroys the very basis of faith which has been handed on. Because, however, the baptismal catechesis and liturgy are tied entirely
to the Creed (Nicene), the possibility that the formula of Chalcedon
be used in baptismal instruction itself is denied, as we have already
seen.[100] Only the bishops should occupy themselves with it—and
this above all in the battle against the heretics. Such a determined
attitude is interesting. It permeates more or less the whole of the
Codex encyclius. This means that the usual global judgement that with
Chalcedon the Church fell prey to Hellenistic formulas and an abstract
theology is not correct. The study of the *Codex encyclius* can provide
worthwhile assistance in creating a change of opinion here.

Though this kerygmatic, pastoral attitude of the bishops of the
Codex encyclius is so important, it still has its problems, which the
bishops themselves cannot escape. Not all of the bishops cope successfully with them. In their reflection on the validity of Chalcedon
and its 'new' definition of faith, the bishops fall into two groups:
one conservative, and the other open-minded. Or perhaps better,
two attitudes arise which in some bishops even struggle with each
other: an attitude which is set purely on preservation and one which
is open for what is new. The problem was this: Ephesus had resolved
that no new definition of faith should be drawn up.[101] A new definition
had come which had to prove its justification above all in the struggle
against the Alexandrians. All the bishops of the *Codex encyclius*
acknowledge this fact. There is only one exception that has been
recorded by the Church historians; we shall have occasion to speak
of this again. For all that, only a few of the bishops deal with the
peculiar novelty of this formula or are able to characterise it correctly.
But all of them feel more or less that there was a new formulation
of faith. How is this *novum* to be explained, considering the prohibition of Ephesus? Basil of Seleucia, about whom we have already
spoken, dodges the question by dealing only with the creeds and
letters read out at Chalcedon and by not examining the new formula.
Other bishops attempt to cope with this fact by giving prominence
to their 'conservative' function. Thus in several letters there is talk
of Chalcedon's formula of faith signifying no 'addition', but also
no 'diminution' of the faith of Nicaea.[102] Its function is that of con-

---

[100] Cf. above the comments of CE 31 and 36 and the texts cited in n. 75–79.

[101] Conc. Ephesinum, Can. VII: COD (³1973) 65: *Decrevit sancta synodus aliam fidem nulli licere proferre vel conscribere vel componere praeter definitam a sanctis patribus qui Nicaeam per Spiritum sanctum convenerunt . . .*

[102] Here are some references to a few texts of this kind with their main catch-phrases: CE 14: ACO II 5, p. 27, 4–9 (*nec augmentum quoddam vel detractionem fecerit*); CE 13 (above n. 58); CE 33: ACO II 5, p. 65, 9–16 (*nec aliquod augmentum aut detractionem in symbolo sancto fecisse cognovimus*).

firming anew Nicaea and the other previous councils. This is the sense in which all those bishops speak who attribute to it a function which is purely *relative*, i.e. relative to Nicaea, and who hardly acknowledge the autonomous act of the Council of 451. But would Nicaea itself have been possible, if the bishops at that time had not had the courage to make an *additio* to an older baptismal creed or to introduce a new language for the interpretation of the old kerygma? The *homoousios* of 325 was likewise felt to be an extra, as later the 'two natures' was. Emphasising that Chalcedon signifies no addition or diminution to the faith in Christ which had been handed on is principally concerned with the content of the confession, not its linguistic formulation. To look at the concepts and formulas suits very few of the bishops of the *Codex encyclius*.

Nevertheless, we find some considerations on the reciprocal relationship of the texts of the two Councils of 325 and 451. In the letters just cited, the word *interpretatio* has already emerged. Chalcedon is a new 'interpretation' of Nicaea, and, indeed, in the first place negative: it is not a misinterpretation.[103] Beyond that this interpreting has a positive content: Chalcedon is the *revelatio*, the laying open of the intention of the Nicene Council, as CE 25 says, but not without once again referring to the conservative function of Chalcedon.[104] The whole abundance of words at this Council had no other purpose than being a 'broader interpretation' of the Creed of Nicaea, as Basil of Seleucia has already told us.[105] From a contemporary viewpoint the word interpretation (ἑρμηνεία) indicates the problem clearly or even shows the way in which two councils and their formulations can be determined. Chalcedon intends—in the sense of the bishop just named—to guarantee a correct *understanding* of the Creed of Nicaea. For this reason an accomodation of the old creed from the fourth century to the situation of the fifth century is also needed. Basil does not deign to deal with the problem of the new linguistic style used for interpreting the incarnation or to deduce the contribution of Chalcedon from the newly composed formula of faith. Thus his remark about the '*interpretatio latior*' promises more than it contains.

The monk Baradatus tackles the problem of the development or of the advance in Christian proclamation and teaching in a more resolute manner. He is riled by the Alexandrians who say that 'the

---

[103] Cf. CE 14 (above n. 102).

[104] CE 25 (from the bishops of *Phoenice*): ACO II 5, p. 43, 24–26 (above in n. 95). In l. 31–33 they say that Chalcedon has brought no *augmentum*, no *correctio*, no *imminutio* and no *decisio* (mutilation) to the old decisions.

[105] See above n. 66. How he understands this 'interpretation' has already been indicated.

Council which was held at Nicaea is sufficient for them and they will in no way give their assent to Chalcedon'.[106] It is noticeable that this monk does not fear to use the word *adiectio* for the history of doctrine. He cites various examples for this. Thus the apostles (without Paul) gathered at Jerusalem and collaborated to write the book 'the acts of the apostles', 'an account of faith in our Lord Jesus Christ'. (We probably have here a particular 'version' of the legend of the origin of the Apostles' Creed which was not known in the East.) But afterwards at Antioch Paul ventured to rebuke Peter before the whole assembly on account of his behaviour among the Gentile Christians.

Peter and the other apostles did not contradict Paul, but they accepted the words of Paul with gratitude and remained in true faith, which through Paul had been supplemented for them.[107]

In this way the supporters of Timothy were also to accept the teaching of the holy Council and of Emperor Marcian and everything that had been defined at Chalcedon about the true faith. Just as there is a development from the Old and to the New Testament and both have their validity before God, in the same way Nicaea and Chalcedon are also related. Just as the sacrifice of Abraham and the sacrifice of Job, although both were very different, pleased God, so also did the legislation of the earlier and the later councils. Abraham and Job were not baptised and still found the favour of God. In spite of all differences we also belong to them; 'all of us are also sons of Abraham, called to one faith',[108] There is thus a legitimate development; there is unity in genuine diversity. The monk Baradatus ventured to break the grip of an absolute commitment to a formulation once passed down or to a single council. He takes the middle path between an affirmation of the Council bound up with the complete reduction of Chalcedon to Nicaea on the one hand, and the rejection of this Council as an illegitimate *novitas* on the other hand. In his letter Baradatus urges that one calmly admit that Chalcedon signifies a development. But it is not the loss of unity with Nicaea, and beyond that with the gospels and the prophets. This monk's presentation

---

[106] CE 21: ACO II 5, p. 37, 18–22. The supporters of Timothy had indeed written to the Emperor (CE 9: ACO II 5, p. 22, 1–2): 'Nor does the symbol of faith of the said holy Fathers need any explanation (*interpretatione*), since it is interpreted through itself and preaches clearly the mysteries of devotion'.

[107] Ibid., p. 37, 28–30.

[108] Ibid., p. 38, 8–12: 'And a short time ago (*dudum*) the holy and venerable archbishops presented in writing to Your Tranquillity the true faith and wrote about [Nicaea and] Chalcedon; for they are similar in the eyes of God, just as for God the old and the new covenant are similar; and as the sacrifice of Abraham in the early period (*prius*), and that of Job in the middle period (*medio*), and that of the saints in the most recent times (*novissime*) were [pleasing] in the eyes of God, in the same way God accepts the legislation of the earlier and of the later holy Councils'.

of christology is archaic and clumsy[109]; but on his side is a native theological understanding.

If in Baradatus Chalcedon is acknowledged as a stage in a development of Church doctrine, in the words of Bishop Sebastian it appears to be simply the final point of this development.

> Just as nothing is lacking to the sun in its proof that it is the sun, so also of everything good absolutely nothing is lacking to that great holy and general Council of Chalcedon; it does not need anything to be added, nor taken away, because it is seasoned as with heavenly salt by the Holy Spirit.[110]

For this reason the Emperor should make his own the judgement of such a legitimate and reliable Council.

> Let the Council of Chalcedon be sufficient for you, because taken by itself it contains all the old councils of the orthodox in the power of the Holy Spirit.[111]

These words are directed against efforts of the Alexandrians to summon a new council which was intended to eliminate Chalcedon. If they succeeded in this the whole previous history of the councils would be extinguished.

We have seen that with regard to method, at least in one part of the letters of the *Codex encyclius*, the way is opened for an assessment of Chalcedon which is both positive and concerns content. There is also 'development' and 'history' for Christian doctrine. At least in relation to the all-dominating Council of Nicaea, its proclamation is no longer fixed at one stage. Yet if we were to seek, for instance, a presentation of the state of christological teaching in these open-hearted letters, we would be quickly disappointed. If we learn anything about this state at all, it is mostly from letters which adopt a critical stance towards Chalcedon.

Particularly in the regions far removed from Byzantium, knowledge of the new definition of faith of 451 was extremely slight. The Mesopotamian bishops know only that the Council dismissed the various heretics in the history of the Church and confirmed the proclamation of the 'trinitarian (sic!) faith' in accord with the Scriptures and the tradition of the Fathers.[112] Bishop Alypius of Caesarea in Cappadocia, one of the successors of the great Basil, feels himself entirely foresaken. He does not know what happened at Chalcedon, because he was not present at the Synod. In order to give an answer to the Emperor, he calls together his two bishops. One of them is sick and cannot come, but he does send an explanation in writing.

---

[109] Cf. esp. ibid., p. 36, 1–37, 18.

[110] CE 17: ACO II 5, p. 30, 21–25. In the apparatus Schwartz indicates that Facundus later takes over this passage (l. 21–29) in another translation.

[111] Ibid., p. 31, 8–9.

[112] Cf. CE 24: ACO II 5, p. 42, 14–19.

As Thalassius, the bishop at the time of the Council, brought nothing of the *acta* of Chalcedon with him, Alypius could read nothing other than the 'definition'. He looked into it thoroughly, read it repeatedly, accepted it and, as he believed, understood and recognised its orthodoxy. Because of this he can bring no charge against the Council.[113] Out of the whole *Codex encyclius*, it is really only in four of five letters that anything of the definition or the christology of Chalcedon can be discovered. Basil, the metropolitan of Antioch, together with the bishops of *prima Syria*, cites the text in quite some detail, no doubt in recollection of the Antiochene participation in the Formulary of Reunion of 433 and the definition of Chalcedon which endorsed this.[114] But even here we hear only a little of the two-nature formula so welcome to the Antiochenes. They give a paraphrase of the definition in which important expressions appear, as e.g. *'unus idemque'*, the twofold *'consubstantialis'* (consubstantial). It is interesting how they introduce the word *'natura'* without citing literally the *'in duabus naturis'*. In the same way they remain silent about the 'one *hypostasis*' or the 'one *prosopon*', as they also leave unmentioned the 'perfect in divinity' and 'perfect in humanity', as well as the 'unseparated'. The Chalcedonian line is not abandoned for the benefit of a weaker Antiochene formulation. What the Council intended, viz. to express the unity and difference in Christ, is successfully achieved by them. But they make no attempt, for instance, to justify or interpret the two-nature formula against the one-nature formula. They give no thought to the task of building a bridge to the Alexandrians and their one-nature formula by an explanation of the offensive two-nature formula. The bond is to be rather the christology of the *Council of Nicaea*. For Basil first of all expounds the doctrine of the incarnation as it was presented at Nicaea and later at Constantinople in agreement with the Scriptures. The principal statements of these Councils con-

---

[113] CE 28: ACO II 5, p. 76, 5–24. Because this passage sheds a great deal of light on the situation after Chalcedon, we shall cite some sentences from it. 'About the Council of Chalcedon I say only this, because I did not know what happened (*gesta*) at Chalcedon, not having been at the Synod ... The things which were particularly examined and done (*gesta*) by the bishops gathered in the city of Chalcedon I have not read about (for nothing more of what is known to have happened there was brought back here by the bishop of the time, Thalassius of holy memory); I could only examine the definition set forth by that holy Council which was brought back by him; in rereading this with profit and accepting it sympathetically, in understanding it also, as I think, with the right frame of mind and examining it as it should be, I have found out with certainty that it does not disagree with right faith'.

[114] CE 20: ACO II 5, p. 33, 37–34, 7: '.., they [the Fathers of 451] taught that [Jesus Christ] is one and the same Son both as to his divine and human nature, the same from the Father as to his divinity, the same from his mother as to his humanity, as God impassible, as man passible, the same according to what was taken from us is consubstantial with us, the same according to his birth from the Father is consubstantial with his begetter; and what he was before the ages is manifest in his nature (*natura manifestantem*), and what he assumed into himself he has in truth preserved in these last days; by these expressions they did not indicate now this one and then that one, but they glorified becomingly the same Son, Lord and God, whatever is said about him'.

cern the unity and equality in being of the Son with the Father and the true incarnation. Chalcedon corroborates these propositions of Nicene faith. Against those who slander the divine nature of the Only-begotten by saying that it is passible[115], they reply by positing the contrary, and teach that the divine substance is unconvertable (i.e. cannot change from divinity into humanity) and unchangeable.[116] Against those who deny to the Only-begotten the first-fruits of our nature (i.e. do not allow him to be really man), they argue on the basis of the same Creed by explaining the text.

For what concerns becoming flesh and becoming man, it [the Creed] has pointed to nothing other than the assumption and the uniting of our nature [with the Only-begotten of the Father].[117]

It is a matter of the true uniting of divinity and humanity in the one Christ, without mingling. With this teaching the Alexandrians must also declare themselves to be in agreement.

The most interesting comment of the *Codex encyclius* from a christological viewpoint is the letter of Epiphanius and the bishops of Pamphylia. He alone deals expressly with the offensive point of Chalcedon, the two-nature formula.[118] Why was the perception expressed here not held up by the Emperor and his successors as a model of a conciliatory view of things, instead of being allowed to perish? In addition to what is already known to us of his attitude, Epiphanius declares:

The unity of the two natures or substances in the one Christ we find explained well in very many holy and illustrious Fathers who have lived with us ... (but because simple believers take offence at this two-nature formula, let Pope Leo explain that his letter to Flavian and also the definition of Chalcedon are not a creed, but rather a word of reproach to the heretics) and also the in two natures [formula] which they used and which can perhaps be recognised as a cause of uncertainty for them [the simple faithful], while it was put forward by the Father [Pope Leo] on account of those who deny the true incarnation of the God-Logos. This should be indicated more openly in these discourses, in such a way, however, that there be no harm done to the holy Synod in any respect. For it is completely the same whether one says 'unmingled unity of two natures' or in the same way emphasises 'out of two natures'. But even if one says 'one nature of the Logos', adding, however, 'which has become flesh', this signifies nothing different, but explains the same only in a more elegant fashion. For we find that holy Fathers in the empire of Your Devoutness have said repeatedly what it signifies.[119]

[115] Here one may think at first of the Arians; but it is probably more the Eutychians, as the 'successors' of the Apollinarians, who are intended; to them was ascribed the teaching of the metamorphosis of the godhead and its passibility.
[116] This calls to mind the 'without confusion' and 'without change' of the definition of 451.
[117] Cf. CE 20: ACO II 5, p. 33, 35–37.
[118] CE 31: ACO II 5, p. 59ff. (cf. n. 76 above). In what follows we shall gather together everything that is said about the 'two natures'. This text is already included in JdChr I² (1982), but not in CCT I².
[119] Ibid., p. 59, 7–24: we hear here of '*in duabus naturis*', of '*duarum naturarum unitas inconfusa*', of '*ex duabus naturis*', and of '*una verbi natura*' as '*incarnata*'.

The ecumenical significance of the text is obvious. It is the first of its kind, if we take no account of Basil of Seleucia, whose christology will also be mentioned briefly here. Epiphanius deals with the two-nature teaching of Chalcedon and acknowledges it as a legitimate interpretation of the tradition concerning the *oikonomia Christi*, admittedly with certain restrictions which are already known to us. According to him this formula has primarily an anti-heretical function: to refute Eutyches. The bishop emphasises, however, that the expressions 'unmingled unity of two natures' and 'from two natures' are identical in meaning. The famous dilemma of the imperial officials at the Council of Chalcedon, 'Leo or Dioscorus'[120], does not harass Epiphanius. For he regards both the 'from two natures' and the *mia physis* formula itself as orthodox. This is correct and can be shown from the development of doctrine both immediately before Chalcedon as well as in the long period after Chalcedon. All the same, the structure and terminology of the Chalcedonian definition are not broached. The significance of these consisted precisely in the fact that the concepts '*hypostasis*' (person, *prosopon*) and '*physis*' (nature, essence) were distinguished. One deliberately wanted to distinguish between the level on which the unity and the level on which the diversity in Christ are to be sought. In practice Epiphanius brackets the concept of the '*hypostasis*' (taken in its Chalcedonian meaning).[121] He harks back to pre-Chalcedonian terminology, even if he acknowledges the 'two-natures formula' and consequently distinguishes himself from the Alexandrians.

VI. THE CHALCEDONIAN DECISION AS *NOVUM*

1. *Basil of Seleucia*

In our first volume we have already investigated other examples of the equivalent use of Cyrillian and Chalcedonian language immediately before Chalcedon. This equivalent use, however, did not preclude what would be new in the Chalcedonian definition. We have in mind some texts of Basil of Seleucia which, in comparison with the letter of Epiphanius, would have been better for bridging the gap with the Alexandrians. Unfortunately Basil did not include his insights once again in his report to Emperor Leo.[122] First of all it

---

[120] Cf. CCT I², 543; JdChr I², 753. I. Ortiz de Urbina, 'Das Symbol von Chalkedon', *Chalkedon* I, 396–397.

[121] By translating the Latin text of Epiphanius (ACO II 5, p. 59, 7–8: *duarum namque naturarum sive substantiarum unitatem*) back into Greek, it is seen that the concepts *physis* and *hypostasis* = *substantia* are taken by him as synonymous.

[122] Essentially we follow the studies referred to above in n. 63, especially those of T. Šagi-Bunić. In addition see the analysis of the definition of Chalcedon in JdChr I², 755–759, where we follow the article of A. de Halleux referred to there.

can be established that Basil did not put forward the formula 'in two natures' just by chance; it could almost be regarded as his own personal discovery, admittedly only if one also takes note of the word γνωρίζεσθαι which passed into the definition of Chalcedon. He acquired this formula by following Cyril of Alexandria closely, a fact which is particularly important for present dialogue with the Oriental Orthodox Church. Precisely on account of this ecumenical significance—also in view of our later presentation of Monophysitism—the stages or logical steps in Basil's development we explain here once more.

(1) At the Home Synod of 12 November, 448, Basil put forward a *professio fidei* which followed closely the *Laetentur* letter of Cyril and contained as its most important sentence: 'We adore our Lord Jesus Christ known in two natures'.[123]

(2) Behind this sentence are the problems which arose from the Formulary of Reunion of the Antiochenes taken up by Cyril in the *Laetentur* letter. In the Formulary of Reunion there was talk of the 'perfect God and perfect man' and of 'the uniting of two natures'. Cyril made of this: 'perfect in the divinity, one and the same perfect also in the humanity'. Basil understood this sentence as if what was written were: 'one and the same existing in perfect divinity and in perfect humanity' and, although only one concrete subject is before us, also knowable in both of these natures.

(3) On the basis of these premises it seems that the process of Basil's thought was the following. The *'duo perfecta'* are 'divinity' and 'humanity'. According to a statement of Cyril's *Obloquuntur* letter, divinity and humanity are precisely those different natures which, without the abolition of their difference, have come together into unity. Furthermore, according to the statement of the *Laetentur*, 'the difference of the natures from which the unity is accomplished is not unknowable, but knowable'. On the basis of these two statements the conclusion follows: 'the one Christ or Lord is known in two natures'[124], and this for the reason that, according to Cyril, Christ is 'one and the same in perfect divinity and perfect humanity'.

(4) Finally also, Basil had taken over from the *Obloquuntur* letter the formulation that the Word assumed from Mary the human nature and had united this to himself καθ᾽ ὑπόστασιν.[125] This means that in Christ a unity *in being* of divinity and humanity is to be admitted,

---

[123] ACO II 1, 1, p. 117, 22: προσκυνοῦμεν τὸν ἕνα κύριον ἡμῶν ᾽Ιησοῦν Χριστὸν ἐν δύο φύσεσιν γνωριζόμενον.

[124] See JdChr I², 733.757; T. Šagi-Bunić, *'Deus perfectus et homo perfectus'* (above n. 63) 191–193. Cf. ACO I 1, 1, p. 27, 1–5; II 1, 1, p. 105, 17–20 (from Cyril's *obloquuntur* letter); ACO I 1, 4, p. 17, 18–19; ACO II 1, 1, p. 110, 6–7.

[125] ACO II, 1, 1, p. 117, 24.

and not just a *iuxtapositio*. But in order not to fall prey to the mistake of mingling the two natures, Basil stresses the 'knowability' of the fact that the one Lord is 'in two natures'. In other words, this much is certain: both true divinity as well as true humanity are discernible in the one Lord, without anything being able to be stated about the how of the ontic connexion. It is remarkable that the accent is constantly on the 'in two natures' and that Basil does not reflect on the conceptual distinction between *physis* and *hypostasis*. But for all this, it can be seen how, through a close following of Cyril, the formula of 'knowable in two natures' could be discovered. In our opinion this is of great significance ecumenically. There is something more to be added:

(5) One should not be upset if at Ephesus II (449), under pressure from Dioscorus, Basil accepted the *mia physis* formula and conceived it in such a way—completely in the sense of Cyril—that the 'in two natures' was not excluded.[126] He omitted, of course, the positive statement about the 'two natures'—and hence neglected an opportunity to bring his good interpretation of Cyril into play.

(6) Without compromising himself too much, at Chalcedon Basil could thus repeal his anathema of 449 and accept once again the knowability of the two natures in the one Christ.[127]

After all these changes and the memories associated with them it is not a cause for wonder if in his letter to Emperor Leo Basil no longer deals with these formulations. But we also see that—apart from this confession to 'in two natures'—the terminological step forward is not reflected upon. Here the nimble-minded bishop fails. He does not attempt to bridge the gap towards Alexandria. The battle of words which would continue for a long time begins, a fact which the bishops of *secunda Armenia* sense and criticise.[128]

---

[126] ACO II 1, 1, p. 179, nr. 850. Reproached because of his acknowledgement of the *two natures*, he made the confession: 'and I adore the one nature of the divinity of the Only-begotten, who became man and assumed flesh'. Even Flavian of Constantinople, in a *professio fidei* which he gave to Emperor Theodosius II, had acknowledged the *mia physis* formula as orthodox or as capable of being interpreted as such (ACO II 1, 1, pp. 35–36).

[127] ACO II 1, 1, p. 93, nr. 172. Here Basil says: 'Anathema to him who divides [Jesus Christ into two sons]; anathema to him who separates the two natures after the union; but anathema also to him who does not recognise the property of the natures'. At the intervention of Bishop Eusthathius of Berytos Basil added: 'We recognise (γνωρίζομεν) the two natures, we do not separate them. We say they are neither "separated" nor "mingled"' (ibid., p. 143, nr. 532).

[128] CE 37: ACO II 5, p. 74, 8–15: 'If indeed some attempt to stir up wars and strife against the Churches by plucking out syllables that belong together and arrangements of words, God has opposed them [the supporters of Timothy are meant here]; [the method of the undersigned is, however:] by examining the intention and frame of mind of those who expound the faith, however, we do not depart from the arrangements of words, but we also regard the holy Fathers gathered at Chalcedon as defenders of doctrines and perfect custodians of the faith of the 318 Fathers, and we honour them in the same way as the 318 Fathers themselves. For by adding nothing to the Creed of those [Fathers] they condemned the mouth which is guilty on many counts'. To seek out the 'intention of a statement' behind words and formulas is good hermeneutics, which Vatican II in *Dei Verbum* Ch. III, art. 12, could ˄lso recommend.

2. A homily of Diadochus of Photike

A final word of warning is still called for. It would miss the mark to equate the entire christological knowledge and speech of the episcopate in the period after 451 with what the *Codex encyclius* reveals. This was a response to a particular question, which enjoined neither the complete presentation of the faith in Christ of the episcopal Churches nor the display of their understanding of the formula of Chalcedon. That there could be more in the heads of individual bishops than what is revealed in the letters of the *Codex encyclius*, which were either composed by them or to which they added their signature, is a lesson already given to us by Basil of Seleucia. Another modest but pertinent example of background knowledge which is not incorporated in the *Codex encyclius* is the delightful homily of Diadochus of Photike which he delivered the feast of the ascension of Christ. Diadochus is a bishop who added his signature to CE 46, i.e. the letter of the bishops of *Epirus Vetus* with their metropolitan Eugenius of Nicopolis.[129] A comparison of the two documents shows that Diadochus no doubt played a considerable part in the composition of CE 46. In this letter a profession of Leo's letter to Flavian as well as of the Council of Chalcedon is unambiguous, without, however, any particular discussion of the point at issue between Chalcedon and Alexandria, i.e. the one-nature or two-natures formula. But this is just what Diadochus produces in his homily, and this in such a way that shows that the Chalcedonian terminology has already penetrated the minds of his hearers. Yet he still remains completely in the kerygmatic style which draws its proofs from the biblical language of the Old Testament, but makes full use of them for the doctrine of Chalcedon. His starting-point is Ps 68, 19 as this is cited in Eph 4, 8 (Ἀναβὰς εἰς ὕψος . . .; what is important for him is the key word 'he ascended', thus an autonomous action)(PG 65, 1144A). In contrast to this he places Ps 8, 2, and this in the reading of the LXX with the key phrase: 'your majesty was raised above the heavens (ἐπήρθη, thus passive). Added to this is Ps 57, 6 as well: 'Raise yourself above the heavens, O God . . .'. For Diadochus, there is in the distinction between the *activum divinum* and the *passivum humanum* reference to the divinity and the humanity of Christ, i.e. the two natures. Even this 'technical' language is introduced in a completely uncomplicated manner.

The prophets have thus proclaimed one and the same Lord and they have in no way mingled, as some are introducing, the form of his incarnation (τῆς δὲ σαρκώσεως αὐτοῦ τὸ σχῆμα; cf. Phil 2, 7b) in one nature. Rather they have brought

[129] Diadochus Phot. eppus, *sermo de ascensione D.N.I.Chr.*: PG 65, 1141–1148. His name appears under CE 46: ACO II 5, p. 95, 11, in the sixth place.

out wonderfully the characteristics which befit his divinity, while what belongs to the body they have expressed in human fashion to teach us clearly that the *one ascending* or the Lord *raised* above the heavens—the former exists with what he is from the Father, the latter came from the Virgin, remains man, being one in form and in hypostasis (εἰς ὢν ἐν εἴδει καὶ εἰς ἐν ὑποστάσει). For the unbodily, having given himself a visible form in the assumption of the flesh, in this form ascends visibly to the place whence invisibly he descended and assumed flesh ... Thus let no one suppose, brothers, that the tangible human nature which the holy Logos of God really appropriated for himself and is known by (ἐγνώρισται) is altered because of the rays of his divine and sublime essence, as far as the undivided truth of each of the two natures in him is concerned.[130]

We find here exactly the Chalcedonian conception and language about Jesus Christ: in the one concrete subject, the one *hypostasis*, in the one *eidos* both natures, the divine and human reality, are knowable. The one who ascends to heaven 'radiates' his divine glory, and this happens in the unchanged human nature—a picture of Christ which we have already discovered in Theodoret.[131] There has been no advance on Chalcedon in the application of the concept of *hypostasis*, even if there were some references to Cyril's language (οὐσιωδῶς κοινωνήσας: 1145D 8–9).

Chalcedon is thus accepted by the overwhelming majority of the bishops.[132] Yet for a good number of them, in their acceptance of it, the conviction gleams through that the Council, as far as content goes, was not necessary, as Nicaea had already said everything for them. A condemnation of Eutyches would have been sufficient, or even a re-confirmation of Nicaea, 'the greatest of all synods'. Even if the bishops themselves deal so little with the new terminology and its exegesis, Timothy as well ought not to have made such a fuss about it and staged a 'battle of words' about something where all were fundamentally one. This is the opinion of the bishops of

---

[130] PG 65, 1145BC (§§ V and VI).
[131] See JdChr I², 696 from Theodoret, *In Ez. 11,22.23*: PG 81, 901CD. Cf. PG 82, 401B. Whereas Theodoret speaks of the 'two natures in one *prosopon*', Diadochus puts in lieu of it 'one in the *hypostasis*' with the 'undivided truth of each of the two natures' (PG 65, 1145C, 2–3; D 11–12).
[132] See the recapitulatory judgement of Theophanes, *Chronogr.* A. M. 5952: De Boor I, 111,29–112,3: 'They [the bishops] ratify unanimously and with one voice that the Synod of Chalcedon is holy and they accept the *horos* proclaimed by it, but they unanimously condemn Timothy as a murderer and heretic'. In the CE itself the idea that the universal reception of Chalcedon is the pre-condition of its validity is best expressed by CE 45 (from Anastasius of Ancyra in *Galatia II*): ACO II 5, p. 91, 24–32: 'Consequently we preserve the teachings (*dogmata*) of the holy Fathers and acknowledge the holy Council of Chalcedon which namely preserved for the Churches the riches of the teachings of the Fathers. But those who cut themselves off from that Council do not know that, in denying the Council of Chalcedon in name at least, in reality without doubt they separate themselves from the whole college of bishops of the entire world. That [Council] was celebrated by all (*omnibus celebratum est*): not one of those who were gathered there inwardly disagreed, and even if a certain few because of some exigences remained in their provinces, they were drawn into its communion, because it is recognised that the old teachings of the Church are preserved'. Hence with respect to Chalcedon there exists a consensus in both a horizontal and vertical sense. It stands in the line of the whole Nicene tradition and it is accepted in the whole Church.

secunda Armenia, although they declare themselves in favour of the words of the Council (see above n. 128).

The idea of Emperor Leo I to call upon the bishops of the empire to give their opinion with regard to Chalcedon allows us a look at the state of reflection on the largest council of the early Church. The process of its reception has begun[133], but at the same time the crisis is ushered in which the Church had to endure for the sake of the expression of the one faith.

---

[133] Because the main theme in the CE is the 'reception' or 'non-reception' of a council, we find there rather an abundance of terms for reception or rejection. We shall give a brief survey of these. The numbers in brackets are page and line references to ACO II 5. 1. Terms for reception: *amplecti* (*iudicium concili* or *synodum*) CE 17 (30, 30); CE 28 (50, 24); *cognoscere et amplecti syn.* CE 27 (48, 32); cf. *conplecti*: CE 16 (29, 23). The constructions with *communicare* are interesting: *communicare generali concilio*: CE 7 (14, 36); CE 8 (20, 2); *c. synodis*: CE 9 (22, 17–18); CE 29 (52, 33; 54, 10); *communicatores sancti concili*: CE 7 (15, 7–8); CE 29 (52, 3); *ad communionem concili αδτραηι*: CE 45 (91, 31). *Concordare* CE 14 (26, 36); *concordem esse sancitis ab universali concilio*: CE 30 (56, 32). The expressions *firmare, confirmare* (the opposite: *infirmare*) are frequent: (*consensu suo definitiones*) *firmare*: CE 18 (31, 27); (*suscipere atque*) *firmare*: CE 39 (78, 8); CE 36 (70, 6.9.15); *confirmare*: CE 23 (40, 35); CE 36 (70, 10); CE 41 (86, 2); CE 42 (87, 34); CE 43 (88, 11); *confirmare-roborare*: CE 37 (75, 4). *Consentire*: CE 18 (31, 24 together with *credere*); CE 21 (37, 36); CE 39 (77, 36); CE 14 (26, 36–37 together with *concordare*). *Custodire*: CE 20 (34, 7.10); CE 29 (55, 3). *Roborare*: CE 36 (70, 15); CE 37 (73, 21; 75, 4). *Servare*: CE 29 (42, 15); CE 36 (70, 4); CE 39 (77, 37); as well *conservare*: CE 40 (84, 1). *Sequi fidem concili*: CE 29 (42, 13); CE 37 (75, 17); CE 45 (93, 9). *Subscribere*: CE 39 (77, 37). The most significant term, however, is *suscipere*: CE 9 (22, 21); CE 21 (37, 33; 38, 12: *deus suscipit legislationem ... concili*); CE 29 (54, 11); CE 31 (59, 3); CE 35 (68, 6); CE 36 (70, 21); CE 39 (78, 8 *suscipere-firmare*); CE 41 (85, 3); CE 45 (92, 37). *Tenere*: CE 16 (30, 2); CE 19 (32, 16: *tenere et possidere*); CE 29 (55, 2–3: *rectae fidei symbolum suscipere, fidem trecentorum XVIII sanctorum patrum immobiliter tenere et custodire*); moreover, *concilium optinere et servare*: CE 24 (42, 15). Furthermore, there are some circumlocutions: *laudare-mirari concilium*: CE 27 (49, 22–23); *adquiescere legibus* (*concili*): CE 27 (49, 24); *synodum salutarem esse decernere*: CE 28 (50, 24–25); *perdurare in fide* (Nicaea) together with *tenere, observare*: CE 16 (30, 2–3); *non denegare tantum concilium*: CE 40 (84, 2); significant is: *synodum popriam iudicare*: CE 36 (70, 6). On this expression cf. A. Grillmeier, 'Konzil und Rezeption', idem, *Mit ihm und in ihm* (1978²) (303–334) 317. 2. Terms for non-reception: this can be expressed through the negation of *recipere, suscipere* etc.; e.g. CE 29 (52, 35); CE 37 (75, 1). The special words for non-reception predominate, however: *abdicare concilium*: CE 20 (34, 18–20); *abicere*: CE 39 (78, 11); *abrenuntiare*: CE 8 (20, 4); *sese abscindere ex concilio*: CE 23 (40, 23); CE 45 (91, 27); *anathematizare concilium*: CE 30 (57, 2); *denegare synodum*: CE 27 (48, 34); CE 42 (86, 23–24); CE 42 (87, 4); as well simply *negare*: CE 32 (62, 28); *derogare synodo*: CE 37 (74, 39); *destruere ea, quae a concilio decreta sunt*: CE 26 (45, 7); *expellere*: CE 30 (57, 9); *sese extraneum facere a fide* (Nicaena), *a sancto concilio*: CE 37 (75, 3); CE 41 (85, 19); *ignorare* (*penitus*): CE 29 (52, 33); CE 35 (68, 8); *inferre contumelias concilio*: CE 30 (57, 9); *infirma iudicare* (*ea quae a concilio sancita sunt*): CE 26 (45, 7); *refutare synodum*: CE 35 (68, 15); *relinquere*: CE 26 (45, 5); *reprobare*: CE 39 (78, 10); *repugnare*: CE 39 (78, 9); CE 42 (86, 39); [*se*] *separare a concilio* (*non separare*): CE 23 (40, 39); CE 42 (86, 33); *se separare*: CE 45 (92, 36).

CHAPTER FOUR

SUBSTITUTE FOR A COUNCIL—AN 'ECUMENICAL' EXPERIMENT

THROUGH the tenacious struggle and the persistent propaganda of Timothy Aelurus and his supporters the division of the Byzantine imperial Church became more and more a manifest fact. Nevertheless Constantine's principle of an imperial Church remained in force—the welfare of imperial rule demanded religious unity. The only point contested was towards which party the search for this unity should be directed and what means were to be employed. The Byzantine Emperors seized the initiative. But while Emperor Leo I (457–474) in his stance with regard to Chalcedon took his bearings from the judgement of the bishops of the *oikumene* and the outcome of the discussion between the Church parties, two of his successors, the usurper Basiliscus (475–476) and Emperor Zeno (474–475. 476–491), deigned to intervene in the conflict between the supporters and opponents of the Fourth Council with their own decrees. In this way they hoped to create an overarching unity. This intention was especially pronounced in Emperor Anastasius I (491–518), the successor of Zeno. Unfortunately in the period between 475 and 518 theology retreated behind ecclesiastical politics. The real gain that it produced consisted in the 'ecumenical' insights which—*mutatis mutandis*—are valid even today.

I. THE ENCYCLICAL AND THE ANTENCYCLICAL OF BASILISCUS (475–476)

Before Emperor Leo I died in 474 he installed his grandson Leo as co-regent and thus as his successor. Leo II was the son of the Isaurian Zeno (originally, Tarasis Kodissa[1]), who was hated by the people, and Leo's daughter Ariadne. From 9 February, or as early as 29 January, 474, Zeno was at first a co-regent of Leo II, and then, after the latter's early death (November 474), the sole ruler.

---

[1] On this form of the name and its meaning see R. M. Harrison, 'The emperor's Zeno's real name', *ByzZ* 74 (1981) 27–28. In 466 there came to Constantinople an Isaurian leader (chieftain) whose name has been handed down as 'Tarasicodissa Rousoumbladiotes'. The additional word seems to be an ethnic descripton. In the proper name there is no doubt that of the father 'Kodisas', the genitive of which is 'Kodisa'. Since the name 'Tarasis' is evidenced in Isauria, it would be permissable to interpret the proper name as: 'Tarasis son of Kodisas'.

The Emperor's widow Verina, however, was not pleased by this. Zeno had to flee to Isauria to escape her intrigues (9 January, 475). Yet it was not her favourite, Patricius, the *magister officiorum*, who acceded to the throne, but her brother, Basiliscus, who had been defeated in the war against the Vandals in 468. The hour had sounded for a new drive against the Fourth Council. An anti-Chalcedonian delegation of Egyptian monks and clergy soon sought to effect the recall of Timothy Aelurus, who had been banished to Cherson. The attempt was successful. After sixteen years of exile the banished patriarch was jubilantly fetched by sailors who were at anchor just off Constantinople. The churches of the imperial city, however, remained closed to him. Only in the houses of supporters could he celebrate the eucharist.[2] Unbroken in his hostility to Chalcedon, Timothy proposed an imperial edict which was to eliminate the Fourth Council. Paul the Sophist, a member of the Alexandrian delegation, was to compose it. One should note that by acting in this way Timothy integrated himself into the system of the imperial Church, admittedly only on the condition that Chalcedon be rescinded. Timothy's initiative resulted in the 'Encyclical' of Emperor Basiliscus,[3] to which was attached a constitution of Theodosius II against

[2] Simplicius ppa, *ep. ad Zenon. aug.*; JW nr. 573: CA nr. 56, p. 126, 1–4; id., *ep. ad Acacium ep. Const.*; JW nr. 572: CA nr. 58, p. 131, 9–10; id., *ep. ad presb. et archim. Const.*; JW nr. 574: CA nr. 59, p. 134, 26. By way of anecdote the failure of Timothy's procession to the churches is depicted in the epitome of the HE of Theodore Lector, §404: Hansen 113. Zacharias reports an initial readiness on the part of Acacius to accept Timothy (HE V 1: Hamilton-Brooks 104): 'And at first Acacius was preparing a lodging for him at the church called *Irene*; and he was setting apart some of his own clergy for his retinue and service. But afterwards, because he thought that they were forming a plan to make Theopompus bishop at the royal city instead of him, Acacius was distressed and indignant; and he endeavoured to put a stop to Timothy's coming. However, he did not succeed. For he returned, and was welcomed with great state by the Alexandrian sailors and the people who happened to be then in Constantinople. And he went to lodge in the king's palace. And large numbers were coming to him to be blessed, and to be sanctified, and to receive healing from him.'

[3] The Encyclical is preserved in two versions: 1. The shorter one is addressed to Timothy (Aelurus), Archbishop of Alexandria, and it is transmitted in Zacharias Rh., HE V 2: Brooks 1: CSCO 83 (T), 87 (V), 146–147; Hamilton-Brooks 105–107; Greek: Evagrius, HE III 4: Bidez-Parmentier 101–104; cf. P. Allen, *Evagrius Scholasticus* 122–124; Nicephorus Callistus, HE XVI 3; PG 147, 121–125; English translation in Coleman-Norton, *State & Church* 3, nr. 524, p. 915–920. The exemplar which Timothy had preserved in Constantinople is the basis of the shorter text in Evagrius. 2. The longer version is addressed: 'To the metropolitans and peoples of the whole *oikumene*'. It is transmitted in the collection which originated in Alexandria at the time of Peter Mongus: Cod. Vat. gr. 1431; cf. E. Schwartz, 'Codex Vaticanus gr. 1431', nr. 73, pp. 49–51; for the text ibid., 133–137. Here Schwartz held the opinion that the shorter version in Evagrius was an adaptation of the longer text undertaken by Acacius of Constantinople. According to him, Acacius expunged everything that was against the see of Constantinople (Canon 28 of Chalcedon) in the longer text. In PS 186, n. 4, he relinquishes this opinion and sees the original text in Evagrius. The consequence of this is that the other version presents an expansion of the shorter one through which are attacked not only Leo's Tome and the teaching of Chalcedon, but also the ecclesiastical order as this had been created to the advantage of the see of Constantinople by Canon 3 of the Council of Constantinople (381) and Canon 28 of the Council of Chalcedon—against Canon 6 of Nicaea (325). This longer text, which also defended the Council of Ephesus (449), was available for the first time to the bishops whom Timothy gathered around himself in Ephesus in 475. On the whole matter see Schwartz, PS 185–191. Besides these two works of Schwartz already mentioned see E. Stein, *Histoire*

Nestorius and his supporters.[4] We shall present the new document here in a translation of the Greek text of Evagrius.[5]

1. The text of the Encyclical of the usurper Basiliscus

Emperor Caesar Basiliscus, Pious, Victor, Triumpher, Greatest, Ever-August, Augustus, and Marcus, Noblest Caesar to Timothy, the most reverend and most God-beloved archbishop of the Alexandrians' megalopolis.

As many laws in behalf of the correct and apostolic faith as the most pious emperors before us—all who have persevered correctly in worshipping the Blessed, Ageless, and Life-giving Trinity—have ordained, these we wish to be invalid for no time at all, for reason of having been always in the past salutary for the whole world, but rather we promulgate them as our own personal laws.

` We, preferring before every effort concerned with human affairs piety and zeal in behalf of our God and Saviour Jesus Christ, who has created and glorified us, believing also that the unifying bond of Christ's flocks is the salvation of us and of every subject, both an unbroken foundation and an unshattered wall of our Empire, consequently incited reasonably by godly zeal of intention and bringing to our God and Saviour Jesus Christ the unity of the holy Church as the first-fruits of our reign, ordain that the basis and the security of human well-being, that is, the creed of the 318 holy fathers, who assembled long ago in Nicaea with the Holy Spirit, into which both we and all believers before us have been baptized, only should govern and should prevail over the orthodox people in all God's holiest churches as the only definition of the precisely fixed faith and sufficient for the destruction of every heresy entirely and for the utmost unity of God's holy churches—the acts in this royal city by the 150 holy fathers for the confirmation of the sacred symbol itself against those who blaspheme against the Holy Spirit and, besides, all the acts in the Ephesians' metropolis against the impious Nestorius and those who afterward were of that one's mind, of course, having their own validity.

But the things which have divided the unity and the good order of God's holy churches and all the world's peace, manifestly Leo's so-called *Tome* and all the things which in Chalcedon have been said and have been transacted for an innovation against the mentioned holy creed of the 318 holy fathers[6] [and of the whole ecclesiasti-

du Bas-Empire I, French edition published by J.-R. Palanque (Paris 1959) 361–364; R. Haacke, 'Die kaiserliche Politik in den Auseinandersetzungen um Chalkedon (451–553)', *Chalkedon* II (95–177) 112–116; A. Michel, 'Der Kampf um das politische oder petrinische Prinzip der Kirchenführung', *Chalkedon* II (491–652) 526–528; W. H. C. Frend, *The Rise of the Monophysite Movement* (Cambridge 1972) 169–174; J. Jarry, 'Hérésies et factions dans l'Empire Byzantin du IVᵉ au VIIᵉ siècle' = *RechPhilHist* XIV (Le Caire 1968) 241–253.

[4] Probably this is the Constitution which had already been published in 435 and had been read out at the Synod of Ephesus (449). It is preserved in: 1. The *acta* of the Council of Ephesus of 449 (Syriac), ed. J. Flemming with G. Hoffmann's German translation = *AbhGöttGW* Phil.-hist. Kl. NS 15, 1 (Göttingen 1917) 151; 2. Latin: Coll. Casin., ACO I 3, p. 181; 3. Greek: Coll. Vat. III, ACO I 1, 3 p. 68; 4. In a form which suffered interpolation by Justinian: ACO IV, 1 nr. 25, pp. 91–92; the comparison between this and the Ephesian version of the Constitution is drawn by R. Devreesse, *Essai sur Théodore de Mopsueste* = ST 141 (Città del Vaticano 1948) 235–6; 5. A shortened form in the Cod. Theod. XVI 5, 66 and Cod. Iust. I 5, 6. An English translation of the Greek version is given by Coleman-Norton, *State & Church* 2, nr. 402.

[5] Evagrius, *HE* III 4: Bidez-Parmentier 101–104; Zacharias Rh., *HE* V 2: Brooks 1: CSCO 87, 146–147: E. Schwartz, 'Codex Vaticanus gr. 1431', 49–51. On the individual titles of the Emperor see G. Rösch, ONOMA ΒΑΣΙΛΕΙΑΣ = Byzantina Vindobonensia X (Wien 1978), Greek and Latin index.

[6] The Egyptian opponents of Chalcedon had even declared in the *Codex encyclius* of Emperor Leo I: '*synodum uero centum quinquaginta nescimus*' (ACO II 5, p. 22, 18). With regard to this Schwartz

cal, i.e. canonical order and for the consolidation of the evil teaching of the ungodly Nestorius][7] in definition of the faith or in exposition of the creed or of interpretation or of instruction or of discourse, we ordain that they should be anathematised both here and everywhere in every church by the most holy bishops everywhere and that they should be committed to fire, wherever they may be found, because concerning all heretical dogmas Constantine and Theodosius the Younger (the emperors who were of pious and blessed lot before us) so have ordained; and that, since they thus have become invalid, they should be discarded from the one and only Catholic and Apostolic Orthodox Church as repealing the everlasting and saving definitions of the 318 holy fathers and those of the blessed fathers who in the Holy Spirit declared decrees at Ephesus; and that, in short, it should never be permitted to anyone be he priest or layman to devise for himself any deviation from that most sacred statute of the holy creed; and that with all the innovations made in Chalcedon against the sacred creed there should be anathematized also the heresy of those not confessing that the Only-Begotten Son of God in truth was made into flesh and assumed man's nature from the Holy Spirit and from Mary, the Holy and Ever-Virgin and Mother of God, but talking marvels—that he was either from heaven or according to fantasy and appearance; in short, every heresy, and whatever other thing at whatever time and in whatever manner and at whatever place of the whole world had been devised as an innovation in respect to thought and word toward the transgression of the sacred creed.

But since it is the property of royal providence from its predictive inspection to lavish upon its subjects security, not only for the present but also for the future time, we ordain that the most holy bishops everywhere should suscribe to this our sacred encyclical epistle, when shown to them, distinctly declaring that they

writes: 'The Alexandrian hierarchy had their reasons for not treasuring the memory of the imperial Synod of Constantinople... [the elimination of the cynic Maximus, the Alexandrian candidate for the see of the Imperial City, and his condemnation in Canon 4 of 381],... they would have had to have approved the third canon, which assigned to Constantinople as the New Rome the second position behind Old Rome. These embarrassing memories make it understandable that in Alexandria and the Egyptian ecclesiastical province C [= the Creed of Constantinople] did not have the validity which was lawfully due to it. Theophilus and Cyril did not venture to fight against it publicly... a public opposition against the creed ratified by the Emperor would only have caused harm, but nothing prevented them from ignoring it. If N [=the Creed of Nicaea] had the same value as it, they could employ it exclusively and were sure, nevertheless, that C was not played off against N; indeed, because they were legally on a par, N could not be confuted by C. Hence it is understandable that Cyril in his public activity cites only N in its pure form and that at the Synod of Ephesus (431), which was dominated by him, only N as norm was taken as the basis... Dioscorus continued Cyril's politics, only more forcibly and with less caution. Basing himself on the decisions of the first Synod of Ephesus, at the second he allowed the validity of N alone to be proclaimed in order to eliminate the Formulary of Reunion (433)'. Thus Schwartz, 'Das Nicaenum und das Constantinopolitanum auf der Synode von Chalkedon', *ZNW* 25 (1926 (38–88), 83–84. The Eutychians of Constantinople who had been subpoenaed by the Council of Chalcedon also wanted to acknowledge only N (ibid. 84). 'Timothy Aelurus himself and his successors did not participate in these politics of the moment. As the former refused to have communion with the Eutychians in Egypt and Constantinople... and Eutyches was from that moment on considered to be a heretic in the Egyptian anti-Chalcedonian Church, so on the other hand C was consistently acknowledged; apart from the combination of N and C in the cod. Brit. Mus. 12156, this is shown particularly by the Encyclical of Basiliscus and the Henoticon of Emperor Zeno. In contesting C one would have separated oneself definitively from the imperial Church, and Timothy and his successors wanted this on no account; rather they fostered the hope of attaching themselves once again to the imperial Church, if only the sole obstacle, the Council of Chalcedon, were taken away' (E. Schwartz, art. cit., 85). It seems, however, that with the acceptance of C Canon 3 of 381 was not thought about. Apparently the silence in Alexandria about the Council of 381 had allowed the canons to be forgotten. The situation was different in Antioch. Cf. below on Jacob of Sarug.

[7] Encyclical: Schwartz, 'Cod. Vat. gr. 1431' (n. 3 above) 50, 21–22 (a later addition).

submit to only the sacred creed of the 318 holy fathers, which the 150 fathers confirmed, as it seemed best by definition also to the most holy fathers who subsequently
convened in the Ephesians' metropolis that it is necessary to agree to only the holy
creed of the 318 holy fathers for a definition of faith, while they anathematize every
obstacle for the orthodox people produced in Chalcedon and entirely eject these
from the churches as being obstructive to the world's and our welfare.

(In the final paragraph the absolute prohibition against the propagation of the
innovation of Chalcedon by speech and writing is again expressed, and the sanctions
which Emperor Theodosius had already imposed against infractions are reiterated
as well.)[8]

2. The theological content of the Encyclical

The *theological* content is expressed more negatively than positively.
With the decided no to Chalcedon, the conciliar development and
the christological statement are whittled down to Nicaea or the baptismal faith of the 318 Fathers. For this faith, as the unique definition
of inerrant faith, is sufficient to refute every heresy and to unite the
Churches. What is significant is that the inspirers of Basiliscus also
recognise the Creed and Council of Constantinople, together naturally with the Council of Ephesus (431). The Alexandrians displayed
elsewhere no inclination to speak of the Council of 381. To give
prominence to this Synod was rather in the interests of the bishop
of Constantinople. The sharp reproach with regard to Chalcedon
and Leo's Tome was based on the fact that these were a novelty
vis-à-vis the Creed of 325 and the whole ecclesiastical and canonical
order, and were a ratification of the teaching of Nestorius, as the
longer version emphasises. Condemnation and burning of the decisions of Chalcedon were to be carried out everywhere.

The Encyclical does not forget to condemn with their docetism
the Eutychians who, as we already know, were preparing serious
troubles for the returning exile.[9] The imperial decree wishes to pin
down the bishops of the Empire for all time to the restoration of
anti-Chalcedonianism, and hence they are all ordered to subscribe.
An irrevocable swearing on the Creed [and canons] of Nicaea (thus
the longer version) would be demanded throughout the whole
Empire, and in addition to this a commitment to the faith of the
150 Fathers of Constantinople (381) and the First Council of Ephesus
(431). Furthermore, the stipulation of the First Council of Ephesus,
that no new creed going beyond that of Nicaea was to be formulated,
is called to mind.[10] Everything that happened at the Council of 451
was to be anathematised as a seduction of orthodox believers and

[8] Evagrius, *HE* III 4: Bidez-Parmentier 103, 27–104, 19; E. Schwartz, ibid., 51, 14–30.
[9] Evagrius, *HE* III 4: Bidez-Parmentier 103, 2–10. Schwartz, ibid., 51, 2–5.
[10] DOC 65 = Can. Eph. VII, which follows the reading out of the *Symbolum Nicaenum*.

as a danger to 'ecumenical' and imperial well-being.[11] With reference to Emperor Theodosius II and his attached constitution sanctions were finally imposed on those who contravened these directives. Thus from the point of view of theology as well as the history of councils everything is reduced to the state of 431 (449). It is to be noted that no commitment to the *mia physis* formula, for instance, occurs and also that no mention is made of the two-natures formula. Nevertheless the purely Alexandrian tradition was clearly intended. As far as its theological statement as such was concerned the Encyclical was tolerable, this resulting particularly from the fact that the christological teachings of the Eutychian monks were expressly rejected.[12] Yet in it there was a strong theological challenge; this, however, occurred in the way in which it understood the Church and councils. As an imperial declaration of war against a Council which was already generally accepted and which was in force as imperial law, the Encyclical necessarily aroused serious ecclesiastical confusion. Similar to the imperial Synod of Ephesus (449), it demonstrated as clear as lightning the dangerous nature of the principle of the imperial Church.

For with the Encyclical a further step was taken in Constantinian policy for the imperial Church. Once again we find reference to the Constantinian principles of the welfare of the Empire, this time, however, with the demand that a Council be annulled which had already found approval both from the side of the bishops as well as from that of several Emperors, with the exception of a minority at and after the Council. On the basis of the very same principles of the imperial Church there occurred, with the co-operation of the Emperor, a drive which had the aim of annulling history in accord with the mind of the minority. Timothy Aelurus himself and his helpers sought, with the cooperation of Basiliscus, to render effective for themselves the very same principles of the imperial Church which had been employed against them at and after the Council of Chalcedon. This must be taken into account when the question regarding the motives of the Alexandrian reaction against Chalcedon is posed. We do not discover any aversion to the system of the imperial Church as such or any Egyptian nationalism, even if Constantinople's striving for ecclesiastical precedence in the sense of Canon 28 of Chalcedon was felt by the Alexandrian side to be an attack on its own rights,

[11] Evagrius, *HE* III 4: Bidez-Parmentier 103, 11–26; Schwartz, 'Cod. Vat. gr. 1431', 51, 5–14, where in 1. 9 Canon 6 of Nicaea is called to mind—this is not found in Evagrius.

[12] Evagrius, *HE* III 4: Bidez-Parmentier 103, 2–6. The Eutychians of Constantinople then were also not satisfied with the Encyclical. Cf. Zacharias Rh., *HE* V 4: Hamilton-Brooks 109–112. For this reason they separated themselves from Timothy and his supporters; their intrigues with Zenonis, the wife of Basiliscus, led to the rapid departure of Timothy.

as the history of Canon 3 from 381 has already shown. What characterises the combined undertaking of Basiliscus and the Alexandrians
is the fact that they wanted to give absolute authority to their christological tradition, through the exclusion of all developments which
had occurred after 431, by putting the apparatus of the imperial
Church into operation.

The new initiative seemed to be blessed with amazingly quick success. Admittedly Timothy Aelurus had to leave Constantinople;
though the immediate reason for this was his being threatened by
the radical Eutychians, nevertheless it was also certainly caused by
Chalcedonian resistance to the Encyclical.[13] At Ephesus, however,
he successfully made a greater incursion into the Chalcedonian front
at a synod which had been summoned by him there. He proclaimed
the imperial document with certain additions which would restore
again to the metropolis of the province of Asia the rights which
it had lost to Constantinople. Through an interpolated reference to
the imperial Council of 449—this in conjunction with the prominence
given to the Council of 431 which was already in the original Encyclical—the old conciliar city received back its standing which allegedly
had been damaged by Chalcedon.[14] The names of the leaders at both
Councils—Cyril of Alexandria, Celestine I of Rome and Dioscorus—
which were likewise interpolated, were intended to show the bond
that the Churches of Asia had with those of Alexandria and Rome.
Constantinople with its new claim to the patriarchate was isolated.[15]
Thus it is understandable that 500 bishops subscribed the imperial
document.[16] The anti-Chalcedonian movement, with Paul of Ephesus
and the bishops who subscribed, had conquered such a wide area
that it could already credit itself with the majority of the sees in
the East. This happened within the framework of the imperial Church
system, even indeed with its help.

3. The miscarriage of the Encyclical

If the Encyclical of Basiliscus, nevertheless, quickly foundered,
even before West Rome could intervene, then this was the work
of Patriarch Acacius of Constantinople (472–489). He could depend

---

[13] Zacharias Rh., ibid.

[14] Cf. Schwartz, 'Cod. Vat. gr. 1431', 50 13-15.

[15] Ibid., 50, 15.

[16] Evagrius, HE III 5: Bidez-Parmentier 104, 29· 'about 500'; F. Nau, 'Documents pour servir
à l'histoire de l'Église Nestorienne', PO 13, 166, where a text from BM Add. 12.155, f. 108^{rv}
with an indication of the supporters of the Encyclical is given: '... with Timothy, Peter of Antioch,
Paul of Ephesus, Anastasius of Jerusalem and all the bishops of their regions who, as the report
has it, were 700, united in the true faith which was in the Encyclical'. The same names with the
same number are found in Zacharias Rh., HE V 2: Hamilton-Brooks 107; see further Michael the
Syrian, Chron. IX 5: Chabot II, 145-146.

upon a strong party among the monks, the clergy and the people. The military and political circumstances came to his aid. He himself had refused to subscribe the Encyclical. Vis-à-vis the Council of 451 itself, however, his heart was divided. As would soon become evident, he was ready to compromise on the doctrinal question. But to be able to maintain his claims to the patriarchate he did need the Council of 451. For it was against these claims that those additions were directed which the longer version of the Encyclical exhibits, namely the emphasis on the Canons of Nicaea (Canon 6 of Nicaea (325)) and various references to the long-established order which was threatened by Canon 28 of Chalcedon and by that Council in general.[17] If and when the longer version of the Encyclical was seen by the Patriarch of Constantinople cannot be decided. In itself the original form of the Encyclical was sufficient to reveal to him its danger for his claims. In any case Acacius could realise from the proceedings in Ephesus what was in store for him. It is likely that he already knew Basiliscus' intention of making Theopompus patriarch in his stead. Theopompus was a member of the Alexandrian delegation and brother of the Emperor's personal physician, Theoctistus.[18]

Hence Acacius had to act rapidly.[19] When Zeno advanced against the capital with his army in 476, the clergy, people and the monks there were greatly disturbed, a state of affairs which quickly developed into a revolt against the 'heretic Basiliscus'.[20] One can conclude from the *Epitome* of Theodore Lector[21] that because of this Acacius became frightened and sided with their fanaticism (ζήλῳ), 'after it had been rumoured previously that he was of the opposite persuasion'. He now preached from the ambo against the usurper in favour of Zeno. He ordered the throne and altar of his church be draped in black (according to the *Vita* of the stylite Daniel, this was to happen in all churches). Commissioned by him, a deputation of the most important archimandrites of the city had to go to this stylite at Anaplous on the Bosporus. Daniel had already enjoyed the confidence of

---

[17] Cf. E. Schwartz, 'Cod. Vat.gr. 1431', 50, 7.11.16. 19–20, 21–22, 31–32, 33; 51, 9.12; cf. Evagrius *HE* III 4.

[18] Cf. Zacharias Rh., *HE* V 1: Brooks I: CSCO 87, 145, 22–24; Hamilton-Brooks 103–5; on the whole matter see W. H. C. Frend, *The Rise of the Monophysite Movement* 169–174.

[19] On Acacius see the information with regard to sources and literature in V. Grumel, *Regestes* I 1 (Paris 1972²) 112–126, nr. 148–172. The whole picture of his attitude to Chalcedon can be presented only in connection with the Henoticon. A Jacobite synaxarium (3 Hatour) (PO 3, 246) and the *History of the Patriarchs* I 2 13 (PO I 446) mention for the time of Basiliscus one or more letters of Acacius to Peter Mongus, in which he supposedly confessed the one-nature formula against the two-nature formula. At this time, however, Acacius was still an opponent of Peter and a supporter of Chalcedon, at least in so far that a confession of the one-nature formula was out of the question.

[20] Zacharias Rh., *HE* V 5: Brooks I: CSCO 87, 151–152; Hamilton-Brooks 112–114. Cf. H. Bacht, 'Die Rolle des orientalischen Mönchtums in den kirchenpolitischen Auseinandersetzungen um Chalkedon (431–519)', *Chalkedon* II (193–314) 261–264.

[21] Theodore Lector, *Epitome*: Hansen 113, nr. 406 and 407.

Emperor Leo I and Patriarch Gennadius (458–471). In imitation of the self-humiliation of Christ in the incarnation the saint was to descend from his column and come to the aid of the bride of Christ, the Church.[22] Daniel descended and was received ceremoniously by the Patriarch in Constantinople.[23] The Emperor had to condescend to meet the saint in the presence of the Patriarch and before a concourse of the people. This provided Basiliscus with the opportunity to have read aloud before the multitude a *mandatum* in his defence. In this he professed his faith in the 'trinity in one nature' in which he was baptised and brought up; at the same time he confessed his inability, as a soldier, to judge in matters of faith. In this way the stylite saint, the people and the Patriarch were placated. 'Thus did our Master God bring the enemy of His Holy Church to His feet'.[24] The final act in the theological adventure was the Antencyclical, in which Basiliscus retracted the Encyclical.[25] In this was expressed the condemnation of Nestorius and Eutyches and all their supporters, which met the wishes of the friends and foes of Chalcedon alike. Furthermore, no new synod was to be summoned nor was any further investigation to be carried out. The plans of Timothy Aelurus for another council which were feared equally by Constantinople and Rome were thus rejected. The privileges of his see, which had not been exercised for very long, were guaranteed to Acacius; he understood these in the sense of Canon 3 of 381 and Canon 28 of 451, not that reference was made to these canons. The usurper explained that the *status quo* prior to the Encyclical was to be restored.[26] Significantly, there is no talk of the doctrine of Chalcedon.[27] What mattered to the Patriarch was the practical recognition of Canon 28.

The short anti-Chalcedonian interlude was not, however, to be underestimated in its effect. Insurrection had been put to the test.

---

[22] Theodore Lector, ibid., nr. 407; *Vita S. Danielis Stylitae*, c. 72, ed. H. Delehaye, *AnBoll* 32 (1913) 189; E. Dawes and N. H. Baynes, *Three Byzantine Saints* (Oxford 1977) 50–51.

[23] *Vita S. Danielis Stylitae*, cc. 72–73: H. Delehaye 189–190; Dawes and Baynes 50–52.

[24] Ibid., c. 84: Delehaye 199, 23–24; Dawes and Baynes 58–59.

[25] Evagrius, *HE* III 7: Bidez-Parmentier 107; Niceph. Call. *HE* XVI 7: PG 147, 129; E. Schwartz, 'Cod. Vat. gr.1431', nr. 74, 52.

[26] Evagrius, *HE* III 7: Bidez-Parmentier 107, 18–19: ἀλλὰ ταῦτα μένειν ἀρραγῆ καὶ ἀσάλευτα.

[27] A veiled attack on Chalcedon is certainly to be found in the sentence; the Emperor leaves it to the readers to examine: 'wherefore those who have composed this writing [= Acacius, Daniel the Stylite and the archimandrites of Constantinople] have relegated the Council of Nicaea to forgetfulness'. Cf. E. Schwartz, 'Cod. Vat. gr.1431', 135; somewhat more reserved in PS 188 f. In the judgment of Basiliscus Timothy apparently offered the better guarantee of maintaining Nicaea. The Council of Nicaea itself was characterised as 'what restrains the rule of the ungodly' (τὸ κατέχον—a modification of 2 Thess 2, 6.7); it was in danger of being taken away by Zeno, who was drawing near. According to Zacharias Rh., *HE* V 5: Brooks 1: CSCO 87, 152, 1–3; Hamilton-Brooks 113; Theodore Lector, *Epitome* nr. 412: Hansen 114, Basiliscus was moved to publish the Antencyclical by the news of the imminent approach of Zeno, i.e. 'the ungodly' (*anomos*). The *Vita* of Peter the Iberian, Raabe 77, also sees the Antencyclical and the return of Zeno as a new approach of 'ungodliness'.

The vision of the unity of the Empire on an anti-Chalcedonian basis seemed to be within attainable reach—at least for the greater part of the East, for Asia, Syria and Palestine, but particularly for Egypt. The West was only brought into play when this became necessary for the interests of Acacius. The utmost joy at the new situation prevailed in Palestine and Egypt. A new synod was to be summoned in Jerusalem.[28]

At the court of Byzantium, however, in no way were all dignitaries for the Encyclical and the Alexandrians.[29] There was strong resistance on the part of the clergy, monks and people. Yet what is striking is that at first the Roman Pope was not called in at all. For fifteen years West Rome no longer had any opportunity to intervene in the affairs of East Rome. In his predicament Acacius sought, through the mediation of monks, to establish links with Pope Simplicius (468–483), who was no Leo I. The Patriarch seems to have written himself.[30] The Pope immediately addressed letters to Basiliscus,[31] Acacius[32] and the presbyters and archimandrites of Constantinople.[33] The Emperor (Basiliscus or Zeno) was to order that what the predecessors of the Pope had sent in letters to Constantinople be sought out in his archives. The Pope writes that in these the mystery of the incarnation is completely and clearly presented.[34] It is interesting that Simplicius also draws attention to the *Codex encyclius* of Emperor Leo I, in which 'the bishops of the whole of the East had unanimously' expressed themselves.[35] This was not a useless reminder, for in this collection there was a very informative confirmation of the *consensus*

---

[28] *Petrus der Iberer*, Raabe 76: 'And it was [on account of the Encyclical] a feast of exultation and spiritual joy which raised the souls of those who feared God'. On the summoning of a new council in Jerusalem: according to the *Chronicle* of John of Nikiu, 88, 33 (translation Charles 112; Zotenberg (French) 478) Basiliscus himself had promised Timothy Aelurus to summon a council in Jerusalem, but did not keep this promise. Zacharias Rh., *HE* V 5: Brooks 1: CSCO 87, 151, 28–31: Acacius learnt that the Synod of Jerusalem was directed against him. Cf. Michael Syr., *Chron.*: Chabot II 146. From the last two authors it is not clear whether an imperial Synod was to be summoned. See L. Perrone, *La chiesa di Palestina e le controversie cristologiche* (Brescia 1980) 125.
[29] On the various forces and parties which were involved in the overthrow of Basiliscus see J. Jarry, 'Hérésies et factions' 250–264.
[30] Simplicius, *ep. ad presb. et archim.*, 10 Jan., 476; JW 574: CA nr. 59 §7, p. 135. He speaks of Acacius' silence on the question of Timothy Aelurus' return and of a new council. The Pope will not attribute this to him, however, for he is convinced that Acacius had not made what he was silent about his own opinion. Gelasius I, *ep. ad eppos Dardaniae*; JW 664: CA nr. 95 §47, p. 385, 20–22; it is attested that during the time of Basiliscus Acacius took the trouble to send a report to Rome (*ad apostolicam sedem referre curavit*). The first letters of Pope Simplicius to Acacius (JW 572 and 575: CA nr. 57–58) from January 476 say nothing of a report about Basiliscus. Yet he is acquainted with the fact that Acacius closed the churches of Constantinople to Timothy: CA nr. 57, p. 130, 7–10; nr. 58, ibid., 131, 9–10; cf. nr. 59, ibid., 134, 26.
[31] CA nr. 56, 10 Jan., 476; JW 573. On the address see Schwartz, PS 161, nr. 5–6; Guenther in CA p. 124 (apparatus).
[32] CA nr. 57; JW 575, perhaps from 31 Jan., 476; CA nr. 58, JW 572.
[33] CA nr. 59; JW 574.
[34] CA nr. 56 §9, p. 127.
[35] Ibid.

of the bishops after Chalcedon. Finally the Pope refers to Scripture and the Petrine tradition of the Roman see. For these reasons the rejection of Timothy and his supporters is for him a 'catholic matter'.[36] Hence all attempts to achieve a *retractacio* of the Fourth Council had to be repulsed. Rome had once again an occasion to advance its theory of a council. Weeds which the evangelical sickle, wielded by apostolic hand, has cut down can never again sprout up; even less can this occur when the cutting down happens with the assent of the universal Church (*ecclesiae universalis adsensu*).[37] Added to this is an appeal, made on the principle of the imperial Church, to ensure the welfare of the Empire by doing what is pleasing in the eyes of God.[38] In all the Pope's letters there is the exhortation not to permit a new council.[39]

Pope Simplicius is original neither in his christology nor in his theology of a council. His intention was directed at the preservation of the *status quo* which for him, however, did not include the precedence of Constantinople that was striven for in Canon 28 of Chalcedon.[40] His letters to the East contained severe demands vis-à-vis the anti-Chalcedonian bishops. Time and again their deposition and banishment were insisted upon.[41] In the course of Basiliscus' cam-

---

[36] Ibid. §§ of 11–12, pp. 128–9.

[37] Ibid. §10, p. 128, 11–12.

[38] Ibid. §12, p. 129. Cf. JW 575: CA nr. 57, p. 130: Acacius was to say to the Emperor that the sure and sole firmness of his rule was the inviolate observance of the Council of bishops who had gathered in the Holy Spirit for the sake of the faith (*causa fidei*).

[39] Cf. Simplicius, *ep. ad Acacium*, 10 Jan., 476; JW 572: CA nr. 58 §6, p. 132; whoever strives for a retractation (*retractatio*) of Chalcedon ought no longer count himself among the number of the faithful; JW 574: CA nr. 59 §2, p. 133: opposition to Chalcedon will be punished with banishment by the Emperor. Thus ecclesiastical excommunication (*ab ecclesiae corpore*) and banishment in the civil domain (*a coetu hominum exiliis corpore*) belong to the one *damnatio* (*unitae sententiae damnatio*). JW 576: CA nr. 60 §7, p. 138: Chalcedon and Leo's Tome cannot be retracted, nor can Timothy be once again accepted, for he is to be regarded 'as one who has been condemned by the one mouth of catholic truth everywhere' (cf. the *Codex encyclius* of Emperor Leo). Simplicius, *ep. ad Acacium*, Oct. 477; JW 577: Schwartz PS 122: Chalcedon is irrevocable, 'because that is upheld by the indissoluble observance through the whole world which was established by all of the bishops together (*universitas*) and so often corroborated by the confirmation of heavenly revenge, as has become clear'. There follows a reference to the divine judgment, as we shall encounter this repeatedly in all these documents (especially in regard to the Acacian schism). The same divine revenge was, however, also 'prophetically' threatened to Basiliscus by Timothy and his companions if he gave up his Encyclical: John of Nikiu, *Chronicle* 88, 30: Charles 112; Michael Syr., *Chron.* IX 5: Chabot II 147a.

[40] At the beginning of his pontificate Pope Simplicius had made Emperor Leo I aware that Canon 28 was not accepted by him (JW nr. 569). Pope Gelasius reports this in *ep. 26 ad eppos Dardaniae*; JW 664: CA nr. 95 §57, p. 389.

[41] Cf. Simplicius, *ep. ad Acacium*; JW 577: Schwartz, PS 121, 32–33, with 27–30: Acacius was to press with the Emperor that Timothy with his followers be taken to a place of exile without the chance of return (*ad inremeabile . . . exilium*); as well Paul of Ephesus, Peter the Fuller of Antioch and all those consecrated either by him or by those bishops consecrated by him were to be ousted from their sees. Simplicius repeated to Emperor Zeno his demand for banishment with regard to Peter Mongus. Cf, CA nr. 62 §4, p. 141 (and CA nr. 63 §4, p. 144): banishment, carried out by imperial power, appeared to be the only way of preserving the Churches from the infection of heresy and of maintaining the *sinceritas 'quam sola tenere potest imperialis auctoritas'*. The preservation of orthodoxy no longer appears as the effect of a self-cleansing process of the Church. Cf. also

paign various episcopal sees were occupied by supporters of the Enyc-lical: Timothy Aelurus returned to Alexandria, Peter the Fuller came to Antioch (for the first time in 471; then 475; 477, however, ousted by John Codonatus; for the third time 485–488). We shall speak of Jerusalem presently. It becomes more and more obvious that Acacius played a double game in Constantinople, something that Pope Felix III(II) (483–492) had to reproach him with.[42] At this juncture we come to a new document of the imperial Church behind which Aca-cius stood, just as much as Timothy Aelurus did behind the Encyclical.

II. The Henoticon of Emperor Zeno (482) and its Significance in the East

After an absence of twenty months Emperor Zeno, with the assis-tance of his countryman Illus, once again entered Constantinople in August 476.[43] Basiliscus and his wife were immediately removed, Armatus some time later. In letters to Patriarch Acacius of Constanti-nople (472–489) and Pope Simplicius, the Emperor praised both bishops for their assistance against the heresy. The Pope in Rome trusted the orthodoxy of Zeno[44] and believed that—in pursuing the attitude of his predecessor, Hilary (461–468)[45]—he would be able to restore Chalcedon to its rights. In three letters he emphasised,

---

CA nr. 64 §2, p. 145. Acacius is also commissioned—though in vain—to effect the banishment of Peter Mongus: CA nr. 65 §2, p. 146; cf. p. 148. It was, indeed, he himself who had proposed Peter Mongus as bishop of Alexandria (CA nr. 68 §3, p. 152). See too CA nr. 66, §§2 and 6 (from the year 479 or 482?); pp. 147 and 149.

[42] Felix, *ep. ad Acacium:* JW 599: *Coll. Veron.* 5: Schwartz, PS 6–7.

[43] On Emperor Zeno see W. Barth, *Kaiser Zenon* (Diss. Basel 1894); E. W. Brooks, 'The Emperor Zeno and the Isaurians', *EngHistRev* 30 (1893) 209–238; E. Stein, *Histoire du Bas-Empire* II 7–76 (with list of sources); R. Haacke, *Chalkedon* II, 117–124; C. Capizzi, *L'imperatore Anastasio I (491–518)* = OCA 184 (Roma 1969) 61–72, 93–95, 157–161; A. Lippold, Art. 'Zenon (2)': *Kl. Pauly* 5 (1979) 1498; L. Perrone, *La chiesa di Palestina* 132–134, 151–152. In spite of the hatred of the 'Romans' for the Isaurians, the supporters of Chalcedon preferred the Isaurian Zeno to the 'monophysite' Basiliscus (Brooks, op. cit., 216 f.). From 484, however, the *Henoticon* provided the opportunity for Verina, Leo's widow, with the assistance of the Isaurian Illus, to proclaim the general Leontius of Dalisandos as anti-emperor (Brooks, op. cit., 225–227). He was to be a 'Christian Emperor'. The ties of Illus to the pagan neo-Platonist Pamprepius contributed to the complication of relationships into which was also drawn the Antiochene Patriarch Calandion (479 [482]–484), who sought contact with John I Talaia, the Chalcedonian anti-patriarch of Alexandria. Cf. Zacharias Rh., *HE* V 9: Hamilton-Brooks 124–126. The whole plan failed, both politically and ecclesiastically. Leontius and Illus were seized and beheaded. The see of Antioch passed to Peter the Fuller (Cnapheus), who had already occupied it from 475 to 477. In Alexandria Peter Mongus (482–490) was successful. Emperor Zeno was thus driven into the arms of the opponents of Chalcedon. See the brief survey of the course of events in Joshua the Stylite, *Chronicle* §§XII–XVII: Wright pp. 9–12; John of Antioch, frg. 214: FHG IV (1851) pp. 620–621. According to Brooks, op. cit., 230, John of Antioch, with his report of heavenly signs and the sudden death of the executioners of Leontius and Illus, wanted to present these as martyrs for Chalcedon, for which there were no grounds.

[44] Gelasius I, *ep.* 26 *ad eppos Dardaniae;* JW 664: CA nr. 95 §48, p. 386; ibid., §64, p. 392, 1, where it is emphasised that the Emperor himself declared that he followed the advice of Acacius. Felix tells of Zeno's praise for Pope Simplicius; *ep. ad Zenon. aug.:* Schwartz, PS 65, 15–23; Simplicius, *ep. ad Zenon. aug.* from 6.4.477; JW 576: CA nr. 60 §5, p. 137.

[45] Cf. *Liber Pontificalis,* cited in Thiel I, 173 (IX).

at first in a negative way, that no new council should be allowed as the anti-Chalcedonian party was demanding. He said that on this point there was no *retractatio*.[46] He wanted to maintain the line of Leo I and for this reason reminded the Emperor that the latter had in his archives letters from his great predecessor. The Emperor and Patriarch Acacius were also referred to the testimony of the *Codex encyclius*.[47] The Pope wrote that in this it is testified that Chalcedon is the result of an 'assent of the universal Church' (*universalis ecclesiae adsensus*).[48] This declaration has its weight and should not be lost sight of for the following development. The Pope stated that the task of the Emperor was to destroy the enemies of the Empire and of the Church.[49] At the same time the Petrine office of the bishop of Rome was emphasised, and consciousness of his own responsibility for the Church was also demanded of Patriarch Acacius.[50] On the whole the letters of Pope Simplicius remain within the framework already given by Leo I, thus repeating the judgement passed on Alexandrian monophysitism which was gaining more and more ground.[51] Eutyches and Dioscorus were put on a par;[52] this assessment would remain effective for a long time, although at that stage all Eastern anti-Chalcedonians had already clearly dissociated themselves from the condemned archimandrite. The bond which since Constantine had been established between the welfare of imperial rule and strict unity in faith was also emphasised time and again by Simplicius and

---

[46] The three letters are from 10 Jan., 476: JW 572–574: 1. To the Emperor (Basiliscus or Zeno): CA nr. 56, pp. 124–129, esp. §10, p. 128; 2. To Acacius: CA nr. 58, pp. 130–133; 3. To the presbyters and archimandrites of Constantinople: CA nr. 59, pp. 133–135. In addition 4. *Ep. ad Zenon. imp.* from 6 April or 9 Oct. 477: JW 576; CA 60, pp. 135–138. Acacius had turned to Pope Simplicius for help when under Emperor Basiliscus Timothy Aelurus wanted Ephesus as patriarchal see in place of Constantinople. Cf. Evagrius, *HE* III 5: Bidez-Parmentier 104–105; expressed more clearly in Zacharias Rh., *HE* V 4: Hamilton-Brooks 110: 'To him [Bishop Paul] Timothy canonically restored the rights of his see, which the Council of Chalcedon had snatched from it, and had given by partiality to the throne of the royal city' (i.e. in the so-called Canon 28). See also, the Antencyclical of Basiliscus: Schwartz, 'Cod. Vatic. gr. 1431', nr. 74, p. 52, which speaks in favour of Constantinople. When Pope Simplicius demanded of Patriarch Acacius that he prevent a new council which the party of Timothy Aelurus wanted, Acacius did this gladly, but for the sake of Canon 28 not on account of the question of faith.
[47] Simplicius, *ep. ad Basiliscum (Zenon.) imp.* from 10 Jan., 476; JW 573: CA nr. 56, §9, p. 127; *ep. ad presb. et archim. Constant.*: JW 574: CA nr. 59, §4, p. 134.
[48] Simplicius *ad Zenon. imp.* from 6 April or 9 Oct. 477: JW 576: CA nr. 60, §6, p. 138; (*quod tot tantique pontifices et cum egregiis orthodoxisque principibus universalis ecclesiae decrevit adsensus*).
[49] Simplicius, *ep. ad Acacium*; JW 577: Schwartz, PS 121–122. The Pope insists that Timothy Aelurus '*cum sequacibus suis ad inremeabile dirigatur exilium*'. No doubt the Pope had no concrete idea how such a demand could be carried out.
[50] Simplicius, *ep. ad Acacium* from 15 July, 482; JW 586: CA nr. 68, pp. 151–154, §§1–2.
[51] Simplicius, *ep. ad Acacium* from 15 July, 482; JW 586: CA nr. 68, §5, p. 153: '. . . *unde haereticorum mentium crescit funesta dominatio et catholicorum succedit miseranda captivitas*'. On the Alexandrian 'heresy' see the earlier letters, CA nr. 56 (10 Jan., 476); ibid., nr. 57 (from 31 Jan., 476); ibid., nr. 58 (10 Jan., 476) (to Emperor Zeno and Patriarch Acacius).
[52] Simplicius, *ep. ad Zenon. imp.* from Oct., 478; JW 579; CA nr. 62, esp. §2, p. 140. Similarly Felix III (II), *ep. ad Zenon. aug.* from the year 490; JW 612: Schwartz, PS 83, 31 (*Coll. Berol.* nr. 34).

his successors.[53] To the style of the period and to the policy of the imperial Church belonged also the call made on the Emperor to send Peter Mongus into exile and to employ all the juridical means of the state in the fight against the heretics.[54]

At first it seemed that everything in the East was proceeding in accord with these ideas. On 17 December, 476, Emperor Zeno issued a constitution which restored to Constantinople and the other provinces the *status quo* as it had been before his flight.[55] According to various reports three edicts to the clergy and people of Alexandria were issued one after the other. According to the testimony of Pope Felix III(II) and Pope Gelasius I,[56] Zeno demanded from the episcopate and clergy of Egypt that 'within two months they should renounce what they had in mind from the very beginning against the Canons, the Churches of God and right faith'; they should resume communion with Timothy Salophaciolus (Patriarch of Alexandria— first 460–475, then 477–482), who had been ousted on the return of Timothy Aelurus (475). Should they refuse to do this they would be driven out of Alexandria, even out of Egypt. For whoever separated himself from the universal Church (*ab ecclesia quae ubique terrarum est*) should not, in the judgement of the Emperor, be invested with any episcopal or other ecclesiastical dignity. At Antioch Peter the Fuller was again banished (at the end of 476 or the beginning of 477),[57] as after three months was his monophysite successor, John Codonatus, who once before had succeeded in taking the see from Peter. A synod at Constantinople (end of 476 or beginning of 477) under Acacius condemned the heads of the anti-Chalcedonian opposition, thus Peter the Fuller, John Codonatus, Peter Mongus (who later, as Peter III, was patriarch from 482 to 490), Paul of Ephesus and above all Timothy Aelurus.[58] After the murder of the Chalcedonian

---

[53] Simplicius, *ep. ad Zenon. imp.* from 10 Jan., 476; JW 573: CA nr. 56, §12, p. 129. Simplicius speaks of '*verae confessionis pax*', which because of Zeno's concern was to extend over the whole *orbis* of his rule. Similarly in the letter to Acacius from 31 Jan., 476; JW 575: CA nr. 57, §2, p. 130. Felix III (II) (Gelasius), *ep. 1 ad eppos Orient.* (488–89); JW 611: Thiel p. 303, §29.

[54] Simplicius, *ep. ad Zenon. aug.* (c. 21 Oct., 478); JW 581: CA nr. 64, pp. 144–145. For the banishment of Peter Mongus, Patriarch Acacius was also to plead with the Emperor. Cf. Simplicius, *ep. ad Acacium* from Oct. 582: CA nr. 65, §2, p. 146; cf. CA 66, §2, pp. 147–148 (*extra metas vestri pelleretur imperii*). This demand that Peter Mongus be banished is also raised in the synodal letter of the Roman Synod of 5 October, 485, to the presbyters and archimandrites of Constantinople and Bithynia. Cf. Thiel I, p. 253, §2 with reference to the repeated campaigning of Simplicius.

[55] *Cod. Iust.* I 2, 16: Krueger 14; English translation in Coleman-Norton, *State & Church* nr. 526, pp. 922–924.

[56] Felix, *ep. ad Zenon. aug., Coll. Berol.* 10 and 22, Schwartz, PS 66, 6–13 and 74, 6–14. *Gesta de nomine Acacii*: CA nr. 99, Guenther 447, 14; Gelasius, *De vitanda communione Acacii*: *Coll. Veron.* 11, Schwartz, PS 34, 6 and 16 ff.

[57] On Peter the Fuller (Cnapheus) see the *Gesta de nomine Acacii*: CA nr. 99, Guenther 449, 17–451, 3; Schwartz, PS 162, Urkunde 19; ibid., 182–183 (first episode of Peter the Fuller in Antioch); 192–193 (second episode).

[58] See the evidence in Grumel, *Regestes* (1972²) nr. 150.

patriarch of Antioch, Stephen II (477–479), Acacius, at the command of the Emperor, ordained as bishop the Chalcedonian Calandion, who could assume his office, however, only after some time. Many bishops who subscribed the Encyclical of Basiliscus addressed a common letter to Acacius with an apology for their misdemeanour and a confession of Chalcedon. With this the Chalcedonian restoration seemed to be in sight, especially as Timothy Aelurus died on 31 July, 477 (according to E. Stein, on either 31 or 30 August).

But Peter Mongus, who was of like mind, had already been consecrated in secret. Obviously no longer was a purely Chalcedonian policy able to prevail as the imperial Church's profession of unity. Hence in 478 the necessary conditions were fulfilled which allowed this goal (i.e. the imperial Church's profession of unity) to be steered for by means of a compromise. Preliminary work for this had already been performed in Jerusalem. At the beginning of July, 478, the anti-Chalcedonian patriarch, Anastasius (458–478), died there. He had subscribed to the Encyclical of Basiliscus and was opposed to its retraction in the Antencyclical. But he had not made the first document the 'criterion of orthodoxy', nor had he made it the absolute criterion for communion with those bishops who made a pilgrimage to Jerusalem. Jerusalem was to be an 'open city' for the whole of Christendom, at least externally, even if internally a certain effort was needed to keep the agitation of monophysite groups under control. The successor of Anastasius, Patriarch Martyrius (478–486), could reap the benefits of this attitude.[59] On the occasion of a synod of the Palestinian bishops he created, with the special assistance of the monophysite monk Marcian, a new (second) union, whose formula of faith would become the model for the document that was to overcome the division between Chalcedonians and anti-Chalcedonians and guarantee unity in the sense of the imperial Church. The fundamental ideas on this subject were to be culled from an address which Patriarch Martyrius delivered in the Anastasis church in Jerusalem to the clergy, monks and people shortly after the union had been achieved. Zacharias Rhetor has transmitted this address, even if only in excerpts.[60]

Everybody should be convinced of the fact 'that we have no other true definition of the faith but that into which we have been and are being baptised. For thus have they been baptised, and believe as we do.

[59] See the detailed depiction of the development in Palestine under the Patriarchs Anastasius (458–478) and Martyrius (478–486) in L. Perrone, La chiesa di Palestina 116–127, 127–139; cf. E. Schwartz, Kyrillos von Skythopolis 371–372, where the different conditions for a union, in both Jerusalem and Egypt, are described.
[60] Zacharias Rh., HE V 6: Brooks I: CSCO 87, 153; Hamilton-Brooks 115–116. E. Schwartz, Kyrillos von Skythopolis 367–368 with a translation back into Greek of the extracts from the address of Patriarch Martyrius; idem., Vita Euthymii p. 66, 18–67, 20.

Whosoever, then, holds or has held or learned doctrine contrary to this definition of the faith which was framed by the three hundred and eighteen holy fathers, the bishops assembled at Nicaea; to which definition the one hundred and fifty believing and true bishops, assembled in the royal city, adhered, ratifying and confirming the same, as did also the Synod held in Ephesus: whosoever (I say) holds or has held or learned what is contrary to this definition, let him be accursed, if he have any other teaching or doctrine defined elsewhere, whether in Rimini, or in Sardica, or in Chalcedon, or in any other place whatsoever, according to the saying of the apostle, "If any man preaches to you more than what we have preached to you, let him be accursed" '

(And he continued in the following terms):

'If any man teaches, or brings in as new, or thinks or interprets, or holds any other definition or faith contrary to this approved and orthodox doctrine of faith of the three hundred and eighteen holy bishops and the one hundred and fifty, and them of Ephesus, he is an alien to the holy Church... But the confession, signed with your own signatures, lo, it is recorded in Heaven above! And you shall give account before the fearful and righteous Judgement-Seat, if you accept anything more or less than the true faith. I am clear from your blood; I have not desisted from speaking unto you'.

Here a compromise was traced out 'on the basis of a formula which, like the Second Council of Ephesus, recognised only three synods, and which did not curse the Council of Chalcedon, but sterilised it'.[61] The condemnation of the letter of Leo I was also dispensed with. Admittedly, one could have completely negative thoughts about the Council (and the Tome) when Chalcedon is named together with Rimini, Sardica and 'any other teaching or doctrine defined elsewhere'. A model of union had thus already been devised when Patriarch Acacius set to work at Constantinople to compose that document which would go down in history first as 'Zeno's edict', and later as the 'Henoticon'. One can justly conjecture that he had the Palestinian Henosis as his model.[62] The difference between the two projects lies in the fact that the union of Jerusalem was purely ecclesiastical, while the document from Constantinople was an instrument of the imperial Church, to which Acacius could contribute as the instigator (or even partly as author), but not in a formal legal sense as an ecclesiastical authority. One must notice first of all that the new edict was addressed to the Churches of Egypt and that it received its universal significance (significance for the imperial

[61] E. Schwartz, Kyrillos von Skythopolis 369–370.

[62] Ibid., 370. Schwartz emphasises in n. 2 that it is better to consider the politics of Acacius with respect to the Henoticon from the point of view of Jerusalem and in general of the East, and not in the first place from the polemic of the Popes Felix and Gelasius 'which is usually pushed to the forefront and as a consequence the historical perspective is distorted. The Church of the East must not be viewed from the point of view of the West'. On Acacius as the inspirer and composer (no doubt with the cooperation of the imperial chancellery) see Evagrius HE III 13: Bidez-Parmentier 110; Theophanes, Chronogr. ad A.M. 5976: De Boor 130, 13–15.

Church) only through the ecclesiastical policy of Emperor Anastasius I. It is of the utmost importance to distinguish between an unbiassed interpretation of the text and its actual employment by the various parties. We shall first cite the text, then give its history in the Eastern provinces, and finally in the relationship between Constantinople and Rome.

1. Zeno's Edict [Autumn 482][63]

(1) Emperor Caesar Zeno, Pious, Victor, Triumpher, Greatest, Ever-August, Augustus to the bishops and people throughout Alexandria and Egypt and Libya and Pentapolis.

(2) Considering the source and the constitution and the power and the invincible shield of our Empire as the only right and true faith, which through divine intervention the 318 holy Fathers, assembled in Nicaea, expounded and the 150 holy Fathers, convened similarly in Constantinople, confirmed,

(3) by night and by day we have employed every prayer and effort and the laws, that through the holy catholic and apostolic Church, the incorruptible and immortal mother of our imperial sceptres, may be increased everywhere and that the pious laymen with most holy bishops and most God-fearing clergy and archimandrites and solitaries, continuing in peace and concord with respect to God, may offer acceptable supplications in our Empire's behalf. For, while the great God and our Saviour Jesus Christ, who was incarnate and was born from Mary, the holy Virgin and *theotokos*, approves and receives readily our laudation from harmony and worship, the enemies' races will be erased and will be obliterated, all will bend their own necks to our power after God, peace and its blessings and kindly temperature of the air and abundance of fruits and other benefits will be lavished on human beings.

(4) Since the faultless faith preserves both us and the affairs of Rome, to us have been brought petitions from archimandrites most pleasing to God and hermits and

---

[63] With regard to the *Henoticon*: 1. the designation at first reads Ἤδικτον Ζήνωνος. Thus only in the Cod. Vat. gr. 1431: Schwartz p. 52. The name *'Henoticon'* is found for the first time in Zacharias Rh., *HE* V 8: Hamilton-Brooks 121, and elsewhere; further in Severus of Antioch. Evagrius, *HE* III 14, 'who copies Zacharias' (E. Schwartz, PS 197, n. 3), made it popular. 2. The TEXT: (a) Greek: E. Schwartz, 'Cod. Vat. gr. 1431', nr. 75, pp. 52–54; somewhat abbreviated in Evagrius, *HE* III 14: Bidez-Parmentier 111–114; Niceph. Call., *HE* XVI 12: PG 147, 136D–140C. (b) Latin: Liberatus, *Breviar.*, 17: ACO II 5, 127–129; Schwartz, 'Cod. Vat. gr. 1431', 54–56. (c) Syriac: Zacharias Rh., *HE* V 8: Brooks 1: CSCO 83, 227–231 = Latin tr. CSCO 87, 157–159; English tr. Hamilton-Brooks 121–123; *Incerti Chronicon ps.-Dionysianum vulgo dictum*, ed. I.-B. Chabot, CSCO 91 (V 121) 231–234; French tr. by F. Nau, 'Analyse de la seconde partie inédite de l'Histoire Ecclésiastique de Jean d'Asie', *ROC* 2 (1897) 481. (d) Coptic: F. Amélineau, 'Lettres d'Acace et de Pierre Monge', *Mémoires publ. par les membres de la mission archéol. Franc. au Caire* IV (1888–1895) 216–220. (e) Armenian (partial tr.) (English tr. in F. Conybeare, 'Anecdota Monophysitarum', *AmerJourTheol* 9 (1905) 739–740); reference is made to the Armenian variants in Coleman-Norton, *State & Church* 3, nr. 527, pp. 924–927, together with his tr. of the text of Evagrius. 3. On the SIGNIFICANCE of the *Henoticon*: Facundus Herm., *Pro def. trium cap.* XII 4: PL 67, 845B–849A (with fundamental remarks concerning the Emperor's right to speak in questions of faith); S. Salaville, 'L'hénotique', *DTC* 6, 2153–2178; idem, 'L'affaire de l'Hénotique ou le premier schisme byzantin au Vᵉ siècle', *EO* 18 (1918) 255–266, 389–397; 19 (1920) 49–68, 415–433; W. T. Townsend, 'The Henoticon Schism and the Roman Church', *JRel* 16 (1936) 78–86; further *ByzZ* 36 (1936) 501 f.; Schwartz, PS 197–201 (Acacius' intention); R. Haacke, *Chalkedon* II, 117–124; W. H. C. Frend, *The Rise of the Monophysite Movement* 174–183; P. T. R. Gray, *The Defense of Chalcedon in the East (451–583)* (Leiden 1979) 28–34. The paragraph division as it appears in our tr. was made by Th. Becker, Frankfurt-M.

other venerable men, beseeching with tears that there should be unity for the holiest Churches and that members should be united to members, which the hater of good from most distant times has bustled to sever, knowing that, when warring against the Church's complete body, he will be conquered. For it happens from this that there are uncounted generations, as many as time in so many years has withdrawn from life, that some, deprived of the washing of regeneration, have departed, that others, not having partaken of the divine communion, have been transported to the inexorable departure of mankind, that myriad murders have been undertaken and by the amount of blood-sheddings, not only the earth but also as well the very air have been polluted. Who would not pray that these things should be transformed into good?

(5) Therefore we have been eager for you to know that both we and the most holy orthodox Churches everywhere neither have held nor hold nor shall hold nor know anyone who holds another creed or teaching or definition of faith or faith save the aforesaid holy creed of the 318 holy Fathers, which the said 150 holy Fathers also confirmed, and if anyone should hold such, we consider him an alien.

(6) For we have confidence that this alone (as we said) preserves our Empire and all the peoples, when they obtain this alone, are baptised, after they are deemed worthy of salutary enlightenment. And this all the holy Fathers who were convened in the Ephesians' city followed, who also deposed the impious Nestorius and those who later were of that one's mind. And this Nestorius with Eutyches and the persons who have thoughts opposed to what has been said we also anathematise, receiving also the said *Twelve Chapters* from Cyril, whose memory is pleasing to God, the archbishop of the Alexandrians' catholic Church.

(7) We also confess that the Only-Begotten Son of God, also God, who according to truth was made man, our Lord Jesus Christ, consubstantial with the Father in respect to godhead and himself consubstantial with us in respect to manhood, having descended and having been incarnate from the Holy Spirit and Mary, the Ever-virgin *theotokos*, is one son and not two, for we say that both his miracles and his sufferings, which he willingly underwent in the flesh, are of one person, the Only-Begotten Son of God. For we do not accept at all the persons who divide or combine or introduce an apparition, inasmuch as according to truth the sinless incarnation from the *theotokos* has not made an addition of a son, for the Trinity has remained a Trinity, even after one of the Trinity, God and Word, became incarnate.

(8) Knowing, then, that neither God's most holy orthodox Churches everywhere nor the priests most pleasing to God who preside over these nor our Majesty have been content with nor are content with a creed or a definition of faith other than the said holy teaching, unite yourselves without any wavering.

(9) These things we have written, not devising a new faith, but fully assuring you. But every person who has thought or thinks anything else, either now or at any time, either in Chalcedon or in any synod whatever, we anathematise, especially the aforesaid Nestorius and Eutyches and the persons who are of their mind.

(10) Be you joined, therefore, to the spiritual mother, the Church, by enjoying in her the same holy communion with us according to the aforesaid one and only definition of the faith of the same holy Fathers. For our all-holy mother, the Church, awaits to embrace you as genuine sons and yearns to hear your long-delayed and dear voice.

Therefore urge yourselves, for by doing these things you will also draw to yourselves the good will of Christ our Saviour and God, and by our Majesty you will be praised.

Being steadfast in the Lord, pray for us, most devoted brothers.

2. The theology of the Henoticon

Let us once again characterise the position of the main actor in the whole undertaking—Acacius (472–489). He fought against Basiliscus and Timothy Aelurus, not so much for the dogmatic formula of Chalcedon, but rather for the prerogatives of his see which were the objective of Canon 28. What makes the *Henoticon* theologically significant is the combination of what it suppresses and what it formulates positively.

(*a*) The negative aspect. The document does not contain any formal execration of the *Tomus Leonis* as a whole or of the Council of Chalcedon itself. It is true that a sentence of the Tome is clearly criticised and rejected, but this sentence as such was not included in the definition of 451. We are referring to Leo's phrase—'the one shines through miracles [viz. the divine nature of Christ], the other is subject to abuse [viz. the human nature of Christ]'—which seemed to insinuate a division into two persons. Placed in positive contrast to this phrase is: 'For we say that both his miracles and his sufferings, which he willingly underwent in the flesh, are of one person, the Only-Begotten Son of God' (§7). The Alexandrian principal formula—'the one incarnate nature of the God-Logos'—found no approval. On the other side as well nothing is said against the expression that was so detested by the Alexandrians—'knowable in two natures'. It is to be noted that the annulled imperial Council of Ephesus (449) is also not mentioned. It could not be considered an invitation to unity, because it had favoured Eutyches too much.

(*b*) The positive aspect. The common foundations of the faith are, according to §6, only the Council of Nicaea (325) and the Council of Constantinople (381), Synods to which the Council of Ephesus (431) also showed allegiance, but not Nestorius and Eutyches, who on that account are anathematised as well. This had been the starting-point of the Council of Chalcedon too. It is here that the feelings of Acacius became divided. He was certainly still grateful even at this time, and precisely at this time, that Marcian's Synod reminded the Alexandrians of the Council of 381; during the period up to Cyril they had readily suppressed this memory. That at this moment Canon 3—in contradistinction to the Creed—was more important to Acacius does not need to be hammered at. If one considers in more detail the relationship of the *Henoticon* to the formula of faith of 451, three points can be established.

(i) In principle a Chalcedonian could agree that distinction and union in the relationship of divinity and humanity in Christ were expressed with words that were reminiscent of the 'unmingled' and 'undivided' of 451 (§7). The emphasis on Christ's twofold consubstan-

tiality, viz. 'consubstantial with the Father in respect to godhood
and himself consubstantial with us in respect to manhood', seems
even more clearly to take up the text of 451. But these words were
already in the Formulary of Reunion (433) which was adopted into
the *Laetentur* letter of Cyril that was so highly esteemed. Let us also
call to mind once again how much this twofold 'consubstantiality'
could bind together Chalcedon, Leo I and Timothy Aelurus. Common property were also the phrases about the sinless incarnation
from the *theotokos* Mary or about the sinlessness of Christ in general,
phrases which had a special significance for Chalcedon.

(ii) The suppression of the formula of the one hypostasis or person
in two natures (the great vexation of the Alexandrians) resorted to
a position anterior to that of Chalcedon. This was to be a sacrifice
for the sake of unity, just as on the other side the *mia physis* formula
does not occur.

(iii) If here a balance, so to speak, is attained, still one cannot
fail to recognise a weighting in favour of the Alexandrian monophysite christology. Various details need to be mentioned here. (1) If
both Eutyches and Nestorius are rejected, still in justifying this the
Henoticon falls back on an old Apollinarian argument that is found
in the work 'That Christ is one', an argument directed against Paul
of Samosata (or better, against Photinus and his teacher, Marcellus
of Ancyra).[64] Whoever accepts two sons in Christ makes the Trinity
into a quaternity. For in that way a foreign fourth hypostasis of
a different kind is added to the three. By implication the monophysite
argument could also be voiced in this: whoever accepts two *natures*
in Christ accepts two sons, and hence the quaternity. (2) If one recalls
the reserve which the Council of Ephesus and even Chalcedon showed
with regard to the twelve *cephalaia* or anathemas of Cyril, if one
thinks of the difficulties which they had caused for the Alexandrians,
then their explicit recognition is to be equated with the demand that
the intensified Cyrillian christology of union be accepted generally
(cf. §6). This still did not signify a rejection of the doctrine of Chalcedon as such which was also capable of being expressed without the
'terminology' of the 'two natures'. (3) There seems to be only *one*
step away from an open rejection of Chalcedon when it is said in
§9: 'But any person who has thought or thinks anything else, either
now or at any time, either in *Chalcedon* or in any synod whatever,
we anathematise'. This could be the thin edge of the wedge for all

---

[64] Ps.-Athanasius, *Quod unus sit Christus* 3–4 = CPG 3737: Lietzmann, *Apollinaris von Laodicea*
(Tübingen 1904) 296, 8–297, 8; this accusation became a topos against Chalcedon. Cf. John Rufus,
Plerophories LXXII: PO 8, 128: 'L'église de ces partisans des quatre (dieux)'.

those who saw an explicit condemnation of the Fourth Council expressed in the *Henoticon*. (4) Finally a new point of conflict is heralded by the formula: 'One of the Trinity, God the Word, became incarnate' (§7). In this form it ought not have caused any excitement. For this to happen it needed only to be intensified; this did not take long to occur.

Although a concept of the Church, capable of carrying out what was required of it, was expressed in the *Henoticon* with talk of the one universal 'mother, the Church' (§10) and of the necessity of baptism and the eucharist (§4), still in the dispute about the Edict the validity of the administration of the sacraments and of episcopal consecrations was contested from time to time. In the process of the Edict's gaining acceptance it was not the genuine ecclesiastical elements which came to the fore, but purely the pragmatic, political principle of unity, enshrined in the imperial Church. This fact also contributed to the theological poverty of the next decades. Acacius himself, as author, had particular difficulties in safeguarding his own interests. Peter Mongus wanted to be patriarch in Alexandria. The Patriarch of Constantinople was determined to achieve the recognition of his see as the seat of a patriarchate, and as second in stature. To achieve this he had to work through Zeno. Peter Mongus would have to pay a price for his elevation to patriarch, not in relation to the doctrinal part of Chalcedon, but with regard to its canonical legislation. It was Canon 28 in particular that Acacius was concerned about. Acceptance of the Canons, but not of the doctrinal definitions—this we shall also encounter in the Syrian region. That the Bishop of Constantinople was so easily prepared to dispense with the new formulas of Chalcedon—even if only in the sense of suppressing them—robbed the supporters of the *Henoticon* of an effective instrument for fighting the still active virulence of docetist, Manichaean and Apollinarian tendencies, which even Timothy Aelurus in fact had not completely overcome.[65] The later history of anti-Chalcedonianism in the East will demonstrate this.

In what follows we need no longer be concerned with the *Henoticon* as a 'christological' document. But the conflict around it reveals, nevertheless, an important side of the system of the imperial Church, the emergence of new theological forces. Finally, the whole affair provides excellent material for a study of 'ecumenism' in its modern meaning—the presence or the absence of it. The lines of argument that we encounter here played a rôle right up to the discussion about 'religious freedom' at the Second Vatican Council.

---

[65] See Chapter V below.

3. 'Schisms' instead of 'henosis'. The Henoticon policy as an 'ecumenical' problem

Section One: In the Eastern patriarchates

With a laconic sentence, Facundus of Hermiane highlighted the major error of the *Henoticon*: 'He [Emperor Zeno] did not understand that confusion does not create unity'.[66] This could be a heading for much 'ecumenical' dialogue.

Schisms everywhere was the immediate result of the Emperor's attempt to end the conflict about Chalcedon by a theologically pragmatic compromise. The situation of the Churches at the time of Emperor Zeno's death (491) is vividly described by Evagrius Scholasticus.[67] The Church historian begins by giving prominence to the irenically conservative character of Zeno's successor, Emperor Anastasius I (491–518), who wanted to keep the Church and his own reign free from all disturbance. With upright intentions the new Emperor also took over the *Henoticon* as the guarantee of unity. This he did with tenacious stamina. The result, however, was entirely contrary to his intentions, even if Evagrius in his presentation passes over the last years of the Emperor (see *Ad Fontes*):

> The Council of Chalcedon, accordingly, was during these times neither openly acknowledged in the most holy Churches, nor yet rejected by all, but each of the bishops acted according to his own opinion. There were some who very resolutely abided by what had been expounded at the Council and would not give in to the extent of one syllable of its definitions, nor would they admit the change of even a single letter, but they rejected all contact and absolutely refused to countenance communion with those who did not accept the matters expounded by the Council. There were others who not only did not accept the Council of Chalcedon and the matters defined by it, but also anathematised both it and the Tome of Leo. Others adhered to the Henoticon of Zeno, and this although they were at variance with one another on the point of the one or two natures, some being taken in by the way the document was composed, others inclining rather towards a peaceful situation.[68]

Evagrius found the result disappointing:

> The upshot was that all the Churches were divided into separate groups and that the bishops were not in communion with each other. From this there arose a great number of divisions throughout the Eastern and Western parts [of the Empire] and throughout Libya; the bishops of the East were not on peaceful terms with those of the West, nor again those of Libya with those of the East. The situation became more absurd: neither did the presidents of the East communicate with each other, nor yet those in charge of the sees of Europe or Libya, much less with those from far off.[69]

---

[66] Facundus Herm., *Pro def. trium cap.* XII 4: PL 67, 845B: *nec intellexit quod non confusio faciat unitatem.*
[67] Evagrius, *HE* III 30: Bidez-Parmentier 126, 5–30.
[68] Ibid., 126, 5–21.
[69] Ibid., 126, 21–30.

In order to characterise the situation we shall present the various party groupings in detail, in so far as this can be ascertained.[70]

(a) Positions on the anti-Chalcedonian side

(i) Moderate supporters of the *Henoticon*, without a condemnation of Chalcedon or the Tome of Leo I.

Alexandria. Here the leading figure was Peter III Mongus (482–490), who as early as 477 was proposed for the patriarchal see by his supporters (to replace Timothy Salophaciolus). He assumed communion with Acacius of Constantinople and received ratification from Emperor Zeno, whereas John I Talaia, the Chalcedonian rival and Rome's candidate, was not given a chance. The two subsequent patriarchs, Athanasius II (490–497) and John II Hemula (497–505), kept to the line of Peter Mongus, as Severus of Antioch reports.[71]

Jerusalem. As we have already pointed out, the union of Jerusalem under Patriarch Martyrius (478–486) and its document was taken as the model for the *Henoticon*.[72] What such a start signified for later development will deserve special consideration (see Vol. II/2).

Antioch. Here Patriarch Calandion was deposed in 485; Peter the Fuller, who had already occupied the see in 471 and 475–477, returned as patriarch (+488). Thus it seemed that Acacius of Constantinople had guided the patriarchates of the East together through the *Henoticon*. Zacharias Rhetor has transmitted the synodal letters of Acacius, Peter the Fuller and Martyrius. Through these they had once again resumed ecclesiastical communion with each other.[73]

Thus the East seemed to be relatively unanimous in standing behind the idea of the *Henoticon*; according to E. Schwartz, this was a victory

---

[70] A short exact survey of the development in the period we are concerned with is given by E. Honigmann, *Évêques et évêchés* 3–18: Le monophysisme jusqu'à l'accession de Sévère au patriarcat (475–512). On the divisions see J. Lebon, *Le monophysisme sévérien* (Louvain 1909) 31–36; C. Capizzi, *Sul fallimento di un negoziato di pace ecclesiastica fra il papa Ormisda e l'imperatore Anastasio I (515–517)* (Firenze 1980) 28–29.

[71] Severus Ant., Letter to the Presbyter Ammonius: Brooks, *Select Letters* II(V), IV 2, p. 255: . . . 'contented with the Henoticon only, as Peter and Athanasius and John who succeeded the latter had been, without requiring reference to be made in actual words to the impious things done at Chalcedon or to the impious Tome of Leo'. On John Talaia and his clumsy measures see F. Hofmann, *Chalkedon* II, 41–44 and passim; Schwartz, PS 195–199; E. Stein, *Histoire du Bas-Empire* II, 22 ff.

[72] See L. Perrone, *La chiesa di Palestina* 127–139. Perrone characterises the period introduced by Martyrius as 'l'epoca del "calcedonismo minimale".'

[73] Zacharias Rh., *HE* V 10: Brooks 1: CSCO 87, 161–164; Hamilton-Brooks 126–128; (*a*) the Synodal letter of the assembly of Antioch under Peter the Fuller (reminder of Jesus bar Nun, the leader of Israel into the promised land; cf. A. Grillmeier, JdChr 1², 57–58, 63–65; and of the Petrine tradition in Antioch; reference to the first three Councils and the Twelve Anathematisms of Cyril). (*b*) ibid., V 11: Brooks 1: CSCO 87, 162–164; Hamilton-Brooks 128–130 (cf. Liberatus, *Breviar.* 17: ACO II 5, 129, 17–21; CA, p. 795, §14). Hamilton-Brooks 129: the Emperor Zeno is compared with the star of Bethlehem which leads to Christ, and with David, the conqueror of Goliath. On the intentions which moved Acacius in the *Henoticon* question see Schwartz, PS 198–199. (*c*) ibid., V 12: Brooks 1: CSCO 87, 164; Hamilton-Brooks 130–131: Martyrius of Jerusalem to Peter Mongus.

for Constantinople in the field of ecclesiastical politics. By means of Zeno's Edict Patriarch Acacius wanted to ensure for himself supremacy over the Eastern patriarchates. The idea of unity of faith was not prominent to the same extent. This unity was achieved through subtractions from and a thinning out of what the Union of 433 and the definition of 451 had contributed to the vigorous theology of the Fathers. This surrogate (E. Schwartz: stopgap) was bound, then, to have the effect of dissolving rather than of unifying.

(ii) Radical opponents of the *Henoticon* on the anti-Chalcedonian side.

In Egypt, Palestine and Syria there arose strong opposition to the *Henoticon*, particularly in monastic circles. At the head was Peter the Iberian and his large group of supporters, about whom we are informed by John Rufus.[74] The latter names the *Henoticon* neither in his *Vita* of Peter the Iberian nor in the *Plerophoriai*, a fact which reference to the detailed index in F. Nau can demonstrate. Emperor Zeno is mentioned only briefly. In contrast John Rufus reverts to the Encyclical of the ursurper Basiliscus, which was the work of Timothy Aelurus. This is characterised as *the* orthodox document and as the support of right faith. On the other hand the Antencyclical is looked upon as a regression and is deeply lamented.[75] In a legendary report it is depicted how a 'judgement of God' intervened in the decision between the Encyclical and the definition of Chalcedon. Both documents were thrown into the fire. Only the former withstood the glow of the fire.[76] In Egypt Peter Mongus also experienced fierce opposition. A group of extremists separated themselves from him because they could not find a clear rejection of Chalcedon and Leo's Tome in the *Henoticon*. They demanded from their patriarch an oral or written condemnation of both nightmares. When they did not receive this they formed their own party and, because they had no episcopal head, they were called 'the acephalists'[77] or simply 'the aposchists' (separatists; E. Schwartz: 'Sonderbündler' which has a

---

[74] Cf. E. Schwartz, 'Johannes Rufus ein monophysitischer Schriftsteller', = *SbHeidAk*, Phil.-hist. Kl. 1912 (Heidelberg 1912) 1–28; John Rufus composed: 1. the *Life* of Peter the Iberian: R. Raabe, *Petrus der Iberer* (Leipzig 1895) (corrections in Schwartz, op. cit., 27); 2. *Plerophories*, ed. F. Nau, *Jean Rufus, Évêque de Maiouma, Plérophories*: PO 8 (1912) I, pp. 11–183 with indices (185–205). Cf. M. Cramer-H. Bacht, 'Der antichalkedonische Aspekt im historisch-biographischen Schrifttum der koptischen Monophysiten (6.–7. Jh.)', *Chalkedon* II, 315–338.

[75] So in John Rufus, *Plerophories*, §45: PO 8, 98; §82: 137, 14–138, 9; §83: 138, 12; §86: 140, 1–2; on the Encyclical itself, ibid., §22: 47, 7; §45: 98, 1.10.14.

[76] Ibid., §46: 98, 5–16.

[77] Cf. S. Vailhé, 'Acéphales', *DHGE* I (1912) 282–288; Zacharias Rh., *Vie de Sévère*: PO 2 (1907) 107 (application of the name *acephaloi* to Isaurian bishops); A. de Halleux, *Philoxène de Mabbog* (Louvain 1963) 207–208. On the discontent of the Egyptian monks and faithful see H. Bacht, *Chalkedon* II. 267–269; Schwartz, PS 199–200.

contemptuous meaning). We recall that even Timothy Aelurus, who certainly did not hesitate to condemn Chalcedon, had great difficulties with the radical supporters of Eutyches in Egypt. Finally Peter Mongus had no other option than to expel the ringleaders from their monasteries.[78]

If we bear in mind this fanaticism and the zealous propagandist activity of these monastic groups as well as the powerful influence of Peter the Iberian, then we realise without further ado that the *Henoticon* had no chance of creating *henosis*. Such a form of anti-Chalcedonianism admits no compromise.

(b) Differences on the fundamentally pro-Chalcedonian side

(i) The attempt at a synthesis between the *Henoticon* and Chalcedon

The readiness of those who were fundamentally supporters of Chalcedon to accept the *Henoticon* was not exactly widespread, but it was still present. The reason for this was either the *bonum pacis* for the universal Church in one case or the unconditional obedience to the Emperor in the other. Pope Felix III refers to certain monks who hoped to be able to combine both. They belonged to the party of Acacius.[79] There was even success in getting some papal legates who had been sent to Constantinople to convert Acacius to the Roman, purely Chalcedonian standpoint to opt for this synthesis, i.e. to do a volte-face. This became a great scandal in Rome.[80] It is difficult to determine to what extent the Eastern bishops as a whole were inclined to accept this synthesis. A section of the East Illyrian episcopacy which either rejected the *Henoticon* or indeed accepted it, but in such a way that the anti-Chalcedonian point seemed to be removed, constitutes a unique case.[81]

What appeared to be most harmless in a doctrinal sense was the practice of rejecting the *Henoticon* as such, but at the same time mentioning living or already deceased supporters of this document at liturgical celebrations, i.e. entering their names in the so-called diptychs. In this regard Rome was sensitive, particularly with respect to the names of Acacius and Peter Mongus. For both of these were considered by Rome to be heretical and anathematised, as was really the case for every supporter of Zeno's Edict. Their being mentioned

[78] Cf. Zacharias Rh., *HE* VI 1–2: Brooks 2: CSCO 88, 1–2 (the monks Theodore and Nephalius); Hamilton-Brooks 132–136; cf. H. Bacht, *Chalkedon* II, 268 with n. 12.

[79] Felix III, *ep.* 12 = *Coll. Berol.* nr. 29: Schwartz, PS 78, 4: *non est dubium nonnullos ex monasteriis vestris esse deceptos atque inimicos dei seu sponte seu necessitate transisse . . .* See, however, the synodal letter of Peter Mongus to Fravitta of Constantinople, below n. 82 and 83.

[80] Cf. H. Bacht, *Chalkedon* II, 269–270. Those involved were the bishops Vitalis and Misenus and the *defensor* Tutus: Schwartz, PS 77, 18–78, 14.

[81] On East Illuricum see C. Capizzi, *L'imperatore Anastasio I*, p. 105, n. 73, with numerous illustrations from papal letters.

in the diptychs thus meant the fundamental acceptance of a heresy, and consequently separation from Rome.

But one could attempt to combine an affirmation of the *Henoticon* with an affirmation of the Fourth Council, and moreover also live in schism with one of the Eastern patriarchs or bishops who professed the *Henoticon*, because in the East the recognition of Zeno's Edict was interpreted as an open rejection of Chalcedon or was tied to an anathema against the Fourth Council. Hence there were unstable relations of *communio* between Constantinople, Antioch, Alexandria and Jerusalem, *communio* being dependent upon the stance of the patriarchs who succeeded each other. We shall consider the situation by studying two people who were of special significance for Constantinople. This situation, especially for the relationship to Rome, could only arise because nothing at all was said about the content of the *Henoticon*. This Edict of the Emperor was not conveyed at all to the West—initially, indeed, it affected only Constantinople and Alexandria; hence juridically it had to be considered as non-existent. For this reason during the Acacian Schism (484–519) christological discussion in official documents was to a great extent obstructed.

(ii) Resolute defenders of Chalcedon without compromise

In the East the *acoimetoi*[82] stood out as such. They also started an extensive collection of documents which were extremely important for Chalcedonian propaganda for many years after that. Their archimandrite, Cyril, even found that Rome under Pope Felix was too slack in this matter. But other monasteries of the Imperial City were also determined supporters of the Fourth Council. Later we shall have to deal with a special figure, who from being an opponent of Chalcedon became a supporter of it, even if in his own way—the monk Nephalius.[83] In Palestine the supporters of Chalcedon gathered around the archimandrite Sabas of the great Lavra (439–532), who was the disciple and successor of St. Euthymius (+473).[84] According

[82] Cf. H. Bacht, *Chalkedon* II, 269 with n. 20, with reference to J. Pargoire, Art. 'Acémètes', *DACL* I (1924) 307–321 (fundamental) and criticism of Schwartz, PS 205–212. According to Zacharias Rh., *HE* VII 7: Brooks 2: CSCO 88, 26; Hamilton-Brooks 168, the Sleepless Monks numbered about one thousand. They worked together with the archimandrites of one section of the monasteries in Constantinople, with Egyptian pro-Chalcedonian refugees, but above all, by supplying information, with the Popes in Rome. Their power increased after the death of Patriarch Acacius (+ 26.9.489), who had known how to exercise hegemony over the Eastern imperial Church and to dominate Emperor Zeno and the bishops. Their first success was that once again they had dealings with Rome. See now Fr. Halkin, *AnBoll* 86(1968) 271–321.
[83] Cf. Schwartz, PS 199–200. See below.
[84] See H. Bacht, *Chalkedon* II, 282; E. Schwartz, *Kyrillos von Skythopolis, Vita Sabae*, esp. §50: pp. 85–200; tr. by A.-J. Festugière, *Les moines d'Orient*, 3, 2: *Les moines de Palestine* (Paris 1962) (13–130); P. Devos, 'Cyrille de Scythopolis', *AnBoll* 98 (1980) 25–38. L. Perrone, *La chiesa di Palestina* 144–145.

to his biographer, Cyril of Scythopolis, he was 'the most solid support of catholic faith in Palestine'. Commissioned by Patriarch Elias of Jerusalem, Sabas went to Emperor Anastasius in Constantinople in order to plead the cause of right faith, without, however, accomplishing anything.[85] Yet what power Sabas, together with the holy man Theodosius, had, manifested itself at the end of Emperor Anastasius' reign. His great opponent was Severus of Antioch, whose theology we still have to consider in detail. During his sojourn in Constantinople (508–511) Severus had won the confidence of Emperor Anastasius, and could initiate a movement about him which was supported by an increasing crowd of monks from Palestine and Syria and some Eastern bishops. It had no other goal than to lead the battle against the Council of Chalcedon to victory and to eliminate the compromise of the *Henoticon* once and for all[86] (see below). After the great Synod of Antioch (513)[87] had ratified his intentions, Severus also hoped to win over Patriarch Elias and to enter into communion with him. But Elias did not accept the *synodica* of Severus which had been brought to him by official courier. At the call of St. Sabas the monks from the Kedron valley and from the desert of Judea gathered around their patriarch. Together with the inhabitants of the city they adopted such a threatening attitude that the delegates of Severus had to go away without accomplishing anything. This in fact cost Elias the patriarchal see. But his successor, John III (516–524), who had been installed by Emperor Anastasius, continued to be kept to the Chalcedonian line by Sabas and Theodosius to such an extent that imprisonment in Caesarea by the Emperor did not break him, indeed it even led to an unexpected triumph in the Holy City. This was brought about by the two holy men and 10,000 of their monks who, together with the people of Jerusalem, organised a massive demonstration

---

[85] See Cyril of Scythop., *Vita Sabae* §§50–54: Schwartz, op. cit., p. 139, 20–147, 9; Festugière, op. cit., 66–75; Perrone, *La chiesa di Palestina* 157–158. Patriarch Elias gave to the delegation a letter addressed to the enraged Emperor Anastasius: 'Voici l'élite des bons et fidèles serviteurs de Dieu qui gouvernent tout le désert, et, parmi eux, mon seigneur Sabas, fondateur et administrateur du désert et mon diocèse, lumière de toute la Palestine. Je vous les ai adressés pour qu'ils supplient Votre Majesté impériale' (Festugière 67). §50 contains an excellent summary of the relationships of communion between the various patriarchates around 493–494 (Festugière 66–67).

[86] See H. Bacht, *Chalkedon* II, 279, 285.

[87] On the Synod of Antioch in 513 see below. Jacobite historians report a Synod of Tyre which was similarly structured. They are followed by E. Honigmann, *Évêques et évêchés* 16–18 (date: 514–515); E. Schwartz and L. Duchesne (513); E. Stein (514). Through a comparison of the sources (*a*) Zacharias Rh. cont. VII 10; VII 12; (*b*) John of Ephesus (ad a. 826); (*c*) Anonymous of 846 (CSCO 3/4), A. de Halleux, *Philoxène de Mabbog* 81–85 comes to the conclusion that the description fits exactly the great Synod of the Orientals at Antioch in 513. On the other hand, such a synod could not have taken place in Tyre before 514–515 because the Chalcedonian bishop, Epiphanius, was in office there. Certainly after his deposition Severans could have arrived in Tyre to confirm the deposition and to install a successor. It is quite understandable if on that occasion the anathemas of 513 were repeated. The source common to the Syrian historians had no doubt confused the great Synod of Antioch (513) with the assembly of bishops in Tyre in 514–515, which had the purpose indicated.

for the Council of Chalcedon in St. Stephen's church. The result was a declaration by Patriarch John against Severus and his party. The representative of the Emperor, the *dux Palestinae*, took to flight. The Emperor's nephew, Hypatius, who was also a delegate, protested that he had nothing to do with Severus. The attempt of the Emperor after this to have all three, John and the two holy men, deposed, foundered on the tenacious opposition of the monks, who drew up a statement addressed to the Emperor in which they protested against any coercion to assume *communio* with Severus and declared themselves ready even to shed their blood for their cause.[88] This will suffice to sketch the position of the intransigent defenders of Chalcedon in Eastern monasticism under Emperor Anastasius. It is more important for us to determine more clearly the attitude of the three patriarchs of Constantinople.

(iii) Three patriarchs of Constantinople caught between the Emperor, the Pope and the Eastern patriarchates

Patriarch Fravitta (December 489–March 490).[89] In his notification of election to Pope Felix III at the end of 489, he attempted to resume contact with Rome. Peter is recognised as head of the apostles, as the rock of faith and the possessor of the power of the keys. In the text (which is lost today) it seems, according to the testimony of various sources, that the desire for *communio* in right faith with the Pope was expressed, as well as the refusal of *communio* with Peter Mongus.[90] At the same time *synodica* were sent to Alexandria in which communion was taken up.[91] Whereas Fravitta did not mention the *Henoticon*, Peter Mongus in his reply[92] did not miss the opportunity,

[88] The petition of Theodosius and Sabas to the Emperor is found in Cyril Scyth., *Vita Sabae* I 57: Schwartz 152, 21–157, 24; Festugière, op. cit., 82–85. It is to be noted how in this and in other Palestinian documents the position of Jerusalem vis-à-vis the other Churches is brought into play in the argumentation against the Byzantine Emperor. The most recent patriarchal see is distinguished by the fact that 'Sion is the mother of all the Churches, the place where the salvation of the world, this great mystery of religion, was accomplished, salvation which, beginning in Jerusalem, was made the light of truth to the ends of the earth by divine and apostolic preaching'. Reference is made to 'the precious and supernatural mystery of Christ which here unfolded through the instrument of the victorious and precious cross, the life-giving resurrection' (153, 3–9).

[89] See Grumel, *Regestes* I 1², nr. 173–174, pp. 128–129.

[90] Ibid., nr. 173 (list of sources).

[91] Ibid., nr. 174; the synodal letter is preserved only in Syriac in the extract in Zacharias Rh., *HE* VI 5: Brooks 2: CSCO 88, 6–7; Hamilton-Brooks 140–142. Evagrius, *HE* III 23: Bidez-Parmentier 121, 2–5, following the documents before him, also witnesses to the assumption of communion; in his letter of reply Peter discussed Chalcedon. Theophanes, *Chronogr.* A. M. 5981: De Boor 133, 8–14 speaks in a stronger tone of a double game: 'Fravitta ... writes to Felix that he has communion with him, but not with Peter Mongus; to Mongus, however, he writes that he has communion with him and that he is turning his back on Felix of Rome. Felix, however, received through orthodox believers a copy of the letter to Mongus, and because just then the *apocrisiarii* of Fravitta were departing, he dismissed them unceremoniously with the Synodals'.

[92] Zacharias Rh., *HE* VI 6: Brooks 2, CSCO 88, 7–9; Hamilton-Brooks 142–145. This reply no longer reached Fravitta, who had died after three months in office, but the Patriarch Euphemius, who immediately broke off communion with Peter.

after an otherwise completely orthodox presentation of his faith, to praise the *Henoticon* expressly as Emperor Zeno's special work of union and to interpret it as a condemnation of Chalcedon and Leo's Tome.[93] 'And we consent to this same document; and we preach it, by word of mouth and by writing, to the believing nations...'.[94] Fravitta, like Peter Mongus, presents no clear-cut picture. It must remain an open question how much of the picture we have is due to the Syrian redaction of Zacharias Rhetor's *Church History*.

Patriarch Euphemius (490–496),[95] the clear, but unappreciated supporter of Chalcedon. His image in the eyes of the Pope was marred by the shadow that fell on him because of Acacius. Rome ought to have supported him with all its strength against Emperor Anastasius I (491–518). Even before Anastasius' accession to the throne, when he was still *silentiarius* at court, Euphemius opposed him as a 'heretic and of like mind to Eutyches' and he drove him from the pulpit of the old Hagia Sophia where he sought to proclaim his teachings.[96] When this *silentiarius* was designated after Emperor Zeno's death as candidate for Emperor, the Patriarch raised objections 'by calling [Anastasius] a heretic and unworthy for the Christians'.[97] When the appointment could no longer be avoided the Patriarch forced from the new imperial candidate, 'who through his faith (*fide*) but much more through his perfidy had already attracted attention in his foreign homeland [Dyrrhachium]', a documented promise 'to do nothing to the detriment of apostolic faith and the Synod of Chalcedon'. The Bishop took the 'written homology' and deposited it in the Church's archives. The Council of Chalcedon was to be received as a 'definition of faith', something which Anastasius also said he did.[98] Only then did the Bishop crown the Emperor. The former,

---

[93] Zacharias Rh., *HE* VI 6: Brooks 2: CSCO 88, 9, 4–7; Hamilton-Brooks 144, 3–7: 'for the sake of the unity of the people, and that we might be established in power and in the truth, by what he wrote so faithfully in the Henoticon, anathematised all the rash thoughts and words of Chalcedon and the Tome of Leo'. Cf., however, n. 68 above. Did Peter Mongus favour a more radical stance? Severus appears to know nothing of this.

[94] Zacharias Rh., *HE* VI 6: Brooks 2, CSCO 88, p. 9, 7–8; Hamilton-Brooks 144, 8–9.

[95] Grumel, *Regestes* I 1², nr. 174a–180a.

[96] Theodore Lector, *Epit.* 441: Hansen 123, where in frg, 33 Suda, s.v. φατρία is quoted with the same content. Cf. Theoph., *Chronogr.*, A.M. 5981: De Boor 134, 19–24. He contrasts the 'wholly orthodox' Euphemius with Anastasius 'who later ruled badly'.

[97] Theodore Lector, *Epit.* 446: Hansen 125, 25–27.

[98] Theodore Lector, *Epit.* 446: Hansen 125 f.; frg. 39: Hansen 126. Hence it is not correct when A.-J. Festugière, *Les moines d'Orient* III 2, 131, referring to Stein, *Histoire du Bas-Empire* II 77 (where there is talk of a 'document par lequel il s'engageait à maintenir intacte l'Église catholique et à ne rien innover en matière religieuse') interprets the context of the promise extracted from the Emperor as being 'donc, en fait à suivre l'Hénotique'. Then the Emperor would not have placed such value on having the document once again in his hands. Cf. Stein, *Histoire du Bas-Empire* II, 38–39. Stein says here that Euphemius was fundamentally a supporter of Chalcedon and that he had given up communion with Peter Mongus. His stance on the question of the diptychs must not be interpreted as falling in with the line of Acacius.

however, reckoning with the 'cunning' (*calliditas*) of the new ruler, summoned a synod (*synodos endemousa*) and ratified the decrees of the Council of Chalcedon.[99] Euphemius maintained this decision of his right up to his deposition and exile in 496.[100] Before these events the Emperor still tried to recover the document which he had signed— but without success.[101] He repeated the attempt with the new patriarch.[102]

Although the stance of Euphemius on Chalcedon was so unambiguous, still the announcement of his election was not well received by Pope Felix III (483–492) in October 490 or at the beginning of 491. Only one announcement was sought—that Acacius, who had been anathematised by Rome, was removed from the diptychs. Because this announcement was not found, Euphemius was not recognised as bishop of Constantinople, but only as an 'orthodox man'.[103] Even a letter to Pope Gelasius I (492–496) (sent after the month of March)[104] could not effect any change. From him Euphemius had not received even notification of his election. Even the request that the baptisms and ordinations performed by Acacius be recognised and that his inclusion in the diptychs be approved was not granted.[105] A new letter to Rome from the end of 492 or the beginning of 493[106] wanted to take things up at a deeper level, viz. with the argument that the anathematisation of Acacius was invalid, because the charge of heresy could not be upheld. Euphemius also indicated that the people of Constantinople would not accept the removal of their former patriarch from the diptychs. This attempt to tone down the *Henoticon* affair was also not acknowledged in Rome.[107]

---

[99] On the crowning see W. Enßlin, *Zur Frage nach der ersten Kaiserkrönung durch den Patriarchen und zur Bedeutung dieses Aktes im Wahlzeremoniell* (Würzburg n.d.) 24–25. On the Synod of Constantinople (492): Theodore Lector, *HE*, frg. 41 (Victor of Tunnuna ad a. 492) (2): Hansen 127, 2–3; *Epit.* 451: ibid., 18–19; cf. *Synodicon Vetus* 108: Duffy-Parker 93, with n. 117. The synodical of 490 or 491 which was sent to Pope Felix is incorrectly combined with this synod of 492. On this Synod cf. Cyril of Scyth., *Vita Sabae*: Schwartz 140, 8–15; Theophan., *Chronogr.* A. M. 5984: De Boor 137, 11–13. On the bounds of competence of patriarch and synod see R. Potz, 'Patriarch und Synode in Konstantinopel. Das Verfassungsrecht des ökumenischen Patriarchats' = *Kirche und Recht* 10 (Wien 1971) 25–31.

[100] Theodore Lector, *HE*, frg. 45; *Epit.* 455 and 457: Hansen 128; A. Schönmetzer, *Chalkedon* II, Zeittafel nr. 251; R. Haacke, ibid., 128.

[101] Theodore Lector, *HE*, frg. 40; *Epit.* 447: Hansen 126; Theophan., *Chronogr.* A.M. 5987–5989: De Boor 139–140; John of Nikiu, *Chron.* 89, 46: Charles 126.

[102] E. Stein, *Histoire du Bas-Empire* II, 169; different in P. Charanis, *Church & State* 26.

[103] Theodore Lector, *Epit.* 442: Hansen 123, 18 ff.

[104] Grumel, *Regestes* I 1², nr. 178.

[105] Gelasius I, *ep. ad Euphem.*: JW 620; *Coll. Veron.* 12: Schwartz, PS 51, 16–24; Thiel I 315–316. For the self-justification of the Pope see PS 54, 12–30; Thiel I, 319.

[106] Grumel, *Regestes* I 1², nr. 179, p. 135.

[107] Cf. above, n. 95: Schwartz 55, 2–10; Thiel 320: he writes that the shepherd must not allow himself to be led on the false path by an errant flock. The Pope concludes with a reference to the judgment of God which awaits both of them in this matter.

In short, Patriarch Euphemius was a sincere professor of Chalcedon who with regard to the Emperor clearly rejected the *Henoticon*, but he was also a man who advised moderation. What distinguished his position from that of Rome was the troublesome question of the diptychs.[108] Whether a union between Euphemius and Rome would have been accepted and tolerated by the Emperor remains a moot point. For on the question of unity the latter's gaze was directed particularly to Alexandria.

Patriarch Macedonius of Constantinople (496–511)[109]—a man of compromise. It was hoped that the *Henoticon* would bring about peace. Instead a crisis ensued which, through the debate for and against, shook the Byzantine imperial Church most severely during the period of office of Patriarch Macedonius, the successor of Euphemius. The play of forces in this struggle was concentrated particularly on him, even if Patriarch Flavian of Antioch (498–512) and, to a lesser extent, Patriarch Elias of Jerusalem (494–516) entered the line of fire as well. The Emperor, the Pope, the monks, the people, but above all the two leaders of the anti-Chalcedonian movement who emerged at that time, Philoxenus of Mabbog and Severus (512–518 the patriarch of Antioch), all of these expected the bishop of Constantinople to conform to their line. During this period the spectrum of these lines would manifest variations that were more marked. Yet everything was to remain, insofar as the Eastern patriarchates were concerned, within the framework of an 'interpretation' of the *Henoticon*, even if this framework had already been sundered. We shall present a brief survey of the individual forces at play and the initiatives undertaken by each of them.

(c) The play of forces

(i) *Emperor Anastasius* ordered Patriarch Macedonius to subscribe the *Henoticon*, this no doubt being in connexion with his ordination.[110] He prevented Macedonius from sending Pope Anastasius II

---

[108] Thus with regard to Patriarch Euphemius the judgment of Theodore Lector, who cites John Diakrinomenos, is too severe when he writes without reservation concerning the stance of the patriarchs of the East: 'while all the patriarchs assented to Zeno's *Henoticon*, Felix of Rome alone did not condescend to assume communion'. Cf. *Epit.* 549: Hansen 155, 24–25.

[109] See Grumel, *Regestes* I 1², nr. 181–192, pp. 138–142; R. Janin, Art. 'Macedonius II', Bibl. SS 8 (Roma 1967) col. 442–444. M. Richard in: *Chalkedon* I, pp. 733/4.

[110] Theodore Lector, *Epit.* 456: Hansen 128, 21: καθυπέγραψεν; Theophan., *Chronogr.* A.M. 5988 and 6004: De Boor 140, 15–16; 154, 29–155, 24 (reprimanding); Nicephor. Call., *HE* XVI 26: PG 147, 165C–168A: he admits the fact, but speaks of a signature obtained by deceit; John of Nikiu, *Chron.* 89, §§46–47: Charles 126, says more strongly that Macedonius took Zeno's edict from the hand of the Emperor, expressed himself (openly) against the Council of Chalcedon, but in his heart thought otherwise. There is a variation in Zacharias Rh., *Vita Severi*: PO 2, 113: 'At the time of his consecration Macedonius promised to accept the *Henoticon* and to maintain communion with the bishops. Later, however, he spurned the significance of this document and refused to have communion with Egypt'. In the same way Flavian is said to have dealt with Antioch.

(496–498) *synodica* which in 497 the former wanted to transmit to Rome through Theodoric's ambassador, Festus, to have the Pope ratify Chalcedon.[111] On the other hand, Festus had given the Emperor hope that Anastasius II, who had reconciliation in mind, could easily be moved to accept the *Henoticon*. If this undertaking were indeed honestly intended, still it came to nothing at all on account of the sudden death of the Pope. Nevertheless there were certain indications that the Emperor and the Pope were drawing closer during this short pontificate.[112] The *Liber Pontificalis*[113] refers to the re-establishment of *communio* between the Pope and the deacon Photinus of Thessalonica who was Acacian-minded, as well as to the readiness of Rome to restore Acacius to the diptychs. In the eyes of the author of the *Liber Pontificalis* this was, of course, a break with the policy of Popes Felix III and Gelasius I. He especially reproached Anastasius II for not having agreed his plan with presbyters, bishops and clergy. The tensions which were present in Rome manifested themselves then also in the so-called Laurentian Schism (498. 501–505).

That Macedonius as well showed a certain readiness to accept the *Henoticon* may perhaps be taken from an account of a synod (*synodos endemousa*) of 497 (1) which is found in Theodore Lector. It is reported that at this synod the Patriarch condemned even the supporters of Chalcedon, and not only the defenders of Nestorius and Eutyches.[114] However, this can already be an 'interpretation' of a less suspicious state of affairs. For short accounts in Zacharias Rhetor let it be seen that for Macedonius the 'condemnation of Chalcedon' says nothing more than what is already contained more or less in the text of the *Henoticon*. In that case what is rejected is the introduction of a 'quaternity' in place of the 'Trinity', such as was seen to be present in the teaching of the two natures (see above, *Henoticon* §7). At this time the alleged execration of Chalcedon can still be understood as the usual monophysite interpretation of §9 of the Edict.[115]

(ii) The pro-Chalcedonian monks in and around Constantinople
About 499 the Emperor wanted the Patriarch to win over the pro-

---

[111] Theodore Lector, *Epit.* 461: Hansen 130 f.: Nicephor. Call., *HE* XVI 35: PG 147, 192 BC. Already in 496 a synodical letter had been sent to Patriarch Elias in Jerusalem; cf. Cyril of Scyth., *Vita Sabae* §50: Schwartz 140, 15–24; Festugière, *Les moines d'Orient* III/2, 66–67, a fact which 'confused the Emperor not a little. Thus there came to be concord (*homonoia*) between Macedonius and Elias, and after the death of Palladius with Flavian [of Antioch]'—a '*symphonia*' which in no way pleased Anastasius I, so that he was determined to proceed against it.
[112] Cf. Anastasius pp. II, *ep.* 1 *ad Anastas. imp.* from the year 496: JW 744 = Thiel 615–623; a short account in F. Hofmann, *Chalkedon* II, 66–67; cf. 66–70.
[113] *Liber Pontificalis* LII: Duchesne I 258–259.
[114] Theodore Lector, *HE*, frg. 46 (Victor Tunn.): Hansen 129. On this see the remarks in Grumel, *Regestes* I 1², p. 139, nr. 185.
[115] Cf. Zacharias Rh., *HE* VII 8: Brooks 2: CSCO 88, 28, 22–25; Hamilton-Brooks 170.

Chalcedonian monasteries of Constantinople and nearby Bithynia for the *henosis*. Whether Macedonius undertook this out of conviction or simply from outward obedience, in any case he came to feel the unconquerable opposition of the monks.[116] This made an impression on the Emperor, for he had a high opinion of monasticism.[117] With this tail-wind it was obviously the time for Macedonius to steer a more open pro-Chalcedonian course. Thus he was able to wrest from the Emperor his agreement to the summoning of a synod (*synodos endemousa*) at which the 'right decrees' of Chalcedon (τὰ ἐν Χαλκηδόνι καλῶς δογματισθέντα) were to be acknowledged in writing. This was also placed on record. However, with this emphasis on the 'right decrees' of Chalcedon is it perhaps insinuated that the Council also enacted 'wrong decrees'? It could not be in the interests of the see of Constantinople to annul the Fourth Council absolutely. That Macedonius had ulterior motives with regard to the manner or extent of Chalcedon appears, however, to be ruled out by the reaction of the monasteries of Dion, Bassianus, of the *acoimetoi* and of Matrona, all of which were for taking up *communio* with the Patriarch 'after they had cut themselves off on account of the *Henoticon* of Zeno'.[118] If one may let these reports and their interpretation stand, then at this time the pro-Chalcedonian stance of Macedonius was externally at its apex. The *acoimetoi* were his friends; that says a great deal. Indeed, at this time the Patriarch could venture to stipulate conditions to the Emperor for the recognition of John of Nikiu as patriarch of Alexandria (506–516) after the death of John Hemula (+505) and for the assumption of communion with him; the *quid pro quo* was the recognition of Chalcedon as 'mother and teacher'.[119] With this recognition was it that the *Henoticon* was eliminated, or did it only make clear that the *Henoticon* could also be interpreted in 'pro-Chalcedonian way'? Neither of these two positions was in the minds of those men who would become of decisive importance

---

[116] Theodore Lector, *Epit.* 459: Hansen 129; Theophan., *Chronogr.* A.M. 5991: De Boor 141, 19–21.

[117] He receives from Cyril of Scyth., *Vita Sabae* 51: Schwartz 142, 20; Festugière, *Les moines d'Orient* III/2, 69, 3–4, the epithet *'philomonachos'*. Festugière: 'De fait, il aimait les moines, même s'il avait été poussé par quelques scélérates à lutter contre la foi orthodoxe'. See too the Anonymous, *Vita Danielis Stylitae*, c. 43 (written about 493): Festugière, op. cit., 157–158 n. 22 ff.; Dawes and Baynes 64. In one of Daniel's visions Emperor Anastasius is described as 'a man who loved Christ' and a man who 'would surpass all those who had reigned at any time'. 'Throughout his reign he will grant peace and confidence to the holy Churches and to the order (*tagma*) of monks'. It is said that all of these predictions were fulfilled after his election. Cf. also c. 44 (the Emperor's donations after Daniel's death).

[118] Theodore Lector, *Epit.* 459: Hansen 129, 15–20; Theophan., *Chronogr.* A.M. 5991: De Boor 141, 19–142, 5.

[119] Theodore Lector, *Epit.* 477: Hansen 136, 17–20. Cf. Zacharias Rh., *Vita Severi*: PO 2, 113 (for the text see n. 110 above). John of Nikiu went further in interpreting the *Henoticon* in an anti-Chalcedonian sense than his predecessors Athanasius (490–497) and John Hemula (497–505) had done.

for Macedonius from this time on. In order to judge the theological value of the dispute that was about to flare up, one has to ask oneself quietly each time whether the text of the *Henoticon* is really being discussed and interpreted, or whether each of the parties that were being formed imposes its own preconceived reading or position, so that on that account the Edict of Zeno could really be forgotten.

(iii) The anti-Chalcedonian activity in Constantinople and Antioch of *Bishop Philoxenus of Mabbog*, and *Severus*, the subsequent patriarch of Antioch.

The scope for a pro-Chalcedonian restoration in Constantinople was palpably restricted by the time of the second journey of Bishop Philoxenus of Mabbog, whose christology we shall have to present in detail later. Here we are concerned only with his position on the *Henoticon*. When he made his first journey to Constantinople (either in the spring or summer of 484), the two originators of the *Henoticon*, Emperor Zeno and Patriarch Acacius, were still living, and he was certain of a good reception from them. The second journey was undertaken in 507[120] at the invitation of the Emperor, but it did not meet with the approval of Patriarch Macedonius. The latter refused *communio* to the opponent of Chalcedon. Indeed, such a protest erupted among the monks and the people that Anastasius I was forced to send Philoxenus home finally in secret. In 508, however, came the monk Severus who was able to keep a low profile for many years, and as compensation brought down Patriarch Macedonius. We shall arrange our presentation of the anti-Chalcedonian interpretation of the *Henoticon*, in the formation of which Philoxenus and Severus played leading rôles, by looking in turn at four synods and a new important document of this period, the so-called *Typus* of Emperor Anastasius. In the latter, according to the intention of its author, the monk-presbyter Severus, the *Henoticon* was to be allowed only a wholly general function in bringing about union; Chalcedon would to all intents and purposes be liquidated, and the Cyrillian, pre-Chalcedonian tradition—in its Severan interpretation—adorned with the imperial seal. The four synods are: Constantinople (507), Antioch (509), Sidon (511) and Antioch (513) (a synod allegedly summoned

---

[120] On the journeys of Philoxenus to Constantinople see A. de Halleux, *Philoxène* 60–63, against Honigmann, *Evêques et évêchés* 7, n. 8–14, who postulates five journeys: 482 or 484 and 507, which is tenable, but in addition 508–509 (before the Synod of Antioch), 511 (in connexion with the 'typus' of the Emperor), the end of 511 to Nov. 512 to take legal action against Flavian of Antioch. A. de Halleux, however, refers to the letter to the monks of Senoun (521), in which Philoxenus speaks expressly of his two journeys to the Imperial City: CSCO 232 (V), p. 79, 7–9 with further list of sources in n. 8, viz. Theophan., *Chronogr.* A.M. 5999: De Boor 150, 4–8; Zacharias Rh. cont., *HE* VII 8 (letter of the presbyter Simeon): Brooks 2: CSCO 88, 28–33; Hamilton-Brooks 170–176.

in Tyre in 513 or 514–5 we can exclude); the document referred to, the *Typus*, is to be situated between the Synods of Antioch (509) and Sidon (511). This chronological sequence will be the order of our exposition.

(1) *Constantinople (507)*

On the suggestion of Philoxenus Emperor Anastasius I ordered that a synod (*synodos endemousa*) be summoned by Patriarch Macedonius. We are correct in relegating an event which Victor of Tunnuna recorded for 499 to 507.[121] Whether the Bishop of Mabbog himself still took part in it cannot be clearly established. In any case a confession of faith was read out in his name before the assembly,[122] as, according to the continuator of Zacharias Rhetor, the presbyter Symeon reported in a letter. Together with the report of Victor of Tunnuna, from this there emerges a uniform picture: the same *names* are condemned, viz. Diodore of Tarsus, Theodore of Mopsuestia, Nestorius (omitted by Victor of Tunnuna), Theodoret, Ibas of Edessa, Andrew of Samosata, John of Aigai, Eutherius of Tyana (Victor of Tunnuna: Eucherius). Their *fault* is: preparing for (setting up) the Council of Chalcedon, accepting Leo's Tome, dividing the unity of the Word Incarnate into two natures (and into two forms, i.e. splitting or apportioning the properties, as Victor and Zacharias say, supplementing each other), refusing the formula 'one of the Trinity was crucified' (Victor of Tunnuna). All this was to be understood as interpreting the *Henoticon*, as Zacharias Rhetor explicitly says. In short, it was a question of condemning the whole Antiochene and Leonine tradition[123] as this had passed into Chalcedon, even if it were in no way the sole determining tradition. The response of Patriarch Macedonius is summed up as follows: 'When Macedonius was required to do this, he anathematised them [the names (?)] under compulsion; but after that he used secretly to celebrate their memory in the monastery of Dalmatus, as has been written above'.[124] Whether an explicit execration of Chalcedon and the names cited was put on record at

---

[121] Theodore Lector, *HE*, frg. 54: Hansen 135. With Tillemont and Assemani, A. de Halleux, *Philoxène* 62 f. claims that the synod of 499 took place in 507. Reports of this Synod are found in Michael Syr., *Chron.* IX 8: Chabot II 160 and Barhebraeus, *Chron. Eccles.* I 41: Abbeloos-Lamy I, col. 187–188.

[122] Zacharias Rh. cont., *HE* VII 8: Brooks 2: CSCO 88, 33, 2–18; Hamilton-Brooks 176–177. De Halleux takes the word *synkletos* (= senate) to mean '*synodos endemousa*'. Is Philoxenos' confession of faith in 507, which is mentioned in the text, identical with that which he had submitted to Emperor Zeno (Vaschalde, *Three Letters*, Letter C: pp. 90–92 (analysis); 118–126 (V), 163–173 (Syr.); de Halleux, op. cit. 171–173)? Presumably it is only the repetition of the *event* of reading out a credo.

[123] Zacharias Rh. cont., *HE* VII 8: Brooks 2: CSCO 88, 33, 3–18; Hamilton-Brooks 176–177.

[124] Letter of the presbyter Symeon etc. in Zacharias Rh. cont., *HE* VII 8: Brooks 2: CSCO 88, 33, 16–18; Hamilton-Brooks 177.

the Synod is not clear from the text. Presumably this is an interpretation of the letter-writer, because Emperor Anastasius would hardly have permitted a direct condemnation of the Fourth Council.

(2) Antioch (509) under Patriarch Flavian II (498–512)

The object of attack that was closer to Philoxenus was the patriarch of Antioch at that time, Flavian II. His overthrow was resolutely striven for. But this could be effected only with the help of the Emperor. In this process there emerged new variations in the relationship between Chalcedon and the Henoticon. Through the metropolitan Constantine of Seleucia (Isauria), the Metropolitan of Mabbog had success in having a rejection of Chalcedon demanded from Flavian of Antioch and Elias of Jerusalem.[125] Yet at the same time the activity of the monk-priest Severus in Constantinople should not be forgotten.

In 509 one of the two synods which it was the custom to hold each year was devoted to the question just referred to. Philoxenus was present. We possess two reports about this: one from Palestinian monks, written for the metropolitan Alcison in Illyria,[126] and the other from Philoxenus himself, this being addressed to (the) monks in Palestine.[127] From these reports important shades of difference in the Henoticon question emerge.[128]

Patriarch Flavian accepted the Henoticon as ratification of Cyril's twelve anathemas—this also corresponds to the text of the Henoticon itself (see the text §6)—, but not as a rejection of Chalcedon. Taking into account the Fathers who could be cited as witnesses for the formula of the 'two natures' in Christ, the Patriarch refused simply to condemn the 'diphysites'. He believed that it was only in this

---

[125] Following Theophan., Chronogr. A.M. 6001: De Boor 151, 19–21.

[126] Letter of the Palestinian monks to Alcison: Evagrius, HE III 31: Bidez-Parmentier 127–129; tr. Festugière, Byz 45 (1975) 337–341; P. Allen, Evagrius Scholasticus 147–149; Theophan., Chronogr., A.M. 6001: De Boor 151, 27–31. According to the letter of the monks to Alcison, Philoxenus prevented the imminent collapse of the anti-Chalcedonian party. Cf. Evagrius, HE III 31, p. 127, 18–26. On the basis of this letter three phases in Philoxenus' anti-Chalcedonianism are to be distinguished, with each of which an extension of the persons or groups to be anathematised runs parallel. See on this A. de Halleux, Philoxène 85–88. 1. At first Philoxenus contents himself with the demand that Nestorius be condemned. 2. Because his opponent, Flavian of Antioch, meets this demand, Philoxenus extends his range. The following persons are to be condemned: Diodore of Tarsus, Theodore of Mopsuestia, the entire party of Orientals at the Council of Ephesus (431), thus Theodoret, Eutherius of Tyana, Ibas of Edessa, Andreas of Samosata, Alexander of Hierapolis (Mabbog), Irenaeus of Tyre, Cyrus of Hierapolis, John of Antioch, Acacius of Seleucia, Barsauma of Nisibis. Cf. Evagrius, HE III 31: Bidez-Parmentier 127, 28–31; Philoxenus, ep. ad monachos Palaest. II: Mus 75 (1962) 41 (V); idem, Catalogus haeresium in Budge II, p. CXXXVI s.; idem, ep. ad omnes monachos orthodox. Orientis, frg. 2: ed. and tr. J. Lebon, Mus 43 (1930) 207 (T), 218 (V). 3. In the final phase Philoxenus demands the condemnation of Chalcedon itself, as well as Leo's Tome and the two-natures teaching in general, this being fundamentally his goal all along. Cf. Evagrius, HE III 31: Bidez-Parmentier 128, 18–129, 4; cf. Philoxenus, Letter to the monks of Senoun: CSCO 232 (V), pp. 13,14–14,23.

[127] Philoxenus of Mabbog, Letter to the monks of Palestine, Syriac with French tr. ed. by A. de Halleux, 'Nouveaux textes inédits de Philoxène de Mabbog I': Mus 75 (1962) 31–62; to be added to this is a fragment from the 'Lettre liminaire' from the synodicon of Ephesus: ibid., 39 (V 45).

[128] See A. de Halleux, Mus 75 (1962) 53.

way that he could counteract the 'phantasy teaching', i.e. the docetism of Eutyches. From the letter of Philoxenus, however, one can detect above all initial moves towards a new christological synthesis in Flavian's position; we shall be concerned with these later under the heading 'Neo-Chalcedonianism'. The point at issue was to emphasise the connexion between Chalcedonian-Antiochene and Alexandrian-Cyrillian christology and terminology. Certainly the following were 'condemned': naturally Nestorius with his teaching, but as well all those who divide Christ into (two) *prosopa*, *hypostases*, sons, lords. Above all there were 'positive' concessions: recognition of Cyril's anathemas, acceptance of the *Henoticon* as well as of catch-phrases and formulas which were so important for the old Alexandrian theology, such as *theotokos* (in the meantime, however, generally accepted), 'the God-Logos became body and flesh' and the more recent formula 'one of the Trinity . . .'. Indeed, the synodal letter contained, in addition to its confession of Christ as the 'one *prosopon* and the one *hypostasis*', also the controversial basic formula of the Cyrillians—'the one incarnate nature of the God-Logos'.[129]

This interpretation of the *Henoticon* clearly went beyond the literal sense of the text and made great concessions to the party of Philoxenus. Nevertheless, he was not yet satisfied with what he had achieved. He missed the *explicit* condemnation of the 'two natures' and found in Flavian's acceptance of the *Henoticon* a crafty interpretation of the document itself. It is worthwhile citing his words:

[III] Again he [Flavian] professes that he, with us, accepts the document called 'Henoticon'; [but if] we adhere to it, then it is for the sole reason that [this document] has anathematised and rejected the addition introduced at Chalcedon against the faith of the Fathers; whereas [the Patriarch, though] saying he approves this document, has not consented to reject the innovation which gave rise to it [the Edict], but has written openly in his letters [= his synodal letter] that it was composed as a ratification of the chapters of blessed Cyril. [Thus] there where he ought to have shown that he holds the [chapters] as true, by anathematising and rejecting what the heretics have written against them, he did not consent to do it; [but] touching on a document [produced] for the purpose of suppressing the innovation which was brutally [or maliciously: see the Syriac text] introduced into the faith, he devised [the ploy] of saying that [this document] was composed to ratify the [twelve] chapters.[130]

From these words it emerges that for Philoxenus the *Henoticon* had only one function, viz. to discredit the 'two natures' as an *additio*. He was not interested in the positive content of it which was meant as a basis for union. That being his attitude he came nowhere near the intention of the Edict, and in the same way also contradicted the moderate interpretation which Emperor Anastasius gave to this document.[131] Admittedly, it was not Philoxenus himself, but his sup-

---

[129] Ibid., p. 36, 88–91 (Syr.); French §IV, p. 42.

[130] Philoxenus, *Letter to the monks of Palestine*: Mus 75 (1962) pp. 35,76–36,98 (Syr.); French §III, p. 42.

[131] See the important comments on Emperor Anastasius in A. de Halleux, *Philoxène* 51–52, with n. 14: the Syrian monophysites enjoyed the Emperor's good pleasure only as long as they supported his moderate *Henoticon* policy. The cleverness of the Syrians consisted in the fact that they made this *charta unionis* the instrument of their theological aggression and, in doing so, averred that they were working towards nothing else than its 'sincere' acceptance.

porters, who here advocated an absolute rigorism. Philoxenus wanted to hold on to the *Henoticon* and found monophysite christology expressed in it. For peace among the Churches his supporters demanded the anathema against Chalcedon and the admission of monophysite formulas exclusively. They became the counterpart of the Alexandrian 'acephalists'. During the patriarchate of Severus (512–518) this radical wing of the Isaurian supporters of Philoxenus separated themselves from him.[132] (On the name 'acephalists' for these rigorists, see note 77.)

(3) The *Typus* of Emperor Anastasius (between Antioch [509]) and Sidon [511])

From 509 there was a more powerful opponent of Chalcedon than Philoxenus in Constantinople: Severus, the monk and presbyter from the school of Peter the Iberian in Palestine. The monk quickly became the real leader of the anti-Chalcedonian movement and its theology. He came from a Christian family in Sozopolis in Pisidia. Through his studies of Greek and Latin grammar and rhetoric at Alexandria and of law at Berytus (Beirut), he laid the foundations for his later importance as a theologian of the movement which was directed against the Fourth Council.[133] It was only in 488 that he was baptised. Through friends he was made aware of Peter the Iberian (+1.12.491), who in 490 came in person to Berytus. But it was only in 494, under the influence of Evagrius of Samosata, on a pilgrimage to Jerusalem, that the highly educated man decided to become a monk. He betook himself to the monastery of Theodore, the successor of Peter the Iberian, which lay between Gaza and Maiuma, spent some time in

---

[132] Cf. A. de Halleux, *Philoxène* 53, with n. 22; 87. There was disagreement between Severus and Philoxenus. The former was of the opinion that the *Henoticon* was undoubtedly sufficient to bring about the *general* reunion of the Church; for one's own *personal* confession one must not be content with it. The latter emphasised that the edict 'lacked nothing' and he did not want to take over the rigorism of the Isaurians, which was again something that Severus did not sanction. See the letter to the Alexandrian presbyters: PO 12, 297. The difference, however, is not great. Philoxenus too was convinced of the necessity of condemning explicitly the following: (*a*) Chalcedon (*b*) the Tome of Leo (*c*) the diophysites. Philoxenus championed this already at the Synod of Antioch (513): cf. the letter to the presbyter Simeon of Tele'adā, frg. 4: Lebon, 'Textes inédits de Philoxène de Mabboug', *Mus* 43 (1930) 181 (Syr.); 192, 14–19 (V): *satis autem nobis fuit quoad totam rem quod nobiscum subscriberent depositioni Flaviani et anathematizarent sicut nos synodum atque Tomum, et nobiscum sincere, non autem dolose ut Flavianus et Macedonius etiam scriptum Henoticon reciperent, quemadmodum synodus quoque dioeceseos Aegypti illud recipit magnaque ecclesia Alexandriae.* Cf. also Severus, *Letter to Hippocrates*: PO 12, n. 46, p. 321. Philoxenus has this attitude even under Emperor Justin; cf. the letter to all monks of the Orient, frg. 6, de Halleux, *Mus* 76 (1963) 8–9; similarly the letter to the monks of Senoun: CSCO 231–232, 95 (79, 5–6). The disagreement between Philoxenus and Severus arises only with regard to whether one must see the condemnation of Chalcedon's two-natures teaching already implied in the *Henoticon* or not (cf. A. de Halleux, *Philoxène* 88).

[133] On the studies of Severus see Zacharias, *Vita Severi*: PO 2, 46–47; Brooks, SL II 1 (1903), Introduction V–XI; Lebon, *Le monophysisme sévérien* (1909) 118–175 (polemical writing); Schwartz, PS 238–244; idem, 'Johannes Rufus, ein monophysitischer Schriftsteller': *SBHeidAkW* 16 (1912) 6–7.

the desert of Eleutheropolis and then found acceptance in the monastery of Romanus which was located there. In the neighbourhood of Maiuma he founded his own monastery. At this time he also combined with his asceticism further study, which meant particularly canonical law and the writings of Cyril of Alexandria. He was ordained priest by Epiphanius of Perge in Pamphylia, who for a time had been bishop of Magydon but, because he supported the Encyclical of Basiliscus under Emperor Zeno, had had to leave his diocese, and who then joined the circle of Peter the Iberian.[134] As he had the necessary qualities, things augured well for activity at the imperial court. The opportunity for this came through the persecution and expulsion of the monks from monasteries around Maiuma; this persecution and expulsion was instigated by the monk Nephalius and ordered by Patriarch Elias of Jerusalem (508).[135] Severus was the ideal man, as *apocrisiarius* of the monks, to present their case to Emperor Anastasius in the imperial capital.[136] A huge crowd of monks accompanied him.

At this time the question whether the *Henoticon* would become more the instrument of the anti-Chalcedonian cause than that of the pro-Chalcedonians was still undecided. Indeed, it seemed that the second alternative was gaining ground as a result of the bond between the three patriarchs, Macedonius II of Constantinople, Flavian II of Antioch and Elias of Jerusalem.[137] In this context the aim of Severus and his friends had to be to check, with the assistance of the Emperor, the persecutions in Palestine, but even more to establish the unity of the Churches in the East on the basis of an anti-Chalcedonian interpretation of the *Henoticon*. The first aim was quickly fulfilled by the Emperor. The dispossessed monks received back their monastery. The monks returning to their monasteries received a 'doctrinal letter',[138] addressed to the archimandrites of the persecuted, in which recourse is had to the pre-Chalcedonian, Cyrillian formula 'from two natures', but the exhortation was also given to bear in mind the peace of the Churches. This refers to the Emperor's desire to make the *Henoticon* the guiding rule in the re-established monasteries.

---

[134] The opponents of Severus seek to contest his consecration as being uncanonical. Cf. Severus, SL I 1, *Letter to Bishop Constantine*: Brooks II, 7–8 (V); Honigmann, *Évêques et évêchés* 132–133.

[135] Zacharias Rh., *Vita Severi*: PO 2, 103, 10–14; Evagrius, *HE* III 33: Bidez-Parmentier 132; Schwartz, *Kyrillos von Skythopolis* 377–378; Perrone, *La chiesa di Palestina* 149–151.

[136] Zacharias Rh., *Vita Severi*: PO 2, 103–109; L. Perrone, op. cit., 151–173. Theodore, the successor of Peter the Iberian, also came to Constantinople: PO 2, 107, 1–2.

[137] On the critical situation of the anti-Chalcedonians at this time see Evagrius, *HE* III 31: Bidez-Parmentier 127, 18–23; Severus, *ep.* 38 to Peter and Ammonius..., PO 12, nr. 38, pp. 294–295. Severus admits for this period (513–516): 'we, the few in number and small'. See L. Perrone, op. cit., 152, n. 22.

[138] Zacharias Rh., *Vita Severi*: PO 2, 105, 6–10.

With the help of powerful patrons in the capital and of like-minded local monks who had journeyed there, Severus resolutely built up opposition against Macedonius, Flavian and Elias.[139] With regard to the Patriarch of Antioch, however, he showed, in contrast to Philoxenus, a certain moderation. A special instrument in this attack was to be a text which is called the *Typus* of Emperor Anastasius, but which was composed by Severus on the instruction of the Emperor.[140] The text as a whole is lost; it is preserved only in two Armenian extracts, one in the 'Book of Letters' and the other in the 'Seal of Faith'. J. Lebon[141] drew the attention of scholars to these fragments and made a Latin translation of them. His student, C. Moeller, has published and interpreted the shorter version (following the text of the 'Seal of Faith').[142] We shall give an English translation of this, but recourse must be had to the scholarly apparatus of Moeller.

From the letter of Emperor Anastasius against all schismatics, written after the forty-first year of the Council of Chalcedon:[143] 'We accept only one definition of faith, that of the 318 Fathers who gathered at Nicaea, which shows that one of the holy Trinity is our Lord Jesus Christ, the Word of God, which assumed flesh from the holy *theotokos* and virgin Mary and became man. That definition was maintained by the 150 holy Fathers who gathered at Constantinople through the Holy Spirit. According to that also the holy synod of those who gathered at Ephesus and anathematised the schismatic Nestorius and all those who think and believe as he did, as also does the letter which is called the Henoticon of Zeno, the orthodox Emperor, and as well the letter of John [of Nikiu (510–516)], the archbishop of Alexandria,[144] which shows [these things] in the same way in which it anathematises Leo's Tome and those who transgress that definition [of Nicaea] and defined two natures after the union for the one Christ.

We, as we have received from the holy Fathers, do not say two natures, but we confess the Word of God as one nature become flesh, and we anathematise the Synod of Chalcedon and with it also Leo and his Tome and those who say Christ is two sons, one before the ages and the other at the end of the ages. But those who say, after professing the unity, [that there are] two natures, and two persons and two forms and two properties, and [that] the distinguishing characteristics also are the work of each of the two natures, we reject and anathematise, because [this] is found to be contrary to the twelve chapters of blessed Cyril.[145]

---

[139] Zacharias Rh., *Vita Severi*: PO 2, 107, 12–108, 7 (Flavian and Elias); 109, 14–110, 13 (Macedonius).

[140] See Severus, *Letter to Bishop Constantine*: SL I 1, Brooks II, 3–4 (V).

[141] See J. Lebon, 'Les citations patristiques dans le Sceau de la Foi', *RHE* 25 (1929) 5–32; *Le sceau de la foi*, ed. K. Ter-Mekerttschian (Etschmiadzin 1914) 128; *Le livre des Lettres*, ed. J. Ismireantz, Bibl. Sahag Mesrobienne 5 (Tiflis 1901) 277–278.

[142] Ch. Moeller, 'Un fragment du Type de l'empereur Anastase I', *StudPat* III 1 = TU 78 (1961) 240–247. Text on p. 242 from the 'Seal of Faith' in the Latin translation of J. Lebon, collated with the text from the 'Book of the Letters', p. 243.

[143] This date (= 492) is incorrect.

[144] In the longer recension of the 'Book of the Letters' John of Nikiu is already characterised as 'blessed'. Hence this recension is posterior to the text-form in the 'Seal of Faith'.

[145] See the continuation of the text of the 'Book of the Letters' in Moeller, op. cit., 242 f., n. 3.

This *Typus* of Emperor Anastasius must not be placed on the same level as the Encyclical of the usurper Basiliscus and the Edict of Zeno. It is rather to be regarded as an expert opinion requested by the Emperor of a theologian, precisely the priest-monk Severus, which would be useful for the interpretation of the *Henoticon*. Through this the *Henoticon* was to be more acceptable for all the Churches. At the Synod of Sidon (511), with which we shall become more closely acquainted shortly, the redactor of the document spoke of it as a 'profession de foi individuelle' (see below). In contrast the *Henoticon* was regarded also by him as an official document, indeed of an 'ecumenical' character, but still only on the smallest possible common basis.[146] In the mind of the Emperor the expert opinion that he desired was not to exceed, as far as content was concerned, the framework of the *Henoticon*, especially not in the direction of a condemnation of Chalcedon. He had no doubt feared something like this. For this reason he sent the zealous monk to the *magister militum*, Patricius, for the purpose of meeting there Bishop John of Claudiopolis in Isauria, as Severus himself reports in a letter.[147] Apparently the *Typus*, 'the formula of satisfaction', had already been composed before this meeting. The Isaurian bishop then tried to introduce a compromise proposal as a 'statement' into the *Typus*, but according to Severus this was equivalent to emptying the *Typus* of meaning. The proposal—made in the sense of Flavian of Antioch—was to make a partial acceptance of Chalcedon possible, this being negative in character, viz. the rejection of Nestorius and Eutyches; at the same time the terminological and conceptual innovation of the Council was to be bracketed and got around:

> ... 'We receive the synod at Chalcedon, not as a definition of faith, but as a rejection of Nestorius and of Eutyches'. Thus both those that are pleased with the Synod will not be angry, and you [Severus and his supporters] will receive contentment in that the doctrines which offend you are rejected.[148]

The attempt foundered on the resoluteness of Severus who discovered a logical contradiction in it—though only on the basis of his presuppositions:

> If the Synod of Chalcedon introduced the doctrine of Nestorius into the churches ... how can we say that it rejected the opinion of Nestorius? But, if the formula of satisfaction [= the *Typus*] in so many words rejects the doctrines of the Synod

---

[146] See the letter of Severus to Bishop Constantine below.
[147] Severus, *Letter to Bishop Constantine*: SL I 1, Brooks II 4–5. In the letter rather long portions of the dialogue between Severus and John of Claudiopolis are cited, and for that reason the letter is to be considered an important source in evaluating the '*typus*'.
[148] Severus, op. cit., 5, 1–6; cf. Zacharias Rh. cont., IX 20 ad fin., from the letter of Severus from the year 536 to the Oriental Presbyters and monks: Brooks 2: CSCO 88, 95–96; Hamilton-Brooks 268–270.

and the impious Tome of Leo, which are the life blood of the abomination of Nestorius, how can we honestly say that we accept this synod as against Nestorius?[149]

In the eyes of Severus Chalcedon is essentially 'Nestorianism'. Thus there is no division in the acceptance or rejection of the Synod respectively. Severus viewed the defenders of Chalcedon fundamentally as people who wanted to drive out the devil of Eutychianism with the Beelzebul of Nestorianism. This identification of Chalcedon and Nestorianism was really so clear that the concession that Severus went on to make no longer had a sound foundation. He discovered in the supporters of the Fourth Council after all 'a certain part of the sound faith' (probably the rejection of Eutyches is meant). But according to him they mixed this remnant of orthodoxy with the vanity of their profane, impious words and seduced so many (pp. 6–7). Even the Encyclical of Basiliscus 'repudiated the impiety that was confirmed at Chalcedon' (p. 7).

During his mission in Constantinople Severus was, according to Zacharias Rhetor, the focus of the whole struggle about the unity of the catholic Church, for the major figures of the capital as well as for bishops and monks who journeyed there. He won over the Isaurian bishops who were denounced as dissidents (acephaloi). He and his Palestinian companions were successful, according to his biographer, in leading radical monks from Antioch, who took pleasure in appalling excommunications and thus were an obstacle to the union of the Churches, from the low level of the assurances (plerophoriai) of Flavian to the height of his teaching. He was able to move the radicals to moderation, without thereby deviating from the right doctrine. In this way every reason the bishops who were put off by the extremists had for refusing the union was removed.[150] This important paragraph in his biography closes with the comment:

and he requested the Emperor to ordain that the union take place in this way. Flavian of Antioch and Elias of Jerusalem, as also certain [other] opponents of these things, did not want to obey him and caused great troubles for themselves and the people.[151]

It is to be taken from this statement that according to the opinion of Severus the Typus was more suitable for the establishment of unity than the Henoticon was. But whether this can be said of the text of the extant Armenian fragments is questionable. However much the extant fragmentary version corresponds to the personal wishes of the monk, still it would no doubt have been too strong for the

[149] Severus; SL I 1, Brooks II 5, ll. 10–19. Even the condemnation of Eutyches rests on the Nestorianism of Chalcedon.
[150] Zacharias Rh., Vita Severi: PO 2, 106–108.
[151] Zacharias Rh., ibid., 108.

Emperor, at least in the period between 508 and 511. Rather a chronological setting between 512 and 518 (the patriarchate of Severus)
would suggest itself.[152] For the years of his sojourn in Constantinople
one can concur with the judgement of A. de Halleux:

> The whole cleverness of the future Patriarch of Antioch thus consisted in clothing
> a text that was really and profoundly anti-Chalcedonian in a formulation that was
> mollifying.[153]

Severus could credit himself with a first manifest success. On 20
July, 511, he was able to confront Patriarch Macedonius II before
a tribunal appointed by the Emperor himself in a disputation about
the 'doctrines'. There he was certainly able to employ all his education
as a rhetorician, lawyer and theologian. Whether this disputation
was formally about the text of the *Typus* is hard to clarify on the
basis of the extant reports. But there is no doubt that with respect
to the matter of the disputation the whole anti-Chalcedonian line
concerning the *Henoticon*, the *Typus* and the Council of 451 was
unfolded.[154] Macedonius was not able to be successful against Severus.
He overtly approved the 'dogmata' of his opponent, whether by
this word the text or a form of the text of the *Typus* is meant or
not.[155] The agitation among the Chalcedonian monks of the capital
was so great that at Bēth Dalmata Macedonius retracted immediately
the concessions he had made to Severus (probably as early as 21
July, 511).[156] The monks of the monastery resumed *communio* with
him. The disfavour of the Emperor was revealed, however, on 22
July at the Feast of Dedication in the *martyrium* at Hebdomon, when
the Emperor and Empress did not accept gifts from him, but rather
hard words were to be heard from the Emperor. On Sunday, 24
July, the monks of Bēth Dalmata stuck by him, to the chagrin of
the Emperor. On Monday, 25 July, followed the response of the
monks opposed to him. They handed over to the *magister militum*,
Patricius, a document for the Emperor in which the patriarch was
accused of having commemorated Nestorius. On 27 July, the
Emperor called a secret council at which he announced to the
patricians the Patriarch's retraction at Bēth Dalmata. The patrician

---

[152] A. de Halleux, *Philoxène* 68, n. 32.
[153] A. de Halleux, ibid., 69, with reference to Liberatus, *Breviar.*: ACO II 5, p. 133, where
it is said that for Severus union was to occur on the basis of the condemnation of Chalcedon.
Later this will be more nuanced (see below).
[154] Zacharias Rh., *Vita Severi*: PO 2, 109, 14–16.
[155] See Schwartz, PS 243: *Chalkedon* II, 131, 281.
[156] See Theodore Lector, *Epit.* 488: Hansen 139, 1–5; Zacharias Rh. cont., *HE* VII 8: Brooks
2: CSCO 88, 29, 16–19; Hamilton–Brooks 171–172; Ahrens–Krüger 122–123, with an accurate chronology of the course of events.

ize.

Clementinus cried out before all: 'May God Himself cast him out from his priesthood who has lied unto God'.[157]

With this the cue was given. On 6 August, Macedonius was deposed and on 7 August was led away into exile in Euchaita.[158] His successor was Patriarch Timothy I (511–518).

(4) *The Synod of Sidon* (October 511)[159]

Once again the *Henoticon* was the centre of interest when Emperor Anastasius summoned a synod at Sidon. The Edict of Zeno was to prove its ecumenical function, i.e. its ability to unite all the Churches in accordance with the will of the Emperor by bringing together the Eastern patriarchs of that time, viz. Timothy of Constantinople, Flavian of Antioch, Elias of Jerusalem and John of Nikiu from Alexandria. Philoxenus wanted, however, to achieve more[160] than the Emperor wished. The latter had complained in a letter to John of Nikiu (patriarch of Alexandria 505–516) that he (John) was not satisfied with the *Henoticon* alone, as were his predecessors Peter Mongus (482–490), Athanasius II (490–497) and John II Hemula (497–505), but demanded 'that reference be made in actual words to the impious things done at Chalcedon or to the impious Tome of Leo'.[161] Behind this moderate warning of the Emperor stood, according to Severus, the *apocrisiarii* of Alexandria in Constantinople, Dioscorus and

---

[157] Zacharias Rh. cont., *HE* VII 8: Brooks 2: CSCO 88, 29, 20–22; Hamilton-Brooks 172.
[158] Ibid.: Brooks 2: CSCO 88, 32, 19–20; Hamilton-Brooks 176. According to Brooks 2: CSCO 88, 31, 11–29; Hamilton-Brooks 174, 12–16, the Emperor had arrested the 'Nestorians' who confessed 'that they had some forged books of this heresy'. It is a question of an 'ornamental' book which Macedonius had, allegedly with extracts from 'Fathers' who had taught two natures *after* the incarnation. This book was a florilegium of Diodorus, Theodore of Mopsuestia and the five books of Theodoret against Cyril, thus from the famous Antiochenes. Cf. on this M. Richard, 'Les florilèges diphysites du Ve et du VIe siècle', *Chalkedon* I, 721–748 (= *Opera Minora* I, 3), esp. 729–736 (florilegia from the time of the *Henoticon*). The Emperor ordered the book to be burnt. From this there arose a story that the Emperor ordered that the original of the *acta* of Chalcedon be taken from the Patriarch shortly before his banishment. See Schwartz, PS 243 f., n. 3, with reference to Theodore Lector in the edition of Hansen, 139 (*Epit.* 491) with apparatus.; Marcellinus Comes, *Chron.* ad a. 511: Mommsen II, 97. The *Chronicle* of Edessa LXXXIII: L. Haller, TU IX, 1 (Leipzig 1903) 121–122 knows even of the opening of the sarcophagus of Euphemia the martyr in which the *acta* of Chalcedon were said to have been placed. But fire which leapt forth prevented the attempt to take them out and burn them.
[159] See 1. Marcellinus Comes, *Chronicon*: Mommsen, 98 §8, ad a. 512: *Porro redintegrata Anastasius pravitate infamem et irridendam synodum apud Sidonem civitatem, cuius de nomine in ridiculis nomina praeponuntur, octoginta ferme perfidorum episcopis congregatis* [a number which is certainly wrong] *adversum orthodoxorum episcopos fieri imperavit.* 2. Philoxenus, *Letter to the Presbyter Simeon of Tele'ada*: Lebon, 'Textes inédits' frg. 4, *Mus* 43 (1930) 179–180 (T), 190 (V), ll. 19–20:. *Et nos decem ex omnibus Orientis illi* [sc. Flaviano] *adversati sumus Sidone.* On the date: Honigmann, *Évêques et évêchés* 12; Duchesne, *VI siècle* 27–28; Devreesse, *Antioche* 68; de Halleux, *Philoxène* 70 are in favour of 511. Lebon, *Le monophysisme sévérien* 51; 'Christologie' 426, n. 3; Bury, *Later Empire* I, 450, n. 5; Bardy, 'Anastase' 313; Tisserant, 'Philoxène', *DTC* 12 (1935) (1509–1532) 1514 are in favour of 512.
[160] Cf. Zacharias Rh. cont., *HE* VII 11: Brooks 2: CSCO 88, 36–37; Hamilton-Brooks 181–183: petition of the Oriental monks and of Cosmas of Qennešrīn.
[161] Severus, *Letter to Ammon* (513–516 AD), SL IV 2: Brooks II, 255–256.

Chaeremon.[162] For this reason the result could hardly be to the taste of the Metropolitan of Mabbog and Severus, both of whom regarded the Synod as a disgrace for their party.[163] Philoxenus described his opposition to Flavian of Antioch, with which his suffragans, with the exception of three, sided.[164] In several letters from this period Severus, however, admits that 'the complete union of the holy churches... needs a lawful concession on certain points'. But if it is a question of a union which seizes the whole man on the personal level, then this must be comprehensive, i.e. it must be achieved in every respect. The *Henoticon* has thus only a very limited function in the service of unity.[165] From this it is clear that there was a profound difference between the Emperor and Severus in their understanding of the reunion of the Churches. The value of Zeno's Edict is strongly played down when the most that is conceded is that it contains 'a right confession of faith', but then it is immediately emphasised: 'on its own it is devoid of all healing power in relation to what is necessary'.[166] Looking back the Patriarch of Antioch says in a letter (516–517) to his Alexandrian colleague that over and above the *Henoticon*, which does contain a 'right confession' and is a 'repudiation' of the outrage which was perpetrated on the faith at Chalcedon, more is needed for converts to the true faith (in the sense of Severus), viz.

a formula which condemns by name [i.e. explicitly] what happened at Chalcedon against the orthodox faith... as well the evil Tome of Leo... and those who describe our one Lord and God Jesus Christ as two natures after the divine and unutterable union.

Although the Edict, or *Henoticon*, may be taken as

a rejection of these things, I [Severus] do not consider it, however, as sufficiently convincing.[167]

---

[162] Severus, ibid., 255. He calls them 'hirelings and hucksters of piety'. Cf. Honigmann, *Évêques et évêchés* 9, 122, 123; P. Peeters, 'Jacques de Saroug appartient-il à la secte monophysite?', *AnBoll* 66 (1948) 175, 179, 183, 189, 190, n. 1.

[163] Severus, ibid., 255 f. [289]; Philoxenus, *Letter to Presbyter Simeon of Tele'adā* frg. 4: Lebon, 'Textes inédits', *Mus* 43 (1930) 189, 15–193, 19 (V), esp. 190.

[164] Cf. de Halleux, *Philoxène* 71, n. 52 on the names.

[165] Severus, *Letter to Solon*: SL I 2: Brooks II 15–16. He refers to the more radical Bishop Constantine of Seleucia (Isauria), who had taken part in the Synod of Antioch (509). He passed over the *Henoticon* in his Church as 'superfluous': 'for if it does not touch the stumblingblocks that sprang up at Chalcedon and separated the churches, what is the use of mentioning it?' Severus then discusses in more detail the intentions of Emperors Anastasius and Zeno with regard to the *Henoticon*.

[166] Severus, *Letter to Hippocrates*: PO 12, nr. 46, p. 320.

[167] Severus, *Letter to Patriarch Dioscorus II* (516–7 AD): PO 12, nr. 49, p. 324. He writes that at a Synod of Alexandria also it was explained in this way. By comparison the *typus* is designated as a 'formula of satisfaction' (*plerophoria*); thus in the letter to Bishop Constantine: SL I 1: Brooks II, 4–5. This points to Severus as the author of the *typus*. Cf. the important letter to Oecumenius (from the years 508–512): PO 12, 175–186. Here also Severus speaks of the *typus*, if the interpretation of E. W. Brooks, PO 12, 185, n. 6 is correct.

Hence it is clear why neither Philoxenus nor Severus could be satisfied with the Synod of Sidon. But just one year later both were in a completely changed situation. Patriarch Flavian II, who was able to guide the Synod of Sidon to this result so undesired by his opponents, was deposed (November 512), and on 6 November Severus became his successor as patriarch of Antioch. What was to become of the *Henoticon*?

(5) *Severus of Antioch. Consecration (512) and the 'Oriental Synod' (513)*

With the very consecration of the new patriarch on 16 November, 512, a new direction was manifested. Among the twelve consecrating bishops was Philoxenus of Mabbog, as well as four comrades-in-arms whom Severus had won over on his journey to the Synod of Sidon (511) and in addition five of his suffragans.[168] Nevertheless, opponents of Severus also took part, in particular Dionysius of Tarsus. The address (*prosphonesis*) of the new patriarch in the Great Church after his consecration has been handed down. It contained a profession of faith. Despite all the obscurity surrounding where it was delivered and who subscribed it, at least this much is certain: the christological position of the newly consecrated bishop in the conflict about the *Henoticon* is depicted.[169] He professed the first three Councils, and the *Henoticon* of Emperor Zeno which was sanctioned by Emperor Anastasius. Anathematised, however, were all heretics, especially Nestorius and Eutyches, Chalcedon, Leo's Tome and all supporters of the 'two natures after the union',[170] and every distribution of activities and properties in the one incarnate Logos to 'two' (natures), which meant for Severus the profession of two persons. Chalcedon

---

[168] Cf. Honigmann, *Évêques et évêchés* 13, 15; de Halleux, *Philoxène* 78 with n. 21. These names are contained in various documents. Cf. M. A. Kugener, 'Notices relatives à Sévère': PO 2, 317–321, IV–VII. The jubilation of the people at the reception of the Patriarch is depicted by Zacharias Rh., *Vita Severi*: PO 2, 241–242.

[169] See M. A. Kugener, 'Allocution prononcée par Sévère après son élévation sur le trône patriarcal d'Antioche', *OrChr* 2 (1902) 265–282; on the various other MSS containing the confession of faith see ibid., 272, n. 1; idem, 'Notices relatives à Sévère': PO 2, 316–325; Severus, *Homily* 1: PO 38, 254. Honigmann, op. cit., 15, following Mansi X, 1116C and XI 273, places this *prosphronesis* in the martyrium of St. Euphemia at Daphne, which would be a particular hit at Chalcedon. According to the text edited by Kugener, based on BM Add. 14.533, it was held 'in the cathedral after the elevation of Severus as patriarch, before the archimandrites and Oriental (monophysite) monks, and also signed there after his consecration'. See the title of the text in PO 2, §VIII, p. 322. On the signatures see ibid., 324–325. A repetition of the *prosphonesis* (with the act of signing) in various churches is not excluded. In any case it was once again delivered on 18 November in the martyrium of St Romanus. See Severus, *Homily* 1: PO 38, 254–268 (Coptic), 255–259 (Syriac). Both versions are not literally identical, but only in the strict sense of the word. Of all places, it is in the MS which presents the *prosphonesis* with the list of the consecrators who signed that the name of the first, Bishop Dionysius of Tarsus, is missing; in its place is that of Severus himself. Cf. PO 2, 324–325.

[170] See *Homily* 1, just referred to: PO 38 (Coptic), pp. 261–263, §§14–16. This is a clear profession of the *mia physis* formula; it goes beyond the *Henoticon*, just as much as it does the condemnation of Chalcedon.

had stirred up an even more furious storm than Nestorius had (Coptic §10, p. 258). At this Council the new Jews assembled (Coptic §14, pp. 260–261). The word 'two' dissolves the unity. According to the Coptic text, Severus at this time openly advocated the formula of the 'one person, the one hypostasis, the one nature of the incarnated Word in accord with the formula which the holy inspired Fathers handed on to us' (Coptic §15, pp. 162–163; as well §21, pp. 264–265). Naturally the reproach that Chalcedon signified a 'fourness' in the Trinity instead of a threeness also turned up again (§22, pp. 264–265). In the Syriac text all the names of the Antiochenes familiar to us, beginning with Diodore of Tarsus and proceeding on to the Persian Barsauma, are anathematised, especially those who had written against the twelve anathemas of Cyril. Finally Severus professed *communio* with John of Nikiu and Timothy of Constantinople, the successor of the deposed Macedonius.

In April or October 513 the great *Oriental Synod* was held, at which the new patriarch presided.[171] Philoxenus, seconded by his supporters, demanded a vote on the following points: (1) the legitimacy of the new patriarch, Severus, and the validity of Flavian's deposition; (2) the anathema against Chalcedon and Leo's Tome, and—as the obverse of this—the ratification of the orthodoxy of the opponents of the Council and the Tome; (3) the restoration of the peace of the Church on this basis. The *Henoticon* was accepted, yet not 'hypocritically in the manner of the deposed patriarchs Flavian and Macedonius', but 'honestly'. This was accentuated by a profession of faith and the signing of a charter condemning the teaching of 'two natures'. The result of the Synod was communicated in synodal letters to Timothy of Constantinople and John of Nikiu.[172]

What reactions to this important Synod, which clearly transcends the *Henoticon*, can be established? Severus himself gave reports of

---

[171] See Honigmann, *Évêques et évêchés* 15–17; A. de Halleux, *Philoxène* 79–85. Sources: 1. *Philoxenus, Letter to the Presbyter Simeon of Tele'adā*: 'Fragments inédits', nr. 4: *Mus* 43 (1930) 192 (V) 1–4: quod nobis curae esset, ut (scilicet) vel ordinatio (Severi) confirmaretur vel verbum pro recta fide (factum) stabiliretur vel anathemata lata adversus haereticos rata haberentur vel Ecclesia in pace et concordia permaneret'. *Letter to all the monks of the East*, frg. 6: *Mus* 76 (1963) 8 (V). Epiphanius, Bishop of Tyre, brother of the deposed Flavian, did not participate in the Synod of Antioch: *Letter to the monks of Senoun*: CSCO 232 (V) 63, 14. 2. *Severus: Letter to Hippocrates*: PO 12, nr. 46, p. 321; *Letter to Musonius and Alexander* (513–516 AD): SL I 27, Brooks II 88 (V) ('the whole synod of the God-loving bishops of the East is united in the right doctrines and anathematizes all the heresies', among which are included: the division of Christ into two natures after the union; Chalcedon ('the stronghold of this evil heresy') and the Tome of Leo ('the cleaver of peace') 3. *Jacob of Sarug, ep.* 17: Olinder, *The Letters of Jacob of Sarug. Comments on an edition I* (Lund-Leipzig 1939) nr. 17, 46–48; ed. Martin, ZDMG 30 (1876) 258–262 (T); 262–265 (V), §IV, 264 (V).

[172] Severus, *Letter to Hippocrates*: PO 12, nr. 46, frg. p. 321 (synodal letter to Timothy is mentioned). *Letter to Musonius and Alexander*: SL I 27, Brooks II 88 (John of Nikiu): '... we have now drawn up a synodical letter addressed to the God-loving archbishop of the Alexandrians, inviting him to unanimity and pure communion'. Further despatches are announced.

these. He acknowledged that after the Synod of 513 he saw himself exposed to 'an immense number of attacks', even from a side whose judgement could not be a matter of indifference to him, viz. from the side of Emperor Anastasius. According to Theodore Lector (Chalcedonian) and John Diacrinomenos (Monophysite) the new patriarch had committed himself before his consecration to refrain from a condemnation of Chalcedon in his new position. To all intents and purposes he was bound by oath to the *Henoticon*. On the day of his consecration, however, according to Theodore Lector, he had done the very opposite of this, for at the insistence of his supporters he anathematised the Council from the ambo of the church where he was consecrated.[173] It was not so much by this fact (alone), but (really only) by the Synod (513) held immediately after it, that the imperial capital was thrown into the state of agitation which Severus himself describes as follows:[174]

And, when all the bishops of the East were present at Antioch, and anathematised the synod in writing, and we addressed a synodical letter to Timothy the prelate of the royal city, we anathematised what was done at Chalcedon against the orthodox faith, and the Jewish Tome of Leo, and those who call our one Lord and God Jesus Christ two natures after the incomprehensible union. And afterwards, when innumerable attacks were made upon me, insomuch that the glorious Asterius, the ex-prefect of the city, who held the office called *a secretis*,[175] was sent after me,

---

[173] Theodore Lector, *Epit.* 499 and 561: Hansen 142 and 157.

[174] Severus, *Letter to Hippocrates*: PO 12 nr. 46, 321.

[175] According to Brooks, op. cit., n. 3, Asterius was only to be called ex-prefect when Severus wrote Letter 46. Thus the prefecture must have fallen between 513 and 516. Schwartz, PS 247 is of the opinion that the prefect of Antioch (Asterius) sent his secretary to collect the patriarch. There is also a translation back into Greek of the words above: χειμάζεται ἡ Ῥωμαίων βασιλεία διὰ τοῦτο. The Syriac is literally ἐν χειμῶνι. The initiative to reprimand, however, no doubt came from Rome, as the text says. Severus' reply also went to the Emperor himself. The latter, at the insistence of the moderate Alexandrian *apocrisiarii*, Dioscorus and Chaeremon, had written a letter of reproach to John of Nikiu, as Severus himself in his letter to Ammonius, presbyter of Alexandria, says (SL IV 2: Brooks II 255): 'which contained no small complaints, on the ground that he had not been contented with the Henoticon only [as had Peter III (Mongus), Athanasius II and John II Hemula, his successor], without requiring reference to be made in actual words to the impious things done at Chalcedon as to the impious Tome of Leo' (the whole of the rest of the letter is interesting for Severus' appreciation of the *Henoticon* at the time of the Synod of Sidon (511). Even at the Synod of Constantinople under Patriarch Menas in 536 the scant regard that Severus had for the *Henoticon* is expressed in a play on words. This appraisal, certainly exaggerated but in many ways hitting the mark, occurs in a *Libellus Monachorum*, a deposition made by monks who were led by the archimandrite Marianus of Dalmata, the exarch of the monasteries of the Imperial City. 'He [Severus] stood before his acephalous sect and did not accept the *Henoticon*, but characterised it as *Kenoticon* (κενωτικόν) [i.e. *purgativum*; Mansi VIII 1000D translates '*novativum*', presupposing καινωτικόν] and as the instrument of division, and condemned it in his own writings. When he was successful in snatching the undefiled see of Theoupolis [Antioch], he did quite the reverse and feigned to accept it; in this manner he wormed his way into the favour of the archbishop of Alexandria [John of Nikiu] and assumed Peter, named Mongus, who at the very time of the *Henoticon* seized the see of Alexandria, into the diptychs of the holy Church of Antioch. By this action he left in the lurch all those who, deceived by him, had been instructed that Peter of the Alexandrian Church must be cut off [because he had merely accepted the *Henoticon* without condemning Chalcedon, and it was for this purpose that the party of the *acephaloi* had been formed]. But he did not even rest here. For he was out to generate commotions, yet then not to admit it' (ACO III, nr. 14, p. 40, 30–41, 1). Severus is then made a supporter, indeed the leader of the acephalous movement which was once directed against Peter Mongus, but which pretended to accept the *Henoticon*.

I was not in the least frightened, nor did I fear, nor yield to the time, though he said, 'The kingdom of the Romans is in a turmoil (*cheimon*) on account of this', but I plainly said, 'I am ready to leave the city and resign the see, rather than upset one stroke of what I wrote from the beginning in the synodical words addressed to Timothy': and this I did not say without writing it down, but I expressed myself with freedom (*parrhesia*) in writing to the religious king also.

We can infer from this letter that Emperor Anastasius had certainly been informed by Patriarch Timothy about the proceedings in Antioch and that apparently he was severely enraged about Severus. The fact that he was enraged is also a proof that the Emperor wanted to uphold the policy of the *Henoticon* (as this had been understood until then) and also that the so-called *Typus*, as Severus was determined to formulate it, did not find favour with him. It was also Patriarch Timothy's intention to pursue this line with the Emperor.

(6) An anti-Chalcedonian Synod of Tyre (513 or 514–5)?

Three Jacobite historians who did not know of the great Oriental Synod of Antioch (513) reported a council in Tyre in the years 513 or 514–15 which dealt with the same topics as the Synod of Antioch (513).

> The three historians in question are: 1. *Zacharias Rhetor (cont.)*, HE VII 10: CSCO 83(T), p. 51; CSCO 87(V), p. 35, 22–29; VII 12: CSCO 87, p. 38, 15–28; Hamilton-Brooks 179–180 (VII 10) and 183–184 (VII 12). 2. *Anonymous of 846*: CSCO 3(T) and 4(V), p. 221 and 168, 30–32 respectively. 3. *John of Ephesus = Ps.-Dionysius of Tellmaḥrē*, Chronicle: CSCO 91 (T) and 121 (V) (I); CSCO 104 (T), an. 826 (II), pp. 13–14.

According to A. de Halleux[176] the four depictions have their origin in *one* source because they are almost completely identical in their reports about the summoning of the (alleged) synod and its course. The differences concern details which can be explained as interpolations or later corrections. According to the four reports mentioned this Synod of Tyre brought together the Oriental episcopate on the order of Emperor Anastasius I and at the instigation of the anti-Chalcedonians. They state that Severus and Philoxenus of Mabbog were the ones who presided. At the Synod it was shown that Chalcedon was in contradiction to the *Henoticon* and for that reason was also condemned as an 'addition' to the faith which had been handed on. They wrote that letters of *communio* were sent to John of Alexan-

---

[176] References with texts in A. de Halleux, *Philoxène* 81–82; for his argumentation see 81–85; idem, 'Nouveaux textes inédits de Philoxène de Mabbog': *Mus* 76 (1963) 5–26. The date is given by the different authors as either 513 or 514–5. (1) 513: Duchesne, *VIe siècle*, 31, n. 1; cf. Schwartz, PS 255; P. Peeters, 'Hypatius et Vitalien', *Mélanges H. Grégoire* 2 (1950) (5–51), n. 1; (2) in favour of 514–5 are J. Lebon, *Le monophysisme sévérien* 62; P. Charanis, *Anastasius I* 70; Tisserant, art. 'Philoxène', *DTC* 12 (1935) (col. 1509–1532) 1515; C. Capizzi, *Anastasio I*, 122, n. 125.

dria, Timothy of Constantinople and Elias of Jerusalem. This description corresponds so clearly to the great Oriental Synod of 513 depicted above, that it can only be a question of one and the same assembly which officially interpreted the *Henoticon* in an anti-Chalcedonian sense and re-established *communio* with Egypt. Thus according to A. de Halleux one has to choose between speaking of a Synod of Tyre or of a Synod of Antioch (513).[177] There is one weighty reason why Tyre has to be excluded. No monophysite synod of significance could have convened in the Phoenician metropolis as long as the episcopal see there was occupied by an archbishop who was a determined diphysite, 'indeed the most passionate of all the opponents of Severus', viz. the brother of the deposed Flavian II of Antioch.[178] The Synod could not have been held before 514–515, the date which John of Ephesus gives. But at that time it was no longer necessary, as the Antiochene Synod of 513 had already fulfilled all the desires of the anti-Chalcedonians. Perhaps after Epiphanius had been deposed there was another assembly of bishops in Tyre to celebrate the elimination of the opponent and the installation of his 'successor' and at the same time to repeat the anathemas of 513. Admittedly Epiphanius could return to Tyre once more in 518.

(7) On the position of the *Henoticon* in these years let us add two further voices from the Syrian region: (1) a judgement of Philoxenus of Mabbog from the year 521 and (2) one of Bishop Jacob of Sarug. After the turn of events of 518–519 Philoxenus, in a letter written from Philippopolis where he lived in exile, looked back at the long development of the theme 'God suffered' and determined the place of the *Henoticon*.[179]

There [then] is what blessed Cyril also wrote who follows in everything the path of the holy Fathers, his precursors, without wandering either to the left or to the right from the royal highway along which they advanced. [For] he himself also says: the virginal conception is [that] of God [is to be expressed of Jesus Christ as God]; the birth is of God; the resemblance to us in all things is of God; the passion is of God; the resurrection from the dead is of God; the ascension into heaven is of God. And [it is] because Nestorius departed from this way [in order to] show another one, new and strange, already trodden before him by the feet of heretics, I mean Diodore, Theodore [of Mopsuestia] and those of their persuasion, [that] he was anathematised with [his] doctrine, first by the holy Council held at Ephesus, *then by all the bishops and archbishops who subscribed the unifying Edict [Henoticon]*. These anathematised, apart from Nestorius, the erring Eutyches and his own heresy which is Manichaean. And they condemned also those who had assembled at Chalcedon, who even before the *Henoticon* had fallen under the anathema through the decision taken at the holy Council held at Ephesus where these words were

---

[177] A. de Halleux, *Philoxène*, 83.
[178] Ibid., 83 f.
[179] Philoxenus, *Letter to the monks of Senoun*: CSCO 232, p. 38, 25–39, 9.

officially sanctioned: 'Anyone who shall produce a definition of faith other than the august and holy [definition] coming from the Fathers of Nicaea, let him be anathema'.

Thus in the recollection of Philoxenus the *Henoticon* has an eminent position—completely in opposition to the conception of Severus from 508 to 513. It is the decisive condemnation of Chalcedon and all the (heretical) preparation for it. Only Canon VII of Ephesus (431) (DOC p. 65) can be compared to it, because in a very real sense this canon had made Chalcedon proleptically impossible by its ban on 'presenting, compiling or composing another formula of faith other than that of the holy Fathers who gathered at Nicaea in the Holy Spirit...'. In his eyes the Council of Antioch (513) also had brought nothing new, as the same letter to the monks of Senoun testifies in a passage which offers nothing short of an ecumenical survey of the various positions on the *Henoticon*. On account of its significance we shall cite it completely, following CSCO 232, p. 63, 4–17:

Know, then, I beseech you, venerable sons, that for our part we do not accept the [teachings] which have come from Rome and that we do not approve those who sent them, for all those who have occupied this see since Leo are Nestorians and work to have the cause of this heretic approved. And we no longer side with what has been invented at Jerusalem, whatever may be their pretence to confess the virgin [as] Mother of God, for they have thrown out this word as bait to catch the simple by means of it, without really accepting it.* But we shall share completely the tradition and the communion of the Council of the diocese of Egypt† and of [those] of our [Council], that of the East, which met a short time ago in Antioch, [a tradition] which moreover all the bishops from everywhere had approved forty years [ago] by subscribing the document *Henoticon* and the anathema of the Council of Chalcedon and the Tome of Leo.

* Philoxenus is presumably alluding to the attempt at union by Patriarch Martyrius which we have already presented.

† What council is meant by this remains unclear. Cf. A. de Halleux, CSCO 232, p. 63 n. 3.

Whatever significance the last years of Bishop Jacob of Sarug may have had for his attitude to Chalcedon (see below), still the judgement of T. Jansma on his position with regard to the *Henoticon* is valid:

His whole theological activity was in the spirit of this document; it was only *vi coactus* that he openly professed it (Ep. XVI and XVII). In a real sense even the Henoticon was superfluous. Indeed, in Nicaea and Constantinople everything that could be said on the creed had already been said.[180]

[180] T. Jansma, 'The Credo of Jacob of Sĕrūgh', *Nederlands Archief voor Kerkgeschiedenis* 44 (1960–61) (18–36) 28, with copious references. He emphasises that 'Jacob in his Christology had not written a single positive word that is not to be found in Cyril of Alexandria as well' (p. 33). Jacob is primarily a Cyrillian and has no intrinsic relationship either to Chalcedon or to the *Henoticon* or even to the creed of Severus from the beginning of his patriarchate. He remains true to himself in his conceptions. Cf. *ep*. XIV: Olinder, CSCO 110 (1952) 58, 19–21, with *ep*. XVII: p. 85,

Letter XVII to the monks of Mar Bassus[181] shows most clearly Jacob's position with regard to the *Henoticon*. From this we shall cite §§IV and V:

IV_ Severus . . . spoke the truth openly at the great assembly of the Oriental Synod, and what was done in the document *Henoticon* with hints and enigmas he [then] said with open words before the great multitude [of the city] of the daughter of the day whom Peter betrothed to the Crucified [= Antioch]. And since then it is proper for everyone who is a believer to speak openly, without shame, while adhering to the document *Henoticon* which rejects the Council covertly and with a hint. And [one] also adheres now to the public confession that was proclaimed at the Oriental Synod which was gathered around the great, holy and blessed Severus, when the Council [held] in Chalcedon was anathematised, which [Council] had been anathematised by the Alexandrians and the other countries from the [very] beginning, but since the document *Henoticon* onwards by the whole world. Now, however, the meaning of the document *Henoticon* has become manifest through saintly Severus the Patriarch.

V For myself. . . neither have I learned from the document *Henoticon* something I did not [already] know nor have I added anything to my faith from the confession of Severus. For I am now what I was before, all the time anathematising with the whole Church Nestorius and his teaching, those of his opinion and the Council of Chalcedon, because this [Council] also employed words which accord with the opinion of Nestorius, the anathematised [one]. As for Diodore, Theodore, Theodoret, Ibas and the Tome of Leo, they are anathematised by [the very fact] that one says: 'I anathematise Nestorius and those of his opinion'. And because these men evidently adhere to the opinion of Nestorius, they are anathematised with him since they are of his opinion.

The assertion of T. Jansma that the concluding section of the *Henoticon* (i.e. §7 in our division) is a summary of Jacob's christology is quite correct. According to Jansma this christology is tied into the doctrine of the Trinity in an unusually strong way and is understood as a part of this. 'The belief in the Trinity suffices. In this the whole Church is one. Nothing can be added to faith, charity can be added to indefinitely'. Love is also the bringer of the longed-for peace (*Ep.* XVI) which no edict can effect.[182]

This survey of the position of the East with regard to the *Henoticon* shows that it was never able to unite the anti-Chalcedonians. It was

---

14–18. But what is added in the course of time is (*a*) the readiness to express more and more anathemas, which runs counter to the intentions of Emperor Anastasius. In *ep.* XIII there is still none; *ep.* XIV anathematises Nestorius and Eutyches, but Chalcedon is also intended by this (CSCO 110, p. 61, 14 ff.) without its being mentioned. *Ep.* XVI: anathemas against Nestorius, Eutyches, Chalcedon and Leo's Tome; and (*b*) the increasingly more accurate determination of his doctrinal position: in *ep.* XIII and XIV there are still no controversial formulae; in *ep.* XVI he refers to Cyril's anathemas and Zeno's *Henoticon*; *ep.* XVII: the interpretation of the *Henoticon* by Severus. See further the art. by T. Jansma, 'Credo (Encore) de Jacques de Saroug', *OrSyr* 10 (1965) 75–88; 193–236; 331–370; 475–510, and our exposition of the Christology of the Syrians.
[181] Jacob Sar., *ep.* XVII (*ep.* II *ad mon. Mar Bassus*): ZDMG 30 (1876): French 262–265 (written after the elevation of Severus to the patriarchate of Antioch [512] and after the Oriental Synod of 513). Cf. T. Jansma, art. cit., *Nederl. Arch. v. Kerkgesch.* 44 (1960–61), Appendix I, 33–34.
[182] T. Jansma, art. cit., ibid., 28.

Emperor Anastasius who had most clearly delimited the document as an 'ecumenical' starting-point and emphasised at the same time that it was not an annulment of Chalcedon; the East, however, did not follow him in this, as we have just seen.[183] This will become quite manifest when now we go on to depict the conflict with the West. Unfortunately the 'Acacian Schism' was the prelude to the *status schismatis* between East and West.

Section Two: The *Henoticon* and the first schism between the Pope and the Patriarchate of Constantinople

From the time of Leo I the following was true for West Rome: 'unconditional adherence to the Council of Chalcedon without any regard for the Patriarchate of Constantinople or for the situation in Alexandria and Egypt'.[184] Though this attitude was unambiguous and had its indispensible significance for the whole Church, conversely it showed little awareness of the autonomous and different development of the various local Churches. On account of the constricting effect of the conflict between 482 and 518 this period is theologically poor, at least in the exchange of documents between East and West. Because the *Henoticon*, itself of slight theological content, at first concerned only Constantinople and Alexandria, it did not go officially to Rome. For this reason it was ignored there and a discussion of its contents was simply passed over. The sole passage in which the name '*Henoticon*' surfaces is a forgery.[185] Thus other questions are focused on, if we do not take into consideration the treatise of Gelasius I on the 'two natures'. Tight limits were placed on dialogue between the two sides, insofar as a dialogue took place at all. For the opponents of the Council of 451, the Council, Leo's Tome and its defenders were 'Nestorian'. On the Chalcedonian side we encounter time and again the placing on a par of Manes, Apollinar-

---

[183] Gelasius I, *De vitanda communione Acacii missa ad orientales episcopos* (= *De vitanda communione*): *Coll. Veron.* nr. 11, Schwartz, PS 36, 25–26: '... we have in our safekeeping a *sacra* (but we do not believe that it is from a catholic Emperor [i.e. Anastasius I] in which he solemnly declares that he firmly adheres to the catholic faith and the definition of the Synod of Chalcedon'. Emperor Anastasius I to Pope Hormisdas: CA nr. 125 = CSEL 35 II, 539: 'Yet we wonder why You [= Hormisdas] wanted to write to us something about the holy Fathers who gathered at Chalcedon as long as what was decided by them is shown to have been confirmed by various decrees of our predecessors'. Cf. Schwartz, PS 198 f., who remarks that with this declaration there was not bound up the opinion 'that [the] Chalcedonian [statement] is the formula of faith which is definitive, beyond discussion and can in no way be supplemented'. This is an observation which presupposes an appreciation of the historical character of the Christian proclamation of faith, an appreciation that could be more or less strongly developed.

[184] See Schwartz, PS 202. On the attitude of the Popes with regard to Chalcedon cf. F. Hofmann, *Chalkedon* II, 13–94. To this study corresponds that of R. Haacke, ibid., 95–177. These two expositions, with their rich array of references, allow us to be brief. Cf. further A. Grillmeier, 'Die Rezeption des Konzils von Chalkedon in der römisch-katholischen Kirche', in idem, *Mit ihm und in ihm* (Freiburg-Basel-Wien 1978²) 335–370, esp. 340–344.

[185] Cf. Schwartz, PS 197 n. 3; 203 n. 2.

ius, Eutyches, Dioscorus, Timothy Aelurus and Peter Mongus. Apart from a brief interlude under Anastasius II (496–498) these *idées fixes* were not shaken. They became more rigid every time there was a wrestle about the occupation of a vacant episcopal or patriarchal see and a conflict about mentioning the names of dead or living in the liturgy (on the so-called 'diptychs'). For the Popes the mere mention of the name of an 'heretical' bishop or patriarch was to profess his teaching.[186]

(a) The breach

At the time of Pope Simplicius' succession to Pope Felix III(II) new events were enacted in the East which called for energetic reaction from the side of Rome. In Antioch Patriarch Calandion (479[482]–484) was exiled and Peter the Fuller was installed for a third time (471; 475–477; 485–490). This meant that all Eastern patriarchates were occupied by bishops who were in favour of the *Henoticon*.[187] West Rome could gather information about the *Henoticon* from John Talaia, who on account of his claim to the see of Alexandria intended to appeal to Pope Simplicius and for that reason came to Rome. He had a letter of recommendation from Patriarch Calandion of Antioch and a detailed indictment against Peter Mongus.[188] He requested a letter from Pope Simplicius to Patriarch Acacius, which in fact was made out and reached the addressee. In his reply Acacius, according to Liberatus, made reference to the *Henoticon* and on this basis established *communio* with Peter Mongus of Alexandria.[189] For this he was reproached by Rome because he had assumed communion with a 'heretic'. For Rome it was not sufficient that Peter Mongus profess Church communion on the basis of Zeno's Edict, 'but it was necessary that he [Peter Mongus] embrace communion in accordance with the decision of Chalcedon and Leo's Tome'.[190] This is Liberatus' account. Simplicius certainly knew of the *Henoticon*. The notification of election of Pope Felix III(II), the successor of Pope Simplicius, also points in this direction. In this the new Pope deals

---

[186] Cf. Felix II (III) (Gelasius), *ep. 14 ad Flavitam ep. Constant.* (490), JW 613: Schwartz, PS 112, 7–21 (*Coll. Berol.* nr. 44); idem, *ep. ad Zenon. imp.* (490) JW 612: Schwartz, PS 82–85 (*Coll. Berol.* nr. 34); *ep. ad Rufin., Hilar. et Thalass.* (490) JW 614: Schwartz, PS 78, 29–79, 3 (*Coll. Berol.* nr. 30); esp. idem, *ep. 17 ad Vetranion. eppum* (490) JW 615: Schwartz, PS 79–81 (*Coll. Berol.* nr. 31); in the schism with Acacius the point at issue is the question of truth.

[187] On the situation in Jerusalem and on the preliminary work which had been done there for the *Henoticon*, to which we have already referred, see L. Perrone, *La chiesa di Palestina* 141–144.

[188] Cf. Liberatus, *Breviar.* 17: ACO II 5, p. 129, 11–130, 3. For the whole picture of the course of events see F. Hofmann, *Chalkedon* II, 43–51.

[189] Cf. Liberatus, *Breviar.* 17: ACO II 5, p. 129, 17–21: *Acacius vero susceptis epistolis simpliciter rescripsit ei quia Iohannem quidem Alexandriae ignoraret episcopum, Petrum vero mongum suscepisset in communionem* in Zenonis principis unitivo *[= Henoticon] et [ut] hoc citra eius egisset sententiam propter unitatem ecclesiarum, principis iussione suscipiens Petrum.*

[190] Liberatus, *Breviar.* 17: ACO II 5, p. 129, 21–27.

with a complaint of Emperor Zeno, a complaint which is expressed only in the *Henoticon* (see the text §4 above): through the annulment of communion for the sake of Chalcedon many had already died without baptism and outside the ecclesial community; this state of affairs would be removed by the *Henoticon*.[191] The Pope refrained from a direct attack on the Edict.

(b) The 'Undivided *tunica Christi*'

The open breach came in connexion with a Roman synod of seventy-seven bishops in 484. Peter Mongus and Acacius of Constantinople were anathematised and declared to be deposed and excommunicated. In the sixth letter of Pope Felix to Acacius of 28 July, 484 (the synodal letter) the *crimina* of Acacius are listed. In this letter he is depicted as a harmful member of the body of Christ and as a 'destroyer of the one catholic Church' (*unam dei catholicam ecclesiam dissipans*):[192] 'How could it ever happen that one who has rent the *tunica Christi*, which the crucifiers of Christ did not dare to divide, still be counted among the number of the faithful?'.[193] Compared with the gloomy idea his predecessor had of Alexandrian christology,[194] his language to Acacius may even be characterised as moderate. In order to uphold the Council of 451, he pulls out all stops in his efforts to persuade. He refers to the *Codex encyclius*[195] and the authority of a Council 'which was held [decided] by the elders for everybody'.[196] Emperor Zeno is reminded of his world-wide responsibility as the *representative of God* ('may you preside over the world as the representative of God').[197] He is said to be constituted as the

---

[191] The agreement between *Henoticon* §4 (see above) and Felix III, *ep. ad Zenon, imp.*: JW 591 from March (?) 483: Thiel I, p. 230, §13 with n. 44; Schwartz, PS 68, 16–17 (*Coll. Berol.* nr. 20), is unmistakeable.

[192] Synodal letter of the seventy-seven Bishops under Felix III (II) from 28 July, 484 to Acacius; JW 599: CA nr. 70, pp. 155–161; cf. esp. 157 f.: 'We have found that also Acacius, who is bound to the members of Christ to their ruin, and scatters the one catholic Church of God over towns and provinces, is no longer to be counted among the holy bishops and Christians' (CA nr. 70, §6).

[193] See CA 70, §6 (previous note): *scindens tunicam Christi*. This picture of the 'divided tunic' of the Lord is found before this in Felix III (II), *ep. 1 ad Zenon. Aug.* from March, 483: Schwartz, PS 64 (*Coll. Berol.* 20), ll. 11–14. Cf. John 19, 23. 24. See Cyprian, *De cath. eccles. unitate* 7: CSEL III, 1, 207–233; Augustine, In Joh. 19, 23. 24, tr. 13, 13: PL 35, 1499. Gelasius I, who composed the letters of Felix III, is fond of this image. Cf. H. Koch, 'Gelasius im kirchenpolitischen Dienste seiner Vorgänger' = *SbMünchAkW* 1935; Gelasius, *Tr.* 2, 8; Thiel 525; Anastasius II, *ep. ad Anastasium imp.* 1, 1: Thiel 616. On the other side the anti-Chalcedonians accused the Council of this rending of Christ's tunic: Zacharias Rh. *HE* III 1: Hamilton-Brooks 41. See further instances in A. Michel, *Chalkedon* II, 491–562, esp. 555, n. 327, with reference to his study, *Amalfi und Jerusalem im griechischen Kirchenstreit* (1054–1090) = OCA 121 (Roma 1939) 10 with n. 1–5.

[194] Simplicius, *ep. ad Acacium*; JW 587: CA nr. 68 §§2–6, pp. 151–154.

[195] Felix III (II), *ep. ad Acacium*: JW 593: Schwartz, PS 75, 9–11 (*Coll. Berol.* nr. 23).

[196] Idem, *ep. 1 ad Zenon. aug.* from March, 483: JW 591: Schwartz, PS 68, 9 (*Coll. Berol.* nr. 20): '*a veteribus universaliter decisum*'.

[197] Idem, Schwartz, PS 69, 8–11 (*Coll. Berol.* nr. 20): '*et ad tuae gloriae cumulum ita vice dei praesideas mundo, ut veraciter existas divinitatis imitator* atque adhuc in rebus temporalibus constitutum iam experiaris et munus in aeternam tibi beatitudinem praeparatum'.

imitator of God and inspired by God.[198] In thanksgiving for regaining his throne the Emperor should 'prove himself the disciple of the Master and lead back to communion with holy Peter the see of the blessed evangelist Mark, with the surrender due to its servants'.[199] The motives which move the Pope here should be recognised: 'For an error against which resistance is not offered finds its approval, and the truth which is not defended at all perishes'.[200] If Chalcedon is abandoned, the whole Church suffers damage.[201] Pope Felix saw the division coming, as he wrote to Acacius: 'the scandal of the Churches which we see becoming divided must be cleared away'.[202] In his opinion the fault was completely on the side of Acacius, 'whose soul misconducts itself badly and has arrived at the state of second death'.[203] 'He is the one who throws into disorder the whole Church of the East (*perturbator totius Orientalis ecclesiae*)', because he is 'the defender and patron of the plague of Eutychian heresy'.[204] The Acacius question is not only a matter of whether *communio* should be assumed or rejected. Rather it concerns truth.[205]

Were the positions really so different? In his first letter to Emperor Zeno from March 483, i.e. after the publication of the *Henoticon*, Felix III renders the substance of Chalcedon in a way which dispenses with the controversial two-nature formula, and so approaches the *Henoticon* which attempts the same, though less carefully and in a context which endangered the Council. We shall cite the most important sentences here:[206]

For you see, venerable Emperor, that as the clear-cut defence of the Synod of Chalcedon is the elimination (*elisio*) of those who are hostile to it, so on the contrary an open attack on it proves to be taking sides (*electio*) with the enemies of the venerable Council itself. The memorable assembly, as the divine words instruct us, transgressed neither to the right nor to the left the bounds of right ordering (*dispositio*), but by proceeding, as it is written, along the royal middle way [Num 21, 22; cf. Is 30, 21], denouncing on this side and on that the sacrilegious inventions of Nestorius and Eutyches it thus preaches the mystery of great devotion (*Magnae pietatis . . . sacramentum*; cf. 1 Tim 3, 16): the consubstantial and co-eternal Word of the omnipotent God and Father which without change to its divinity descended and became

---

[198] See above, Chapter II, section 4.
[199] Felix III (II), *ep. 1 ad Zenon. aug.*; JW 591: Schwartz, PS 69, 5–7 (*Coll. Berol.* nr. 20).
[200] Felix III (II), *ep. 2 ad Acacium*, from March 483; JW 592: Schwartz, PS 72, 1–2 (*Coll. Berol.* nr. 21): '*error enim cui non resistitur, approbatur et veritas cum minime defensatur, opprimitur.* Cf. p. 73 2–3 (Acacius is guilty by omission).
[201] Felix III (II), *ep. 2 ad Acacium*; JW 592: Schwartz, PS 73, 1–11 (*Coll. Berol.* nr. 21).
[202] Idem, *ep. 3 ad Acacium* from March 483; JW 593: Schwartz, PS 75, 20–23 (*Coll. Berol.* nr. 23): '*Amotis scandalis ecclesiarum, quas scindi videmus*'.
[203] Idem, *ep. 11* (Synodal letter from 5 Oct., 485): Thiel 252–257; CA 70, p. 160, §11.
[204] Ibid., §8, p. 158, 15 and §7, p. 158, 6.
[205] Idem, *ep. 16 ad Rufin., Hilar. et Thalass.* from 1 May, 490; JW 614: Schwartz, PS 79, 1–3 (*Coll. Berol.* nr. 30).
[206] Idem, *ep. 1 ad Zenonem aug.*; JW 591: Schwartz, PS 67, 12–25 (*Coll. Berol.* nr. 20).

flesh from the very moment of the ineffable conception which it [the Word] power-fully began for itself in the womb of the virgin mother; [the Council preaches that] one and the same Jesus Christ God and Lord, one and the same God and man, one and the same unconfused and undivided (*inconfuse indivise*) truly remaining God and man, of undefiled birth subjected to the law, became visible in this world, performed acts at the same time divine and human; he dies, and rising from the dead sits at the right hand of the Father whence he will come as he was seen to go into heaven . . . .

These words are remarkable in more than one respect. They present a parallel to §4 of the *Henoticon* (see above) and hence would have been able to provide a good basis for a dialogue on the question of union. For the faith in the *oikonomia* of the incarnation is presented in both texts in such a way that all that is important is said against Eutyches as well as against Nestorius, without the controversial for-mulas of the 'one nature' or the 'two natures' arising. Thus one would have been able to discover what was held in common in this question; if this had been achieved, then the difference of the formulas need not have signified any particular scandal. The successor of Pope Felix III, Pope Gelasius I (492–496), believed, however, that the difference had to be emphasised more than the unity.

(c) Gelasian integralism and imperial immobility

During the pontificate of Pope Gelasius I there arose an extremely intense polarisation between the Pope and the Emperor on the one hand, and between the Pope and the patriarch of Constantinople on the other, insofar as the *Henoticon* was concerned. The style and language of the new Pope, who described himself as a 'Roman by birth'[207] but who certainly stemmed from North Africa,[208] reminds

---

[207] Gelasius I, *ep.* 12 *ad Anastas. imp.*; JW 632; Thiel I, 350, with n. 5.

[208] Thus according to the *Liber Pontificalis*, ed. Mommsen 116; L. Duchesne, *VI⁵ siècle* 12 ff., which compares Gelasius with Tertullian with respect to talent, temperament and speech. H. Koch, op. cit., 43 ff., gives prominence to the many similarities between Gelasius and Cyprian. On Gelasius see E. Caspar, *Geschichte des Papsttums* II. (Tübingen 1933) 44–81; C. Capizzi, op. cit., 110–113; F. Hofmann, *Chalkedon* II, 52–66, with lists of sources and secondary literature; V. Monachino, 'Gelasio I', Bibl.SS 6 (Roma 1965) 90–93; W. Ullmann, *Das Papsttum an der Wende der Spätantike zum Mittelalter = Päpste und Papsttum* 18 (Stuttgart 1981). In this study (Chs. V–VII, pp. 108–216), Ullmann analyses the different fundamental orientations of West Rome and East Rome respectively at the time of the Acacian schism. For Pope Gelasius I, who already under Popes Simplicius and Felix III was the chancellor of the Roman curia (pp. 116–127), what was particularly important was the upholding of the order and security of law on the basis of his legal conservatism. What was characteristic of Gelasius was that faith and law combined to form a new social order (138). The East on the other hand was more dominated by theology and subtle speculation (137–150). According to Ullmann there was the sharpest contrast between 'a Roman world oriented to law and a Greek world oriented to theology'. There were no longer two 'halves of the one Empire', but 'two unities which, in spite of many common ties, were divorced from each other' (150). It remains true, nevertheless, that Acacius attempted with his *Henoticon* policy to extend the rights of his patriarchate, particularly with regard to Alexandria, and that he pursued practical interests to a great extent. We shall presuppose the exposition of Ullmann and limit ourselves to christology and to what could be achieved on the basis of it to bring about understanding between Rome, Constantinople and Alexandria. In this area the disagreement between Rome and Constantinople was to be quickly settled after the death of Emperor Anastasius I, while Alexandria was no longer to be gained.

one of Tertullian's polemic. That juridical, canonical manner of dealing with East Rome, which became predominant later in the era of Gregory VII, announced its arrival. First of all we shall discuss only the way in which Gelasius I tackled the question of the *Henoticon* and the schism. In this regard we shall take into consideration the following writings:

(a) *Gesta de nomine Acacii*, written about 485–486, thus still under Pope Felix III(II): CA nr. 99, 440–453, together with the Epitome in Appendix II—III: CA 791–800; CLP 1670.

(b) *De vitanda communione Acacii*, written about 488–489: Schwartz, PS 33–49 (*Coll. Veron.* nr. 11); Thiel I, 287–311.

(c) Letter to the bishops of Dardania, 1 February, 496: CA nr. 95, 369–398, with Appendix I: CA 774–790; Thiel I, 392–413; 414–422.

(d) Letter to the bishops of the Orient: Thiel I nr. 27, 422–435; JW 665; Schwartz, PS 24–32 (*Coll. Veron.* nr. 10) in which the reasons for the condemnation of Acacius are presented. (The so-called *Tractatus* II of Pope Gelasius I, in Schwartz, PS 106–11 (*Coll. Berol.* nr. 43), is neither from Gelasius nor from any other Roman Pope; cf. Schwartz, loc. cit.). We shall conclude our study with a sketch of the Pope's christology on the basis of his important treatise 'On the two natures'. But first we have to deal with the question whether Gelasius, independently of his doctrinal position, brought with him the necessary qualities for furthering the possibilities of winning back the Church of Alexandria and for settling the schism with Constantinople. Thus what rôle did he play in the history of the *oikumene* (in the modern sense)? We are concerned here only with a few points which determined the Pope's judgement and method of proceeding with regard to the East:

(i) his heresiology, i.e. the reduction of the christology of all the supporters of the *Henoticon* to Eutychianism;

(ii) his understanding of a council or his conception of the effect of a conciliar condemnation and its extention;

(iii) his conception of and praxis regarding the question of assuming or refusing *communio* with its liturgical expression in the so-called diptychs;

(iv) his doctrine of the two natures.

(i) The heresiological positions of Pope Gelasius

In Treatise I (a. 486), designated as *Gesta de nomine Acacii*,[209] Gelasius gives an outline of the history of christological errors since the

[209] See CPL 1670; CA nr. 99, 440–453. An epitome was made of this: CA, Appendices nr. 2, 791–800. It contains once again the history of Eutychianism, finishing with the deposition of Patriarch Calandion of Antioch (484); Thiel I, 510–519; *Chalkedon* II, 60. Tr. I is contemporaneous with the letter of Felix III to the Oriental bishops: JW 611.

appearance of Nestorius and Eutyches. By means of this an 'historical foundation' (E. Caspar II, 41) was created for the papal polemic. As Nestorius was viewed in the line of Paul of Samosata and Photinus, so Eutyches was fitted into the series of those theologians at whose head was Apollinarius. In the fight against Nestorius, Eutyches fell into the opposite trap by affirming

> that Christ was not true man, as in him also two natures ought not to be accepted, but only one which is namely that of the God-Logos, even if it became flesh. But that is not the nature of a man, but is only human (*quam quidem non esse hominis perhibuit sed humanam* [sc. *naturam*]), whereby it is more the similarity with the human body than its reality (*veritas*) which is insinuated.[210]

In his way the Pope briefly weaves in the Chalcedonian conception of the person of Christ which could recommend itself as the middle solution between Eutyches and Nestorius, more than the *Henoticon* could:

> Against this the catholic faith confesses that Christ, the Son of God, is true God and true man, not of one nature, but of one existence and person.[211]

In the writings of Gelasius what strikes one is the urgency with which he brings up the teaching of Eutyches and the Eutychians. Certainly Manichaeism, which was still a threat in Rome in the fifth century, played a part in this. 'Eutychianism' signified for the Pope not only *a* heresy, but a whole collection of errors which had an unwholesome effect on the Christian conception of the economy of salvation. For on the reality of the incarnation, which was denied by Marcion, Manes and Eutyches, depended the truth of all the mysteries of the life of Jesus as a whole.[212] It must have been harsh on Greek ears to hear:

> Among the Greeks, who undoubtedly abound in a multitude of heresies, there arose now almost forty-five years ago a dispute about the incarnation of our Lord Jesus Christ with Eutyches, at one time a presbyter of Constantinople, blasphemously saying that we ought to believe that in our Lord Jesus Christ there is but one nature or substance, i.e. solely that of the godhead, with the complete abolition of the truth of the assumed flesh.[213]

---

[210] CA nr. 99, p. 440 f., §§2-3.

[211] Ibid., p. 441, §3: *non unius naturae sed unius existentiae atque personae*. This formula also reappears in the epitome = Appendix II: CSEL 35, p. 796, 3, with the one difference that in this *essentiae* is written instead of *existentiae*. On these readings see Thiel, *Tr.* I, p. 511, n. 4. He places the reading of the CA, cod. Vat. 4961 *existentiae*, in the apparatus and decides on *essentiae*, for which Petrus Coustant in his edition would prefer *substantiae*. This would presuppose the Greek *hypostasis*. Whether one is to read *essentiae* or *substantiae* is of little consequence for Thiel, because according to him both terms are here synonymous with *persona*. The conjecture of Cousant should be noted. One may perhaps refer to the translation of the Chalcedonian acta by Rufinus and his rendition of *hypostasis* by *subsistentia* (cf. his work *Contra Acephalos*: PL 67, 1238B; *Chalkedon* II, 819-821).

[212] Gelasius, *ep.* 3 *ad eppos Dardaniae*: JW 623; CPL 1608; PLS 3, 740; CA nr. 79, p. 221, §5. Cf. *ep.* 1 *ad Euphem.*: JW 611 from 492 AD; Schwartz, PS 49-55 (*Coll. Veron.* 12). For the Pope there is a line which stretches from Eutyches through Dioscorus, Timothy Aelurus, Peter Mongus and the anti-Chalcedonian Alexandrians in general. Even the rejection of Eutyches by Patriarch Euphemius will not be acknowledged by Gelasius. The fact of communion with Peter Mongus is in his eyes the recognition of Eutyches. Cf. PS 53.

[213] Gelasius, *ep.* 3 *ad eppos Dardaniae*: JW 623; CA nr. 79, p. 220, §4.

Somewhat later, however, the Pope admitted that the Greeks of his time did not themselves confess the pestilence of Eutyches, but made themselves guilty of this error by assuming *communio* with Eutychians.[214] Wandering preachers also sought to propagate this error in Dardania (ibid. §9). In their reply the bishops from there emphasised their vigilance against Eutyches, Peter Mongus, Acacius and their accomplices, and their own obedience to the Apostolic See which for them was a *sedes angelica*.[215]

Acacius of Constantinople came off particularly badly in the *commonitorium*[216] which had also been given to the papal emissary Faustus at the end of 493 while he was under way. In *ep.* 11 to the bishops of Dardania, of 3 August, 494,[217] the Eutychian pollution of the East was once again given strong emphasis. This state of affairs called for a condemnation which could not be more scathing. In this condemnation it was not so much a question of the past as of the present, for the later supporters of a heresy could be just as unwholesomely seized by it as its originators:[218]

Because just as in [the case of] any heresy catholic integrity ought to avoid with the condemned author of the deformity his successors and accomplices and indeed adherents of the kind who have commingled with them in defiled communion, so [it is that] with Eutyches one is to disown completely Dioscorus together with Timothy Aelurus, Peter of Alexandria and Acacius who was in communion with him, likewise Peter of Antioch with his partners....

The fact that one was not in fact a heretic (which really should have been the heart of the matter) was not sufficient for Gelasius I. Whoever inscribed the names of heretics in the diptychs remained in communion with those who erred, as the Pope emphasised in *ep.* 11. He never departed from this opinion.

(ii) The deposition of Patriarch Acacius and Pope Gelasius I's understanding of a council

For the West Acacius was considered to be deposed from 484. In the East this assumption was contested. According to the thesis of the supporters of the Patriarch he could only be deposed at an imperial synod which had been summoned especially for this purpose.[219] Such legal protection could least of all be denied to the bishop

[214] Ibid., CA nr. 79, p. 222, §8.
[215] CA nr. 80, p. 224, §§2 and 4: even without the warning from Rome they would have had this attitude.
[216] Gelasius, *ep.* 4 (*commonitorium*): JW 622; Schwartz, PS 16–19 (*Coll. Veron.* nr. 7).
[217] Gelasius, *ep.* 11 *ad appos Dardaniae*: JW 638; CA nr. 101, 464–468.
[218] Ibid., CA nr. 101, p. 465, §4.
[219] Cf. Schwartz, PS 224–225; Gelasius, *ep. ad eppos Dardaniae* from 1 Feb. (or 13 May?), 496: CA nr. 95, p. 369, 15 (§2); pp. 374–375 (§§16–17); *commonitorium* = *Coll. Veron.* nr. 7: PS 16, 33; 17, 10–23.

of the imperial residence.[220] In this context Gelasius developed his conception of a council: a council continues to have an effect which is not of limited duration. In the case of Acacius a new synod was not necessary for the reason that the work of the Council of 451 extended also to him. Thus he was deposed *de facto* 'by a council'. This negative effect the Patriarch drew upon himself because he assumed *communio* with Peter Mongus who was considered a heretic (Eutychian).[221] Gelasius illustrated his idea for the bishops of Dardania by referring to the history of Arius and the Arians.[222] But this rule applies to any heresy one cares to think of at any time whatsoever. For each time at a unique assembly the orthodox Fathers decided so clearly about faith and truth, about catholic and apostolic *communio* according to scripture and tradition that a distortion of their words was impossible. They were so definitive that there could be no possibility of either a *retractio* or an *iteratio*. Rather the phrase *positae semel synodalium regulae* (synodal rules are imposed once and for all) is applicable here.[223] Thus there was no necessity for a new synod or for a further condemnation of heretics of the same pedigree.[224] Gelasius had already presented this point of view in *ep.* 15 which was sent to the Oriental bishops in 495. With a condemnation such as in the case of Eutyches are included each time 'all those who are accomplices, supporters or fellow-travellers (*omnes complices, sectatores, communicatores*) of a deformity (*pravitas*) which had once been condemned'.[225] Hence just as Timothy Aelurus and Peter Mongus were condemned as supporters (*sectatores*) of such a man as Eutyches without a new assembly of bishops, the same is also true of Acacius, who did not invent a new error but only took up an old one by assuming *communio* with Peter Mongus.[226] Gelasius referred to his

---

[220] Gelasius, *ep. ad eppos Dardaniae*: CA nr. 95, p. 370, §2; p. 387, 16–17 (§53), which is formulated very harshly: *Risimus autem quod praerogativam volunt Acacio comparari quia episcopus fuerit regiae civitatis.* The intention in this is to expose Canon 28 of Chalcedon to ridicule.

[221] Gelasius, *ep.* 15 *ad eppos Orientis de Acacio* (AD 495); JW 665: Thiel, *ep.* 27, pp. 422–435; Schwartz, PS 26, 8–9 (*Coll. Veron.* nr. 10): *nihil enim nobis commune cum hominibus communionis externae*; ibid., p. 26, 26: (Petrus Mongus) *in haereticorum collegio perdurasse.* The Antiochene, Peter the Fuller, is judged in the same way: p. 31, 29–31: *Haec illa mixtura, haec est illa confusio quae per Orientem totum inter catholicam haereticamque communionem nulla discretio est.* On the contrary, whoever wants to disassociate himself from this group is considered a heretic. On p. 32, 22–23 Gelasius makes an unwarranted sweeping judgment: *Graeci . . . apud quos nulla est veri falsique discretio.* On the Pope's idea of a council see H. J. Sieben, *Die Konzilsidee* 270–305. Gelasius distinguishes between well and badly conducted synods (*bene-male gesta synodus*) on the basis of determined criteria (CA, p. 380, §31).

[222] Gelasius, *ep.* 13; JW 664 (1 Feb. or 13 May, 496): CA nr. 95, pp. 369–398 (with Appendix I), esp. p. 371, §7.

[223] Ibid.: CA nr. 95, p. 370, §§3–4.

[224] Ibid., p. 381, §34: to be *complex erroris* means *particeps eiusdem damnationis.*

[225] Gelasius, *ep.* 15 *ad eppos Orient. de Acacio*; JW 665: Schwartz, PS 25,36–26,6; Thiel, *ep.* 27.

[226] Ibid.: Schwartz, PS 26, 5–6: *Qui Petro communicavit Acacius ut criminis particeps, ita consors sit factus et poenae.*

predecessor, Felix III(II), who for his part helped an older decision gain acceptance.[227]

(iii) The *communio* between the Churches and its liturgical expression

One form of the declaration of *communio* was the assumption of the name (of a patriarch or bishop) into the diptychs, i.e. into the ancient writing tablets (*sacrae tabulae*). The profane sphere also knew of such entries; in this sphere such a practice concerned personages who had done great service (for public welfare). In the ecclesiastical realm the motive for entering someone's name was 'orthodoxy', seen each time from the standpoint of the one making the entry.[228] The opposite of this was striking somebody from the sacred tablets. Thus Acacius himself had erased the names of the bishops of West Rome from his diptychs and hence made manifest his breach with the Pope. From that point on there was no longer an exchange of correspondence between Acacius and the Roman Popes. On this question of the diptychs came to grief attempts made to heal the division by two successors of Acacius, both of whom were completely prepared to establish peace with West Rome, Fravitta (489–490) and Euphemius (490–496). Although the latter proved his loyalty to Chalcedon and even dissolved his *communio* with Peter Mongus, the lifting of the schism failed only because of the fact that the Patriarch did not want to erase the name of Acacius from the diptychs for the sake of the people.[229] Such rigidity is incomprehensible to us today. But Gelasius and even his predecessor Felix III(II) had a clear reason for this: the question about *communio* is a question about faith and truth. In this no *confusio* is allowed.[230]

(iv) *'Unus-integer-verus'*: the two-nature teaching of Pope Gelasius I

In the thoughts and writings of Pope Gelasius I, occasioned as

---

[227] Gelasius, *Commonitorium*: Schwartz, PS 17, 3–4: *executorem fuisse veteris constituti, non novae constitutionis auctorem.*

[228] On the diptychs see esp. *DACL* 4 (1920) 1045–1170, esp. 1055–1058; J. A. Jungmann, *Missarum Sollemnia* (Wien 1950) Bd. 2, 194ff.; *Chalkedon* III, Index s.v. Diptychen; Augustine, *ep.* 78: PL 33, 269–270: *liber vitae.*

[229] See the four letters in JW nr. 612 and 613 (Fravitta) and 614–615.

[230] The formula *'communio enim ad fidem pertinet'* (the question of being in communion is a question of faith): (*a*) This is found already in Felix III: Thiel, *ep. Gelasii* 1, p. 296, 17. See CPL 1165 and 1667; JW 611 (anno 489?; according to Thiel it was conceived by Gelasius I. (*b*) Cf. Gelasius, *Commonitorium* (= JW 622: Thiel, *ep.* 10; Schwartz, PS 16–19, esp. 17, 6–9. (*c*) Gelasius, *De vitanda communione Acacii* (ca. 488–9): Schwartz, PS 38, 15. (*d*) With the originator of a heresy are also condemned the *communicatores*, i.e. all who assume communion with him: Gelasius, *ep.* 26 *ad eppos Dardaniae*; JW 664; CA nr. 95, p. 371, §5; p. 381, §34: one can incur the punishment of a condemned heretic by being a *complex* of his error either through taking it over by way of infection or also, however, through *communio* or *consortium* with him. Ibid., p. 371, §5: both are revealed for what they are, either through a confession (*professione*) or through *communio*. It is for this reason that the question of diptychs is so important.

they were by the polemic around the unpleasant schism between East and West, the Western teaching of two natures found its most significant presentation since the two Tomes of Leo the Great. Admittedly, this was not in the pastoral style of his predecessor, but rather in the sharp and sometimes gruff language of the African Tertullian. The most important document in this regard is the so-called Third Treatise *de duabus naturis* (concerning the two natures).[231] On occasions the language finds dialectical formulations which aim at the one point: how can there be in Christ 'truth' and 'wholeness' (integrity) of the two natures of God and man, and yet he can still be 'one' (*unus*)?

The starting-point is the good news of the incarnation of the Son of God in the womb of the virgin, wherein the redemptive unity between God and man, the divine and the human nature, is established. We immediately recognise a pattern which Leo I could sketch for the eyes of his faithful in such a comprehensible way: Eutyches recognised only the divine nature, Nestorius only the human nature. For this reason the Church's teaching must proclaim the continued existence of the two natures against Eutyches' doctrine of mingling; with regard to Nestorius it must be emphasised that these two natures are from the very beginning unseparated, but this in such a way that both *sine confusione qualibet atque defectu* come together, and thus the properties of each of the natures also remain preserved in the union. Were the union of the two to mean the annulment of the human reality, then there would be rather a consumption (*consumere, consumpta*; Feuerbach would say: *maceratio*) than a fulfilling glorification of our nature. The old arguments against the *mia physis* doctrine of the anti-Chalcedonians recur in such a kind of 'becoming man' God would be subjected to change, whether this be seen as a transformation of the godhead into flesh or a transformation of flesh into the godhead. For Gelasius the synthesis lies in the designation *'deus-homo'*, 'God-man', for which he formulated one of the most powerfully expressive passages in Latin patristic writings:

> *Quamvis enim unus atque idem sit dominus Iesus Christus, et totus deus homo et totus homo deus, et quicquid est humanitatis, deus homo suum faciat et quicquid est dei, homo deus habeat, tamen ut hoc permaneat sacramentum nec possit ex aliqua parte dissolvi, sic totus homo permanet esse quod deus est, ut totus deus permaneat esse quod homo est, ne si aliquid, quid absit, vel divinitatis vel humanitatis inde cessaverit, sequatur ineffabilis resolutio sacramenti et, quod dictu audituque fugiendum est, vel homo deus esse iam desinat, si sola illic humanitas, non etiam deitas perseverat, vel deus homo consequenter esse desistat, si sola illic divinitas, non etiam humanitas unita permaneat nec glorificata videatur nostra conditio unitione deitatis, sed potius esse consumpta, si non eadem subsistit in gloria, sed sola existente deitate humanitas illic esse iam destitit (De duab. nat.: PS p. 87, 8–18).*

('Although the Lord Jesus Christ is one and the same, both the whole God being man and the whole man being God, and although whatever is of humanity the God-man makes his own and whatever is of God the man-God possesses, nevertheless in order that this mystery remain and not be able to be dissolved in any way, thus the whole man in Christ remains what God is so that the whole God remains what man is; lest if anything be lacking, anything either of the

---

[231] Gelasius I, *De duabus naturis in Christo adv. Eutychen et Nestorium*: Thiel I, 530–557 (*Tr*. III); Schwartz, PS 85–106. Details on this are to be found above in the text. On the expression *deus-homo* see A. Grillmeier, art. 'Gott-Mensch (Patristik)', RAC XII (1982) 312–366, esp. 332–334. There I neglected to refer specifically to Gelasius, *De duabus naturis*.

divinity or of the humanity disappear from it, the dissolution of the ineffable mystery would follow; and, what one must shun from saying or hearing, either man would now cease to be God if there only the humanity and not also the divinity persists, or God would consequently cease to be man if there the divinity alone and not also the humanity united with it were to remain; and our nature would not appear glorified through union with the divinity, but rather would be consumed, if it does not continue to be the same in glory, but with the continued existence of the divinity the humanity there now ceased').

The inversion 'God–man'—'man–God', this play on words which recurs constantly, is typical for Gelasius and does not occur in any other Latin Father. By means of this the Pope intends to elucidate the formula of the one person in two natures and to exclude any mingling, dissolution or diminution of the divine and the human reality in Christ (cf. ibid., p. 89, 27–34; 90, 1–4). One time he looks from the divinity to the humanity (*deus-homo*), another time from the humanity to the divinity (*homo-deus*).

On this divine-human unity is based the possibility of a truly human suffering of the cross on the one hand, and its redemptive effect on the other (so that paradise is opened to the robber). This divine-human unity is demonstrated by the quaking of the earth and by the resurrection which was effected by the God in the God-man, by the visible appearance before the disciples though the doors were closed, through the showing of his hands and feet throughout forty days, through the ascension of the God-man into heaven, his sitting at the right hand of the Father and the promise of his return. The whole series of the mysteries of Jesus' life is thus gone through under the motto 'God–man'—'man–God' (ibid., p. 90, 11–31). 'The same natures truly remain, *out of which* or *in which* one and the same true man-God and the true God–man exists' (ibid., 1. 28–31).

Gelasius avoids repeating the phrase from Leo's Tome to Flavian which was so offensive to the Alexandrians (v. 94: *agit enim utraque forma cum alterius communione quod proprium est*). He paraphrases it clearly, however, with his 'God–man'—'man–God' terminology. 'Indeed when we say of our Lord who is one and the same, what he said and did as God, and what as man, or even if we say "this he said or did as God–man and this he said and did as man–God", I ask whether,—either when we say that something was said and done as man, or the God–man did or said something,—whether, [I say] the man in him is true or false' (ibid., p. 92, 24–28). Gelasius has the same picture of Christ as Leo I: he views the one Lord in his undivided, unmingled total form as God and as man, but he accepts with Chalcedon that both natures are knowable as such in their actions and expressions (the important *gnorizomenoi*). Admittedly in his writings the accent is on the discernibility of the totality of the human, this being against Manes, Apollinarius, Marcion and other 'still more pernicious' varieties of such teachings which were rife at that time (ibid., p. 92, 28–31). By the latter the Alexandrians are meant.

With this emphasis on the '*Deus-homo*' in the unity of the person and duality of the natures, the insufficiency of the argument for the one-nature formula which the Alexandrians deduced from the comparison of the union of divinity and humanity in Christ with the anthropological unity of body and soul is obvious. Although man is composed of two parts which are essentially different, yet from both there is still *one* nature. Certainly according to Gelasius this is also the analogy, taken from the created sphere, which is most appropriate for the God–man Jesus Christ. He also admits that the scriptures speak of an 'inner' and 'outer' man without wanting to abolish in this way the unity of the person or of the one man. 'Surely then, although man consists of body and soul which undoubtedly are two natures, through a union of nature man is one person and one' (ibid., p. 94, 11–13): is this not the best proof for the *mia physis* formula? Gelasius faces up to this objection, but immediately emphasises the disparity of this analogy. Later scholastic theology would say: in man two 'incomplete natures' (*naturae incompletae, duo principia incompleta*) are united. The result is thus *'una natura'* in the strict sense, and, because a spiritual principle, i.e. the spiritual soul, is involved, also a person. Soul and body are *from their very nature* ordered to each other. That is not at all the case in the unity of God and man in Christ. Gelasius does not use the chance of this distinction. He has a weaker solution: *interior et exterior [homo] ad significantiam dicitur* **qualitatum,** *non ad evidentiam* **personalem** *duorum* ('the inner and outer man serve only to characterise qualities, not to express the personal unity of two [natures]') (ibid., p. 94, 15–16). The Pope increases his difficulties vis-à-vis the Alexandrians when he goes beyond Leo's Tome and attributes a special rôle to the word *'integer'* in order to put an end to the Eutychian, monophysite contraction (as he understands it) of Christ's human reality. It is precisely by doing this that he exposes himself to the reproach of Nestorianism, i.e. a doctrine of two persons. For the Pope still feels that in Alexandrian theology that principle is active which Ps.-Athanasius, *C. Apollinar.* I 2 (PG 26, 1096B) formulated in this way: 'Two perfect things cannot become one'. 'But rather they themselves profess that they affirm a Christ who is not whole by attempting to take away in the same mystery (*sacramentum*) something from those things in which it consists as a whole' (ibid., p. 94, 4–5). Then follows the important sentence: *itaque nos magis unum dicimus, qui integrum profitemur, et illi partem removendo de his ex quibus integer et unus existit, ita unum non habent, sicut nec integrum, et sicut integrum non habent, ita non verum. quapropter cum nobis obiciunt dyo fysis, sine quibus integer unus et verus Christus omnino non constat, aperiant sui oculos cordis et videant quod ipsi potius mone fysis rectius imputetur, per quam non integer Christus, ergo nec unus nec verus apud eos esse doceatur* (PS, p. 94, 6–11). ('Hence it is we who call him more the one, we who confess him as whole, than those who, by taking away one of the parts out of which he exists as whole and one, do not consider him as one just as they do not consider him as whole, and just as they do not consider him as whole so neither do they consider him as true. Wherefore, when they reproach us with *dyo fysis* without which the whole, one and true Christ does not abide at all, let them open the eyes of their hearts and see that one may rather reproach them with their *mone fysis*, whereby neither the whole Christ, and hence neither the one nor the true Christ, is taught by them to exist').

Thus according to Gelasius the unity in Christ of God and man must preserve three things so that the *deus-homo* does not become a half (*dimidius*) Christ. He must be one, whole, true. The word 'one' concerns the rejection of the Nestorian two persons, which the Chalcedonian two-natures teaching was interpreted as being. The words 'whole' and 'true' refer above all to the integrity and reality of Jesus' humanity which the Pope finds denied by the Eutychians and Alexandrians, these groups not being distinguished. All three predicates are necessary for the *deus-homo* and *homo-deus* if he is to be confessed in the sense of right faith. They condition each other reciprocally.

In order to be one he must be whole; in order to be whole he must be one and the same; and in order to be one and the same there remain preserved in him without ambiguity both natures out of which and in which he exists (*persistit*) as one and the same (ibid., p. 93, 27–30).

This is no doubt a more complicated language than the one the Council of Chalcedon itself used. Let us think only of the 'one and the same perfect in godhead, the same also perfect in manhood'. But the fact is that the more technical language of 'one nature and two natures' had been in discussion for decades and Gelasius could not by-pass this, for the 'two natures' were for the other side 'two persons'. The Pope suspected behind the *mone fysis* the principle of Ps.-Athanasius, *C. Apollinar.* I 2 already cited above: 'Two complete things [*dyo teleia*, or in the language of Gelasius: *duo integra*] cannot become one'. They cannot form an *unum*. It is on this account that both the Arians and the Apollinarians destroyed the *integritas* of the human reality of Christ by excluding a human soul (cf. Ps.-Athanasius, *C. Apollinar.* II 3: PG 26, 1136C–1137A). For Gelasius this was also the mistake of Eutyches and all supporters of the *mia physis* formula, though with the distinction that they denied the reality of the flesh (see above PS, p. 94, 6–8). In the eyes of the *mia physis* theologians it is nothing short of a contradiction when 'wholeness out of two' and 'one' are called for in the same breath. It is to be noted that with the expression 'out of two and in two' Gelasius goes beyond the terminology of Chalcedon, which consciously rejected the 'out of two natures' (cf. PS, p. 93, 27). We have here already an intimation of the dialectic of Maximus the Confessor, who saw the highest degree of unity realised precisely there where two extremes unite as 'one'. One could also say for Gelasius: the more that godhead and manhood in Christ are taken in their fulness, the more 'unity' is realised in him.

As proof of his claim the Pope then goes into the so-called anthropological-christological comparison: godhead and manhood form in Christ a unity as body and soul form one man (ibid., p. 94, 11ff.). He does not succeed, however, in making the similarity and dissimilarity in this relationship clear: Godhead and manhood in Christ form a unity in the same way as body and soul result in one man. Two linguistic forms of the comparison make up the starting-point: (*a*) soul and body = one man; (*b*) inner and outer man = one man. He concedes that in the first form each of the two terms, i.e. soul and body, is a 'nature'. But because both natures result in *one* man, and this by way of a 'natural uniting' (*adunatione naturali*), so the two natures of Christ in the Chalcedonian sense result in *one* Christ (ibid., p. 94, 11–13). The later scholastic anthropology was here more ingenious; but it was just because of this that it took the ground from Gelasius' comparison. For scholastic anthropology body and soul are '*naturae incompletae*', i.e. incomplete partial principles which are ordered to each other. With this conception the Arian-Apollinarian

principle 'two perfect things cannot become one' is implicity acknowledged, at least on the level of the relationship of *natura completa*
to *natura incompleta*. The analogy in the form in which Gelasius
employs it turns against him whether he expressly or tacitly takes
body and soul as *natura completa* or *incompleta*. When he allows godhead and manhood in Christ to be united through an *adunatio naturalis*,
he takes over Cyrillian or even Apollinarian terminology which was
so much detested by the Antiochenes. One immediately recognises
behind the Latin expression the *henosis physike* of Cyril. In a certain
respect one could thus describe the Pope as a Neo-Chalcedonian,
were not the irreconcilability of the one-nature formula with the
two-nature terminology so decidedly maintained by him. Gelasius
did not see through the dangerous implications of his presentation
and interpretation of the anthropological comparison. His anthropology is in itself just as imprecise as its application to the divine-
human unity.

With the second form of the anthropological analogy the Pope
makes things even worse for himself. Had he had the previous philosophical and theological history of the teaching on 'inner' and 'outer'
man in sight, he would have done better to have dispensed with
its use. On the one hand the Platonic and neo-Platonic interpretation
of the relationship between body and soul (the soul is in the body
like a sailor in his craft) weakens the emphasis on unity, the *one*.
On the other hand the statement of Ps. Athanasius, *C. Apollinar.*
II 3 (PG 26, 1136C–1137A) that the Arians used this comparison
to set the Logos (in their understanding) in the place of the 'inner'
man would of necessity have alarmed him. Because of this they could
also take over the *mia physis* formula. Thus there is no longer that
very thing which Gelasius accentuated so sharply: no longer is there
any *integritas*. But if he takes the 'inner' and 'outer' man as natures,
then once again it is difficult to make the unity understandable.
Gelasius sidesteps: both concepts (cf. Rom 7) are not employed to
depict two persons (*non ad evidentiam personalem duorum*), but to describe qualities. But with this move he no longer does justice to the
other two terms of the comparison, viz. God and man in Christ.
Probably the Pope saw himself justified in taking this way out by
the phrase in Leo's Tome to Flavian '*salva proprietate utriusque naturae*',
for he cites it in the immediate context (PS 94, 17). In other words,
it is once more to be emphasised that God and man in Christ as
natures remain preserved in their integrity, but nevertheless become
unus. Yet *how* this happens he cannot explain. For it is a matter of
an '*ineffabilis adunatio indivisibilis*', of an ineffable, indivisible union
(ibid., 1. 16). Hence Gelasius also makes no attempt to explain the

event of the *adunare*, of the uniting, although he contrasts well *adunatio* as the way to the result against the result itself, i.e. the *unus* with the *unio* as the united unity.

The intention of explaining the one Christ in two natures leads the Pope to another theological analogy, the doctrine of the eucharist. Here once again it is a question of the christological *unum, integrum, verum*. In the eucharist there is also intact duality in unity. The 'truth' here also has two poles. (1) We find a *'divina res'*, i.e. the reality of Christ's flesh and blood which allows the *incarnation* (sic) to become food and us to become sharers in the divine nature. The mention of the incarnation is directed at the 'docetism' of Eutyches and his reputed supporters. (2) On the other side the *'substantia vel natura panis et vini'* (substance or nature of the bread and wine) persists. The duality that Gelasius is driving at lies in the coexistence of the *'res divina'* and the earthly realities of bread and wine. For him there is clearly a duality in the unity. We ought not gauge his conception against the Tridentine teaching of transsubstantiation. J. Betz[232] refers to the affinity between Gelasius' conception and the interpretation of Theodoret of Cyrus. This reference is also justified by the fact that Gelasius produces as an appendix to his treatise a florilegium (PS 96–106)—whether this be complete or incomplete—which is taken from the fourth book of the lost *Pentalogus* of Theodoret. The sixty one testimonies correspond more or less felicitously to the line of proof which dominates the whole treatise—the *unus-integer-verus*. Through the Antiochene-Eustathian character of its terminology the florilegium was bound to nettle the opponents rather than convince them. According to the intention of the compiler the collection was to substantiate the distinction of godhead and manhood in Christ, this being aimed against the theopaschism of the Apollinarians and of the *mia physis* formula. The natures are distinguished, however, on the basis of the quality of the works. In particular some texts from Gregory of Nazianzus (e.g. nr. 18.19.27.61 in Schwartz, PS 98–106) well suited the aim of the Pope. We ought not expect more from the intense effort of the Pope than what is valid in general for the discussion at that time: the essence of the understanding of Christ which had been handed on is maintained when these three things are emphasised—integrity of manhood and godhead, truth of the human reality, and yet one Christ. Emperor Anastasius just

---

[232] See J. Betz, *Eucharistie* = HDG IV, 4a (1979) 155 f., with translation from *De duabus naturis* = PS 94, 22–34; PLS 3, 773 f. On Theodoret of Cyrus see ibid., 156 and 121 f. On the florilegium of Theodoret (*Pentalogus*), which Gelasius takes over, see the Chapter 'Ad Fontes' above II 5 and III, and Chapter IV 1. The texts in Schwartz, PS 96 ff., esp. nrs 7, 20, 45, 58, betray the Antiochene terminology (*homo assumptus, homo deum ferens, templum*, etc.).

as much as Acacius and the Alexandrians was bound to agree on this, if one does not take into account those extreme groups whom we encounter with the Manichaeans in West and East and the gnostic, docetist radicals in Egypt and elsewhere. Timothy Aelurus will portray for us the type of those who advocated the *mia physis* formula but who fought against it with just as much resolution as Leo I and Gelasius I, save for the difference that he, on account of his pledge to precisely this Apollinarian formula, could not root up the seed with its roots. The weed sprang up again and again.

The Two Natures-Doctrine and the Two Powers-Doctrine

Is there a parallel between the model used in christology and that applied to the imperial Church? One could be tempted to look for the christological model of the combination of duality in unity or, in Chalcedonian language, of 'unmingled and undivided' in the famous teaching of Gelasius on the two powers.[233] The defence both of the Latin teaching on the Church and of the Greek Chalcedonian teaching of two natures against Emperor Anastasius I led, indeed, to the formula which has become classical:

> *Duo quippe sunt, imperator auguste, quibus principaliter mundus hic regitur: auctoritas sacrata pontificum, et regalis potestas...*[234].
>
> *Christus memor fragilitatis humanae ... sic actionibus propriis dignitatibusque distinctis officia potestatis utriusque discrevit ... ut et Christiani imperatores pro aeterna vita pontificibus indigerent, et pontifices pro temporalium cursu rerum imperialibus dispositionibus uterentur, quatenus spiritalis actio a carnalibus distaret incursibus et ideo militans Deo minime se negotiis saecularibus implicaret [2 Tim 2, 4] ac vicissim non ille rebus divinis praesidere videretur qui esset negotiis saecularibus implicatus, ut et modestia utriusque ordinis curaretur, ne extolleretur utroque subfultus, et competens qualitatibus actionum specialiter professio aptaretur. Quibus omnibus rite collectis, satis evidenter ostenditur a saeculari potestate nec ligari prorsus nec solvi posse pontificem.*[235]

('There are two things, august Emperor, by which this world is principally governed: the sacred authority of the bishops, and kingly authority...'.

---

[233] On Gelasius' teaching of two powers see the texts in G. Pilati, *Chiesa e stato nei primi quindici secoli* (Paris 1961) 53–55 with notes; Thiel, *Epistolae*: Gelasius, *ep*. 12, 349–358; Schwartz, PS 19–24; II 1–6 of *ep*. 12 in H. Rahner, *Kirche und Staat* 254–263. The perspectives opened up here could lead beyond the happy acceptance of the imperial Church by the bishops of the CE (see Ch. III, above), but this would once again soon be eclipsed, as Pope Anastasius II demonstrates. On the teaching of two powers see E. Caspar, *Geschichte des Papsttums* II 10–81, esp. 63 ff.; W. Ullman, op. cit., (n. 208, above), esp. 198–212; W. Kissling, *Das Verhältnis zwischen Sacerdotium und Imperium nach den Anschauungen der Päpste von Leo dem Großen bis Gelasius I. (440–496)* (Paderborn 1920) 123–147. *Ep*. 43, cited in ibid., 138, which is addressed to the Bishops of Syria with a harsh censure of Emperor Anastasius for the *Henoticon*, is not genuine (cf. Schwartz, ACO III, 218–220; idem, PS 126–130; Thiel I, 58 f.; F. Dvornik, *Early Christian and Byzantine Political Philosophy, Origin and Background* (Dumbarton Oaks 1966) 804–809; H. J. Sieben, *Die Konzilsidee* 275–289; C. Capizzi, op. cit., 111–112.

[234] Gelasius I, *ep. ad Anast. aug.* (494 AD); JW 632: Thiel I, 350–351.

[235] Gelasius, *De anathematis vinculo: Coll. Veron.* nr. 6, Schwartz, PS 14, 14–24.

'Christ, mindful of human weakness, ... thus separated the functions of each of the two powers through the actions which are proper to each and through their different dignities ... so that Christian emperors need the bishops for eternal life, and the bishops use imperial directions for the running of temporal matters, so that spiritual action may stand apart from carnal attacks. Hence someone who is fighting for God should not involve himself at all in temporal affairs [2 Tim 2, 4], and in turn he who is involved in temporal affairs should not appear to preside in divine matters, both so that the restraint of each of the two orders be fostered, lest one borne by both [powers] become proud, and so that each special calling correspond to the qualities of each of its actions. When all these things have been correctly taken together it will be sufficiently evident that the *pontifex* can neither be directly bound by the secular power nor freed from it'.)

As much as the delimitation of 'both powers' is ascribed to Christ in these texts, yet in complete contrast to this the Pope does not call to mind the Chalcedonian model of the two-natures. Naturally theological reflection is not debarred from drawing the parallel. Precisely if the 'autonomy'[236] of the secular as well as the ecclesiastical spheres in the unity of a Christian society, as the Popes and Emperors at that time considered it, is taken as the point of departure, could christology have gained quite a lot. The Gelasian concept of the *integritas* of the *homo* in Christ would have been capable of being extended into the region of freedom of decision. But at that time no one thought of this, or if someone did, it was only by way of intimation. Even for Maximus the Confessor the leap over the ditch was not completely successful. From such a position the distinction of the two powers would also have been established christologically. Without realising it, Gelasius had written words of enormous explosive force. They signified nothing other than the destruction of the Eusebian-Constantinian principle of the imperial Church. Admittedly from time to time the Popes shook its structure when it became too confined for them. If the Emperors protected the *auctoritas sacrata pontificum* without surrendering this principle, the Pontifices could also as a consequence subject themselves without reservation to the *regalis potestas*, oscillating between joy and sorrow as the Justinian era will show us; indeed even the immediate successor of the great Pope Gelasius I already provides a good example of this.

(d) An inconsistent compromise proposal. Pope Anastasius II (496–498)

The successor of Pope Gelasius I would have liked to consider the fact that Emperor and Pope shared the same name—a coincidence

---

[236] On the topic 'autonomy' in the relations of Church and state, Church and the world see Vatican II, *Const. past. Gaudium et spes* nr. 36, 2–36, 3.

which he alluded to in his notification of election to the Emperor[237]—
an indubitable help (*non dubium . . . auxilium*) in the undertaking to
restore the unity of the Lord's tunic which had been divided on account of one who was dead.[238] What did the Pope offer and what
was the Emperor to give in return? One is surprised to see how
the position of the Emperor in the imperial Church, even in questions
of faith, is emphasised, as though there had never been a Gelasius I.

The breast of Your clemency is the sanctuary of public happiness so that at your
ínsistence (*instantiam*), you whom God has ordered to preside on the earth as his
vicar (*sic*), stubborn pride may not resist the evangelic and apostolic commands,
but so that what is salvific may be fulfilled through obedience.[239]

The depiction of the Emperor as the *vicarius Dei* and the custodian
of general welfare signifies an unconditional affirmation of the principle of the imperial Church which, however, in the very *Henoticon*
itself had become extremely questionable.

The conclusion drawn for the Emperor's procedure in striving for
the renewal of ecclesiastical unity sounds even more strange:

Nevertheless this in particular I make known to Your serenity, most glorious
and most clement son Augustus, so that, because the concerns of the Alexandrians
have reached your ears, you may bring it about by authority, wisdom and your
divine warnings that they return to sincere and catholic faith. For if you also have
commanded what must be held in the catholic religion according to the definitions
of the Fathers and the preaching of all the bishops (*sacerdotum*) who have flourished
in the Church, we shall refresh the memory of it for those who know by writing
(*transmittendo*), and for those who do not know we shall offer it to be learnt on
the basis of our teaching office (*pro officio nostrae instructionis*).[240]

To be sure the Pope upholds his superiority vis-à-vis the Emperor
in spiritual matters in a twofold way. He describes him as 'son',
as Pope Gelasius had done.[241] The Emperor also does not receive
the right to determine the content of faith which the Alexandrians
were to accept. But he was ascribed, in virtue of his imperial-sacral
authority, the possibility of demanding (or forcing) obedience with
regard to the proclamation of the bishops (Chalcedon is meant by
this as well). Without doubt there is reference here to the *Henoticon*,
the Emperor's reply to the *causa* of the Alexandrians. The contents
of the *Henoticon* itself are not acknowledged; nevertheless the Emperor

---

[237] Anastasius II, *ep.* 1 *ad Anast. imp.* (496 AD): Thiel I, p. 616, §1: *consonantia in me augustissimi
nominis tui non dubium praestat auxilium*. On the few letters of this Pope see CPL 1677; see Schwartz,
PS 226–30, on the Pope's policy with reference to the Church; likewise F. Hofmann, *Chalkedon*
II, 66–70; on the Pope's unjustified accusations see ibid., 69; C. Capizzi, op. cit., 286–288.
[238] Anastasius II, *ep.* 1 *ad Anast. imp.*: Thiel I, 616.
[239] Idem, ibid. cap. VI: Thiel 620 (§7).
[240] Ibid., cap. V, §6: Thiel I, 619.
[241] On addressing the Emperor as 'son' see H. Rahner, op. cit., 252–255 (following Thiel I, 292 f.:
Pope Gelasius).

is ascribed the competence to implement it. Thus the Pope offers his services to compose a new presentation of tradition, but it is his intention to leave it to the Emperor to force through the acceptance of this confession amongst the Alexandrians (and naturally also in the other patriarchates).

That Pope Anastasius II had not already appended a confession of faith to his announcement of election attracted attention. According to E. Schwartz, the Pope's reason for this was that 'he wanted to negotiate in Constantinople and did not want to tie himself down'.[242] Warned, however, by bishops who had become uneasy, the Pope made haste to make up for what he had neglected. In doing this he ventured to deal with the Chalcedonian formulas more than Pope Felix III(II) had done in his letter to Emperor Zeno cited above. He submitted a doctrinal interpretation 'which at no point offends against the Council of Chalcedon, containing even the controversial ἐν δύο φύσεσιν...'.[243] The Pope despatched legates to Constantinople. Through the mediation of the Thessalonian deacon, Photinus, who acted as interpreter, these made contact with the Alexandrian *aprocrisiarii* who were residing there. In spite of all this the expectation of the Pope that the *Henoticon* would be replaced by a letter promoting unity which he himself had composed amounted to nothing.[244] After certain errors that had found their way into the Greek translation of Leo's Tome had been clarified, the Alexandrians handed to the papal legates the official exposition of the faith (ἔκθεσις πίστεως) of their Church. It was nothing other than—the *Henoticon*. Only a few small changes were made: it was mentioned that at the Council of Ephesus Pope Celestine had assented to the condemnation of Nestorius. What was more significant was that in §9 of the *Henoticon* the naming of 'Chalcedon' was omitted and replaced by a neutral formulation. The dangerous formulation had read: 'But every person who has thought or thinks anything else, either now or at any time, either in Chalcedon or in any synod whatever, we anathematise...'. 'Either in Chalcedon' became 'at any place'.[245] The initiative had passed to the Alexandrians.

The legates took official notice of this document and declared that they would submit it to the Pope; he was said to be prepared, should an Alexandrian delegation be sent to Rome, to give it information about how he stood with regard to the submitted *ekthesis* [thus the slightly changed *Henoticon*]. They added that Dioscorus, Timothy Aelurus and Peter Mongus were opponents of this confession and hence their names had to be struck from the (Alexandrian) diptychs.[246]

This was naturally rejected. What came to Rome was this *ekthesis*,

---

[242] Schwartz, PS 228.   [243] Ibid.   [244] Ibid., 228–229.   [245] Ibid., 229.
[246] Ibid.

thus the slightly changed *Henoticon*, furnished with a report of the *aprocrisiarii*, brought by the *patricius* Festus and the two bishops whom Pope Anastasius had despatched. In the minds of the Alexandrians the Pope was to communicate his opinion about it to the Alexandrian patriarch either through a letter or a go-between.

> They [the Alexandrians] are said to be prepared to send legates to Rome to negotiate about the reunification of the Churches if the Pope upholds (it is thus insinuated that he has not deviated from it) the confession of the orthodox faith (only the *Henoticon* can be meant by this).[247]

The way the Pope had imagined he could impose upon the separated Alexandrians a Chalcedonian formula of faith composed by him was excluded. The death of the Pope on 19 November, 498 saved him from the disappointments which a look into the documents of his legates would have caused him. He would have been still more disappointed if the senator Festus, the leader of the mixed delegation assembled by Theodoric and the Pope, had attempted to carry out his unauthorised promise to move the Pope to accept the *Henoticon*. Such behaviour would have turned the mission of the (papal) legates into its precise opposite.[248] It was intended that the schism be healed in the other direction. Instead of the one division, there came to be two.

(e) *Clarae Ecclesiae Disciplinae*: Pope Symmachus (498–514)[249]

After the death of Anastasius II a legitimate majority elected the Sardinian Symmachus as his successor. The senator Festus with a smaller following attempted, on the other hand, to put the archpriest Laurentius on the papal throne, no doubt also with the hope of bringing his plans for the *Henoticon* to fulfilment. Thus there was added to the East-West schism a Roman one as well, the so-called 'Laurentian schism'. Only in 505 could a synod of 115 bishops ratify Symmachus, whose part King Theodoric I had taken from the start. Already in the period from 498 to 505 the new Pope had complained to Emperor Anastasius I about his proceeding with military power against the opponents of the *Henoticon* in the East.[250] Every possible means of having Zeno's Edict accepted was resolutely utilised. In the person of Flavian II, Patriarch Palladius of Antioch (+498)

---

[247] Ibid.

[248] Theodore Lector, *Epitome* 461: Hansen p. 130, 13–15: 'Festus, however, as the story goes, secretly promised the Emperor that he would persuade the Bishop of Rome to sign Zeno's *Henoticon*. But when he arrived in Rome he found the Pope already dying. For this reason he hastened to achieve what he sought [i.e. the signature] by a schism'. Cf. Theophanes, *Chronogr.*, A.M. 5993; De Boor 143. It is the beginning of the so-called Laurentian schism that is referred to.

[249] Symmachus ppa, *ep.* 13 *ad Orientales* (8 Oct., 512); JW 763: Thiel I, §5, p. 720; CA nr. 104, §13, p. 491, 10.

[250] Idem, *ep.* 10 *ad Anastasium imp.*; JW 759: Thiel I, p. 705, §11; Schwartz, PS 156, 3–5.

received a successor who acknowledged the *Henoticon* but who, unlike Palladius, did not assume communion with the Alexandrian patriarch, John Hemula, because the latter had anathematised Chalcedon and the Tome of Leo.[251] After the end of three years' war with the Persians which had tied up the Emperor's military forces, the pressure on Flavian II by the opponents of Chalcedon, led by Philoxenus of Mabbog, increased; this resulted in the Synod of Antioch (509), with which we are already familiar. The anger of the Emperor was directed, however, particularly against West Rome, to which he addressed a letter 'full of invective against the Pope',[252] who was described as a 'Manichaean', which meant a great deal in the old Roman imperial tradition. The Pope's ordination was put in doubt. It was said that in conspiracy with the Senate he had even excommunicated the Emperor. The reply was a sharp letter from Pope Symmachus; this letter is included by H. Rahner among documents concerned with the struggle for the freedom of the Church.[253] Anastasius I is reminded that he is a 'Christian prince' who has to listen to the voice of the 'apostolic bishop'.

You assert that I am a Manichaean. Am I a Eutychian or do I defend the Eutychians whose madness greatly favours the Manichaeans? Rome is my witness and the archives can prove whether I deviated in any point from the catholic faith which, on my conversion from paganism, I received in the see of the blessed apostle Peter ... And you who take to yourself the Alexandrian Peter [Mongus], are you not zealously striving to contemn the blessed apostle Peter in his successor, be he as he may. Is it that I would make a better [bishop], if I were to countenance the Eutychians, if I were to place the name of Acacius in the diptychs? The purpose behind these allegations of yours cannot be concealed.[254]

For West Rome there were also hopeful signs that the name of the 'dead Acacius' (i.e. the *Henoticon*) no longer had the power to form a united front against Chalcedon. This is shown by a letter to Pope Symmachus from a group of bishops in the Eastern Balkans.[255] If, since 482, there had ever been a possibility of building a bridge to the East, then it was through this group. Although they quite clearly professed Chalcedon, for tactical reasons they did not want to assent to the condemnation of a patriarch of the Imperial

[251] C. Capizzi, op. cit., 115 with n. 104.
[252] Ibid., 115 with n. 103. Shortly after 506 Emperor Anastasius published a *libellus* full of 'invective and insults' against Pope Symmachus. This document as such is lost, but its content can be inferred from Symmachus, *ep.* 10, *Apologia adv. Anastasium imp.*: Thiel 700–708; Schwartz, PS 153–157; commentary 249. Cf. F. Hofmann, *Chalkedon* II, 70–73.
[253] H. Rahner, op. cit., 264–277 (Latin-German).
[254] Ibid., 268 and 269; Thiel 702 f.; PS 154.
[255] *Inter epp. Symmachi ppae* 12: Thiel 709–717; F. Hofmann, *Chalkedon* II, 71, n. 175; V. Schurr, *Die Trinitätslehre des Boethius im Lichte der 'skythischen Kontroversen'* = FCLDG 18, 1 (Paderborn 1935) 108–127, furnishes proof that this group was made up of non-deposed supporters of the *Henoticon* in the Eastern Balkans.

City. Because of this they brought upon themselves the whole wrath of the Pope against the evil 'schismatics'.[256] He wrote that he could not bestow the religious comfort which they expected upon those who still lacked the 'full perfection of instruction' (*institutionis... plena perfectio*).[257] With the utmost severity these allies of the Church of Constantinople were rebuked for that city's history of heresy, as well as that of the Churches of Alexandria, Antioch, Apamea and Tyre. In the eyes of the Pope continued communion with Acacius and his allies put all these Churches which had communion with each other in the camp of the Eutychian heresy:

> Therefore let us undaunted proclaim with great confidence the clear teachings of the Church... Let us shun the sacrilegeous error of Eutyches which concurs with the Manichaean malice. For the same reason let us avoid the communion of those raised by them who now, as though infected by a disease, attempt to force their way into the Churches of your regions.[258]

Only someone who breaks with the whole fraternity—Eutyches, Dioscorus, Timothy Aelurus, Peter Mongus, Acacius—can return to unity with Rome (ibid. §8: Thiel 722).

The unrelenting attitude of the Pope left these bishops in their crisis of conscience and missed the opportunity of bridging the gap. Admittedly the Roman experiences with the Manichaeans ought not be forgotten.

(*f*) A new council in place of the *Henoticon*?

The last phase of Emperor Anastasius I's struggle with the Popes of West Rome during his period of office came with Pope Hormisdas (514–523). We can forego a depiction of the complete course of events.[259] We shall stress only two interrelated measures undertaken to restore the unity of the Church: the exchange of delegations and the attempt to summon and hold a new council.

In the period from January 515 to July 517 the last attempt to bring about unity between the Emperor and the Pope was made. Two papal and two imperial delegations[260] went back and forth between Rome and Constantinople. According to Evagrius, *HE* III 30, Emperor Anastasius I was for deposing all bishops who either

---

[256] Symmachus ppa, *ep.* 13 *ad Orientales*; JW 763: Thiel I, 717–722; CA nr. 104, 487–493.
[257] Ibid.: Thiel p. 718, §1; CA nr. 104, §2, p. 488.
[258] Ibid.: Thiel p. 720, §§5–6; CA nr. 104, §§12–15, p. 491–492.
[259] Cf. A. Schönmetzer, Zeittafel, *Chalkedon* II, 959–961; C. Capizzi, art. cit., *Critica storica* XVII (1980) 23–54. Altogether Capizzi discusses four failed attempts in the years 490, 492, 496 and 515–517. See ibid., 24, n. 4; F. Hofmann, *Chalkedon* II, 73–84.
[260] (*a*) Sources: *Liber Pontificalis*; Marcellinus Comes, *Chronicon*: Mommsen 60–108; papal letters, CPL 1683; JW 101–104; Schwartz, PS 169–170: Urkunden. (*b*) Studies: W. Haacke, *Die Glaubensformel des Papstes Hormisdas im Acacianischen Schisma* (Romae 1939) 19–22; See also the article by J. Speigl, 'Die Synode von Heraklea 515', *AHC* 12 (1980) 47–61.

expressly condemned Chalcedon or positively sanctioned it against the prevailing will of their diocese. In saying this the Church historian still ignored or overlooked the case of Patriarch Elias of Jerusalem (494–516).[261] The measures taken by the Emperor in the direction alluded to were only curbed by the insurrections of Vitalian[262], who took advantage of the religious excitement during and after the dangerous uprising of the people of Constantinople in 512 to have himself appointed *magister militum* and commander-in-chief of all troops in Thrace. On his (second) march against Constantinople he wrested from the Emperor the promise that a council would be summoned in Heraclea in Thrace (cf. Theodore Lect., *HE* frg. 66, *Epitome* 509: Hansen p. 145). Pope Hormisdas was to assume the presidency. The goal of the council was to be the uniting of the separated Churches, prescinding from the re-installation of the bishops who had been unjustly deposed. In Vitalian's mind this was no doubt thought of as an ecumenical council, an imperial synod, by means of which the *Henoticon* was to be eliminated.

On 28 December, 514, Emperor Anastasius forwarded to Pope Hormisdas the formal invitation to the newly-planned council; this arrived in Rome, however, only on 14 May, 515.[263] A second message, sent on 12 January, 515, reached its destination more quickly.[264] Beyond doubt it was with the knowledge of the Emperor that Bishop Dorotheus of Thessalonica, a supporter of the *Henoticon*, also wrote to the Pope. In his letters of invitation the Emperor displayed a striking tendency to limit the reason for summoning the council and to restrict its goal to a particular group. He spoke only of clearing away the obvious resistance in Thrace which as the last obstacle in the rejection of the *Henoticon* would have to be overcome: the ulterior motives of the Emperor may be interpreted in this way.[265] Already in the letter of 28 December, 514 the only matter that concerned him was 'certain doubts with regard to the orthodox religion

---

[261] Evagrius, *HE* III 30: Bidez-Parmentier 125–127; P. Allen, *Evagrius Scholasticus* 145–147.

[262] C. Capizzi, art. cit., *Critica storica* XVII (1980) 34–35, sketches the pro-Chalcedonian reaction which was triggered off by this in 511, 512 and 513 (Vitalian); on this W. Enßlin, *PWK* II 17. Halbb. (1961) 374–378. In March, 514, by means of an armed uprising, Vitalian attempted to force the re-installation of the deposed and banished bishops and the summoning of a Council under the presidency of the Pope. The opening of the Council was planned for 1 July, 515, and the Council was to be held in Heraclea in Thrace. Cf. *ep. Anastasii imp.* 1 *ad Hormisdam* (28 Dec., 514): CA nr. 109; *ep.* 2 (12 Jan., 515: CA nr. 107. The question of the Council has been fully treated recently by J. Speigl, art. cit. (n. 260); for further reference see in particular V. Schurr, op. cit., (n. 255) 127–135.

[263] C. Capizzi, art. cit., 35 f.

[264] Anastasius imp., *ep. ad Hormisdam* 2: CA nr. 107, p. 499–500. The letter of Bishop Dorotheus of Thessalonica was certainly written with the knowledge of the Emperor: CA nr. 105. Both these letters, conveyed by Patricius, arrived in Rome as early as 28 March, 515.

[265] CA nr. 107, p. 500, 2–4.

in the region of Scythia'.[266] This restriction, however, is certainly conditioned by the addressee, Pope Hormisdas, together with the Churches placed under his charge in Thrace (*de ecclesiis sub sui sacerdotii cura constitutis*). We hear of the inclusion of the Eastern Church only from Severus of Antioch who decidedly refused to participate.[267] If it was the Emperor's aim to have the *Henoticon* definitively accepted by wanting to have the Patriarch of Antioch retract or refrain from the anathema against Chalcedon, then the council was doomed to failure from the very beginning. Of course this is true as well from the Roman side, for falling into line with such a policy with regard to the *Henoticon* was unthinkable for Hormisdas.

The Pope was also concerned about the date. Only on 4 April, 515 did he write to the Emperor[268], and at first requested merely further information about the reason for summoning the assembly (*causa congregationis*) (CA nr. 108, §6). He wrote that only then could he give an 'exhaustive reply' (*plenissimum responsum*). At the same time he called a Roman synod[269] to discuss the sending of legates. Moreover, Hormisdas journeyed with Vitalian's negotiators to Ravenna to inform King Theodoric and to hear his opinion, as one can well assume. Nevertheless, we know nothing about the result of the negotiations. The delegation which set off for the East on 11 August, 515 also had only a preparatory function, but it was well armed for this purpose. It carried the following documents: (1) a letter to the Emperor,[270] (2) an *indiculus* with precise instructions for the negotiations[271] and (3) the famous *libellus fidei* of the Pope which all the bishops were to subscribe if they wanted to assume communion with Rome.[272] This last document contains the counter-proposal to the *Henoticon*:

'The beginning of salvation is to preserve the rule of right faith and not to deviate at all from the decisions of the Fathers'. [The words of Christ 'You are Peter...' are confirmed by the fact that the catholic religion has constantly been preserved unstained by the Apostolic See]. 'Therefore not in the least desiring to separate ourselves from this hope and faith... we anathematise all heresies, their teachings and their supporters [expressly mentioned are: Nestorius, Eutyches, Dioscorus, Timothy Aelurus, Peter Mongus, Acacius; the inclusion of Peter the Fuller of Antioch is new], whereas we accept and approve all the letters which holy Pope Leo wrote about the Christian religion. Following in everything the Apostolic See and proclaiming all its propositions of faith... we promise that the names of those excluded

---

[266] CA nr. 109, §2, p. 502. See ibid., 2–3 on the location of the Synod: *Heracleotana civitas provinciae Europae.*
[267] Severus, *ep. ad mag. off.* (between 514 and 518): Brooks, SL II, I, 21, p. 73.
[268] Hormisdas ppa, *ep. 2 ad Anastas. imp.*; JW 771: CA nr. 108, a reply to nr. 107.
[269] *Liber Pontificalis*, Mommsen 126.
[270] Hormisdas ppa, *ep. 8 ad Anastas. imp.*; JW 775: CA nr. 115, pp. 510–513.
[271] 'Indiculus' together with 'Capitula singularum causarum': CA 116 with 116 a, pp. 513–520.
[272] *Exemplum 'Libelli'*: CA nr. 116b, pp. 520–522, cited here following *Chalkedon* II, 76–77.

from the community of the catholic Church... will no longer be mentioned at the celebration of the sacred mysteries. This profession of mine I sign with my own hand and give it to you, Hormisdas, the holy and venerable Pope of the city Rome'.

The delegation of two bishops, a priest, a deacon and a notary arrived in Constantinople about the middle of September 515.

In the meantime the Emperor was freed from political pressure with regard to the council by the failure of Vitalian's third attack on Constantinople (autumn 515). Consequently, the carrying out of the plans for the council depended only on himself and Pope Hormisdas. That the Emperor was serious about the council is evidenced by the fact that in the summer and autumn of 515 some two hundred bishops turned up in Constantinople;[273] a journey to the capital was in any case a pleasure for many a prelate. In this number Severans also were not missing, despite the decided refusal of their leader.[274] Nevertheless, a council did not eventuate; it was not even opened.[275]

The origins of this turn of events lie elsewhere. As early as summer 515 a group of forty bishops from the Balkan provinces separated themselves from the metropolitan in Thessalonica and established relations with Pope Hormisdas. The 'Henoticon party' fell away to the left (the extremism of the anti-Chalcedonians) and to the right (return to Chalcedon). On 11 September in a letter to Caesarius of Arles,[276] Pope Hormisdas could report overjoyed about the initiative of the 'forty'. On the other hand, the anti-Chalcedonian party with the well-known leading names (now including Peter the Fuller) is condemned in this letter (§2) in the sharpest language: it is written that in the eyes of the catholics they bear impressed on them the marks of eternal damnation (*infixa aeternae damnationis stigmata*). They no longer have any right to call themselves Christian. This conclusion was reached because Hormisdas considered them as representatives of the 'Manichaean fantasy', and hence as the absolute negators of the reality of the incarnation.

---

[273] Theodore Lector, frg. 67, from the book 'Concerning schisms', §8: Hansen 146; Theophanes, *Chronogr.*, A.M. 6006: De Boor 161; J. Speigl, *AHC* 12 (1980) 47–61, with a survey of secondary literature; Severus, SL I 24: Brooks 83.

[274] See J. Speigl, *AHC* 12 (1980) 55 f.

[275] Ibid., 56: 'The sources are not adequate for even considering as assured that the Council was opened in Heraclea or that it was transferred to Constantinople. It remains a moot point how many bishops came to the city of Heraclea at all and how many remained in Constantinople from the outset. Nevertheless, the fact that bishops from various provinces sojourned in Constantinople for many months cannot be doubted. Admittedly nothing happened during this time for someone like Theodore Anagnostes, who had expected the re-installation of the deposed bishops. In other respects there must have been a great deal of theological discussion as well'.

[276] Hormisdas ppa, *ep. 9 ad Caesar. Arel.* (11.9.515); JW 777: Thiel 758–761, §2: *episcopi tam Dardani quam Illyrici pene omnes nec non Scythae.*

The contemporary chronicler Marcellinus Comes portrays the reaction of the Emperor to this secession in his chronicle for the year 516.[277] He writes that a number of these bishops, among whom was Alcison (who is known to us from the letter of the monks from Palestine [Evagrius *HE* III 31]), came to Constantinople, where two of them died. They would have liked to have mediated in some way between the Emperor and the papal delegation, which was then on the point of arriving. But this failed. On their return to Rome in the winter of 515–516 they carried with them a letter from the Emperor which, though a disappointment to the Pope, is still of great importance for determining the Emperor's interpretation of the *Henoticon*. We shall emphasise only the most important points and cite some sections word for word.[278]

The way in which he describes the economy of the incarnation in §§2–6 is reminiscent of §7 of the *Henoticon* and even more of Pope Felix III's letter of March 483 to Emperor Zeno (see above), but especially of the periphrastic presentation of the doctrine of the incarnation at Chalcedon with its confession of the twofold *homoousion* (cf. §3). The reference to the return of Christ sounds decidedly devout: 'Our nature (*substantia*), however, was assumed without diminution or confusion of our body in such a way that the Son of God will come in the same flesh to judge the world, showing to the eyes of all the signs of the wounds and the nails (*vulnerum et clavorum indicia*), as it is written: "they will look on the one whom they have pierced" [Joh 19, 37]' (§4). He affirms that this was his faith from the beginning of his life and that on this his rule is founded. The Emperor may be believed and exonerated definitively of the suspicion of monophysitism.

Particularly significant are §§7–9: 'Yet we wonder why you wanted to write to us something about the holy Fathers who gathered at Chalcedon as long as what was decided by them is shown to have been confirmed by various decrees of our predecessors, and since no other synod has been held by means of which the ordinances of that Synod (*quae ab illa disposita sunt*) were made of no consequence, and no law has been enacted by us through whose novelty (*novitas*) the statutes of the said episcopal Council would be annulled, especially since the Synod itself said that anyone who wanted to teach another faith than that which the three hundred and eighteen venerable Fathers established at Nicaea or to change [that faith] ought to be anathema. In addition they also condemned those whom we mentioned above, i.e. Nestorius and Eutyches, whom we also condemn. For the divine [imperial] letters, which not just once but repeatedly were addressed to Alexandria, are for us also testimonies on behalf of the same cause. In these we rebuked [the Alexandrians], [asking] why they did not consider that they could be satisfied with the direct teaching of the faith, refraining from anathematising the Synod of Chalcedon or the venerable memory of Bishop Leo. For this purpose we [exerted] no little effort, and this intention also continues now, insofar as we can divert the same ones [the Alexandrians] from a superfluous anathema and unite [them] to the holy universal Church'.

It was not without reason that the Emperor gave such a vivid

[277] Marcellinus Comes, *Chron.* a. 516, §3: Mommsen 99.
[278] Anastasius I imp., *ep. ad Hormisdam*: CA nr. 125, pp. 537–540.

description of the picture of Christ as the returning judge who, as he wrote, will bear on him the signs of the wounds and nails for all to see. Without doubt he wanted in this way to express unambiguously that for him the man Christ was no Manichaean fantasy, but reality. But it is particularly his understanding of the *Henoticon* and his rôle in the uniting of the Churches which is clear here. (1) He declares unambiguously that Chalcedon is in no way annulled, rather that it has often been expressly confirmed by the Emperors. (2) He can also truthfully say that he was wholly displeased with the enthusiasm with which the Alexandrians (but especially the Antiochene Severus) had expressed the positive anathema against the Fourth Council. What he had in mind was the 'direct teaching of the faith' which should have been presented on both sides (without the formulas which divided and without mutual condemnation). That this might have been possible, we have demonstrated by various examples which expressed the doctrine of the incarnation by reference to Cyril's *Laetentur* letter and the definition of Chalcedon itself, without employing either the formula of the 'one nature' or that of the 'two natures'. With such an interpretation of the *Henoticon*—indeed dogmatically acceptable; in practice, however, idealised—the Emperor stood virtually alone. Neither the anti-Chalcedonians nor the Pope could declare that they agreed with it. The actual interpretation of the document by the estranged parties made any attempt at mediation impossible. In the last resort the whole discussion again ended up in the direct recognition or rejection of Chalcedon.

Nothing of this was changed by the last exchange of delegations in the years 516–517. On 16 July, 516 an imperial delegation to Pope Hormisdas departed for West Rome with an imperial *sacra*.[279] The legates also had a letter to give to the senate.[280] In the latter Anastasius returned strikingly to the old imperial title *pontifex*.[281] In his reply the Pope certainly declared his desire for peace, but as before he expected one thing from the Emperor—the condemnation of Patriarch Acacius. The Roman senate endorsed this.[282] Was there another attitude possible here without putting the faith in danger? When the counter delegation from West to East set out, Pope Hormisdas once again demanded that Acacius be condemned.[283] On their way his delegates had to involve themselves in extensive activity

[279] Id., *ep. ad Hormisdam*: CA nr. 111, pp. 503–504; C. Capizzi, art. cit., 39–41.
[280] *Anastasius I imp. Senatui Urbis Romae*: CA nr. 113, pp. 506–507.
[281] Ibid., p. 506, 20.
[282] Hormisdas ppa, *ep. ad Anastas. Imp.*; JW 779: CA nr. 112, pp. 504–506; the Senate: CA nr. 114, pp. 508–509.
[283] Papal embassy to Constantinople on 3 April, 517 with letters 11–16; JW 789–794, to the Emperor, Patriarch Timothy and others.

in and around Constantinople.[284] At the end one had not really come a single step closer in the search for what could unite everybody in a more profound knowledge of Jesus Christ. If one does not take into account the ambivalent 'use' of the principle of the imperial Church, one may humanly consider the last words which the Emperor wrote to Pope Hormisdas as the expression of a Christian tragedy:

> Even if silence is considered to be something great, it is necessary, however, that those who admire the mercy of God make frequent assiduous use of speech, especially because the beginning of the faith which the Lord and God, our Saviour Jesus Christ, taught us lies pre-eminently in the forgiveness of sins is held not to be unknown to anybody... If it is true, as some endeavour to show, that certain [people who derive their office] from the apostles themselves neglect through disobedience to fulfill such pious teaching, we do not know where the teaching office of the merciful Lord and great God can encounter us... but from now on we hold back in silence our demand, because we consider it unreasonable to bring the goodness of requests to those who do not wish to be asked and stubbornly reject [every request]. For we can put up with being insulted and regarded as nothing; to be given orders—that we can not.[285]

Thus on 11 July, 517 Emperor Anastasius broke definitively with Pope Hormisdas, who for his part had made everything dependent on subscribing the *Libellus fidei* and was prepared to assume communion solely on this basis.[286] This stance can only be explained on the basis of the Pope's conviction that the question of truth had priority over all other acknowledgements; that is, the conviction that faith in the true incarnation of Christ was definitively abandoned with the *Henoticon* and the assumption of communion with its defenders and the opponents of Chalcedon in general.[287] The great omission between 482 and 518 was this: the common basis, which was actually present, was not taken advantage of, nor was it discussed thoroughly by both sides. This accusation is indeed easy to make; but our experiences with ecumenical discussions today should temper the demands we make on that period. For with the question of truth were combined extremely difficult topics which likewise had to be discussed thoroughly. (In many ways these are under discussion even today). These were: (1) the suitability of the system of the imperial Church as a whole, a system from which the Popes attempted to escape on various occasions without remaining consistent in their attitude;

---

[284] See A. Schönmetzer, Zeittafel, *Chalkedon* II, 960, nr. 307–309: CA nr. 126–130, pp. 540–552; C. Capizzi, art. cit., 40–43 with a summary of the event.

[285] Anastasius imp., *ep. ad Hormisdam*: CA nr. 138, pp. 564–565. The last sentence reads: '*iniuriari enim et adnullari sustinere possumus, iuberi non possumus*'.

[286] Cf. *Liber Pontificalis*: Mommsen 126–128; *Chalkedon* II, 83 and 137.

[287] That this conviction on the Roman side was sincere cannot be doubted. We have emphasised sufficiently that this view was too narrow and too black and white.

(2) the question of the authority of such a great Council as Chalcedon was—if one retreated behind such a great event or kept silent about its results, its linguistic prescriptions and its reception by the great majority of the bishops, as Emperor Anastasius wished to achieve through having everybody bind himself by oath to the *Henoticon*, then the logical consequence of this was to put the Church's autonomy and its understanding of itself in question. Sooner or later the advance to a new level of theological reflection would perforce have to be made. In the following chapters the necessity of this advance will be shown by the fact that it was precisely within the traditionalist group which maintained the *mia physis* theology that schisms continued to emerge, whereas the development within Chalcedonian theology was relatively continuous.

In short, the *Henoticon* showed itself to be the wrong way to unity The return to Chalcedon after the death of the Emperor permitted a broader attempt to be made. This was rendered all the more possible since the anti-Chalcedonian position around 518 had already been so explicated by its major authors that the central differences could be expressed openly without being camouflaged. In this perspective we can already look ahead to the discussion which dominated the seventh century, ending with the Council of Constantinople (680–681).

CHAPTER FIVE

'A PERFECT FEAST FOR THE CHURCH'
THE CHALCEDONIAN RESTORATION UNDER
EMPEROR JUSTIN I (518–527) AND IN THE FIRST
YEARS OF THE REIGN OF EMPEROR JUSTINIAN I
(527–565)

DURING the night 8/9 July 518, Emperor Anastasius I died. On the same day, 9 July, the commander of the *excubitores*, i.e. the palace guards, Justin, from Berediana in Dardania (East Illyria), was 'unexpectedly' elected emperor.[1] The decision in his favour was supported by the senate, the army, the demes and also by the Church. He was crowned immediately in the hippodrome by Patriarch John II. Even the circus parties, the Greens and the Blues, agreed on him. As an Illyrian with Latin as his mother tongue he, as well as his wife, the new Empress Euphemia, possessed certain qualifications that were favourable for ties with West Rome;[2] but, as Emperor Anastasius had shown, such qualifications did not automatically produce results.

(A) THE UNQUALIFIED PROFESSION OF THE COUNCIL OF CHALCEDON

The new Emperor quickly championed the cause of Chalcedon. One must presume that even before his elevation to the throne he was a supporter of the Council. The change of rule revealed how strong the Chalcedonian party was in the imperial city, this partly as a result of the influence of Vitalian, but more because of that of the monks, particularly the Acoimetoi.[3]

---

[1] See Evagrius, *HE* IV, 1–4: Bidez-Parmentier 153–155; on this P. Allen, *Evagrius Scholasticus the Church Historian* (Louvain 1981) 171–175. Evagrius names the candidates for the throne from the side of the clientele of Anastasius. Theocritus, the favourite of the powerful Amantius, was selected. He could not get a chance (cf. Evagrius IV 2). On the following: A. A. Vasiliev, *Justin the First* (Cambridge/Mass. 1950) 68–82; ibid. 9–42 the sources for Justin's religious policy. E. Stein-J. R. Palanque, *Histoire du Bas-Empire* II (Paris-Bruxelles-Amsterdam 1949) 219–273; R. Haacke, 'Die kaiserliche Politik in den Auseinandersetzungen um Chalkedon (451–553)', *Chalkedon* II 141–152; F. Hofmann, 'Der Kampf der Päpste um Konzil and Dogma von Chalkedon von Leo d. Gr. bis Hormisdas (451–519)', ibid. 84–94.
[2] Cf. Zacharias Rh. cont. *HE* VIII 1: CSCO 88 (V) 42: *sententiam filiorum Romae participavit, synodum et Tomum Leonis proclamari imperiose iussit.* Hamilton-Brooks 190: 'he shared the opinions of the inhabitants of Rome....'.
[3] Cf. H. Bacht, 'Die Rolle des orientalischen Mönchtums...', *Chalkedon* II (193–314), 269–271.289; J. Pargoire, 'Acémètes', *DACL* 1 (1924) 318–321. Important is F. Halkin, 'La vie ancienne de saint Marcel l'Acémète', *AnBoll* 86 (1968) 271–321; see in particular the introduction.

I. *Vox populi—Vox Dei*

When the liturgy was celebrated in the old Hagia Sophia on 15 July, the first Sunday after the coronation of the Emperor, spontaneous demonstrations showed that it was above all the people who pressed for swift action with regard to the policy concerning the Council. Patriarch John II (518–520), just elected under Anastasius I and devoted to him, was to be the first to experience this. Under pressure from the faithful who had no intentions of stopping their acclamations, he had to make himself the instrument for carrying the change in religious policy. The suggestive mysticism of the *ekboeseis*, the acclamations, had its great hour. We have a detailed report of an ear- and eye-witness for the days of 15 and 16 July 518.[4] According to this report the people were unyielding in making the following demands: (1) proclamation of the 'holy Synod' of Chalcedon; (2) banishment of Severus of Antioch, who was more than once depicted as a 'Manichaean' (i.e. as one who denied the reality of the incarnation), although this in no way corresponded to the truth; (3) recognition of the title *Theotokos* for Mary, a title, however, which was no longer a matter of controversy. John II[5] had to ascend the ambo in order to pacify the applauding throng which kept the doors of the church closed and were prepared to hold out to the end. He professed orthodoxy, which he cleverly described as acceptance of the first four Synods from 325 to 451, so that he was spared from having to profess the Fourth Council on its own, something which no doubt would have been even more difficult for him. Above all he placed Nicaea with the creed of the 318 Fathers in the forefront,[6] this being regarded as a special proof of orthodoxy. For all that he also acknowledged Chalcedon as a 'synod that cannot be abandoned'.[7] Furthermore he emphasised that he wanted to hold fast to the traditions of the Fathers, which he had already done before 'with the

---

[4] See the *Collectio Sabbaitica*: Schwartz, ACO III, nr. 27, pp. 71–74; on the origin of the CS, ibid. VIII–XI; a full translation of nr. 27 in Vasiliev, *Justin the First*, 136–141. These acclamations were noted down (and counted) and were to be submitted to the Emperor; cf. ACO III, 76, 2–3. Considerable attention was also paid to these by the Synod of 20 July in its report to Patriarch John II: ACO III, nr. 25, p. 62, 27–28; 63, 7–8.12–15 (where reference was made to the sustained shouts from the 'people with wives and family', the dignitaries, the army and the monks); in addition p. 63, 33–34; 64, 11; the monks for their part made reference to them in their *libellus* to the *synodos endemousa*, ibid., nr. 25, p. 67, 38–40.

[5] On John II, the Cappadocian (519–520), see *Regestes* I 1², nr. 206–216. When Victor of Tunnuna reports ad a. 517 (Hansen, *Theodoros Anagnostes* 76, p. 151; *Regestes* nr. 206) that John, in accord with the will of Emperor Anastasius, had to curse the Council of Chalcedon, then this does not correspond to the real procedure of the Emperor. Indeed at the consecration of the Patriarch on 17 April 518 the people had demanded the condemnation of Severus and the restoration of orthodoxy. Cf. Theophan., *Chron.* A.M. 6010: De Boor I, p. 164, 13. Thus the ground had already been laid for the events of 15 and 16 July 518.

[6] Cf. ACO III, nr. 27, p. 73, 9–14.

[7] Ibid., p. 75, 11–29.

hope of uniting the separated Churches'. We must assume that this was a sincere motive for the Patriarch, as well as for Emperor Anastasius I. After the Emperor's policy with regard to the *Henoticon* had foundered, John II could combine his hope for the union of the Churches only with a reaffirmation of Chalcedon. The people had their own conception of how this should happen. In prolonged shouts they demanded the special proclamation of the Fourth Council in the setting of 'a synaxis of the Synod of Chalcedon', thus a liturgical celebration, which was to take place on the following day, 16 July.[8] This was the important step that introduced a feast of Chalcedon, which became a permanent institution in the ecclesiastical calendar of the Church of Constantinople.[9]

II. *The feast of Chalcedon*

On Monday, 18 July 518, this Chalcedonian synaxis was celebrated in Hagia Sophia.[10] As soon as the Patriarch entered, the people demanded 'a perfect feast for the Church'.[11] By this was meant nothing other than a total settlement of the post-Chalcedonian crisis with its problems of faith and of persons. In any case the whole matter was to be dealt with. In the course of the three days, 15, 16 and 20 July, this became all the clearer. As the setting of the liturgical celebration on 16 July showed, the Chalcedonian theme was to be broached first of all in the reading out of the diptychs. In accord with the demand of the people the following would have to be named in these: (1) the 'four Synods' (this already represented an extension of the acclamation of the previous day. Apparently the proposal of their Patriarch that the Fourth Council be named together with the first three had appealed to the acclaimers);[12] (2) the names of the deposed Patriarchs Euphemius and Macedonius, as well as that of Pope Leo I of Rome. Through the binding together of both forms, the naming of synods and persons, the confessional character of incorporation in the diptychs became clear. The original *memoria* of persons became a *memoria* of important ecclesial events which here signified a special statement of faith. To give outward expression

---

[8] Ibid., p. 73, 17–21.27–34.
[9] See S. Salaville, 'La fête du concile de Chalcédoine dans le rite byzantin', *Chalkedon* II, 677–695, where the development and the content of the liturgical celebration is described in detail. Here we shall point out only what is most important.
[10] ACO III, nr. 27 p. 74, 18–76, 25.
[11] Ibid., p. 75, 2: τελείαν ἑορτὴν τῇ ἐκκλησίᾳ, which is then further developed on pp. 74–75.
[12] Cf. ACO III, nr. 27, p. 75, 3. A.-J. Festugière, *Les moines d'Orient* (4 Vols) (Paris 1961–1965), III/2, 90, n. 190, is of the opinion that there is talk of the *memoria* of the four Synods only because of a manner of speech that was too terse (this occurring in *Vita Sabae*, LX: Schwartz, 162, 2–19; Festugière, op. cit., 90, 2–19). In reality, 'les diptyques sont des listes de noms de personnes (vivants et morts), non de listes de conciles'. On account of the witnesses from Constantinople which we have mentioned, this assertion cannot be sustained.

to the rehabilitation of the patriarchs of Constantinople who had formerly been deposed, it was ordered that their mortal remains should be translated. Conversely, the leading opponents of Chalcedon and other 'heretics', the Nestorians and Eutychians as a whole, had to be condemned. If those in question were already dead, then their remains had to be scattered. On 16 July the repudiation of Nestorius, the condemnation of Severus of Antioch and his supporters, especially the *praepositus sacri cubiculi*, Amantius, were demanded. The latter soon met his death, as Theocritus, who had been regarded as a 'monophysite' candidate for the throne after the death of Emperor Anastasius,[13] had even before. Once all the wishes of the people, so far as these were directed to the Patriarch, had either been fulfilled on the spot or their fulfilment was firmly promised, the Benedictus and Sanctus could be sung and the liturgical celebration duly brought to a conclusion.[14] Thus on 16 July 518 the feast of Chalcedon (in conjunction with the *memoria* of the three other Synods) had its première in the Constantinopolitan liturgy.[15] In this feast the Byzantine liturgical reception of the decisive Synods of the early Church was expressed in impressive fashion. The Churches of Antioch and Jerusalem were called upon, in letters addressed to each, to adopt this celebration (see II/2).

III. *A synodal act*

It was natural that the new initiative received synodal reinforcement, a procedure easily carried out in Constantinople thanks to the institution of the *synodos endemousa*. Without delay it met on 20 July 518 to examine the decisions demanded by the people; the Patriarch, however, was not present.[16] Even the Chalcedonian monks of Constantinople advocated the recognition of the 'four Synods' with a *libellus*.[17] The result was five synodal resolutions which were presented to the Patriarch:[18]

(1) the assumption into the diptychs of Patriarchs Euphemius and Macedonius who had died in exile; (2) the same for all four Synods from Nicaea to Chalcedon;

---

[13] On the rôle of Theocritus and Amantius at the time of the change of Emperors and on their murder, see Zacharias Rh. cont. *HE* VIII 1: CSCO 88 (V), 42; Hamilton-Brooks 189–190; Stein-Palanque, *Bas-Empire* II, 223–224.

[14] ACO II, nr. 27, p. 76, 4–25.

[15] For the further history of this celebration and its extension to seven synods, see S. Salaville, art. cit., 687–690. The first synod to be added (as number five) was the Council of Constantinople (536), at which Severus of Antioch, Peter of Apamea, Anthimus of Constantinople and the monk Zoaras were condemned. At this Synod the reports about the proceedings of 15 and 16 July 518 were read out.

[16] ACO III, nr. 25, pp. 62–66; Vasiliev, op. cit., 146–148.

[17] Ibid., nr. 26, pp. 67–71; Vasiliev, op. cit., 145–146.

[18] Ibid., nr. 25, pp. 63–64.

(3) in addition, the names of Leo I of Rome and Cyril of Alexandria; (4) the reinstatement of all those banished on account of their loyalty to the two Patriarchs, and the return of their confiscated goods; (5) the anathematisation of Severus of Antioch. The last demand was pressed by the submission of a special complaint of the Chalcedonian monks and clerics of Antioch which had been lodged with Patriarch John II and which contained a whole list of accusations.[19]

(B) A New Attempt to Unite the Church on the Basis of Chalcedon

The dogged effort of Emperor Anastasius I to unite the imperial Church by means of his *Henoticon* policy had failed. Such a policy was out of the question for the supporters of Chalcedon, but also for the radical opponents of the Council. With the disappearance of this artificial basis of the *Henoticon* the polarisation in the Eastern Church became all the more acute. Could it be hoped at all that the unity of the Church could still be established on the basis of the Fourth Council? This goal which Emperor Justin boldly attacked demanded two steps: (1) the elimination of the Acacian schism between East and West Rome, and (2) the bridging of the much deeper separation between the supporters of the Council and its opponents, whose leader was still considered to be Severus. While the reconciliation between Pope, Emperor and Patriarch could be brought about quickly, the definitive division of the Eastern imperial Church into the Byzantine Chalcedonian Church and the old Oriental anti-Chalcedonian Church in Egypt and Syria began after 518 with varying speed. Though after the Council of Ephesus (431) the radical Nestorians had been forced across the border of the Empire, the anti-Chalcedonian Orientals remained inside it until they became swift prey for the Islamic conquerors in the seventh century.

I. *The conclusion of peace between East and West Rome*

On 1 August 518 the new Emperor informed Pope Hormisdas of his election in a short letter which was answered in the name of the 'catholic Church' in October or November the same year.[20] The negotiations on union thus began and quickly led to success.

---

[19] *Petitio clericor. et monach. Antioch. ad Ioann. Patr. et Synodum Cp.*: ACO III, nr. 24, pp. 60–62 (subscribed by twenty-six representatives of the Church of Antioch). The main reproach was the raid made by Severans on a group of pilgrims who were Syrian Chalcedonian monks. During this attack, which occurred in the neighbourhood of the Symeon monastery in Syria Prima in autumn 517, 350 monks were killed on the spot. Cf. E. Honigmann, *Évêques et Évêchés*, 60–61; the report of the survivors to Pope Hormisdas in CA nr. 139, 5: CSEL 35 II, 566–567; on 9 February 518, Pope Hormisdas sent a letter of condolence to the survivors: CA nr. 140 (Latin and Greek), pp. 572–585; Thiel I, 820–830.

[20] See *Iustin. Aug. Hormisdae ppae.*: CA nr. 141; CSEL 35 II, 586; the reply of the Pope, ibid., nr. 142; CSEL 35 II, 586–587.

Here we can take for granted the detailed exposition of the individual steps and the analysis of the corresponding exchange of letters between Emperor and Pope,[21] as not very much of what arises from that pertains to christology. It will be sufficient to give prominence to the concluding of peace and its major document, the *formula of Hormisdas*. A brief chronology, however, may help in following the course of events:

9.7.518	Emperor Justin requests a papal delegation to resolve the schism (letters of Justin, Justinian and Patriarch John II: CA nr. 143.147.146)
1/2.519	Papal delegation despatched to Constantinople with many letters (JW nr. 802–814)
25.3.519	The arrival of the delegates in Constantinople (CA nr. 148–150)
28.3.519	Under the influence of the Emperor, Patriarch John accepts Hormisdas' formula of faith, though this is editorially assumed into a letter to his 'colleague in office' (*comministrator*) who was, however, acknowledged as the encumbent of a see which at all times was a steadfast protector of the catholic faith (CA nr. 159)
31.3.519	On the feast of Easter Emperor Justin declares that ecclesiastical unity has been restored. End of the Acacian schism (484–519). The papal legates communicate with the Patriarch and the bishops present in Constantinople, who likewise subscribe the formula of Hormisdas (CA nr. 159.167.223)
24.4.519	Large mail despatch to Pope Hormisdas (CA nr. 160–165)
519/520	Through legislation of Justin the army is pledged to Chalcedon: Jacob Edess., *Chronicon* (cf. *Chalkedon* II, 148, n. 26)
9.7.520	Return journey of the papal delegates from Constantinople with letters to the Pope (CA nr. 192.194–198)
25.3.521	Letters of Pope Hormisdas to Emperor Justin (CA nr. 236: CSEL 35 II, 716–722)

From our point of view the most important act and the decisive document is the formula of Pope Hormisdas and its acceptance in the East, particularly by Patriarch John II.[22] In a positive christological sense subscription of the *libellus* means nothing more than

---

[21] See F. Hofmann, art. cit., *Chalkedon* II, 84–94 (from the papal side); R. Haacke, art. cit., ibid., 141–149 (from the imperial side).

[22] See *Exemplum Libelli Iohannis ep. Constantinop.*: CA nr. 159: CSEL 35 II, 607–610 = DS nr, 363–365; CPL nr. 1684; *Regestes* I 1², nr. 210. The basic text of this formula of Hormisdas is already present in the *libellus* which on 11 August 515 he gave to his legates who were destined for the planned Council of Heraclea. Cf. CA nr. 116b: CSEL 35 II, 520–522. See the excerpt in Ch. IV, n. 272. The bishops of the Synod were to subscribe it. The Synod, however, did not take place. In the winter 515/516 the legates returned to Rome with the letter of Emperor Anastasius: CA nr. 125: CSEL 35 II, 537–540. The other exemplars of the *libellus* are listed by Guenther in CSEL 35 II, Appendix IV, p. 800. Apart from CA nr. 159, the important ones are: (1) the exemplar which Justinian subscribed for Pope Agapetus on 16 March 536 = CA nr. 89: CSEL 35 I, 338–340. In contrast to CA nr. 159 there is in §3 (p. 339) of this an addition which includes the main text of the definition of 451 in the *libellus*. (2) The exemplar which Patriarch Menas gave to Agapetus: CA nr. 90: CSEL 35 I, 340–342, with the same addition in §3. On the transmission of the text, see E. Caspar, *Papsttum* II, 764–765; W. (=R.) Haacke, *Die Glaubensformel des Papstes Hormisdas im Acacianischen Schisma* = AnGreg 20 (Roma 1939); for a critique of this see H. Koch, ThLZ 65 (1940) 256–260.

acceptance of the definition of 451 and 'all the letters' of Pope Leo I.[23] No attempt is undertaken to give a concentrated exposition of the Chalcedonian definition which had been in dispute since 451, although this might have seemed called for after the numerous misunderstandings and violent controversies. In lieu of it there are anathemas directed against the most important opponents of Chalcedon, or of Ephesus in the past: Nestorius, Eutyches, Dioscorus, Timothy Aelurus, Peter Mongus, Acacius of Constantinople, Peter the Fuller (CA nr. 159 §3–4). Such a listing of names must give food for thought. Severus of Antioch is not named in this list, nor even in the exemplars of the formula which were subscribed on 16 March 536 (CA nr. 89 and 90), although at the Synod of Constantinople from 2 May to 4 June 535 anathemas were pronounced against Severus as well as against Patriarch Anthimus of Constantinople.[24] Pope Hormisdas looked beyond Constantinople towards the whole East. In numerous letters which continued to go to the Imperial City, to Justin, Justinian, Patriarch John II and others,[25] or in instructions for his delegates to the East,[26] the mandate was given to look after the Churches of Antioch and Alexandria in order to lead them back to the Chalcedonian confession or to confirm them in it. For the Patriarch of Constantinople what was most difficult was to renounce his dead predecessors in office and to strike their names from the diptychs. The work of union was here brought to an unnecessary crisis. Time and again Pope Hormisdas returned to this point and was intransigent. His main reason for this was already expressed in January 519 in a letter to Patriarch John II:[27] 'To receive the Council of Chalcedon and still to continue to defend the name of Acacius, that is to maintain things that are irreconcilable'. But what is not understandable at all is that finally the removal of the names of the Patriarchs Euphemius and Macedonius and of a series of other bishops in the East was demanded as well. On 9 September 520 Emperor Justin complained rightfully and powerfully about the severity of the papal letter regarding the diptychs, because on this question one of the Pope's predecessors, Pope Anastasius (496–498), had been

---

[23] CA nr. 159: CSEL 35 II, 6, p. 609: *unde probamus et amplectimur epistolas omnes beati Leonis papae urbis Romae, quas conscripsit de recta fide.*

[24] See ACO III, *Coll. Sab.*, nr. 5, pp. 178–182. The creed which Emperor Justinian subscribed and presented to Pope Agapetus: CA nr. 91, §§8–22, from 18 March 536, makes no reference to Severus (CSEL 35 I, 344–347).

[25] Cf. JW nr. 819–821.

[26] Cf. JW nr. 827.841.842.

[27] See *Hormisdas ppa, ep.* 47, 2 (JW nr. 803), January 519: Thiel I, 837; CA nr. 145: CSEL 35 II, 589–591. The sentence cited: p. 590, §4. It is remarkable what a problem of conscience Hormisdas makes out of the assumption of *communio*: ibid., p. 590, §7: ... *libellum ... subscriptum ad nos dirige, ut sine conscientiae formidine unam communionem, sicut oramus, habere possimus.* Cf. in addition JW 804–808.

much milder in his action,[28] demanding only the removal of the name of Acacius.

There is no doubt that the real agitator in the diptychs question was the Alexandrian deacon, Dioscorus. In the middle or at the end of January 519 he was assigned as unofficial adviser and interpreter to the papal delegation to the East, which consisted of the bishops Germanus and John, the priest Blandus and the deacon Felix. He gained more and more influence over the delegation. On 22 April 519 he sent to Pope Hormisdas a *suggestio* of his own[29] which reached Rome on 19 June 519. In this it is reported that after peace had been concluded in the capital, even apart from Acacius, the names of the patriarchs between 489 and 518 in general (thus Fravitta, Euphemius, Macedonius and Timothy) and the names of the Emperors Zeno and Anastasius were removed from the diptychs, no doubt under pressure from the papal delegates.[30] The Church of Constantinople had coped with this. Thus the unity between East and West was established for nearly half a millenium.

The same severity which Hormisdas and his deacon Dioscorus had applied to the relationship between the *sedes Romana* and the *sedes Constantinopolitana* ought to be extended, according to the said *suggestio*, to the question of *communio* between Constantinople and the Eastern patriarchates and episcopal sees. Rome ought to stipulate precise conditions for this. Such a procedure had to endanger the work of union, particularly if the question of the diptychs was pressed without any consideration of differences.[31] It was only under Patriarch Epiphanius (520–535), the successor of Patriarch John II, that Pope Hormisdas, while still emphasising his *libellus*, condescended to concede to the Church of Constantinople greater freedom of choice in granting or refusing *communio*.[32] The exhortations of Justin which we mentioned thus had some effect.

After the *Henoticon* had ceased to be a possible basis for *communio* between Constantinople and Alexandria, for which purpose it had been devised in the first place, the supporters and opponents of the

[28] See *Justin. Aug., ep. ad Hormisdam*: CA nr. 232; CSEL 35 II, 701–703 (9 September 520). The Emperor did not insist on retaining the names of Acacius, Peter Mongus, Peter the Fuller, Dioscorus and Timothy Aelurus. He asked the Pope: 'Is it better for the sake of small things [= the diptychs] that such large numbers of Christians be completely cut off from us, or through concessions and an overlooking of small things that that which is greater and must be absolutely attained be corrected?' (loc. cit. §4, p. 702).

[29] *Suggestio Dioscori diac. per Pullionem subdiac.*: CA nr. 167; CSEL 35 II, 618–621.

[30] See ibid., §11, p. 620.

[31] On this action regarding the diptychs Dioscorus says: *et non solum hoc in ipsa sola ecclesia, in qua episcopus manet, verum etiam per omnes ecclesias cum grandi diligentia deo adiutore suggerimus fuisse factum* (p. 620, §11).

[32] Cf. *Hormisdas ppa, ep. ad Epiphan. Constant.*, 26 March 521: JW 861; CA nr. 237; CSEL 35 II, 726–728, §§5–7.

Council of Chalcedon were again facing each other in the open on the decisive point at issue: one nature or two natures in Christ. With regard to the *Henoticon* the West had remained aloof, since for it the document did not exist or it was simply placed on a par with 'monophysitism'. Was there then for the future no possibility of bringing about the unity of the separated groups? In the view of the imperial Church the method which offered itself immediately was that pursued, at least partially, by Emperor Marcian after Chalcedon. This was to force the 'dissidents' to obey and so prevent division by employing imperial power in combination with the threat or imposition of ecclesiastical anathematisation, in accord with the Constantinian principle of unity. Was it not bound to be fact that what could serve as the proper and only way to restore unity and *communio* was the *theological* elaboration of the differences in the various traditions? Was this possibility seen at all in the first phase of the Chalcedonian restoration under Emperor Justin and Pope Hormisdas?

II. *The limits of the imperial-papal restoration under Justin I*

1. The accent of the imperial-papal work for unity lay on *authoritative decrees and measures* which were intended to bring about acceptance of the Fourth Council or the exclusion of those who refused. Insofar as only East Rome and West Rome were directly concerned, this was not so repressive, as in Constantinople too the majority of the people and the monks remained loyal to Chalcedon and of their own accord desired the conclusion of peace between Emperor and Pope. The situation was different for the patriarchates of Antioch and Alexandria. In these there existed strong majorities against Chalcedon and for the old Alexandrian tradition in the sense of Cyril. It was in these that the number and severity of the interventions by the imperial Church rapidly increased. This negative process, however, was not supported solely by the Emperor and the Pope, but by various other forces.

If on 15 July 518 the people of Constantinople had demanded a 'perfect feast for the Church', what was explicitly meant by this was the instrument of the anathema against the opponents of Chalcedon. Severus in particular was in their sights. In this regard Dioscorus, the Alexandrian deacon whom we have mentioned already, became prominent. At the end of his *suggestio* to Pope Hormisdas he insinuated to him that in letters to Patriarch John II he demand the condemnation of Severus and all those whom the Pope had named in his letter to the monks John and Sergius in Syria Secunda.[33] It

---

[33] See the *Suggestio Dioscori diac.* §17: CA nr. 167; CSEL 35 II, 621. For the letter to the Syrian monks see CA nr. 140, 10 February 518, §15; CSEL 35 II, 580–582. Here the persons to be condemned

was not without reason that Pope Hormisdas attempted to put this Alexandrian deacon in the place of the anti-Chalcedonian Patriarch Timothy of Alexandria (517–535).[34] Egypt, of course, could dodge imperial influence to a great extent. For the next fifty years it would become the centre of the resistance against Chalcedon. Severus could flee there and immediately be regarded as the great saint and real patriarch of the Coptic Church. During his lifetime no encumbent of the see of St Mark, whether Melkite or anti-Chalcedonian, could compete with him. Nevertheless even while Justin was Emperor there arose there amongst the opponents of Chalcedon themselves that schism which damaged the authority of Severus for the rest of his years, although it could not impair his posthumous fame in the same way.[35] This was the profound conflict between Severus and Julian of Halicarnassus who, like the deposed Patriarch of Antioch, had also fled to Egypt and had found refuge in the monastery of Ennaton.

The method of solving crises through anathemas increasingly necessitated the employment of civil power. Vitalian's action after April 519 is the worst instance of this trend; he, however, met his death at the end of July 520 at the instigation of Justinian, the nephew of Justin I.[36] In his way the Antiochene Patriarch Paul II (519–521) also participated in the violent proceedings. After two years, however, he had to resign on account of his bad personal life. Numerous episcopal sees were occupied afresh. In the patriarchate of Antioch roughly forty bishops had to surrender their office because they wanted to remain loyal to Severus. 'Particularly affected were the two Eastern provinces, Euphratensis and Osrhoëne. More than half of the bishops in Euphratensis and more than three-quarters in Osrhoëne lost their sees'.[37] In 519 fell the second strongest pillar of the anti-Chalcedonian Syrian Church after Severus—Philoxenus of Mabbog. He died in December 523 in Philippopolis, the metropolis of Thrace.

were named as: (a) for Alexandria: Dioscorus, Timothy Aelurus, Peter Mongus; (b) for Constantinople: Acacius with supporters; (c) for Antioch: Peter the Fuller, Severus, Philoxenus of Mabbog, Cyrus of Edessa, Peter of Apamea.

[34] See *Hormisda ppa. Dioscoro diac.*, 3 December 519: CA nr. 175 §§2/3; CSEL 35 II, 631–632. The Pope had already informed the deacon that he would write to Emperor Justin: *ut te Alexandrinum episcopum debeat ordinare. iustum est enim, ut ea doctrina vel moderatione tua corrigatur ecclesia, in qua praecipue ab istis aetatis tuae principiis militasti* (2). On the other hand Emperor Justin wanted to make Dioscorus the patriarch of Antioch; Hormisdas considered this to be false planning.

[35] Cf. W. E. Crum, 'Sévère d'Antioche en Égypte', *ROC* 23 (1922/23) 92–104; J. Maspéro, *Histoire des Patriarches d'Alexandrie* (Paris 1923) 65–101, especially 86–88; A. Guillaumont, 'Histoire du site des Kellia ...', F. Daumas- A. Guillaumont, *Kellia I. Kom 219* (Le Caire 1969) 10–11.

[36] Cf. E. Stein- J. R. Palanque, *Bas-Empire* II, 230–233.

[37] See J. Speigl, 'Das Religionsgespräch mit den severianischen Bischöfen in Konstantinopel im Jahre 532', *AHC* 16 (1984) 264–285, 264. Speigl refers to the important article of S. Brock, 'The conversations with the Syrian Orthodox under Justinian (532)', *OCP* 47 (1981) 87–121. We shall have occasion to return to this article in II/2.

The bishops who had fled or been banished retained, however, a power which was capable of depriving Justin's restoration program of its results, despite ten years' efforts. Those who had been deposed ordained new clerics for the area which they had left and thus began to build a new hierarchy. They were supported by numerous monks who had been roused to passionate opposition against the new policy of the Church; the severity of Paul II of Antioch had been the cause of this. Even under the more mild Patriarch Euphrasius of Antioch (521–526) they offered dogged resistance. As a result of this they had to get out of the way into the desert, where they founded new coenobia.

The time for a new policy had come. However, when Emperor Justin's nephew, Justinian, was named as co-emperor on 1 April 527, recourse was had once again to the policy of coercion. Patriarch Ephraem (527–545), who had been installed in Antioch in the same year, also joined in this policy. But in 531 Justinian relaxed the persecution of the anti-Chalcedonians and rescinded certain laws. Those who had been banished could return. Numerous bishops proceeded to Constantinople under the protection of Empress Theodora, Emperor Justinian's wife, who was of anti-Chalcedonian mind. On the Persian border Justinian himself came into contact with bishops in exile and discovered that the way which could lead to the goal of unity was not that of expulsion, but rather of discussion. It was obviously from this experience that there emerged the proposal for the *religious conference of 532 in Constantinople*. 'The Emperor himself had sufficient open-mindedness for such talks, and he had his special reasons for them in the ineffectiveness of the previous policy and in the stabilisation which the region (the problem provinces on the Persian border and the patriarchate of Antioch) needed'.[38] Thus a *commissio mixta* was formed in which, following the idea of the Emperor, both sides were to be represented equally, each by six bishops who were selected in accord with a cleverly devised scheme. We shall be content here merely to register the fact of this religious conference, as we still have to evaluate it in detail (in II/2). By way of restriction we must say even now that Justinian was animated by only one concern, to lead the anti-Chalcedonians back into the unity of the imperial Church by means of the discussion of faith. 'The talks of the two groups of bishops had not been negotiations between people on the same footing. Rather the Emperor brought the bishops who were adverse to his imperial confession into contact with representatives of his own side, in order to find out how the

[38] J. Speigl, art cit., 264–265.

dissidents could be led back to unity'.[39] For all that a compromise seemed to be suggested which at this point, against the background of the history of discussion about the *Henoticon*, deserves to be mentioned.

According to a Syrian report about the religious conference the Syrians had formulated their own ideas on the assumption of communion, and submitted these to the Emperor. 'They laid down the following conditions. Those who accept the two natures after the union must be anathematised. The same anathema must apply to the letter of Leo and to everything the Council of Chalcedon did against right faith. And above all the *libelli* of the Roman Popes (Hormisdas), which all the bishops are to subscribe, must be suppressed as well ... After receiving the Syrian conditions, Justinian for his part made proposals with compromise formulas and solutions. They [the Syrians] were to anathematise Diodore, Theodore of Mopsuestia, Theodoret, Ibas, Nestorius and Eutyches and were to accept the Twelve Chapters of Cyril, while everything that had been written against them was to be anathematised. They [the Syrians] were *obliged to confess one nature of the incarnate Word of God* [my italics], but apart from that they were to anathematise those who speak of two natures after the miraculous union, while they had also to anathematise those who, in the sense of Nestorius, divide Christ into two natures. They were to accept the Synod of Chalcedon, insofar as this Synod concerned the anathematisation of Eutyches, but they did not have to accept the definition of faith which had been made there. They were to renounce their anathema of Leo's Tome, and the *libelli* of the Romans were not to be annulled ... In order to save a recognition of the Council of Chalcedon and communion with Rome, apparently some names were to be condemned in a kind of exchange transaction. If we may trust the Syrian report even to some extent, the greatest significance of the meeting of 532 lay in the fact that Emperor Justinian made compromise proposals for a solution, proposals which herald the beginning of the Three Chapters dispute'.[40]

Thus the way of discussion had also opened up no prospect of unity. Obviously the time was not yet ripe to analyse the theological language used by both sides in their formulas, to define the concepts and to contrast what was really meant with the linguistic and conceptual expression, so that in that way true disagreement and genuine agreement could be established. The situation called for the new theological and philosophical methods which mark the beginning of the Byzantine scholasticism of the sixth century (see Ad Fontes, Part V). Emperor Justinian himself soon reverted to the employment of force as the way to restore unity.

At a Synod in the Imperial City (2 May–4 June 536) Severus of Antioch and Patriarch Anthimus of Constantinople (535–536) were anathematised.[41] Novel 42 of Justinian[42] ratified the decisions of this

---

[39] Ibid., 279.
[40] Ibid., 282–283.
[41] On the Synod of Constantinople (536), see ACO III, *Coll. Sab.* nr. 5, 126–130.
[42] An imperial constitution of 6 August 536 prohibited Patriarch Anthimus and Patriarch Severus with his followers from remaining in Constantinople. See Stein-Palanque, op. cit., 383 with notes 2 and 3.

Synod. All the leaders of the opponents of Chalcedon had to be expelled from the larger cities; the works of Severus, however, had to be destroyed. In the winter of 536/7 the persecution of the anti-Chalcedonians came to life again in Antioch, being personally directed by Patriarch Ephraem. Patriarch Theodosius of Alexandria (535/6. +566], with whose story we still have to concern ourselves (II/2), was taken from Egypt to Dercos near Constantinople because he refused to accept Chalcedon. From 539, however, he could dwell in the capital city itself, where until his death he worked as the recognised head of the anti-Chalcedonians and replaced Severus, who died on 2 August 538 at Xois in the Nile delta.

Finally, in spite of all hindrance the restoration or the establishment of the anti-Chalcedonian hierarchy could take place, this occurring particularly through Bishop John of Hephaistopolis, who from the end of 536 stayed in Constantinople as an exile. On secret journeys into the East, even to Egypt, he could ordain bishops and priests. On an even larger scale this was done by Jacob Baradaeus—under the protection of Empress Theodora—, and by Theodore of Arabia. As wandering bishops they created a new 'monophysite' clergy, and from 542 decisively promoted the consolidation of the 'old Oriental' confession.[43] The employment of force adopted by the imperial Church thus did not attain its goal.

This can suffice as a survey of the outward course of the Chalcedonian restoration under Emperor Justin and Pope Hormisdas. It will be our task (in II/2) to pursue in all its details the *theological* unfolding of christology in the whole Church without, however, being able to separate this from an account of events as a whole, the centre of which will be the Council of Constantinople (553). It can also be shown that it was precisely Chalcedon which was an effective source of theological ideas.

2. Still let us attempt, on the basis of the documents of Pope Hormisdas, to settle the question, whether and to what extent the *theological* side of the Chalcedonian restoration and reconciliation was seen or promoted. The starting-point of the division concerning Chalcedon was the disparity between the Alexandrian Cyrillian tradition with its linguistic and conceptual tools and the Antiochene-Constantinopolitan christology with its world of ideas. Time after time we were forced to the conclusion that ecclesiastical authority and the theologians lacked the insight or the ability to look sufficiently behind language and formulas and to judge from that vantage point whether there was mutual disagreement or consensus. In his *Laetentur* letter

---

[43] Cf. A. van Roey, 'Les débuts de l'Église jacobite', *Chalkedon* II, 339–360, and the further exposition in II/2.

and at the Union of 433 Cyril had, of course, already pointed in this direction. In this respect we could also name some bishops who expressed themselves in the so-called *Codex encyclius* of Emperor Leo I. And there were some Africans, whom we still have to encounter (II/2), who had an eye for seeing how far the tag 'Eutychian' or 'Manichaean' applied to the opponents of Chalcedon as a whole. Most of all one should expect such a talent for discrimination to be present where ecclesiastical authority was to be employed, as in the work of reunion in the years after 518. Of course in authoritative documents, such as the formula of Pope Hormisdas, theological expositions are not to be expected. But the more decisively subscription to these is demanded, so much the more must consideration be given to a person's state of conscience. This is true particularly in the case of the bishops of the East with another tradition. Certainly the intention that Hormisdas had with his demands can be reduced in its christological statement to a global content, that really could and had to be presupposed as common: i.e. the truth and reality of the incarnation of God in Christ. On the other hand, in Constantinople and Egypt there were not lacking strong groups of extremists around Eutyches, whose members were not the like of Dioscorus, Timothy Aelurus and Severus, but rather were combatted by all the anti-Chalcedonian patriarchs of Alexandria themselves. Apart from Nestorius, Pope Hormisdas proscribed one name only from which all distanced themselves in the same way, viz. Eutyches. Nevertheless in his formula Hormisdas put on the same level with him: Dioscorus, Timothy Aelurus, Peter Mongus (all from Alexandria), Peter the Fuller of Antioch, and finally Acacius of Constantinople. It will be shown (II/2) that these were decided opponents of Eutyches, not his friends. Yet with his macroscopic assessment of the anti-Chalcedonian movement Pope Hormisdas was not alone. The people and monks of Constantinople and all the Chalcedonians amongst the patriarchs and clergy as well could not distinguish between Dioscorus and Manes, between Dioscorus and Eutyches. Only the catch-phrase *mia physis* was heard, and by this was understood without further ado the denial of the truth of the incarnation.

But if Hormisdas sought and expected with his formula the winning back of the Alexandrian Church and its partisans, then the demand of the hour would have had to have been to clarify the differences in language between Chalcedon and Cyril and to make apparent the common faith behind them. At the least the knowledge of the differences and the willingness to speak about these would have had to come to light. Unfortunately Patriarch Acacius as well had not known how to enlighten West Rome about the true circumstances in Alexandria and Antioch. For this he had to incur the Pope's severe judgement contained in his formula:

itemque ... condemnamus ... et anathematizamus Acacium Constantinopolitanum quondam episcopum ab Apostolica Sede damnatum, eorum [Eutyches etc.] complicem atque sequacem, vel qui in eorum communionis societate permanserint; quia]Acacius] quorum se communioni miscuit, ipsorum similem meruit in damnatione sententiam. This final sentence is formulated more generally in the text which Emperor Justinian gave to Pope Agapetus: quorum enim quis communionem amplectitur, eorum et similem sententiam in condemnatione consequitur. ('likewise we condemn and anathematise Acacius, the former bishop of Constantinople, who had been condemned by the Apostolic See, as their [Eutyches etc.] accomplice and follower and also those who have remained in communion with them; because [Acacius] joined himself to their communion he has deserved the same judgement of condemnation as theirs'). Expressed more generally: ('For whoever embraces communion with them, shares as a consequence their sentence of condemnation').[44]

Certainly there is much truth in that statement, if it is kept in general terms. *In concreto* all of those who were accused in this way were opponents of Eutyches and advocates of unqualified belief in the truth of the incarnation. Of course the opponents of Chalcedon also did not use kid gloves when they made their reproaches, which mainly concerned the question of the unity in Christ. The Pope rightly defended the Council of Chalcedon and Pope Leo I against the reproach of Nestorianism, thus of propounding two persons and of introducing a 'fourth person' into the Trinity.

On 26 March 521 he wrote in a letter to Patriarch Epiphanius in this way: unam enim patris profitemur esse personam, unam filii dei cum assumpta carne ('we profess that there is one person of the Father, one [person] of the Son of God with the assumed flesh').[45] Thus a fourth person in the Trinity is excluded. In a letter to Emperor Justin, 26 March 521: idem enim deus et homo, non, ut ab infidelibus dicitur, sub quartae introductione personae sed *ipse dei filius deus et homo*, idem virtus et infirmitas, humilitas et maiestas, redimens et venditus, in cruce positus et caeli regna largitus, ita nostrae infirmitatis ut possit interimi, ita ingenitae potentiae ne possit morte consumi.. ('For the same is God and man, not, as is taught by unbelievers, by the introduction of a fourth person [into the Trinity], but the Son of God himself is God and man, the same is power and weakness, humility and majesty, redeeming and sold, placed on the cross and bestowing the kingdom [on the good thief], so sharing our weakness that he could be slain, so possessing uncreated power that he could not be destroyed by death').[46] He could rightly recommend Chalcedon and the letters of Leo to the priests, deacons and archimandrites of Syria Secunda with the words: in his vexillum fidei, in his propugnacula veritatis, in his Christus agnoscitur, in his redemptionis nostrae spes et causa servatur ('In these is the standard of faith, in these the bulwarks of truth, in these Christ is acknowledged, in these the hope and cause of our redemption is preserved').[47]

---

[44] *Libellus fidei Hormisdae ppae*, cited here following DS nr. 364. Also CA nr. 89, 5; CSEL 35 I, 340.
[45] *Hormisda Epiphanio eppo Const.*: CA nr. 237, 10; CSEL 35 II, 730.
[46] *Hormisda Iustino aug.*: CA nr. 236, 12; CSEL 35 II, 720.
[47] *Hormisda Presbyt., Diacon. et Archim. Syr. secund.*: CA nr. 140, 12; CSEL 35 II, 578.

Thus Chalcedon is once again fundamentally established in its rights in the imperial Church. The phase of the *Henoticon* is definitively over. Unfortunately only the schism between East Rome and West Rome has been removed; the cleavage, however, between the supporters of the pre-Chalcedonian, Cyrillian, Alexandrian tradition and those who profess the Council of Chalcedon has not been eliminated. The representatives of the two traditions in what was substantially the one faith in the incarnation of God in Christ had already become so estranged that they could discover in each other only what was opposed, no longer what they had in common.

(C) A FINAL 'ECUMENICAL' REFLECTION

At the end of this investigation of the history of faith during the first epoch after Chalcedon a fundamental 'ecumenical' meditation suggests itself. In view of the squabbling about formulas and diptychs, which is at least in part unintelligible, and the joy of anathematising those who thought differently, the aversion to ecclesiastical definitions of doctrine, which today is so widespread, will easily result in the question: Why did the Church not venture the way of the *Henoticon* and dispense with formulas of faith which experience had taught had not been assimilated, and for that reason gave rise to divisions? The following reasons could point to this line of argument.

I. *Reasons for an agreement which dispenses with difficult formulas*

1. *A spontaneous observation and declaration after the Council of Chalcedon by bishops conscious of their responsibility*. In the so-called *Codex encyclius* of Emperor Leo I we found an important testimonial of Bishop Epiphanius of Perge (CE 31) (above Ch. III). From this it emerges first of all that the Council of 451 was not popular among the simple clergy and the people, at least in the 'province'. It had made too high demands on the mind. Its formulations sounded too erudite, and for that reason did not seem suitable for the 'kerygma', for preaching. The bishop is to the point when he comments that Chalcedon signifies a *new type* of council, which could not be employed pastorally in the same way as the previous councils. Nicaea and Constantinople had made their decision in the form of a creed which could be the basis for baptismal catechesis and for *traditio* and *redditio symboli*. The Council of Ephesus as well had referred to Nicaea and had produced no definition of its own. Although Chalcedon likewise built on Nicaea and Constantinople and had both texts read out twice, it created over and above these a longer text of its own

which it prescribed as the norm of faith. By this measure a new step was taken in the history of councils which would be of great significance for the future, but would also become the bone of contention between opponents and supporters of the Council. This meant for Epiphanius that the doctrine of the 'unity of two natures or substances' could not be employed as material for instruction or as a creed in baptismal catechesis, but could only render assistance in the repulsion of heresies, and then a help only for the bishops (cf. above Ch. III, with notes 74–80). Hence the Council ought indeed remain as it was, since its formula was well attested in tradition, but all the same it ought to have only a restricted function. With this thought Epiphanius had proposed a possible compromise which avoided all the biases and dangers of the *Henoticon*, yet allowed some freedom in a person's stance with regard to the Fourth Council which could take account of the pastoral situation.

2. We have seen that in the Church of Jerusalem a certain openness to a compromise could maintain peace, this compromise becoming at the same time the model for the *Henoticon*. On the other hand this middle position made easier the return to the definitive recognition of Chalcedon in 518 under the influence of the great holy men, Sabas and Theodosius (see Palestine II/2). Thus the *Henoticon* had a certain chance.

3. Chalcedon itself made its statement on different levels: in the way of a *kerygmatic* emphasis of the true divinity and true humanity in the one Christ, and at the same time the expression of this in language borrowed from Greek *philosophy*, whereby the stress could lie entirely on the first. If then a clear confession of the mystery of the incarnation was possible in the first manner, why in addition to that should the more difficult statement be demanded as *articulus stantis et cadentis ecclesiae*? In this connexion the condition had to remain, that the two-natures formula of the Council would not be condemned as heretical and, as a consequence, the more kerygmatic manner of expression placed in doubt, as the radical opponents of Chalcedon in fact did.

4. A further possibility for peace could be opened up if both traditions, the *mia physis* language and the two-natures formula, were accepted as valid, without each declaring that the other was heretical. But this would have to happen on the basis of an unambiguous recognition of the true incarnation of God in Christ, of the one Son of God in true divinity and genuine humanity. Each tradition could serve as a check on the other. In this case a new formula, such as the '*Henoticon*' presented, would be dispensed with, and thus new disagreement avoided. We have seen that Emperor Justinian made

a suggestion along these lines in connexion with the religious conference of 532, nevertheless without results. Such a solution, however,
presupposes an intrinsic comprehension, matured in the course of
dialogue, of the fundamental conceptions and the formulas of both
sides. This situation did not exist around 532. How far the theology
of the period was on its way to such an understanding must still
be examined in detail. It would seem that it is only today that the
doors for this have been opened.[48]

II. *Reasons against the way of the historical* Henoticon

1. Chalcedon was historical reality, occasioned by concrete negative experiences of the *mia physis* christology, experiences associated
with the name 'Eutyches'. The situation which gave rise to the Council
would remain acute for a long time, as the history of the Churches
of Constantinople, and especially Alexandria can teach us. This experience was the realisation that the *mia physis* formula, which itself,
by way of literary forgeries, had found entry into ecclesiastical tradition through Apollinarian circles, was constantly open to grave misunderstandings.

2. On the basis of these negative experiences this formula had
to be discussed and examined to see if it were able to depict the
mystery of Christ. After the development which had taken place
before 451, especially in Antioch and Constantinople, the counter-
formula of the 'one hypostasis in two natures' was found and accepted
as useful, as Bishop Epiphanius of Perge, whom we cited above,
pointed out. But it must be conceded that such language could be
reciprocated only by a limited number of the faithful, even in the
Greek region. At least for these it could perform the function of
helping them say on what level in Christ the unimpaired *unity* was
to be expressed, and on what level the *distinction* between God and
man. Christians who were more sophisticated and critical needed
such linguistic means in order to be able to give a certain personal
justification of their faith.

---

[48] See the joint report of the second meeting of the *Joint Commission of the Catholic Church and
the Coptic Orthodox Church* (Cairo, 27–31 October 1975) in *Dokumente wachsender Übereinstimmung . . .*,
edited and introduced by H. Meyer, H. J. Urban, L. Vischer (Paderborn 1983) 538. Also the declaration of the same *Joint Commission* on christology at its meeting in Vienna, 26–29 August 1976,
ibid., 541–542. In particular: 'When the *Orthodox* confess that our Lord's divinity and humanity
are united *in one nature*, then they understand by "nature" not purely a simple nature, but *rather
one single composed nature*, in which divinity and humanity are united without division and without
confusion. And when the *Catholics* confess Jesus Christ as *one in two natures*, they do not divide
the divinity from the humanity, not even for a single instant; they strive rather to exclude the
mingling, confusion, falsification or change of the one by the other . . . This is our faith in the
mystery of the incarnation of our Lord Jesus Christ and in the salvific plan (oikonomia) of our
redemption. In this faith we all concur'. In view of the long struggle from 451 to the end of
the patristic period, we can accord historical significance to such a document.

3. As we shall see (II/2), even apart from Eutyches, the *mia physis* formula gave rise to new grave misunderstandings, which caused the moderate bishops and theologians of the anti-Chalcedonian party a great deal of trouble as well. For the moment let us refer merely to the quarrels with Julian of Halicarnassus, the tritheism of John Philoponos and finally to monenergism and monothelitism in the seventh century. New synods were necessary to stave off this false interpretation of the picture of Christ, and in these the recourse to Chalcedon was quite explicit. Maximus Confessor pointed the way into the future.

4. Thus for the Church Chalcedon had a mission that could not be surrendered. The Alexandrian picture of Christ expressed by Cyril, especially when it was intensified by taking over the *mia physis* language, needed constant correction. For this picture of Christ was top-heavy, since it was conceived too one-sidedly from above. As will become even clearer in the case of Severus of Antioch, the principle of the hegemony of the Logos dominated the presentation of Christ's humanity in such a way that an adequate appreciation of the 'earthly' Jesus in his human, adult mental life, in his knowing and willing and in his freedom, was not possible. According to this theological conception all spiritual movement in Christ flows from above downwards. In spite of the fundamental recognition of the human soul in Christ by Cyrillian-Severan christology, this christology, in its intrinsic understanding of the spiritual movements in Christ, of his knowing and willing, was in a disquieting manner already on the way to monenergism and monothelitism. This connexion will have to be substantiated expressly (see II/2).

5. Once the Fourth Synod, despite certain reservations and resistance, had nevertheless been received by a convincing majority of the Eastern Church and by the whole of the Latin West, a retreat behind the Council would not have been possible without a great convulsion of the universal Church. The epoch between 451 and 518 had taught just this. In 517, shortly before the change had come about, the archimandrite Theodosius had coined the catch-cry: 'If someone does not accept the four Councils even as the four Gospels, let him be anathema'.[49] That this should have happened in Jerusalem of all places, where decades before one had pointed in the direction of a compromise such as was formulated in the *Henoticon*, shows that the future could not belong to a weak solution favouring the

---

[49] See Cyril Scyth., *Vita Sabae*, LVII: E. Schwartz, *Kyrillos v. Skythopolis* = TU 49, 2 (Leipzig 1939) 152; A.-J. Festugière, *Les Moines d'Orient* (4 Vols) (Paris 1961–1965) III/2, 81; further discussion is to be found in II/2 in the section on Palestine.

middle, but to a deepening of the *fides chalcedonensis*. But this *fides chalcedonensis* had to face the challenge posed by the Alexandrian-Cyrillian–Severan tradition. This process began and it made clear what possibilities the offensive formula of Chalcedon contained.

SELECT BIBLIOGRAPHY

The reader is also referred to works appearing in the list of abbreviations.

Abramowski, L.-Goodman, A. E. (ed., trans.), *A Nestorian Collection of Christological Texts.* Vols I–II (Cambridge 1972)

Allen, P., 'Zachariah Scholasticus and the *Historia Ecclesiastica* of Evagrius Scholasticus', *JTS* NS 31 (1980) 471–488

—— *Evagrius Scholasticus the Church Historian* = SpicSLov 41 (Louvain 1981)

Arens, H., *Die christologische Sprache Leos des Großen. Analyse des Tomus an den Patriarchen Flavian* = FrThSt 122 (Freiburg–Basel–Wien 1982)

Aßfalg, J., 'Die christlichen Literaturen des Orients', *KLL* VII, 72–74

Atiya, A. S., *A History of Eastern Christianity* (London 1968)

Bacht, H., *Das Vermächtnis des Ursprungs. Studien zum frühen Mönchtum.* 2 Vols (Würzburg 1972/1985)

Bartelink, G. J. M., 'Die literarische Gattung der Vita Antonii. Struktur und Motiv', *VigC* 36 (1982) 38–62

Brock, S., 'The Conversations with the Syrian Orthodox under Justinian (532)', *OCP* 47 (1981) 87–121

Capizzi, C., *L'imperatore Anastasio I (491–518)* = OCA 184 (Roma 1969)

—— *Sul fallimento di un negoziato di pace ecclesiastica fra il papa Ormisda e l'imperatore Anastasio I (515–517)* (Firenze 1980)

Chitty, D. J., *The Desert a City. An Introduction to the Study of Egyptian and Palestinian Monasticism under the Christian Empire* (Oxford 1966)

Chrysos, E., 'Konzilsakten und Konzilsprotokolle vom 4. bis 7. Jahrhundert', *AHC* 15 (1983) 30–40

Degen, E., 'Daniel bar Maryam, ein nestorianischer Kirchenhistoriker', *OrChr* 52 (1968) 45–80

Dieten, J.-L. van, 'Synodicon Vetus. Bemerkungen zu einer Neuausgabe (J. Duffy und J. Parker)', *AHC* 12 (1980) 62–108

Dumas, F.-Guillaumont, A., *Kellia I Kom 219* (Le Caire 1969)

Ebied, R. Y.-Wickham, L. R., 'A Collection of unpublished Syriac Letters of Timothy Aelurus', *JTS* NS 21 (1970) 321–369

Feldmann, E., 'Christus-Frömmigkeit der Mani-Jünger. Der suchende Student Augustinus in ihrem Netz', E. Dassmann-K. S. Frank (Ed.), *Pietas* = FS B. Kötting (Münster 1980) 198–216

Festugière, A.-J., *Les Moines d'Orient.* Vols I–IV (Paris 1961–65)

—— 'Évagre Histoire Ecclésiastique', *Byz* 45, 2 (1975) 187–471

Frank, K. S., *Mönche im frühchristlichen Ägypten* (Düsseldorf 1967)

Frend, W. H. C., *The Rise of the Monophysite Movement* (Cambridge 1972)

Garijo, M., 'Der Begriff der "Rezeption" und sein Ort im Kern der katholischen Ekklesiologie', P. Lengsfeld-H.-G. Stobbe (ed.), *Theologischer Konsens und Kirchenspaltung* (Stuttgart 1981) 97–109

Gray, P. T. R., *The Defense of Chalcedon in the East (451–553)* (Leiden 1979)

Grillmeier, A., *Mit ihm und in ihm. Christologische Forschungen und Perspektiven* (Freiburg–Basel–Wien 1978)

—— Art. 'Gott-Mensch' (Patristik), *RAC* XII (1982) Col 312–366

Hage, W., *Die syrisch-jakobitische Kirche in frühislamischer Zeit* (Wiesbaden 1966)

Halleux, A. de, *Philoxène de Mabbog. Sa vie, ses écrits, sa théologie* (Louvain 1963)

Hespel, R., *Le florilège Cyrillien réfuté par Sévère d'Antioche. Étude et édition critique* = BiblMus 37 (Louvain 1955)

Honigmann, E., *Évêques et évêchés monophysites d'Asie anterieure au VIᵉ siècle* = CSCO 127 (Louvain 1951)

—— 'Juvenal of Jerusalem', *DOP* 5 (1950) 211–279

Irmscher, J., 'Geschichtsschreiber der Justinianischen Zeit', *WZUnivRostock* 18 (1969) 469–474

Jalland, T. G., *The Life and Times of St. Leo the Great* (London 1941)

Jossua, J.-P., *Le salut, incarnation ou mystère pascal, chez les Pères de l'Église de saint Irénée à saint Léon le Grand* (Paris 1968)

Klinkenberg, H. M., 'Papsttum und Reichskirche bei Leo d. Gr.', *ZSavSt.K* 38 (1952) 37–112

Lauras, A., 'Saint Léon le Grand et la Tradition', *RSR* 48 (1960) 166–184

—— 'Saint Léon le Grand et le manichéisme romain', *StudPat* XI = TU 108 (Berlin 1972) 203–209

Lebon, J., *Le monophysisme sévérien. Étude historique, littéraire et théologique sur la résistance monophysite au concile de Chalcédoine jusqu'à la constitution de l'Église jacobite* (Louvain 1909)

Lefort, T., 'Catéchèse christologique de Chenouté', *ZÄS* 80 (1955) 40–45

Martorell, J., *Mysterium Christi (León Magno)* (Valencia 1983)

Maspéro, J., *Histoire des patriarches d'Alexandrie depuis la mort de l'impereur Anastase jusqu'à la reconciliation des églises Jacobites* (Paris 1923)

Orlandi, T., 'A Catechesis against Apocryphal Texts by Shenute and the Gnostic Texts of Nag Hammadi', *HThR* 75 (1982) 85–95

Parys, M. van, 'L'évolution de la doctrine christologique de Basile de Séleucie', *Irén* 44 (1971) 493–514

Perrone, L., *La chiesa di Palestina e le controversie cristologiche. Dal concilio di Efeso (431) al secondo concilio di Costantinopoli (553)* (Brescia 1980)

Ries, J., 'Jésus-Christ dans la religion de Mani. Quelques éléments d'une confrontation de saint Augustin avec un hymnaire christologique manichéen copte', *Augustiniana* 14 (1964) 437–454

Roldanus, J., 'Die Vita Antonii als Spiegel der Theologie des Athanasius und ihr Weiterwirken bis ins 5. Jahrhundert', *TheolPhil* 58 (1983) 194–216

Rondeau, M.-J., *Les commentaires patristiques du Psautier (IIIᵉ–Vᵉ siecles)*. Vol. I Les travaux des Pères Grecs et Latins sur le Psautier. Recherches et bilan = OCA 219 (Roma 1982); Vol. II Exégèse prosopologique et théologie = OCA 220 (Roma 1985)

Rose, E., *Die manichäische Christologie* = Studies in Oriental Religions 5 (Wiesbaden 1979)

Sieben, H. J., *Die Konzilsidee der Alten Kirche* (Paderborn 1979)

Speigl, J., 'Die Synode von Heraklea 515', *AHC* 12 (1980) 47–61

—— 'Das Religionsgespräch mit den severianischen Bischöfen in Konstantinopel im Jahre 532', *AHC* 16 (1984) 264–285

Schnitzler, T., *Im Kampfe um Chalcedon. Geschichte und Inhalt des Codex Encyclius von 458* = AnGreg 16 (Roma 1938)

Schurr, V., *Die Trinitätslehre des Boethius im Lichte der 'skythischen Kontroversen'* = FCLDG 18, 1 (Paderborn 1935)

Schwartz, E., 'Johannes Rufus, ein monophysitischer Schriftsteller' = *SbHeidAkW*, Phil.-hist. Kl. 16 (Heidelberg 1912)

—— 'Codex Vaticanus gr. 1431, eine antichalkedonische Sammlung aus der Zeit Kaiser Zenos' = *AbhMünchAkW*, Philos.-philol. u. hist. Kl. XXX, Bd. 6A (München 1927)

—— *Kyrillos von Skythopolis* = TU 49, 2 (Leipzig 1939)

Stein, E., *Geschichte des spätrömischen Reiches.* Bd. 1 (Wien 1928)

—— *Histoire du Bas-Empire.* Tom II (éd. par J.-R. Palanque) (Tournai 1959)

Stockmeier, P., *Leo I. des Großen Beurteilung der kaiserlichen Religionspolitik* (München 1959)

Studer, B., 'Die Einflüsse der Exegese Augustins auf die Predigten Leos des Großen', *Forma futuri. Studi in onore del Cardinale M. Pellegrino* (Turino 1975) 915–930

Tetz, M., 'Zum Streit zwischen Orthodoxie und Häresie an der Wende des 4. und 5. Jahrhunderts', *EvTh* 20 (1961) 354–368

—— 'Athanasius und die Vita Antonii. Die literarischen und theologischen Relationen', *ZNW* 73 (1982) 1–30

Ullmann, W., *Gelasius I. Das Papsttum an der Wende der Spätantike zum Mittelalter* = Päpste und Papsttum 18 (Stuttgart 1981)

Veilleux, A., 'Chénouté ou les écueils du monachisme', *CollCist* 45 (1983) 124–131

Vries, W. de, *Rom und die Patriarchate des Ostens* (Freiburg–München 1963)

—— *Orient et Occident* (Paris 1974)

Wallace-Hadrill. *Christian Antioch. A Study of early Christian Thought in the East* (Cambridge 1982)

Weiss, H.-F., 'Zur Christologie des Schenute von Atripe', *BSAC* 20 (1969) 177–209

Winkelmann, F., 'Geschichtsschreibung in Byzanz', *WZUnivRostock* 18 (1969) 475–481

—— 'Kirchengeschichtswerke im oströmischen Reich', *ByzSlav* 37 (1976) 1–10. 172–190

Woitowytsch, M., *Papsttum und Konzile von den Anfängen bis zu Leo I. (440–461). Studien zur Entstehung der Uberordnung des Papstes über Konzile* = Päpste und Papsttum 17 (Stuttgart 1981)

Wolfinger, F., 'Ecumenical Councils and the Reception of their Decisions', *Conc* 167 (7/1983) 79–84